Scott Foresman
Science

The Diamond Edition

PEARSON
Scott
Foresman

Grade 2 Teacher's Edition • Volume 1
Editorial Offices: Glenview, Illinois • Parsippany, New Jersey • New York, New York
Sales Offices: Boston, Massachusetts • Duluth, Georgia • Glenview, Illinois •
Coppell, Texas • Sacramento, California • Mesa, Arizona

ISBN-13: 978-0-328-31019-7 (ISBN-10: 0-328-31019-0)
This product may appear as part of package ISBN-13: 978-0-328-32089-9 (ISBN-10: 0-328-32089-7).

Scaffolded Inquiry™
Soar on toward inquiry success.

Our program is built on three levels of inquiry. All three engage students in activities that build a strong science foundation and help them develop a full understanding of the inquiry process.

3

Students take the lead in conducting the experiment.
Teacher facilitates Full Inquiry.

2

Students take more ownership of the inquiry process.
Teacher guides the activity.

1

Students learn process skills and follow step-by-step instructions.
Teacher directs the activity.

Research Says: *As students progress through the three stages of inquiry, support from the teacher diminishes and student ownership increases. This developmental process is crucial for students to reach the ultimate goal of conducting science investigations independently—engaging in Full Inquiry.*

Karen L. Ostlund, Ph.D.
UTeach Specialist, College of Natural Sciences, The University of Texas at Austin

Lab zone **Full Inquiry**

Experiment Which bird beak can crush seeds?

Look at the heron's beak. Look at the cardinal's beak. How are the beaks alike? How are they different?

Materials

Ask a question.
Which bird uses its beak to crush seeds? **Use models** to learn more.

2 Use the heron's beak.
Pick up a seed. Try it again.

3 Use the cardinal's beak.
Pick up a seed. Try it again.

models of seeds

model of a heron's beak

Lab zone **Guided Inquiry**

Investigate How can an octopus use its arms?

An octopus has suction cups on its 8 arms. It can use its arms to pick things up. Billye the octopus uses its arms to solve a problem. Billye can open a jar to get a fish inside.

Materials   **What to Do**

3 Work with your group. Take turns. Try to open the jar with suction cups. Where should you put them?

4 How many suction cups did you predict? How many did you use?

How many suction cups will open a jar?							
Predict							
Test							

1 2 3 4 5 6 7 8
Number of Suction Cups

Explain Your Results
Communicate Tell how you used the suction cups.

Go Further
What other problems can you solve using suction cups? Try to solve the problems!

133

Lab zone **Directed Inquiry**

Explore How are worms and snakes alike and different?

Materials

short tape

long tape

7 cotton squares

pipe cleaner

14 pieces of pasta

What to Do
Make models of a worm and a snake.

Worm

1 Roll up.
Pinch the ends.

Snake

2 String the pasta.

3 Roll up.
Pinch the ends.

Process Skills
Models show how animals are alike and different.

Explain Your Results
Feel the **models**. Tell about them.

More Activities Take It to the Net

57

How to Read Science
Discover the cross-curricular link.

Every chapter features pictured vocabulary words for you to build background plus target reading skills so you can teach students how to read science.

Student Edition (Grade 2)

Build Background
- Begin with an essential question.
- Introduce key concepts and vocabulary with a picture.
- Reinforce every vocabulary word four times per chapter.

35

How to Read Science

Reading Skills

Alike and Different

Alike means how things are the same.
Different means how things are not the same.

Science Article

Worms and Snakes

Worms are long and thin. Worms do not have bones. Worms use their bodies to crawl. Snakes are long and thin. Snakes have bones. Snakes use their bodies to crawl.

Apply It!

Tell how a worm and a snake are alike and different. Use your **models** to help you.

Alike	Different

37

How to Read Science

• Teach a target reading skill.
• Practice with an authentic example of science genre—similar to your state test.
• Apply the skill using a graphic organizer.
• Practice each target reading skill four times per chapter.

Differentiated Instruction
Connect with all students through *Content* Leveled Readers.

Content Leveled Readers for every Student Edition chapter **teach the same science concepts, vocabulary, and reading skills—at each student's reading level—**and allow students to read and explore the wonders of nonfiction.

Student Edition (Grade 2)

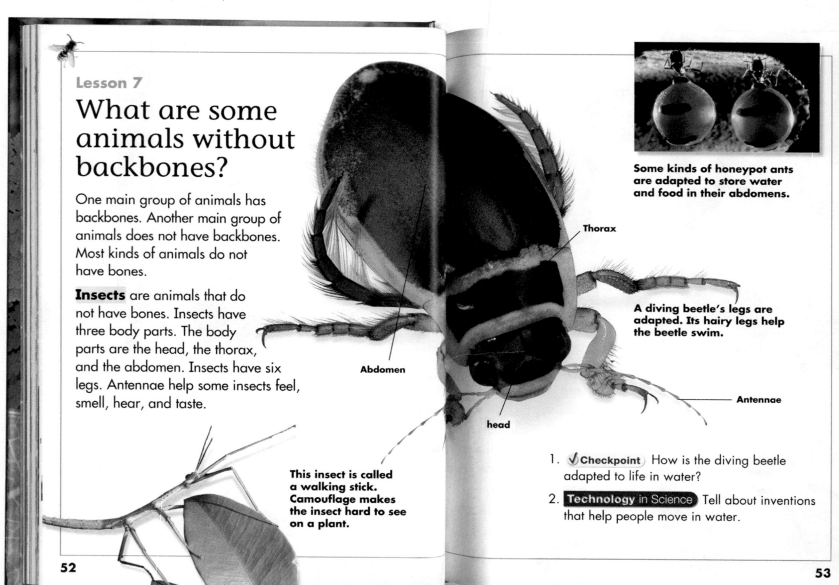

Lesson 7
What are some animals without backbones?

One main group of animals has backbones. Another main group of animals does not have backbones. Most kinds of animals do not have bones.

Insects are animals that do not have bones. Insects have three body parts. The body parts are the head, the thorax, and the abdomen. Insects have six legs. Antennae help some insects feel, smell, hear, and taste.

Abdomen

This insect is called a walking stick. Camouflage makes the insect hard to see on a plant.

Some kinds of honeypot ants are adapted to store water and food in their abdomens.

Thorax

A diving beetle's legs are adapted. Its hairy legs help the beetle swim.

head

Antennae

1. ✓**Checkpoint** How is the diving beetle adapted to life in water?

2. **Technology** in Science Tell about inventions that help people move in water.

52

53

Content Leveled Readers

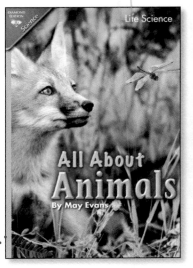

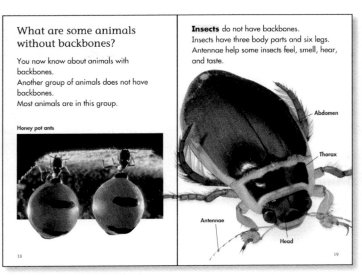

What are some animals without backbones?

You now know about animals with backbones.
Another group of animals does not have backbones.
Most animals are in this group.

Honey pot ants

Insects do not have backbones. Insects have three body parts and six legs. Antennae help some insects feel, smell, hear, and taste.

Abdomen

Thorax

Antennae

Head

18   19

Below-Level teaches the same content and standards as the
Student Edition, but at a grade level below.

There's more!

- *Content* Leveled Reader Teacher's Guide
- Leveled practice for each reader
- Vocabulary cards, songs, activities, and more

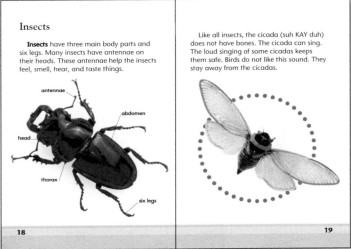

Life Science

Animal Groups

By Carol Levine

Insects

Insects have three main body parts and six legs. Many insects have antennae on their heads. These antennae help the insects feel, smell, hear, and taste things.

antennae

head

thorax

abdomen

six legs

Like all insects, the cicada (suh KAY duh) does not have bones. The cicada can sing. The loud singing of some cicadas keeps them safe. Birds do not like this sound. They stay away from the cicadas.

18   19

On-Level teaches the same concepts and standards as the Student Edition
through additional examples and written slightly below grade level.

Life Science

Nocturnal Animals

by Ann M. Rossi

Fireflies

Fireflies also fly around at night looking for food. These nocturnal insects live in many habitats, but most fireflies are found in warm damp places.

Fireflies mostly live near streams and ponds. They spend their days sleeping in bushes near the water. The fireflies on the right live in a cave.

At night, young fireflies look for earthworms, snails, and slugs to eat. Older fireflies eat plant nectar.

Have you ever seen a firefly at night? Flickering lights can be seen as they zip through the night sky. They have body parts that can give off a light signal. This light helps them warn away predators. It also helps them communicate with other fireflies.

12   13

Advanced expands on the content taught in the Student Edition
to offer enrichment for advanced students and written above grade level.

Time-Saving Strategies
Create extra time in your day.

30-Second Lab Setup

It's that quick! The materials you need for each activity come in their own chapter bag. With the Activity Placemat and Tray™, activity setup takes only 30 seconds instead of 15 minutes. Add it up. You'll easily save 56 hours in a year! What will you do with all that extra time?

1 ### Equipment Kit

Rollable cart contains all the materials you'll need for one year.

2 ### Unit Module Box

Labeled box contains chapter bags with materials for that unit.

3 ### Chapter Bag

The chapter bag includes materials you'll need for each chapter's activ

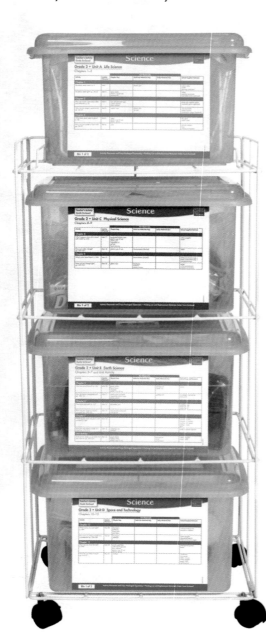

It's all about saving time! We've built strategies right into the Teacher's Edition that will save you hours of time in lesson preparation.

Content Leveled Readers

Save time by integrating your science standards in your reading group.

4 Activity Placemat and Tray™

This handy placemat shows students the materials to gather for each activity.

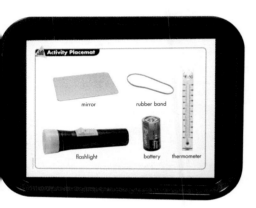

Quick | Teaching Plan

If time is short...
- Build Background, pp. 34–35
- Explore Activity, p. 36
- How to Read Science, p. 37
- Lesson 1, pp. 38–41
- Lesson 2, pp. 42–43
- Lesson 7, pp. 52–55

Other quick options...

Quick ACTIVITY

TE pp. 34, 38, 42, 44, 46, 48, 50, 52, 58

Quick SUMMARY

TE pp. 38, 40, 42, 44, 46, 48, 50, 52, 54

Quick Teaching Plans
Teach the standards even when class time is short.

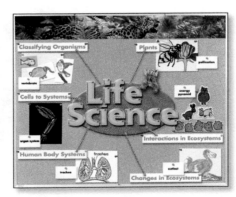

Premade Bilingual Bulletin Board Kits
Save time by creating attractive bulletin boards quickly and easily. No more measuring, no more cutting.

Success ✿ Tracker™

pearsonsuccessnet.com

Save time by having everything in one place—Student Edition, Teacher's Edition, quizzes, games, and lots more.

Reading & Science
Save time by practicing target reading skills in science class.

Professional Development DVDs
Save time by learning at a pace that fits your schedule with high-interest DVDs.

Technology

Scott Foresman brings teaching and learning together in one convenient spot—your computer. From **Success Tracker™** to educational CDs and DVDs, we've created a variety of interactive tools to help support, extend, and enrich your classroom instruction.

For the Teacher

Success Tracker™

 **Online Teacher's Edition** gives you access to the same printed content, so you can plan lessons with the customizable Lesson Planner from your computer at home or at school.

 **Online Science Success Tracker™** helps you meet Adequate Yearly Progress (AYP) for all your students through our Teach & Learn Cycle™—assess, report, diagnose, prescribe, and teach.

 *Content* **Leveled Reader Online Searchable Database** offers you a way to search for Leveled Readers (by content, title, or level) to find just the right topic and level of instruction for every student.

 Activity DVDs guide you through all activities, including preparation, demonstration, and materials needed. Plus professional development.

 Discovery Channel™ Professional Development DVDs give you the science background you're looking for in high-interest DVDs.

 ExamView® Test Generator CD lets you create your own online and printed tests in your state test format.

For the Student

Success Tracker™

 **Online Student Edition** allows students, teachers, and parents to access the content of the textbook from computers at school or at home.

 **Take It to the NET** includes Web activities specific to every unit in the program.
- LabZone alternative activities
- E-Journal
- eTools
- SciLinks

 **Discovery Channel School™ Student DVDs** reinforce the content in every unit of the student book. Previewing and postviewing questions help students focus on the material in each video.

 **Science Games CD** *Powered by KnowledgeBox®* includes a dynamic video, an interactive software activity, and a print activity.

 MindPoint™ Quiz Show CD lets students answer questions about each chapter in a game-show format, providing challenging fun.

 AudioText CD reads the contents of the student book to emerging readers, auditory learners, and students with limited English proficiency.

 Science Songs Audio CD keeps the lessons interesting and upbeat with two consecutive versions of each song: one vocal, the other instrumental.

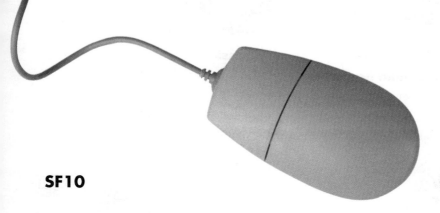

Research-Based Curriculum

From our extensive research and analysis, we know what works best in the science classroom. This research is the foundation for *Scott Foresman Science* and continues to guide our instructional design.

Before (Underlying Research)

Research Base

Experienced authors provided expertise in synthesizing and contributing to a rich body of scientific evidence. Research-based techniques were carefully embedded into the program's instructional materials, assessments, and professional development.

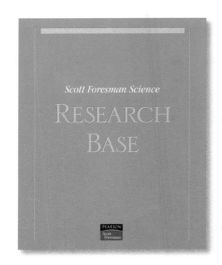

During (Formative Research)

Formative Field Testing

Eighty-three classroom teachers and their 1,675 students from 15 districts across the nation participated in field testing, which helped to shape the instructional design and pedagogical approach of our program.

Independent Field Testing with Treatment and Control Groups

An independent research group conducted additional third-party field testing. Preliminary results showed highly favorable preferences for *Scott Foresman Science* ©2009.

Market Research

Scott Foresman conducted market research through "blind focus" studies with hundreds of teachers where participants were unaware of the sponsorship. The research carried out in these studies focused on ease of use and instructional design.

After (Summative Research)

Third-Party Longitudinal Validation Studies

Using treatment and control groups, these studies test the efficacy of our program with teachers and students and are conducted under the strict guidelines of the What Works Clearinghouse standards.

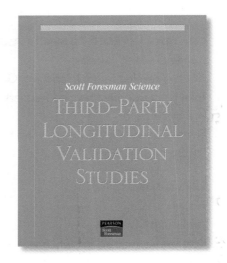

Components

RESOURCES

		K	1	2	3	4	5	6
6	Activities Flip Chart	•	•	•	•	•	•	•
3	Activity Book	•	•	•	•	•	•	•
4	Activity Book Teacher's Guide	•	•	•	•	•	•	•
1	Workbook		•	•	•	•	•	•
2	Workbook Answer Key		•	•	•	•	•	•
5	Assessment Book		•	•	•	•	•	•
15	Quick Study		•	•	•	•	•	•
10	Every Student Learns Teacher's Guide		•	•	•	•	•	•
18	Vocabulary Cards	•	•	•	•	•	•	•
14	Science Content Transparencies		•	•	•	•	•	•
17	Graphic Organizer & Test Talk Transparencies	•	•	•	•	•	•	•
16	Quick Activity Transparencies		•	•	•	•	•	•
7	Human Body Modules		•	•	•	•	•	

CONTENT LEVELED READERS AND LITERATURE

		K	1	2	3	4	5	6
8	*Content* Leveled Readers	•	•	•	•	•	•	•
9	*Content* Leveled Reader Teacher's Guide	•	•	•	•	•	•	•
19	Take-Home *Content* Leveled Readers	•	•	•	•	•	•	•
30	Literature Library	•	•	•	•	•	•	•
35	Science Songs Big Book	•	•	•				
36	Big Book Collection	•	•	•				

TECHNOLOGY

		K	1	2	3	4	5	6
22	Activity DVDs	•	•	•	•	•	•	•
38	AudioText CD		•	•	•	•	•	•
24	Discovery Channel School™ Student DVDs	•	•	•	•	•	•	•
25	Discovery Channel™ Professional Development DVDs	•	•	•	•	•	•	•
23	ExamView® Test Generator CD		•	•	•	•	•	•
11	Online Teacher's Edition	•	•	•	•	•	•	•
27	Online Student Edition		•	•	•	•	•	•
26	Science Games CD *Powered by KnowledgeBox®*	•	•	•	•			
29	MindPoint™ Quiz Show CD		•	•	•	•	•	•
31	Science Songs and Activities Package	•	•	•				
33	Take It to the NET—LabZone, E-Journal, eTools, SciLinks	•	•	•	•	•	•	•
32	*Content* Leveled Reader Online Searchable Database		•	•	•	•	•	•
34	Online Science Success Tracker™		•	•	•	•	•	•

EQUIPMENT KITS

		K	1	2	3	4	5	6
12	Classroom Kit	•	•	•		•		•
20	Unit Module		•	•	•	•	•	•
21	Teacher's Demonstration Kit	•	•	•		•		•
37	Replacement Kit	•	•	•		•	•	•
13	Safety Kit	•	•	•		•	•	•

Pre-K Now Available!

Illinois

Scott Foresman
Science

The Diamond Edition

PEARSON
Scott
Foresman

Editorial Offices: Glenview, Illinois • Parsippany, New Jersey • New York, New York
Sales Offices: Boston, Massachusetts • Duluth, Georgia • Glenview, Illinois
Coppell, Texas • Sacramento, California • Mesa, Arizona
www.pearsonsuccessnet.com

Series Authors

Dr. Timothy Cooney
Professor of Earth Science and Science Education
University of Northern Iowa (UNI)
Cedar Falls, Iowa

Dr. Jim Cummins
Professor
Department of Curriculum, Teaching, and Learning
University of Toronto
Toronto, Canada

Dr. James Flood
Distinguished Professor of Literacy and Language
School of Teacher Education
San Diego State University
San Diego, California

Barbara Kay Foots, M.Ed.
Science Education Consultant
Houston, Texas

Dr. M. Jenice Goldston
Associate Professor of Science Education
Department of Elementary Education Programs
University of Alabama
Tuscaloosa, Alabama

Dr. Shirley Gholston Key
Associate Professor of Science Education
Instruction and Curriculum Leadership Department
College of Education
University of Memphis
Memphis, Tennessee

Dr. Diane Lapp
Distinguished Professor of Reading and Language Arts in Teacher Education
San Diego State University
San Diego, California

Sheryl A. Mercier
Classroom Teacher
Dunlap Elementary School
Dunlap, California

Karen L. Ostlund, Ph.D.
UTeach Specialist
College of Natural Sciences
The University of Texas at Austin
Austin, Texas

Dr. Nancy Romance
Professor of Science Education & Principal Investigator
NSF/IERI Science IDEAS Project
Charles E. Schmidt College of Science
Florida Atlantic University
Boca Raton, Florida

Dr. William Tate
Chair and Professor of Education and Applied Statistics
Department of Education
Washington University
St. Louis, Missouri

Dr. Kathryn C. Thornton
Former NASA Astronaut Professor
School of Engineering and Applied Science
University of Virginia
Charlottesville, Virginia

Dr. Leon Ukens
Professor Emeritus
Department of Physics, Astronomy, and Geosciences
Towson University
Towson, Maryland

Steve Weinberg
Consultant
Connecticut Center for Advanced Technology
East Hartford, Connecticut

Maps
MapQuest, Inc.
Photographs
Every effort has been made to secure permission and provide appropriate credit for photographic material. The publisher deeply regrets any omission and pledges to correct errors called to its attention in subsequent editions. Unless otherwise acknowledged, all photographs are the property of Scott Foresman, a division of Pearson Education. Photo locators denoted as follows: Top (T), Center (C), Bottom (B), Left (L), Right (R), Background (Bkgd)
Earth Science: 1 Mark Gibson/Index Stock Imagery; 2 Carolina Biological Supply Company/Phototake; 3 (CL) Phil Degginger/Alamy Images, (B, T) E.R. Degginger/Bruce Coleman Inc.; 4 David Bell/Corbis
Life Science: 1 John G. Shedd Aquarium; 2 (T) Adam Jones/ Photo Researchers, Inc., (B) Kevin Schafer/Corbis; 3 Illinois Department of Natural Resources; 4 John G. Shedd Aquarium
Physical Science: 2 (T) ©Mark E. Gibson Stock Photography, (BL) ©Robert Frerck/Odyssey/Chicago ; 3 Getty Images
Space and Technology: 2 (TL) Harold Theissen/Alamy Images, (TR) Peter Cade/Getty Images, (BL) Barry Runk/Grant Heilman Photography, (BR) Dan Lim/Masterfile Corporation; 3 NASA; 4 Richard Cummins/Corbis

Consulting Author

Dr. Michael P. Klentschy
Superintendent
El Centro Elementary School District
El Centro, California

Science Content Consultants

Dr. Frederick W. Taylor
Senior Research Scientist
Institute for Geophysics
Jackson School of Geosciences
The University of Texas at Austin
Austin, Texas

Dr. Ruth E. Buskirk
Senior Lecturer
School of Biological Sciences
The University of Texas at Austin
Austin, Texas

Dr. Cliff Frohlich
Senior Research Scientist
Institute for Geophysics
Jackson School of Geosciences
The University of Texas at Austin
Austin, Texas

Brad Armosky
McDonald Observatory
The University of Texas at Austin
Austin, Texas

NASA Content Consultants

Adena Williams Loston, Ph.D.
Chief Education Officer
Office of the Chief Education
Officer

Clifford W. Houston, Ph.D.
*Deputy Chief Education Officer
for Education Programs*
Office of the Chief Education
Officer

Frank C. Owens
Senior Policy Advisor
Office of the Chief Education
Officer

Deborah Brown Biggs
*Manager, Education Flight Projects
Office*
Space Operations Mission
Directorate, Education Lead

Erika G. Vick
*NASA Liaison to
Pearson Scott Foresman*
Education Flight Projects Office

William E. Anderson
*Partnership Manager
for Education*
Aeronautics Research Mission
Directorate

Anita Krishnamurthi
Program Planning Specialist
Space Science Education and
Outreach Program

Bonnie J. McClain
Chief of Education
Exploration Systems Mission
Directorate

Diane Clayton, Ph.D.
Program Scientist
Earth Science Education

Deborah Rivera
Strategic Alliances Manager
Office of Public Affairs
NASA Headquarters

Douglas D. Peterson
*Public Affairs Officer,
Astronaut Office*
Office of Public Affairs
NASA Johnson Space Center

Nicole Cloutier
*Public Affairs Officer,
Astronaut Office*
Office of Public Affairs
NASA Johnson Space Center

Dr. Jennifer J. Wiseman
*Hubble Space Scientist
Program Scientist*
NASA Headquarters

iii

Reviewers

Dr. Maria Aida Alanis
Administrator
Austin ISD
Austin Texas

Melissa Barba
Teacher
Wesley Mathews Elementary
Miami, Florida

Dr. Marcelline Barron
Supervisor/K-12 Math
and Science
Fairfield Public Schools
Fairfield, Connecticut

Jane Bates
Teacher
Hickory Flat Elementary
Canton, Georgia

Denise Bizjack
Teacher Dr. N. H. Jones
Elementary
Ocala, Florida

Latanya D. Bragg
Teacher
Davis Magnet School
Jackson, Mississippi

Richard Burton
Teacher
George Buck Elementary
School 94
Indianapolis, Indiana

Dawn Cabrera
Teacher E.W.F. Stirrup School
Miami, Florida

Barbara Calabro
Teacher
Compass Rose Foundation
Ft. Myers, Florida

Lucille Calvin
Teacher
Weddington Math &
Science School
Greenville, Mississippi

Patricia Carmichael
Teacher
Teasley Middle School
Canton, Georgia

Martha Cohn
Teacher
An Wang Middle School
Lowell, Massachusetts

Stu Danzinger
Supervisor
Community Consolidated
School District 59
Arlington Heights, Illinois

Esther Draper
Supervisor/Science Specialist
Belair Math Science
Magnet School
Pine Bluff, Arkansas

Sue Esser
Teacher
Loretto Elementary
Jacksonville, Florida

Dr. Richard Fairman
Teacher
Antioch University
Yellow Springs, Ohio

Joan Goldfarb
Teacher
Indialantic Elementary
Indialantic, Florida

Deborah Gomes
Teacher
A J Gomes Elementary
New Bedford, Massachusetts

Sandy Hobart
Teacher
Mims Elementary
Mims, Florida

Tom Hocker
Teacher/Science Coach
Boston Latin Academy
Dorchester, Massachusetts

Shelley Jaques
Science Supervisor
Moore Public Schools
Moore, Oklahoma

Marguerite W. Jones
Teacher
Spearman Elementary
Piedmont, South Carolina

Kelly Kenney
Teacher
Kansas City Missouri
School District
Kansas City, Missouri

Carol Kilbane
Teacher
Riverside Elementary School
Wichita, Kansas

Robert Kolenda
Teacher
Neshaminy School District
Langhorne, Pennsylvania

Karen Lynn Kruse
Teacher
St. Paul the Apostle
Yonkers, New York

Elizabeth Loures
Teacher
Point Fermin
Elementary School
San Pedro, California

Susan MacDougall
Teacher
Brick Community Primary
Learning Center
Brick, New Jersey

Jack Marine
Teacher
Raising Horizons Quest
Charter School
Philadelphia, Pennsylvania

Nicola Micozzi Jr.
Science Coordinator
Plymouth Public Schools
Plymouth, Massachusetts

Paula Monteiro
Teacher
A J Gomes Elementary
New Bedford, Massachusetts

Tracy Newallis
Teacher
Taper Avenue Elementary
San Pedro, California

Dr. Eugene Nicolo
Supervisor, Science K-12
Moorestown School District
Moorestown, New Jersey

Jeffry Pastrak
School District of Philadelphia
Philadelphia, Pennslyvania

Helen Pedigo
Teacher
Mt. Carmel Elementary
Huntsville Alabama

Becky Peltonen
Teacher
Patterson Elementary School
Panama City, Florida

Sherri Pensler
Teacher/ESOL
Claude Pepper Elementary
Miami, Florida

Virginia Rogliano
Teacher
Bridgeview Elementary
South Charleston, West
Virginia

Debbie Sanders
Teacher
Thunderbolt Elementary
Orange Park, Florida

Grethel Santamarina
Teacher
E.W.F. Stirrup School
Miami, Florida

Migdalia Schneider
Teacher/Bilingual
Lindell School
Long Beach, New York

Susan Shelly
Teacher
Bonita Springs Elementary
Bonita Springs, Florida

Peggy Terry
Teacher
Madison Elementary
South Holland, Illinois

Jane M. Thompson
Teacher
Emma Ward Elementary
Lawrenceburg, Kentucky

Martha Todd
Teacher
W. H. Rhodes Elementary
Milton, Florida

Renee Williams
Teacher
Bloomfield Schools
Central Primary
Bloomfield, New Mexico

Myra Wood
Teacher
Madison Street Academy
Ocala, Florida

Marion Zampa
Teacher
Shawnee Mission
School District
Overland Park, Kansas

Science

See learning in a whole new light

How to Read Science xx

Science Process Skills xxii

Using Scientific Methods xxvi

Science Tools xxviii

Safety in Science xxxii

v

Unit A Life Science

How do plants live in their habitats?

Life Science in Illinois

Chapter 1 • All About Plants

Build Background How do plants live in their habitats? . . . 2

Directed Inquiry Explore Do plants need water? . . 4

How to Read Science Predict 5

Chapter 1 Song "Plants" 6

Lesson 1 • What are the parts of a plant? 7

Lesson 2 • How are seeds scattered? 10

Lesson 3 • How are plants grouped? 12

Lesson 4 • How are some woodland plants adapted?. . 16

Lesson 5 • How are some prairie plants adapted? . . . 20

Lesson 6 • How are some desert plants adapted? . . . 22

Lesson 7 • How are some marsh plants adapted? . . . 24

Guided Inquiry Investigate Do plants need light?. 26

Math in Science Leaf Patterns 28

Chapter 1 Review and Test Prep. 30

Biography Mary Agnes Chase 32

Chapter 2 • All About Animals

Build Background How are animals different from each other?. 34

Directed Inquiry Explore How are worms and snakes alike and different? 36

How to Read Science Alike and Different . . . 37

Chapter 2 Song "What Has Backbones?" 38

Lesson 1 • What are some animals with backbones? . . 39

Lesson 2 • What are some ways mammals are adapted? 42

Lesson 3 • What are some ways birds are adapted? . . 44

Lesson 4 • What are some ways fish are adapted? . . . 46

Lesson 5 • What are some ways reptiles are adapted? . 48

Lesson 6 • What are some ways amphibians are adapted? 50

Lesson 7 • What are some animals without backbones? 52

Guided Inquiry Investigate How can an octopus use its arms? 56

Math in Science Sorting Animals. 58

Chapter 2 Review and Test Prep 60

NASA Life Along the Ice. 62

Career Wildlife Rehabilitator. 64

How are animals different from each other?

Unit A Life Science

How do living things help each other?

Chapter 3 • How Plants and Animals Live Together

Build Background How do living things help each other?. 66

Lab zone **Directed Inquiry Explore** What does yeast need to grow?. 68

How to Read Science Cause and Effect 69

Chapter 3 Song "Good Partners" 70

Lesson 1 • What do plants and animals need? 71

Lesson 2 • How do plants and animals get food in a grassland? 74

Lesson 3 • How do plants and animals get food in an ocean?. 78

Lesson 4 • What can cause a food web to change? . . 82

Lesson 5 • How do plants and animals help each other? 84

Lab zone **Guided Inquiry Investigate** How can you model a food web?. 90

Math in Science Measuring Length. 92

Chapter 3 Review and Test Prep. 94

Career Farmer 96

viii

Chapter 4 • How Living Things Grow and Change

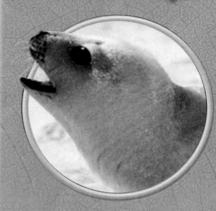

How do living things grow in different ways?

Build Background How do living things grow in different ways? 98

Lab zone Directed Inquiry Explore Which hand do different children use to write? 100

How to Read Science Infer 101

Chapter 4 Song "Hi Little Turtle!" 102

Lesson 1 • How do sea turtles grow and change? . . 103

Lesson 2 • What is the life cycle of a dragonfly? . . . 108

Lesson 3 • What is the life cycle of a horse? 110

Lesson 4 • How are young animals like their parents? 112

Lesson 5 • What is the life cycle of a bean plant? . . 114

Lesson 6 • How are young plants like their parents? . 116

Lesson 7 • How do people grow and change? 118

Lab zone Guided Activity Investigate How does a caterpillar grow and change? 122

Math in Science Measuring Time. 124

Chapter 4 Review and Test Prep. 126

Biography Mario J. Mota 128

Unit A Test Talk 129

Unit A Wrap-Up 130

Lab zone Full Inquiry Experiment Which bird beak can crush seeds? 132

End with a Poem "Little Seeds" 134

Science Fair Projects: Temperature and Seeds; Jumping Insects. 136

Unit B · Earth Science

Earth Science in Illinois

Chapter 5 • Earth's Land, Air, and Water

What are Earth's natural resources?

Build Background What are Earth's natural resources? . . 138

Directed Inquiry Explore How are soils different? 140

How to Read Science Picture Clues 141

Chapter 5 Song "Natural Resources" 142

Lesson 1 • What are natural resources? 143

Lesson 2 • What are rocks and soil like? 146

Lesson 3 • How do people use plants? 150

Lesson 4 • How does Earth change? 152

Lesson 5 • How can people help protect Earth? . . . 154

Guided Inquiry Investigate How do worms change the soil? 160

Math in Science Recycling Bar Graph 162

Chapter 5 Review and Test Prep 164

NASA Looking out for Earth 166

Career Forester 168

Chapter 6 • Earth's Weather and Seasons

Build Background How does weather change? 170

Directed Inquiry Explore How much rain falls?. 172

How to Read Science Draw Conclusions. . . 173

Chapter 6 Song "What's the Weather?" 174

Lesson 1 • What are some kinds of weather? 175

Lesson 2 • What is the water cycle? 178

Lesson 3 • What is spring? 180

Lesson 4 • What is summer? 182

Lesson 5 • What is fall? 184

Lesson 6 • What is winter? 186

Lesson 7 • What are some kinds of bad weather? . . 188

Guided Inquiry Investigate How can you measure weather changes? 194

Math in Science Charting Favorite Seasons. 196

Chapter 6 Review and Test Prep. 198

Career Atmospheric Scientist. 200

How does weather change?

Unit B Earth Science

How can people learn about the Earth long ago?

Chapter 7 • Fossils and Dinosaurs

Build Background How can people learn about the Earth long ago? 202

Directed Inquiry Explore Which fossils match the plants and animals? 204

How to Read Science Retell 205

Chapter 7 Song "Go Find A Fossil" 206

Lesson 1 • How can we learn about the past? 207

Lesson 2 • What can we learn from fossils? 210

Lesson 3 • What were dinosaurs like? 212

Lesson 4 • What are some new discoveries? 216

Guided Inquiry Investigate How can you make a model of a fossil? 218

Math in Science Measuring Fossil Leaves 220

Chapter 7 Review and Test Prep 222

Biography Susan Hendrickson 224

Unit B Test Talk 225

Unit B Wrap-Up 226

Full Inquiry Experiment Does gravel, sand, or soil make the best imprint? 228

End with a Poem "The Spring Wind" 230

Science Fair Projects: Water Evaporates; Measuring Temperature 232

xii

Unit C — Physical Science

Physical Science in Illinois

Chapter 8 • Properties of Matter

What are some properties of matter?

Build Background What are some properties of matter? . 234

Directed Inquiry Explore What happens when oil is mixed with water? 236

How to Read Science Draw Conclusions. . . 237

Chapter 8 Song "They're All Matter" 238

Lesson 1 • What is matter? 239

Lesson 2 • What are the states of matter? 242

Lesson 3 • How can matter be changed? 248

Lesson 4 • How can cooling and heating change matter? 252

Guided Inquiry Investigate How can water change? 256

Math in Science How Can You Measure Matter? . . . 258

Chapter 8 Review and Test Prep 260

Space Food 262

Career Material Scientist. 264

Chapter 9 • Energy

Build Background What are some kinds of energy? . . . 266

Lab zone **Directed Inquiry Explore** Which color heats faster? 268

How to Read Science Infer 269

Chapter 9 Song "Where Do We Get Energy?" 270

Lesson 1 • What is energy? 271

Lesson 2 • How do living things use energy? 274

Lesson 3 • What are some sources of heat? 278

Lesson 4 • How does light move? 282

Lesson 5 • What are other kinds of energy? 286

Lab zone **Guided Inquiry Investigate** How can you change light? 290

Math in Science Measuring Shadows 292

Chapter 9 Review and Test Prep 294

Career Lighting Operator 296

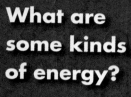

What are some kinds of energy?

xv

Unit C Physical Science

How do forces cause objects to move?

Chapter 10 • Forces and Motion

Build Background How do forces cause objects to move? 298

Lab zone **Directed Inquiry Explore** How can you measure force? 300

How to Read Science Put Things in Order . . 301

Chapter 10 Song "Use Some Force!" 302

Lesson 1 • How do objects move?. 303

Lesson 2 • What is work?. 308

Lesson 3 • How can you change the way things move? 310

Lesson 4 • How can simple machines help you do work? 314

Lesson 5 • What are magnets? 318

Lab zone **Guided Inquiry Investigate** What can magnets do? 322

Math in Science Measuring Motion 324

Chapter 10 Review and Test Prep 326

NASA **Biography** Luther Jenkins 328

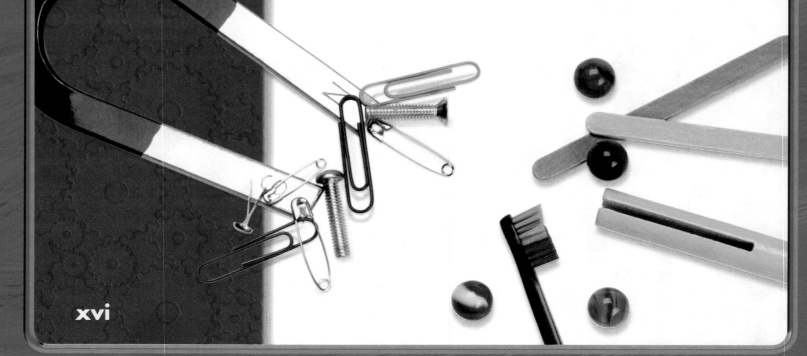

Chapter 11 • Sound

Build Background How is sound made?. 330

Lab zone **Directed Inquiry Explore** How can you make sound? 332

How to Read Science Important Details . . . 333

Chapter 11 Song "Listen to the Sounds!" 334

Lesson 1 • What is sound? 335

Lesson 2 • What is pitch?. 338

Lesson 3 • How does sound travel? 340

Lesson 4 • How do some animals make sounds? . . . 342

Lesson 5 • What are some sounds around you? . . . 344

Lab zone **Guided Inquiry Investigate** How can you change sound? 346

Math in Science Measuring Sounds 348

Chapter 11 Review and Test Prep 350

Biography Alejandro Purgue 352

Unit C Test Talk 353

Unit C Wrap-Up 354

Lab zone **Full Inquiry Experiment** What kinds of objects reflect light clearly? 356

End with a Poem "Apple Shadows" 358

Science Fair Projects: Energy in My Terrarium; Listening to Sound Through Matter. 360

How is sound made?

Unit D • Space and Technology

What are some ways the Earth moves?

Space and Technology in Illinois

Chapter 12 • Earth and Space

Build Background What are some ways the Earth moves? 362

Directed Inquiry Explore What causes day and night? 364

How to Read Science Alike and Different . . 365

Chapter 12 Song "The Sun" 366

Lesson 1 • What is the Sun? 367

Lesson 2 • What causes day and night? 370

Lesson 3 • What causes seasons to change? 374

Lesson 4 • What can you see in the night sky? 376

Lesson 5 • Why does the Moon seem to change? . . 380

Lesson 6 • What is the solar system? 382

Guided Inquiry Investigate How can you make a model of a constellation? 384

Math in Science Planets in Orbit 386

Chapter 12 Review and Test Prep 388

NASA Mission to Mars 390

NASA Career Astronomer 392

Chapter 13 • Technology in Our World

Build Background What are some ways technology helps us? 394

Directed Inquiry Explore How can you move the ball? 396

How to Read Science Retell 397

Chapter 13 Song "Technology Helps Us All" 398

Lesson 1 • What is technology? 399

Lesson 2 • How does technology help us? 402

Lesson 3 • How do we use technology to communicate? 404

Lesson 4 • What are some other ways we use technology? 406

Lesson 5 • How do people make things? 408

Guided Inquiry Investigate How can you make a maze? 410

Math in Science Technology in Your School 412

Chapter 13 Review and Test Prep 414

Biography Shonte Wright 416

Unit D Test Talk 417

Unit D Wrap-Up 418

Full Inquiry Experiment Which tissue is the strongest? 420

End with a Poem "This Happy Day" 422

Science Fair Projects: Phases of the Moon; Flying Better 424

Metric and Customary Measurement EM1

Glossary EM2

Index EM22

Credits . . . . EM 30

What are some ways technology helps us?

How to Read Science

Explain to children that they will be more successful in learning science if they understand what is written on each page. That is, they need to know how to read science. Tell them that there are certain skills that make reading easier. In each chapter, they will practice one of these reading skills.

Before Reading

Tell children that for each chapter, they will have the chance to preview what they will read. Begin with the "Build Background" pages. Have children look at the vocabulary introduced on these pages along with the pictures and think about what they will be learning. Discuss what they might already know about the subject of the chapter.

Have children follow along as you walk through the chapter. Have them look at the pictures and read the captions with you. Have them discuss what they think the chapter is about and what they think they will be learning. The "How to Read Science" page identifies a target reading skill that will be revisited throughout the chapter.

Target Reading Skill

Demonstrate for children how to identify the target reading skill. (It is always located at the top of the page next to a target icon.) Discuss with children the target reading skill for the chapter. If children are unfamiliar with the chapter target reading skill, provide some explanation and elaboration. Tell children that they will get more practice with the target reading skill throughout the chapter. Inform children that the target reading skills they will encounter in the science chapters are the same reading skills they will be learning about and practicing in Reading.

In each chapter, children receive introductory instruction in a reading skill, have two opportunities to practice the skill, and are assessed on the skill over the course of the chapter. By connecting science skills with reading skills, improved scores and comprehension in both Reading and Science can be achieved.

Real-World Connection

Explain to children that there are a variety of ways in which science information can be presented and learned. These ways include stories, diagrams, and pictures. In each How to Read Science feature, one of these ways will be used to present science information to children. A story usually consists of several sentences about a topic. It is often accompanied by a picture. Sometimes information is presented entirely in a picture. Often a diagram with labels is used to explain a concept. Tell children that being familiar with each of these ways will help them learn.

Each chapter in your book has a page like this one. This page shows you how to use a reading skill.

Before reading

First, read the Build Background page. Next, read the How To Read Science page. Then, think about what you already know. Last, make a list of what you already know.

Target Reading Skill

Each page has a target reading skill. The target reading skill will help you understand what you read.

Real-World Connection

Each page has an example of something you will learn.

Graphic Organizer

A graphic organizer can help you think about what you learn.

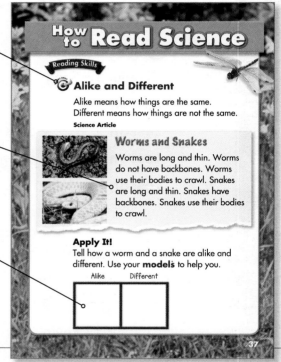

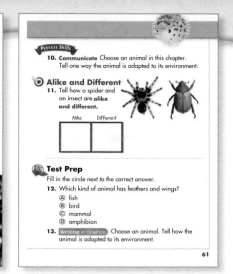

Reptiles are animals with backbones. Most reptiles have dry skin. Scales cover and protect a reptile's body. Some reptiles hatch from eggs. Snakes and turtles are two kinds of reptiles. Look at the picture of the reptile.

Amphibians are animals with backbones. Amphibians live part of their life in the water and part of their life on land. Most amphibians have smooth, wet skin. Amphibians hatch from eggs. Frogs and toads are amphibians.

✓ **Lesson Checkpoint**
1. Which kinds of animals have backbones and scales?
2. 🔘 How are an amphibian and a reptile **alike** and **different?**

amphibian

reptile

Process Skills
10. **Communicate** Choose an animal in this chapter. Tell one way the animal is adapted to its environment.

🔘 **Alike and Different**
11. Tell how a spider and an insect are **alike** and **different.**

Alike	Different

🐚 **Test Prep**
Fill in the circle next to the correct answer.
12. Which kind of animal has feathers and wings?
   Ⓐ fish
   Ⓑ bird
   Ⓒ mammal
   Ⓓ amphibian
13. *Writing in Science* Choose an animal. Tell how the animal is adapted to its environment.

61

🎯 **During reading**
Use the checkpoint as you read the lesson. This will help you check how much you understand.

🎯 **After reading**
Think about what you have learned. Compare what you learned with the list you made before you read the chapter. Answer the questions in the Chapter Review.

Target Reading Skills

These are some target reading skills that appear in this book.

- Cause and Effect
- Alike and Different
- Put Things in Order
- Predict

- Draw Conclusions
- Picture Clues
- Important Details

xxi

Graphic Organizer

Tell children that a graphic organizer is a way for them to organize their thoughts about what they have read or seen. A graphic organizer identifies the important ideas and shows how they are related. Explain to children that there is a graphic organizer for each chapter target reading skill and that it can be used to help them understand what they have read or seen.

During Reading

Tell children that answering questions you ask as they read the lesson is a good way for them to check their understanding of what they have read. Ask children questions as they read so that you and they can assess their level of understanding.

Tell children that it is always a good idea for them to think about what they have learned in one lesson before going on to another lesson. In this way they can be sure they have understood what has been presented. Suggest that children share what they have learned with a partner and/or the class. Tell children that they can check what they have learned by answering the checkpoint questions.

After Reading

After children have finished reading the chapter, ask them to think about what they have learned. Have them answer the questions in the "Chapter Review and Test Prep." You may want to preview the target reading skills in the chart to assess children's knowledge of these concepts.

Science Process Skills

Read aloud the introductory paragraph on page xxii. Remind children that a process is a way of doing things.

Observe

Tell children that their five senses are seeing, hearing, smelling, touching, and tasting. Explain that scientists use their five senses to find out about objects, events, and living things. Ask children to use words to tell about the picture. (Possible answers: Red land, rocks on the land, a machine made of metal, no living things) What sense did you use to observe the picture? (Seeing) Caution children that when they are doing science activities, they should not taste or smell things unless you specifically tell them to.

Classify

Explain to children that properties are things that can be observed, such as how something looks, feels, or acts. Scientists classify things based on how they are alike or not alike. Scientists might classify the rocks in the picture. What else might scientists classify in the picture? Choose some common classroom objects, and ask children to classify them into groups based on properties such as size, shape, or color. Ask volunteers to tell their method of classification.

Estimate and Measure

Tell children that two ways to measure are by using a standard measure, such as a meter or an inch, or by using a nonstandard measure, such as paper clips. Ask: **What things might scientists estimate and measure in the picture?** (Possible answers: The rocks, the size of the machine) Provide children with different nonstandard units and metric and standard rulers. Ask them to measure the length of different classroom objects using both standard and nonstandard units.

Infer

Tell children that since scientists do not see any plants in this picture, they might infer that no animals could survive here. Ask children what else scientists might infer. Have them explain their inferences. Help children understand the meaning of infer by doing the following activity: Ask a volunteer to come to the front of the class. Tell the volunteer to shut his or her eyes. Place an easily identifiable object, such as an apple or a toy car, in the child's hands. Ask the child to use his or her other senses to gather information about the object. After the child has gathered information, ask him or her to infer what the object is.

Science Process Skills

Scientists use process skills to find out about things. You will use these skills when you do the activities in this book. Suppose scientists want to learn more about space. Which process skills might they use?

Observe

A scientist who wants to find out more about space observes many things. You use your senses to find out about things too.

Classify

Scientists classify objects in space. You classify when you sort or group things by their properties.

Estimate and Measure

Scientists build machines to explore space. First scientists make a careful guess about the size or amount of the parts of the machine. Then they measure each part.

Infer

Scientists are always learning about space. Scientists draw a conclusion or make a guess from what they already know.

Space

Science Background

You Are a Scientist!

The word *science* comes from the Latin word *scire,* which means "to know." Scientists observe the world around them in order to know more about it. They observe, question what they see, wonder what makes the world the way it is, and try to find answers to their questions. Anyone who observes the world around them and questions what they see is a scientist!

Predict

First scientists tell what they think will happen. Then they do an experiment.

Make and Use Models

Scientists might make and use models of a machine to use in space. Models show what scientists already know.

Make Definitions

Scientists use what they know to tell what something means.

xxiii

Predict

Discuss what the word *predict* means. Explain that scientists use what they observe and what they can infer to help them predict. Tell children that scientists can predict how the machine will move based on what they know about the machine. Tell children that they can predict too. Hold up an eraser and ask: **What do you predict will happen if I let go of this eraser?** (Possible answer: It will fall to the floor.)

Make and Use Models

Explain that a model is something that can be used to represent an object, event, or living thing. A model can even represent a place or idea. Scientists might have made many models of this machine before they sent the machine into space. Explain that scientists often make and use models to represent or learn about real things. Tell children that even pictures or drawings are kinds of models because they are used to represent something. Explain to children that many toys are models. Ask children for examples of models they have seen. (Accept all reasonable answers.)

Make Definitions

Ask children where they find definitions. (In a dictionary) Explain that scientists make definitions. Scientists use observations and investigations to help make definitions. The machine in the picture moves, or wanders around the surface of the planet. Scientists might define the machine as "something that wanders about, or roams."

Science Process Skills

Make Hypotheses

Tell children that a hypothesis should be in the form of an "If…/then…" statement. Ask children what questions the scientists in the picture might have about space. Write the questions on the board. Ask children to change each question into a hypothesis by making it an "If…/then…" statement. (Possible answers: Why do scientists wear spacesuits? If scientists wear spacesuits, then they will be able to breathe and stay safe in space.)

Collect Data

Explain to children that data are facts or information. Tell children that it is important to record what they observe and measure when they do science activities. Recording what you observe and measure is called *collecting data.* The scientists in the picture are collecting data about space. Graphs, charts, pictures, words, lists, diagrams, and tables can be used to help collect data.

Interpret Data

Tell children that *interpret* means "to explain the meaning of something." Making charts or graphs help scientists to interpret the data they collect. The scientists in the picture will interpret the data they are collecting while they are outside their spacecraft.

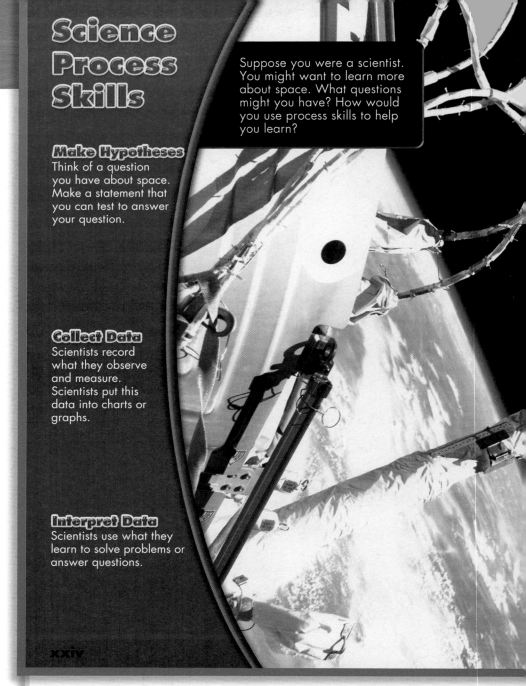

Science Process Skills

Suppose you were a scientist. You might want to learn more about space. What questions might you have? How would you use process skills to help you learn?

Make Hypotheses
Think of a question you have about space. Make a statement that you can test to answer your question.

Collect Data
Scientists record what they observe and measure. Scientists put this data into charts or graphs.

Interpret Data
Scientists use what they learn to solve problems or answer questions.

xxiv

Science Background

Experimental Variables and Controls

- In all scientific experiments, only one factor can be tested at one time. This factor is called the variable. It is the only part of the experiment that can be changed. By testing only one variable at a time, a scientist can be fairly certain that the experimental results are caused by one and only one factor.

- All scientific experiments must have a control experiment. A control experiment is set up exactly like the one that has the variable, but it does not have the variable. Nothing in the control experiment changes. Setting up a control experiment eliminates the possibility of hidden or unknown variables.

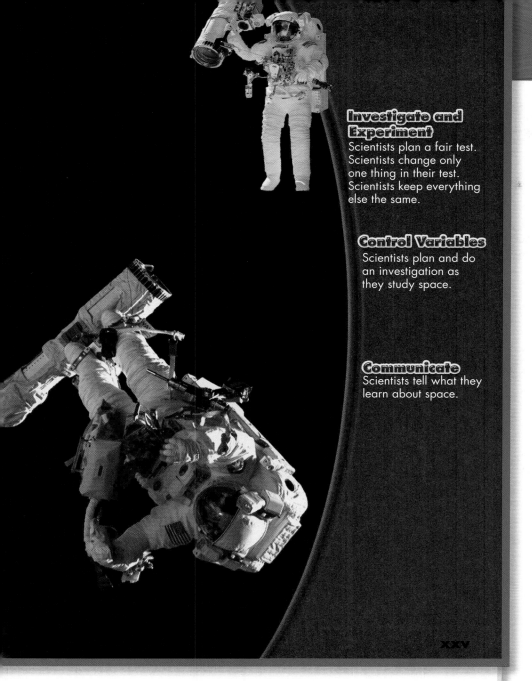

Investigate and Experiment

Tell children that scientists investigate many different things while they are in space. Scientists in the picture might investigate how fast or slow they move in space. What are some other things scientists might investigate while they are in space? (Answers might include: Learning about different planets) The methods scientists use to investigate and experiment are discussed further on pages xxvi–xxvii.

Control Variables

Explain that variables are things that can change or be different. Remind children that scientists change only one thing in their test. Scientists change one thing because they want to find out what the effect of that one thing alone is. The scientists in the picture might change what they use to help them move in space.

Communicate

Scientists use words, pictures, charts, and graphs to share information about their investigation. The scientists in the picture will share what they learn with other scientists. Have children communicate with their classmates. Tell children to draw a picture of something they did today on a piece of paper. Ask volunteers to share their drawings. Tell children that talking, writing, drawing pictures, or making charts are all ways to communicate. Explain that learning to be a good listener and reader is important too.

Science Misconception

It Takes a Community

Children may think that if a scientist's conclusions support a hypothesis, then the hypothesis is accepted by other scientists. That is not the case. Before a hypothesis can be accepted by the scientific community, the experiment must be repeated and the results checked many times by scientists around the world.

Science Background

The Nature of Science

- The results from a single experiment are not sufficient to reach a conclusion. An experiment must be run over and over again, with data collected each time. Only after multiple repetitions of the experiment and collection of substantial data can the data be considered accurate and used to reach a conclusion.

- It is quite often the case in science that the answer to one question leads to new questions. In this way, the cycle of discovery goes on and on.

Tell children that scientists use scientific methods. Read aloud the introductory paragraph on page xxvi to children. Explain to them that they will use scientific methods when they do the **Full Inquiry** activities and the Science Fair Projects at the end of each unit in their book.

Ask a Question

Science often starts with a question. The question may be about something you observe, a problem you notice, or something you want to know. Read the question in the example: *Do seeds need water to grow?*

Make Your Hypothesis

Review with children the meaning of hypothesis. (A statement that a scientist can test to answer a question) Remind children that a hypothesis must be an "If…/then…" statement. Tell children to look at the picture of the two pots. Ask: **What is the hypothesis being tested?** (If seeds are watered, then they will grow.)

Plan a Fair Test

Tell children that planning a fair test means controlling the variables. Remind them that only one thing can change. Everything else must be kept the same. Ask: **Which variable is being changed?** (Water) **What do you think are some variables that are being kept the same?** (Possible answers: Soil, sunlight, temperature)

Scientific methods are ways of finding answers. Scientific methods have these steps. Sometimes scientists do the steps in a different order. Scientists do not always do all of the steps.

Ask a question.

Ask a question that you want answered.

Do seeds need water to grow?

Make your hypothesis.

Tell what you think the answer is to your question.

If seeds are watered, then they will grow.

Plan a fair test.

Change only one thing.

Keep everything else the same.

Water one pot with seeds.

water

no water

xxvi

Science Misconception

Scientific Method

- Scientists use the scientific method to find answers to their questions. The scientific method is a systematic approach to problem solving comprised of a number of basic steps. Although the steps of the scientific method are often presented in a fixed sequence, it is misleading to think that they must be done in that order. The steps of the scientific method do not have to be followed in a strictly linear fashion. Indeed, scientists do not always perform all the steps in the scientific method. The nature of a question determines which steps will be followed and in what order.

- To reinforce the idea that there is not one established scientific method that must be followed in a fixed sequence, scientists often refer to the problem-solving steps they follow as "a scientific method," emphasizing that it may be one of several scientific methods.

Do your test.

Test your hypothesis. Do your test more than once. See if your results are the same.

Collect and record your data.

Keep records of what you find out. Use words or drawings to help.

Tell your conclusion.

Observe the results of your test. Decide if your hypothesis is right or wrong. Tell what you decide.

Seeds need water to grow.

no water

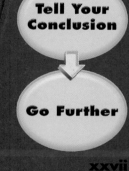

water

Go further.

Use what you learn. Think of new questions or better ways to do a test.

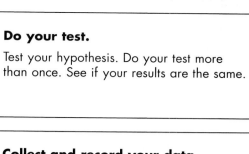

Ask a Question

Make Your Hypothesis

Plan a Fair Test

Do Your Test

Collect and Record Your Data

Tell Your Conclusion

Go Further

xxvii

My Science Journal

Using the Scientific Method

Present the following question to children: Do plants need sunlight to grow? Ask children to follow the steps of the scientific method to explain how they would answer the question. Help children write their answers in their science journals.

Do Your Test

Tell children that scientists test a hypothesis by doing an experiment. Ask children why it is important to do a test more than once. (To see if the results are the same)

Collect and Record Your Data

Explain to children that as scientists do an experiment, they observe what is happening and record important data. Data includes observations and measurements. Ask volunteers to name different ways data can be recorded. (Answers include lists, charts, tables, graphs, diagrams, or written words) Ask: **What data might the person doing this experiment record?** (Possible answers: Amount of water, type of seeds, amount of sunlight) Tell children that the person doing this experiment will then interpret his or her data.

Tell Your Conclusion

Tell children that scientists make conclusions based on interpreting the data and by comparing the results of the experiment with the hypothesis. Scientists decide if the hypothesis they tested is right or wrong. If the hypothesis is correct, the scientist will communicate the results to other scientists. If the hypothesis is not correct, the scientist may decide to do a new experiment that tests a different variable. Ask: **Was the hypothesis about seeds correct?** (Yes)

Go Further

Tell children that scientists always have more questions. These questions can begin a new cycle of investigation and experimentation. Ask: **What are some other questions you might ask about seeds and plants?** (Possible answers: Will using other kinds of seeds affect how the seeds grow? Will seeds grow in the dark? Will seeds grow where it is very cold?)

Science Tools

Children should be familiar with and be able to use appropriate tools and simple equipment/instruments to safely gather scientific data. As children read the pages identifying tools, make sure they know what the tool is used for and how to use it safely. Demonstrate each tool and its safe use.

Safety goggles

Explain to children that it is essential they protect their eyes when performing certain activities. Safety goggles or safety glasses provide such protection.

Demonstrate the use of safety goggles and discuss when they should be worn. Generate a class list of appropriate times. Make a poster of this information to display in the classroom.

Hand lens

Demonstrate the safe use of a hand lens to children. Provide a variety of objects, including newspaper print, for children to examine using a hand lens. Ask children to describe how each object looks under the hand lens.

Clock

Make sure children know how to use a clock to tell time. Discuss how many minutes there are in an hour. Point out the second hand if the clock has one, and explain that there are 60 seconds in one minute.

Science Tools

Scientists use many different kinds of tools.

Safety goggles
You can use safety goggles to protect your eyes.

Hand lens
A hand lens makes objects look larger.

Clock
A clock measures time.

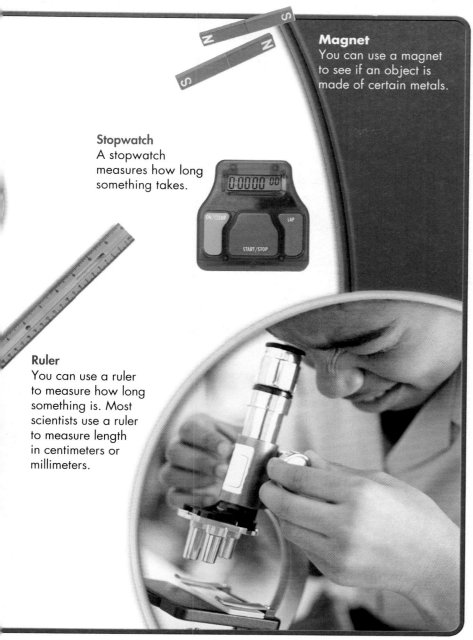

Magnet
You can use a magnet to see if an object is made of certain metals.

Stopwatch
A stopwatch measures how long something takes.

Ruler
You can use a ruler to measure how long something is. Most scientists use a ruler to measure length in centimeters or millimeters.

xxix

Science Background

Note About Magnets

- Magnets have poles.
- The magnets in the picture have a north pole (N) and a south pole (S).
- The rule of poles states that like poles repel and unlike poles attract.

Magnet

Provide magnets, objects containing iron, and objects not containing iron for children to experiment with. Have children identify what objects contain iron and explain how they came to that conclusion. Have children place like and unlike poles together and observe the results.

Stopwatch

Tell children that most stopwatches measure time in hours, minutes, seconds, and parts of seconds. Have children use stopwatches you provide to measure how long it takes several volunteers to make one circuit around the classroom. Demonstrate for children how to start and stop the stopwatch.

Ruler

Tell children that most rulers they will use provide both metric and customary units of length. A ruler is 12 inches (1 foot) or 30.48 centimeters long. Each centimeter is divided into 10 equal parts, or millimeters.

Science Tools

Meter stick

Explain to children that a meter stick is similar to a ruler in that it is used to measure length. Point out that a meter stick is about three feet (one yard) long. Have children examine a meter stick to see the centimeter and millimeter subdivisions.

Ask children to measure the length of the classroom using a meter stick.

Measuring cup

Most scientists use containers marked with milliliters (mL) or cubic centimeters (cc). One mL equals one cc. Some measuring cups also provide customary units.

Explain to children that when they use a measuring cup, they should find the milliliter line on the cup that they want to measure to. Then they should put the measuring cup on a flat surface and move their heads so that their eyes are even with that line. They should pour water into the measuring cup until it is even with the line.

Balance

Demonstrate the use of a balance to children. Have children practice measuring mass with a balance by first choosing two objects and predicting which one has more mass. Then have children put an object on each side of the balance. Have them observe which side of the balance is lower. Have them determine which object has more mass and explain their thinking.

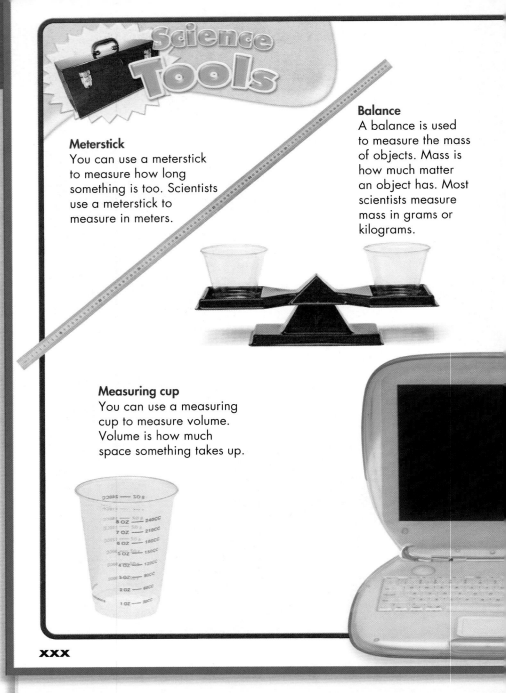

Science Tools

Meterstick
You can use a meterstick to measure how long something is too. Scientists use a meterstick to measure in meters.

Balance
A balance is used to measure the mass of objects. Mass is how much matter an object has. Most scientists measure mass in grams or kilograms.

Measuring cup
You can use a measuring cup to measure volume. Volume is how much space something takes up.

xxx

Science Background
Notes About Tools

- One meter equals 39.36 inches.

- The volume of a liquid can be measured using a measuring cup or a graduated cylinder. The unit of volume is the liter (L). Smaller volumes are measured in milliliters.

- The volume of a regular solid can be found by multiplying its length by its width by its height (Volume = length × width × height). The unit of volume for a regular solid is cubic meters or cubic centimeters.

- The volume of an irregular solid can be measured by water displacement.

- A balance measures mass, or the amount of matter in an object. The unit of mass is the kilogram (kg). Smaller masses are measured in grams (g) and milligrams (mg).

- Mass is not the same as weight. Weight is a measure of the force of Earth's gravity on an object. An object has weight because it has mass. On Earth, mass and weight are used interchangeably. The unit of weight is the newton (N).

- 0 °C (32 °F) is the freezing point of water. 100 °C (212 °F) is the boiling point of water. To convert Celsius to Fahrenheit, use $F = \frac{9}{5}C + 32°$. To convert Fahrenheit to Celsius, use $C = \frac{5}{9}(F - 32°)$.

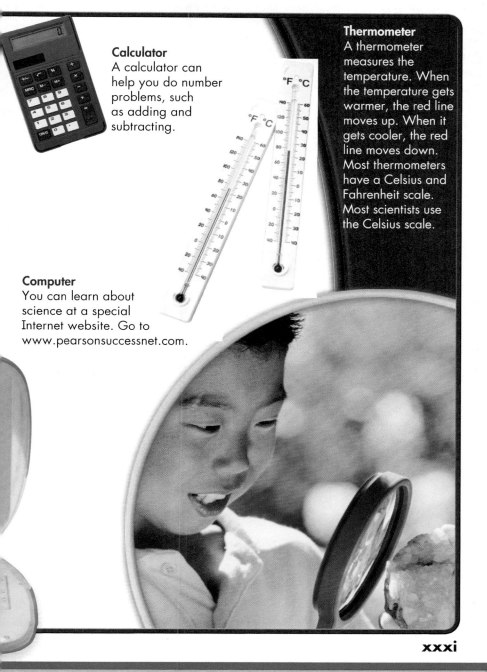

Calculator

A calculator can help you do number problems, such as adding and subtracting.

Thermometer

A thermometer measures the temperature. When the temperature gets warmer, the red line moves up. When it gets cooler, the red line moves down. Most thermometers have a Celsius and Fahrenheit scale. Most scientists use the Celsius scale.

Computer

You can learn about science at a special Internet website. Go to www.pearsonsuccessnet.com.

Thermometer

Demonstrate to children the safe use of a thermometer. Point out the Fahrenheit (F) and Celsius (C) scales. Ask children to determine at what temperature the Fahrenheit and Celsius readings are the same (−40°).

Have children measure temperature with a thermometer by doing the following activity. Put a thermometer in a cup of cold water. Have children observe the red line in the thermometer and record the temperature it indicates. Put the thermometer in a cup of warm water. Again have children observe the red line and record the temperature it indicates. Ask children to describe how the red line and the temperature changed.

Calculator

Supervise children as they use calculators you provide to add and subtract numbers. Explain to them what specific keys mean and how to use them. Then write a series of numbers between 4 and 18 on the board and have children use their calculators to find the total.

Computer

Supervise children as they access and explore **pearsonsuccessnet.com** by having them use the mouse to click on their grade, find a topic they would like to learn about and click on that topic, click on another arrow to go to another page or click on words with lines under them, and write three sentences about what they have learned at the Web site.

Safety in Science

Safety in Science

Communicate to children that learning about science can be an exciting experience. But it can also be a dangerous one if proper safety rules are not followed. Emphasize that conducting science activities requires an awareness of potential hazards and the need for safe practices. This means that appropriate safety procedures must be followed when completing scientific investigations.

Tell children that to have a safe year doing activities, they must be familiar with the safety tips listed on page xxxii. Have children follow along as you read each tip aloud. Then have children read each tip on their own. Have them explain what they have learned about safety in science to a partner.

The following safety guidelines are provided for your information as you plan and implement the activities in this book.

- Be sure children always follow such safety rules as keeping a clean work area, never tasting substances without permission, wearing safety goggles or glasses, and safely handling glue, scissors, rulers, toothpicks, straws, and spools.

- Discuss with children the need to apply safe and appropriate techniques for handling, manipulating, and caring for materials, living organisms, scientific equipment, and technology. For example, children should identify ways to care properly for fish in an aquarium. Children should understand that fish need food and clean water and should be kept out of direct sunlight. Be sure that children understand that to protect native wildlife, they should not release live materials after completing an activity. If necessary, biologists suggest freezing them in a sealed container, and then disposing of the container.

- Be sure children understand what the basic tools for gathering information are. (See pp. xxviii–xxxi.) Discuss with children how to select the appropriate tools and use them safely.

- Discuss with children the need to exercise appropriate safety precautions during severe weather. Identify types of severe weather (thunderstorms, tornadoes, hurricanes, and blizzards) and examples of safety procedures (seeking shelter in safe locations, heeding sirens, listening to TV and radio broadcasts, heeding watches and warnings, developing a personal safety plan).

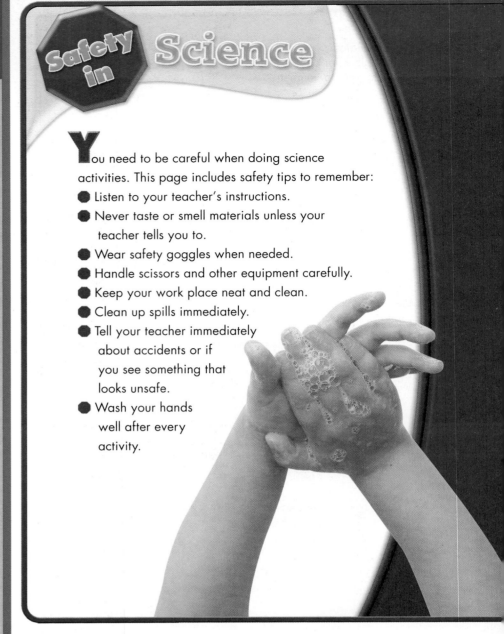

Safety in Science

Y ou need to be careful when doing science activities. This page includes safety tips to remember:

- Listen to your teacher's instructions.
- Never taste or smell materials unless your teacher tells you to.
- Wear safety goggles when needed.
- Handle scissors and other equipment carefully.
- Keep your work place neat and clean.
- Clean up spills immediately.
- Tell your teacher immediately about accidents or if you see something that looks unsafe.
- Wash your hands well after every activity.

xxxii

Safety Tips Art Link

Have children work in small groups to create a Science Safety Poster to display in the classroom. Provide children with appropriate materials to make their posters. Suggest that groups focus on one safety tip for their posters. Display all the posters as a collage of safety tips for the science classroom.

Science Background

Notes About Safety

- As children study astronomy, they will be asked to compare and contrast the characteristics of the Sun, Moon, and Earth. Children should be aware that looking at the Sun without protective eyewear is dangerous and not recommended. They should also be aware of the danger of Sun exposure and should use sunscreen.

- Children should be aware of the danger of exposure to sounds of high decibel levels. They should limit their exposure to such sounds, move further away from the source of such sounds, or use protective ear wear.

- Talk with children about fire safety. For example, make sure children understand that if their clothing catches on fire, they should stop, drop, and roll. Emphasize to children that they should never run.

Unit A

Life Science in Illinois

ILLINOIS

Did you know that you can learn about sea animals in Chicago? The Oceanarium at the Shedd Aquarium is the largest indoor aquarium in the world.

Life Science in Illinois

How are wildflowers, bobcats, and fish alike? They can all be found in Illinois. You will learn more about the science behind them in Unit A.

Woodland Wildflowers

You can see wildflowers during the spring in Illinois. Many wildflowers grow after winter. Wildflowers can be different colors and sizes. You will learn more about plants in Chapter 1.

Badgers, Beavers, and Bobcats

Badgers live in grasslands. Beavers live near water. Bobcats live in forests. They are all mammals in Illinois. They live in different environments that meet their needs. You will learn more about animals and their needs in Chapter 2.

Argyle Lake State Park

Argyle Lake State Park is near Colchester. Bass, trout, and catfish live in Argyle Lake. Some people catch the fish to eat. Some fish are food for birds and other animals. You will learn more about how plants and animals live together in Chapter 3.

2 • Life Science in Illinois

ISAT Prep

Answer the questions below. Write your answers on a separate sheet of paper.

Multiple-Choice Questions

1 Which animal lives in Illinois forests?
- **A.** badger
- **B.** beaver
- **C.** bat
- **D.** bobcat

2 In which season do many Illinois wildflowers grow?
- **A.** winter
- **B.** spring
- **C.** fall
- **D.** summer

3 Fish from Illinois lakes are NOT food for
- **A.** people
- **B.** birds
- **C.** other animals
- **D.** wildflowers

Short-Response Questions

4 Name three kinds of fish that live in Argyle Lake.

5 What are three mammals that live in Illinois?

Life Science in Illinois • **3**

Field Trip
Shedd Aquarium

You can learn how plants and animals live together at the Shedd Aquarium in Chicago. Many of the fish and other animals are from places that are far from Illinois. You can learn about coral reefs and places with rocks. You can also learn about fish and other animals living in lakes and rivers in Illinois.

Find out more:

Research to find out more about the different fish at the Shedd Aquarium.
- Draw a picture of a fish.
- Write the name of the fish.
- Write about what the fish eats and where it lives.

CARIBBEAN REEF

4 • Life Science in Illinois

Answers to ISAT Prep

1. D
2. B
3. D

4. Three kinds of fish that live in Argyle Lake are bass, trout, and catfish.
5. Badgers, beavers, and bobcats.

ILLINOIS Field Trip
Shedd Aquarium

Find out more:

- Children should choose a fish from Shedd Aquarium, draw and label its picture, and then describe what the fish eats and where it lives in the wild.

- Children may want to include other information about the fish in their descriptions, such as the color of the fish and length of the average adult male and female fish.

Art in Science

- Have children make an illustrated brochure that encourages others to visit Shedd Aquarium.

- Information should include costs, permanent exhibits, and any special programs available to visitors.

Set Up Unit A

Getting Started	A2
Activity Connections	A4
Professional Development	A6
Reaching All Learners	A8

Chapter Pages

1 All About Plants — 1–32

Planning Chapter 1	1A
Lab zone **Directed Inquiry** **Explore** Do plants need water?	4
Lesson 1 What are the parts of a plant?	7
Lesson 2 How are seeds scattered?	10
Lesson 3 How are plants grouped?	12
Lesson 4 How are some woodland plants adapted?	16
Lesson 5 How are some prairie plants adapted?	20
Lesson 6 How are some desert plants adapted?	22
Lesson 7 How are some marsh plants adapted?	24
Lab zone **Guided Inquiry** **Investigate** Do plants need light?	26

2 All About Animals — 33–64

Planning Chapter 2	33A
Lab zone **Directed Inquiry** **Explore** How are worms and snakes alike and different?	36
Lesson 1 What are some animals with backbones?	39
Lesson 2 What are some ways mammals are adapted?	42
Lesson 3 What are some ways birds are adapted?	44
Lesson 4 What are some ways fish are adapted?	46
Lesson 5 What are some ways reptiles are adapted?	48
Lesson 6 What are some ways amphibians are adapted?	50
Lesson 7 What are some animals without backbones?	52
Lab zone **Guided Inquiry** **Investigate** How can an octopus use its arms?	56

3 How Plants and Animals Live Together — 65–96

Planning Chapter 3	65A
Lab zone **Directed Inquiry** **Explore** What does yeast need to grow?	68
Lesson 1 What do plants and animals need?	71
Lesson 2 How do plants and animals get food in a grassland?	74
Lesson 3 How do plants and animals get food in an ocean?	78
Lesson 4 What can cause a food web to change?	82
Lesson 5 How do plants and animals help each other?	84
Lab zone **Guided Inquiry** **Investigate** How can you model a food web?	90

4 How Living Things Grow and Change — 97–128

Planning Chapter 4	97A
Lab zone **Directed Inquiry** **Explore** Which hand do different children use to write?	100
Lesson 1 How do sea turtles grow and change?	103
Lesson 2 What is the life cycle of a dragonfly?	108
Lesson 3 What is the life cycle of a horse?	110
Lesson 4 How are young animals like their parents?	112
Lesson 5 What is the life cycle of a bean plant?	114
Lesson 6 How are young plants like their parents?	116
Lesson 7 How do people grow and change?	118
Lab zone **Guided Inquiry** **Investigate** How does a caterpillar grow and change?	122

Wrap-Up Unit A

Test-Taking Strategies	129
Unit A Wrap-Up	130
Lab zone **Full Inquiry** **Experiment** Which bird beak can crush seeds?	132
Lab zone **Full Inquiry** **Science Fair Projects**	136

Unit A
Getting Started

Bulletin Board Kit

Includes:
- illustrated border
- punch-out picture
- label cards in English and Spanish
- suggestions for use

Big Book Collection

- *Jump Into the Jungle* by Theresa Volpe, ISBN 0-328-11789-7

Literature Library

- *Why Do Cats Meow?* by Joan Holub ISBN 0-14-056788-7
- *Feathers, Flippers, and Feet* by Deborah Lock ISBN 0-7566-0264-5
- *AB Sea* by Bobbie Kalman ISBN 0-86505-725-7

All About Plants

flower

How Plants and Animals Live Together

food web

Life Science

All About Animals

amphibian

How Living Things Grow and Change

life cycle

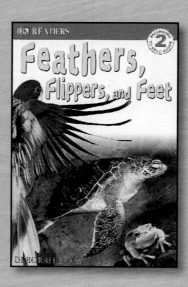

JOAN HOLUB
Why Do Cats Meow?

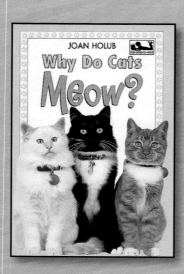

DK READERS
Feathers, Flippers, and Feet

AB Sea

Integrating Your Day

Integrate the following cross-curricular ideas into your lessons as you teach this Life Science unit.

Social Studies in Science

Social Studies in Science, SE/TE, pp. 19, 23, 85
Your State Flower, TE, p. 13
The Sargasso Sea, TE, p. 80
Horses Helping People, TE, p. 111
Different Countries and Peoples, TE, p. 120

Math in Science

Math in Science, SE/TE, pp. 17, 55, 77, 89, 105, 115
Sorting Animals, pp. 58–59
How Many Legs? TE, p. 53
Math in a Food Web, TE, p. 81
Measuring a Remora Fish, TE, p. 88
Measuring Length, pp. 92–93
Symmetry in Nature, TE, p. 19
Measuring Time, pp. 124–125
Counting Animals, TE, p. 113
Saguro Arms, TE, p. 117

Reading and Writing in Science

Writing in Science, SE/TE, pp. 9, 49, 51, 61, 79, 81, 87, 95, 111, 113, 127
My Science Journal, TE, pp. 8, 11, 14, 17, 19, 23, 35, 40, 45, 54, 67, 72, 75, 81, 83, 86, 88, 99, 104, 106
Reading Strategy, Predict, p. 5, 11, 25, 31
Reading Strategy, Alike and Different, p. 37, 41, 45, 61
Reading Strategy, Cause and Effect, pp. 69, 73, 83, 95
Reading Strategy, Infer, pp. 101, 109, 111, 121, 127
Writing Link, TE, pp. 51

Technology in Science

Technology in Science, SE/TE, pp. 21, 53
Technology Link, TE, pp. 21, 85
NSTA *SciLinks,* SE, pp. 16, 114
Rocket Science Student CD-ROM
Discovery Channel School DVD
Web Game
Students may access the Online Student Edition at **pearsonsuccessnet.com**

Health in Science

Health in Science, SE/TE, p. 13
Seafood, TE, p. 91

Art in Science

Art in Science, SE/TE, pp. 14, 43, 75, 117
Habitats, TE, p. 18
Fish, TE, p. 47

Scaffolded Inquiry

Levels of Inquiry

Find three levels of inquiry in the pages of the Student Edition. All three levels of inquiry in Scott Foresman Science engage students in activities that build a strong science foundation.

Equipment Kit

- chapter bags
- multi-use materials
- activity placemats
- bulky materials box
- Teacher's Activity Guide

	Student/Teacher Role	What Happens
Directed Inquiry 	Students learn process skills and follow step-by-step instructions. Teacher directs the activity.	Students are introduced to the process of inquiry through Directed Inquiry activities. A Directed Inquiry activity is explicitly directed by the teacher. As students are engaged in the activity, they learn process skills. They also have a positive inquiry experience they can draw upon as they move toward more independence.
Guided Inquiry 	Students take more ownership of the inquiry process. Teacher guides the activity.	Teachers provide structure, and students take more ownership in Guided Inquiry activities. The teacher's role is that of a guide rather than a leader. Students are encouraged to think about variables, and they learn to plan for variables that may affect the outcome of an investigation
Full Inquiry 	Students take the lead in planning and conducting the experiment. Teacher facilitates the inquiry.	Students apply the skills and knowledge developed in Directed and Guided Inquiry to Full Inquiry activities. Students follow the steps of the scientific method as they conduct the experiment shown. Then students are encouraged to identify new answerable questions, plan for variables, and develop their own experiments using available materials.

Materials List

	Activities	Kit Materials	School-supplied Materials
Chapter 1	**p. 4** Do plants need water?	plastic jars, 16 oz.	celery stalk water
	pp. 26–27 Do plants need light?	grass seeds plastic cups, 9 oz. potting soil	water washable paints (optional)
Chapter 2	**p. 36** How are worms and snakes alike and different?	self-adherent red tape cotton squares pipe cleaners	dried mini rigatoni pasta washable paints (optional)
	pp. 56–57 How can an octopus use its arms?	suction cups plastic jars, 16 oz.	Activity Master 1 scissors construction paper (optional)
Chapter 3	**p. 68** What does yeast need to grow?	granulated sugar plastic cups, 9 oz. plastic spoons	dry yeast water
	pp. 90–91 How can you model a food web?	yarn	Activity Masters 2–9 masking tape crayons or markers white paper
Chapter 4	**p. 100** Which hand do different children use to write?		construction paper black crayons scissors tape white chart paper
	pp. 122–123 How does a caterpillar grow and change?	butterfly habitat with caterpillars	transparent tape
Unit A Experiment Activity	**pp. 132–133** Which bird beak can crush seeds?	clothespins craft sticks plastic straws	glue

Unit A
Professional Development

Essential Questions

- overarching questions that tie questions and concepts together
- cannot be answered in single sentence
- help students develop a richer understanding of science

Chapter 1

How do plants live in their habitats?

Plants need water, air, sunlight, space, and nutrients to live. Parts such as roots, stems, leaves, flowers, and seeds help plants survive. Plants can be grouped into two kinds, those with flowers and those without flowers. Plants have adaptations that help them live in different environments such as the woods, prairie, or desert. These adaptations may help plants live in hot, cold, wet, or dry environments.

Tip!

Facilitate Understanding

- Have children name plants they may find in the woodland and in the desert. Ask children to compare and contrast the plants.

- Have children describe woodlands and the desert. Guide them by asking questions about the climate and the types of animals found in each place. Have children discuss how the plants they named are adapted to live in each environment.

Chapter 2

How are animals different from each other?

Animals differ from one another in many ways. Some animals have backbones and some animals do not have backbones. Mammals, birds, fish, reptiles, and amphibians all have backbones. Insects and other animals, such as octopuses, do not have backbones. Animals live in different places and are adapted to their environments in different ways.

Tip!

Facilitate Understanding

- Help children create a T-chart to contrast any two animals.

Frog	Spider

Chapter 3

How do living things help each other?

Living things help each other in different ways. Animals eat plants and/or other animals for food. Animals may get shelter from plants such as trees or they may use smaller plant parts to build nests. Animals may provide protection to plants and other animals.

Facilitate Understanding

- Have children discuss different ways that a bird may use parts of a tree.
- Encourage children to think of other pairs of living things (plants and plants, plants and animals, animals and animals) that help one another. List the pairs on the board and have children describe how they help each other.

Chapter 4

How do living things grow in different ways?

Living things have different life cycles. A life cycle is the way a living thing grows and changes. Some plants grow from seeds. Young plants eventually grow into adult plants. Some animals hatch from eggs and some grow inside of their mothers and are born live. Some young animals look like their parents. Other young animals, such as young insects, look different from their parents.

Facilitate Understanding

- Help children create a Venn diagram to compare and contrast animal life cycles.

Cow   Chicken

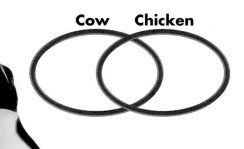

Technology Resources

for Professional Development

Background information is available on the Life Science volume of the *Discovery Channel Professional Development DVD.* Relevant segments include:

Classification of Living Things

Characteristics of Organisms

Continuation of Life

Ecological Organization

Additional Resources

Additional content support is available online at **http://www.nasa. gov**

Also refer to these technology resources:

at pearsonsuccessnet.com

Unit A
Reaching All Learners

Meeting Individual Needs

These suggested strategies can help you customize instruction for children with individual needs.

English Learners

Lead a class conversation about the meaning of selected vocabulary words.

Speaking of Science

 10 minutes whole class

Model correct, natural usage of words, phrases, and idioms from the lesson. Pantomime and demonstrate to help establish meaning. Use sentence frames—common sentence patterns—and call attention to everyday words in the sentences.

- **Beginning** Write one vocabulary word on the board. Ask: *What is _____?* Use gestures and simple but correct English to explain and demonstrate its meaning. Model its use in a short sentence that you write on the board. Help children understand each word in the sentence.

- **Intermediate** Choose 1–3 vocabulary words. For each one, ask: *What does _____ mean?* Have volunteers answer. Repeat answers, modeling correct English. Invite other children to define additional vocabulary words.

- **Advanced** Focus on 3–5 vocabulary words. Ask children for definitions. Provide a dictionary so children may look up unfamiliar words. Repeat key sentences, modeling correct English.

Advanced Learners

Help children extend their thinking as they focus on essential questions for Life Science.

Essential Question: How are living things similar and different?

Play a sorting game.

 20 minutes   small groups

- Show children pictures of various plants and animals from textbooks or other sources. Have children classify the living things according to their shared characteristics.

- Begin by having children sort the living things into plants and animals. Then have children think of other ways to group the plants and the animals.

- Have children explain their groups to the class. Groups will vary and may include categories such as plants that live in the desert, or reptiles, birds, fish, and so on.

Special Needs

Utilize visuals to reinforce concepts throughout the unit. Select a variety of visuals, such as pictures, graphic organizers, and real objects.

Look-Write-Discuss

 20 minutes   whole class

- Have children study a visual for one minute.

- Remove the visual and have children describe it in as much detail as possible. Use their descriptions as a basis for discussion.

- Finally, help children compare their descriptions to the visual for accuracy.

Leveled Readers and Leveled Practice

Leveled Readers deliver the same concepts and skills as the chapter. Use Leveled Readers for original instruction or for needed reteaching.

Below-Level

Life Science

All About Plants

by Leslie Ann Rotsky

Leveled Practice

Leveled Reader Teacher's Guide

On-Level

Life Science

Plants

by Christine Wolf

Leveled Practice

Leveled Reader Teacher's Guide

Advanced

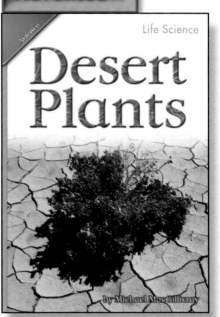

Life Science

Desert Plants

by Michael MacGillivray

Leveled Practice

Leveled Reader Teacher's Guide

Below-Level Leveled Reader has the same content as Chapter 1, but is written at a less difficult reading level.

On-Level Leveled Reader has the same concepts as Chapter 1, and is written at grade level.

Advanced Leveled Reader is above grade level and enriches the chapter with additional examples and extended ideas.

Leveled Reader Database
Scott Foresman
pearsonsuccessnet.com

Use the online database to search for additional leveled readers by level, title, content, and skill.

Key Content and Skill in Leveled Readers and Chapter 1

Content	Vocabulary		Target Reading Skill	Graphic Organizer
All About Plants	nutrients roots stem leaves	flower environment adapted prairie	Predict	

Chapter 1 Planning Guide

Essential Question: What do living things need?

Lesson/Activity	Pacing	Science Objectives
Build Background pp. 2–3	20 minutes	• The student identifies words and constructs meaning from text, illustrations, graphics, and charts, using the strategies of phonics, word structure, and context clues.
Lab zone Flip Chart Activity What are the parts of a flowering plant?		
Lab zone Flip Chart Activity How are a cactus and a fern alike and different?	15 minutes	
Lab zone Directed Inquiry		• The student knows that people use scientific processes including hypothesis, making inferences, and recording and communicating data when exploring the natural world.
Explore Do plants need water? p. 4	5 minutes for setup, 5 minutes day 2, 10 minutes day 3	
How to Read Science p. 5	20 minutes	• The student uses a variety of strategies to comprehend text (for example, self-monitoring, predicting, retelling, discussing, restating ideas).
1 What are the parts of a plant? pp. 6–9	30 minutes	• The student knows the basic needs of all living things. • The student knows the main parts of plants (stems, leaves, roots, flowers).
2 How are seeds scattered? pp. 10–11	20 minutes	• The student understands that structures of living things are adapted to their function in specific environments.
3 How are plants grouped? pp. 12–15	30 minutes	• The student knows that the structural characteristics of plants and animals are used to group them.
4 How are some woodland plants adapted? pp. 16–19	30 minutes	• The student understands that structures of living things are adapted to their function in specific environments. • The student understands that living organisms need to be adapted to their environment to survive.
5 How are some prairie plants adapted? pp. 20–21	20 minutes	• The student understands that the amount of food, water, space, and shelter needed is dependent on the size and kind of living things.
6 How are some desert plants adapted? pp. 22–23	20 minutes	• The student knows that animals and plants can be associated with their environment by an examination of their physical characteristics.
7 How are some marsh plants adapted? pp. 24–25	20 minutes	• The student understands that structures of living things are adapted to their function in specific environments. • The student knows that plants and animals are adapted to different ranges of temperature and moisture.
Lab zone Guided Inquiry		• The student knows that people use scientific processes including hypothesis, making inferences, and recording and communicating data when exploring the natural world.
Investigate Do plants need light? pp. 26–27	30 minutes	
Wrap-Up Chapter 1 pp. 28–32 Math in Science: Leaf Patterns Chapter 1 Review and Test Prep Biography: Mary Agnes Chase	20 minutes 20 minutes 20 minutes	• The student recognizes, extends, generalizes, and creates a wide variety of patterns and relationships using symbols and objects.

Vocabulary/Skills	Assessment/Intervention	Resources/Technology
	• Chapter Review, SE, pp. 30–31	• Science Content Transparency 1 • Workbook, p. 1 • Graphic Organizer Transparency 1 • Vocabulary Cards • Activity Book, pp. 31–32
Process Skills: Make and Use Models, Observe		
Process Skill: Predict **Target Reading Skill:** **Predict**	• Explain Your Results, SE, p. 4 • Activity Rubric **Predict,** SE, p. 5	• Activity Book, pp. 27–28 • Activity DVD • Activity Placemat 1 • Workbook, pp. 2–3 • Every Student Learns, p. 1
nutrients roots stem leaves flower	• Scaffolded Questions, TE, pp. 7, 9 • Checkpoint Questions, SE, p. 9 • Chapter Review, SE, pp. 30–31	• Workbook, p. 4 • Quick Study, pp. 2–3 • Every Student Learns, p. 2
	• Scaffolded Questions, TE, p. 11 • Checkpoint Questions, SE, p. 10 **Predict,** SE, p. 10	• Workbook, p. 5 • Quick Study, pp. 4–5 • Every Student Learns, p. 3
	• Scaffolded Questions, TE, pp. 13, 15 • Checkpoint Questions, SE, pp. 13, 14	• Workbook, p. 6 • Quick Study, pp. 6–7 • Every Student Learns, p. 4
environment adapted	• Scaffolded Questions, TE, pp. 17, 19 • Checkpoint Questions, SE, pp. 17, 18 • Chapter Review, SE, pp. 30–31	• Workbook, p. 7 • Quick Study, pp. 8–9 • Every Student Learns, p. 5
prairie	• Scaffolded Questions, TE, p. 21 • Checkpoint Questions, SE, p. 20 • Chapter Review, SE, pp. 30–31	• Workbook, p. 8 • Quick Study, pp. 10–11 • Every Student Learns, p. 6
	• Scaffolded Questions, TE, p. 23 • Checkpoint Questions, SE, p. 22	• Workbook, p. 9 • Quick Study, pp. 12–13 • Every Student Learns, p. 7
	• Scaffolded Questions, TE, p. 25 • Checkpoint Questions, SE, p. 24 **Predict,** SE, p. 24	• Workbook, p. 10 • Quick Study, pp. 14–15 • Every Student Learns, p. 8
Process Skill: Observe	• Explain Your Results, SE, p. 27 • Activity Rubric	• Activity Book, pp. 29–30 • Activity DVD • Activity Placemat 2
Math Skill: Patterns	• Scaffolded Questions, TE p. 29 **Predict,** SE p. 31 **ExamView®** Chapter 1 Test **Success Tracker** pearsonsuccessnet.com/ successtracker	• Workbook, pp. 11, 13–14 • Assessment Book, pp. 1–4

Quick | Teaching Plan

If time is short...
• Build Background, pp. 2–3
• Explore Activity, p. 4
• How to Read Science, p. 5
• Lesson 1, pp. 6–9
• Lesson 3, pp. 12–15
• Lesson 4, pp. 16–19
• Lesson 5, pp. 20–21

Other quick options...

Quick ACTIVITY

TE pp. 2, 6, 10, 12, 16, 20, 22, 24, 28

TRANSPARENCIES 1, 2, 3, 4, 5, 6, 7

Quick SUMMARY

TE pp. 6, 8, 10, 12, 14, 16, 18, 20, 22, 24

Chapter 1 Activity Guide

Children learn to ask and answer scientific questions as they progress to greater independence in scaffolded inquiry.

Directed Inquiry   A Directed Inquiry activity begins each chapter.

Guided Inquiry   A Guided Inquiry activity closes each chapter.

Full Inquiry   Experiments and Science Fair Projects at the end of each unit provide opportunities for Full Inquiry.

Lab zone Directed Inquiry

Explore   Do plants need water? p. 4

Time   5 minutes for setup, 5 minutes on day 2; and 10 minutes on day 3.

Groups   small groups

Advance Preparation   Cut a 10 in. long piece of celery for each group. Fill each pouring container with about $\frac{2}{3}$ c water.

Materials   1 fresh cut stalk of celery with leaves; 1 clear plastic jar, 16 oz; water (about $\frac{2}{3}$ c); pouring container for water

Alternative Materials   Large clear plastic cups can be used instead of clear plastic jars.

What to Expect   After a day, the stalk of celery will droop because the celery lost water. When water is added the celery stalk will absorb water and begin to stand upright again.

Safety Note   Have paper towels handy for water spills.

Activity DVD   Unit A, Chapter 1

Activity Placemat   Mat 1

Lab zone Guided Inquiry

Investigate   Do plants need light? pp. 26–27

Time   30 minutes for setup and then 10 minutes daily for 1 week

Groups   small groups

Advance Preparation   Plant seeds about 10 days in advance. Cover seeds with a thin layer of soil. Keep soil moist. Fill pouring containers.

Materials   2 clear plastic cups, 9 oz; grass seeds for each cup; potting soil, about $1\frac{1}{4}$ c; water (about $\frac{1}{4}$ c); pouring container for water; washable paints (optional)

Science Center   This activity can be set up in your Science Center for students to work on throughout the day.

What to Expect   The grass in the dark place will look paler green and less healthy.

Safety Notes   Have paper towels handy for water spills. Check for plant allergies in advance.

Activity DVD   Unit A, Chapter 1

Activity Placemat   Mat 2

Other Resources
The following Resources are available for activities found in the Student Edition.

Demonstration Kit If you wish to rehearse or demonstrate the Chapter 1 activities, use the materials provided in the Demonstration Kit.

Classroom Equipment Kit Materials shown in *italic print* are available in the Classroom Equipment Kit.

Activity Placemats The Equipment Kit includes an Activity Placemat for each activity, a work surface that identifies the materials that need to be gathered.

Quick **ACTIVITY**

Transparencies Each lesson starts with a Quick Activity. Use the Quick Activity Overhead Transparencies to focus children's attention on each task.

Teacher's Activity Guide For detailed information about Inquiry Activities, access the Teacher's Activity Guide at **pearsonsuccessnet.com**.

Activity Flip Chart

What are the parts of a flowering plant?

This activity supports the chapter as a whole.

Process Skills make and use models

 Time 20 minutes

 Grouping individual or pairs

Materials plastic foam, variety of shapes such as half-ball and rectangles; construction paper of several colors; clay; white glue; marker; string; pipe cleaners; scissors; index cards

Procedure
- Teacher should make a model of a plant and label its parts. Review the parts and the function of each part with the class.
- Help children **make a model** of a flowering plant using the materials listed.
- Have children **use a model** to point out plant parts to classmates.

What to Expect Children will make a model of a plant and label its parts. Students will communicate the function of each plant part.

Think About It
1. roots, a stem, leaves, and flower.
2. The leaf makes food for the plant. The flower makes seeds. The root takes in water and holds the plant in the ground. The stem holds the plant up and brings water up from the roots.

Activity Flip Chart

How are a cactus and a fern alike and different?

Use this center activity after teaching Lesson 6 of the chapter.

Process Skills observe

 Time 15 minutes

 Grouping pairs

Materials fern in a pot; cactus in a pot; hand lens or magnifying glass

Procedure
- Discuss different types of plants that live in the desert and how they adapt to the climate. Use a Venn diagram to compare and contrast the plants.
- Children will **observe** both plants and record observations in the chart that compares and contrasts both plants.

What to Expect Students will observe both plants and record.

Think About It
1. They are both plants. They both have roots, stems, and leaves.
2. Cactuses have thick stems and sharp leaves that are spines. Ferns have thin stems and wide leaves divided into many parts.

Chapter 1 Workbook Support

Online **Teacher's Edition**
pearsonsuccessnet.com

Use the following Workbook pages to support content and skill development as you teach Chapter 1. You can also view and print Workbook pages from the Online Teacher's Edition.

Use with Build Background, pp. 2–3

Name _____ Vocabulary Preview
Use with Chapter 1.

Draw a picture or write a sentence to go with each word.

flower	environment
leaves	stem
nutrients	adapted
roots	prairie

Directions: Read the words and draw pictures to illustrate them or write sentences about them. Cut out the boxes to use as word cards.
Home Activity: Ask your child to identify the words that name parts of a plant (flower, leaf, roots, stem) and then explain how roots and nutrients, adapt and environment, and environment and prairie are related.

Workbook   Vocabulary Preview **1**

Workbook, p. 1

Use with How to Read Science, p. 5

Name _____ How to Read Science
Use with Chapter 1.

Ⓒ Predict

Read the science story.

Pine Cones
Pine trees do not grow flowers. They grow cones. Their seeds grow inside the cones. When the seeds are ready, the cones open and the seeds drop out of the cones. The seeds fall to the ground.

2 How to Read Science   Workbook

Workbook, p. 2

Use with How to Read Science, p. 5

Name _____ How to Read Science
Use with Chapter 1.

Apply It!
Predict what will happen to the pine tree seeds next. Fill in the graphic organizer.

I Know	**I Predict**
Possible answers: New plants grow from seeds. Seeds can grow in soil. Not all seeds grow into plants.	Possible answer: Some of the pine tree seeds will grow into new pine trees.

Directions: Read the Science Story and look at the pictures. Think about what you know about seeds and plants and write those facts in the I know box. Then write your prediction in the I predict box.
Home Activity: Your child learned about predicting. Put a pot of water on the stove and turn on the burner. Ask your child to predict what will happen to the water. Discuss how your child used what he or she knows about stoves and water to predict.

Workbook   How to Read Science **3**

Workbook, p. 3

Use with Lesson 1, pp. 6–9

Name _____ Think, Read, Learn
Use with pages 7–9.

What are the parts of a plant?

Before You Read Lesson 1

Read each sentence. Do you think it is true? Do you think it is not true? Circle the word or words after each sentence that tell what you think.

1. Plants get water and nutrients from the soil.   True   Not True
2. Roots make food for the plant.   True   Not True
3. The stem is one of the main parts of a plant.   True   Not True

After You Read Lesson 1

Read each sentence again. Circle the word or words after each sentence that tell what you think now. Did you change any answers? Put an **X** by each answer that you changed.

1. Plants get water and nutrients from the soil.   (True)   Not True
2. Roots make food for the plant.   True   (Not True)
3. The stem is one of the main parts of a plant.   (True)   Not True

Home Activity: Together talk about your child's answers. Have your child explain why his or her answers may have changed after reading the lesson.

Workbook   Think, Read, Learn **4**

Workbook, p. 4

Use with Lesson 2, pp. 10–11

Name _____ Think, Read, Learn
Use with pages 10–11.

How are seeds scattered?

Before You Read Lesson 2

Read each sentence. Do you think it is true? Do you think it is not true? Circle the word or words after each sentence that tell what you think.

1. *Scatter* means "to break into small pieces."   True   Not True
2. Seeds grow inside of fruits.   True   Not True
3. Air and water can carry seeds to new places.   True   Not True

After You Read Lesson 2

Read each sentence again. Circle the word or words after each sentence that tell what you think now. Did you change any answers? Put an **X** by each answer that you changed.

1. *Scatter* means "to break into small pieces."   True   (Not True)
2. Seeds grow inside of fruits.   (True)   Not True
3. Air and water can carry seeds to new places.   (True)   Not True

Home Activity: Together talk about your child's answers. Have your child explain why his or her answers may have changed after reading the lesson.

Workbook   Think, Read, Learn **5**

Workbook, p. 5

Use with Lesson 3, pp. 12–15

Name _____ Think, Read, Learn
Use with pages 12–15.

How are plants grouped?

Before You Read Lesson 3

Read each sentence. Do you think it is true? Do you think it is not true? Circle the word or words after each sentence that tell what you think.

1. All plants have flowers.   True   Not True
2. Plants with flowers grow only in gardens.   True   Not True
3. Some seeds grow inside cones.   True   Not True
4. Some plants do not make seeds.   True   Not True

After You Read Lesson 3

Read each sentence again. Circle the word or words after each sentence that tell what you think now. Did you change any answers? Put an **X** by each answer that you changed.

1. All plants have flowers.   True   (Not True)
2. Plants with flowers grow only in gardens.   True   (Not True)
3. Some seeds grow inside cones.   (True)   Not True
4. Some plants do not make seeds.   (True)   Not True

Home Activity: Together talk about your child's answers. Have your child explain why his or her answers may have changed after reading the lesson.

Workbook   Think, Read, Learn **6**

Workbook, p. 6

Use with Lesson 4, pp. 16–19

How are some woodland plants adapted?

Before You Read Lesson 4

Read each sentence. Do you think it is true? Do you think it is not true? Circle the word or words after each sentence that tell what you think.

1. Plants live in many different places.   True   Not True
2. Only trees live in a woodland.   True   Not True
3. Plants can adapt to live in a cold or wet place.   True   Not True

After You Read Lesson 4

Read each sentence again. Circle the word or words after each sentence that tell what you think now. Did you change any answers? Put an **X** by each answer that you changed.

1. Plants live in many different places.   (True)   Not True
2. Only trees live in a woodland.   True   (Not True)
3. Plants can adapt to live in a cold or wet place.   (True)   Not True

 Home Activity: Together talk about your child's answers. Have your child explain why his or her answers may have changed after reading the lesson.

Workbook   Think, Read, Learn   **7**

Workbook, p. 7

Use with Lesson 5, pp. 20–21

How are some prairie plants adapted?

Before You Read Lesson 5

Read each sentence. Do you think it is true? Do you think it is not true? Circle the word or words after each sentence that tell what you think.

1. A prairie has lots of trees and a little grass.   True   Not True
2. Summers on a prairie can be hot and dry.   True   Not True
3. Prairie plants have adapted to keep the water they need.   True   Not True

After You Read Lesson 5

Read each sentence again. Circle the word or words after each sentence that tell what you think now. Did you change any answers? Put an **X** by each answer that you changed.

1. A prairie has lots of trees and a little grass.   True   (Not True)
2. Summers on a prairie can be hot and dry.   (True)   Not True
3. Prairie plants have adapted to keep the water they need.   (True)   Not True

 Home Activity: Together talk about your child's answers. Have your child explain why his or her answers may have changed after reading the lesson.

Workbook   Think, Read, Learn   **8**

Workbook, p. 8

Use with Lesson 6, pp. 22–23

How are some desert plants adapted?

Before You Read Lesson 6

Read each sentence. Do you think it is true? Do you think it is not true? Circle the word or words after each sentence that tell what you think.

1. Deserts are very dry.   True   Not True
2. Desert plants do not need water.   True   Not True
3. A cactus holds water in its stem.   True   Not True

After You Read Lesson 6

Read each sentence again. Circle the word or words after each sentence that tell what you think now. Did you change any answers? Put an **X** by each answer that you changed.

1. Deserts are very dry.   (True)   Not True
2. Desert plants do not need water.   True   (Not True)
3. A cactus holds water in its stem.   (True)   Not True

 Home Activity: Together talk about your child's answers. Have your child explain why his or her answers may have changed after reading the lesson.

Workbook   Think, Read, Learn   **9**

Workbook, p. 9

Use with Lesson 7, pp. 24–25

How are some marsh plants adapted?

Before You Read Lesson 7

Read each sentence. Do you think it is true? Do you think it is not true? Circle the word or words after each sentence that tell what you think.

1. Some marsh plants get nutrients from water.   True   Not True
2. Some marsh plants get nutrients from insects.   True   Not True
3. The soil in a marsh has all the nutrients plants need.   True   Not True

After You Read Lesson 7

Read each sentence again. Circle the word or words after each sentence that tell what you think now. Did you change any answers? Put an **X** by each answer that you changed.

1. Some marsh plants get nutrients from water.   (True)   Not True
2. Some marsh plants get nutrients from insects.   (True)   Not True
3. The soil in a marsh has all the nutrients plants need.   True   (Not True)

Home Activity: Together talk about your child's answers. Have your child explain why his or her answers may have changed after reading the lesson.

Workbook   Think, Read, Learn   **10**

Workbook, p. 10

Use with Math in Science, pp. 28–29

Making Patterns

Anna collected maple and beech leaves. She arranged the leaves in two patterns.

Here is how Anna arranged the leaves.

Use what you know about Anna's patterns. Predict what two leaves Anna will add next. Draw two more leaves in each pattern.

 maple beech leaf leaf

 beech maple leaf leaf

Directions: Look closely at Anna's patterns. Note what the pattern is and when it repeats. Then draw the next two leaves in each pattern.
Home Activity: Your child learned about patterns. After your child explains how he or she continued the patterns on the page, use pennies and nickels to make two patterns like the leaf patterns.

Workbook   Math in Science   **11**

Workbook, p. 11

Chapter 1 Assessment Support

Use the following Workbook pages to support content and skill development as you teach Chapter 1. You can also view and print Workbook pages from the Online Teacher's Edition.

Assessment Options

Formal Assessment

- Chapter Review and Test Prep, SE pp. 30–31
- Assessment Book pp. 1–4
- Prescriptions for remediation are shown on TE p. 31

Performance Assessment

- Unit Wrap-Up, SE pp. 130–131

Ongoing Assessment

- Diagnostic Check, TE pp. 7, 13, 15, 17
- Scaffolded Questions, TE pp. 7, 9, 11, 13 15, 17, 19, 21, 23, 25, 29

Portfolio Assessment

- My Science Journal, TE pp. 8, 11, 14, 17, 19, 23

 **Success Tracker**

- Data management system to assess Adequate Yearly Progress (AYP) and provide intervention

ExamView®

- Alternative test formats are available online or through ExamView CD-ROM

Chapter 1 Test

Name _____   [Chapter 1 Test]

Read each question and choose the best answer. Then fill in the circle next to the correct answer.

1 Choose the best word to complete the sentence. Plants need food, water, air, space, and _____.
Ⓐ fruit
Ⓑ seeds
Ⓒ flowers
Ⓓ sunlight

2 Look at the picture of a plant.

Why is the circled part important?
Ⓕ It grows into the soil.
Ⓖ It makes food for the plant.
Ⓗ It takes water from the soil.
Ⓘ It carries water to the leaves.

Assessment Book   Chapter 1 Test **1**

Assessment Book, p. 1

Chapter 1 Test

Name _____   [Chapter 1 Test]

3 Look at the picture of a maple seed.

How do maple seeds travel?
Ⓐ by air
Ⓑ by water
Ⓒ by animals
Ⓓ by getting stuck on fur or feathers

4 Why does a Venus's-flytrap trap insects inside its leaves?
Ⓕ to get water
Ⓖ to make seeds
Ⓗ to get sunlight
Ⓘ to get nutrients

2 Chapter 1 Test   Assessment Book

Assessment Book, p. 2

Chapter 1 Test

Name _____   [Chapter 1 Test]

5 Read the chart.

Groups of Plants	
Plants with Flowers	**Plants without Flowers**
Fruit trees	Plants with cones
Cactus	Mosses
	Ferns

What is this chart about?
Ⓐ pine cones
Ⓑ plants that grow from seeds
Ⓒ plants grouped by their parts
Ⓓ plants with flowers that grow seeds

6 What makes up a plant's environment?
Ⓕ only animals
Ⓖ only living things
Ⓗ only nonliving things
Ⓘ both living and nonliving things

7 Which word completes the sentence? Plants that grow near rivers and streams are adapted to live where it is very _____.
Ⓐ hot
Ⓑ dry
Ⓒ wet
Ⓓ dark

Assessment Book   Chapter 1 Test **3**

Assessment Book, p. 3

Chapter 1 Test

Name _____   [Chapter 1 Test]

8 Look at the tree in the picture. Notice that it has lost its leaves.

The plant is adapted to its environment. Which environment is it from?
Ⓕ a river or stream
Ⓖ a woodland that gets cold in winter
Ⓗ a desert that is dry most of the year
Ⓘ a prairie that sometimes gets little water

Write the answers to the questions on the lines.

9 Choose a plant that grows on the prairie when there is little rain. Tell how the plant is adapted to the prairie. (2 points)
Answers should tell about goldenrod or prairie smoke. For example: Prairie smoke has fuzz that helps keep water in the plant.

10 Tell how the spines on an octopus tree help the plant's leaves keep the water they need. (2 points)
The spines protect the leaves from animals that try to eat them.

4 Chapter 1 Test   Assessment Book

Assessment Book, p. 4

You Will Discover

- how each part of a plant helps the plant live.
- where different kinds of plants live.

Chapter 1

All About Plants

online
Student Edition
pearsonsuccessnet.com

1

Chapter 1

All About Plants

⭐ **Science Objectives**

- The student knows that life occurs on or near the surface of the Earth in land, air, and water.
- The student understands that structures of living things are adapted to their function in specific environments.
- The student knows that there are many different kinds of living things that live in a variety of environments.
- The student knows that animals and plants can be associated with their environment by an examination of their structural characteristics.
- The student knows that people use scientific processes including hypothesis, making inferences, and recording and communicating data when exploring the natural world.

Quick | **TEACHING PLAN**

If time is short...
Use Build Background page to engage children in chapter content. Then do Explore Activity, How to Read Science, and Lessons 1, 3, 4, and 6.

💿 ## Professional Development

To enhance your qualifications in science:
- preview content in Life Science DVD Segments *Classification of Living Things* and *Characteristics of Organisms.*
- preview activity management techniques described in Activity DVD Unit A, Chapter 1.

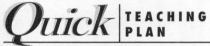
Take It to the NET

To access student resources:
1. Go to **www.pearsonsuccessnet.com.**
2. Click on the register button.
3. Enter the access code **frog** and your school's zip code.

Chapter 1 Concept Web

roots
stems ⟩— have four main parts
leaves
flowers

Plants —need— water / air / sunlight / space / nutrients

can be grouped as

having flowers   **not having flowers**

live in environments such as

woodlands   prairies   deserts   marshes

Children can create a concept web to organize ideas about plants.

Build Background

Science Objective

- The student identifies words and constructs meaning from text, illustrations, graphics, and charts, using the strategies of phonics, word structure, and context clues.

Chapter 1 Vocabulary Words

nutrients, p. 7
roots, p. 8
stem, p. 8
leaves, p. 8
flower, p. 9
environment, p. 16
adapted, p. 16
prairie, p. 20

1 | Introduce the Concept

Quick ACTIVITY

Explain to children that a habitat is a place where living things grow. Ask: **What might be living in a habitat?** Different plants and animals **Are all habitats the same?** Brainstorm a list of different kinds of habitats in the world, such as forests, deserts, ponds, and rivers. You may wish to show children pictures of different kinds of habitats. Point out that cities and towns are habitats too.

Discuss Essential Question

Many science vocabulary words are abstract. Use the pictures and labels on these pages to help you open a discussion about science concepts and build academic language.

Read the Chapter 1 Essential Question to children, **How do plants live in their habitats?** Use the pictures of the prairie, roots, and leaves to guide discussion. Ask questions such as: **What kind of habitat does the picture show? What do the flowers need to grow? What do the other pictures show? What are roots and leaves? How do parts of a plant help a plant live in its habitat?** Accept and discuss all answers. Tell children they will find out how plants live in their habitats.

Revisit the essential question with children as they work through this chapter.

stem

flower

nutrients

Nutrients are materials that living things need to live and grow.

2

roots

Build Background Resources

Workbook, p. 1

Graphic Organizer Transparency 1

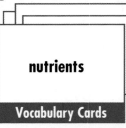

nutrients

Vocabulary Cards

ELL Support

Access Content Before reading the chapter text, lead children on a picture/text walk.

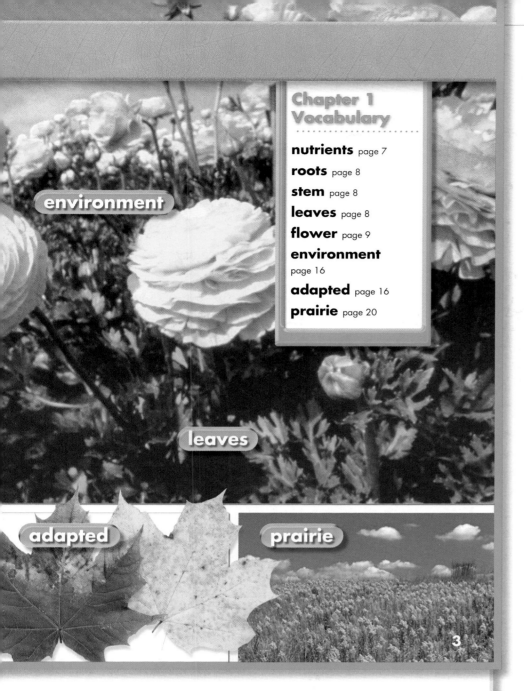

Chapter 1 Vocabulary

nutrients page 7

roots page 8

stem page 8

leaves page 8

flower page 9

environment page 16

adapted page 16

prairie page 20

environment

leaves

adapted

prairie

3

Science Misconception

Living Things and Nonliving Things

Some children may believe that only animals are living things, and that plants are not. Two characteristics shared by all living things are their need for food and their ability to grow. To help children understand that plants are living things, generate a discussion about what plants need to live and grow. (Sunlight, water, nutrient-rich soil, air) Emphasize that sunlight, water, and air are used by plants to make food.

Science Background

Minerals in Soil

Soil contains various minerals and decaying plant and animal matter. Plants take up minerals in soil through their roots. To be healthy, plants need soil that contains the minerals nitrogen, potassium, and phosphorus.

2 | Introduce Vocabulary

Use the following K-W-L chart provided on **pearsonsuccessnet.com** or Graphic Organizer Transparency 1.

	K What I Know	W What I Want to Know	L What I Learned
nutrients			
roots			
stem			
leaves			
flower			
environment			
adapted			
prairie			

List vocabulary words under the first column. Explain to children that you will fill in the "K" and "W" columns of the chart together.

- Pronounce each word. Solicit information from children as you fill in the "K" column. For example, children may have prior knowledge that roots grow into the ground.
- Guide children as you fill in the "W" column of the chart. A possible question might be, "What are some nutrients?"
- Encourage children to add a note in the "W" column when they learn what they wanted to know.
- Tell children they will fill in the last column after reading the chapter.

Word Recognition Use the Vocabulary Cards to reinforce recognition of each written word and its definition.

3 | Practice

Vocabulary Strategy: Which Word?

Using the Vocabulary Cards, read the definition of a vocabulary word aloud. Ask: **Which word is that?**

Ask students to participate in a form appropriate to their level of skill:

- choral response
- telling a partner
- pointing to the word in the pictures
- selecting the word from the Vocabulary Cards

Explore Do plants need water?

⭐ Science Objective

- The student knows that people use scientific processes including hypothesis, making inferences, and recording and communicating data when exploring the natural world.

1 | Build Background

Children observe plants not watered and predict effect of watering plants.

Managing Time and Materials

Time:	5 minutes for set up, 5 minutes on Day 2, 10 minutes on Day 3
Groups:	small groups
Materials:	1 stalk of celery with leaves; *1 clear plastic jar, 16 oz*; water (about $\frac{2}{3}$ c); pouring container

Materials listed in *italics* are kit materials.

Advance Preparation

Cut a 10 in. long piece of celery for each group. Fill each pouring container with about $\frac{2}{3}$ c water.

2 | What to Do

Engage Review the activity objective together.

Explore Observe a celery stalk with no water for a full day. Predict the effect of water added.

Explain Ask groups to explain what happened to the celery stalks on the second and third days.

Extend Cut the celery stalk to show the tubes.

Evaluate Have children describe the importance of water to the survival of plants.

3 | Explain Your Results

The stalk will droop because it loses water.

Process Skills

Tell children to use what they know about plants and what they observed to help them **predict**.

Explore Do plants need water?

Materials

celery

jar

water

What to Do

1 Put celery in the jar. Look at the celery.

2 Wait 1 day. How did the celery change?

3 Put water in the jar. **Predict** what will happen to the celery.

4 Wait 1 day. How did the celery change? Why did it change?

Explain Your Results

Predict What will happen if you take the celery out of the water?

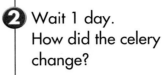
Process Skills

You **predict** when you tell what you think might happen.

 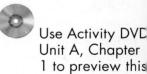

Activity Resources

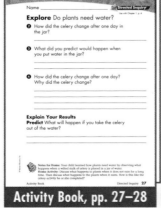

Activity Book, pp. 27–28

Activity Rubric

Use Activity DVD Unit A, Chapter 1 to preview this activity.

Call 1-888-537-4908 with activity questions.

More Lab zone Activities Take It to the Net
pearsonsuccessnet.com

Find more about this activity at our Web site.

- See the **Teacher's Activity Guide** for more support.
- An alternative activity is also available to download.

Reading Skills

Predict

Predict means to tell what you think might happen next.

Science Story

Workers plant celery seeds in little pots. When the seeds begin to grow, farmers move the young plants to fields. The farmers cut the celery when it is grown.

Apply It!

Predict what will happen to the celery next. Make a graphic organizer to help you.

I Know → I Predict

5

How to Read Science Resource

Workbook, pp. 2–3

ELL Support

For more practice on **Predict,** use **Every Student Learns Teacher's Guide,** p. 1.

Predict

Reading Objective

• The student uses a variety of strategies to comprehend text (for example, self-monitoring, predicting, retelling, discussing, restating ideas).

About the Target Skill

The target skill for *All About Plants* is **Predict.** Children are introduced to the skill as you guide them through this page.

1 | Introduce

Ask children to think about what they would do if they were thirsty and were handed a glass of water. Ask: **What do you think you would do next?** Drink the water Say: **You can predict that you would drink the water because you know that thirsty people drink something if they have the chance.**

2 | Model the Skill

Read the Science Story as a class. Ask: **What is the story about?** Growing celery **What did you learn about growing celery?** Farmers grow celery from seeds to plants. Then they cut the plants. Say: **Now think about what you know about foods after they have been grown and picked.**

3 | Practice

Graphic Organizer

Look at the Graphic Organizer together. Work with children to complete the Graphic Organizer using the facts from the Science Story.

Apply It!

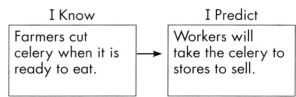

I Know → I Predict

| Farmers cut celery when it is ready to eat. | Workers will take the celery to stores to sell. |

What are the parts of a plant?

 Science Objective

- The student knows the basic needs of all living things.

1 Introduce

Quick ACTIVITY | **TRANSPARENCY 1**

Ask children to name a plant that grows outside. (Possible answers: trees; grass; bushes; flowers) Ask: **How are these plants alike?** Possible answers: They are green. They grow. They are pretty.

Access Prior Knowledge

Ask children to think about the plants they just named. Ask: **What do you think plants need in order to live?** Possible answers: water, soil, air, sunlight **How do you think plants get these things?** Accept reasonable answers.

Set Purpose

Tell children they are going to read about plants and their parts. Help them set a **purpose for reading,** such as finding out how different parts of plants help plants get what they need to live.

2 Teach

Quick SUMMARY

- Plants need water, air, sunlight, nutrients, and space to grow.
- The parts of a plant help the plant get what it needs.

Sing or play "Plants" for children. Read page 7 together. On the board, list things plants need. Say: **Plants are living things. They need water, air, sunlight, and space to grow. They also need nutrients.** Tell children that nutrients are materials that plants get from the soil. Nutrients contain important minerals such as nitrogen, potassium, and phosphorus. Explain to children that bigger plants need more nutrients, water, air, space, and sunlight.

♪ Plants

Sung to the tune of "Where, Oh, Where Has My Little Dog Gone?"
Lyrics by Gerri Brioso & Richard Freitas/The Dovetail Group, Inc.

Plants have roots that grow in soil,
And hold the plant in place.
The roots take in water and nutrients,
And carry them up to the stem.

6 Science Songs ♪♪♫

Lesson 1 Resource

Workbook, p. 4

 Science Songs ♪♪♫

Use the Science Songs CD to play "Plants" for the class.

Lesson 1

What are the parts of a plant?

Plants need water, air, and sunlight. Plants need space to grow. Plants need nutrients. **Nutrients** are materials that living things need to live and grow. Many plants get nutrients from soil and water.

The parts of a plant help it get food, water, air, and sunlight.

7

ELL Leveled Support

Taking Care of Plants

Beginning Show a living plant to children.
Say: ***This is a plant***. Have children repeat after you. Encourage discussion about what plants need by helping children fill in the cloze sentence: ***Plants need _____.*** (air, water, sunlight, food, space). Point to these things in the classroom or in a picture to check for understanding.

Intermediate Help children create a checklist on the board that would be given to a friend who will be taking care of a plant.

Advanced Help children create a list of full-sentence "do's and don'ts" on the board for a friend coming to care for a plant.

Assign Quick Study pp. 2–3 to children who need help with lesson content.

Guide Comprehension

Ask children the following scaffolded questions to assess understanding.

Scaffolded Questions

1 **Define** ***What are nutrients?*** Materials that living things need to live and grow

2 **List** ***What do all plants need?*** Water, air, sunlight, space, nutrients

3 **Predict** ***Suppose you are taking care of a plant in a pot. If the pot tipped over and the soil fell out, what would happen to the plant?*** The plant could not live.

Extend Vocabulary

Tell children that the word **nutrient** comes from a Latin word that means "feed or keep alive." Children may know other words from the same root. These words include *nutrition*, which means "food or nourishment," and *nutritious*, which means "having value as a food." Write the words on the board, and say each aloud. Invite students to make up sentences using the words.

Diagnostic Check

If... children have difficulty understanding what plants need to grow,

then... point out that plants are living things, like animals. Ask: ***What does a lion need?*** Water, air, food, space ***Does a big lion need more things such as food than a lion cub? Why?*** Yes. It is bigger.

⭐ Science Objective

- The student knows the main parts of plants (stem, leaves, roots, flowers).

2 Teach (continued)

Quick SUMMARY

- The four main plant parts are roots, stem, leaves, and flowers.
- Different plant parts help the plant in different ways so that the plant can live, grow, and make new plants.

Tell children that all living things grow and make new living things. The new living things are like the living things they come from. To grow and make new living things, plants need food, water, and air. Read pages 8–9 with children. Use the illustrations to discuss how each plant part helps the plant meet its needs. Ask: **How do water and nutrients from the soil move through the plant?** Roots take water and nutrients from the soil and carry them to the stem. The stem carries water and nutrients to the leaves.

Plant Parts

Plants have different parts. The four main parts are the roots, stem, leaves, and flowers.

Roots grow down into the soil. Roots hold the plant in place. Roots take water and nutrients from the soil to the stem.

1 The **stem** carries water and nutrients to the leaves. The stem holds up the plant.

3 Green **leaves** take in sunlight and air. They use sunlight, air, water, and nutrients to make food for the plant.

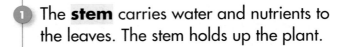

Leaves

Roots

8

My Science Journal

Plant Parts

Have children make a two-column chart. The first column should list the four plant parts. The second column should tell what each part does.

Science Misconception

Roots

- Roots don't always grow into the ground. For example, a banyan tree has aerial roots that grow into the air and catch rainwater.
- Roots can store water and nutrients. Root vegetables include yams, carrots, radishes, and turnips.

ELL Support

Multiple Meanings

The word *plant* has three different meanings. It can name something that grows. It can also describe the action of "putting something in the ground to grow." *Plant* can also refer to a building having machinery to produce something.

Many plants have flowers. A **flower** makes seeds. These seeds might grow into new plants.

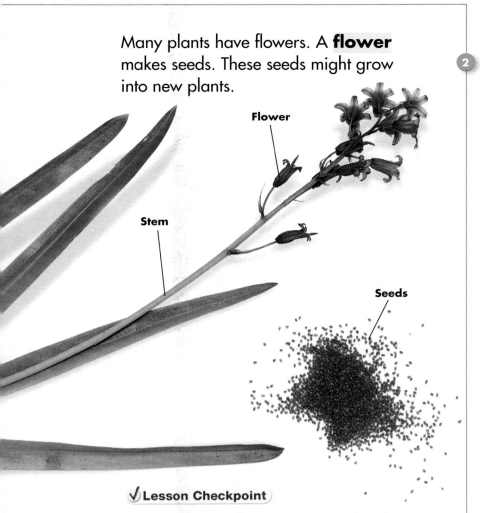

Flower

Stem

Seeds

②

✓ **Lesson Checkpoint**

1. What are the four main parts of a plant?

2. Writing in Science
   Write a sentence in your journal. Tell why the stem of a plant is important.

9

ELL Leveled Support

Describe Parts of a Plant

Beginning On the board, write the names of plant parts: roots, stem, leaves, flower. Below this, draw a simple diagram of a sunflower showing its roots, stem, leaves, and flower. Point to each part. Ask children to name it.

Intermediate On the board, draw a simple diagram of a sunflower showing its roots, stem, leaves, and flower. Prepare four cards. They should contain the names of the plant parts, one part per card. Call on volunteers to pick a card. Have the child match that name with the correct part on the drawing on the board.

Advanced Tell children to draw a plant, showing the roots, stem, leaves, and flower. They should label each part. Below the drawing, they should write a sentence about each part to tell what it does.

For scaffolded instruction about plant parts, use **Every Student Learns Teacher's Guide,** p. 2.

Guide Comprehension

Ask children the following scaffolded questions to assess understanding.

Scaffolded Questions

① **Identify** *What part holds up the plant?* Stem

② **Explain** *Why is a flower important?* It makes new seeds that might grow into new plants.

③ **Process** *What plant part makes new food for the plant? How does it do this?* Leaves make new food for the plant. They use sunlight, air, and water to make food.

Extend Vocabulary

Tell children that some words can have more than one meaning. Write the word **roots** on the board. Remind children that roots can be the part of a plant that grows under the ground. Explain that roots can also be where people's families come from, or where people grew up. Many Americans have their roots in places throughout the world, such as in Europe, Africa, or Asia. Call on volunteers to tell what their family's roots are, such as a specific continent, country, or town.

3 | Assess

✓ **Lesson Checkpoint**

1. The four main parts of a plant are the roots, stem, leaves, and flower.

2. Writing in Science Have children write their answers in their science journals. The stem holds up the plant. The stem carries water and nutrients to the leaves.

Lesson 2

How are seeds scattered?

 Science Objective

- The student understands that structures of living things are adapted to their function in specific environments.

1 | Introduce

Ask children: **What are some ways that seeds travel?** Then tell children that they will build a model to demonstrate how seeds travel by wind. Show Quick Activity Transparency 2. Give a strip of paper and a paperclip to each child or a pair. Tell them to fold the paper in half, put a paperclip over the fold, and fold the ends down. Then have them toss the paper in the air. Ask: **How might this paper model of a seed travel in the wind?** Explain that the folded paper has "wings" like some seeds.

Access Prior Knowledge

Use the pictures to discuss different fruits and predict how they travel. Ask: **Do all the fruits look alike? Which looks like it has wings? Which looks like it can float? Which might get stuck on an animal?**

Set Purpose

Tell children you are going to read to them about some different kinds of seeds and how they travel. Help them set a **purpose for listening,** such as to discover ways that seeds travel.

2 | Teach

Quick SUMMARY

- Different fruits have different shapes that help them travel to new places.
- Fruits travel by air, by water, and by getting stuck on people and animals that travel.

Read pages 10–11 to children. Use the pictures to point out ways that the shapes of the different fruits help them travel.

Lesson 2

How are seeds scattered?

Many new plants grow from seeds. Suppose you plant seeds. You would scatter the seeds in the soil. Scatter means to spread out. The seeds have space to grow.

Fruits cover and protect seeds. When fruits travel, the seeds inside are scattered. Some fruits are scattered by air or water. Some fruits get stuck on the fur or feathers of animals. Scattering helps carry seeds to new places where they might grow.

✓ **Lesson Checkpoint**

1. Name 3 ways that seeds travel.

2.  **Predict** A maple tree fruit spins to the ground. It lands in an open field. What do you think might happen next?

10

Lesson 2 Resource

Workbook, p. 5

ELL Support

For scaffolded instruction about how seeds travel, use **Every Student Learns Teacher's Guide**, p. 3.

The fruits of a maple tree are shaped like wings. This shape helps them travel through the air.

The fruits of the water lily float on lakes and streams.

Burrs are fruits. Burrs travel by sticking on clothing or fur. This dog has burrs stuck to its fur.

11

My Science Journal

Plant Seeds

Have children observe each of the three fruits and make simple drawings of them. Then have them write a caption for each drawing. The caption should name the fruit and tell how it travels.

Science Background

An Idea From Nature

The idea for the nylon hook-and-loop fastener used in place of zippers and other fasteners was suggested by burrs, which stuck firmly to the clothing of George de Mestral, a Swiss mountain climber. His invention was originally called "locking tape."

ELL Support

Fruits

Children may think that the word *fruit* refers only to edible fruits. Explain that a fruit is the part where the seeds are. Ask students to name fruits. Then discuss what kinds of seeds each fruit has.

Focus children's attention on the three images. Ask: **Which fruit is scattered by air? Which is stuck to an animal's fur?** The maple; the burr
Assign Quick Study pp. 4–5 to children who need help with lesson content.

Guide Comprehension

Ask children the following scaffolded questions to assess understanding.

Scaffolded Questions

1 Compare *In what ways are fruits different?* They have different sizes, shapes, and travel in different ways.

2 Dramatize *Show how the fruit of a maple tree travels through the air.* The child should spin with arms outstretched.

3 Analyze *How might a small seed get from one island to another?* Possible answers: float on water, be carried by wind, be carried by a bird

Extend Vocabulary

Write the words *fur* and *fir* on the board. Have children say the words aloud. Ask: **In what way are the words the same?** Sound the same **How are the words different?** Spelled differently, have different meanings Tell children that words that sound alike but are spelled differently and have different meanings are called homophones. Tell children that a *fir* is a plant. It is a kind of evergreen tree. *Fur* is a body covering. Ask children to write a sentence using each word correctly.

3 Assess

✓ Lesson Checkpoint

1. Seeds travel by water, wind, and by getting hooked onto fur, feathers, or clothes.

2. ◉ **Predict** If there is soil in the open field, the fruit might go into the soil and the seed might begin to grow.

Lesson 3

How are plants grouped?

 Science Objectives

- The student knows that the structural characteristics of plants and animals are used to group them.
- The student understands different ways in which living things can be grouped (for example, plants/animals, edible plants/non-edible plants).

1 Introduce

Quick ACTIVITY | TRANSPARENCY 3

Bring a variety of fruits to class, such as an apple, plum, peach, and bell pepper. Cut each to reveal the seeds. Display the fruits and their seeds. Have children describe what they see.

Access Prior Knowledge

Tell children to describe their favorite fruit. Ask if they know where the seeds are. Point out that fruits come from flowering plants.

Set Purpose

Tell children they are going to read about flowering plants. Help them set a **purpose for reading,** such as to discover how seeds are protected by fruits.

2 Teach

Quick SUMMARY

- There are two groups of plants. One group has flowers. The other group does not have flowers.
- Flowers form fruits that cover and protect the seeds inside.
- Cactus plants grow in the desert. Their flowers form seeds.

Read pages 12–13 with children. Ask: **How are all the plants in this lesson alike?** They all have flowers. Explain to children that flowers become fruits as a result of a process called *pollination.* Bees and birds help in this process.

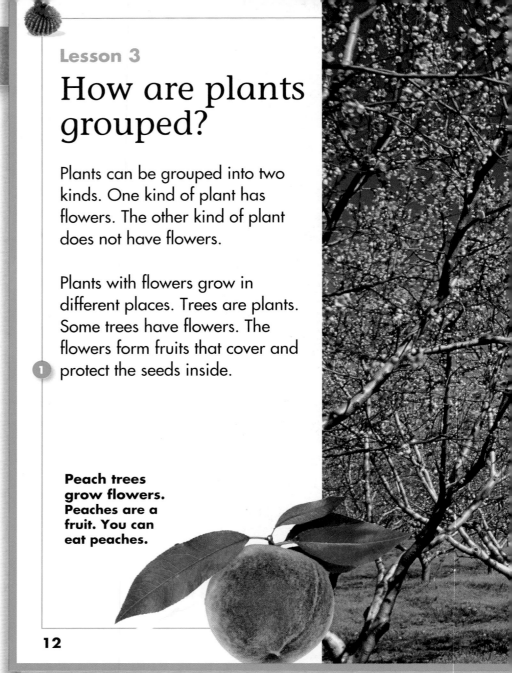

How are plants grouped?

Plants can be grouped into two kinds. One kind of plant has flowers. The other kind of plant does not have flowers.

Plants with flowers grow in different places. Trees are plants. Some trees have flowers. The flowers form fruits that cover and protect the seeds inside.

Peach trees grow flowers. Peaches are a fruit. You can eat peaches.

12

Lesson 3 Resource

Workbook, p. 6

Cactus plants grow in the desert. Their flowers form seeds. Some seeds fall into the sand. New cactus plants might grow.

Saguaro cactus flowers open during cool nights.

1. ✓**Checkpoint** How are plants grouped?

2. **Health** in Science Name some fruits that you can eat.

Social Studies Link

Your State Flower

Have children use the Internet or other resources to find out about their state flower. Ask them to write about it in their science journals, telling the name of the flower and describing what it looks like. They can also draw a picture of the flower.

Science Background

More About the Saguaro

- The saguaro flower is the state flower of Arizona. The saguaro cactus is the largest cactus of the United States. It stores water in its thick stem and branches.

Edible and Nonedible Plants

- Another way to group plants is whether or not parts of the plants can be eaten. Examples of edible plants are broccoli, chives, lettuce, and soybeans.

Assign Quick Study pp. 6–7 to children who need help with lesson content.

Guide Comprehension

Ask children the following scaffolded questions to assess understanding.

Scaffolded Questions

1. **Name** *Which plant part protects seeds?* Fruit

2. **Predict** *What might happen if violet seeds fall into soft soil?* New violet plants might grow.

3. **Understand** *How do flowers make it possible for the plant to make more plants?* The flowers form seeds. The seeds can grow into new plants.

Extend Vocabulary

On the board, write *one flower/two _____.* Say: **When you write about more than one, you have to use the plural form of a word. What is the plural form of flower?** Write *flowers* on the blank. Repeat with *one stem, two _____, one fruit, two _____, one tree, two _____,* and *one plant, two _____.* Help children generalize the rule that to form the plural of many nouns, add *–s.*

Diagnostic Check

If... children have difficulty understanding that many plants have flowers,

then... display pictures of plants that do not have showy flowers. For example, show the flowers on clover, pea and onion plants, and local weeds.

3 | Assess

1. ✓**Checkpoint** Plants can be put into two groups. One group has flowers, the other group does not have flowers.

2. **Health** in Science Accept reasonable answers.

 Plants Without Flowers

Not all plants have flowers. Some plants have cones. Seeds grow inside the cones. When a cone opens, the seeds fall out. Some seeds grow into new trees.

Mosses are tiny plants that do not have flowers. Mosses do not make seeds or fruits. Mosses do not have leaves, roots, or stems.

Ferns do not have flowers. Ferns do not make seeds. Ferns have leaves, roots, and stems.

✓ Lesson Checkpoint

1. What grows inside cones?
2. **Art** in Science Draw a forest. Label trees, mosses, and ferns.

14

★ Science Objective

- The student knows that the structural characteristics of plants and animals are used to group them.

2 Teach (continued)

Quick SUMMARY

- Plants that do not have flowers include cone-bearing trees, mosses, and ferns.
- Cone-bearing trees have cones that hold seeds.

Read pages 14–15 with children. Point to the pictures of the pine trees and pinecone on page 15. Ask: **What grows inside a pinecone?** Seeds Look at the pictures of moss and fern. Ask: **How are pine trees, mosses, and ferns alike?** They do not have flowers.

My Science Journal

Plants Without Flowers

Have children write one or two questions they have about plants without flowers and how they might find answers to their questions.

ELL Support

Language Detectives: Comparative Forms

Provide the following sentence frames and comparative forms of *big, tall,* and *small.* Help children choose the appropriate form of each word to go in each sentence.

This tree is _____.

This tree is _____ than that tree.

This is the _____ tree in the forest.

For scaffolded instruction about plants that have no flowers, use **Every Student Learns Teacher's Guide,** p. 4.

Pine trees have cones. ①

Mosses often grow on wet rocks. ③

Some ferns live in warm, shady, wet places. ②

15

Lesson 4

How are some woodland plants adapted?

 Science Objectives

- The student understands that structures of living things are adapted to their function in specific environments.
- The student knows that plants and animals are adapted to different ranges of temperature and moisture.
- The student understands that living organisms need to be adapted to their environment to survive.

1 | Introduce

Quick ACTIVITY   TRANSPARENCY 4

Review with children the names of the four seasons. Point out that in some parts of the country, the weather changes a great deal with each season.

Access Prior Knowledge

Ask children what they do to keep themselves warm when the weather gets chilly. Then ask how they stay cool when the weather gets warm. Point out that these are different ways to adapt to different environments. Tell children that plants are adapted to the different environments in which they are found. Some of these adaptations can be seen in the structures of the plants.

Set Purpose

Tell children you are going to read to them about how some woodland plants are adapted. Help them set a **purpose for listening,** such as to discover these ways.

2 | Teach

Quick SUMMARY

- A plant's environment includes all the living and nonliving things around it.
- Living things have adapted, or changed, to live in their environment.

How are some woodland plants adapted?

Plants live almost everywhere. A plant's **environment** is all the living and nonliving things around it.

Living things have **adapted,** or changed, to live in their environment.

Many kinds of plants grow in a woodland environment. Pine trees are adapted to live in cold weather. Pine trees have small leaves that are shaped like needles.

Pine tree leaves are adapted to keep from drying out in cold weather.

Lesson 4 Resource

Workbook, p. 7

SciLinks Take It to the Net
pearsonsuccessnet.com

Technology Link

Children can go online to discover more about **environment** by using the NSTA SciLink available at **pearsonsuccessnet.com.**

Maple tree leaves turn color in the fall. ②

Maple trees are adapted to live where summers are warm and winters are cold. Maple trees have large flat leaves. The maple tree loses its leaves in winter. This helps the tree keep the water it needs to live in winter. ③

1. ✓**Checkpoint** How are pine trees adapted to their environment?

2. **Math** in Science Find a leaf outside. Use paper clips and counters to measure it.

17

My Science Journal

Predict Plant Changes

Have children name or describe different plants in the area. Discuss any changes in the plants' appearance during the different seasons. Have children write a prediction about what is likely to happen to one of the plants in the next two seasons.

Math Link

Symmetry in Nature

- Fold a sheet of paper in half. Cut half of a heart shape along the fold. Unfold the paper and ask children to identify the figure. Ask how each side of the fold is like the other side. Explain that when you fold something in half and the two halves match, there is symmetry.

- Divide the class into groups of four or five. Give each group several differently shaped leaves to examine to see if they have symmetry. Groups should then compare findings.

Read pages 16–17 to children. Use the pictures to point out different seasons.

Explain that pine trees are evergreens—trees that are green all year. Like other evergreens, pine trees have leaves that are adapted to cold weather. Point out that weather is part of a plant's environment.

Assign Quick Study pp. 8–9 to children who need help with lesson content.

3 | Assess

1. ✓**Checkpoint** Their leaves are adapted to keep from drying out in cold weather.

2. **Math** in Science Assess children's answers. Children can also use counting bears.

Science Objectives

- The student understands that structures of living things are adapted to their function in specific environments.
- The student knows that plants and animals are adapted to different ranges of temperature and moisture.
- The student understands that living organisms need to be adapted to their environment to survive.
- The student knows that animals and plants can be associated with their environment by an examination of their structural characteristics (for example, physical structures are adaptations that allow plants and animals to survive, such as gills in fish, lungs in mammals).

2 | Teach (continued)

Quick SUMMARY

- Some plants are adapted to the wet habitats along river and stream banks.
- Structures that help these plants survive include roots, sharp hairs, and thin leaves.

Read pages 18–19 to children. Ask: **Where do these plants live?** On the banks of rivers and streams Use the pictures to point out that the plants are living in a wet environment in the woods. Ask: **How is the cardinal plant adapted to the wet environment?** Its roots are adapted to get nutrients from the moist soil. Note the shape of the fanwort leaves. Ask: **How is the plant adapted to its environment?** Water moves easily through the leaves. Discuss how the stem of the nettle helps the plant survive.

Plants That Live Near Water

Some plants in a woodland environment live near rivers and streams.

 Plants that grow near rivers and streams are adapted to live where it is very wet.

This red plant is called a cardinal plant. The roots of a cardinal plant are adapted to get nutrients from the moist soil in a woodland.

Cardinal plant

✔ Lesson Checkpoint

1. How is a fanwort adapted to its wet habitat?

2. **Social Studies** in Science
Look at a map. Find a river or stream in your state.

18

Science Background

Nettles

The stinging nettle grows along rivers and streams. Most animals will not eat this plant because the nettle's stem and leaves have hairs that give animals a painful rash. People should be careful around the stinging nettle too. The sharp hairs of the nettle are hollow. When they break off in a person's skin, they inject a stinging liquid.

Art Link

Habitats

Have children work in groups of four. Assign each group a different habitat, such as a forest, a stream, or a garden. Briefly discuss each habitat. Have each group work to create a picture of its habitat. Then have children determine how the habitats are alike and different.

The stinging nettle has tiny, sharp hairs on its stem. The hairs protect the plant from animals that want to eat it.

The fanwort is adapted to live in water. Water can move through the thin leaves of the plant.

My Science Journal

Danger: Stinging Nettles

As a class, write a catchy two or three sentence warning about the danger of getting too close to a stinging nettle. Then have children write one of their own.

ELL Support

Language Detectives: Building Vocabulary

Tell children that rivers and streams are two environments that have water. Ask children to name others. (Lake, pond, brook, sea, ocean, waterfall) List children's responses on the board. Then ask children to use words to describe each place. Point out that each of these places has plants that are adapted to live in wet environments.

For scaffolded instruction about plants adapted to wet environments, use **Every Student Learns Teacher's Guide,** p. 5.

Lesson 5

How are some prairie plants adapted?

 Science Objectives

- The student understands that the amount of food, water, space, and shelter needed is dependent on the size and kind of living things.
- The student knows that plants and animals are adapted to different ranges of temperature and moisture.
- The student knows that animals and plants can be associated with their environment by an examination of their structural characteristics (for example, physical structures are adaptations that allow plants to survive, such as gills in fish, lungs in mammals).

1 | Introduce

Quick ACTIVITY — TRANSPARENCY 5

Ask children: **What is a prairie?** Tell them to look at the pictures on pages 20–21. Then have them draw a picture of a prairie.

Access Prior Knowledge

Use the pictures to elicit a discussion about prairies. Ask **What can you find out about prairies from looking at the pictures?**

Set Purpose

Tell children you are going to read to them about plants on the prairie. Help them set a **purpose for listening,** such as to discover ways that plants are adapted to live on prairies.

2 | Teach

Quick SUMMARY

- Prairies are places with lots of grass and few trees. Many prairies have summers that can be hot with little rain.
- The physical characteristics of prairie plants help them keep water they need.

Lesson 5

How are some prairie plants adapted?

A **prairie** is flat land with lots of grass and few trees. Many prairies have hot summers with little rain. Some prairie plants are adapted to keep water when there is not enough rain.

Goldenrod plants have stiff stems and leaves. The stems and leaves help the plants keep the water they need to live.

Goldenrod

✓ Lesson Checkpoint

1. How are goldenrod plants adapted?

2. **Writing** in Science Write a sentence in your **science journal.** Tell how prairie plants are different from woodland plants.

20

Lesson 5 Resource

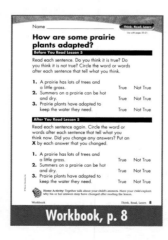

Workbook, p. 8

ELL Support

Plant Clues

Tell children that the name of a plant may be a clue to the way the plant looks. Discuss which part of the prairie smoke might look like smoke.

Prairie smoke has fuzz on its stems and leaves. The fuzz helps the plant keep the water it needs.

Prairie grasses have thin leaves. The leaves help the plants keep the water they need.

3

21

Read pages 20–21 to children. Use the pictures to point out how the plants are adapted.

Say: **Look at the goldenrod and grasses. What are their leaves like?** Long and narrow Point out that the slender leaves are able to catch light but lose little water. Point out the fuzzy hairs on the prairie smoke, which trap air and help keep the plant moist.

Assign Quick Study pp. 10–11 to children who need help with lesson content.

Guide Comprehension

Ask children the following scaffolded questions to assess understanding.

Scaffolded Questions

1 **Name** *What kind of environment has lots of grass, few trees, and little rain in summer?* Prairie

2 **Describe** *How does goldenrod look?* Possible answer: It has stiff stems and leaves and yellow flowers.

3 **Invent** *If you were inventing a new kind of plant that would grow well on the prairie, what would it be like? Describe its parts.* Possible answer: It would have stiff, narrow leaves with fuzz on them.

Extend Vocabulary

Remind children that prairie plants are adapted to very hot weather and little rain. Ask children what the word *little* means in that sentence. (Not much) Write the word *little* on the board. Ask children if they know another word that means the same, or almost the same as *little*. (Small, tiny) Tell children that words that mean the same or almost the same are called synonyms. Ask children to name synonyms for the word *big*. (Large, huge, gigantic)

3 | Assess

✓ Lesson Checkpoint

1. The plant's stiff stems and leaves help it keep water.

2. Possible answer: Woodland plants are adapted to live where it is very wet while prairie plants are adapted to keep water when there is little rain.

Science Background

More About Prairies

- Prairie land is flat or rolling grassland, bordered by woodlands.
- Many prairie plants have extensive root systems. About two-thirds of the plants' growth may be underground. This helps protect the plant from the Sun and the heat of prairie fires.
- The American prairies are rich farmland.

Technology Link

Find Out About Prairies

Children can go to this Web site to find an article about the prairies. **http://www.bellmuseum.org/distancelearning/prairie/index.html**

ELL Support

For scaffolded instruction about how prairie plants are adapted, use **Every Student Learns Teacher's Guide**, p. 6.

Lesson 6

How are some desert plants adapted?

 Science Objectives

- The student understands that structures of living things are adapted to their function in specific environments.
- The student knows that plants and animals are adapted to different ranges of temperature and moisture.
- The student knows that animals and plants can be associated with their environment by an examination of their structural characteristics (for example, physical structures are adaptations that allow plants to survive, such as gills in fish, lungs in mammals).

1 | Introduce

Quick ACTIVITY | TRANSPARENCY 6 |

Show children some desert pictures, including the picture on pages 22–23. Ask: **What do you know about a desert?** Have children draw a picture of something that can be found in a desert.

Access Prior Knowledge

Ask children what happens to the soil and plants when there are long periods without rain. (Soil gets dry and plants begin to droop.)

Set Purpose

Tell children they are going to read about plants that live in the desert. Help them set a **purpose for reading,** such as to discover ways that plants are adapted to live in a desert environment.

2 | Teach

Quick SUMMARY

- Desert plants are adapted to keep needed water in the sunny, hot, and dry environment.
- The saguaro cactus holds water in its stem.

Lesson 6
How are some desert plants adapted?

Many deserts are sunny and hot during the day. Deserts can be cool at night. Very little rain falls in a desert environment.

Some desert plants are adapted to hold water for a long time. The desert almond has leaves that grow in different directions. Some leaves get less sunlight than others. Leaves that get less sunlight can keep the water they need to live.

Desert almond

✓ Lesson Checkpoint

1. Tell about the leaves of a desert almond.

2. **Social Studies** in Science
   Find Arizona on a map. Name a desert in Arizona.

22

Lesson 6 Resource

How are some desert plants adapted?

Workbook, p. 9

The saguaro cactus has a long, thick stem that holds water.

The octopus tree has long spines. The spines protect the plant from animals that want to eat the leaves.

My Science Journal

Write About Environments

Tell children they have learned about different environments: woodlands, woodlands near water, prairie, and desert. In their science journals, have them write what they have learned about each environment and the kinds of plants that grow there. Invite them to illustrate their descriptions. They can also tell if they live in or near any of these environments.

ELL Support

Holding Water

Children may find the word *hold* confusing here. Point out that *hold* means not only "to pick up and keep something in your hand" but also "to keep something where it is." A cactus stem that holds water keeps water inside.

For scaffolded instruction about desert plants, use **Every Student Learns Teacher's Guide,** p. 7.

Read pages 22–23 with children. Use the pictures to discuss adaptations of the plants to the desert environment.

Assign Quick Study pp. 12–13 to children who need help with lesson content.

Guide Comprehension

Ask children the following scaffolded questions to assess understanding.

Scaffolded Questions

1 Identify *What protects the leaves of an octopus tree?* Spines

2 Explain *How can having parts in the shade help a desert plant?* It loses less water. Sunlight dries a plant.

3 Predict *Suppose you planted a plant from a wet environment in the desert. How would it do? Explain.* Possible answer: It would dry out and die. It is not adapted to the dry environment.

Extend Vocabulary

Write the word *desert* on the board and ask a volunteer to pronounce it. Point out that another word has the same spelling but a different history and meaning. Also, it is pronounced differently. The word is *desert* (di ZERT), which means "to go away and leave a person or place." Tell children that words that look the same but have different histories and meanings are called *homographs*. Write these examples on the board: *bow* (a weapon, an action); *live* (being alive; existing); *wind* (moving air; turn). Discuss the words and have children use them in sentences.

3 | Assess

✓ Lesson Checkpoint

1. They grow in different directions. Some are always in the shade and can hold more water.

2. **Social Studies** in Science The Sonoran Desert

Lesson 7

How are some marsh plants adapted?

 Science Objectives

- The student understands that structures of living things are adapted to their function in specific environments.
- The student knows that plants and animals are adapted to different ranges of temperature and moisture.
- The student knows that animals and plants can be associated with their environment by an examination of their structural characteristics (for example, physical structures are adaptations that allow plants and animals to survive, such as gills in fish, lungs in mammals).

1 | Introduce

Quick ACTIVITY | TRANSPARENCY 7 |

Display a picture of a marsh or similar wetland. Have children draw a picture of a desert and a marsh. Ask: ***How is a marsh different from a desert?*** A marsh is very wet, and a desert is very dry.

Access Prior Knowledge

Ask children what they would do to adapt to living in a marsh. (Wear boots, build bridges) Point out that marsh plants are adapted to this environment.

Set Purpose

Tell children they are going to read about plants that live in a marsh. Help them set a **purpose for reading,** such as to discover ways that plants are adapted to live in a wet environment.

2 | Teach

Quick SUMMARY

- In marsh environments, soil may not have the nutrients plants need.
- Some plants are adapted to get nutrients in other ways.

How are some marsh plants adapted?

A marsh is an environment that is very wet. The soil in a marsh may not have the nutrients plants need. The plants in a marsh are adapted to get nutrients in other ways.

Cattails are plants. Cattails are adapted to grow in very wet soil. Cattails get the nutrients they need from the water.

Cattails

✔ **Lesson Checkpoint**

1. How does a sundew plant trap insects?

2. **Predict** An insect lands on the leaf of a Venus's-flytrap. Predict what will happen next.

24

Lesson 7 Resource

How are some marsh plants adapted?

Before You Read Lesson 7

Read each sentence. Do you think it is true? Do you think it is not true? Circle the word or words after each sentence that tell what you think.

1. Some marsh plants get nutrients from water. | True   Not True
2. Some marsh plants get nutrients from insects. | True   Not True
3. The soil in a marsh has all the nutrients plants need. | True   Not True

After You Read Lesson 7

Read each sentence again. Circle the word or words after each sentence that tell what you think now. Did you change any answers? Put an **X** by each answer that you changed.

1. Some marsh plants get nutrients from water. | True   Not True
2. Some marsh plants get nutrients from insects. | True   Not True
3. The soil in a marsh has all the nutrients plants need. | True   Not True

Home Activity: Together talk about your child's answers. Have your child explain why his or her answers may have changed after reading the lesson.

Workbook   Think, Read, Learn **10**

Workbook, p. 10

A sundew plant gets some nutrients from insects. The plant has sticky hairs on each leaf. Insects land on a leaf and stick to the hairs. ②

A Venus's-flytrap also gets some nutrients from insects. An insect lands on the plant's leaves. Then the leaves snap shut.

25

Science Background

Flowers and Plants

- Other plants that get nutrients from digesting insects or tiny animals include pitcher plants, bladderworts, and butterworts.

- Most plants get nitrogen from the soil in which they grow. Plants that trap insects are unable to do this, because they grow in environments where there is little nitrogen-rich soil. In order to survive, animal-trapping plants have adapted to make use of the nearest source of nitrogen in their environment: insects and other small animals. These plants are adapted to attract insects, trap them, and digest them.

ELL Support

Word Meanings

Point out that the word *trap* can be used as a noun and as a verb. For example: Some plants *trap* insects. The insect goes into a *trap*.

For scaffolded instruction about plants that adapt to marsh environments, use **Every Student Learns Teacher's Guide,** p. 8.

Have volunteers read the paragraphs and captions on pages 24–25 aloud. Use the pictures to discuss the different ways plants adapt to living in a marsh. Focus children's attention on the picture of the sundew plant on page 25. Explain that the tiny hairs make sticky drops. When an insect lands in these drops, it sticks to the hairs.

Assign Quick Study pp. 14–15 to children who need help with lesson content.

Guide Comprehension

Ask children the following scaffolded questions to assess understanding.

Scaffolded Questions

① **Recall What wet environment has many plants such as cattails and sundew plants?** Marsh

② **Draw Conclusion Why do some plants trap animals?** To get nutrients

③ **Predict What will happen to a plant if it does not get the nutrients it needs?** It will die or not grow as well.

Extend Vocabulary

Write the word *digest* on the board. Tell children that *digest* means "change food into a form that the body can use." Explain that plants that trap animals digest the animal. However, plants do not chew their food like people or many animals. After the leaf of the plant traps an insect, the leaf gives off juices that digest the insect. These juices slowly turn the soft parts of the insect into nutrients. Have children illustrate their ideas of this concept.

3 | Assess

✓ Lesson Checkpoint

1. The plant makes sticky drops that look like water. The drops, which are on the hairs, attract insects. The insects get stuck in the hairs.

2. ⊙ **Predict** The leaves of the Venus's-flytrap will snap shut and trap the insect.

SCAFFOLDED INQUIRY

Investigate Do plants need light?

⭐ **Science Objective**

• The student knows that people use scientific processes including making inferences, and recording and communicating data when exploring the natural world.

1 | Build Background

This activity encourages children to observe what will happen to plants if they are not given sunlight.

Managing Time and Materials

Time:	30 minutes for setup and then 10 minutes daily for 1 week
Groups:	Small groups
Materials:	*2 clear plastic cups, 9 oz; grass seeds for each cup; potting soil per cup, 5 oz;* water (about $\frac{1}{4}$ c); pouring container for water; washable paints (optional)
Center:	This activity can be set up in your Science Center for children to work on throughout the week.

Materials listed in *italic* are kit materials.

Advance Preparation:

Plant seeds about 10 days in advance. Cover seeds with a thin layer of soil. Keep soil moist. Fill each pouring container with about $\frac{1}{4}$ c water.

Teaching Tip:

Be careful not to overwater seeds.

2 | What to Do

Encourage Guided Inquiry

Preview the activity and the materials with children. Ask: **What might happen to a plant kept in a dark room?**

Guide children to write an If.../then... statement such as: **If I put a plant in the dark, then it will not grow as well as a plant in the light.**

Investigate Do plants need light?

Plants need water, air, sunlight, and nutrients to live and grow. What might happen if plants do not get light?

Materials

2 cups with grass

water

What to Do

1 Water both plants.

You can paint your cups!

2 Put one plant in sunlight.

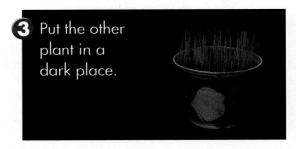

Process Skills

You **observe** when you look closely at the plants.

3 Put the other plant in a dark place.

Activity Resources

Investigate Do plants need light?

Fill in the chart. Draw pictures to show the plants each day.

	Sunlight	Dark
Day 1		
Day 2		
Day 3		
Day 4		
Day 5		

Activity Book, pp. 29–30

Activity Rubric
Investigate: Do plants need light?

Scoring Criteria	1	2	3	4
Student followed directions to complete this activity.				
Student stayed on-task during this activity.				
Student **observed** both plants daily.				
Student recorded **observations** by filling in the chart with drawings.				
Student **inferred** that a plant will die if it does not get sunlight.				

Scoring Key
4 points correct, complete, detailed
3 points partially correct, complete, detailed
2 points partially correct, partially complete, lacks some detail
1 point incorrect or incomplete, needs assistance

Activity Rubric

Use Activity DVD Unit A, Chapter 1 to preview this activity.

Call 1-888-537-490 with activity questions.

 **More Lab zone Activities** Take It to the Net pearsonsuccessnet.com

Find more about this activity at our Web site.

• See the **Teacher's Activity Guide** for more support.
• An alternative activity is also available to download.

4 How do you think the plants will look after 1 week? **Observe** the plants every day for 1 week.

	Sunlight	**Dark**
Day 1		
Day 2		

5 Fill in the chart. Draw pictures to show the plants each day.

Explain Your Results
1. Which plant grew better?
2. **Infer** What will happen if a plant does not get sunlight?

Go Further
What will happen if you move the plant from the dark place to a sunny place? Try it and find out.

Engage Ask children to brainstorm a list of things that produce light. (Sun, lightbulb, fluorescent light, fire, flashlight.)

Explore Ask children what they think will happen to the plants stored in the darker area and the plants stored in the lighter area.

Explain Ask children to explain what happened to the plants grown with and without light.

Extend Have children complete the *Go Further* and move the shaded plants into the sunlight. Observe what happens to them over several days.

Evaluate Have children review their Investigation question answers. Based on their drawings, would they change them?

3 | Explain Your Results

Use these questions to help children review evidence and develop explanations.

- Give children an opportunity to reflect on the data, or evidence, they have gathered in the investigation.
- Have children use the evidence gathered to develop their explanations. Accept reasonable, logical explanations.
1. The plant in the sunlight.
2. **Infer** The plant will not grow. It will die.

Go Further

Children may propose any number of modifications to the experiment to determine the importance of light to a plant. Children may wish to place some of the grass plants in sunlight and some of them under different types of light such as a plant light, fluorescent light, and an incandescent lightbulb.

Post other questions children have about how plants grow. Encourage children to investigate on their own.

Process Skills

Observe

Discuss the importance of being able to make observations. Explain to children that observations are bits of information that are gathered with the senses. You can use the Process Skills sheet on Observing at this time.

Science Background

Light

- The speed of light in a vacuum (empty space) is about 300,000 kilometers per second or 186,000 miles per second. It takes light from the Sun about 8.3 minutes to reach Earth. The speed of light depends on the material that the light is traveling through.
- Light from the Sun or a lightbulb contains all of the colors of the rainbow (red, orange, yellow, green, blue, indigo, and violet.) Light can be split into its different colors by sending it through a triangular piece of glass called a prism. The light slows down as it enters the solid prism and separates into the various colors. Rainbows occur because water droplets act like small prisms to produce bands of colored light.

ELL Support

Access content before beginning the activity. Conduct an inventory of materials with children. Solicit other names for each item. Accept labels in English and the children's home languages.

Leaf Patterns

 Science Objective

- The student recognizes, extends, generalizes, and creates a wide variety of patterns and relationships using symbols and objects.

1 | Introduce

Quick ACTIVITY

Write the following sequence on the board: 1 1 2 2 3 3 4 4. Ask children to identify the pattern. (The numbers appear twice and in sequence.) Ask: **What numbers do you expect to see next if this pattern were to continue?** 5 5 6 6

2 | Teach the Skill

Read pages 28–29 with children.

Ask children to name the two trees shown. Have them describe the leaves of the ash tree and then the leaves of the beech.

Help children recognize that the leaves have different patterns.

- Ash tree leaves grow directly across from each other. They form a symmetrical pattern. Review the term *symmetry*, which means "a regular, balanced form or arrangement on opposite sides of a line or around a center."

- Beech tree leaves also grow on opposite sides of a stalk, but they are not symmetrical.

Math in Science

Leaf Patterns

① **Ash tree leaves**

Leaves grow on branches in different patterns. Ash tree leaves grow in pairs. Two leaves grow across from each other. One leaf is on one side of a stalk. One leaf is on the other side.

Beech tree leaves grow in a different pattern. One leaf grows on one side of a stalk. Farther down, another leaf grows on the other side of the branch. This pattern repeats.

Beech tree leaves ②

28 **e Tools** Take It to the Net
pearsonsuccessnet.com

Activity Resource

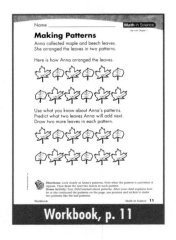

Workbook, p. 11

 **e Tools** Take It to the Net
pearsonsuccessnet.com

Copy the leaf pictures below. Use what you know about leaf patterns. Predict where the next two leaves will grow. Draw two more leaves on each stalk.

3

29

Lab zone Take-Home Activity

Take your drawings home. Discuss what you have learned about the way leaves grow with your family.

Take-Home Activity

Tips for Success

- Assist children in labeling each drawing with the name of the tree whose leaf pattern it represents.

- Suggest that children look around their neighborhoods and try to find other leaves with predictable patterns. Encourage them to try to learn the name of the plants by asking friends, family members, or other knowledgeable people.

Point out the leaf pictures on page 29. Make sure children understand that they show the leaf patterns discussed on page 28. Say: **Look at the leaf pattern on the left. Where are the first two leaves?** Directly across from each other **What pattern will the rest of the leaves have?** The same pattern, directly across from each other

Have children copy the leaf pictures on a piece of paper. Have them predict and then draw where the next two leaves will go on each leaf picture.

Guide Comprehension

Ask children the following scaffolded questions to assess understanding.

Scaffolded Questions

1 **Inspect** **Look at the first pair of ash leaves on page 28. How do they grow?** Across from each other

2 **See Relationships** **Now look at the beech tree leaves. How are these like the ash leaves?** Beech leaves grow on both sides of the stalk, but beech leaves do not grow across from each other in pairs.

3 **Apply Mathematics** **Draw where you predict the next beech leaf will be.** Children's drawings should show the leaf below and on the opposite side of the stalk.

3 | Assess

Review children's drawings to make sure the patterns continue correctly.

Chapter 1 Review and Test Prep

Vocabulary

1. D
2. A
3. E
4. B
5. C

What did you learn?

6. Nutrients are materials that living things need to live and grow.
7. A plant's environment is all the living and nonliving things around it.
8. Its stem helps it keep water.

Chapter 1 Review and Test Prep

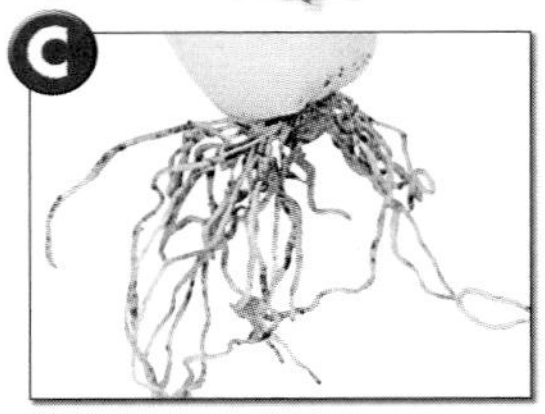

Vocabulary

Which picture goes with each word?

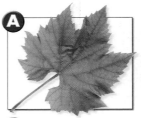

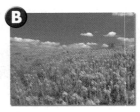

1. stem
2. leaf
3. flowers
4. prairie
5. roots

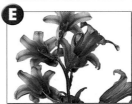

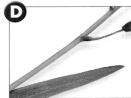

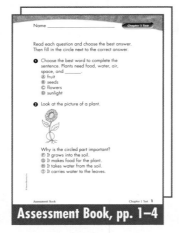

A

B

C

D

E

What did you learn?

6. What are nutrients?
7. What is a plant's environment?
8. How is prairie smoke adapted to live on a prairie?

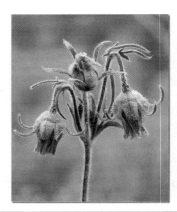

Assessment Resources

Name ______ Chapter 1 Test

Read each question and choose the best answer. Then fill in the circle next to the correct answer.

1. Choose the best word to complete the sentence. Plants need food, water, air, space, and ______.
Ⓐ fruit
Ⓑ seeds
Ⓒ flowers
Ⓓ sunlight

2. Look at the picture of a plant.

Why is the circled part important?
Ⓕ It grows into the soil.
Ⓖ It makes food for the plant.
Ⓗ It takes water from the soil.
Ⓙ It carries water to the leaves.

Assessment Book Chapter 1 Test 1

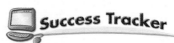

Assessment Book, pp. 1–4

MindPoint Quiz Show

MindPoint enables children to test their knowledge of the chapter in a game format.

ExamView® Use ExamView as a print or online assessment tool.

Success Tracker

Data management system to track Adequate Yearly Progress (AYP) and provide intervention online at **pearsonsuccessnet.com/successtracker**

Take-Home Booklet

Children can make a Take-Home Booklet using Workbook pp. 13–14.

9. Infer What might happen if a plant does not get enough space to live and grow?

◉ Predict

10. The leaves on a maple tree change color from green to red. **Predict** what will happen next.

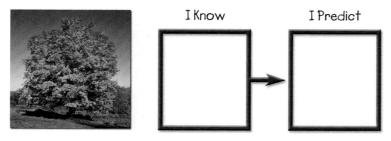

I Know → I Predict

Test Prep

Fill in the circle next to the correct answer.

11. Which part of a plant brings water up to the leaves?

Ⓐ stem
Ⓑ cone
Ⓒ roots
Ⓓ flower

12. **Writing** in Science Name the 4 main parts of a plant. Tell how each part helps the plant.

31

9. Infer It would die.

◉ **Predict**

10.

I Know		I Predict
Leaves change color in the fall.	→	The leaves will drop off the tree.

Test Prep

11. A

12. **Writing** in Science Roots hold the plant in place. They carry water and nutrients to the stem. The stem carries water and nutrients to the leaves. The leaves use sunlight, air, and water to make food for the plant. A flower makes seeds that can grow into new plants.

Intervention and Remediation

Science Objectives	Review Item	Student Edition Pages	Teacher Edition Resources				Ancillary Resources		
			Guide Comprehension	Extend Vocab	Diagnostic Check	Vocab Cards	Quick Study	Workbook Pages
The student knows the basic needs of plants.	6, 9	6–7	7	7	7	7	2	4
The student knows the main parts of plants (stem, leaves, roots, flowers).	11, 12	8–9	9	9	13	8, 9		
The student identifies ways that seeds travel.		10–11	11				4	5
The student knows that the structural characteristics of plants and animals are used to group them.		12–15	13, 15		13, 15		6	6
The student understands that structures of living things are adapted to their function in specific environments.	7, 8	16–25	17, 19, 21, 23		17	16, 20	8, 10, 12, 14	7, 8, 9, 10
The student knows that plants and animals are adapted to different ranges of temperature and moisture.	8, 10	16–25	15, 17, 19, 21, 23	15, 19, 21	17	16, 20	8, 10, 12, 14	7, 8, 9, 10
The student understands that living organisms need to be adapted to their environment to survive.	7, 8, 9	16–19	17, 19, 21, 23, 25	25	17	16		7
The student knows that animals and plants can be associated with their environment by an examination of their structural characteristics (for example, physical structures are adaptations that allow plants and animals to survive, such as gills in fish, lungs in mammals).	7, 8	18–19	19, 23					
The student understands that the amount of food, water, space, and shelter needed is dependent on the size and kind of living things.	9	20–21			7	20	10	8

Biography

Mary Agnes Chase

 Science Objective

- The student explores and identifies career opportunities in plant science.

1 Introduce

Build Background

Ask children to brainstorm a list of important uses of plants and plant parts. Possible answers may include food, wood for building houses and making campfires, decorations in yards and parks, and medicines. Explain to children that a plant scientist is a person who studies plants.

2 Teach

Quick SUMMARY

- Mary Agnes Chase was a plant scientist who studied and drew plants from all over the world.

Read page 32 with children. Have children look at the photographs of Mary Agnes Chase. Explain that Mary Agnes Chase lived a long time ago when cars were first being produced and not available to many people. She had to travel by horse or by foot to get to the plants she wanted to study. Tell children that Mary Agnes Chase liked to study grasses most.

3 Explore

Remind children that Mary Agnes Chase was a plant scientist. Ask children: **Besides drawing plants, what other jobs do you think a plant scientist might do?** Possible answers might include developing new plants, finding cures for plant diseases, finding ways to make plants grow faster, making medicines from plants, and taking care of plant exhibits in zoos and other places.

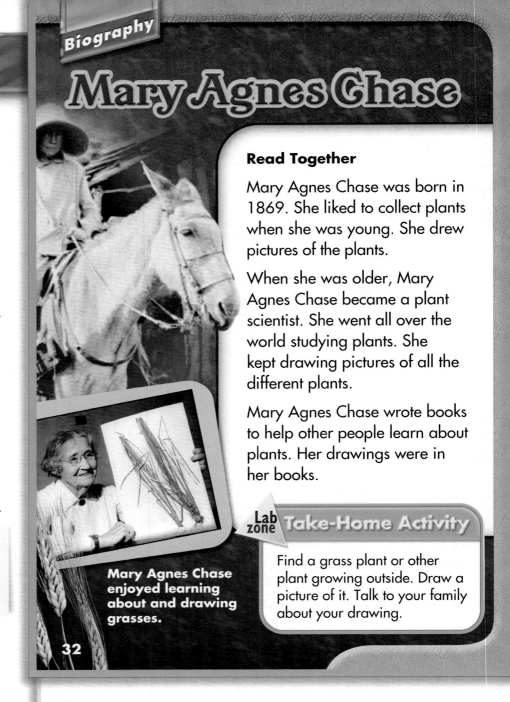

Biography

Mary Agnes Chase

Read Together

Mary Agnes Chase was born in 1869. She liked to collect plants when she was young. She drew pictures of the plants.

When she was older, Mary Agnes Chase became a plant scientist. She went all over the world studying plants. She kept drawing pictures of all the different plants.

Mary Agnes Chase wrote books to help other people learn about plants. Her drawings were in her books.

Mary Agnes Chase enjoyed learning about and drawing grasses.

32

Lab zone Take-Home Activity

Find a grass plant or other plant growing outside. Draw a picture of it. Talk to your family about your drawing.

Take-Home Activity

Tips for Success

- Review the physical characteristics of grasses before children start to look for plants. Show several photographs of different types of grasses and show children the common characteristics that make these plants grasses.

- Have children share their drawings with classmates.

Leveled Readers and Leveled Practice

Leveled Readers deliver the same concepts and skills as the chapter. Use Leveled Readers for original instruction or for needed reteaching.

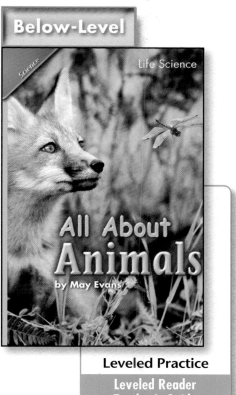

Below-Level

Life Science
All About Animals
by May Evans

Leveled Practice
Leveled Reader Teacher's Guide

On-Level

Life Science
Animal Groups
by Carol Levine

Leveled Practice
Leveled Reader Teacher's Guide

Advanced

Life Science
Nocturnal Animals
by Ann M. Rossi

Leveled Practice
Leveled Reader Teacher's Guide

Below-Level Leveled Reader has the same content as Chapter 2, but is written at a less difficult reading level.

On-Level Leveled Reader has the same concepts as Chapter 2, and is written at grade level.

Advanced Leveled Reader is above grade level and enriches the chapter with additional examples and extended ideas.

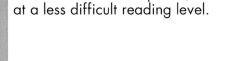

Leveled Reader Database
Scott Foresman
pearsonsuccessnet.com

Use the online database to search for additional leveled readers by level, title, content, and skill.

Key Content and Skill in Leveled Readers and Chapter 2

Content	Vocabulary		Target Reading Skill	Graphic Organizer
All About Animals	mammal bird reptile camouflage	gills fish amphibian insect	Alike and Different	

Chapter 2 Planning Guide

Essential Question: How are animals different from each other?

Lesson/Activity	Pacing	Science Objectives
Build Background pp. 33–35	20 minutes	• The student identifies words and constructs meaning from text, illustrations, graphics, and charts using the strategies of phonics, word structure, and content clues.
Lab zone **Flip Chart Activity** How does camouflage help an animal survive?		
Lab zone **Flip Chart Activity** Why does a backbone have many parts?		
Lab zone **Directed Inquiry**		• The student compares and describes the structural characteristics of plants and animals.
Explore How are worms and snakes alike and different? p. 36	20 minutes	• The student understands similarities and differences across texts (for example, topics, characters, problems).
How to Read Science p. 37	20 minutes	
1 What are some animals with backbones? pp. 38–41	30 minutes	• The student knows that the structural characteristics of plants and animals are used to group them. • The student compares the characteristics of things that live on land, in the water, and in the air.
2 What are some ways mammals are adapted? pp. 42–43	20 minutes	• The student knows some characteristics of the vertebrate groups (mammals, reptiles, birds, amphibians, fish).
3 What are some ways birds are adapted? pp. 44–45	20 minutes	• The student knows some characteristics of the vertebrate groups (mammals, reptiles, birds, amphibians, fish). • The student knows that animals and plants can be associated with their environment by an examination of their structural characteristics.
4 What are some ways fish are adapted? pp. 46–47	20 minutes	• The student knows some characteristics of the vertebrate groups (mammals, reptiles, birds, amphibians, fish).
5 What are some ways reptiles are adapted? pp. 48–49	20 minutes	• The student knows some characteristics of the vertebrate groups (mammals, reptiles, birds, amphibians, fish).
6 What are some ways amphibians are adapted? pp. 50–51	20 minutes	• The student knows some characteristics of the vertebrate groups (mammals, reptiles, birds, amphibians, fish). • The student understands that living organisms need to be adapted to their environment to survive.
7 What are some animals without backbones? pp. 52–55	30 minutes	• The student understands that structures of living things are adapted to their function in specific environments.
Lab zone **Guided Inquiry**		• The student understands that structures of living things are adapted to their function in specific environments.
Investigate How can an octopus use its arms? pp. 56–57	15 minutes	
Wrap-Up Chapter 2 pp. 58–64 Math in Science: Sorting Animals Chapter 2 Review and Test Prep NASA Feature: Warm Water and Penguins Career: Wildlife Rehabilitator	20 minutes 20 minutes 20 minutes 20 minutes	• The student uses mathematical language to read and interpret data on a simple concrete graph, pictorial graph, or chart. • The student knows that the activities of humans affect plants and animals in many ways.

Vocabulary/Skills	Assessment/Intervention	Resources/Technology
Process Skills: Make and use models, Infer	• Chapter Review, SE, pp. 60–61 (1–8, 12)	• Science Content Transparency 2 • Workbook, p. 15 • Graphic Organizer Transparency 2 • Vocabulary Cards • Activity Book, pp. 39–40 • Web Game
Process Skill: Models ⊙ Target Reading Skill: **Alike and Different**	• Explain Your Results, SE, p. 36 ⊙ **Alike and Different,** SE, p. 37	• Activity Book, pp. 35–36 • Activity Rubric • Workbook, pp. 16–17 • Every Student Learns, p. 10 • Activity DVD • Activity Placemat 3
mammals birds reptiles fish amphibians	• Scaffolded Questions, TE, pp. 39, 41 • Checkpoint Questions, SE, p. 41 • Chapter Review, SE, pp. 60–61 (2, 3, 5, 7, 8, 14, 15) ⊙ **Alike and Different,** SE, p. 41	• Workbook, p. 18 • Quick Study, pp. 16–17 • Every Student Learns, p. 11
camouflage	• Scaffolded Questions, TE, p. 43 • Checkpoint Questions, SE, p. 43 • Chapter Review, SE, pp. 60–61 (2, 6)	• Workbook, p. 19 • Quick Study, pp. 18–19 • Every Student Learns, p. 12
	• Scaffolded Questions, TE, p. 45 • Checkpoint Questions, SE, p. 45 • Chapter Review, SE, pp. 60–61 (7, 14) ⊙ **Alike and Different,** SE, p. 45	• Workbook, p. 20 • Quick Study, pp. 20–21 • Every Student Learns, p. 13
gills	• Scaffolded Questions, TE, p. 47 • Checkpoint Questions, SE, p. 47 • Chapter Review, SE, pp. 60–61 (4, 5, 10)	• Workbook, p. 21 • Quick Study, pp. 22–23 • Every Student Learns, p. 14
	• Scaffolded Questions, TE, p. 49 • Checkpoint Questions, SE, p. 49	• Workbook, p. 22 • Quick Study, pp. 24–25 • Every Student Learns, p. 15
	• Scaffolded Questions, TE, p. 51 • Checkpoint Questions, SE, p. 51 • Chapter Review, SE, pp. 60–61 (3)	• Workbook, p. 23 • Quick Study, pp. 26–27 • Every Student Learns, p. 16
insects	• Scaffolded Questions, TE, pp. 53, 55 • Checkpoint Questions, SE, p. 53, 55 • Chapter Review, SE, pp. 60–61 (1, 13)	• Workbook, p. 24 • Quick Study, pp. 28–29 • Every Student Learns, p. 17
Process Skills: Communicate, Predict	• Explain Your Results, SE, p. 57	• Activity Book, pp. 37–38 • Activity Rubric • Activity DVD • Activity Placemat 4
Math Skill: Make a Graph	⊙ **Alike and Different,** SE, p. 61 ⊙ **ExamView®** Chapter 2 Test 🖥 **Success Tracker** pearsonsuccessnet.com/successtracker	• Workbook, pp. 25, 27–28 • Assessment Book, pp. 5–8

Quick | Teaching Plan

If time is short...
• Build Background, pp. 34–35
• Explore Activity, p. 36
• How to Read Science, p. 37
• Lesson 1, pp. 38–41
• Lesson 2, pp. 42–43
• Lesson 7, pp. 52–55

Other quick options...

Quick ACTIVITY

TE pp. 34, 38, 42, 44, 46, 48, 50, 52, 58

TRANSPARENCIES 8, 9, 10, 11, 12, 13, 14

Quick SUMMARY

TE pp. 38, 40, 42, 44, 46, 48, 50, 52, 54

Chapter 2 Activity Guide

Children learn to ask and answer scientific questions as they progress to greater independence in scaffolded inquiry.

Directed Inquiry   A Directed Inquiry activity begins each chapter.

Guided Inquiry   A Guided Inquiry activity closes each chapter.

Full Inquiry   Experiments and Science Fair Projects at the end of each unit provide opportunities for Full Inquiry.

Lab zone — Directed Inquiry

 Explore   **How are worms and snakes alike and different?** p. 36

 Time   20 minutes

Grouping   small groups

Advance Preparation   Cut one 6 inch strip and one 13 inch strip of self-adherent first-aid tape for each group.

Materials   *red self-adherent tape* (one 6 inch strip, one 13 inch strip); *7 cotton squares; pipe cleaner* (12 in.); *14 pieces of dried mini rigatoni pasta; washable paints (optional)*

Alternative Materials   Paper towels may be substituted for cotton squares. Fold and cut the paper towels to make 2 x 4 in. and 2 x 10 in. strips. Plastic wrap many be used in place of self-adherent/first-aid tape. Plastic beads may be used instead of pasta.

Activity DVD   Unit A, Chapter 2

Activity Placemat   Mat 3

Lab zone — Guided Inquiry

 Investigate   **How can an octopus use its arms?** pp. 56–57

 Time   15 minutes

Grouping   small groups

Advance Preparation   Make copies of the paper fish using Activity Master 1 from the Activity Book Teacher's Guide, p. T23. You may wish to copy the master onto colored construction paper.

Materials   *clear plastic jar with lid (16 oz); 8 suction cups* ($1\frac{1}{4}$ in. diam.); *Fish (Activity Master 1); safety scissors; construction paper (optional; to make copies of activity master)*

What to Expect   This activity is open-ended and there are several possible solutions, but most groups will figure out that one child needs to steady the sides of the jar with suction cups as another child unscrews the lid. Many children will find that it is possible to open the jar with three or four suction cups (1 or 2 on the lid and 1 on each side of the jar).

 Activity DVD   Unit A, Chapter 2

 Activity Placemat   Mat 4

Other Resources
The following Resources are available for activities found in the Student Edition.

Demonstration Kit If you wish to rehearse or demonstrate the Chapter 2 activities, use the materials provided in the Demonstration Kit.

Classroom Equipment Kit Materials shown in *italic print* are available in the Classroom Equipment Kit.

Activity Placemats The Equipment Kit includes an Activity Placemat for each activity, a work surface that identifies the materials that need to be gathered.

Quick ACTIVITY

Transparencies Use a transparency to focus children's attention on the Quick Activity for each lesson.

Teacher's Activity Guide For detailed information about Inquiry Activities, access the Teacher's Activity Guide at **pearsonsuccessnet.com**.

Activity Flip Chart

How does camouflage help an animal survive?

Use this center activity after teaching Lesson 2 of the chapter.

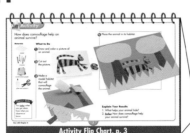
Activity Flip Chart, p. 3

Process Skills make a model, infer

 Time 20 minutes

 Grouping individual

Materials paper, crayons, construction paper, glue, scissors

Procedure
- Discuss what camouflage means and how it helps an animal survive. Tell children that camouflage may be patterns as well as color.
- Children draw an animal and **make a model** of a habitat to camouflage the animal. They place their animal in the habitat so it is hard to find.
- Children should **infer** that camouflage helps hide an animal so that it is hard for other animals to see it.

What to Expect Students should build a habitat with colors and patterns that make it difficult to clearly see the animal they drew.

Think About It
1. It blends into its surroundings.
2. It helps the animal so that it is hard for other animals to see it.

Activity Flip Chart

Why does a backbone have many parts?

Use this center activity after teaching Lesson 7 of the chapter.

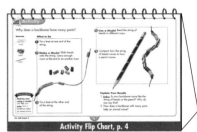
Activity Flip Chart, p. 4

Process Skills make and use models, infer

 Time 20 minutes

 Grouping individual

Materials foot-long piece of string; about a dozen plastic or wooden beads; pencil

Procedure
- Review with children what a backbone is—the bone running the length of their back. Have them feel this bone in their lower back.
- Help children **make a model** of a backbone by sliding beads onto the string and tying a knot at the other end of the string.
- Have children compare how the string of beads moves to how a pencil moves. Children should **infer** that a backbone is like a string of beads because it bends and moves in different ways.

What to Expect Children will understand that a backbone is made of many bones that give an animal flexibility.

Think About It
1. String of beads because your body bends like a string of beads.
2. It helps the animal bend its body and move in different ways.

Chapter 2 Workbook Support

online **Teacher's Edition**
pearsonsuccessnet.com

Use the following Workbook pages to support content and skill development as you teach Chapter 2. You can also view and print Workbook pages from the Online Teacher's Edition.

Use with Build Background, pp. 34–35

Name _____ **Vocabulary Preview**
Use with Chapter 2.

Draw a picture or write a sentence to go with each word.

reptile	mammal
bird	amphibian
fish	camouflage
gills	insect

Directions: Read the words and draw pictures to illustrate them or write sentences about them. Cut out the boxes to use as word cards.
Home Activity: Review the word cards *reptile, bird, fish, mammal, amphibian,* and *insect* with your child. Look through magazines together. Help your child find an example of each kind of animal.

Workbook   Vocabulary Preview **15**

Workbook, p. 15

Use with How to Read Science, p. 37

Name _____ **How To Read Science**
Use with page 37.

Alike and Different

Read the science article. Fill in the chart. Tell how honey bees and spiders are alike and different.

Honey Bees and Spiders

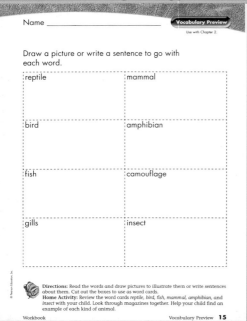

Honey bees do not have bones. They have three body parts and six legs. They have wings. They can walk and fly.

Spiders do not have bones. They have two body parts and eight legs. They cannot fly. They do not have wings. They walk.

Apply It!

Use the chart on the next page. Tell how a honey bee and spider are alike and different.

16 How to Read Science   Workbook

Workbook, p. 16

Use with How to Read Science, p. 37

Name _____ **How To Read Science**
Use with page 37.

Alike	Different
Both do not have bones. Both have legs and body parts. Both can walk.	Honey bees have 3 body parts. Honey bees have 6 legs. Honey bees have wings. Honey bees can fly. Spiders have 2 body parts. Spiders have 8 legs. Spiders have no wings. Spiders cannot fly.

Directions: Read the science article. Think about how honey bees and spiders are alike. Write your ideas in the chart under *Alike*. Then think about how honey bees and spiders are different. Write your ideas in the chart under *Different*.
Home Activity: Your child learned about the concept of alike and different. Find pictures of two different animals in a magazine. Discuss with your child how the animals are alike and different.

Workbook   How to Read Science **17**

Workbook, p. 17

Use with Lesson 1, pp. 38–41

Name _____ **Think, Read, Learn**
Use with pages 39–41.

What are some animals with backbones?

Before You Read Lesson 1

Read each sentence. Do you think it is true? Do you think it is not true? Circle the word or words after each sentence that tell what you think.

1. Mammals are one group of animals with bones.   True   Not True
2. Only birds hatch from eggs.   True   Not True
3. Both fish and reptiles have scales. True   Not True
4. Amphibians do not have bones.   True   Not True

After You Read Lesson 1

Read each sentence again. Circle the word or words after each sentence that tell what you think now. Did you change any answers? Put an **X** by each answer that you changed.

1. Mammals are one group of animals with bones.   (True)   Not True
2. Only birds hatch from eggs.   (True)   Not True
3. Both fish and reptiles have scales. (True)   Not True
4. Amphibians do not have bones.   True   (Not True)

Home Activity: Together talk about your child's answers. Have your child explain why his or her answers may have changed after reading the lesson.

Workbook   Think, Read, Learn **18**

Workbook, p. 18

Use with Lesson 2, pp. 42–43

Name _____ **Think, Read, Learn**
Use with pages 42–43.

What are some ways mammals are adapted?

Before You Read Lesson 2

Read each sentence. Do you think it is true? Do you think it is not true? Circle the word or words after each sentence that tell what you think.

1. Mammals can change to live in their environment.   True   Not True
2. Camouflage is all the living and nonliving things around an animal. True   Not True
3. A mule deer's fur changes color from brown in summer to gray in winter.   True   Not True

After You Read Lesson 2

Read each sentence again. Circle the word or words after each sentence that tell what you think now. Did you change any answers? Put an **X** by each answer that you changed.

1. Mammals can change to live in their environment.   (True)   Not True
2. Camouflage is all the living and nonliving things around an animal. True   (Not True)
3. A mule deer's fur changes color from brown in summer to gray in winter.   (True)   Not True

Home Activity: Together talk about your child's answers. Have your child explain why his or her answers may have changed after reading the lesson.

Workbook   Think, Read, Learn **19**

Workbook, p. 19

Use with Lesson 3, pp. 44–45

Name _____ **Think, Read, Learn**
Use with pages 44–45.

What are some ways birds are adapted?

Before You Read Lesson 3

Read each sentence. Do you think it is true? Do you think it is not true? Circle the word or words after each sentence that tell what you think.

1. All birds use their wings to fly.   True   Not True
2. Some birds use camouflage to hide in their environment.   True   Not True
3. A hummingbird's beak is adapted for sipping liquid from flowers.   True   Not True

After You Read Lesson 3

Read each sentence again. Circle the word or words after each sentence that tell what you think now. Did you change any answers? Put an **X** by each answer that you changed.

1. All birds use their wings to fly.   True   (Not True)
2. Some birds use camouflage to hide in their environment.   (True)   Not True
3. A hummingbird's beak is adapted for sipping liquid from flowers. (True)   Not True

Home Activity: Together talk about your child's answers. Have your child explain why his or her answers may have changed after reading the lesson.

Workbook   Think, Read, Learn **20**

Workbook, p. 20

Use with Lesson 4, pp. 46–47

Name _____ 〔Think, Read, Learn〕

Use with pages 46–47.

What are some ways fish are adapted?

Before You Read Lesson 4

Read each sentence. Do you think it is true? Do you think it is not true? Circle the word or words after each sentence that tell what you think.

1. Gills and fins help fish live in the water.   True   Not True
2. Gills are body parts that help fish swim.   True   Not True
3. Some fish can change their shape to protect themselves.   True   Not True

After You Read Lesson 4

Read each sentence again. Circle the word or words after each sentence that tell what you think now. Did you change any answers? Put an **X** by each answer that you changed.

1. Gills and fins help fish live in the water.   (True)   Not True
2. Gills are body parts that help fish swim.   True   (Not True)
3. Some fish can change their shape to protect themselves.   (True)   Not True

 Home Activity: Together talk about your child's answers. Have your child explain why his or her answers may have changed after reading the lesson.

Workbook   Think, Read, Learn **21**

Workbook, p. 21

Use with Lesson 5, pp. 48–49

Name _____ 〔Think, Read, Learn〕

Use with pages 48–49.

What are some ways reptiles are adapted?

Before You Read Lesson 5

Read each sentence. Do you think it is true? Do you think it is not true? Circle the word or words after each sentence that tell what you think.

1. Reptiles get cold when the air is cold and warm when the air is warm.   True   Not True
2. A chameleon uses its long, sticky tongue to catch food.   True   Not True
3. Snakes use teeth to chew their food.   True   Not True

After You Read Lesson 5

Read each sentence again. Circle the word or words after each sentence that tell what you think now. Did you change any answers? Put an **X** by each answer that you changed.

1. Reptiles get cold when the air is cold and warm when the air is warm.   (True)   Not True
2. A chameleon uses its long, sticky tongue to catch food.   (True)   Not True
3. Snakes use teeth to chew their food.   True   (Not True)

 Home Activity: Together talk about your child's answers. Have your child explain why his or her answers may have changed after reading the lesson.

Workbook   Think, Read, Learn **22**

Workbook, p. 22

Use with Lesson 6, pp. 50–51

Name _____ 〔Think, Read, Learn〕

Use with pages 50–51.

What are some ways amphibians are adapted?

Before You Read Lesson 6

Read each sentence. Do you think it is true? Do you think it is not true? Circle the word or words after each sentence that tell what you think.

1. Amphibians live in the water and on land.   True   Not True
2. Most amphibians have dry, rough skin.   True   Not True
3. Toads are amphibians.   True   Not True

After You Read Lesson 6

Read each sentence again. Circle the word or words after each sentence that tell what you think now. Did you change any answers? Put an **X** by each answer that you changed.

1. Amphibians live in the water and on land.   (True)   Not True
2. Most amphibians have dry, rough skin.   True   (Not True)
3. Toads are amphibians.   (True)   Not True

 Home Activity: Together talk about your child's answers. Have your child explain why his or her answers may have changed after reading the lesson.

Workbook   Think, Read, Learn **23**

Workbook, p. 23

Use with Lesson 7, pp. 52–55

Name _____ 〔Think, Read, Learn〕

Use with pages 52–53.

What are some animals without backbones?

Before You Read Lesson 7

Read each sentence. Do you think it is true? Do you think it is not true? Circle the word or words after each sentence that tell what you think.

1. Most kinds of animals have bones.   True   Not True
2. Insects are one group of animals that do not have bones.   True   Not True
3. An octopus uses suction cups on its arms to hold its food.   True   Not True
4. Like beetles, spiders have six legs and no bones.   True   Not True

After You Read Lesson 7

Read each sentence again. Circle the word or words after each sentence that tell what you think now. Did you change any answers? Put an **X** by each answer that you changed.

1. Most kinds of animals have bones.   True   (Not True)
2. Insects are one group of animals that do not have bones.   (True)   Not True
3. An octopus uses suction cups on its arms to hold its food.   (True)   Not True
4. Like beetles, spiders have six legs and no bones.   True   (Not True)

 Home Activity: Together talk about your child's answers. Have your child explain why his or her answers may have changed after reading the lesson.

Workbook   Think, Read, Learn **24**

Workbook, p. 24

Use with Math in Science, pp. 58–59

Name _____ 〔Math in Science〕

Use with Chapter 2.

Sorting Animals

Sort these animals into two groups—animals with bones and animals without bones. Color the graph to show how many animals you put in each group.

 Toad   Walkingstick   Hummingbird

Spider   Fish   Chipmunk   Honeypot Ant

Animal Groups						
Animals with bones						
Animals without bones						
0	1	2	3	4	5	6

 Directions: Decide whether each animal shown on the page is an animal with bones or an animal without bones. (You can look in your book if you need help.) Find the correct row on the graph. Color one box in that row for the animal.
Home Activity: Your child learned how to fill in a graph. Ask your child to explain how he or she filled in the graph on the page. Then together make another graph for the same animals showing how many have fur or feathers and how many do not.

Workbook   Math in Science **25**

Workbook, p. 25

Chapter 2 Assessment Support

Use the following Assessment Book pages and ExamView to assess Chapter 2 content. You can also view and print Assessment Book pages from the Online Teacher's Edition.

Assessment Options

Formal Assessment

- Chapter Review and Test Prep, SE pp. 60–61
- Assessment Book pp. 5–8
- Prescriptions for remediation are shown on TE p. 61

Performance Assessment

- Unit Wrap-Up, SE pp. 130–131

Ongoing Assessment

- Diagnostic Check, TE pp. 39, 53
- Scaffolded Questions, TE pp. 39, 41, 43, 45, 47, 49, 51, 53, 55

My Portfolio Assessment

- My Science Journal, TE pp. 35, 40, 45, 54

Success Tracker

- Data management system to assess Adequate Yearly Progress (AYP) and provide intervention

ExamView®

- Alternative test formats are available online or through ExamView CD-ROM

Chapter 2 Test

Name _____

Read each question and choose the best answer. Then fill in the circle next to the correct answer.

1 Which group of animals has bones and either fur or hair and feeds milk to its babies?
- Ⓐ birds
- Ⓑ fishes
- Ⓒ insects
- Ⓓ mammals

2 What should the title of the list be?

> Dogs
> Cats
> Skunks
> Chipmunks

- Ⓕ Animals with Wings
- Ⓖ Animals with Feathers
- Ⓗ Animals with Backbones
- Ⓘ Animals without Backbones

Assessment Book   Chapter 2 Test **5**

Assessment Book, p. 5

Chapter 2 Test

Name _____

3 Fish live in water. What do fish have that helps them swim in water?
- Ⓐ fins
- Ⓑ bones
- Ⓒ lungs
- Ⓓ scales

4 Read the chart. Use what you learn to answer the question.

Mule Deer Camouflage	
In Summer	**In Winter**
Fur turns brown to blend with their summer environment.	Fur turns gray to blend with their winter environment.

How are mule deer adapted to their environment?
- Ⓕ They have beautiful coats in summer and winter.
- Ⓖ They have more food to eat in summer than in winter.
- Ⓗ The color of their fur changes in summer and winter.
- Ⓘ Their habits change because they like summer better than winter.

6 Chapter 2 Test   Assessment Book

Assessment Book, p. 6

Chapter 2 Test

Name _____

5 Penguins are adapted to living in a cold environment. What does their second layer of feathers help penguins do?
- Ⓐ fly
- Ⓑ swim
- Ⓒ find food
- Ⓓ keep warm

6 Marie noticed that when she wore her black T-shirt in the Sun, she would get hot and sweaty. When she wore her white T-shirt in the Sun, she felt cooler. Look at the picture. Think about what color might help you stay cool.

Think about what Marie learned. Reptiles sit in the sun to get warm. But the Sun is very strong in a desert. What helps a desert iguana from getting too hot?
- Ⓕ bones
- Ⓖ scales
- Ⓗ light skin
- Ⓘ dark skin

Assessment Book   Chapter 2 Test **7**

Assessment Book, p. 7

Chapter 2 Test

Name _____

7 Catfish find food on the bottom of dark rivers. What do catfish have that helps them find food in the dark?
- Ⓐ fins
- Ⓑ gills
- Ⓒ claws
- Ⓓ feelers

8 What helps frogs live in moist environments?
- Ⓕ their light color
- Ⓖ their good eyesight
- Ⓗ their dry, rough skin
- Ⓘ their smooth, wet skin

Write the answer to the question on the line.

9 Look at the picture of a spider in a web. Think about how it gets its food.

Think about what you learned from the picture. Tell how this spider is adapted to life in the air. (2 points)
This spider builds a web to trap insects.

8 Chapter 2 Test   Assessment Book

Assessment Book, p. 8

You Will Discover
- that there are many different kinds of animals.
- how animals are adapted to different kinds of environments.

Chapter 2

All About Animals

Chapter 2

All About Animals

 **Science Objectives**

- The student knows that life occurs on or near the surface of the Earth in land, air, and water.
- The student understands that structures of living things are adapted to their function in specific environments.
- The student compares and describes the structural characteristics of plants and animals.
- The student knows that there are many different kinds of living things that live in a variety of environments.

Quick TEACHING PLAN

If time is short...

Use Build Background page to engage children in chapter content. Then do Explore Activity, How to Read Science, and Lessons 1, 2, and 7.

Web Games
Take It to the Net
pearsonsuccessnet.com

online
Student Edition
pearsonsuccessnet.com

 Professional Development

To enhance your qualifications in science, before beginning this chapter:

- preview the content in Life Science DVD segments *Classification of Living Things* and *Characteristics of Organisms.*
- preview activity management techniques described in Activity DVD Unit A, Chapter 2.

Take It to the NET

To access student resources:
1. Go to **www.pearsonsuccessnet.com.**
2. Click on the register button.
3. Enter the access code **frog** and your school's zip code.

Chapter 2 Concept Web

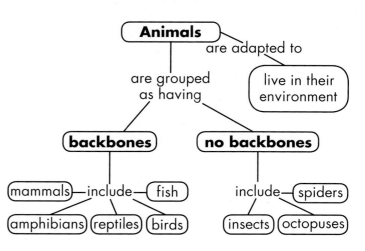

Children can create a concept web to organize ideas about animals.

Build Background

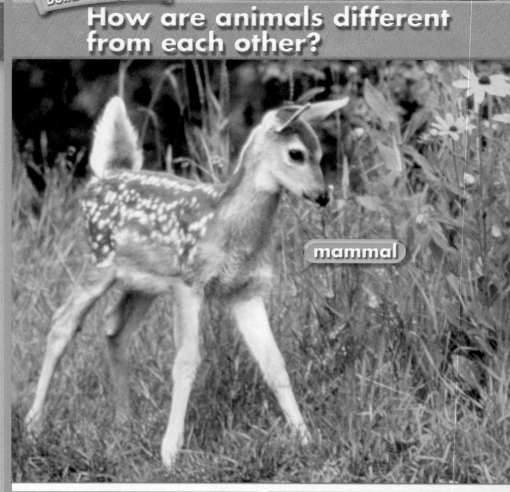

mammal

bird

fish gills

34

Build Background

 Science Objective

- The student identifies words and constructs meaning from text, illustrations, graphics, and charts using the strategies of phonics, word structure, and context clues.

Chapter 2 Vocabulary Words

mammal, p. 40
bird, p. 40
fish, p. 40
reptile, p. 41
amphibian, p. 41
camouflage, p. 42
gills, p. 46
insect, p. 52

1 | Introduce the Concept

Quick ACTIVITY

Ask children: **What pets do you have at home?** Write children's responses on the board. Point to each pet listed and ask: **What does this pet look like?** Children's answers will vary.

Discuss Essential Question

Many science vocabulary words are abstract. Use the pictures and labels on these pages to help you open a discussion about science concepts and build academic language.

Read the Chapter 2 Essential Question to children, **How are animals different from each other?** Have children look at the photos and ask volunteers to identify the animals shown. Invite children to suggest characteristics of the animals that they see. (Reptiles have dry skin, amphibians have wet skin, fish have gills, mammals have fur, insects and birds have wings.)

Revisit the essential question with children as they work through this chapter.

Build Background Resources

Workbook, p. 15

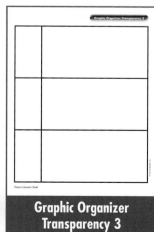

Graphic Organizer Transparency 3

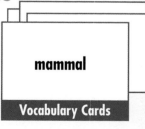

mammal

Vocabulary Cards

ELL Support

Access Content Before reading the chapter text, lead children on a picture/text walk.

Chapter 2 Vocabulary

mammal page 40

bird page 40

fish page 40

reptile page 41

amphibian page 41

camouflage page 42

gills page 46

insect page 52

reptile

amphibian

camouflage

insect

35

My Science Journal

Animal Diary

Have children keep a running list of the animals they see in their daily lives. Encourage children to look in places such as a backyard, park, or school playground. They should record the names of the kinds of animals they see. Next to each name, they can write notes about the animal, such as how it looks and how it moves. In Lesson 7, they will group the animals by shared characteristics.

Science Background

Classifying Animals

Classification helps bring order to the study of all living things. Living things are arranged in groups according to similarities and differences. In the animal kingdom, animals are divided into two major groups: vertebrates and invertebrates. Vertebrates are divided into five groups: mammals, birds, bony fish, reptiles, and amphibians. Animals within each group share similarities.

Invertebrates are divided into seven groups, the largest of which, arthropods, includes insects, spiders, and shrimp.

2 | Introduce Vocabulary

Use the following Graphic Organizer provided on **pearsonsuccessnet.com** or Graphic Organizer Transparency 3.

Word	Prediction	Definition
mammal		
bird		
fish		
reptile		
amphibian		
camouflage		
gills		
insect		

Use Graphic Organizer 3 to introduce the vocabulary words. Provide each child with a copy of the Graphic Organizer. Reproduce the Graphic Organizer on the board. List the vocabulary words in the first column. Have children copy the words on their charts. Explain to children that you will fill in the Prediction column of the chart with them.

- Pronounce each word as you write it in the first column. Ask children for their ideas about the possible meaning of each word as you fill in the Prediction column. For example, children might predict that the word *camouflage* means making something difficult to see.

- Continue to add predictions about each word by asking questions such as **What might all mammals have in common? What kind of animal is a fish?**

- Tell children that they will fill in the last column after reading the chapter.

Word Recognition Use the Vocabulary Cards to reinforce recognition of each written word and its definition.

3 | Practice

Vocabulary Strategy: Word Web

Using the Vocabulary Cards, read the definition of a vocabulary word aloud. Reinforce the definition and identification of the word by creating a word web. Write the word in the center. Invite children to contribute descriptive words, synonyms, and examples that help define the word. Repeat with each vocabulary word from pages 34–35.

SCAFFOLDED INQUIRY

1 Explore How are worms and snakes alike and different?

 Science Objective

- The student knows that people use scientific processes including hypothesis, making inferences, and recording and communicating data when exploring the natural world.

1 Build Background

This activity encourages children to identify and compare the characteristics of different animals.

Managing Time and Materials

Time: 20 minutes
Groups: small groups
Materials: *red self-adherent tape* (one 6 in. strip and one 13 in. strip); *7 cotton squares; pipe cleaner; 14 pieces of pasta (mini rigatoni)*; washable paints (optional)

Materials listed in *italics* are kit materials.

Advance Preparation

Cut two strips of red tape per group.

2 What To Do

Engage Review the activity objective together. Discuss how worms and snakes look and move.

Explore Point to the pictures and describe how to build each model. Tell children to make their models.

Explain Ask groups to discuss how each model represents a worm or a snake.

Extend Have children suggest ways to model other animals and features to include. (Size, shape, feel)

Evaluate Gather as a class to discuss how the models are the same and how they are different.

3 Explain Your Results

The models feel the same on the outside. The worm model is soft inside. The snake model is hard inside.

Process Skills

Have children explain how they made their **models.**

Explore How are worms and snakes alike and different?

Materials

short tape

long tape

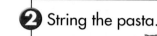
7 cotton squares

pipe cleaner

14 pieces of pasta

Process Skills

Models show how animals are alike and different.

What to Do

Make models of a worm and a snake.

Worm

1 Roll up. Pinch the ends.

Snake

2 String the pasta.

3 Roll up. Pinch the ends.

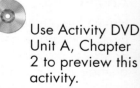

Explain Your Results

Feel the **models**. Tell about them.

36 More lab Activities Take It to the Net
pearsonsuccessnet.com

Activity Resources

Use Activity DVD Unit A, Chapter 2 to preview this activity.

Call 1-888-537-4908 with activity questions.

More lab Activities Take It to the Net
pearsonsuccessnet.com

Find more about this activity at our Web site.

- See the **Teacher's Activity Guide** for more support.
- An alternative activity is also available to download.

How to Read Science

Reading Skills

Alike and Different

Alike means how things are the same.
Different means how things are not the same.

Science Article

Worms and Snakes

Worms are long and thin. Worms do not have backbones. Worms use their bodies to crawl. Snakes are long and thin. Snakes have backbones. Snakes use their bodies to crawl.

Apply It!

Tell how a worm and a snake are alike and different. Use your **models** to help you.

Alike	Different

37

How to Read Science Resource

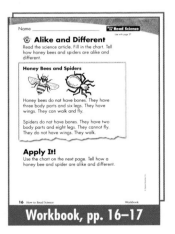

Workbook, pp. 16–17

ELL Support

For more practice on **Alike and Different**, use **Every Student Learns Teacher's Guide,** p. 9.

Alike and Different

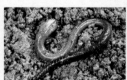

Reading Objective

• The student understands similarities and differences across texts (for example, topics, characters, problems).

About the Target Skill

The target skill for All About Animals is **Alike and Different**. Children are introduced to the skill as you guide them through this page.

1 | Introduce

Show pictures of an apple and a banana, or two other fruits, to the class. Or bring two different fruits to class and place them on your desk or table. Tell children to look at the fruits carefully. Ask: **How are [names of the fruits] alike? How are they different?** Children should note that both fruits are food. However, they differ in size, color, shape, and/or taste.

2 | Model the Skill

Look together at page 37. Read the Science Article as a class. Ask: **What does the Science Article tell you?** Things about worms and snakes **What do you see in each picture?** A worm and a snake **Are there things that look the same? Are there things that look different?**

3 | Practice

Graphic Organizer

Look at the Graphic Organizer together. Work with children to complete the Graphic Organizer using the facts from the Science Article.

Apply It!

Alike	Different
Long and thin Use bodies to crawl	Worms don't have backbones. Snakes have backbones.

What are some animals with backbones?

 Science Objective

- The student knows that the structural characteristics of plants and animals are used to group them.

1 Introduce

Quick ACTIVITY | TRANSPARENCY 8

Display the transparency and discuss how the two animals are alike and how they are different. Have children identify the animals. (a kangaroo and a cat) You might also ask children to look at the pictures on pages 38–39. Discuss how these animals are alike and different.

Access Prior Knowledge

Ask children: **How are a deer and a skunk alike?** Their fur covering, each animal has four legs and a tail Ask: **What other animals are like a deer and a skunk?** Possible answers: mouse, dog, cat, horse

Set Purpose

Tell children they are going to read about different kinds of animals. Help them set a **purpose for reading,** such as finding out how different animals are grouped.

2 Teach

Quick SUMMARY

- There are many different kinds of animals.
- Some animals have backbones.
- Bones give animals shape; they help animals move; they can help protect some animals' body parts.

Sing or play "What Has Backbones?" for children. Then read page 39 together. Discuss different kinds of animals. List the ways bones help animals.

You Are There

♪ What Has Backbones?

Sung to the tune of "There's a Hole In The Bucket"
Lyrics by Gerri Brioso & Richard Freitas/The Dovetail Group, Inc.

There are animals with backbones,
Like mammals.
Yes, mammals.
Dogs and cats,
Skunks and chipmunks,
All have backbones.

38 **Science Songs** ♪♪♪

Lesson 1 Resource

Workbook, p. 18

 **Science Songs** ♪♪♪

Use the Science Songs CD to play "What Has Backbones?" for the class.

Lesson 1

What are some animals with backbones?

There are many different kinds of animals. One main group of animals has backbones.

Bones help give an animal shape. Bones can help an animal move. Bones can help protect some body parts of animals.

A skunk has a backbone.

39

ELL Leveled Support

Which Animal Is It?

Beginning Have children cut pictures of animals from magazines to create a collage. As children work, talk as a class about the names of the animals. Have children write labels for the animals in their pictures.

Intermediate Have children use pictures of animals cut from magazines to create animal name flashcards for the class. If students know the names of some of the animals in their home language, ask them to share these with the class.

Advanced Have children cut pictures of animals from magazines. Then have them label each animal with its name in English. If students know the names of some of the animals in their home language, ask them to share these with the class.

Assign Quick Study pp. 16–17 to children who need help with lesson content.

Guide Comprehension

Ask children the following scaffolded questions to assess understanding.

Scaffolded Questions

1 **Name** *Name one main group of animals.* Animals with backbones

2 **Compare** *How are a deer and a skunk alike?* They have backbones.

3 **Evaluate** *Why is it useful to put animals in groups?* Because there are many different kinds of animals

Extend Vocabulary

Point out the word *different* on page 39. Use Graphic Organizer Transparency 4, a word web, to help children understand the word. Ask: *What does this word mean?* Not alike, or unlike. Ask: *What is the opposite of this word?* Same, or like. Place these answers on the web. To complete the web, encourage children to provide a sentence using the word and examples of things that are different.

Diagnostic Check

If... children have difficulty understanding how animals are grouped,

then... point out the two animals on pages 38–39 (deer and skunk). Tell children that these two animals have backbones. Explain that these animals are in a group of animals with backbones. Review the ways that bones help these animals.

Science Objectives

- The student compares the characteristics of things that live on land, in the water, and in the air.
- The student knows some characteristics of the vertebrate groups (mammals, reptiles, birds, amphibians, fish)
- The student knows that the structural characteristics of plants and animals are used to group them.
- The student knows that animals and plants can be associated with their environment by an examination of their structural characteristics (for example, physical structures are adaptations that allow plants and animals to survive, such as gills in fish, lungs in mammals).

2 | Teach (continued)

Quick SUMMARY

- Birds, fish, reptiles, amphibians, and mammals are animals that have backbones.
- Each of those animals has parts that help it survive in its environment.

Read pages 40–41 with children. Point out that all the animal groups described have backbones. Tell children that animals that have backbones are called vertebrates. Lead children in a discussion of how the animals in each group—mammals, birds, fish, reptiles, and amphibians—are the same and different.

Then look at the pictures. Ask: **What animals do you see?** Help children identify the chipmunk, hummingbird, fish, iguana, and red-eyed tree frog. Focus children's attention on each animal. Ask children to give one characteristic of each animal. Tell children that they will learn more about each of the animal groups pictured in later lessons. Explain that each of these animals has adaptations that help it survive.

Assign Quick Study pp. 18–19 to children who need help with lesson content.

Animals with Backbones

Mammals are animals with backbones. A mammal usually has hair or fur on its body. Young mammals get milk from their mother. Dogs and cats are two kinds of mammals. The chipmunk in the picture is a mammal.

Birds are animals with backbones. Birds have feathers and wings. Birds hatch from eggs.

Fish are animals with backbones. Fish live in water. Most fish are covered with scales. Fish have fins. Most fish hatch from eggs.

③

mammal   bird   fish

40

My Science Journal

A scientist's journal

Ask children to write entries in a scientist's journal about the different animal groups. Entries should include the name of each group, the shared characteristics of each group, and some examples.

Science Misconception

Animal Exceptions

- Not all birds fly. The ostrich, emu, and penguin are birds that don't fly. The ostrich is the largest bird in the world. Native to Africa, it can weigh as much as 300 pounds. Its small wings are useless for flying, but its long, powerful legs enable it to run up to 40 miles per hour. The emu is the second largest bird. It is native to Australia. It is similar to an ostrich, but smaller. It weighs up to 150 pounds, and can run up to 30 miles per hour. The penguin is native to the Southern Hemisphere. Its wings are adapted for swimming.
- Not all amphibians live in wet environments. Frogs and toads, for example, live in all but the most extreme dry or cold environments.

Reptiles are animals with backbones. Most reptiles have dry skin. Scales cover and protect a reptile's body. Some reptiles hatch from eggs. Snakes and turtles are two kinds of reptiles.

Amphibians are animals with backbones. Amphibians live part of their life in the water and part of their life on land. Most amphibians have smooth, wet skin. Amphibians hatch from eggs. Frogs and toads are amphibians.

✓**Lesson Checkpoint**

1. Which kinds of animals have backbones and scales?

2. 🔄 How are an amphibian and a reptile **alike** and **different?**

reptile

amphibian

41

ELL Support

Language Detectives: Building Vocabulary

Provide the following sentence frames for children to complete:

- A _____ has wings and can fly.
- A _____ has fins and can swim.
- A _____ has dry skin and scales.
- A _____ lives in water and on land.

Help children choose the appropriate animal that fits each description and write its name on the blank.

For scaffolded instruction about animals with backbones, use **Every Student Learns Teacher's Guide,** page 10.

For scaffolded instruction about animals with backbones, use **Every Student Learns Teacher's Guide,** page 10.

Lesson 2

What are some ways mammals are adapted?

 Science Objectives

- The student understands that structures of living things are adapted to their function in specific environments.
- The student knows some characteristics of the vertebrate groups (mammals, reptiles, birds, amphibians, fish).
- The student understands that living organisms need to be adapted to their environment to survive.
- The student knows that animals and plants can be associated with their environment by an examination of their structural characteristics (for example, physical structures are adaptations that allow plants and animals to survive, such as gills in fish, lungs in mammals).

1 | Introduce

Quick ACTIVITY | TRANSPARENCY 9

Ask children to draw a picture of an animal they think is a mammal. Use children's drawings to elicit a discussion of different mammals.

Access Prior Knowledge

Ask: **What does an animal need to stay alive?** (Food, water, shelter) Have children discuss how animals meet their needs.

Set Purpose

Tell children they are going to read about some mammals. Help them set a **purpose for reading,** such as to find out how mammals are adapted to live in different environments.

2 | Teach

Quick SUMMARY

- An animal's environment is all the living and nonliving things around it.
- Some animals are adapted to act in ways that let them live.

What are some ways mammals are adapted?

Mammals live almost everywhere in the world. Like plants, mammals have adapted to live in their environment. An animal's environment is all the living and nonliving things around it.

Like many animals, mule deer are adapted to their environment by camouflage. **Camouflage** is a color or shape that makes a plant or animal hard to see.

The mule deer's fur is brown in summer.

In winter, the mule deer's fur turns color. The deer is harder to see in the snow.

summer

winter

42

Lesson 2 Resource

Workbook, p. 19

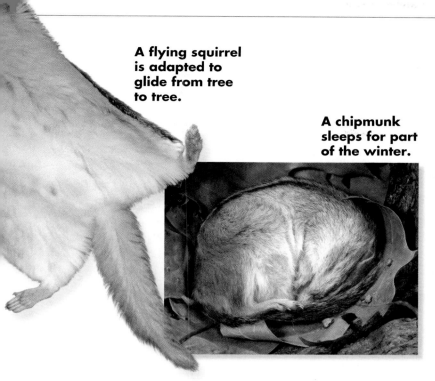

A flying squirrel is adapted to glide from tree to tree.

A chipmunk sleeps for part of the winter.

Some animals are adapted to act in ways that help them live. Chipmunks store some of the food they find in the summer. They sleep for part of the winter. Chipmunks eat some of the food they store every time they wake up.

✓ **Lesson Checkpoint**

1. How does a mule deer's fur change in winter?

2. **Art** in Science Draw a picture of a mammal that you have seen.

43

Read pages 42–43 together. Look at the pictures. Discuss the ways in which each animal is adapted.

Assign Quick Study pp. 18–19 to children who need help with lesson content.

Guide Comprehension

Ask children the following scaffolded questions to assess understanding.

Scaffolded Questions

1 **Name** *What two mammals can you name?* Sample answers: Mule deer and flying squirrel

2 **Infer** *How does camouflage help an animal stay safe from other animals that may want to hunt it?* Possible answer: Camouflage lets an animal blend in with its environment. This makes it hard for the hunter to see it and kill it.

3 **Evaluate** *In what way does a chipmunk plan ahead for winter?* It stores the food it finds in the summer for the winter.

Extend Vocabulary

Tell children to find the word *nonliving* on page 42. Ask: *What does this word mean?* Not living or not alive. Explain to children that the word is made up of the root word living and the prefix *non-*. Ask: *What do you think the prefix non- means?* Not. *How would you define the word nonfattening?* Not fattening *The word nonstop?* Not stopping. Ask children to come up with other words that have the prefix *non-*.

3 | Assess

✓ **Lesson Checkpoint**

1. A mule deer's fur turns color in winter.

2. **Art** in Science Children's drawings should show mammals they have observed when outdoors.

Science Background

Adaptation

Animals don't adapt to their environments. In order to survive in their environments, animals must be adapted to those environments. Adaptation is change that takes place over many generations. Animals that have adapted have a better chance of survival. For example, an animal that blends in with its environment is less likely to be prey than an animal that doesn't blend in. Therefore, it is more likely to survive and pass on its coloring to offspring. Explain to students that another adaptation of the mule deer is the ability to change the color of its coat each summer and winter.

ELL Support

Help children understand camouflage by scattering black and red dots or buttons on a large piece of red cloth. Ask: *Which is easiest to find, the black or the red dots (buttons)? Why?*

For scaffolded instruction about adaptations of mammals, use **Every Student Learns Teacher's Guide,** page 11.

What are some ways birds are adapted?

 Science Objectives

- The student knows some characteristics of the vertebrate groups (mammals, reptiles, birds, amphibians, fish).
- The student knows that animals and plants can be associated with their environment by an examination of their structural characteristics (for example, physical structures are adaptations that allow plants and animals to survive, such as gills in fish, lungs in mammals).

1 Introduce

Quick ACTIVITY   `TRANSPARENCY 10`

Hold up eating utensils, such as chopsticks, a fork, and a straw. Ask: **Which tool would you use to eat spaghetti?** Fork or chopsticks **Which tool would you use to drink a milkshake?** Straw Then ask: **What do birds eat with?** Their beaks

Access Prior Knowledge

Ask children to look at the pictures on pages 44–45. Ask: **How are these birds alike?** They have feathers, wings, beaks. **How are they different?** Children might mention sizes of birds, coloring, sizes and shapes of body parts.

Set Purpose

Tell children you are going to read to them about birds. Help them set a **purpose for listening,** such as to discover ways that birds are adapted to live in different environments.

2 Teach

Quick SUMMARY

- Birds have a variety of adaptations, including camouflage, beaks, and wings.

What are some ways birds are adapted?

Many birds are adapted to fly. Wings and feathers help birds fly.

The nightjar lives in fields. Its feathers look like the ground. This camouflage helps the bird hide from animals that might eat it.

This bird is called a nightjar.

Hmmm! A hummingbird's beak is adapted. A hummingbird uses its beak to drink liquid from flowers.

44

Lesson 3 Resource

Workbook, p. 20

ELL Support

Ask children questions about the pictures on pages 44–45 that require one- or two-word answers. For example, ask: **What camouflages the nightjar?** Feathers

Most penguins live where it is very cold.

A penguin's top feathers are waterproof. These feathers help keep the penguin dry. Tiny feathers below the top feathers trap air. The trapped air helps keep the penguin warm. ③

Penguins do not fly. Their wings are adapted for swimming. ②

✓ Lesson Checkpoint

1. How does camouflage protect the nightjar?

2. 🎯 How are hummingbirds and penguins **alike?** How are they **different?**

45

My Science Journal

Comparing animals

Have children work in small groups of three or four to compare the lists of animals they began on page 35. Encourage children to discuss places they have seen the animals.

Science Background

Nightjars, Hummingbirds, and Penguins

- A nightjar hunts insects at night for food.
- The hummingbird is attracted to the cardinal flower because of its red color and its plentiful nectar. The cardinal flower relies on the hummingbird for pollination.
- Adélie and Chinstrap penguins build nests from pebbles and stones. King and Emperor penguins hold their eggs on their feet.

ELL Support

For scaffolded instruction about bird adaptations, use **Every Student Learns Teacher's Guide,** p. 12.

Read pages 44–45 to children and have children follow along. Ask: **What kind of environment does each bird live in?** Children can use the pictures and text for clues.

Discuss the different adaptations of each bird that help it survive in each kind of environment.

Assign Quick Study pp. 20–21 to children who need help with lesson content.

Guide Comprehension

Ask children the following scaffolded questions to assess understanding.

Scaffolded Questions

① **Recall** **What food does a hummingbird eat?** Liquid from flowers

② **Analyze** **How do a penguin's wings help it survive?** The wings help the penguin swim in the ocean to find food.

③ **Compare** **Both a nightjar and a penguin have special feathers that protect them.** How do each bird's feathers protect it? The nightjar's feathers provide camouflage. The penguin's special feathers keep the penguin warm and dry.

Extend Vocabulary

Write the word *waterproof* on the board. Tell children it is an example of a compound word, or a word made up of two words. Ask: **What are the two words that make up this word?** Water and proof. Tell children that as used here, the word *proof* means "something that protects against." Waterproof feathers protect against water. Ask: **What are some other compound words of proof? What do they mean?** Possible answers: Heatproof: protected against heat; rainproof: protected against rain.

3 | Assess

✓ Lesson Checkpoint

1. Camouflage protects the nightjar by helping it hide from animals that might eat it.

2. 🎯 **Alike and Different** Alike: Both are birds. Different: Hummingbirds have wings that help them fly; penguins have wings that help them swim.

Lesson 4

What are some ways fish are adapted?

 Science Objectives

- The student understands that structures of living things are adapted to their function in specific environments.
- The student knows some characteristics of the vertebrate groups (mammals, reptiles, birds, amphibians, fish).
- The student understands that living organisms need to be adapted to their environment to survive.

1 Introduce

Quick ACTIVITY | TRANSPARENCY 11 |

Ask children to think about a pet or an animal they know about. Ask: **How might this animal act when it wants to protect itself?** Have children write one or two sentences to explain. Possible answers: dogs bark, cats screech.

Access Prior Knowledge

Ask: **Where do fish live?** In water **How do fins help fish?** They help the fish swim.

Set Purpose

Tell children they are going to read about fish. Help them set a **purpose for reading,** such as to find out what different fish do to protect themselves and find food.

2 Teach

Quick SUMMARY

- Fish are adapted to life in the water.
- Gills help fish get oxygen from the water. Fins help fish swim.

Lesson 4

What are some ways fish are adapted?

Fish are adapted to life in the water. Fish have gills. **Gills** are body parts that help fish get oxygen from the water. Fish have fins to help them swim.

This porcupine fish is adapted to protect itself. The porcupine fish can make itself big. Sharp spikes stick out from its body when it is big.

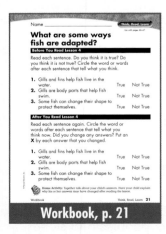

Gill   Fin

This tiny porcupine fish can become very big.

Changing shape protects the porcupine fish.

46

Lesson 4 Resource

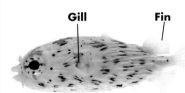

What are some ways fish are adapted?

Before You Read Lesson 4

Read each sentence. Do you think it is true? Do you think it is not true? Circle the word or words after each sentence that tell what you think.

1. Gills and fins help fish live in the water.   True   Not True
2. Gills are body parts that help fish swim.   True   Not True
3. Some fish can change their shape to protect themselves.   True   Not True

After You Read Lesson 4

Read each sentence again. Circle the word or words after each sentence that tell what you think now. Did you change any answers? Put an X by each answer that you changed.

1. Gills and fins help fish live in the water.   True   Not True
2. Gills are body parts that help fish swim.   True   Not True
3. Some fish can change their shape to protect themselves.   True   Not True

Workbook, p. 21

ELL Support

Point to the picture of the sharp spikes sticking out from the porcupine fish. Ask children to use adjectives to describe how these spikes look and how they might feel.

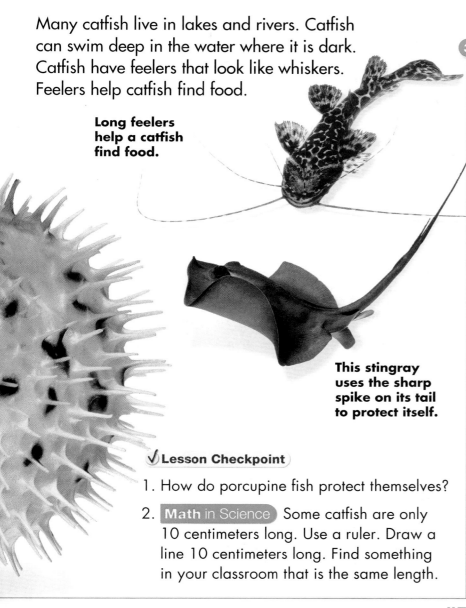

Many catfish live in lakes and rivers. Catfish can swim deep in the water where it is dark. Catfish have feelers that look like whiskers. Feelers help catfish find food.

Long feelers help a catfish find food.

This stingray uses the sharp spike on its tail to protect itself.

✓ **Lesson Checkpoint**

1. How do porcupine fish protect themselves?

2. **Math in Science** Some catfish are only 10 centimeters long. Use a ruler. Draw a line 10 centimeters long. Find something in your classroom that is the same length.

47

Science Background

Porcupine Fish

Porcupine fish have large eyes, beaklike teeth, and spine-covered skin. They can be found in coral reefs in oceans all around the world. Porcupine fish can range in length from three to nineteen inches. The Porcupine fish hunts over the ocean floor at night, using tiny jets of water to uncover its prey.

Art Link

Fish

Have children use classroom books, textbooks, and library resources to locate pictures of different fish. Tell each child to choose one fish and draw a picture of it. In drawing their fish, children should remember to include characteristics that they see in each fish, such as gills and/or fins. Then have children write one or two sentences about the fish they drew. Display children's work.

ELL Support

For scaffolded instruction about adaptations of fish, use **Every Student Learns Teacher's Guide,** p. 13.

Read pages 46–47 with children. Examine the pictures so children can see how each fish is adapted to protect itself or to find food. Tell children to look closely at the two pictures of the porcupine fish, one before and one after it swells up.

Tell children that the spikes of the porcupine fish and stingray help them defend themselves against enemies and survive in their environments.

Assign Quick Study pp. 22–23 to children who need help with lesson content.

Guide Comprehension

Ask children the following scaffolded questions to assess understanding.

Scaffolded Questions

1 Explain *Why does a porcupine fish makes itself big?* To protect itself

2 Appraise *Why are spikes a good adaptation for animal survival?* Enemies don't want to go near an animal with spikes because they might get hurt.

3 Infer *Why does a catfish need feelers to find food?* It is dark at the bottom of the water where the catfish looks for food.

Extend Vocabulary

Write the word *catfish* and *stingray* on the board. Ask: **What two smaller words do you see in each word?** cat/fish, sting/ray Explain that some words in English are made up of two words joined together. Such words are called compound words. Ask: **What kind of fish do people sometimes have as a pet?** (gold/fish)

3 Assess

✓ **Lesson Checkpoint**

1. Porcupine fish can make themselves look big. Sharp spikes stick out from their body when they are big.

2. **Math in Science** Answers will vary. Possible answers: book, pencil

What are some ways reptiles are adapted?

Science Objectives

- The student knows some characteristics of the vertebrate groups (mammals, reptiles, birds, amphibians, fish).
- The student knows that plants and animals are adapted to different ranges of temperature and moisture.
- The student understands that living organisms need to be adapted to their environment to survive.

1 | Introduce

Quick ACTIVITY | TRANSPARENCY 12

Show children pictures of various reptiles. Use the pictures to review what children have learned about the characteristics of reptiles: they have bones, dry, scaly skin, hatch from eggs.

Access Prior Knowledge

Ask children: **What are some reptiles you know about?** Snakes, lizards, turtles, chameleons.

Set Purpose

Tell children they are going to read about reptiles. Help them set a **purpose for reading,** such as to find out ways that different reptiles catch and eat food.

2 | Teach

Quick SUMMARY

- Snakes swallow their food whole.
- The chameleon's good eyesight and long tongue help it catch food.
- The desert iguana's light skin helps it stay cool in the hot sun.

Lesson 5

What are some ways reptiles are adapted?

Reptiles are adapted to changes in air temperature. A reptile's body is cold when the air is cold. A reptile's body is warm when the air is warm. Reptiles can move quickly when they are warm.

Zap!

A chameleon has a long tongue. The chameleon has a sticky ball at the end of its tongue. Food ② **sticks to this ball.**

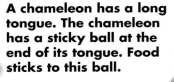

Open wide!

This snake's mouth is adapted to open very wide. This snake can swallow its food whole.

48

Lesson 5 Resource

Name _____

What are some ways reptiles are adapted?

Before You Read Lesson 5

Read each sentence. Do you think it is true? Do you think it is not true? Circle the word or words after each sentence that tell what you think.

1. Reptiles get cold when the air is cold and warm when the air is warm. True Not True
2. A chameleon uses its long, sticky tongue to catch food. True Not True
3. Snakes use teeth to chew their food. True Not True

After You Read Lesson 5

Read each sentence again. Circle the word or words after each sentence that tell what you think now. Did you change any answers? Put an X by each answer that you changed.

1. Reptiles get cold when the air is cold and warm when the air is warm. True Not True
2. A chameleon uses its long, sticky tongue to catch food. True Not True
3. Snakes use teeth to chew their food. True Not True

Home Activity: Together talk about your child's answers. Have your child explain why his or her answers may have changed after reading the lesson.

Workbook, p. 22

ELL Support

Draw children's attention to the adjective *cold* on page 48. Ask children to name other words that have a similar meaning. List the synonyms on the board.

A desert iguana is adapted to live in the hot, sunny desert. Dark colors get hot in the sun. Light colors stay cooler in the sun. The light skin helps the desert iguana keep cool.

desert iguana

✓ Lesson Checkpoint

1. How is a desert iguana adapted to live in its environment?

2. **Writing** in Science Tell one way some snakes are adapted to get food.

49

Science Misconception

Chameleons

Chameleons don't change color to match their surroundings. Instead, they change color in response to temperature or light, or to signal other chameleons.

Science Journal

Tell children that reptiles get warm by sitting in the sun. This is because they absorb heat. Have available a large, cool stone. Allow children to feel the stone. Then put it on a windowsill in the sunlight or under a lamp. Let the stone remain there for several hours. Have children feel the stone. The absorption of energy from the Sun in the form of heat raises the temperature of an object. This is the principle behind solar heating devices. Students should record their observations in their science journals.

ELL Support

For scaffolded instruction about adaptations of reptiles, use **Every Student Learns Teacher's Guide,** p. 14.

Read pages 48–49 with children. Have children look at the pictures and discuss the different adaptations described. Have children tell how the adaptations help reptiles survive in their environments.

Ask: **Why does a snake's mouth open very wide?** So the snake can swallow its food whole

Assign Quick Study pp. 24–25 to children who need help with lesson content.

Guide Comprehension

Ask children the following scaffolded questions to assess understanding.

Scaffolded Questions

1 **Name** *Name three kinds of reptiles.* Snake, chameleon, desert iguana

2 **Tell** *How does the sticky ball at the end of a chameleon's tongue help it catch food?* The food sticks to it.

3 **Predict** *What color do you think most desert animals are?* Light color

Extend Vocabulary

Write the words *whole/hole* on the board. Ask a volunteer to read each word. Ask: **Do these words sound the same?** Yes **Do they mean the same? What does each word mean?** No; *whole* means "entire," *hole* means "an open place." Say: **These words are homophones. Homophones are words that sound the same but are spelled differently and have different meanings.** Ask children to write a sentence using the word *hole* and a sentence using the word *whole.*

3 | Assess

✓ Lesson Checkpoint

1. It has light skin that keeps it cool.

2. **Writing** in Science Snakes open their mouths very wide and swallow their food whole.

Lesson 6

What are some ways amphibians are adapted?

 Science Objectives

- The student knows some characteristics of the vertebrate groups (mammals, reptiles, birds, amphibians, fish).
- The student knows that plants and animals are adapted to different ranges of temperature and moisture.
- The student understands that living organisms need to be adapted to their environment to survive.

1 Introduce

Quick ACTIVITY | TRANSPARENCY 13 |

Have children make a model of where a frog might live. Provide craft materials such as construction paper, glue, and crayons and markers. When children are done, have them describe their models.

Access Prior Knowledge

Have students look at the picture of the frogs on page 50. Ask: **Where might you find frogs?** In water and on land

Set Purpose

Tell children they are going to read about amphibians. Help them set a **purpose for reading,** such as to find out how different amphibians are adapted to their environment.

2 Teach

Quick SUMMARY

- Most amphibians begin life in the water. Many move to land when they are grown.
- Frogs have smooth, wet skin.

Lesson 6

What are some ways amphibians are adapted?

Most amphibians begin their life in the water. Many amphibians move to the land when they are grown. Frogs are amphibians. Frogs often live near water. Smooth, wet skin helps frogs live in moist environments.

These tree frogs have bright red eyes. Other animals want to eat the frogs. The frogs' eyes help scare these animals away.

50

Lesson 6 Resource

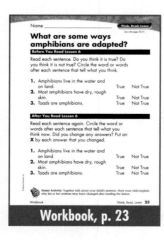

Workbook, p. 23

ELL Support

To reinforce their understanding of how amphibians adapt, have children create a word web that describes amphibians.

Toads are amphibians. Toads begin their life in water. Toads move to the land when they are grown. Toads dig deep into the ground when it is very hot. They look for food at night.

Most toads have dry, rough skin.

✓ **Lesson Checkpoint**

1. Name one way a toad and a frog are different.

2. **Writing** in Science Tell how bright red eyes can help a tree frog.

51

Science Background

Frogs

- Red-eyed tree frogs live in the rain forest. This frog's green color is its camouflage when it sleeps. If it hears another animal, its eyes open. The flash of its red eyes confuses or scares a predator.

- The waterholding frog can wait up to seven years for rain. During that time, it lives in a bubble made with its own shed skin.

Writing Link

Tell children to choose two groups of animals with backbones. Have them write two or three rhyming sentences about each group. Have them read their sentences to the class.

ELL Support

For scaffolded instruction about adaptations of amphibians, use **Every Student Learns Teacher's Guide**, p. 15.

Read pages 50–51 with children. Ask: **What kinds of environments do amphibians live in?** Wet, dry Use the pictures to discuss the different adaptations of the tree frog and toad.

Make sure children understand that most amphibians are born in water and move to land when they are grown. Ask: **Where do amphibians begin their life?** In water **Where do many amphibians move when they are grown?** To land

Assign Quick Study pp. 26–27 to children who need help with lesson content.

Guide Comprehension

Ask children the following scaffolded questions to assess understanding.

Scaffolded Questions

1 **Recall What adaptation helps a frog live in moist places?** Smooth, wet skin

2 **Explain What do toads do when it is hot?** Toads dig into the ground where they can stay for a long time.

3 **Hypothesize Why do you think some amphibians look for food at night?** Possible answer: At night their enemies can't see them easily.

Extend Vocabulary

Tell children that the skin of most amphibians is smooth and wet. Point out that *smooth* and *wet* are descriptive words. They help paint a picture of what amphibians look like. Ask children to provide other words that can describe amphibians. (moist, silky, soft)

3 | Assess

✓ **Lesson Checkpoint**

1. Frogs have smooth, wet skin. Toads have rough, dry skin.

2. **Writing** in Science The tree frog's bright red eyes scare away other animals.

Lesson 7

What are some animals without backbones?

  Science Objectives

- The student knows that the structural characteristics of plants and animals are used to group them.
- The student understands that structures of living things are adapted to their function in specific environments.

1 | Introduce

Quick ACTIVITY | TRANSPARENCY 14 |

Have students work with a partner to brainstorm a list of as many different insects as they can. Then call on volunteer pairs to read their lists aloud.

Access Prior Knowledge

Ask children what they know about ants. Prompt their thinking by asking: **What does an ant look like? Where does it live?**

Set Purpose

Tell children they are going to read about animals without backbones. Help them set a **purpose for reading,** such as to find out ways in which animals without backbones are adapted to their environments.

2 | Teach

Quick SUMMARY

- All insects have three body parts and six legs.
- Some insects have antennae that help them feel, smell, hear, and taste things.

Read pages 52–53 together. Tell children that the biggest group of animals without backbones is the insect group. Note the physical characteristics that all insects share.

What are some animals without backbones?

One main group of animals has backbones. Another main group of animals does not have backbones. Most kinds of animals do not have bones.

Insects are animals that do not have bones. Insects have three body parts. The body parts are the head, the thorax, and the abdomen. Insects have six legs. Antennae help some insects feel, smell, hear, and taste.

Abdomen

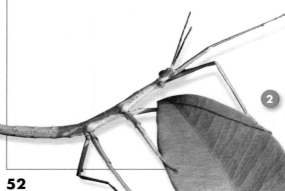

This insect is called a walking stick. Camouflage makes the insect hard to see on a plant.

52

Lesson 7 Resource

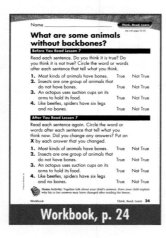

Workbook, p. 24

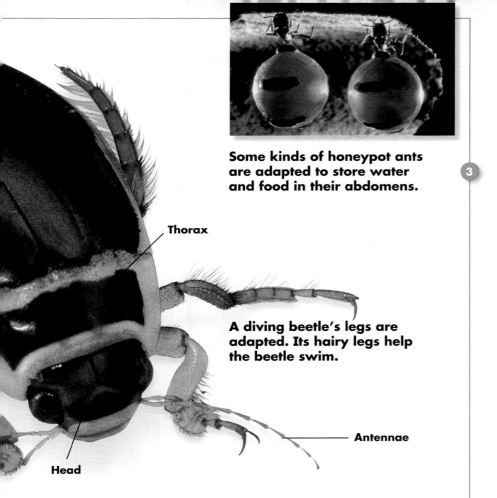

Some kinds of honeypot ants are adapted to store water and food in their abdomens.

3

Thorax

A diving beetle's legs are adapted. Its hairy legs help the beetle swim.

Antennae

Head

1. ✓**Checkpoint** How is the diving beetle adapted to life in water?

2. **Technology** in Science Tell about inventions that help people move in water.

Science Background

Insects

- There are more than 800,000 known species of insects. Many spread diseases and damage plants and crops. However, many insects are also beneficial. They pollinate plants and serve as food for other animals.

- In some countries, honeypot ants are a delicacy. The whole ant or just its swollen abdomen may be eaten.

- Some walkingsticks also have an offensive odor for protection and sometimes their eggs look like seeds.

Math Link

How Many Legs?

Remind children that all insects have three body parts and six legs. Ask: **How many body parts do two insects have in all?** Six Children can use counters or make marks on paper to help them answer. Say: **Write a number sentence.** 3 + 3 = 6

Then ask: **How many legs do two insects have in all?** 12 **Write a number sentence.** 6 + 6 = 12

Assign Quick Study pp. 28–29 to children who need help with lesson content.

Guide Comprehension

Ask children the following scaffolded questions to assess understanding.

Scaffolded Questions

1 **Identify** *How do insects use antennae?* To feel, smell, hear, and taste

2 **Analyze** *In what kind of environment does a walkingstick live? How do you know?* A place with twigs, such as a field or a forest. It would blend with that kind of place.

3 **Judge** *Do you think a honeypot ant lives well with other honeypot ants? Explain.* Yes. Honeypot ants share water and food when needed.

Extend Vocabulary

Use the diving beetle picture on pages 52–53 to discuss insect body parts. Write the words *abdomen* and *thorax* on the board. Using the picture, explain that the abdomen is the back section of an insect's body. The thorax is the part of an insect's body between its head and its abdomen.

Diagnostic Check

If... children have difficulty understanding how insects are grouped,

then... show children pictures of different insects, such as a grasshopper, an ant, and a beetle. Have children count the body parts (3) and the legs (6) of each insect.

3 | Assess

✓**Checkpoint**

1. A diving beetle's legs help it swim.

2. **Technology** in Science Answers will vary.

Science Objective ⭐

- The student knows that the structural characteristics of plants and animals are used to group them.

2 | Teach (continued)

Quick SUMMARY

- An octopus and a spider do not have backbones.
- An octopus is adapted to find and catch food in the ocean.
- A spider can spin a web to trap its food.
- An octopus has eight arms and a spider has eight legs.

Read pages 54–55 with children. Point out that both the octopus and spider are in the group of animals that do not have backbones.

Use the pictures to discuss the different adaptations that help each animal live in its environment.

Other Animals Without Backbones

An octopus lives in the ocean. An octopus is an animal without a backbone.

An octopus is adapted to find and catch food. An octopus has good eyesight. Its eyesight helps it find food. The suction cups on its ① arms help the octopus hold its food.

An octopus has 8 arms.

54

My Science Journal

Grouping Animals

Have children look at the animal lists they began on page 35. Tell children to now group the animals on their lists. Encourage children to use their observations as well as what they have learned about how scientists group animals. Suggest that they use groupings such as backbones/no backbones, live in water/live on land, fins/no fins, and so on.

Science Background

Octopuses

- Octopuses have gills, like fish.
- Octopuses spit out dark ink to hide themselves. Then they gulp water and push the water out fast to escape enemies.
- Octopuses can change color when attacking prey, or as camouflage.

ELL Support

For scaffolded instruction about animals without backbones, use **Every Student Learns Teacher's Guide,** p. 16.

Spiders are animals without backbones. Spiders have eight legs. Spiders are adapted to spin webs. The webs trap insects that spiders eat.

This spider builds a web to trap insects.

✓ **Lesson Checkpoint**

1. Tell how the octopus is adapted to find food.

2. **Math in Science** A spider has 8 legs. How many legs will 2 spiders have in all? Write a number sentence to show your answer.

55

Ask children the following scaffolded questions to assess understanding.

Scaffolded Questions

❶ Recall *What does an octopus use to hold its food?* Suction cups on its arms

❷ Explain *Why does a spider trap flies and other insects?* To eat them

❸ Classify *A spider has 8 legs. Is it an insect or not? Explain.* No, it is not an insect. Insects have 6 legs.

Extend Vocabulary

Remind children they have learned about an *octopus*. Write the word octopus on the board, underlining as shown: <u>octo</u>pus. Say: ***Octo- means "eight." How many legs does an octopus have?*** Eight ***Can you think of any other word that begins with octo-?*** October Explain that long ago, in the Roman calendar, October was the eighth month of the year.

3 | Assess

✓ **Lesson Checkpoint**

1. The octopus has good eyesight and suction cups on its arms that help it find and hold its food in the water.

2. **Math in Science** Two spiders have 16 legs in all. 8 + 8 = 16.

ELL Leveled Support

Comparing Animals

Beginning On the board, write the words *Bird, Fish,* and *Both.* Then read each of the following characteristics aloud. Ask children to call out the word *bird* or *fish* or *both* to match that characteristic.

   Has feathers   Lays eggs   Has bones   Has scales

Intermediate Have children work with partners. Write the headings *Bird* and *Fish* on the board. Have children copy the headings on a sheet of paper. Then have them write descriptions under each group. When they are done, have them circle the characteristics that are the same for each group and write them under the heading *Bird and Fish.*

Advanced Draw a Venn diagram on the board. Tell children that a Venn diagram is a way to show how two things are the same and how they are different. Explain to children how to use the Venn diagram. Have children complete the Venn diagram using the headings *Bird, Fish,* and *Both* and the characteristics Has feathers, Lays eggs, Has bones, and Has scales.

SCAFFOLDED INQUIRY

▉▉ **Investigate** How can an octopus use its arms?

⊛ **Science Objective**

• The student understands that structures of living things are adapted to their function in specific environments.

1 | Build Background

This activity encourages children to figure out how an octopus uses suction cups on its arms.

Managing Time and Materials

Time:	15 minutes
Groups:	Small groups
Materials:	*clear plastic jar with lid (16 oz); 8 suction cups ($1\frac{1}{4}$ in. diam.); Fish (Activity Master 1); scissors; construction paper (optional)*
Center:	This activity can be set up in your Science Center for children to work on throughout the day.

Materials listed in *italic* are kit materials.

Advance Preparation

Copy the fish shape for each group. Use Activity Master 1. You may wish to copy the master onto colored construction paper.

Teaching Tip

Cut construction paper to letter size if copier does not have an adjustable tray.

2 | What to Do

Encourage Guided Inquiry

Preview the activity and materials with children. Ask: **How can you use suction cups to open a jar?**

Guide children to write an If.../then... statement such as **If I use a suction cup on the lid and a suction cup on the side of the jar, then I will be able to open the jar.**

Engage Look at the picture of Billye the octopus. Ask children to tell what they know about an octopus. Then ask why children think an octopus would want to open a jar. (To get food that is inside) Discuss things that people might use to open jars more easily. If possible, bring such devices to class.

Investigate How can an octopus use its arms?

An octopus has suction cups on its 8 arms. It can use its arms to pick things up. Billye the octopus uses its arms to solve a problem. Billye can open a jar to get a fish inside.

Materials

✂ scissors

🐟 fish

🫙 jar

8 suction cups

What to Do

① Cut out the fish.

② Put the fish in the jar. **Predict** how many suction cups you will need to open a jar.

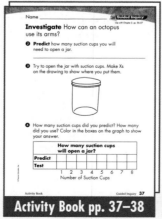

Process Skills

When you share your ideas, you **communicate** with classmates.

Activity Resources

Investigate How can an octopus use its arms?

❷ **Predict** how many suction cups you will need to open a jar.

❸ Try to open the jar with suction cups. Make Xs on the drawing to show where you put them.

❹ How many suction cups did you predict? How many did you use? Color in the boxes on the graph to show your answer.

How many suction cups will open a jar?								
Predict								
Test								
	1	2	3	4	5	6	7	8

Number of Suction Cups

Activity Book | Guided Inquiry **37**

Activity Book pp. 37–38

Activity Rubric

Investigate: How can an octopus use its arms?

Scoring Criteria	1	2	3	4
Student followed directions to complete this activity.				
Student **predicted** the number of suction cups needed to open the jar.				
Student figured out how to place the suction cups.				
Student recorded the **prediction** and result in a bar graph.				
Student **communicated** how the suction cups were used.				

Scoring Key
4 points correct, complete, detailed
3 points partially correct, complete, detailed
2 points partially correct, partially complete, lacks some detail
1 point incorrect or incomplete, needs assistance

T68 Guided Inquiry | Activity Book

Activity Rubric

Use Activity DVD Unit A, Chapter 2 to preview this activity.

Call 1-888-537-4908 with activity questions.

🖥**More** Lab zone **Activities** Take It to the Net pearsonsuccessnet.com

Find more about this activity at our Web site.

• See the **Teacher's Activity Guide** for more support.
• An alternative activity is also available to download.

3 Work with your group. Take turns. Try to open the jar with suction cups. Where should you put them?

4 How many suction cups did you predict? How many did you use?

How many suction cups will open a jar?								
Predict								
Test								

1   2   3   4   5   6   7   8
Number of Suction Cups

Explain Your Results

Communicate Tell how you used the suction cups.

Go Further

What other problems can you solve using suction cups? Try to solve the problems!

Explore As children place the suction cups on the jar, ask how they plan to use the suction cups. Tell children they can work together to open the jar.

Explain After completing the activity, ask how the suction cups helped them open the jar. Have children explain why it was important that the suction cups stuck to the jar. Ask children why it would be harder to open the jar lid if instead it had been covered by a smooth cloth, such as a napkin or scarf. Discuss why an octopus might use its suction cups in the ocean, such as to capture and hold prey.

Extend Challenge children to pick up objects in the classroom using just two suction cups. Have children think about other ways that people use suction cups.

Evaluate Have children compare their predictions with their test. Did they use more suction cups than they expected? Can they figure out a way to use fewer suction cups?

3 | Explain Your Results

Use these questions to help children review evidence and develop explanations.

Communicate Possible Answer: I used two suction cups on the lid to turn it. My partner held the jar steady with two more suction cups.

Go Further

Children may propose any number of modifications to finding out how an octopus uses its suction cups. Guide children to sort questions into those that can be answered with the materials available in the classroom and those that cannot.

Post additional questions children have about how an octopus uses its suction cups. Encourage children to experiment on their own.

Process Skills

Communicate

Discuss the importance of being able to communicate information. When someone communicates, they tell what they know about something to another person. Help children understand that there are different ways to communicate information. For example, they might communicate information by speaking, by writing words, by drawing a picture, or by creating a data table. You can use the Process Skills sheet on Communicating at this time.

Science Background

Octopuses

- Octopuses belong to the class of invertebrates known as cephalopods. These animals are characterized by tentacles attached to their heads. Other cephalopods include squids and cuttlefish.

- Scientists have discovered that cephalopods exhibit intelligent behavior. Octopuses have shown that they can solve problems, learn cues, and remember solutions.

- Biologists who are studying these animals observed Billye, a giant Pacific octopus, open a glass jar to remove a fish. When presented with a jar, Billye learned to grasp the jar, get it into position, and twist off the lid.

ELL Support

Access Content Before beginning the activity, conduct an inventory of materials with children. Solicit other names for each item. Accept labels in English and children's home languages.

Sorting Animals

 Science Objective

- The student uses mathematical language to read and interpret data on a simple concrete graph, pictorial graph, or chart.

1 | Introduce

Quick ACTIVITY

Draw a tally chart on the board. Title one column *Girls* and the other column *Boys*. Take a survey of class members and record the results. Ask: **How is the information in a tally chart recorded?** Have children form smaller groups of about five to six boys and girls. Have each group take a survey of their members and record their results on a tally chart.

2 | Teach the Skill

Read pages 58–59 with children.

Encourage children to name the pictured animals. Children should tell whether each animal has a backbone or does not have a backbone.

Help children understand that whether or not an animal has a backbone determines its placement in the tally chart on page 59.

- The frog, deer, penguin, snake, and porcupine fish have backbones.
- The octopus and diving beetle do not have backbones.

Math in Science

Sorting Animals

Sort these animals into 2 groups. One group has animals with backbones. Count the number of animals with backbones. The other group has animals without backbones. Count the number of animals without backbones.

tree frog

octopus

penguin

deer

diving beetle

58 **e Tools** Take It to the Net
pearsonsuccessnet.com

Activity Resource

Workbook, p. 25

e Tools Take It to the Net
pearsonsuccessnet.com

Make a graph like this one. Color in your graph to show the number of animals in each group.

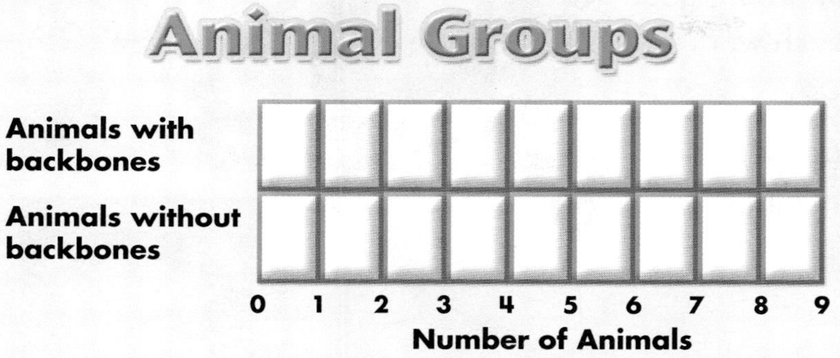

Animal Groups

Animals with backbones

Animals without backbones

0 1 2 3 4 5 6 7 8 9

Number of Animals

1. Which group has the most animals?
2. Which group has the fewest animals?

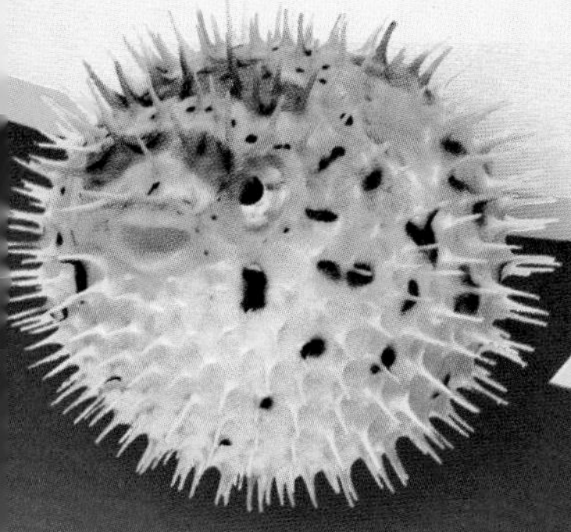

porcupine fish

snake

Lab zone **Take-Home Activity**

Take a nature walk. List all of the animals you see. Sort the animals into groups.

59

Ask: **How do you know that the diving beetle does not have a backbone?** Insects do not have bones.

Ask: **Can you name another animal that does not have a backbone?** Possible answer: bee

Guide Comprehension

Ask children the following scaffolded questions to assess understanding.

Scaffolded Questions

1 Recall **How many animals shown have backbones?** Five **How many animals shown do not have backbones?** Two **How many animals are there in all?** Seven

2 Examine **What does the tally chart show?** The tally chart shows animals with backbones and animals without backbones.

3 Extend **Look at the tally chart. Add two more animals with backbones to the chart. How many animals with backbones are there now?** Seven **How many animals are there in all?** Nine

3 | Assess

1. Animals with backbones
2. Animals without backbones

Take-Home Activity

Tips for Success

- Assist children in creating a tally chart and writing the correct headings (Animals with backbones, Animals without backbones). Also review how to tally data.

- Help children brainstorm the kinds of animals they might see on a nature walk.

- Remind children to sort the animals they list into the identified groups.

- Have children tally the number of listed animals in each group using the tally chart. Have them use this information to count how many animals with backbones they saw and how many animals without backbones they saw. Then have them use the information to count how many more animals with backbones or animals without backbones there are.

- Children can share their tally charts with their family or friends.

Vocabulary

1. C
2. D
3. A
4. E
5. F
6. B

What did you learn?

7. Fish use gills to get oxygen from the water.

8. It makes an animal hard to see.

9. Animals with backbones: mammals, birds, fish, reptiles, amphibians. Animals without backbones: insects, octopuses, spiders.

Vocabulary

Which picture goes with each word?

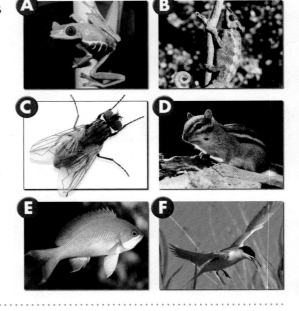

1. insect
2. mammal
3. amphibian
4. fish
5. bird
6. reptile

What did you learn?

7. How do fish use gills?

8. How does camouflage help protect animals?

9. Name 2 kinds of animals with backbones. Name 2 kinds of animals without backbones.

Assessment Resources

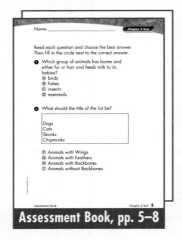

Assessment Book, pp. 5–8

MindPoint Quiz Show

MindPoint enables children to test their knowledge of the chapter in a game format.

ExamView Use ExamView as a print or online assessment tool.

Success Tracker

Data management system to track Adequate Yearly Progress (AYP) and provide intervention online at **pearsonsuccessnet.com/ successtracker**

Take-Home Booklet

Children can make a Take-Home Booklet using Workbook p. 27.

10. Communicate Choose an animal in this chapter. Tell one way the animal is adapted to its environment.

Alike and Different

11. Tell how a spider and an insect are **alike and different.**

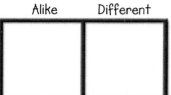

Alike	Different

Test Prep

Fill in the circle next to the correct answer.

12. Which kind of animal has feathers and wings?

Ⓐ fish
Ⓑ bird
Ⓒ mammal
Ⓓ amphibian

13. Writing in Science Choose an animal. Tell how the animal is adapted to its environment.

61

Process Skills

10. Communicate
Answers will vary but may include a penguin's wings are adapted for swimming. Its feathers are adapted to help it stay warm.

Alike and Different

11. Alike: Both are animals that do not have backbones. Different: A spider has 8 legs and an insect has 6 legs.

Alike	Different
Without backbones	Number of legs— insect 6, spiders 8 Insects have antennae

Test Prep

12. B

13. Writing in Science Answers will vary.

Intervention and Remediation

⭐ Science Objectives	Review Item	Student Edition Pages	Teacher Edition Resources			Ancillary Resources		
			Guide Comprehension	Extend Vocab	Diagnostic Check	Vocab Cards	Quick Study	Workbook Pages
The student knows that the structural characteristics of plants and animals are used to group them.	9, 11, 12	38–41, 52–55	39, 41, 55	41, 51, 55	39, 53	40–41, 52	39, 40, 53	18, 24
The student compares the characteristics of things that live on land, in the water, and in the air.	10, 12, 13	40–41		39, 41		40–41	40	18
The student understands that structures of living things are adapted to their function in specific environments.	7, 10, 13	42–47, 52–53, 56–57	43, 45, 47, 49	45		42, 46	43, 45, 47	19, 21, 24
The student knows some characteristics of the vertebrate groups (mammals, reptiles, birds, amphibians, fish)	7, 9, 12	40–51	39, 41	41	39	40–41, 46	40, 43, 45, 47, 49, 51	18, 19, 20, 21, 22, 23
The student understands that living organisms need to be adapted to their environment to survive.	8, 10, 13	42–51	43, 45, 47, 49, 51, 53			42, 46	43, 47, 49, 51	19, 21, 22, 23
The student knows that animals and plants can be associated with their environment by an examination of their structural characteristics (for example, physical structures are adaptations that allow plants and animals to survive, such as gills in fish, lungs in mammals).	7, 10, 13	40–45	41, 45, 53				40, 43, 45	18, 19, 20
The student knows that there are many different kinds of living things that live in a variety of environments.	10	44–45	39	39		40-42	45	20
The student knows that plants and animals are adapted to different ranges of temperature and moisture.	10, 13	48–51	45, 51	39, 45		52	49, 51, 53	22, 23

Life Along the Ice

 Science Objective

- The student knows that living things are found almost everywhere in the world.

1 Introduce

Quick ACTIVITY

Remind children that all living things need certain things in order to survive. Point to the picture of the penguins. Ask children to list things these penguins need to survive (food, water, air, space, shelter). Write the list on the board.

Access Prior Knowledge

Point to the picture of the penguins. Ask: **Do penguins live where it is cold or where it is warm?** (Cold) As a class, make a list of other animals that are adapted to live in cold places. Examples may include polar bears, Arctic hares, Arctic foxes, caribou, whales, elephant seals, and snowy owls. If possible, obtain photos of some of these animals from books, magazines, or the Internet.

2 Teach

Quick SUMMARY

- Many penguins live in the ocean near Antarctica.
- Penguins eat krill that live in areas of melted ice.
- Scientists learn about penguins and other animals using satellites.

Read pages 62–63 with children.

Have children examine the map of Antarctica. Explain that Antarctica is located at the South Pole. Some children may mistakenly believe that the North Pole is cold but the South Pole is hot. Tell children that Antarctica is the coldest, windiest place on Earth. The ground is covered by a sheet of ice throughout the year. Almost 90 percent of the ice on Earth can be found in Antarctica.

Life Along the Ice

Scientists working with NASA use satellites to study animals and their environments. Scientists use satellites to learn about penguins that live near Antarctica.

62

Science Background

Polynyas

Areas of open water or reduced ice cover where one might expect sea ice are called polynyas. They are usually created by strong winds that blow ice away from the coast or by gaps that appear when flowing ice becomes blocked. These openings are important to penguin populations because they host phytoplankton blooms which feed krill. The krill, in turn, are eaten by penguins. NASA researchers have found that Adélie Penguin populations grow when plankton in polynyas are productive. The same penguin populations decline when plankton productivity declines. Along the eastern coast of Antarctica, more than 90 percent of all Adélie Penguin colonies live next to coastal polynyas. This gives them an abundant food source and prevents them from having to travel for food, thereby exposing them to predators and other dangers.

Antarctica is very cold. Most of the ocean water near Antarctica is full of ice. The wind blows holes in the ice. Plants called algae can grow in the holes in the ice. Tiny animals called krill eat the algae. Penguins eat krill.

Scientists have learned that when there are more algae, there are more krill. When there are more krill, there are more penguins. When there are fewer krill, there are fewer penguins.

Krill

Satellites send information about the ocean back to Earth.

Lab zone **Take-Home Activity**

Draw a picture of a penguin. Tell your family how scientists learn about the ocean. Tell them how the amount of krill affects the number of penguins.

63

Explain that in some spots around Antarctica, the ice at the surface of the ocean melts. Tell children that these spots are surrounded by ice so people on land or in boats cannot see them. Only a satellite can see the places where the ice has melted. Point to the satellite image. Tell children that a satellite is a device that is sent into space. It travels around Earth much like the Moon does. A satellite takes different types of pictures of Earth. In some pictures, different colors are used to show places where the temperature is warmer than in other places.

3 | Explore

Explain that plants called algae grow in the places where ice has melted. Tiny animals called krill eat the algae. Penguins and other living things eat krill as food. Ask children: **Where do penguins find krill?** (In places where ice has melted.)

Ask children to look at the picture of krill. Ask children: **Why do the krill look big even though they are very small?** (This picture was made using a microscope.) Then ask: **What do krill look like?** (Some children may know they look like shrimp.) Tell children that krill are found in huge groups called swarms.

Tell children that krill eat tiny plants that float on the ocean. These plants are called plankton. Ask children to draw a food chain showing that penguins eat krill for food and krill eat plants called algae for food. Children should draw tiny plants, krill, and a penguin connected by arrows. Each arrow should point from the food source to the living thing that eats it. Mention that other animals, such as whales and seals, also depend on krill and algae.

Take-Home Activity

Tips for Success

- Have children look at the pictures of the penguin before they begin to draw.
- Ask children to describe in words how scientists learn about the ocean.
- Tell children to show how penguins and krill are related in their pictures and then to explain that warmer water is important to penguins because there is more krill in these waters.

Wildlife Rehabilitator

 Science Objective

- The student knows that the activities of humans affect animals in many ways.

1 Introduce

Build Background

Ask children to think about ways wild animals might become injured. Allow volunteers to describe examples they may have seen on television or in a book or magazine. As a class, discuss why it might be important to help injured animals.

2 Teach

Quick SUMMARY

- Wildlife rehabilitators help animals that are sick or have been hurt.

Read page 64 with children. Examine the picture of the sea turtle. Ask: **How do you think the wildlife rehabilitator took care of this turtle?** Kept it warm and gave it food and water until it was healthy

Explain that wildlife rehabilitators know a lot about different animals. Wildlife rehabilitators also know how to trap an injured animal without hurting the animal or themselves. This is why children should never try to capture an animal, even if they think it needs help. Instead, they should call an adult who can contact a wildlife rehabilitator or other professional.

3 Explore

Ask: **Why does a wildlife rehabilitator release animals back into their habitats?** Explain that the goal of wildlife rehabilitation is to release an animal back into its natural habitat once it is healthy.

Wildlife Rehabilitator

Read Together

What happens when animals that live in forests or oceans are hurt? Are there ways people can help?

Wildlife rehabilitators are people that help hurt or sick animals. They know what animals need to live in their environment. A wildlife rehabilitator can even teach young animals how to hunt for food.

Wildlife rehabilitators know that it is important that animals get the care they need to survive.

A wildlife rehabilitator saved this sea turtle.

64

Lab zone Take-Home Activity

Write about what it would be like to be a wildlife rehabilitator. What kinds of animals would you like to help?

Take-Home Activity

Tips for Success

- Good sources of information about wildlife rehabilitators in your area are the U.S. Fish and Wildlife Service, Department of Animal Control, Humane Society, or a local veterinarian. Another source is the National Wildlife Rehabilitators Association.

- Have volunteers read their writing to the class. Make a list on the board of the animals children would like to help. Make a tally chart to determine the most popular animals.

Leveled Readers and Leveled Practice

Leveled Readers deliver the same concepts and skills as the chapter. Use Leveled Readers for original instruction or for needed reteaching.

Below-Level

Life Science

How Plants and Animals Live Together

by May Evans

Leveled Practice

Leveled Reader Teacher's Guide

On-Level

Life Science

Plants AND Animals

by Evan Allen

Leveled Practice

Leveled Reader Teacher's Guide

Advanced

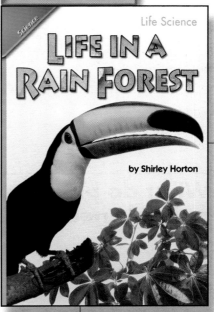

Life Science

LIFE IN A RAIN FOREST

by Shirley Horton

Leveled Practice

Leveled Reader Teacher's Guide

Below-Level Leveled Reader has the same content as Chapter 3, but is written at a less difficult reading level.

On-Level Leveled Reader has the same concepts as Chapter 3, and is written at grade level.

Advanced Leveled Reader is above grade level and enriches the chapter with additional examples and extended ideas.

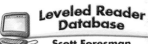

Leveled Reader Database

Scott Foresman
pearsonsuccessnet.com

Use the online database to search for additional leveled readers by level, title, content, and skill.

Key Content and Skill in Leveled Readers and Chapter 3

Content	Vocabulary		Target Reading Skill	Graphic Organizer
How Plants and Animals Live Together	producer consumer food chain	predator prey food web	⟳ Cause and Effect	

Chapter 3 Planning Guide

Essential Question: How do living things help each other?

Lesson/Activity	Pacing	Science Objectives
Build Background pp. 65–67	20 minutes	• The student identifies words and constructs meaning from text, illustrations, graphics, and charts using the strategies of phonics, word structure, and context clues.
Lab zone **Flip Chart Activity** What is a food chain?		
Lab zone **Flip Chart Activity** How does a bird make a nest?		
Lab zone Directed Inquiry		• The student knows that people use scientific processes including hypothesis, making inferences, and recording and communicating data when exploring the natural world.
Explore What does yeast need to grow? p. 68	20 minutes	
How to Read Science p. 69	20 minutes	• The student makes connections and inferences based on text and prior knowledge (for example, order of events, possible outcomes).
1 What do plants and animals need? pp. 70–73	30 minutes	• The student knows the basic needs of all living things. • The student understands that the amount of food, water, space, and shelter needed is dependent on the size and kind of living things.
2 How do plants and animals get food in a grassland? pp. 74–77	30 minutes	• The student understands that there is an interdependency of plants and animals that can be shown in a food web.
3 How do plants and animals get food in an ocean? pp. 78–81	30 minutes	• The student understands that there is an interdependency of plants and animals that can be shown in a food web.
4 What can cause a food web to change? pp. 82–83	20 minutes	• The student knows that human beings cause changes in their environment, and these changes can be positive (for example, creating refuges, replanting deforested regions, creating laws to restrict burning) or negative (for example, introducing toxic organisms, deforestation, littering, contaminating water and air).
5 How do plants and animals help each other? pp. 84–89	40 minutes	• The student knows that plants and animals are dependent upon each other for survival.
Lab zone Guided Inquiry		• The student understands that there is an interdependency of plants and animals that can be shown in a food web.
Investigate How can you model a food web? pp. 90–91	30 minutes	
Wrap-Up Chapter 3 pp. 92–93	20 minutes	• The student uses mathematical language to read and interpret data on a simple concrete graph, pictorial graph, or chart.
Math in Science: Measuring Length	20 minutes	
Chapter 3 Review and Test Prep	20 minutes	
Career: Farmer	20 minutes	

Vocabulary/Skills	Assessment/Intervention	Resources/Technology
Process Skills: Make Definitions Infer, Observe	• Chapter Review, SE, pp. 94–95 (1–3)	• Science Content Transparency 3 • Workbook, p. 29 • Graphic Organizer Transparency 3 • Vocabulary Cards • Activity Book, pp. 47–48
Process Skill: Infer Target Reading Skill: **Cause and Effect**	• Explain Your Results, SE, p. 68 • Activity Rubric • **Cause and Effect,** SE, p. 69	• Activity Book, pp. 43, 44 • Activity DVD • Activity Placemat 5 • Workbook, pp. 30–31 • Every Student Learns, p. 17
producer consumer	• Scaffolded Questions, TE, pp. 71, 73 • Checkpoint Questions, SE, p. 73 • Chapter Review, SE, pp. 94–95 (1, 2, 4, 6) • **Cause and Effect,** SE, p. 73	• Workbook, p. 32 • Quick Study, pp. 30–31 • Every Student Learns, p. 18
food chain food web predator prey	• Scaffolded Questions, TE, pp. 75, 77 • Checkpoint Questions, SE, pp. 75, 77 • Chapter Review, SE, pp. 94–95 (3, 5, 10)	• Workbook, p. 33 • Quick Study, pp. 32–33 • Every Student Learns, p. 19
	• Scaffolded Questions, TE, pp. 79, 81 • Checkpoint Questions, SE, pp. 79, 81 • Chapter Review, SE, pp. 94–95 (3, 10)	• Workbook, p. 34 • Quick Study, pp. 34–35 • Every Student Learns, p. 20
	• Scaffolded Questions, TE, p. 83 • Checkpoint Questions, SE, p. 82 • Chapter Review, SE, pp. 94–95 (4) • **Cause and Effect**, SE, p. 82	• Workbook, p. 35 • Quick Study, pp. 36–37 • Every Student Learns, p. 21
	• Scaffolded Questions, TE, pp. 85, 87, 89 • Checkpoint Questions, SE, pp. 85, 87, 89 • Chapter Review, SE, pp. 94–95 (6, 9)	• Workbook, p. 36 • Quick Study, pp. 38–39 • Every Student Learns, p. 22
Process Skill: Model	• Explain Your Results, SE, p. 91 • Activity Rubric	• Activity Book, pp. 45, 46 • Activity DVD • Activity Placemat 6
Math Skill: Read a Table	• Scaffolded Questions, TE p. 93 • **Cause and Effect,** SE, p. 95 • **ExamView®** Chapter 3 Test • **Success Tracker** pearsonsuccessnet.com/successtracker	• Workbook, pp. 37, 38–39 • Assessment Book, pp. 9–12

Quick Teaching Plan

If time is short . . .
• Build Background, pp. 66–67
• Explore Activity, p. 68
• How to Read Science, p. 69
• Lesson 1, pp. 70–73
• Lesson 2, pp. 74–77
• Lesson 5, pp. 84–89

Other quick options . . .

Quick ACTIVITY

TE pp. 66, 70, 74, 78, 82, 84, 92

TRANSPARENCIES 15, 16,17,18,19

Quick SUMMARY

TE pp. 70, 72, 74, 76, 78, 80, 82, 84, 86, 88

Chapter 3 Activity Guide

Children learn to ask and answer scientific questions as they progress to greater independence in scaffolded inquiry.

Directed Inquiry A Directed Inquiry activity begins each chapter.

Guided Inquiry A Guided Inquiry activity closes each chapter.

Full Inquiry Experiments and Science Fair Projects at the end of each unit provide opportunities for Full Inquiry.

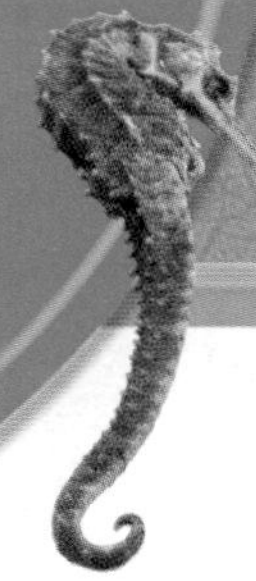

Lab zone Directed Inquiry

Explore What does yeast need to grow? p. 68

Time 20 minutes

Grouping small groups

Advance Preparation Fill a plastic cup with about $\frac{1}{2}$ tsp dry yeast and another cup with 1 tsp sugar for each group. Just prior to start, fill a third cup with about $\frac{1}{3}$ c warm water for each group.

Materials *3 clear plastic cups, (9 oz); sugar* (1 tsp); *plastic spoon;* dry yeast (about $\frac{1}{2}$ tsp); warm water (about $\frac{1}{3}$ c)

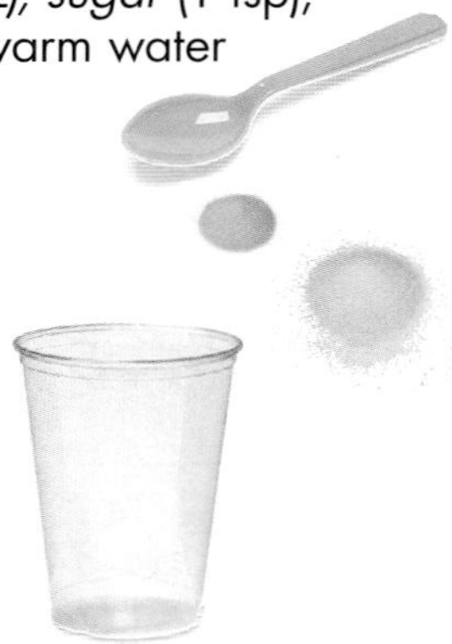

What to Expect Children may immediately see some bubbles rise to the surface as they add the sugar and water to the yeast. In about 15 minutes, a bubbly foam will appear on the surface of the mixture of yeast, water, and sugar.

Activity DVD Unit A, Chapter 3

Activity Placemat Mat 5

Lab zone Guided Inquiry

Investigate How can you model a food web? p. 90–91

Time 30 minutes

Grouping 8 or fewer children

Advance Preparation Make copies of the food web cards for each group. Use Activity Masters 2–9 from the Activity Book Teacher's Guide pp. T25–T32. Make a ball of yarn for each group. Measure 40 yards for each ball.

Materials *yarn* (40 yd; wrapped in a ball); Food Web cards (Activity Master 2–9); tape; crayons or markers

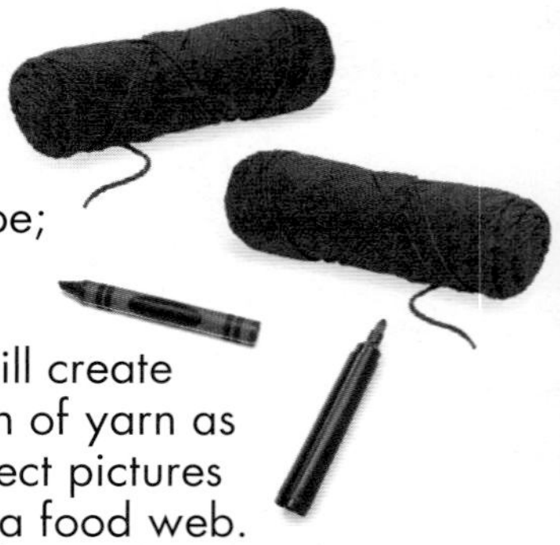

What to Expect Children will create a food web from a single length of yarn as they toss a ball of yarn to connect pictures of consumers and producers in a food web. The complexity of the web reinforces the idea that living things are dependent on one another.

Activity DVD Unit A, Chapter 3

Activity Placemat Mat 6

Other Resources

The following Resources are available for activities found in the Student Edition.

Demonstration Kit If you wish to rehearse or demonstrate the Chapter 3 activities, use the materials provided in the Demonstration Kit.

Classroom Equipment Kit Materials shown in *italic print* are available in the Classroom Equipment Kit.

Activity Placemats The Equipment Kit includes an Activity Placemat for each activity, a work surface that identifies the materials that need to be gathered.

Quick ACTIVITY

Transparencies Use a transparency to focus children's attention on the Quick Activity for each lesson.

Teacher's Activity Guide For detailed information about Inquiry Activities, access the Teacher's Activity Guide at **pearsonsuccessnet.com**.

Activity Flip Chart

What is a food chain?

Use this center activity after teaching Lesson 2 of the chapter.

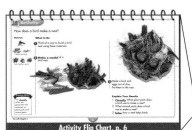

Process Skill make definitions

 Time 20 minutes

 Grouping Individual or pairs

Materials construction paper of several colors; crayons; scissors; 11 × 17 sheet of white paper; white glue (alternate materials: children can do this activity by making clay models instead of drawing pictures).

Procedure
- Refer children to the pictures of a food chain in their textbook for Lesson 2. Have children label the prey and predators in their food chain. Ask children how their food chain model would have to change in order to become a food web.
- Help children **make definitions** of how a food chain works by having them make a paper model of a food chain consisting of four living things.

What to Expect Students will make a model of a food chain showing the correct order in which energy moves through an environment.

Think About It The food chain shows how food passes from the leaf to the owl.

Activity Flip Chart

How does a bird make a nest?

Use this center activity after teaching Lesson 5 of the chapter.

Process Skill infer, classify

 Time 20 minutes

 Grouping Individual or pairs

Materials cardboard; about 8½ × 11 to serve as base for nest model; clay; leaves, both fresh and dried; small twigs and sticks; pieces of bark; feathers; grass clippings

Procedure
- Instruct children to use the clay as the base and support of their bird nest. You might want children to do this outside, especially if they use mud.
- Children **classify** their nest models and **infer** that a bird's nest is made from many different kinds of materials that birds can find in nature.

What to Expect Students will make a model of a bird's nest to show how birds use natural materials to build their nests one piece at a time.

Think About It
1. leaves, sticks, bark, grass
2. feathers
3. A nest protects birds from predators, shelters it from weather, and keeps it and its eggs warm.

online
Teacher's Edition
pearsonsuccessnet.com

Use the following Workbook pages to support content and skill development as you teach Chapter 3. You can also view and print Workbook pages from the Online Teacher's Edition.

Use with Build Background, pp. 66–67

Name _____ Vocabulary Preview
Use with Chapter 3.

Draw a picture or write a sentence to go with each word.

producer	prey
consumer	food chain
predator	food web

Directions: Read the words and draw pictures to illustrate them or write sentences about them. Cut out the boxes to use as word cards.
Home Activity: Pair the words *producer/consumer*, *predator/prey*, and *food chain/food web* and ask your child to explain how the two words are related to each other.

Workbook   Vocabulary Preview **29**

Workbook, p. 29

Use with How to Read Science, p. 69

Name _____ How to Read Science
Use with Chapter 3.

© Cause and Effect
Look at the pictures.
Read the paragraph.
Answer the questions.

Science Activity

Gelatin is sprinkled over hot water in a bowl. The hot water causes the gelatin to dissolve. As the water cools, the gelatin causes the water to become solid.

30 How to Read Science   Workbook

Workbook, pp. 30–31

Use with Lesson 1, pp. 70–73

Name _____ Think, Read, Learn
Use with pages 71–73.

What do plants and animals need?

Before You Read Lesson 1

Read each sentence. Do you think it is true? Do you think it is not true? Circle the word or words after each sentence that tell what you think.

1. Most green plants are consumers. True Not True
2. Consumers cannot make their own food. True Not True
3. Large animals need more food than small animals. True Not True

After You Read Lesson 1

Read each sentence again. Circle the word or words after each sentence that tell what you think now. Did you change any answers? Put an **X** by each answer that you changed.

1. Most green plants are consumers. True (Not True)
2. Consumers cannot make their own food. (True) Not True
3. Large animals need more food than small animals. (True) Not True

Home Activity: Together talk about your child's answers. Have your child explain why his or her answers may have changed after reading the lesson.

Workbook   Think, Read, Learn **32**

Workbook, p. 32

Use with Lesson 2, pp. 74–77

Name _____ Think, Read, Learn
Use with pages 74–77.

How do plants and animals get food in a grassland?

Before You Read Lesson 2

Read each sentence. Do you think it is true? Do you think it is not true? Circle the word or words after each sentence that tell what you think.

1. All food chains start with the Sun. True Not True
2. All food chains have predators and prey. True Not True
3. Predators are animals that are caught and eaten. True Not True

After You Read Lesson 2

Read each sentence again. Circle the word or words after each sentence that tell what you think now. Did you change any answers? Put an **X** by each answer that you changed.

1. All food chains start with the Sun. (True) Not True
2. All food chains have predators and prey. (True) Not True
3. Predators are animals that are caught and eaten. True (Not True)

Home Activity: Together talk about your child's answers. Have your child explain why his or her answers may have changed after reading the lesson.

Workbook   Think, Read, Learn **33**

Workbook, p. 33

Use with Lesson 3, pp. 78–81

Name _____ Think, Read, Learn
Use with pages 78–81.

How do plants and animals get food in an ocean?

Before You Read Lesson 3

Read each sentence. Do you think it is true? Do you think it is not true? Circle the word or words after each sentence that tell what you think.

1. Plants are not part of the food chains in an ocean. True Not True
2. Energy passes through each step in a food chain. True Not True
3. A sea otter can get energy from the Sun. True Not True

After You Read Lesson 3

Read each sentence again. Circle the word or words after each sentence that tell what you think now. Did you change any answers? Put an **X** by each answer that you changed.

1. Plants are not part of the food chains in an ocean. True (Not True)
2. Energy passes through each step in a food chain. (True) Not True
3. A sea otter can get energy from the Sun. (True) Not True

Home Activity: Together talk about your child's answers. Have your child explain why his or her answers may have changed after reading the lesson.

Workbook   Think, Read, Learn **34**

Workbook, p. 34

Name _____ **Think, Read, Learn**

Use with pages 82–83.

What can cause a food web to change?

Before You Read Lesson 4

Read each sentence. Do you think it is true? Do you think it is not true? Circle the word or words after each sentence that tell what you think.

1. Animals and plants may die if a food chain changes.   True   Not True
2. People do not cause changes in a food chain.   True   Not True
3. An oil spill can cause changes in a food chain.   True   Not True

After You Read Lesson 4

Read each sentence again. Circle the word or words after each sentence that tell what you think now. Did you change any answers? Put an **X** by each answer that you changed.

1. Animals and plants may die if a food chain changes.   (True)   Not True
2. People do not cause changes in a food chain.   True   (Not True)
3. An oil spill can cause changes in a food chain.   (True)   Not True

Home Activity: Together talk about your child's answers. Have your child explain why his or her answers may have changed after reading the lesson.

Workbook   Think, Read, Learn **35**

Workbook, p. 35

Name _____ **Think, Read, Learn**

Use with pages 84–89.

How do plants and animals help each other?

Before You Read Lesson 5

Read each sentence. Do you think it is true? Do you think it is not true? Circle the word or words after each sentence that tell what you think.

1. Animals can help plants.   True   Not True
2. Some animals get help from other animals.   True   Not True
3. Squirrels use parts of plants to build nests.   True   Not True
4. Sharks do not help other animals.   True   Not True

After You Read Lesson 5

Read each sentence again. Circle the word or words after each sentence that tell what you think now. Did you change any answers? Put an **X** by each answer that you changed.

1. Animals can help plants.   (True)   Not True
2. Some animals get help from other animals.   (True)   Not True
3. Squirrels use parts of plants to build nests.   (True)   Not True
4. Sharks do not help other animals.   True   (Not True)

Home Activity: Together talk about your child's answers. Have your child explain why his or her answers may have changed after reading the lesson.

Workbook   Think, Read, Learn **36**

Workbook, p. 36

Name _____ **Math in Science**

Use with Chapter 3.

Comparing Lengths

These animals are all predators in ocean food webs. Read the table. Find out how long these animals can grow to be.

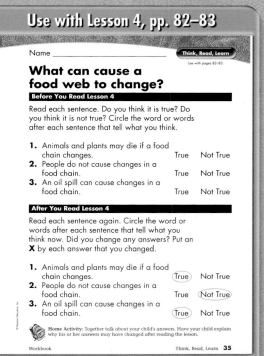

Animal	Length in m
Sea otter	1
Orca	9
Gray whale	13
Marlin	3
Blue shark	4

1. Which animal is the longest? _gray whale_
2. Which animal is the shortest? _sea otter_
3. How much longer is the orca than the blue shark? _5 m_
4. Put the animals in order from longest to shortest.
   gray whale
   orca
   blue shark
   marlin
   sea otter

Directions: Use the information in the table to answer the questions about the animals' lengths. Use what you know about ordering numbers to help you.
Home Activity: Your child learned how to use a table to compare data. Together measure the lengths of several kitchen utensils. Make a table showing the measurements in order from shortest to longest.

Workbook   Math in Science **37**

Workbook, p. 37

Use the following Assessment Book pages and ExamView to assess Chapter 3 content. You can also view and print Assessment Book pages from the Online Teacher's Edition.

Assessment Options

Formal Assessment

- Chapter Review and Test Prep, SE pp. 94–95
- Assessment Book, pp. 9–12
- Prescriptions for remediation are shown on TE p. 95

Performance Assessment

- Unit Wrap-Up, SE pp. 130–131

Ongoing Assessment

- Diagnostic Check, TE pp. 71, 75, 79, 85, 87
- Scaffolded Questions, TE pp. 71, 73, 75, 79, 81, 83, 85, 87, 89, 93

Portfolio Assessment

- My Science Journal, TE pp. 67, 72, 75, 81, 83, 86, 88

Success Tracker

- Data management system to assess Adequate Yearly Progress (AYP) and provide intervention

ExamView®

- Alternative test formats are available online or through ExamView CD-ROM

Chapter 3 Test

Name _____ Chapter 3 Test

Read each question and choose the best answer. Then fill in the circle next to the correct answer.

❶ Look at the picture. Think about the size of each animal.

elephant   warthog   aardvark   prairie dog

Which animal probably needs the most food, water, and space?
Ⓐ warthog
Ⓑ elephant
Ⓒ aardvark
Ⓓ prairie dog

❷ What is a predator?
Ⓕ an animal that is hunted for food
Ⓖ an animal that eats plants for food
Ⓗ an animal that hunts another animal for food
Ⓘ a plant that uses sunlight, air, and water to make food

Assessment Book   Chapter 3 Test **9**

Assessment Book, p. 9

Chapter 3 Test

Name _____ Chapter 3 Test

❸ Read the chart. Use what you learn to answer the question.

A Grassland Food Chain	
Living Things in the Food Chain	**How They Get Food**
corn plant	uses sunlight, air, and water to make food
vole	eats the corn
coyote	eats the vole
mountain lion	eats the coyote

How does the coyote get energy?
Ⓐ by eating corn
Ⓑ by eating a vole
Ⓒ by eating a mountain lion
Ⓓ by making it from sunlight

❹ What is a food web made up of?
Ⓕ the plants in a habitat
Ⓖ the animals in a habitat
Ⓗ the predators in a habitat
Ⓘ the food chains in a habitat

10 Chapter 3 Test   Assessment Book

Assessment Book, p. 10

Chapter 3 Test

Name _____ Chapter 3 Test

❺ What do animals use to build their nests?
Ⓐ parts from plants
Ⓑ feathers and fur from other animals
Ⓒ parts from plants and from other animals
Ⓓ none of the above

❻ Look at the picture. Think about this ocean food chain.

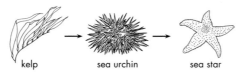

kelp   sea urchin   sea star

Think about what you learned from the picture. Why is the sea urchin a consumer?
Ⓕ It eats kelp.
Ⓖ It makes its own food.
Ⓗ It is eaten by a sea star.
Ⓘ It is eaten by a sea gull.

❼ Who is helped when an egret sits on top of a rhinoceros and eats flies?
Ⓐ the egret
Ⓑ the rhinoceros
Ⓒ the egret and the rhinoceros
Ⓓ none of the above

Assessment Book   Chapter 3 Test **11**

Assessment Book, p. 11

Chapter 3 Test

Name _____ Chapter 3 Test

❽ Look at the picture of cardinal fish and a sea urchin.

Which of the following is true?
Ⓕ The fish and the sea urchin are helping each other.
Ⓖ The sea urchin and the fish are not helping each other.
Ⓗ The sea urchin is helping the fish. The fish are not helping the sea urchin.
Ⓘ The fish are helping the sea urchin. The sea urchin is not helping the fish.

Write the answers to the questions on the lines.

❾ What do animals need to live in a habitat? (2 points)
Enough air, water, shelter, and space.

❿ How can people help save an ocean food web that was harmed by an oil spill? (2 points)
People can wash the oil off the animals. They can also clean the water and make it safe again.

12 Chapter 3 Test   Assessment Book

Assessment Book, p. 12

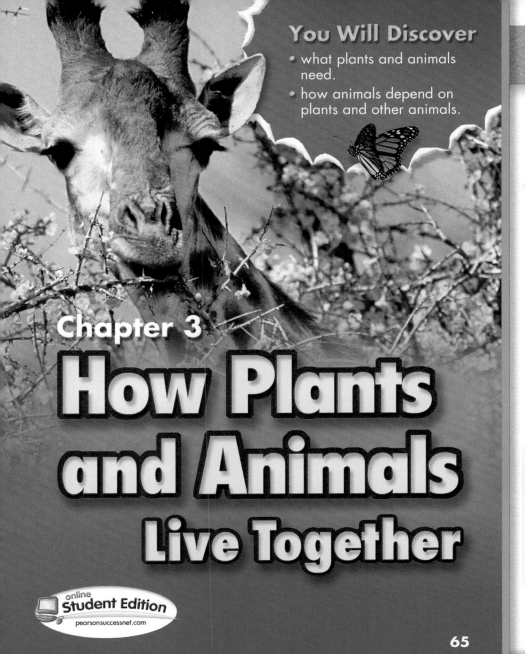

You Will Discover

- what plants and animals need.
- how animals depend on plants and other animals.

Chapter 3

How Plants and Animals Live Together

online **Student Edition**
pearsonsuccessnet.com

65

How Plants and Animals Live Together

 Science Objectives

- The student knows the basic needs of all living things.
- The student knows that plants and animals are dependent upon each other for survival.
- The student knows that if living things do not get food, water, shelter, and space, they will die.
- The student knows that people use scientific processes including hypotheses, making inferences, and recording and communicating data when exploring the natural world.

Quick TEACHING PLAN

If time is short...
Use Build Background page to engage children in chapter content. Then do Explore Activity, How to Read Science, and Lessons 1, 2, and 5.

Professional Development

To enhance your qualifications in science, before beginning this chapter:

- preview content in Life Science DVD Segment *Ecological Organization*.
- preview activity management techniques described in Activity DVD Unit A, Chapter 3.

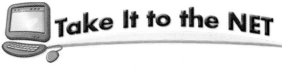 **Take It to the NET**

To access student resources:
1. Go to **www.pearsonsuccessnet.com.**
2. Click on the register button.
3. Enter the access code **frog** and your school's zip code.

Chapter 3 Concept Web

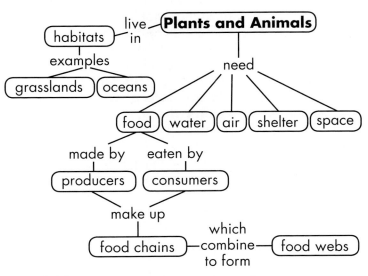

Children can create a concept web to organize ideas about how plants and animals live together.

Build Background

 Science Objective

- The student identifies words and constructs meaning from the text, illustrations, graphics, and charts using the strategies of phonics, word structure, and context clues.

Chapter 3 Vocabulary Words

producer, p. 71
consumer, p. 71
food chain, p. 74
predator, p. 75
prey, p. 75
food web, p. 76

1 | Introduce the Concept

Quick ACTIVITY

Ask children: **Where does milk come from?** A cow **What does a cow eat when it is in the field?** Grass **Is grass a living thing?** Yes **What kind of living thing is grass?** A plant

Discuss Essential Question

Many science vocabulary words are abstract. Use the pictures and labels on these pages to help you open a discussion about science concepts and build academic language.

Read the Chapter 3 Essential Question to children, **How do living things help each other?** Ask children to identify what living things need. (Air, food, water, space) Elicit that living things need food. Have children look at the pictures and ask volunteers to describe what they see. Call children's attention to the series of pictures with arrows that move upward. Say: **This shows how these living things help each other.** Ask: **What do you think the arrows show?** Children's answers will vary. Tell children they will find out more in this chapter.

Revisit the essential question with children as they work through this chapter.

How do living things help each other?

producer
consumer

predator

prey

66

Build Background Resources

Workbook, p. 29

Graphic Organizer Transparency 3

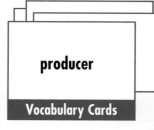

producer

Vocabulary Cards

ELL Support

Access Content Before reading the chapter text, lead children on a picture/text walk.

Chapter 3 Vocabulary

producer page 71

consumer page 71

food chain page 74

predator page 75

prey page 75

food web page 76

food web

Sun

food chain

67

My Science Journal

Write About Plants and Me

Explain to children that they use plants and plant parts every day in one way or another. Suggest some ways, such as for food, clothing, shelter, medicine, and decoration. Have children write about how they use plants or plant parts in one day.

Science Background

The First Plant and Animal Life on Earth

- More than 3.5 billion years ago, single-cell organisms began to develop in the seas covering Earth. Most fed on chemicals in the waters.

- Blue-green algae used sunlight, carbon dioxide, and water to make food. In the process, they produced oxygen. As the blue-green algae population in the oceans increased, Earth's atmosphere changed and began to fill up with oxygen.

- The presence of oxygen made it possible for new organisms to appear. These organisms could not make their own food. However, they produced CO_2, which the algae needed. Thus, a mutually beneficial relationship between plants and animals formed.

2 | Introduce Vocabulary

Use the following Prediction/Confirmation chart provided on **pearsonsuccessnet.com** or Graphic Organizer Transparency 3.

Word	What I Predict It Means	What I Know It Means
producer		
consumer		
food chain		
predator		
prey		
food web		

On Graphic Organizer Transparency 3, list vocabulary words under the first column. Explain to children that you will fill in the What I Predict It Means column of the chart together.

- Pronounce each word. Solicit information from children as you fill in the column. For example, children may predict that a food chain links living things in an environment together.

- Guide children as you fill in the column by asking questions such as, "What kind of web do you think a food web is?"

- Tell children they will fill in the last column after reading the chapter. Encourage them to take notes about information they read that will help them complete the chart.

Word Recognition Use the Vocabulary Cards to reinforce recognition of each written word and its definition.

3 | Practice

Vocabulary Strategy: Which Word?

Using the Vocabulary Cards, read the definition of a vocabulary word aloud. Ask: **Which word is that?**

Ask children to participate in a form appropriate to their level of skill:

- choral response
- telling a partner
- pointing to the word in the pictures
- selecting the word from the Vocabulary Cards

Explore What does yeast need to grow?

 **Science Objective**

- The student knows that people use scientific processes including hypothesis, making inferences, and recording and communicating data when exploring the natural world.

1 Build Background

Children observe what yeast needs to grow.

Managing Time and Materials

Time: 20 minutes

Groups: small groups

Materials: *3 clear plastic cups,* (9 oz); *sugar* (1 tsp); *plastic spoon; dry yeast* (about $\frac{1}{2}$ tsp); warm water (about $\frac{1}{3}$ c)

Materials listed in *italic* are kit materials.

Advance Preparation

Fill a cup with about $\frac{1}{2}$ tsp dry yeast and another cup with 1 tsp sugar for each group. Just prior to start, fill a cup with about $\frac{1}{3}$ c warm water for each group.

2 What to Do

Engage Ask children if they think plants and animals need the same things as people to survive.

Explore Have children add the yeast to a cup with water. Then add the sugar and stir.

Explain Discuss why bubbles form.

Extend Have children look at bread with a hand lens. Yeast is added to bread before baking. The yeast makes the holes in the bread.

Evaluate Have children describe the importance of food and water to the survival of living things.

3 Explain Your Results

Infer Adding food and water.

Process Skills

Children **infer** when they tell why yeast bubbles.

Explore What does yeast need to grow?

Yeast are tiny living things.
They cannot make their own food.
They must get food from where they live.

 Don't slip! Clean up spills.

Materials

cup with yeast

cup with warm water

cup with sugar

spoon

What to Do

1 Put water in the cup with yeast.

2 Add sugar and stir. Watch the yeast.

Look at the tiny bubbles!

3 **Estimate** How long did it take to see tiny bubbles?

Process Skills

You can **infer** from what you observe with your senses.

Explain Your Results

Infer What made the yeast change?

Activity Resources

Activity Book pp. 43–44 | Activity Rubric

 Use Activity DVD Unit A, Chapter 3 to preview this activity.

 Call 1-888-537-4908 with activity questions.

More Lab Activities Take It to the Net pearsonsuccessnet.com

Find more about this activity at our Web site.

- See the **Teacher's Activity Guide** for more support.
- An alternative activity is also available to download.

Reading Skills

 Cause and Effect

A cause is why something happens.
An effect is what happens.

Science Activity

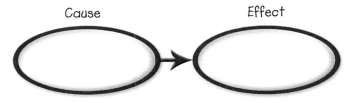

Yeast is added to bread dough. The yeast causes air bubbles to form in the bread dough. The air bubbles make the bread dough rise.

Apply It!

Infer What would happen to the bread dough without the yeast?

Cause   Effect

69

How to Read Science Resource

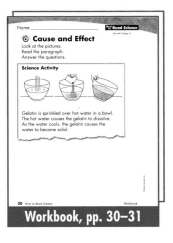

Workbook, pp. 30–31

ELL Support

For more practice on **Cause and Effect,** use **Every Student Learns Teacher's Guide,** p. 17.

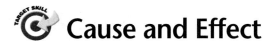
Cause and Effect

⭐ Reading Objective

- The student makes connections and inferences based on text and prior knowledge (for example, order of events, possible outcomes).

About the Target Skill

The target skill for *How Plants and Animals Live Together* is **Cause and Effect.**

Children are introduced to the skill as you guide them through this page.

1 | Introduce

Demonstrate a simple cause and effect. Show children a balloon. Then blow air into it. Ask: **What did I do to the balloon?** Blew air into it **What happened because I blew air into it?** It got bigger.

2 | Model the Skill

Look at page 69 together. Read the Science Activity together. Ask: **What is put into the dough** yeast **What happened to the bread dough?** It rose. **Why did the dough rise?** The yeast caused air bubbles to form in the dough. Point out that adding the yeast is the cause and the dough rising is the effect.

3 | Practice

Graphic Organizer

Look at the Graphic Organizer together. Work with children to complete the Graphic Organizer using the facts from the Science Activity.

Apply It!

Cause   Effect

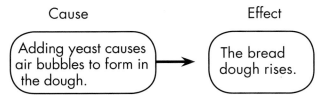

Adding yeast causes air bubbles to form in the dough. → The bread dough rises.

What do plants and animals need?

 Science Objective

- The student knows the basic needs of all living things.

1 | Introduce

Quick ACTIVITY | TRANSPARENCY 15 |

Ask children to name some of the things they need to live and grow. Accept reasonable answers. If necessary, explain the difference between needs and wants.

Access Prior Knowledge

Discuss how people's needs are met. Ask children: ***What do you do when you are thirsty? What do you do when you are hungry?***

Set Purpose

Tell children they are going to read about plants and animals. Help them set a **purpose for reading,** such as finding out about the needs of plants and animals.

2 | Teach

Quick SUMMARY

- Most green plants are producers, while animals are consumers.

- Animals need air, water, shelter, space, and food.

Sing or play "Good Partners" for children. Then read pages 70–71 together. Ask children to describe what they see in the picture. (Different animals around water hole) Ask: ***Why do you think the animals are there?*** Remind children that all living things need water to live and grow.

You Are There

 Good Partners

Sung to the tune of "Frere Jacques"
Lyrics by Gerri Brioso & Richard Freitas/The Dovetail Group, Inc.

Plants and animals
Are good partners.
Yes they are.
Yes they are.

70 Science Songs ♪♪♪

Lesson 1 Resource

Workbook, p. 32

 Science Songs ♪♪♪

Use the Science Songs CD to play "Good Partners" for the class.

Lesson 1

What do plants and animals need?

You learned that plants need air, water, sunlight, nutrients, and space to grow. Most green plants are producers. A **producer** is a living thing that can make its own food.

Animals need air, water, shelter, and space to live. Animals need food. Animals are consumers. A **consumer** cannot make its own food. Consumers get food from their habitat.

①
②
③

These giraffes are consumers.

71

Ask: **What else do living things need?** Food, air, light, shelter, and space Discuss which needs are part of the physical environment (air, water, shelter, light).

Point out that all living things need to make or find food. Remind children that in Chapter 1, they learned that plants need air, water, and sunlight to manufacture their own food. Plants also need minerals, which they get from the soil. Animals get nutrients from food that they eat.

Assign Quick Study pp. 30–31 to children who need help with lesson content.

Guide Comprehension

Ask children the following scaffolded questions to assess understanding.

Scaffolded Questions

① **List** *What do all animals need to live and grow?* Air, water, shelter, space to live, and food

② **Comprehend** *What is the main difference between a producer and a consumer?* A producer makes its own food; a consumer gets food from its habitat.

③ **Hypothesize** *Look at the animals in the picture. What do you think would happen if a lion appeared at the watering hole?* The animals would run away to keep from being eaten.

Extend Vocabulary

Write the words **producer** and **consumer** on the board. Circle the *-er* suffix in each. Explain that those letters are word endings. When *-er* is added to an action verb, it changes the meaning to "one who does" that action. Write the word *produce* and define it: "to make something out of raw materials." Explain that a *producer* makes something out of raw materials. Follow this procedure with the word *consume* ("to eat") and *consumer* ("any living thing that has to eat to stay alive.")

Diagnostic Check

If... children have difficulty understanding the basic needs of all living things,

then... ask: *What would happen to a plant that did not get water? What would happen to an animal that did not get food?* It would not grow. It would die.

ELL Leveled Support

Getting What They Need

Beginning Point to pictures and say: *These animals are drinking water. Animals need water.* Ask: *What do animals need?* Have volunteers fill in the cloze sentence: Animals need _____ (air, water, shelter, space). Point to these things in the classroom or in a picture to check for understanding.

Intermediate Ask: *What is a runner?* (A person who runs) Ask: *What is a walker?* (A person who walks) Explain that these are words with *–er*, a word ending or suffix which means "a person who" or "a thing that." Demonstrate other examples such as
    write + er = writer (a person who writes)
When children have grasped this relationship, introduce this lesson's vocabulary terms
    produce (to make) + er = producer (a maker of food)
    consume (to eat) + er = consumer (an eater of food)

Advanced Offer children words comprised of a verb + the suffix *–er*, which means "a person who" or "a thing that." Ask what *producer*, *consumer*, and *decomposer* mean. Repeat students' responses, using correct English.

Science Objective

- The student understands that the amount of food, water, space, and shelter needed is dependent on the size and kind of living things.

2 | Teach (continued)

Quick SUMMARY

- Plants and animals depend on each other and their habitat to meet their needs.
- Large animals need more food, water, and space than small animals.
- If an environment does not have enough food, some animals might die.

Read pages 72–73 with children. Focus on the picture on page 73. Ask children to answer the caption question: **Which animal do you think needs more water?** The larger animal

Explain that the larger animal is a wildebeest. The smaller animal is a warthog. Ask: **What happens if the habitat does not have enough food or water for all of the animals that live there?** Some of the animals might die.

Different Needs

① Many plants and animals live together in a habitat. Plants and animals depend on each other and their habitat to meet their needs.

② Large animals often need a lot of food, water, and space. Large animals need a large shelter.

③ Small animals often do not need as much to eat and drink as large animals. Small animals can live in small spaces.

These plants and animals live in the same habitat.

72

My Science Journal

How Animals Meet Needs

Have children make a T-chart in their science journals. In the first column, they should list the basic needs of animals. In the second column, have them record what meets those needs. For example, animals' homes meet their need for shelter and space. Whatever the animals eat meets their need for food.

Science Background

Food and Heat

Warm-blooded animals are able to maintain a constant body temperature. If they are in a cold environment, their adaptations (feathers, layers of fat, behaviors) enable them to conserve heat and keep warm. When they are in a hot environment, they cool themselves. Warm-blooded animals generate heat by converting ingested food into energy during digestion and respiration. Much of the food eaten by mammals is used to maintain a constant body temperature.

These animals both need water. Which animal do you think needs more water?

Sometimes a habitat does not have enough food for all of the animals that live there. When this happens, some of the animals might die.

✓**Lesson Checkpoint**

1. What do all animals need?

2. ◎ **Cause and Effect** What might happen if there is not enough food for all of the animals in a habitat?

73

ELL Support

Language Detectives: Comparative Words

Write the words *more* and *less* on the board. Discuss the meaning of each. Then provide the following sentence frames for children to complete using *more* or *less*:

- An elephant needs _____ water than a monkey.
- A dog needs _____ food than a cow.
- A fox needs _____ space than a kitten.
- A small bear needs _____ space than a big bear.

Help children choose the appropriate word to compare animals' needs.

For scaffolded instruction about animals' needs, use **Every Student Learns Teacher's Guide,** p. 18

3 | Assess

✓**Lesson Checkpoint**

1. All animals need air, water, food, space, and a safe place to live.

2. ◎ **Cause and Effect** Some of the animals might die.

How do plants and animals get food in a grassland?

 Science Objective

• The student explains how animals in a grassland habitat depend on plants and other animals for food.

1 | Introduce

Quick ACTIVITY | TRANSPARENCY 16

Use the pictures to elicit a discussion of foods animals eat. Say: ***The small animal at the bottom of page 74 is a vole. What is it eating?*** Corn ***What does the mountain lion eat?*** The coyote. Use Quick Activity Transparency 16 to elicit more discussion on what animals eat.

Access Prior Knowledge

Write the following headings on the board: *Animals That Eat Plants, Animals That Eat Other Animals.* Ask children to help you fill in the headings by giving examples of each.

Set Purpose

Tell children they are going to read about some animals that live in a grassland. Help them set a **purpose for reading,** such as to find out how animals that eat animals get their energy.

2 | Teach

Quick SUMMARY

• Food chains start with energy from the Sun. Plants use sunlight to make food.

• Animals get energy from the food they eat. The energy moves through a food chain.

• A food chain is made up of plants, plant-eating animals, prey, and predators.

Lesson 2

How do plants and animals get food in a grassland?

All living things need food. Most plants make food. Some animals eat plants. Other animals eat those animals. This is called a **food chain.**

③ Food chains start with the Sun. Plants use energy from the Sun to make food. Animals get energy from the food they eat. Look at the pictures of the food chain. Energy passes from sunlight to the mountain lion.

① **The corn plant uses water, air, and energy from sunlight to make food.**

Crunch! The vole eats the corn for energy.

74

Lesson 2 Resource

Workbook, p. 33

All food chains have predators and prey. A **predator** is an animal that catches and eats another animal. **Prey** is an animal that is caught and eaten. Look at the animals in the food chain. The coyote and mountain lion are predators. Which animals are their prey?

1. ✓**Checkpoint** Give an example of a predator and its prey.

2. **Art** in Science Draw a picture of this grassland food chain. Label your picture.

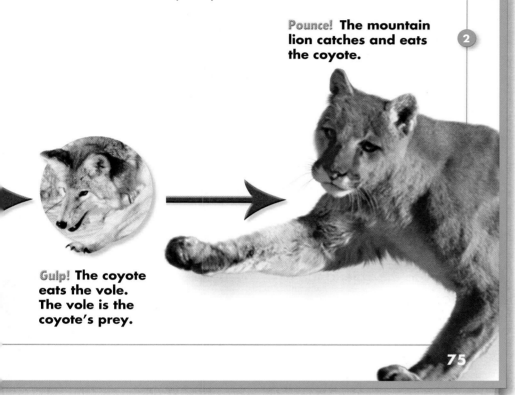

Pounce! The mountain lion catches and eats the coyote.

2

Gulp! The coyote eats the vole. The vole is the coyote's prey.

75

My Science Journal

Food Chains

Tell children that many birds eat sunflower seeds. Have children draw simple food chains showing how energy is passed from the Sun to the birds. Have children include arrows in their drawings.

Science Background

More Than One

There are usually many possible food chains for an organism because most animals eat more than one type of food. Voles, for example, eat not only corn, but also bulbs, tubers, tree bark, and home garden plants. Voles are eaten not only by coyotes, but also by badgers, weasels, cats, and owls. In any particular environment, life forms depend on many other life forms, as well as on nonliving things.

Read pages 74–75 together. Reinforce the idea that a predator is an animal that catches and eats another animal, called the prey. Have children answer the question in the text.

Discuss the food chain. Point out that the arrows show the way energy moves.

Assign Quick Study pp. 32–33 to children who need help with lesson content.

Guide Comprehension

Ask children the following scaffolded questions to assess understanding.

Scaffolded Questions

① **Find** *Where is the plant in the food chain on pages 74–75? Where is the mountain lion?* The corn is at the beginning. The mountain lion is at the end.

② **Scrutinize** *How is the coyote both a predator and prey?* It is a predator when it hunts and eats the vole. It is prey when the mountain lion hunts and eats it.

③ **Apply** *Is the first living thing in a food chain ever an animal? Explain.* No. Food chains must start with plants, because they use energy from the Sun to make food.

Extend Vocabulary

Write the term **food chain** on the board. Show children a metal chain, paper chain, or picture of a chain. Point out that each ring connects to the ring that comes before and after it. Have children discuss how food chains are like metal or paper chains.

Diagnostic Check

If... children have difficulty understanding that all energy passes through a food chain,

then... refer them to the food chain on pages 74–75 and have them trace the movement of energy with their fingers on the page as you describe it.

3 | Assess

1. ✓**Checkpoint** A coyote is a predator. Its prey is a vole.

2. **Art** in Science Pictures should show: Sun/corn/vole/coyote/mountain lion.

- The student understands that there is an interdependency of plants and animals that can be shown in a food web.

2 | Teach (continued)

Quick SUMMARY

- A habitat can have different food chains.
- A food web is made up of food chains in a habitat.

Ask volunteers to read page 76 to the class. Have children follow along. Say: **A food web shows how living things are connected. The arrows show what each animal eats.** Have children follow the arrows to identify the number of food chains in the web. (5) Call on volunteers to identify each living thing in each food chain.

Ask: **How many predators are in the food web? Which animals are they?** 5; Raccoon, hawk, coyote, mountain lion, fox Explain that these animals all live together in one special kind of ecosystem—a grassland. An ecosystem is a place and all the life forms that live there.

A Food Web in a Grassland

Habitats usually have more than one food chain. The food chains in a habitat make up a **food web.** The plants and animals in a food web need each other for energy.

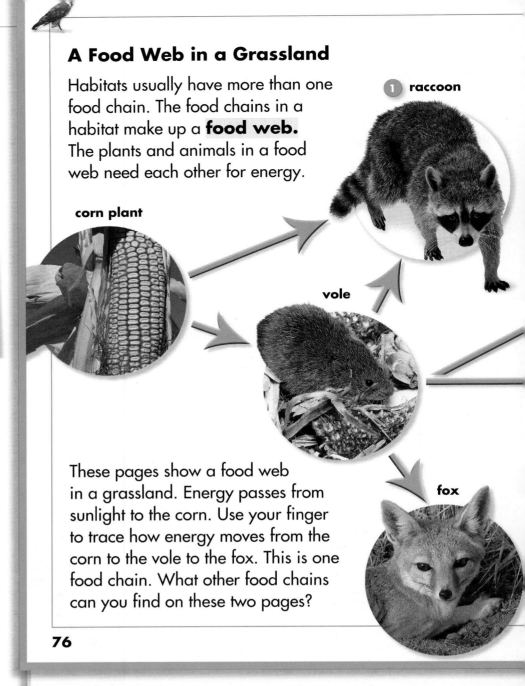

These pages show a food web in a grassland. Energy passes from sunlight to the corn. Use your finger to trace how energy moves from the corn to the vole to the fox. This is one food chain. What other food chains can you find on these two pages?

76

ELL Leveled Support

What Animals Eat

Beginning Show children pictures of different animals, and make a simple sentence about what each animal eats. For example: "The mouse eats seeds." "The squirrel eats a nut." "The shark eats a fish." Then show the pictures again, this time asking children to say what each animal eats.

Intermediate Draw the following food chain on the board: seeds → mouse → owl. Write these sentences next to it:

The _____ eats the seeds. The _____ eats the mouse.

Have children copy the sentences and fill in the blanks with the names of the animals.

Advanced Draw the following simple food web on the board: carrot → rabbit → eagle
↓
wolf

Have children write sentences telling what each animal eats.

hawk

coyote   mountain lion

②
③

✓ **Lesson Checkpoint**

1. Describe a food web.

2. [Math in Science] How many animals in this food web eat the corn? How many animals eat the vole? How many more animals eat the vole than the corn? Write a number sentence.

Science Background

Food Chains and Food Webs

- Food chains overlap and intersect to form complex food webs.
- If one link in a food chain or web becomes depleted, the consumers beyond that break have to look for alternate food sources.
- Organisms usually belong to several food chains.
- Food chains and food webs are examples of energy passing through a system. A terrarium or an aquarium can serve as a model of how energy flows through a system.
- The higher up the food chain, the fewer individuals that food chain supports.

ELL Support

For scaffolded instruction about food chains and food webs, use **Every Student Learns Teacher's Guide**, p. 19.

Lesson 3

How do plants and animals get food in an ocean?

 Science Objective

- The student explains how animals in an ocean depend on plants and other animals for food.

1 Introduce

Quick ACTIVITY | TRANSPARENCY 17 |

Ask children: **What is an ocean like?** Children should recognize an ocean contains a great deal of water. **What lives in an ocean?** Children should respond that both animals and plants live in the ocean. Have children name animals and plants that live in the ocean, and make a list on the board.

Access Prior Knowledge

Have children work in pairs to make lists of plants or animals that live in oceans. Ask: **Why are they part of food chains and food webs?** Accept reasonable answers.

Set Purpose

Tell children you are going to read to them about ocean plants and animals. Help them set a **purpose for listening,** such as to find out how living things in an ocean get their food.

2 Teach

Quick SUMMARY

- An ocean has food chains and food webs.
- Kelp uses energy from sunlight to make food.
- Energy passes through the food chain from the kelp to the animals in the chain.

Read pages 78–79 to children. Ask children to identify the living thing in each picture. (Kelp, sea urchin, sea star, otter) Ask children to explain the food chain.

Lesson 3

How do plants and animals get food in an ocean?

An ocean has food chains and food webs too. Many different plants and animals live in an ocean. The pictures on these pages show an ocean food chain.

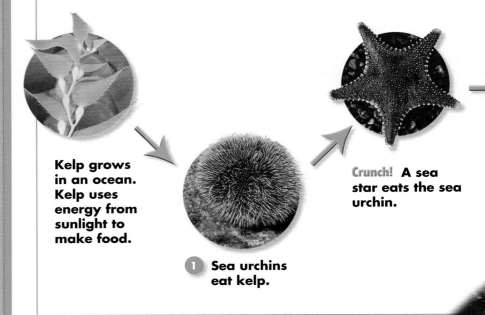

Kelp grows in an ocean. Kelp uses energy from sunlight to make food.

1 Sea urchins eat kelp.

Crunch! A sea star eats the sea urchin.

78

Lesson 3 Resource

Name _____

Think, Read, Learn

How do plants and animals get food in an ocean?

Before You Read Lesson 3

Read each sentence. Do you think it is true? Do you think it is not true? Circle the word or words after each sentence that tell what you think.

1. Plants are not part of the food chains in an ocean.   True   Not True
2. Energy passes through each step in a food chain.   True   Not True
3. A sea otter can get energy from the Sun.   True   Not True

After You Read Lesson 3

Read each sentence again. Circle the word or words after each sentence that tell what you think now. Did you change any answers? Put an **X** by each answer that you changed.

1. Plants are not part of the food chains in an ocean.   True   Not True
2. Energy passes through each step in a food chain.   True   Not True
3. A sea otter can get energy from the Sun.   True   Not True

Home Activity: Together talk about your child's answers. Have your child explain why his or her answers may have changed after reading the lesson.

Workbook   Think, Read, Learn **34**

Workbook, p. 34

Remember that energy is passed through each step in a food chain. Trace how energy in this food chain passes from the Sun to the sea otter.

1. ✓Checkpoint Where does a sea otter get energy?

2. Writing in Science Write 2 or 3 sentences. Tell how energy moves through this food chain.

Chomp! The sea otter eats the sea star. The sea otter gets the energy it needs from the sea star.

79

Science Background

Decomposers

After plants and animals die, organisms break down their final remains. These organisms are called decomposers. Decomposers include bacteria, fungi, and earthworms. Decomposers free the last of the nutrients and chemicals in the dead tissues, recycling them back into the environment.

ELL Support

Ocean Plants and Animals

Ask children if they are familiar with any of the plants or animals pictured. If they are, give them an opportunity to share what they know. Then write the names of the pictured animals on the board. Ask simple questions to elicit discussion, such as "What shape is the sea star?" or "What color is the sea otter?"

For scaffolded instruction about food webs and food chains in the ocean, use **Every Student Learns Teacher's Guide,** p. 20.

Assign Quick Study pp. 34–35 to children who need help with lesson content.

Guide Comprehension

Ask children the following scaffolded questions to assess understanding.

Scaffolded Questions

1 **Name** *What consumer gets its energy from the kelp?* Sea urchin

2 **Classify** *Which life forms in this food chain are consumers?* Sea urchin, sea star, and sea otter

3 **Compare** *How is this food chain like the food chain on the grassland?* Both food chains begin with a living thing that uses energy from sunlight to make food. The other living things do not make their own food. The energy passes along the food chain from living things that make their own food to living things that do not make their own food.

Extend Vocabulary

Write the terms *sea urchin, sea star,* and *sea otter* on the board. Explain that each term is considered a compound word even though the words are not joined. Tell children the terms *food chain* and *food web* are also compound words.

Diagnostic Check

If... children have difficulty understanding how energy is passed through a food chain,

then... have three children stand side by side. Have the first child pass two small balls to the second child. Have the second child keep one ball and pass the other to the third child. Tell children the balls represent the Sun's energy. Have them explain what they have seen.

3 | Assess

1. ✓Checkpoint A sea otter gets energy from a sea star.

2. Writing in Science Have children write their answers in their science journals. Answers should include the following path: Sun/Kelp/Sea urchin/Sea star/Sea otter

- The student understands that there is an interdependency of plants and animals that can be shown in a food web.

2 | Teach (continued)

Quick SUMMARY

- A food web in the ocean has many food chains.

Read pages 80–81 to children. Ask: **Where does kelp get its energy?** From the Sun. Help children recognize that all food chains start with the Sun.

Have children trace over each food chain in the food web with their finger to see how energy passes through the producer to the consumers, and how some chains interconnect.

A Food Web in an Ocean

Look at this simple ocean food web. Energy passes from sunlight to the kelp. Use your finger to trace the food chains. How many food chains can you count?

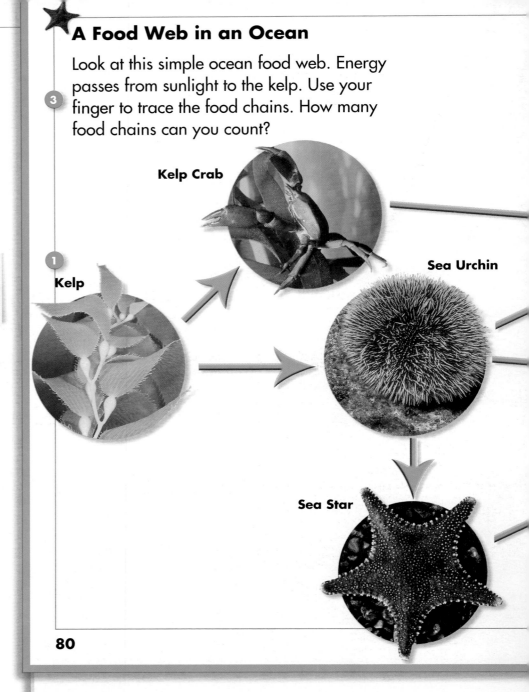

Kelp Crab

Sea Urchin

Kelp

Sea Star

80

Social Studies Link

The Sargasso Sea

One of the most famous of all ocean producers is *sargassum,* a type of brown seaweed. The Sargasso Sea, which lies within the Atlantic Ocean, is named for sargassum, which floats on the surface and covers approximately two million square miles. Christopher Columbus mentioned sargassum after he encountered it during his first trip to North America. Locate the Sargasso Sea for children on a map or globe.

Sea Otter

Orca

Sea Gull

2

1. What eats kelp in this food web?

2. **Writing** in Science   Write one sentence in your journal. Describe one food chain in this ocean food web.

81

My Science Journal

Ocean Food Chain

Have children illustrate one ocean food chain in their science journals. Tell them to start with the Sun. Have them label each picture in the food chain and use arrows to show how the Sun's energy passes from one part of the chain to another.

Math Link

Math in a Food Web

Have children work with a partner. Each pair of children should use the food web to make up a math problem based on the plants and animals shown. For example, a problem might read "How many more living things are in the longest chain than in the shortest chain?" Pairs should exchange their math problems and solve them.

Guide Comprehension

Ask children the following scaffolded questions to assess understanding.

Scaffolded Questions

1 **Visualize relationships** *What is one food chain in the food web in an ocean?* Answers will vary. Possible answer: kelp, sea urchin, sea gull

2 **Calculate** *How many more animals eat sea urchin than sea star? Write a number sentence and solve.* 3 animals eat sea urchin − 1 animal eats sea star = 2 more animals

3 **Tell Why** *What would happen if there were no Sun? Why?* There would be no plants and animals on Earth. All food chains start with the Sun's energy.

Extend Vocabulary

Tell children that many compound words contain the word *sea*. List these words on the board: *seafood, seashell, seashore, seasick, seaside, seawater,* and *seaweed*. Challenge children to guess their meanings. Have them use dictionaries to determine the meanings of any words they cannot define.

3 | Assess

✓ Lesson Checkpoint

1. The crab and the sea urchin both eat kelp.

2. **Writing** in Science   Have children write their answers in their science journals. Possible answers: kelp, kelp crab; kelp, sea urchin, sea star, sea otter, orca; kelp, sea urchin, sea gull.

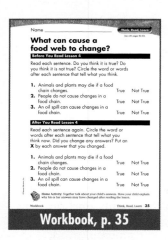

Lesson 4

What can cause a food web to change?

 Science Objective

• The student knows that human beings cause changes in their environment, and these changes can be positive (for example, creating refuges, replanting deforested regions, creating laws to restrict burning) or negative (for example, introducing exotic organisms, deforestation, littering, contaminating water and air).

1 | Introduce

Quick ACTIVITY | **TRANSPARENCY 18**

Ask children to name some birds that swim in water. Then ask what might happen to the bird if oil was spilled in the water. Demonstrate what happens. First dip a feather in a cup of water. Then dip a feather in a cup of oil. Have children draw a picture of how an oil spill might affect a bird.

Access Prior Knowledge

Elicit a discussion of ways that people can cause changes in their habitat. Ask: **What happens to living things in a lake when people throw trash in the water?** Answers will vary.

Set Purpose

Tell children they are going to read about how people can change a food web. Help them set a **purpose for reading,** such as to find out how people can both harm and help a food web.

2 | Teach

Quick SUMMARY

• Changes in a food web make it hard for plants and animals to survive in their habitats.

• People can cause changes in a food web.

• People can also work together to make a habitat safe again.

Lesson 4

What can cause a food web to change?

This ship had an accident. Oil spilled from the ship into the ocean.

2
3

Many things can cause changes in a food web. Some changes may make it hard for plants and animals to survive. Parts of the food web may be harmed or even die.

People can cause a food web to change. The picture shows an oil spill. Many plants and animals were covered with oil.

82

Lesson 4 Resource

Name _____

Think, Read, Learn
Use with pages 82–83.

What can cause a food web to change?

Before You Read Lesson 4

Read each sentence. Do you think it is true? Do you think it is not true? Circle the word or words after each sentence that tell what you think.

1. Animals and plants may die if a food chain changes. True   Not True
2. People do not cause changes in a food chain. True   Not True
3. An oil spill can cause changes in a food chain. True   Not True

After You Read Lesson 4

Read each sentence again. Circle the word or words after each sentence that tell what you think now. Did you change any answers? Put an **X** by each answer that you changed.

1. Animals and plants may die if a food chain changes. True   Not True
2. People do not cause changes in a food chain. True   Not True
3. An oil spill can cause changes in a food chain. True   Not True

Home Activity: Together talk about your child's answers. Have your child explain why his or her answers may have changed after reading the lesson.

Workbook   Think, Read, Learn **35**

Workbook, p. 35

People washed the oil off of this otter's fur.

People worked together to wash the oil off the animals. People helped to clean the water. People made the water safe again for the plants and animals that live there.

✓ Lesson Checkpoint

1. How did people help after the oil spill?

2. 🔄 **Cause and Effect** What is one effect of an oil spill?

My Science Journal

Don't Spoil the Environment

Have children write in their own words what happens to a food web when people make an environment dirty.

ELL Support

Changes in a Food Web

Draw a T-chart on the board. Have children provide an example of one thing people do that hurts a food chain. Write their response in one column. Then have them provide an example of one thing people do to help a food chain. Write their response in the other column. Have children suggest labels for each column.

For scaffolded instruction about how food webs can change, use **Every Student Learns Teacher's Guide,** p. 21.

Read pages 82–83 with children. To help children understand the cause-and-effect relationships, ask questions such as: **What is one way that people can cause a food web to change?** An oil spill **What was the cause of the oil spill?** A ship had an accident. **People washed oil off the fur of the otter. What was the effect?** Its life was saved.

Assign Quick Study pp. 36–37 to children who need help with lesson content.

Guide Comprehension

Ask children the following scaffolded questions to assess understanding.

Scaffolded Questions

1️⃣ **Cause and Effect How do otters get hurt after an oil spill?** Oil gets on their fur.

2️⃣ **Understand the Problem How could an oil spill cause a food web to change?** Animals can die as the result of an oil spill. If many of the same kind of animals die, they won't be around to eat other things or be eaten.

3️⃣ **Tell Why Why should people try to keep water clean?** Possible answer: So plants and animals can survive

---

Extend Vocabulary

Remind children that people should try to keep the waters clean and not make them dirty. Write the words *clean/dirty* on the board. Point out that they have opposite meanings. Ask children to think of other word pairs that have opposite meanings. To elicit responses, you may want to say words such as *heavy* (light), *big* (small), *dark* (light), *full* (empty).

3 | Assess

✓ Lesson Checkpoint

1. People worked together to wash the oil off the animals and clean the water.

2. 🔄 **Cause and Effect** Accept reasonable answers.

Lesson 5

How do plants and animals help each other?

 Science Objective

- The student knows that plants and animals are dependent upon each other for survival.

1 Introduce

Quick ACTIVITY   `TRANSPARENCY 19`

Ask children: **In what kinds of places do people live?** Houses of all kinds, apartment buildings, mobile homes, houseboats **Why do people need to live in homes?** People need homes for shelter, and to protect them from weather. Have children look at Quick Activity Transparency 19. Discuss the picture, and then have children draw some other ways that trees are used as shelter.

Access Prior Knowledge

Point out to children that they have already learned how plants and animals need each other for food. Ask: **What else do living things need?** Space to live, and shelter

Set Purpose

Tell children they are going to read about plants and animals that help each other. Help them set a **purpose for reading,** such as to find out how plants and animals help each other.

2 Teach

Quick SUMMARY

- Some animals get shelter from plants and then protect the plants.
- Some animals get protection from other animals.

Read pages 84–85 with children. Use the pictures and captions to point out how plants and animals help each other survive.

Assign Quick Study pp. 38–39 to children who need help with lesson content.

Lesson 5

How do plants and animals help each other?

Sometimes plants and animals help each other. Some animals get shelter from plants. These ants live inside an acacia plant. The ants protect the acacia plant from animals that might eat it.

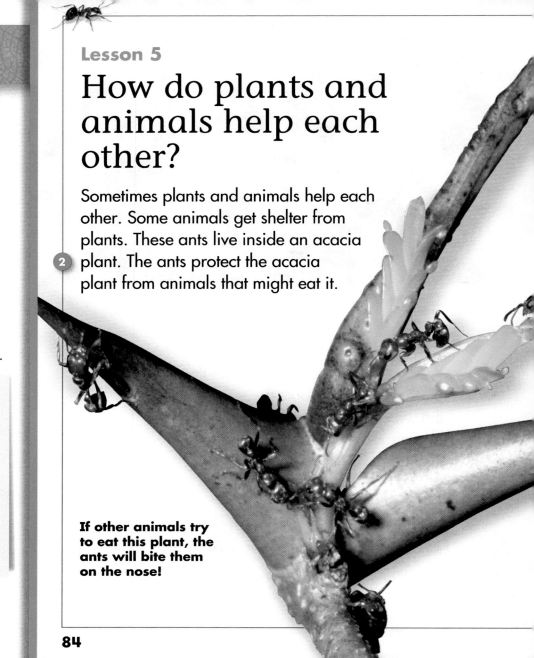

If other animals try to eat this plant, the ants will bite them on the nose!

84

Lesson 5 Resource

Workbook, p. 36

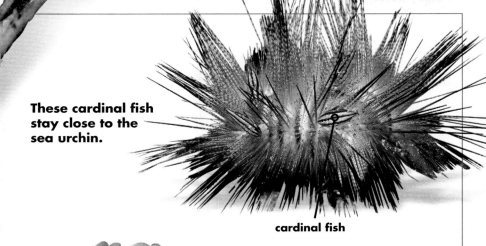

These cardinal fish stay close to the sea urchin.

cardinal fish

Some animals get protection from other animals. Find the cardinal fish in the picture above. Cardinal fish live near sea urchins. The sharp spines of the sea urchin protect the fish. The fish do not help or hurt the sea urchin.

1. ✓**Checkpoint** How do ants protect an acacia plant?

2. **Social Studies** in Science Acacia plants live in Costa Rica. Find Costa Rica on a map. You can find it south of Florida.

85

Science Background

Plants Need Animals

- Plants need animals for pollination. Animals such as bees and hummingbirds transport pollen from flower to flower.
- Plants need animals for seed dispersal.
- Animals give off carbon dioxide that plants need.
- When dead animals decay, nutrients are returned to the soil. Plants use these nutrients.

Technology Link

Find Out About Insects

Have children find an article about insects by going to the following Web site: **http://www.ars.usda.gov/is/kids/contents.htm.** Children can make notes about what they learned in their science journals. They can use their notes to tell what they learned to a partner or the class.

Science Objective

- The student explains how animals depend on plants and other animals for shelter and nesting.

2 | Teach (continued)

Quick SUMMARY

- Animals build nests using materials from plants and other animals.

Read pages 86–87 with children. Discuss why animals build nests (for shelter) and how habitat conditions affect the kind of nesting materials available. For example, ask why a desert owl makes a nest in a cactus. (Cacti live in deserts.) Use the pictures to discuss the different plant and animal parts used to make nests.

Building Nests

Some animals depend on plants and other animals to build nests. Some animals use parts of plants. Some animals use feathers or fur from other animals to build their nests.

Look at the picture of the squirrel's nest. Twigs and leaves are on the outside of the nest. Dried grass, bark, feathers, and wool are on the inside of the nest.

The masked weaver makes a nest from plant parts.

Some owls that live in the desert build their nests in a cactus.

86

My Science Journal

Describing One Animal's Nest

Have children select one nest that they read about or have seen and describe it in their science journals. Children who have pet hamsters, gerbils, or birds may want to describe the nests of their pets. Tell children to write what the nest looks like and what it is made from.

Science Background

What's in That Nest?

Materials found in nature, such as grass, twigs, sticks, and leaves, can be recycled and used again, sometimes in different forms, such as in birds' and other animals' nests. For example, ruby throated hummingbirds use spider webs to help hold their nests together.

1. **✓ Checkpoint** What animal parts does the squirrel use to make its nest?

2. **Writing in Science** Write 2 or 3 sentences in your **science journal.** Tell what you learned about animals that build nests.

87

ELL Support

Nest Materials

Children may be unfamiliar with some of the words on this page. Make a list of such words, which might include twigs, bark, and feathers. Have children work with partners, and assign each pair one word. Have children learn the meaning of that word and then share what they have learned.

For scaffolded instruction about how animals depend on plants and other animals to build nests, use **Every Student Learns Teacher's Guide,** p. 22.

Guide Comprehension

Ask children the following scaffolded questions to assess understanding.

Scaffolded Questions

1 **Recall** *What are two animals that build nests?* Birds and squirrels

2 **Get the Main Idea** *From where do animals get the materials they need to build nests?* From nature

3 **Opinion** *Do you think it is a lot of work for these animals to make their nests?* Possible answer: Yes, it is a lot of work. The nests are made of many different materials. The animal has to find them, carry them to a site, and then build with them.

Extend Vocabulary

Write the word *nest* on the board. Point out that in this lesson the word has been used as a noun that names a place. Explain that *nest* can also be used as a verb. The verb nest means "to build and use a nest." Write other forms of the word, including *nests, nested,* and *nesting.* Then write these sentences on the board:

Some birds nest in trees. One is nested in my yard.

Invite children to read the sentences aloud and then create their own oral sentences.

Diagnostic Check

If... children have difficulty understanding how animals use plant and animal parts to build nests,

then... have children identify each item in the picture of a squirrel's nest on page 87 and say whether it comes from a plant or an animal.

3 | Assess

1. **✓ Checkpoint** The squirrel uses feathers from birds and wool from sheep to make its nest.

2. **Writing in Science** Have children write their answers in their science journals. Answers will vary.

Science Objective

- The student explains how animals depend on plants and other animals for shelter and nesting.

2 | Teach (continued)

Quick SUMMARY

- Some animals form special relationships with other animals for food or protection.
- A remora fish stays close to a blue shark and eats its leftovers.
- An egret sits on a rhinoceros and eats insects around it.
- A boxer crab uses an anemone to sting predators.

Read pages 88–89 with children. Use the pictures to discuss how the animals need other animals for food. Say: **When the shark eats, some of its leftovers float behind it. The remora fish eats these leftovers. The egret eats insects that land on the rhino. The rhino gets food for the bird. As it walks, it moves grasshoppers. The egret sees these and eats them.** Then ask: **What does the anemone do for the boxer crab?** It stings predators.

Animals Need Each Other

Animals need each other for many reasons. The remora fish in the picture below takes a ride with a blue shark. When the shark eats, the remora fish eats the leftovers! The remora does not hurt or help the shark.

The big blue shark scares predators away from the little remora.

88

My Science Journal

How People Help Animals

Ask children to think about different ways that people help pets. For example, they feed them and give them shelter. Then ask for ways people help wild animals. Encourage a variety of responses, such as not throwing out trash that would harm an animal, feeding ducks in a park, or keeping waterways clean. Remind children of the animals that were cleaned after the oil spill. After the discussion, have children write two sentences explaining two ways that people help animals.

Math Link

Measuring a Remora Fish

Say to children: **Look at the picture of the blue shark and the remora. If the blue shark in the picture is about 9 feet long, how long do you think the remora fish in the picture is? Would you measure its length in feet or inches?** Answers will vary, but children should recognize that the remora is much smaller, no longer than 1 foot, and could probably be measured using inches.

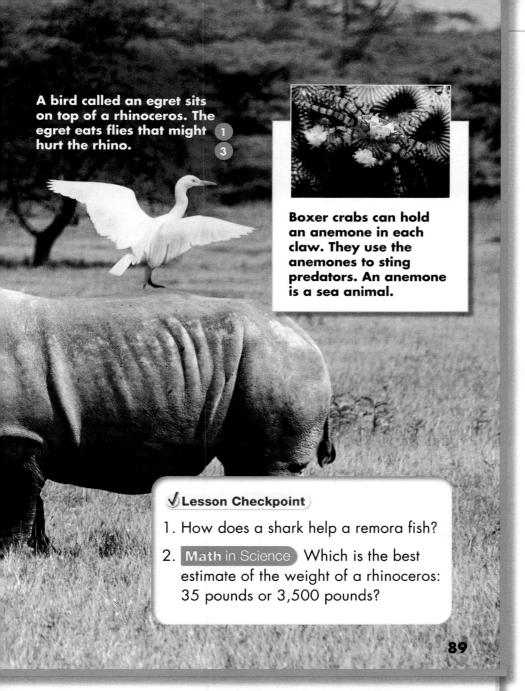

A bird called an egret sits on top of a rhinoceros. The egret eats flies that might hurt the rhino. **1** **3**

Boxer crabs can hold an anemone in each claw. They use the anemones to sting predators. An anemone is a sea animal.

✓ Lesson Checkpoint

1. How does a shark help a remora fish?

2. **Math in Science** Which is the best estimate of the weight of a rhinoceros: 35 pounds or 3,500 pounds?

89

ELL Support

Language Detectives: Where, What, and How

Ask children to answer each of the following riddles. Remind them to reread pages 88–89 if they need help answering the questions.

- Where does an egret sit?
- What does the egret eat?
- How does a boxer crab use an anemone?
- What is an anemone?

If necessary, help children understand the meaning of the words used to form questions: *where, what,* and *how.*

For scaffolded instruction about how animals depend on other animals, use **Every Student Learns Teacher's Guide,** p. 22.

Guide Comprehension

Ask children the following scaffolded questions to assess understanding.

Scaffolded Questions

1 Recall *What does the egret do that helps the rhino?* Eats flies that might hurt it

2 Interpret Picture *What kind of food do you think the rhino eats?* Plants

3 Predict *What do you think would happen to the remora or the egret if the shark or rhino died?* Possible answer: It would look for another shark or rhino to stay with.

Extend Vocabulary

List these words on the board and pronounce them: *remora, egret, rhinoceros,* and *anemone.* Explain to children that although these words may be unfamiliar to them, they can determine the meanings by looking at the pictures in their books. Have children make four vocabulary cards by copying the words onto four small pieces of paper. Challenge children to match each vocabulary card to the correct picture. Explain that this is one way readers learn new words. You may want to demonstrate this with other words and pictures.

3 | Assess

✓ Lesson Checkpoint

1. A shark protects a remora fish from other animals that might want to eat it.

2. **Math in Science** 3,500 pounds

SCAFFOLDED INQUIRY

Investigate How can you model a food web?

 Science Objective

- The student understands that there is an interdependency of plants and animals that can be shown in a food web.

1 | Build Background

This activity encourages children to create a food web and to observe that living things are dependent on one another as they connect pictures of consumers and producers.

Managing Time and Materials

Time: 30 minutes

Groups: 8 or fewer children

Materials: *yarn* (40 yd; wrapped in a ball); Food Web Cards (Activity Masters 2–9); tape; crayons or markers

Materials listed in *italic* are kit materials.

Advance Preparation

Make copies of Activity Masters 2–9. Make a ball of yarn for each group. Measure 40 yards for each ball.

Teaching Tips

Children may need to consult their cards to know which organism is related to the picture they are wearing. You may need to coach children so that all organisms will be included in the web.

2 | What to Do

Encourage Guided Inquiry

Preview the activity and the materials with children. Ask: *What would happen if you removed the kelp from the food web?*

Guide children to write an If.../then... statement such as: **If you remove the kelp from the food web, then the sea urchins may not get enough food to survive.**

Investigate How can you model a food web?

Many different living things make up a food web. All of the animals you see are part of a food web.

Materials

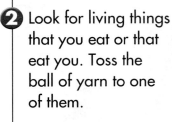

food web cards

tape

yarn

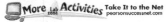

crayons or markers

Process Skills

When you act something out, you **model** it.

What to Do

❶ Choose a card. Tape it on your shirt. Stand in a circle with your group.

❷ Look for living things that you eat or that eat you. Toss the ball of yarn to one of them.

❸ Take turns until everyone is connected. Lay down the yarn and the cards.

Activity Resources

Activity Book pp. 45–46

Activity Rubric

 Use Activity DVD Unit A, Chapter 3 to preview this activity.

 Call 1-888-537-4908 with activity questions.

**More** Lab zone **Activities** Take It to the Net pearsonsuccessnet.com

Find more about this activity at our Web site.

- See the **Teacher's Activity Guide** for more support.
- An alternative activity is also available to download.

4 Draw your food web and write the names of the living things.

My Food Web

Explain Your Results

1. **Infer** What do the web lines mean?
2. How did you **model** a real food web?

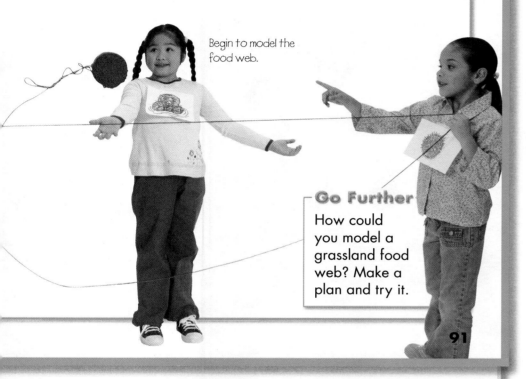

Begin to model the food web.

Go Further

How could you model a grassland food web? Make a plan and try it.

91

Science Background

Food Webs

- Food webs represent a network of interconnected food chains. They express all the possible feeding relationships at a specific level. A food web is a more natural model than a food chain since most organisms depend on more than one species for food.

Health Link

Seafood

- Seafood is an excellent source of protein, fish oils, vitamins B6 and B12, calcium, iodine, phosphorus, and selenium. Many researchers believe that eating seafood once or twice a week may be beneficial in lowering cholesterol and preventing heart disease.

Engage Remind children that a food web is made up of different food chains in a habitat.

Explore Have each child in the group stand in a circle and tape on a different food web card. Give a ball of yarn to one child. Ask the child to hold the end string on the ball and throw the ball to another child with a card that represents a plant or animal that would eat or be eaten by the first child's plant or animal. Children should continue to throw the ball of yarn until they are all connected. Have each group draw and label their food web.

Explain Have children review and explain their food web drawings.

Extend Have children repeat this activity with food webs from other habitats.

Evaluate Compare each group's food web. How are they alike and different?

3 | Explain Your Results

Use these questions to help children review evidence and develop explanations.

- Give children an opportunity to reflect on the data, or evidence, they have gathered in the investigation.
- Have children use the evidence gathered to develop their explanations. Accept reasonable, logical explanations.

1. **Infer** The lines in the web mean that the animal eats the plant or animal to which it is connected.
2. The model shows real-life plants and animals. The lines in the food web show how animals need plants or other animals to live.

Go Further

Children may propose any number of modifications to the activity to understand the importance of food webs. They may wish to expand this food web by including more plants and animals or repeating the activity with other habitats.

Post other questions children have about food webs. Encourage children to investigate on their own.

Process Skills

Model

Discuss the importance of modeling. Remind children that science is a way of learning about the world around us. You can use the Process Skills sheet on Modeling at this time.

Measuring Length

 Science Objective

- The student uses mathematical language to read and interpret data on a simple concrete graph, pictorial graph, or chart.

1 | Introduce

Quick ACTIVITY

Tell children they can measure how long things are. Ask: **What can you use to measure?** (A ruler) Draw a table on the board. Label the first column *Item* and the second column *Length in cm* (if measuring in centimeters). Select classroom items to measure, such as a desk, a pencil, and a book. Enter the results on the table. Ask: **Which is the shortest item? Which is the longest item? How can the table help you compare sizes?**

2 | Teach the Skill

Have children look at the animals pictured on page 92. Ask children to think about how big each animal might be. Ask: **Which animal do you think is the tallest? Which do you think is the shortest?**

Read pages 92–93 with children. Point out that the table shows the name of each animal and its length in centimeters.

Ask: **Which animals are predators?** All the animals, except the vole **Which animal is prey?** Vole

Math in Science

Measuring Length

hawk

These animals are from this chapter. They are some of the predators and prey in a grassland food web.

fox

raccoon

vole

92 ⓔ **Tools** Take It to the Net
pearsonsuccessnet.com

Activity Resource

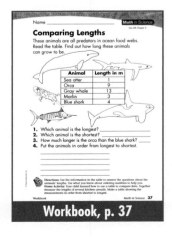

Workbook, p. 37

ⓔ **Tools** Take It to the Net
pearsonsuccessnet.com

Read the table. Find out how long some of the animals can grow to be.

Animal	Length in cm
Raccoon	100 cm
Vole	20 cm
Fox	80 cm
Hawk	60 cm

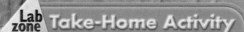

1. Which animal is the shortest?
2. Which animal is the longest?
3. How much longer is the fox than the vole?
4. Put the animals in order from shortest to longest.

Lab zone Take-Home Activity

Use a ruler. Find objects at home that match the length of each animal in the table. List the objects. Share your list with your family.

93

Take-Home Activity

Tips for Success

- Have children copy the table on page 93 on a piece of paper. Have them add one more column to the right of the last column and label this column *Objects at home.* Tell children to take their table home and complete it.

- Remind children that they should find objects at home that match the length of each animal.

- Show children how to visualize the length of each animal on the table by walking the length from the wall for each measurement.

- Tell children they don't have to match the length of each animal exactly, but that the lengths should come close.

- Children can share their lists with their family and friends.

Chapter 3 Review and Test Prep

Vocabulary

1. B
2. A
3. C

What did you learn?

4. All animals need air, water, food, shelter, and space to live.
5. Answers will vary. Possible answers: hawk/vole; mountain lion/coyote; sea otter/sea star
6. Possible answers: They provide food. They provide parts for a nest. They provide protection.

Chapter 3 Review and Test Prep

Vocabulary

Which picture goes with each word?

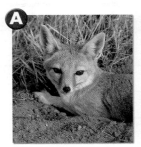

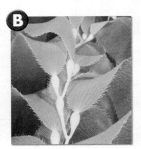

1. producer

2. consumer

3. food chain

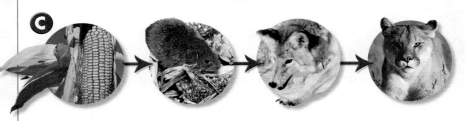

A

B

C

What did you learn?

4. What do all animals need to live?

5. Name a predator from this chapter. What is its prey?

6. What are some ways animals help each other?

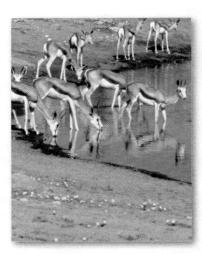

Assessment Resources

Name ______ Chapter 3 Test

Read each question and choose the best answer. Then fill in the circle next to the correct answer.

1. Look at the picture. Think about the size of each animal.

Which animal probably needs the most food, water, and space?
Ⓐ warthog
Ⓑ elephant
Ⓒ aardvark
Ⓓ prairie dog

2. What is a predator?
Ⓕ an animal that is hunted for food
Ⓖ an animal that eats plants for food
Ⓗ an animal that hunts another animal for food
Ⓘ a plant that uses sunlight, air, and water to make food

Assessment Book Chapter 3 Test 9

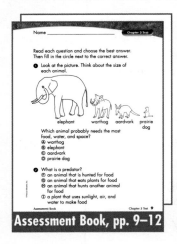

Assessment Book, pp. 9–12

MindPoint Quiz Show

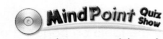

MindPoint enables children to test their knowledge of the chapter in a fun game format.

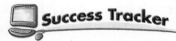

ExamView® Use ExamView as a print or online assessment tool.

Success Tracker

Data management system to track Adequate Yearly Progress (AYP) and provide intervention online at **pearsonsuccessnet.com/successtracker**

Take-Home Booklet

Children can make a Take-Home Booklet using Workbook pp. 39–40.

7. Infer What would happen to an ocean food web if there were no more kelp?

Cause and Effect

8. Read the captions.

It rained all day in this forest.

The mountain lion found shelter from the rain in a cave.

What **caused** the mountain lion to go into the cave?

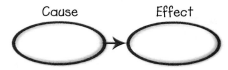

Cause   Effect

Test Prep

Fill in the circle next to the correct answer.

9. Which animal finds shelter in an acacia plant?

Ⓐ masked weaver

Ⓑ egret

Ⓒ cardinal fish

Ⓓ ant

10. **Writing** in Science Describe a food chain from the chapter. Tell how energy passes through it.

95

---

7. Infer The consumers in the ocean food web would have to find a different source of food and energy or they would die.

Cause and Effect

8.

Cause		Effect
It rained all day in the forest.	→	The mountain lion found shelter in the cave.

Test Prep

9. D

10. **Writing** in Science Answers will vary. Possible answer: Corn uses energy from the Sun to make food. A vole eats the corn and energy passes to the vole. Then a hawk eats the vole. Energy passes from the vole to the hawk.

Intervention and Remediation

Science Objectives	Review Item	Student Edition Pages	Teacher Edition Resources				Ancillary Resources		
			Guide Comprehension	Extend Vocab	Diagnostic Check	Vocab Cards	Quick Study	Workbook Pages
The student knows the basic needs of all living things.	4, 8	70–71	71, 73, 81, 85	85	71	71	71	32
The student understands that the amount of food, water, space, and shelter needed is dependent on the size and kind of living things.		72–73	73					
The student explains how animals in a grassland habitat depend on plants and other animals for food.		74–75	75, 89		75	75	75	33
The student understands that there is an interdependency of plants and animals that can be shown in a food web.	10	76–77, 80–81	77, 81	71, 77	79	77		
The student explains how animals in an ocean depend on plants and other animals for food.	7	78–79	79, 81, 83		79		79	34
The student knows that human beings cause changes in their environment, and these changes can be positive (for example, creating refuges, replanting deforested regions, creating laws to restrict burning) or negative (for example, introducing exotic organisms, deforestation, littering, contaminating water and air).		82–83	83	83			83	35
The student knows that plants and animals are dependent upon each other for survival.	5, 7	84–85	73, 89	71	75, 79, 85		84	36
The student explains how animals depend on plants and other animals for shelter and nesting.	6, 9	86–89	85, 87	85, 87	85			

Farmer

 Science Objective

● Explore and identify career opportunities in farming.

1 Introduce

Build Background

Ask volunteers to describe visits they may have had to a farm. Provide children with pictures of farms and farm plants and animals, possibly those found in an area around their community. Have children describe what they see in each of the pictures.

2 Teach

Quick SUMMARY

• Some farmers grow fruits, vegetables, and grains for food.
• Some farmers raise animals that provide milk, eggs, and meat for food.

Read page 96 with children. Have children look at the photographs on page 96. Ask: **What things do farmers need to do to help their plants and animals live and grow?** They need to give the plants water and plant food. They need to give the animals food, water, shelter, and a place to exercise.

3 Explore

Have children look at a map of their state. Show children areas in their state where farming occurs. Bring in pictures or examples of foods produced by local farms for children to examine. Ask: **Which of these foods do you like to eat?** Answers will vary. **Why are these foods good for you?** Foods provide us with energy and the vitamins and minerals we need to keep our bodies healthy.

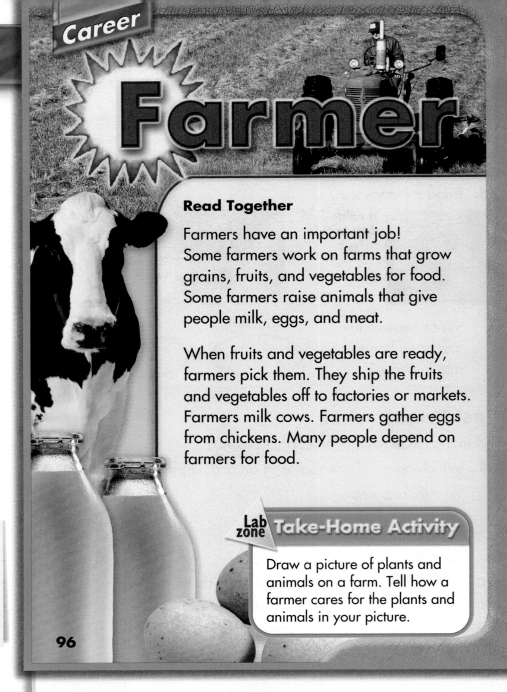

Career
Farmer

Read Together

Farmers have an important job! Some farmers work on farms that grow grains, fruits, and vegetables for food. Some farmers raise animals that give people milk, eggs, and meat.

When fruits and vegetables are ready, farmers pick them. They ship the fruits and vegetables off to factories or markets. Farmers milk cows. Farmers gather eggs from chickens. Many people depend on farmers for food.

Lab zone Take-Home Activity

Draw a picture of plants and animals on a farm. Tell how a farmer cares for the plants and animals in your picture.

96

Take-Home Activity

Tips for Success

• Review the different types of plants and animals that may be found on a farm. Children may ask family members to help them write their stories during their discussion at home.
• Have children share their drawings and stories with classmates.

Leveled Readers and Leveled Practice

Leveled Readers deliver the same concepts and skills as the chapter. Use Leveled Readers for original instruction or for needed reteaching.

Below-Level

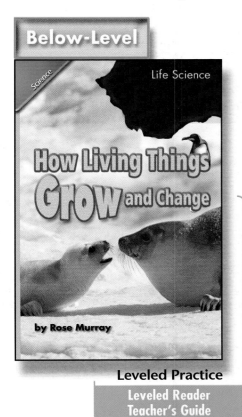

Life Science
How Living Things Grow and Change
by Rose Murray

Leveled Practice

Leveled Reader Teacher's Guide

On-Level

Life Science
Growing and Changing
by Christian Downey

Leveled Practice

Leveled Reader Teacher's Guide

Advanced

Life Science
Animal Eggs
by Molly Fleck

Leveled Practice

Leveled Reader Teacher's Guide

Below-Level Leveled Reader has the same content as Chapter 4, but is written at a less difficult reading level.

On-Level Leveled Reader has the same concepts as Chapter 4, and is written at grade level.

Advanced Leveled Reader is above grade level and enriches the chapter with additional examples and extended ideas.

Leveled Reader Database
Scott Foresman
pearsonsuccessnet.com

Use the online database to search for additional leveled readers by level, title, content, and skill.

Key Content and Skill in Leveled Readers and Chapter 4

Content	Vocabulary		Target Reading Skill	Graphic Organizer
How Living Things Grow and Change	life cycle nymph seed coat	germinate seedling	Infer	

Chapter 4 Planning Guide

Lesson/Activity	Pacing	Science Objectives
Build Background pp. 97–99	20 minutes	• The student identifies words and constructs meaning from text, illustrations, graphics, and charts using the strategies of phonics, word structure, and context clues.
Lab zone **Flip Chart Activity** How common are some traits?		
Lab zone **Flip Chart Activity** What happens when a seed germinates?		
Lab zone **Directed Inquiry**		• The student uses simple graphs, pictures, written statements, and numbers to observe, describe, record, and compare data.
Explore Which hand do different children use to write? p. 100	15 minutes	
How to Read Science p. 101	20 minutes	• The student makes connections and inferences based on text and prior knowledge (for example, order of events, possible outcomes).
1 How do sea turtles grow and change? pp. 102–107	40 minutes	• The student describes how organisms change as they grow and mature. • The student understands that living things can reproduce, and nonliving things cannot reproduce.
2 What is the life cycle of a dragonfly? pp. 108–109	20 minutes	• The student knows that some organisms have adaptations that enable them to move from one medium to another (for example, dragonflies begin life in water, move to land, and then fly in the air).
3 What is the life cycle of a horse? pp. 110–111	20 minutes	• The student knows that living things have offspring that resemble their parents. • The student describes how organisms change as they grow and mature.
4 How are young animals like their parents? pp. 112–113	20 minutes	• The student understands that plants and animals produce offspring with similar characteristics, but individual differences (for example, kittens in a litter may be colored differently).
5 What is the life cycle of a bean plant? pp. 114–115	20 minutes	• The student describes how organisms change as they grow and mature.
6 How are young plants like their parents? pp. 116–117	20 minutes	• The student understands that plants and animals produce offspring with similar characteristics, but individual differences (for example, kittens in a litter may be colored differently).
7 How do people grow and change? pp. 118–121	30 minutes	• The student describes how organisms change as they grow and mature. • The student knows that living things have offspring that resemble their parents.
Lab zone **Guided Inquiry**	10–15 minutes per day; entire growth cycle will take about 3 weeks	• The student describes how organisms change as they grow and mature.
Investigate How does a caterpillar grow and change? pp. 122–123		
Wrap-Up Chapter 4 pp.124–128	20 minutes	• The student adds and subtracts whole numbers to solve real-world problems, using appropriate methods of computing, such as objects, mental mathematics, paper and pencil, calculator.
Math in Science: Measuring Time	20 minutes	
Chapter 4 Review and Test Prep	20 minutes	
NASA Biography: Meet Mario Mota	20 minutes	

Vocabulary/Skills	Assessment/Intervention	Resources/Technology
Process Skills: Observe Predict Collect Data	• Chapter Review, SE, pp. 126–127 1, 2, 3, 4	• Science Content Transparency 4 • Workbook, p. 41 • Graphic Organizer Transparency 3 • Vocabulary Cards • Activity Book, pp. 55–56
Process Skill: ◉ Infer Target Reading Skill: **Infer**	• Explain Your Results, SE, p. 100 • Activity Rubric ◉ **Infer,** SE, p. 101	• Activity Book, pp. 51–52 • Activity DVD • Activity Placemat 7 • Workbook, pp. 42–43 • Every Student Learns, p. 23
life cycle	• Scaffolded Questions, TE, pp. 103, 105, 107 • Checkpoint Questions, SE, pp. 105, 107 • Chapter Review, SE, pp. 126–127 (2, 8)	• Workbook, p. 44 • Quick Study, pp. 40–41 • Every Student Learns, p. 24
nymph	• Scaffolded Questions, TE, p. 109 • Checkpoint Questions, SE, p. 109 • Chapter Review, SE, pp. 126–127 (3, 6, 10) ◉ **Infer,** SE, p. 109	• Workbook, p. 45 • Quick Study, pp. 42–43 • Every Student Learns, p. 25
	• Scaffolded Questions, TE, p. 111 • Checkpoint Questions, SE, p. 111 • Chapter Review, SE, pp. 126–127 (6) ◉ **Infer,** SE, p. 111	• Workbook, p. 46 • Quick Study, pp. 44–45 • Every Student Learns, p. 26
	• Scaffolded Questions, TE, p. 113 • Checkpoint Questions, SE, p. 113 • Chapter Review, SE, pp. 126–127 (11)	• Workbook, p. 47 • Quick Study, pp. 46–47 • Every Student Learns, p. 27
seed coat germinate seedling	• Scaffolded Questions, TE, p. 115 • Checkpoint Questions, SE, p. 115 • Chapter Review, SE, pp. 126–127 (1, 4, 7)	• Workbook, p. 48 • Quick Study, pp. 48–49 • Every Student Learns, p. 28
	• Scaffolded Questions, TE, p. 117 • Checkpoint Questions, SE, p. 117 • Chapter Review, SE, pp. 126–127 (11)	• Workbook, p. 49 • Quick Study, pp. 50–51 • Every Student Learns, p. 29
	• Scaffolded Questions, TE, pp. 119, 121 • Checkpoint Questions, SE, pp. 119, 121 • Chapter Review, SE, pp. 126–127 (5, 11) ◉ **Infer,** SE, p. 121	• Workbook, p. 50 • Quick Study, pp. 52–53 • Every Student Learns, p. 30
Process Skills: Collect and Record Data	• Explain Your Results, SE, p. 123 • Activity Rubric	• Activity Book, pp. 53–54 • Activity DVD • Activity Placemat 8
Math Skill: Measuring	• Scaffolded Questions, TE, p. 125 ◉ **Infer,** SE, p. 127 **ExamView®** Chapter 4 Test **Success Tracker** pearsonsuccessnet.com/ successtracker	• Workbook, pp. 51, 53, 54 • Assessment Book, pp. 13–16

Wrap-Up Unit A

Lab zone **Full Inquiry**

Experiment Which bird beak can crush seeds? pp. 132–133

Lab zone **Full Inquiry**

Science Fair Project p. 136

Quick Teaching Plan

If time is short...

- Build Background, pp. 98–99
- Explore Activity, p. 100
- How to Read Science, p. 101
- Lesson 1, pp. 102–107
- Lesson 4, pp. 112–113
- Lesson 5, pp. 114–115
- Lesson 7, pp. 118–121

Other quick options...

Quick ACTIVITY

TE pp. 98, 102, 108, 110, 112, 114, 116, 118, 124

TRANSPARENCIES 20, 21, 22, 23, 24, 25, 26

Quick SUMMARY

TE pp. 102, 104, 106, 108, 110, 112, 114, 116, 118, 120

Chapter 4 Activity Guide

Children learn to ask and answer scientific questions as they progress to greater independence in scaffolded inquiry.

Directed Inquiry A Directed Inquiry activity begins each chapter.

Guided Inquiry A Guided Inquiry activity closes each chapter.

Full Inquiry Experiments and Science Fair Projects at the end of each unit provide opportunities for Full Inquiry.

Lab zone Directed Inquiry

Explore Which hand do different children use to write? p. 100

Time 15 minutes

Grouping individuals or pairs

Advance Preparation Prepare a classroom graph on chart paper. Make squares large enough for children to attach their paper hands. Fasten the graph to a bulletin board or wall.

Materials construction paper (1 sheet per child); black crayon; safety scissors; tape; white chart paper (whole class use)

What to Expect The majority of the class will have right-handed cutouts. After taping the paper hands to the graph, children should infer that they use different hands to write and that more children use their right hand to write.

Safety Note Tell children to be careful with scissors.

 Activity DVD Unit A, Chapter 4

 Activity Placemat Mat 7

Lab zone Guided Inquiry

Investigate How does a caterpillar grow and change? pp. 122–123

Time 10 minutes observation time per day for about 3 weeks

Grouping whole class

Advance Preparation Use the live materials coupon to order caterpillars 2 weeks in advance. Keep the container at room temperature and out of direct sunlight.

Materials *butterfly habitat (with live materials coupon for 5 Painted Lady caterpillars); transparent or masking tape (teacher use); crayons or markers*

Science Center This activity can be set up in your Science Center for students to work on throughout the day.

What to Expect The Painted Lady larvae will develop into chrysalises in about 7 to 10 days. The caterpillars will climb to the top of the container and hang down from the lid head first. The chrysalises will take another 7 to 10 days to develop into butterflies.

Safety Note To protect native wildlife, do not release living organisms into the environment. After the activity is completed, you can continue to maintain the organisms in the classroom. Adult butterflies will live approximately 2 to 4 weeks. If necessary, biologists suggest freezing the animals in a sealed container and then disposing of the container.

 Activity DVD Unit A, Chapter 4

 Activity Placemat Mat 8

Lab zone Full Inquiry

Experiment Which bird beak can crush seeds? pp. 132–133

Time 20 minutes

Grouping small groups

Advance Preparation Cut 4 pieces of plastic straw for each group. Each piece should be 1 cm long.

Teaching Tips You may wish to have children glue the craft sticks to the clothespin in advance to allow time for the glue to dry. Remind children not to use too much glue. Have children look at the pictures of the cardinal and the heron. Talk about the sizes and shapes of the birds' beaks. You might want to have children talk about the shapes and sizes of their own teeth. Ask them which of their teeth are better for crushing food.

Materials *2 spring-type clothespins; 2 craft sticks; 4 pieces of plastic straw (each 1 cm long); glue*

What to Expect The model of a heron's beak (clothespin with craft sticks attached) will pick up a model of a seed (straw piece) without crushing it. The model of a cardinal's beak (clothespin only) will crush a model of a seed (straw piece). Children should infer that a cardinal uses its beak to crush seeds.

 Activity DVD Unit Experiment

 Activity Placemat Mat 9

Other Resources
The following Resources are available for activities found in the Student Edition.

Demonstration Kit If you wish to rehearse or demonstrate the Chapter 4 activities, use the materials provided in the Demonstration Kit.

Classroom Equipment Kit Materials shown in *italic print* are available in the Classroom Equipment Kit.

Activity Placemats The Equipment Kit includes an Activity Placemat for each activity, a work surface that identifies the materials that need to be gathered.

Quick ACTIVITY
Transparencies Use a transparency to focus children's attention on the Quick Activity for each lesson.

Teacher's Activity Guide For detailed information about Inquiry Activities, access the Teacher's Activity Guide at **pearsonsuccessnet.com**.

Activity Flip Chart

How common are some traits?

Use this center activity after teaching Lesson 7 of the chapter.

Process Skills collect data, observe

 Time 20 minutes

 Grouping Individual

Materials notebook; pencil

Procedure
- Some children may be sensitive to traits, such as a widow's peak or attached earlobes that they may have. Stress that these traits are common.
- Children will observe some of the common physical traits of their classmates. They will **collect data** about these traits by counting the number of children that have each trait and entering this information into a data chart.

What to Expect Students will take a survey to find out how common or uncommon certain traits are among their classmates.

Think About It
1. Answers will vary, but the most common traits are likely to be no widow's peak and detached earlobes.
2. Answers will vary but the least common traits are likely to be widow's peak and attached earlobes.

Activity Flip Chart

What happens when a seed germinates?

Use this center activity after teaching Lesson 5 of the chapter.

Process Skills observe, predict

 Time 20 minutes initially; 5 minutes each day for 3–4 days

 Grouping Pairs

Materials 4 radish seeds; paper towel; plastic sandwich bag; water in spray bottle

Procedure
- Do not leave the towel too wet. It should stay moist in the sealed bag. If necessary, remoisten by spraying water on it.
- Review with children the steps of the germination process described in Lesson 5. Have children **observe** radish seeds for 3–4 days to understand the process of germination.
- Children should **infer** that the root coming out of the radish seed is evidence that the seed is germinating, or growing.

What to Expect After 3–4 days, the seed coats of the radish seeds should open and a root should start growing outward and downward.

Think About It
1. The seed coat breaks open and a root starts growing.
2. Drawings should show a longer root growing downward and a stem and leaves growing upward.

Use the following Workbook pages to support content and skill development as you teach Chapter 4. You can also view and print Workbook pages from the Online Teacher's Edition.

Use with Build Background, pp. 98–99

Name _____ **Vocabulary Preview**
Use with Chapter 4.

Draw a picture or write a sentence to go with each word.

life cycle	nymph
seed coat	germinate
seedling	

Directions: Read the words and draw pictures to illustrate them or write sentences about them. Cut out the boxes to use as word cards.
Home Activity: Have your child use a picture in the chapter to explain the steps in the life cycle of an organism. Then have him or her tell how the terms *nymph, seed coat, germinate,* and *seedling* fit into different life cycles of organisms.

Workbook — Vocabulary Preview **41**

Workbook, p. 41

Use with How to Read Science, p. 101

Name _____ **How to Read Science**
Use with Chapter 4.

Ⓖ Infer

Science Article
Maria planted flower seeds. Little plants soon came up. She watered them, and they grew. The plants made flowers. Later, Maria saw seeds where the flowers had been.

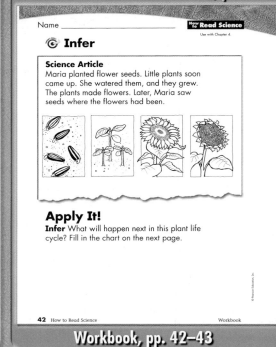

Apply It!
Infer What will happen next in this plant life cycle? Fill in the chart on the next page.

42 How to Read Science — Workbook

Workbook, pp. 42–43

Use with Lesson 1, pp. 102–107

Name _____ **Think, Read, Learn**
Use with pages 103–107.

How do sea turtles grow and change?
Before You Read Lesson 1

Read each sentence. Do you think it is true? Do you think it is not true? Circle the word or words after each sentence that tell what you think.

1. All living things grow and change.   True   Not True
2. Sea turtles lay eggs in the sand.   True   Not True
3. Baby turtles have a tooth.   True   Not True
4. Baby turtles do not look like their parents.   True   Not True

After You Read Lesson 1

Read each sentence again. Circle the word or words after each sentence that tell what you think now. Did you change any answers? Put an **X** by each answer that you changed.

1. All living things grow and change.   (True)   Not True
2. Sea turtles lay eggs in the sand.   (True)   Not True
3. Baby turtles have a tooth.   (True)   Not True
4. Baby turtles do not look like their parents.   True   (Not True)

Home Activity: Together talk about your child's answers. Have your child explain why his or her answers may have changed after reading the lesson.

Workbook — Think, Read, Learn **44**

Workbook, p. 44

Use with Lesson 2, pp. 108–109

Name _____ **Think, Read, Learn**
Use with pages 108–109.

What is the life cycle of a dragonfly?
Before You Read Lesson 2

Read each sentence. Do you think it is true? Do you think it is not true? Circle the word or words after each sentence that tell what you think.

1. Nymphs do not need wings.   True   Not True
2. Nymphs shed their outside cover once.   True   Not True
3. Dragonfly nymphs live in water.   True   Not True

After You Read Lesson 2

Read each sentence again. Circle the word or words after each sentence that tell what you think now. Did you change any answers? Put an **X** by each answer that you changed.

1. Nymphs do not need wings.   (True)   Not True
2. Nymphs shed their outside cover once.   True   (Not True)
3. Dragonfly nymphs live in water.   (True)   Not True

Home Activity: Together talk about your child's answers. Have your child explain why his or her answers may have changed after reading the lesson.

Workbook — Think, Read, Learn **45**

Workbook, p. 45

Use with Lesson 3, pp. 110–111

Name _____ **Think, Read, Learn**
Use with pages 110–111.

What is the life cycle of a horse?
Before You Read Lesson 3

Read each sentence. Do you think it is true? Do you think it is not true? Circle the word or words after each sentence that tell what you think.

1. A baby horse is called a mammal.   True   Not True
2. A foal drinks milk from its mother.   True   Not True
3. A foal looks like its parents.   True   Not True

After You Read Lesson 3

Read each sentence again. Circle the word or words after each sentence that tell what you think now. Did you change any answers? Put an **X** by each answer that you changed.

1. A baby horse is called a mammal.   True   (Not True)
2. A foal drinks milk from its mother.   (True)   Not True
3. A foal looks like its parents.   (True)   Not True

Home Activity: Together talk about your child's answers. Have your child explain why his or her answers may have changed after reading the lesson.

Workbook — Think, Read, Learn **46**

Workbook, p. 46

Use with Lesson 4, pp. 112–113

Name _____ **Think, Read, Learn**
Use with pages 112–113.

How are young animals like their parents?
Before You Read Lesson 4

Read each sentence. Do you think it is true? Do you think it is not true? Circle the word or words after each sentence that tell what you think.

1. Baby penguins have fuzzy feathers.   True   Not True
2. Most animal parents and babies have the same shape.   True   Not True
3. The spots of young and adult giraffes look the same.   True   Not True

After You Read Lesson 4

Read each sentence again. Circle the word or words after each sentence that tell what you think now. Did you change any answers? Put an **X** by each answer that you changed.

1. Baby penguins have fuzzy feathers.   (True)   Not True
2. Most animal parents and babies have the same shape.   (True)   Not True
3. The spots of young and adult giraffes look the same.   True   (Not True)

Home Activity: Together talk about your child's answers. Have your child explain why his or her answers may have changed after reading the lesson.

Workbook — Think, Read, Learn **47**

Workbook, p. 47

Name _____ Think, Read, Learn
Use with pages 114–115.

What is the life cycle of a bean plant?

Before You Read Lesson 5

Read each sentence. Do you think it is true? Do you think it is not true? Circle the word or words after each sentence that tell what you think.

1. A seedling may germinate. True Not True
2. A tiny plant is inside a seed. True Not True
3. Adult plant flowers make seeds. True Not True

After You Read Lesson 5

Read each sentence again. Circle the word or words after each sentence that tell what you think now. Did you change any answers? Put an **X** by each answer that you changed.

1. A seedling may germinate. True (Not True)
2. A tiny plant is inside a seed. (True) Not True
3. Adult plant flowers make seeds. (True) Not True

 Home Activity: Together talk about your child's answers. Have your child explain why his or her answers may have changed after reading the lesson.

Workbook Think, Read, Learn **48**

Workbook, p. 48

Name _____ Think, Read, Learn
Use with pages 116–117.

How are young plants like their parents?

Before You Read Lesson 6

Read each sentence. Do you think it is true? Do you think it is not true? Circle the word or words after each sentence that tell what you think.

1. Parent plants and their young usually look alike. True Not True
2. A young saguaro cactus grows arms. True Not True
3. Some young plants have flowers with different colors than their parents. True Not True

After You Read Lesson 6

Read each sentence again. Circle the word or words after each sentence that tell what you think now. Did you change any answers? Put an **X** by each answer that you changed.

1. Parent plants and their young usually look alike. True (Not True)
2. A young saguaro cactus grows arms. True (Not True)
3. Some young plants have flowers with different colors than their parents. (True) Not True

 Home Activity: Together talk about your child's answers. Have your child explain why his or her answers may have changed after reading the lesson.

Workbook Think, Read, Learn **49**

Workbook, p. 49

Name _____ Think, Read, Learn
Use with pages 118–121.

How do people grow and change?

Before You Read Lesson 7

Read each sentence. Do you think it is true? Do you think it is not true? Circle the word or words after each sentence that tell what you think.

1. To change, people must grow. True Not True
2. People differ in height and eye and hair color. True Not True
3. Children in one family can look different. True Not True

After You Read Lesson 7

Read each sentence again. Circle the word or words after each sentence that tell what you think now. Did you change any answers? Put an **X** by each answer that you changed.

1. To change, people must grow. True (Not True)
2. People differ in height and eye and hair color. (True) Not True
3. Children in one family can look different. (True) Not True

Home Activity: Together talk about your child's answers. Have your child explain why his or her answers may have changed after reading the lesson.

Workbook Think, Read, Learn **50**

Workbook, p. 50

Name _____ Math in Science
Use with Chapter 4.

Measuring Time

The table compares the life cycles of two kinds of flies.

Life Cycles of Housefly and Greenhouse Whitefly Compared		
Stage	**Housefly**	**Greenhouse Whitefly**
Egg	1 day	9 days
Larva	5 to 14 days	30 to 35 days
Pupa	3 to 10 days	11 days
Adult	19 to 70 days	10 to 40 days

Directions: Use the information in the table to answer the questions.

1. How many days does it take a greenhouse whitefly egg to hatch into a larva? _9 days_
2. Which fly hatches from a pupa to an adult quicker? _housefly_
3. Which adult fly usually lives longer? _housefly_
4. A housefly egg hatches into a larva. When is the soonest it could become an adult? Write a number sentence. _5 + 3 = 8 days_

 Home Activity: Your child learned to measure time using a diagram. Discuss the life cycle for people and decide on average time spent as a baby, toddler, child, young adult, and adult. Make a table like the one above. Ask each other questions about the table.

Workbook Math in Science **51**

Workbook, p. 51

Chapter 4
Assessment Support

online Teacher's Edition
pearsonsuccessnet.com

Use the following Assessment Book pages and ExamView to assess Chapter 4 content. You can also view and print Assessment Book pages from the Online Teacher's Edition.

Assessment Options

Formal Assessment

- Chapter Review and Test Prep, SE pp. 126–127
- Assessment Book, pp. 13–16
- Prescriptions for remediation are shown on TE p. 127

Performance Assessment

- Unit Wrap-Up, SE pp. 130–131

Ongoing Assessment

- Diagnostic Check, TE pp. 103, 105, 119
- Scaffolded Questions, TE pp. 103, 105, 107, 109, 111, 113, 115, 117, 119, 121, 125

Portfolio Assessment

- My Science Journal, TE pp. 99, 104, 106

Success Tracker

- Data management system to assess Adequate Yearly Progress (AYP) and provide intervention

ExamView®

- Alternative test formats are available online or through ExamView CD-ROM

Chapter 4 Test

Name _____ | Chapter 4 Test

Read each question and choose the best answer. Then fill in the circle next to the correct answer.

1 Which is a living thing that can grow and be a parent?
- Ⓐ rock
- Ⓑ cloud
- Ⓒ toy turtle
- Ⓓ sea turtle

2 Look at the picture. Think about how the animals are alike and different.

Which sentence is true?
- Ⓕ The mother and baby do not look alike.
- Ⓖ The mother and baby look exactly alike.
- Ⓗ The baby looks like its mother, but its spots are different.
- Ⓘ The baby looks like its mother, but it will grow up to look like another animal.

Assessment Book   Chapter 4 Test **13**

Assessment Book, p. 13

Chapter 4 Test

Name _____ | Chapter 4 Test

3 Which is the first part of the life cycle of sea turtles?
- Ⓐ start life as an egg
- Ⓑ mothers feed their babies milk
- Ⓒ babies grow into adults in shallow water
- Ⓓ babies crack open their eggs using a special tooth

4 Read the chart. Use what you learn to answer the question.

Life Cycle of a Bean Plant	
1	The seed germinates, or begins to grow.
2	The small seedling grows roots, a stem, and leaves.
3	The plant grows taller and thicker.
4	The adult plant grows seeds.

What does a seedling look like?
- Ⓕ a seed
- Ⓖ a tall and thick adult plant
- Ⓗ a tall adult plant with seeds called beans
- Ⓘ a small plant with roots, a stem, and leaves

14 Chapter 4 Test   Assessment Book

Assessment Book, p. 14

Chapter 4 Test

Name _____ | Chapter 4 Test

5 Look at the chart.

Parent	Young plant

What does the chart show?
- Ⓐ All plants have young plants.
- Ⓑ Young plants have shapes like their parents.
- Ⓒ Young plants look just like their parents.
- Ⓓ Young plants look nothing like their parents.

Assessment Book   Chapter 4 Test **15**

Assessment Book, p. 15

Chapter 4 Test

Name _____ | Chapter 4 Test

6 How do teenagers change?
- Ⓕ They grow taller.
- Ⓖ They learn to talk.
- Ⓗ They get a first tooth.
- Ⓘ Their hair changes to gray or white.

7 Where does a dragonfly begin life?
- Ⓐ on land
- Ⓑ in water
- Ⓒ in the air
- Ⓓ in water or on land

Write the answer to the question on the lines.

8 Look at the picture.

Which stage in the life cycle of a horse does the picture show? (2 points)
A foal.

16 Chapter 4 Test   Assessment Book

Assessment Book, p. 16

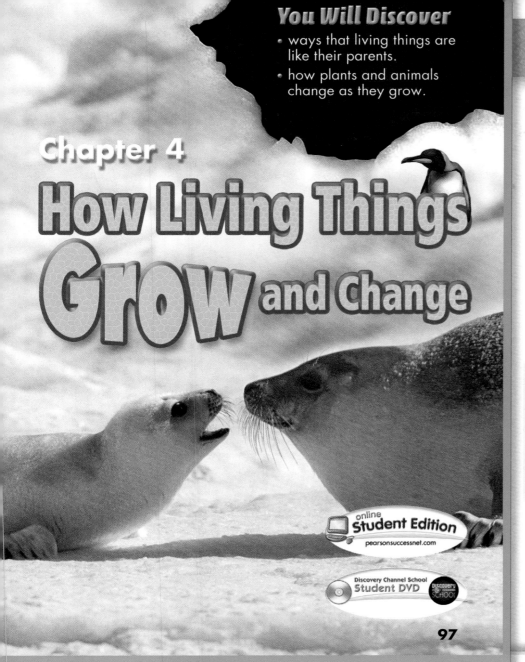

You Will Discover

- ways that living things are like their parents.
- how plants and animals change as they grow.

Chapter 4

How Living Things Grow and Change

online **Student Edition**
pearsonsuccessnet.com

Discovery Channel School
Student DVD

97

Chapter 4

How Living Things Grow and Change

⭐ **Science Objectives**

- The student knows how to apply knowledge about life processes to distinguish between living and nonliving things.
- The student describes how organisms change as they grow and mature.
- The student knows that all living things have offspring that resemble their parents.

Quick | TEACHING PLAN

If time is short...

Use Build Background page to engage children in chapter content. Then do Explore Activity, How to Read Science, and Lessons 1, 4, 5, and 7.

 ## Professional Development

To enhance your qualifications in science:

- preview content in Life Science DVD Segment *Continuation of Life.*
- preview activity management techniques described in Activity DVD Unit A, Chapter 4.

Discovery Channel School
Student DVD ## Technology Link

For additional information on the topics covered in this chapter, have children view the Discovery Channel School DVD *The Lives of Butterflies*

Take It to the NET

To access student resources:
1. Go to **www.pearsonsuccessnet.com**.
2. Click on the register button.
3. Enter the access code **frog** and your school's zip code.

Chapter 4 Concept Web

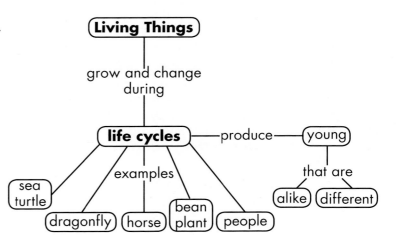

Children can create a concept web to organize ideas about how living things grow and change.

Build Background

 Science Objective

- The student identifies words and constructs meaning from text, illustrations, graphics, and charts using the strategies of phonics, word structure, and context clues.

Chapter 4 Vocabulary Words

life cycle, p. 106
nymph, p. 108
seed coat, p. 114
germinate, p. 114
seedling, p. 114

1 | Introduce the Concept

Quick ACTIVITY

Have children think about a kitten they have seen or bring a picture of a kitten to class to show them. Ask: **What does the kitten look like? What happens to the kitten as it gets older?** Solicit that as the kitten grows up, it gets bigger and turns into a cat.

Then ask: **Has anyone ever seen a seed? What happens after the seed is planted?** Solicit that a seed grows into a plant.

Discuss Essential Question

Many science vocabulary words are abstract. Use the pictures and labels on these pages to help you open a discussion about science concepts and build academic language.

Read the Chapter 4 Essential Question to children, **How do living things grow in different ways?** Remind children that plants and animals are living things. Have children look at the pictures. Ask: **What is happening to the young turtle?** It is becoming a big turtle. **What is happening to the young seed?** It is becoming a plant.

Revisit the essential question with children as they work through this chapter.

How do living things grow in different ways?

life cycle

nymph

seed coat

98

Build Background Resources

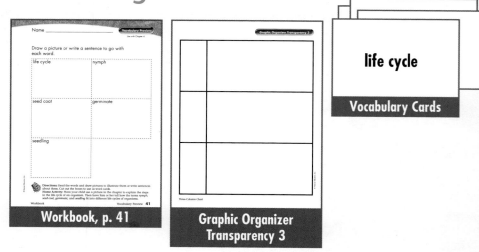

Workbook, p. 41

Graphic Organizer Transparency 3

life cycle

Vocabulary Cards

ELL Support

Access Content Before reading the chapter text, lead children on a picture/text walk.

Chapter 4 Vocabulary

life cycle page 106

nymph page 108

seed coat page 114

germinate page 114

seedling page 114

germinate

Germinate means to begin to grow into a young plant.

seedling

99

My Science Journal

Draw Living Things

On separate pages, have children draw pictures of living and nonliving things they see. One page should be titled *Living Things,* and the other *Nonliving Things.*

Science Background

Living Things and Nonliving Things

Something is either living or nonliving. Dead things were once living and are therefore classified as living. Something that is nonliving has never been alive.

2 | Introduce Vocabulary

Use the following Graphic Organizer provided on **pearsonsuccessnet.com** or Graphic Organizer Transparency 3.

Word	What I think it means	What it means
life cycle nymph seed coat germinate seedling		

On Graphic Organizer Transparency 3, list the vocabulary words under the first column. Explain to children that you will fill in the *What I think it means* column together.

- Pronounce each word. Guide children as they fill in the *What I think it means* column. Children can look at the pictures for clues about the meaning of the word. For example, the picture of the seed coat shows that the seed has an outer cover.

- Help children with their predictions by activating prior knowledge. Ask: **What does the nymph remind you of?**

- Tell children they will fill in the *What it means* column after reading the chapter.

Word Recognition Use the Vocabulary Cards to reinforce recognition of each written word and definition.

3 | Practice

Vocabulary Strategy: Word Maps

Using the Vocabulary Cards, read the definition of a vocabulary word aloud. Ask: **Which word is that?** Have students respond by helping you create a word map on the board. Place the vocabulary word in the center and in each corner place a word or phrase that helps define the vocabulary word. Connect each corner to the vocabulary word with an arrow. Continue until all the vocabulary words have word maps. Tell children they can check the word maps using their books or a dictionary.

Explore Which hand do different children use to write?

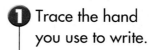 **Science Objective**

- The student uses simple graphs, pictures, written statements, and numbers to observe, describe, record, and compare data.

1 Build Background

This activity encourages children to observe that living things can be alike and different.

Managing Time and Materials

Time: 15 minutes

Groups: individuals or pairs

Materials: construction paper (1 sheet per child); black crayon; safety scissors; tape; white chart paper (whole class use)

2 What To Do

Engage Review the activity objective together. Ask: *What do you know about how children write?*

Explore Have children trace their writing hand on a piece of construction paper, cut it out, and tape it into the appropriate column on the wall graph.

Explain Ask children to explain the wall graph data.

Extend Have children list other characteristics they could compare for classmates on the board.

Evaluate As a class ask and discuss. Ask: *How does the data show one way people can be different?*

3 Explain Your Results

The graph shows that [number] children use their right hand to write and [number] use their left hand.

Process Skills

Tell children that they **infer** when they get ideas from what they know.

Explore Which hand do different children use to write?

Materials

paper

crayon

scissors

tape

chart paper

What to Do

1. Trace the hand you use to write.

2. Write your name in the middle. Cut out the hand.

3. **Collect data** Tape your hand to the graph.

 Be careful!

Scissors are sharp!

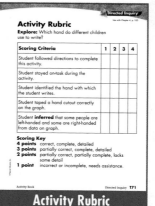 right hand

left hand

Process Skills

You **infer** when you get ideas from what you know.

Explain Your Results
Infer What does the graph show?

Activity Resources

Name _____

Explore Which hand do different children use to write?

Explain Your Results
Infer What does the graph show?

Notes for Home: Your child collected data that showed some children in the class are left-handed and others are right-handed. Your child learned one way in which people are different.
Home Activity: Observe differences in family members such as facial features, hair, or eye color.

Activity Book   Directed Inquiry **51**

Activity Book p. 51–52

Activity Rubric

Explore: Which hand do different children use to write?

Scoring Criteria	1	2	3	4
Student followed directions to complete this activity.				
Student stayed on-task during the activity.				
Student identified the hand with which the student writes.				
Student taped a hand cutout correctly on the graph.				
Student inferred that some people are left-handed and some are right-handed from data on graph.				

Scoring Key
4 points correct, complete, detailed
3 points partially correct, complete, detailed
2 points partially correct, partially complete, lacks some detail
1 point incorrect or incomplete, needs assistance

Activity Book   Directed Inquiry **T71**

Activity Rubric

Use Activity DVD Unit A, Chapter 4 to preview this activity.

Call 1-888-537-4908 with activity questions.

More Lab zone Activities **Take It to the Net** pearsonsuccessnet.com

Find more about this activity at our Web site.

- See the **Teacher's Activity Guide** for more support.
- An alternative activity is also available to download.

How to Read Science

Reading Skills

Infer

Infer means to use what you know to answer a question.

Science Article

Carol is right-handed. She uses her right hand for writing and to drink from a glass. She uses both hands to button her coat. Ben is left-handed.

Apply It!

Infer Which hand do you think Ben would use to cut paper or throw a ball?

I know		I can infer
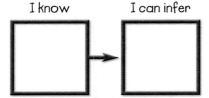	→	

101

How to Read Science Resource

Workbook, pp. 42–43

ELL Support

For more practice on **Infer**, use **Every Student Learns Teacher's Guide,** p. 23.

Infer

 Reading Objective

• The student makes connections and inferences based on text and prior knowledge (for example, order of events, possible outcomes).

About the Target Skill

The target skill for *How Living Things Grow and Change* is **Infer.** Children are introduced to the skill as you guide them through this page.

1 | Introduce

Ask children what happens to ice when it gets warm. (It melts.) Present the following scene to children. **A tray of ice cubes left on the kitchen counter contains mostly water. What do you think happened?** (The ice cubes melted.) Tell children that they have used what they know about ice to answer a question.

2 | Model the Skill

Read the Science Article as a class. Have children look at the pictures and read the information. Say: **Carol is right-handed. What tasks does she do using her right hand?** Write and drink from a glass **Ben is left-handed. Which hand does he use to drink from a glass?** His left hand

3 | Practice

Graphic Organizer

Look at the Graphic Organizer together. Work with children to complete the Graphic Organizer using the facts from the Science Article.

Apply It!

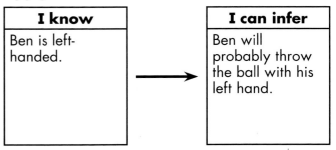

I know		I can infer
Ben is left-handed.	→	Ben will probably throw the ball with his left hand.

How do sea turtles grow and change?

 Science Objective

- The student understands that living things can reproduce, and nonliving things cannot reproduce.

1 | Introduce

Quick ACTIVITY | TRANSPARENCY 20

Point out to children the picture of the sea turtle. Have children describe what the sea turtle looks like. Then have children make a clay model of the sea turtle. Ask: **What does the sea turtle need to live?** Food, water, air, shelter. Ask: **What does the turtle have that provides shelter?** It has a shell.

Access Prior Knowledge

Show children pictures of plants, animals, and nonliving things. Ask: **What living things do you see? Can you tell me about what some living things do?** Answers will vary. **What do living things need?** Food, water, shelter, space, and air

Set Purpose

Tell children they are going to read about sea turtles. Help them set a **purpose for reading,** such as finding out how sea turtles grow and change.

2 | Teach

Quick SUMMARY

- Plants and animals are living things.
- Living things need food and water, they grow and change, they can be parents, some can move on their own.

Sing or play "Hi Little Turtle!" for children. Then read page 103 together. Point out that unlike the toy turtle, the sea turtle will grow and change. Review the characteristics of living things.

You Are There

♪ Hi Little Turtle!

Sung to the tune of "Itsy Bitsy Spider"
Lyrics by Gerri Brioso & Richard Freitas/The Dovetail Group, Inc.

Look at the sea turtle coming from the sea.
Crawling on the sand, looking right at me.
Hey, little sea turtle, I would like to know,
How did you start out and how did you grow?

102 🎵 Science Songs ♪♪♫

Lesson 1 Resource

Workbook, p. 44

🎵 Science Songs ♪♪♫

Use the Science Songs CD to play "Hi Little Turtle!" for the class.

Lesson 1

How do sea turtles grow and change?

Living things need food and water. Living things grow and change. Living things can be parents. Plants and animals are living things.

The sea turtle is an animal. You will learn how a sea turtle grows and changes.

This toy turtle is a nonliving thing. It does not need food and water. It cannot grow and change. It cannot be a parent.

103

ELL Leveled Support

Growing and Changing

Beginning Show children three books of different sizes. Arrange them in order of size. Point to them and say: **Big, bigger, biggest.** Have children repeat after you. Show pictures of children of different ages. Say and have children repeat: **Young, younger, youngest.** Choose volunteers to come to the front of the class. Say and have children repeat: **Tall, taller, tallest.**

Intermediate Say to children: **When you were a baby, you were little. Now you are bigger. You have changed.** Ask volunteers to tell the class other ways they have changed.

Advanced Ask children to talk about how they have changed since they were born. Start them off with sentence frames such as: **When I was little, I _____. As I grew, I _____. Now I _____.**

Assign Quick Study pp. 40–41 to children who need help with lesson content.

Guide Comprehension

Ask children the following scaffolded questions to assess understanding.

Scaffolded Questions

1 List *What do living things need?* Food and water

2 Compare *How are a toy turtle and real turtle alike? How are they different?* Possible answer: Both look like a turtle. A toy turtle is not a living thing.

3 Infer *Explain why plants are living things.* Plants grow and change. Plants need food and water. Plants can be parents.

Extend Vocabulary

Remind children that a sea turtle grows and changes. Write the words *sea* and *see* on the board. Call on a volunteer to read the words aloud. Ask: **What do you notice about how these words sound and look?** Explain that words that sound the same but are spelled differently and have different meanings are called homophones. Ask children to spell the word that means "a body of water." (*s-e-a*) Ask children to spell the word that means "to look at." (*s-e-e*) Have children write a sentence for each word.

Diagnostic Check

If... children have difficulty understanding how living things are different from nonliving things,

then... make a chart on the board comparing some of the characteristics of living and nonliving things.

Living things	Nonliving things
Need food and water	Don't need food and water
Grow and change	Don't grow and change
Can be parents	Can't be parents

Science Objective

• The student understands that living things can reproduce, and nonliving things cannot reproduce.

2 | Teach (continued)

Quick SUMMARY

• Although sea turtles live in the ocean, they crawl to the beach to lay eggs.

• They dig a hole with their flippers, lay eggs in the hole, and cover the hole with sand.

• Baby sea turtles, which hatch after about two months, use a special tooth to help them open the shell.

Read pages 104–105 together. Focus children's attention on the pictures. Ask: **What information do the pictures give?** Children should respond that the pictures show that a sea turtle lays many eggs on the sand and a baby turtle hatches from an egg. Then ask: **Does the baby turtle look like its parent?** Yes

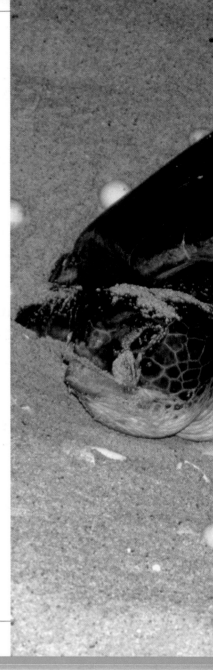

Sea Turtle Eggs

A sea turtle lives in the ocean. A sea turtle crawls onto a beach to lay eggs. A sea turtle uses its flippers to dig a hole in the sand. It lays eggs in the hole. Then the sea turtle covers the ① eggs with sand.

Sea turtles can lay many eggs at one time.

104

My Science Journal

Describe the Order

Write the following sentences on the board. Have children write the sentences in order. Children can also illustrate their sentences.

The young turtle breaks out of the shell. The eggs lay in the sand. A sea turtle lays eggs.

Science Background

More About Sea Turtle Eggs

• A female turtle lays as many as 200 eggs. Each is about the size of an apricot. Predators, animals looking for food, raid the nest. After the turtles hatch, many are eaten by birds, dogs, and lizards. Of the 200 eggs that are laid, only a few will survive.

• Sea turtles are endangered. People work to protect sea turtles' eggs.

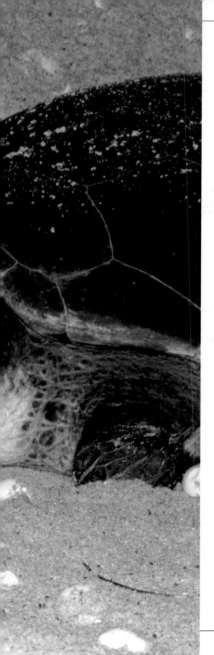

The eggs lay in the sand for about two months. Then the eggs are ready to hatch. ②

Baby turtles have a special tooth. The tooth helps them break open the egg's shell. Later, the tooth falls out. ③

A baby sea turtle hatches from its egg.

1. ✓Checkpoint How do baby sea turtles get out of the egg?

2. Math in Science Suppose 3 sea turtles each laid 100 eggs. How many eggs were laid all together?

105

ELL Support

Using Prefixes

Write the word _nonliving_ on the board, underlining as shown. Tell students that _non_ means "not." Ask: **What does nonliving mean?** Not living Ask children to provide other examples of _non_ words and their meanings to test understanding. (Possible answers: nonfiction/not fiction; nonviolent/not violent; nonstop/not stopping)

For scaffolded instruction about how sea turtles grow and change, use **Every Student Learns Teacher's Guide,** p. 24.

Science Objectives

- The student describes how organisms change as they grow and mature.
- The student knows that living things have offspring that resemble their parents.

2 | Teach (continued)

Quick SUMMARY

- Living things follow a life cycle. They grow and change.
- A young sea turtle looks like its parents.
- When the young sea turtle is grown, it may have young of its own. Then a new life cycle begins.

Read pages 106–107 together. Use the diagram to discuss the life cycle of a sea turtle. Point out that the arrows go from one stage to another. Tell children that after the sea turtle becomes an adult, it may lay eggs of its own and a new life cycle begins for the young. Explain to children that life cycles are not the same for all living things. The sea turtle is just one example of a life cycle.

The Life Cycle of a Sea Turtle

The way a living thing grows and changes ① is called its **life cycle.** Follow the arrows to see the life cycle of a sea turtle.

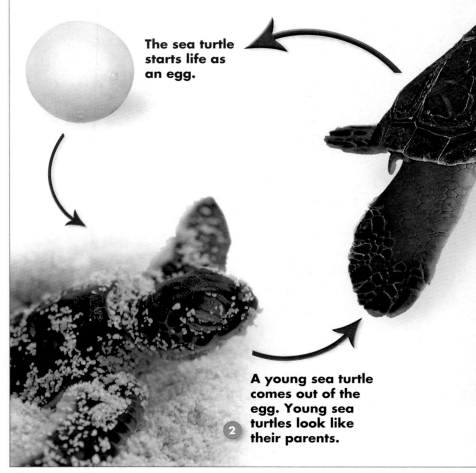

The sea turtle starts life as an egg.

A young sea turtle comes out of the egg. Young sea turtles look like their parents. ②

106

My Science Journal

Write About It

Have children write a fact about sea turtles that they found interesting.

Science Background

More About Sea Turtles

- Female sea turtles return to the beach where they were born to lay their eggs.
- Baby turtles are called hatchlings. After hatching, the young turtles may take three to seven days to dig their way to the surface. They usually wait until night to emerge from their nests to reduce exposure to daytime predators. They head to the water as a group.

One day, the sea turtle may have young of its own. A new life cycle begins. ③

✓**Lesson Checkpoint**

1. How do sea turtles start life?

2. Social Studies in Science Look at a map of the United States. Find some places where sea turtles might lay eggs.

107

Ask children the following scaffolded questions to assess understanding.

Scaffolded Questions

① **Define What is a life cycle?** The way a living thing grows and changes

② **See What does a young sea turtle look like?** It looks like its parents.

③ **Infer Why is a life cycle shown as a circle instead of a line?** The life cycle start over as grown animals have young.

Extend Vocabulary

Write the term **life cycle** on the board. Tell children that a cycle is a continuous, repeating series of events. The events seem to go around and around, as in a circle. Relate this idea to the use of cycle as circle or wheel in the words *bicycle* and *tricycle*.

3 | Assess

✓**Lesson Checkpoint**

1. They start life as eggs.

2. Social Studies in Science Places will vary. They should be on the ocean.

ELL Support

Stages in a Cycle

Make sure children understand how the arrows in the diagram show the order in which the stages happen. Point out that the arrow between the adult and the egg shows where a new life cycle begins.

For scaffolded instruction about the life cycle of a sea turtle, use **Every Student Learns Teacher's Guide,** page 24.

Lesson 2

What is the life cycle of a dragonfly?

 Science Objective

- The student knows that some organisms have adaptations that enable them to move from one medium to another (for example, dragonflies begin life in water, move to land, and then fly in the air).

1 Introduce

Quick ACTIVITY | TRANSPARENCY 21 |

Ask children to think about what a dragonfly might look like based on its name. Ask volunteers to draw it on the board. Then show Quick Activity Transparency 21 and discuss the questions. Have children draw a picture of an imaginary insect.

Access Prior Knowledge

Ask: ***Does a dragonfly have bones?*** No ***How do you know?*** A dragonfly is an insect. Insects do not have bones.

Set Purpose

Tell children you are going to read to them about the life cycle of a dragonfly. Help them set a **purpose for listening,** such as to discover what happens at each stage of a dragonfly's life.

2 Teach

Quick SUMMARY

- Young dragonflies, called nymphs, hatch from eggs.
- Nymphs begin their lives in the water. They look like their parents but have no wings.
- Nymphs shed their coverings many times as they grow. When they become adults, they have wings to fly.

Read pages 108–109 to children. Use the diagram to discuss the stages of a dragonfly's life cycle. Emphasize to children that the life cycle of an insect is different from the life cycle of other animals.

Lesson 2

What is the life cycle of a dragonfly?

The life cycles of insects are different from the life cycles of other animals. Many young insects are called **nymphs.** Nymphs look a lot like their parents, but their wings are still growing. Nymphs shed their outside covering many times as they grow.

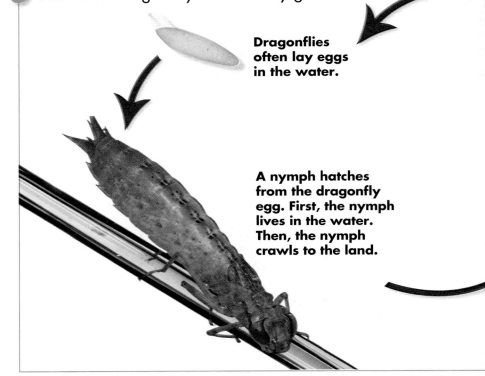

Dragonflies often lay eggs in the water.

A nymph hatches from the dragonfly egg. First, the nymph lives in the water. Then, the nymph crawls to the land.

Lesson 2 Resource

Workbook, p. 45

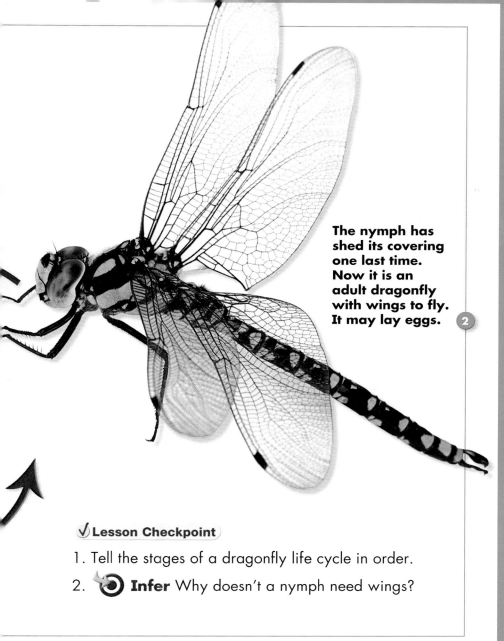

The nymph has shed its covering one last time. Now it is an adult dragonfly with wings to fly. It may lay eggs. 2

☑ **Lesson Checkpoint**

1. Tell the stages of a dragonfly life cycle in order.

2. **Infer** Why doesn't a nymph need wings?

109

Point out the nymph stage of a dragonfly's life cycle. Tell children that the nymph changes into an adult dragonfly. Also point out that the wings of an adult dragonfly allow it to live on land, not in water as the wingless nymph does.

Assign Quick Study pp. 42–43 to children who need help with lesson content.

Guide Comprehension

Ask children the following scaffolded questions to assess understanding.

Scaffolded Questions

1 **Name** *What is a nymph?* A young insect that looks like its parents, but whose wings are still growing.

2 **Compare** *How are a nymph and an adult alike?* A nymph looks like an adult. Both have six legs.

3 **Infer** *Why do you think nymphs shed their outside covering as they grow?* The old covering becomes too small as they grow.

Extend Vocabulary

Discuss how the word *fly* can be both a noun and a verb. Point out that a noun names a person, place, or thing. A verb tells about an action or a state of being. Ask children to make up two sentences, one in which *fly* is used as a noun, and the other in which *fly* is used as a verb. Call on volunteers to read their sentences.

3 | Assess

☑ **Lesson Checkpoint**

1. Egg, nymph, adult

2. **Infer** A nymph does not fly.

Science Background

About Dragonflies

- Nymphs live in the water. They take in oxygen through posterior gills. They shed their skin many times. This allows them to grow bigger.
- Newly emerged dragonflies hang for a while before flying. They pump fluid through the veins in their wings to smooth the wings out.
- Adult dragonflies eat mosquitoes, water fleas, and almost any insect that flies.

ELL Support

Review the picture of a nymph on page 108 to reinforce understanding of this word. Help children pronounce the word by telling them the *y* sounds like short *i* and the *ph* sounds like *f*. Point out that nymphs have no wings and crawl. As adult dragonflies, they will have wings and fly.

For scaffolded instruction about the life cycle of a dragonfly, use **Every Student Learns Teacher's Guide,** p. 25.

Lesson 3

What is the life cycle of a horse?

 Science Objectives

- The student describes how organisms change as they grow and mature.
- The student knows that living things have offspring that resemble their parents.

1 Introduce

Quick ACTIVITY | TRANSPARENCY 22

Tell children to look at the picture of the horse. Ask: **Is a horse a mammal? How do you know?** A horse has a backbone and fur. Tell children that mammals are also warm-blooded. Direct children to put their hand against their neck. Ask: **Does your neck feel warm or cold?** Warm. Ask: **If you were to touch a horse, do you think it would feel warm or cold?** Warm

Access Prior Knowledge

Ask children if they remember all of the characteristics of a mammal. Ask: **Does a mammal hatch from an egg?** No

Set Purpose

Tell children they are going to read about the life cycle of a horse. Help them set a **purpose for reading,** such as to find out what happens at each stage of a horse's life cycle.

2 Teach

Quick SUMMARY

- A young horse grows inside its mother.
- After it is born, it drinks milk from its mother.
- An adult horse can have foals of its own.

Read pages 110–111 with children. Use the pictures to discuss what happens at each stage of a horse's life cycle. Remind children that a horse is a mammal and young mammals grow inside their mothers. Point out how a foal looks like its parents.

Lesson 3

What is the life cycle of a horse?

A horse is a mammal. Most young mammals grow inside their mothers. Young mammals drink milk from their mother.

A young horse is called a foal.
①

The foal grows and grows. It looks like its parents.
②

110

Lesson 3 Resource

What is the life cycle of a horse?

Before You Read Lesson 3

Read each sentence. Do you think it is true? Do you think it is not true? Circle the word or words after each sentence that tell what you think.

1. A baby horse is called a mammal. True Not True
2. A foal drinks milk from its mother. True Not True
3. A foal looks like its parents. True Not True

After You Read Lesson 3

Read each sentence again. Circle the word or words after each sentence that tell what you think now. Did you change any answers? Put an X by each answer that you changed.

1. A baby horse is called a mammal. True Not True
2. A foal drinks milk from its mother. True Not True
3. A foal looks like its parents. True Not True

Workbook, p. 46

ELL Support

Young Mammals

To help children understand the life cycle of a horse, explain that the young horse grows *inside* its mother. Contrast this idea with the way sea turtles and dragonflies lay eggs *outside* the mother.

The foal has become an adult horse. The adult horse is old enough to have foals of its own. **3**

✓ **Lesson Checkpoint**

1. 🔍 **Infer** What is food for a foal?

2. **Writing** in Science Tell what you know about the life cycle of a horse.

111

Science Background

More About Horses

- A foal is weaned at six months. Male foals are called colts. Female foals are called fillies.

- A horse is mature after three years. It is considered an adult at five years.

Social Studies Link

Horses Helping People

Tell children that long ago, there were no cars and machines. Horses helped people in many ways. Have children look on the Internet or in the library for information about how horses helped people living in the United States long ago, and how horses help people today. Children can write what they learned in their science journals.

ELL Support

For scaffolded instruction about the life cycle of a horse, use **Every Student Learns Teacher's Guide,** p. 26.

Assign Quick Study pp. 44–45 to children who need help with lesson content.

Guide Comprehension

Ask children the following scaffolded questions to assess understanding.

Scaffolded Questions

1 **Define** *What is a foal?* A baby horse

2 **See Relationships** *What does a baby horse look like?* Its parents

3 **Sequence** *Think of the life cycle of a horse. What can happen after it becomes an adult?* It can have foals of its own.

Extend Vocabulary

Write the word *newborn* on the board. Ask children: *Which picture shows a newborn horse?* The picture at the left on page 110 Point out that *newborn* is a compound word, or a word that is made of two smaller words put together. Ask: *What two words make up newborn?* New/born Have children use what they know about the meaning of each smaller word to write a definition of *newborn*.

3 | Assess

✓ **Lesson Checkpoint**

1. 🔍 **Infer** A foal gets milk from its mother.

2. **Writing** in Science Possible answer: A young horse grows inside its mother. The foal drinks milk from its mother. It grows and grows until it becomes an adult horse and then it can have foals of its own.

Lesson 4

How are young animals like their parents?

 Science Objective

- The student understands that plants and animals produce offspring with similar characteristics, but individual differences (for example, kittens in a litter may be colored differently).

1 Introduce

Quick ACTIVITY   TRANSPARENCY 23

Show the class several pictures of dogs with their puppies. Say: **Describe the puppies in each picture.** Ask: **Do all the puppies look exactly the same?** Have children identify the ways in which the puppies look different. (Color, markings, size) Then have children draw a picture of how a young penguin and its mother might look.

Access Prior Knowledge

Ask children: **Have you ever been to a zoo? Did you see a penguin? Did you see a giraffe?** Have children look at the pictures of the penguins and giraffes. Ask: **What do you think these pictures show?** Elicit that the pictures show animals with their young.

Set Purpose

Tell children you are going to read to them about some animals and their young. Help them set a **purpose for listening,** such as to find out how some young animals are the same as and different from their parents.

2 Teach

Quick SUMMARY

- Young animals often look like their parents in shape and color.
- Young animals can look different from their parents in ways such as color of fur or patterns on fur.

Lesson 4

How are young animals like their parents?

Young animals often look like their parents in shape and color. Yet some young animals look different from their parents.

Young penguins are covered with fuzzy down feathers. The feathers become white and black as the penguin grows.

3

These kittens all have the same parents. Yet they look different from each other.

112

Lesson 4 Resource

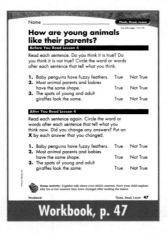

Workbook, p. 47

ELL Support

Parents and Their Young

Children may need help understanding that young animals can look different from their parents and from each other. Use simple sentences to compare animals.

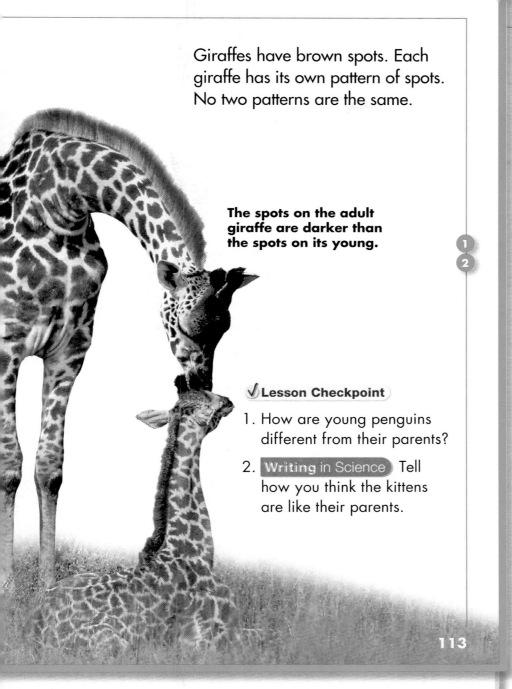

Giraffes have brown spots. Each giraffe has its own pattern of spots. No two patterns are the same.

The spots on the adult giraffe are darker than the spots on its young.

✓ **Lesson Checkpoint**

1. How are young penguins different from their parents?

2. Writing in Science Tell how you think the kittens are like their parents.

113

Science Background

About Giraffes

The spots on giraffes range from regular and geometric in some forms of giraffes to irregular and blotchy, or leaf-shaped, in others.

Math Link

Counting Animals

Have children look at the pictures on pages 112–113. Have them count each kind of animal shown and then calculate how many animals in all are shown. (8) Ask them to write a number sentence for their calculation. (4 kittens + 2 penguins + 2 giraffes = 8 animals) Then have children use the symbols < (less than), = (equal to), and > (greater than) to compare the numbers of each kind of animal. (Possible answer: Number of kittens is > number of giraffes)

ELL Support

For scaffolded instruction about animals and their young, use **Every Student Learns Teacher's Guide,** p. 27.

Read pages 112–113 to children. Examine the pictures of the penguins and the giraffes to discuss the ways in which young animals look the same as and different from their parents. Use the picture of the kittens to discuss how young animals can have the same parents and look different from each other.

Assign Quick Study pp. 46–47 to children who need help with lesson content.

Guide Comprehension

Ask children the following scaffolded questions to assess understanding.

Scaffolded Questions

❶ **Contrast** *How does the young giraffe look different from the adult?* The patterns of spots are different, and the adult's spots are darker.

❷ **In Your Own Words** *How do the young penguin and young giraffe look like their parents?* Possible answers: They have the same body parts as their parents. Their body parts have the same shapes.

❸ **Comprehend** *How will the young penguin look more like its parents as it grows?* Its feathers will become white and black like its parents' feathers. It may grow to be the same size as its parents.

Extend Vocabulary

Write the word *pattern* on the board. Remind children that each giraffe has its own pattern of spots. Explain that a pattern is "a repeating arrangement of colors, shapes, and figures." Have children draw a pattern in their science journals. The pattern can show spots, another shape, or a combination of shapes. Ask children to write a sentence about their patterns.

3 | Assess

✓ **Lesson Checkpoint**

1. Young penguins are covered with fuzzy down feathers, which will become white and black as the penguin grows.

2. Writing in Science Kittens have the same shape as their parents. They are covered with fur and have whiskers like their parents. They may have the same color as their parents.

Lesson 5

What is the life cycle of a bean plant?

 Science Objective

- The student describes how organisms change as they grow and mature.

1 Introduce

Quick ACTIVITY | TRANSPARENCY 24

Have children look at the picture of a bean plant. Ask: **How do the Sun, the rain, and the soil help bean plants grow?** Have children act out their answers.

Access Prior Knowledge

Have children look at the pictures on pages 114–115. Tell them not to read the words. Ask children to describe what they think is happening to the seed. Ask: **What do plants need to grow?** Water, sunlight, air

Set Purpose

Tell children they are going to read about the life cycle of a bean plant. Help children set a **purpose for reading,** such as to find out how a seed grows into a plant that makes new seeds.

2 Teach

Quick SUMMARY

- A seed contains a tiny plant and stored food.
- A seed coat protects a seed.
- As seeds germinate, or begin to grow, roots grow down into the ground and a stem grows up.
- A seedling is a young plant.
- Adult plants have flowers that make seeds.

Read pages 114–115 with children. Ask children if their descriptions of the pictures on pages 114–115 were correct. Use the pictures to describe the life cycle of a plant.

What is the life cycle of a bean plant?

Most plants grow from seeds. A seed has a hard outer covering called a **seed coat.** A seed coat protects the seed.

1 Each seed contains a tiny plant and stored food. The tiny plant uses the stored food as it grows. A seed that gets enough water and air may **germinate,** or begin to grow. Roots from the germinated seed grow **2** down into the ground. A stem grows up. A seedling grows out of the ground. A **seedling** is a young plant.

Seeds are the beginning of a bean plant life cycle.

The bean seed germinates and starts to grow.

A seedling grows from the seed.

Seed coat

Lesson 5 Resource

What is the life cycle of a bean plant?

Before You Read Lesson 5

Read each sentence. Do you think it is true? Do you think it is not true? Circle the word or words after each sentence that tell what you think.

1. A seedling may germinate.   True   Not True
2. A tiny plant is inside a seed.   True   Not True
3. Adult plant flowers make seeds.   True   Not True

After You Read Lesson 5

Read each sentence again. Circle the word or words after each sentence that tell what you think now. Did you change any answers? Put an **X** by each answer that you changed.

1. A seedling may germinate.   True   Not True
2. A tiny plant is inside a seed.   True   Not True
3. Adult plant flowers make seeds.   True   Not True

Home Activity: Together talk about your child's answers. Have your child explain why his or her answers may have changed after reading the lesson.

Workbook   Think, Read, Learn **48**

Workbook, p. 48

SciLinks Take It to the Net
pearsonsuccessnet.com

Technology Link

Children can go on line to discover more about a **seedling** by using the NSTA SciLink available at **pearsonsuccessnet.com.**

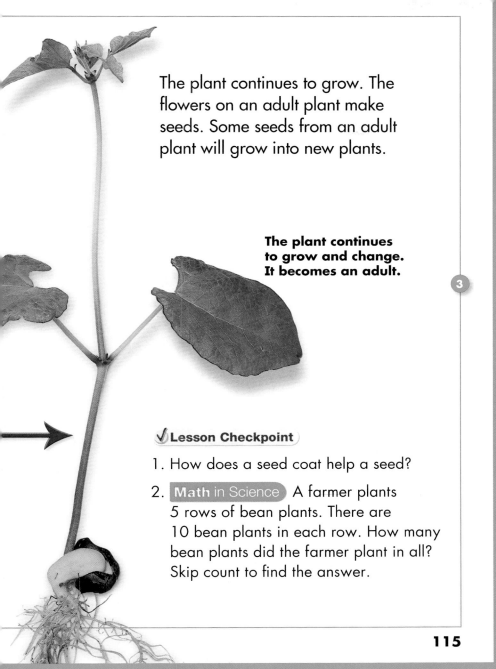

The plant continues to grow. The flowers on an adult plant make seeds. Some seeds from an adult plant will grow into new plants.

The plant continues to grow and change. It becomes an adult.

✓ Lesson Checkpoint

1. How does a seed coat help a seed?

2. Math in Science A farmer plants 5 rows of bean plants. There are 10 bean plants in each row. How many bean plants did the farmer plant in all? Skip count to find the answer.

115

Science Background

Seeds

Seeds contain an embryo (tiny plant) and stored food. The seed sprouts and uses the stored food to grow up and out of the ground. Then it can begin to make its own food by photosynthesis. The stored food in the seed gives it energy to germinate and become a seedling with leaves capable of food making.

ELL Support

Seed Sentences

Give children added support with **seed coat, germinate,** and **seedling** by asking the following questions to elicit one, two, or three word responses. **A seedling is a _____ plant.** (young) **Germinate means to _____.** (begin to grow) **A seed coat _____ the seed.** (protects)

For scaffolded instruction about the life cycle of bean plants, use **Every Student Learns Teacher's Guide,** p. 28.

Point out that the adult plant on page 115 has a flower that will make new seeds. When those seeds drop or are planted in soil, they become new plants and the cycle repeats itself.

Assign Quick Study pp. 48–49 to children who need help with lesson content.

Guide Comprehension

Ask children the following scaffolded questions to assess understanding.

Scaffolded Questions

① **Recall** *What is inside each seed?* A tiny plant and food for the tiny plant

② **Sequence** *What happens after a seed germinates, or begins to grow?* Roots grow down into the ground and a stem grows up.

③ **Infer** *The adult plant makes seeds. Some seeds will grow into new plants. What will those new plants look like?* They will look like the adult plant that made the seeds.

Extend Vocabulary

Write the word **seedling** on the board. Ask children what word they see in the word seedling. (*Seed*) Tell children that the suffix *-ling* means young or small. Ask: **What does a seed grow into?** A plant **What kind of a plant is a seedling?** A young plant Help children think of other words they know with the suffix *-ling*. (*Duckling, hatchling*)

3 | Assess

✓ Lesson Checkpoint

1. A seed coat protects a seed.

2. Math in Science 10, 20, 30, 40, 50; 50 bean plants

Lesson 6

How are young plants like their parents?

 Science Objectives

- The student understands that living things can reproduce, and nonliving things cannot reproduce.
- The student understands that plants and animals produce offspring with similar characteristics, but individual differences (for example, kitten in a litter may be colored differently).

1 Introduce

Quick ACTIVITY | TRANSPARENCY 25 |

Have children look out the window. Direct them to make a list of all the plants they see. Ask: **Can you see any young plants? How do you know these are young plants?** Discuss the different answers with the class.

Access Prior Knowledge

Ask children to compare the two plants on page 116. Ask: **How are they the same?** Possible answer: Same kind of ridges, needles sticking out, same color **How are they different?** The plant on the left is small and round. The plant on the right is tall and has arms.

Set Purpose

Tell children they are going to read about plants and their young. Help them set a **purpose for reading,** such as to find out ways that young plants can be the same and different from parent plants.

2 Teach

Quick SUMMARY

- Young plants usually look like the parent plants, but can be different in some ways.

How are young plants like their parents?

Young plants are usually like the parent plant in color and shape. Young plants can be different from the parent plant in some ways too.

A young saguaro cactus has the same shape as an adult. It has the same color as an adult.

An adult saguaro cactus has arms.

A young saguaro cactus does not have arms.

116

Lesson 6 Resource

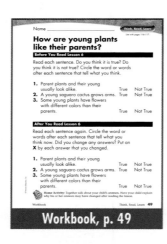

Workbook, p. 49

ELL Support

Saguaro Cactus

Children may have difficulty pronouncing the word *saguaro.* Say it slowly for them, pronouncing each syllable distinctly: suh WAHR uh.

These flowers are called foxgloves. Foxgloves grow leaves during their first year of life. They grow flowers during their second year of life. Look at the picture. ① The foxglove flowers all have the same shape. The foxglove flowers have different colors. ②

117

✓ Lesson Checkpoint

1. How are the foxgloves alike and different?

2. **Art in Science** Draw a young saguaro cactus and an old saguaro cactus. Write how they are different.

Science Background

Foxgloves

- Foxglove got its name because the flowers look like fingers of a glove.
- Foxglove is poisonous. It is used to make digitalis, a heart-stimulating drug.

Math Link

Saguaro Arms

Give children the following problem to solve. Have them write a number sentence. **There are three saguaro plants. Each plant has two arms. How many arms do the three plants have in all?** 6; 2 + 2 + 2 = 6

ELL Support

For scaffolded instruction about plants and their young, use **Every Student Learns Teacher's Guide,** p. 29.

Read pages 116–117 with children. Ask: **In what ways do young plants usually look like the parent plant?** In color and shape **How does the foxglove look different from its parent the first year?** It has no flowers. It has leaves only.

Assign Quick Study pp. 50–51 to children who need help with lesson content.

Guide Comprehension

Ask children the following scaffolded questions to assess understanding.

Scaffolded Questions

① **Explain** *How do you know that the colorful foxgloves on page 117 are not in their first year?* They have flowers.

② **Get the Main Idea** *What general statement can you make about how young plants look compared to their parent plant?* Young plants usually look like their parent plant in shape and color, but they can also look different in some ways.

③ **Estimate** *A saguaro begins to grow arms when it is about 65 years old. How old do you think the big saguaro on page 116 is?* It is more than 100 years old.

Extend Vocabulary

Tell children that a noun can name one or more than one thing. Verbs have to agree with nouns. Write *grow/grows* on the board. Read the following sentences and have children identify which form of the verb completes each sentence. Ask children to explain their choices.

A young cactus _____ straight up from the ground.

Foxgloves _____ leaves in the first year.

3 | Assess

✓ Lesson Checkpoint

1. Alike: They have the same shape. Different: They have different colors.

2. **Art in Science** A young saguaro cactus is round and does not have arms. An old saguaro cactus is tall and has arms.

Lesson 7

How do people grow and change?

 Science Objective

_____ things ha__ _

Lesson 7

How do people grow and change?

People are alike in some ways. All people change as they grow. You used to be a baby. You are a child now. You have lost some of your first teeth. You have grown _____. What _____ _____

This boy has changed since he was a baby. Now he can read and talk.

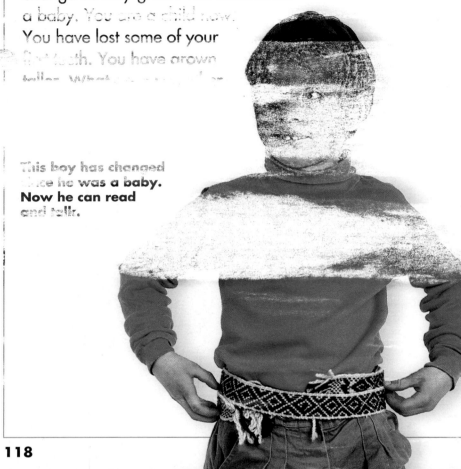

118

1 Introduce

Quick ACTIVITY | TRANSPARENCY 26 |

Have children think back to when they were five. Ask: Are you the same now as you were then? How have you changed? Elicit from children that they have grown. Ask: **How might you look different five years from now?** Show Quick Activity Transparency 26. Have children draw a picture of the child in the picture as an adult. Ask: **How do children change as they become adults?**

Access Prior Knowledge

Ask children to draw three pictures in their science journals. One picture should show a child, one should show a teenager, and one should show an adult. Suggest to children that they concentrate on things such as height, amount of hair, and size of hands and feet. Have children label their drawings.

Set Purpose

Tell children they are going to read about how people grow and change. Help them set a **purpose for reading,** such as to find out ways people change as they grow.

2 Teach

Quick SUMMARY

- All people keep changing as they grow older.
- Children grow taller until they become adults.
- Adults' skin will wrinkle as they get older.

Read pages 118–119 with children. Use the pictures to discuss how people look at different ages, and how they change as they grow.

Lesson 7 Resource

Workbook, p. 50

You will keep changing as you get older. You will get taller. You will become a teenager. Later, you will become an adult. Adults keep changing too. Adults do not grow taller. An adult's skin will begin to wrinkle. The color of an adult's hair may change to gray or white.

The members of this family will keep changing.

1. ☑**Checkpoint** What is one way all people are alike?

2. What are some ways people grow and change?

119

ELL Support

Language Detectives: Building Vocabulary

Provide the following sentence frames for children to complete.

A baby grows and becomes a _____.

A child grows and becomes a _____.

A teenager grows and becomes an _____.

For scaffolded instruction about how people grow and change, use **Every Student Learns Teacher's Guide,** p. 30.

Assign Quick Study pp. 52–53 to children who need help with lesson content.

Assign Quick Study pp. 52–53 to children who need help with lesson content.

Guide Comprehension

Ask children the following scaffolded questions to assess understanding.

Scaffolded Questions

① **Recall** *When do you lose your first teeth, as a child or as an adult?* As a child

② **Understand** *When do people stop growing taller?* When they become adults

③ **Infer** *If you see a person with wrinkled skin, what might you guess about the person's age?* He or she is an adult.

Extend Vocabulary

Write *tall, taller,* and *tallest* on the board. Tell children that these words can be used to describe people. Say: **Use tall *when you tell about one person.* Use taller *when you compare two people.* Use tallest *when you compare three people.*** Have children complete the following sentences with the correct form of *tall.*

The boy is _____. His sister is _____ than he is. The father is the _____ of the three.

Diagnostic Check

If... children have difficulty understanding how people change as they grow,

then... point out that the picture on page 119 shows two children, their parents, and a grandmother. Use the picture to point out ways that people change as they grow.

3 | Assess

1. ☑**Checkpoint** All people grow and change.

2. Answers might include: People get older. They get taller. They become teenagers and then adults. As older adults, their skin wrinkles and their hair may change color.

Science Objectives

- The student describes how organisms change as they grow and mature.
- The student knows that living things have offspring that resemble their parents.

2 | Teach (continued)

Quick SUMMARY

- People can look different in ways such as height, eye color, hair color, and skin color.
- Children in the same family may look alike and different from each other.
- Parents and their children may look alike and different from each other.

Read pages 120–121 with children. Point out that the pictures on page 120 show people from different countries around the world. Explore differences in the way people look. Then bring children's attention to the picture on page 121, which shows how people in the same family can look different from each other.

How People Are Different

People are different in some ways too. Some people are short. Some people are tall. Some people have brown eyes. Some people have blue eyes. People have different hair colors. People have different skin colors.

Look at the many ways these children are different. **2**

120

Science Background

Looking Exactly Alike

- People's characteristics are passed on from one generation to another through genes. With one exception, no two people have the exact same genes. Thus they may show resemblance, but not identicalness. The one exception is identical twins. Because identical twins grow from one fertilized egg, they share identical genes.
- Fraternal twins grow from two different fertilized eggs that develop at the same time. Each egg has a unique set of genetic characteristics.

Social Studies Link

Different Countries and Peoples

Have children use a map to find five countries where people live. Ask children to choose one of the countries and write the name of the country in their science journals. Have children use the Internet or library resources to find out three interesting facts about the country and its people.

Children in the same family might look like each other. They might look different from each other too. How might children in the same family look alike? How might they look different?

Parents and their children may look alike in some ways. They may look different in other ways. Look at the family in the picture on this page. How are the children like their parents? How are they different?

People in a family do not look exactly alike.

✓**Lesson Checkpoint**

1. What are some ways people can be different from each other?

2. 🎯 **Infer** Where did the children in the picture get their dark eyes?

121

ELL Leveled Support

Similarities and Differences

Beginning Show children pictures of people who look very different from each other. Use the pictures to guide children to observe differences.

Intermediate Have children work in pairs. Have each child draw a person and color the drawing. Have children compare their drawing to that of their partner. Have children write sentences that tell how the persons they have drawn look alike and different.

Advanced Have pictures of people available. Tell children to choose two pictures and compare the people. Draw a Venn diagram on the board and tell children to copy it on a piece of paper. Explain how they can use a Venn diagram to tell how the people look alike and different. Guide children as needed to complete their Venn diagrams.

For scaffolded instruction about how people are different, use **Every Student Learns Teacher's Guide,** p. 30.

Ask children the following scaffolded questions to assess understanding.

Scaffolded Questions

1 **List** *What are some things you look at when you describe how people look?* How short or tall they are, their eye, hair, and skin color

2 **Interpret Pictures** *How do all the children on page 120 look alike?* Possible answer: They are all smiling.

3 **Tell Why** *Do you think every person is different, even if they may look like someone else? Tell why.* Answers will vary. Children may answer that everyone is different because they may like different things, have different interests, and can do different things.

Extend Vocabulary

Brainstorm with children words they can use when they describe how a person looks. List responses on the board. Ask: **What words can you use to tell about a person's height?** Possible words: *Short, tall* **What words can you use to describe a person's eyes?** Possible words: *brown, green, blue, big, small, round, oval* **What words can you use to describe a person's hair?** Possible words: *Red, brown, black, blond, straight, curly, wavy*

3 | Assess

✓**Lesson Checkpoint**

1. Answers might include: They can have different heights, eye color, hair color, and skin color.

2. 🎯 **Infer** The children got their dark eyes from both their parents.

SCAFFOLDED INQUIRY

▌▌ Investigate How does a caterpillar grow and change?

⭐ **Science Objective**

- The student describes how organisms change as they grow and mature.

1 | Build Background

In this activity children observe how an organism changes over time.

Managing Time and Materials

Time: 10 minutes for observation each day for about 3 weeks.

Groups: whole class

Materials: *butterfly habitat (with coupon for 5 Painted Lady caterpillars); transparent or masking tape (teacher use); crayons or markers*

Materials listed in *italics* are kit materials.

Advance Preparation

Use the coupon to order caterpillars 2 weeks in advance. Caterpillars will arrive in a clear plastic container with food. Keep the container at room temperature and out of direct sunlight.

Safety Notes

To protect native wildlife, do not release the living organisms into the environment.

Teaching Tips

- Keep the lid on the container. When chrysalises have formed, lift the lid and remove the paper liner with the chrysalises. Use tape to attach the paper liner to the inside wall of the habitat.

- Mix 2 tsp sugar with 1 c water to make food for the butterflies. Put the sugar water on a cotton wick or fresh flowers every day.

2 | What to Do

Encourage Guided Inquiry

Preview the activity and the materials with children. Ask: **What would happen if you observe caterpillars for 3 weeks?**

Egg

Larva

Adult

Chrysalis

Investigate How does a caterpillar grow and change?

Living things change as they grow. Some insects look different from their parents.

Materials

caterpillars

butterfly habitat

crayons and markers

Process Skills

You **collect data** to help you remember information.

What to Do

❶ Observe your caterpillars every day. **Collect data** every day for 3 weeks.

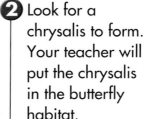

Monday
The caterpillars are little. They don't move a lot.

Tuesday
They look the same. They move a lot. They are eating.

❷ Look for a chrysalis to form. Your teacher will put the chrysalis in the butterfly habitat.

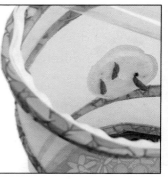

Activity Resources

Name _____

Investigate How does a caterpillar grow and change?
❶ Use this chart to **collect data** on your caterpillars for 3 weeks.

Observations
Week 1
Monday
Tuesday
Wednesday
Thursday
Friday
Week 2
Monday
Tuesday
Wednesday
Thursday
Friday
Week 3
Monday
Tuesday
Wednesday
Thursday
Friday

❷ Predict what will happen next.

Activity Book   Guided Inquiry **53**

Activity Rubric

Investigate: How does a caterpillar grow and change?

Scoring Criteria	1	2	3	4
Student **observed** a butterfly's life cycle every day for three weeks.				
Student **collected data** every day for three weeks.				
Student **predicted** that a butterfly would emerge from the chrysalis.				
Student drew pictures to show the stages of a butterfly's development and described how it changed.				
Student **inferred** that the butterfly developed inside the chrysalis.				

Scoring Key
4 points correct, complete, detailed
3 points partially correct, complete, detailed
2 points partially correct, partially complete, lacks some detail
1 point incorrect or incomplete, needs assistance

T72 Guided Inquiry   Activity Book

Activity Book, pp. 53–54   **Activity Rubric**

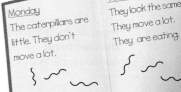

Use Activity DVD Unit A, Chapter 4 to preview this activity.

Call 1-888-537-4908 with activity questions.

 More Lab zone **Activities** Take It to the Net pearsonsuccessnet.com

Find more about this activity at our Web site.

- See the **Teacher's Activity Guide** for more support.
- An alternative activity is also available to download.

3 Continue to collect data. **Predict** what will happen next.

They're alive! Handle with care.

4 Draw pictures that show how the caterpillars changed.

□ → □ → □

Explain Your Results
1. How did the caterpillars change?
2. **Infer** What happens inside a chrysalis?

Go Further
Can you make a model of how a caterpillar grows and changes? Try it.

123

Science Background

More About Butterflies

- The scientific name for the Painted Lady butterfly is *Vanessa cardui*. It is the most widely distributed butterfly in the world. Painted Ladies prefer flying in the daytime and may travel 1,000 miles. The Painted Lady's life expectancy is 2 to 4 weeks. She can lay up to 500 eggs.

- Complete metamorphosis is the way butterflies and other insects such as bees, flies, and beetles develop. Complete metamorphosis has four stages: egg, larva, chrysalis or pupa, and adult. Some insects, such as cockroaches, grasshoppers, and dragonflies, develop by a process called incomplete metamorphosis. Incomplete metamorphosis has three stages: egg, nymph (smaller version of the adult without wings), and adult.

Guide children to write an If.../then... statement such as: **If I observe caterpillars for 3 weeks, then I will observe different stages in the life cycle of a butterfly.**

Engage Have children look at the pictures at the top of page 122. Ask: **What do these pictures show?** (Stages of the life of a Painted Lady butterfly.)

Explore Tell children that they will observe caterpillars every day for 3 weeks. Ask children to predict what they will learn.

Explain After completing the activity, ask children what they learned. Ask: **How are the ways people change different from the ways a butterfly changes?**

Extend Have children compare the life stages of the butterfly to the life stages of a sea turtle.

Evaluate Have children review their answer to the Investigation question. Would they change their answer after finishing their observations?

3 Explain Your Results

Use these questions to review evidence and develop explanations.

- Give children an opportunity to reflect on the data, or evidence, they have gathered in the investigation.

- Have children use the evidence gathered to develop their explanations. Accept reasonable, logical explanations.

1. The caterpillars changed into chrysalises, then into butterflies.
2. **Infer** The wings and other body parts of the butterfly grew inside the chrysalis.

Go Further

Children may propose any number of changes to the activity to fully understand the way a caterpillar grows and changes into a butterfly. Children may wish to investigate the life cycles of other insects.

Post other questions children have about how caterpillars grow and change. Encourage children to investigate on their own.

Process Skills

Collect and Record Data

Discuss the importance of being able to collect and record data. You can use the Process Skills sheet on Predicting at this time.

Measuring Time

 Science Objective

- The student adds and subtracts whole numbers to solve real-world problems, using appropriate methods of computing, such as objects, mental mathematics, paper and pencil, calculator.

1 Introduce

Quick ACTIVITY

Have children think about the cycle of a week, from one Monday to the next. Ask: **How many days in a week?** Seven Then have children think about the cycle of a year. Ask: **How many days in a year?** 365¼, 366 in leap year **How many weeks in a year?** 52 Use a calendar to help children answer the questions.

2 Teach the Skill

Read pages 124–125 with children. Focus children's attention on the pictures showing the life cycles of a butterfly and a frog. Explain that the amount of time between each stage is indicated on the pictures.

Ask: **How many stages are there in the life cycle of a butterfly?** 4 **How many stages are there in the life cycle of a frog?** 3

Point out the labeled arrows between the steps. The labels show the amount of time between the stages.

Explain to children that the life cycles of butterflies and frogs vary by species. Frogs continue to grow and may take up to three years to reach adulthood.

Measuring Time

These pictures show the life cycle of a butterfly and the life cycle of a frog. They show the amount of time between each step in the life cycles.

A butterfly life cycle

1. egg
2. caterpillar
3. pupa
4. butterfly

14 days
4 days
12 days

124 **Tools** Take It to the Net
pearsonsuccessnet.com

Activity Resource

Name _____

Measuring Time
The table compares the life cycles of two kinds of flies.

Life Cycles of Housefly and Greenhouse Whitefly Compared		
Stage	**Housefly**	**Greenhouse Whitefly**
Egg	1 day	9 days
Larva	5 to 14 days	30 to 35 days
Pupa	3 to 10 days	11 days
Adult	19 to 70 days	10 to 40 days

Directions: Use the information in the table to answer the questions.

1. How many days does it take a greenhouse whitefly egg to hatch into a larva? _____
2. Which fly hatches from a pupa to an adult quicker? _____
3. Which adult fly usually lives longer? _____
4. A housefly egg hatches into a larva. When is the soonest it could become an adult? Write a number sentence.

Workbook, p. 51

Tools Take It to the Net
pearsonsuccessnet.com

1. How many days does it take a butterfly egg to hatch into a caterpillar?

2. How many days does it take for a butterfly egg to become a butterfly? Write a number sentence.

3. It takes 2 weeks for frog eggs to hatch into tadpoles. How many days is this? Write a number sentence.

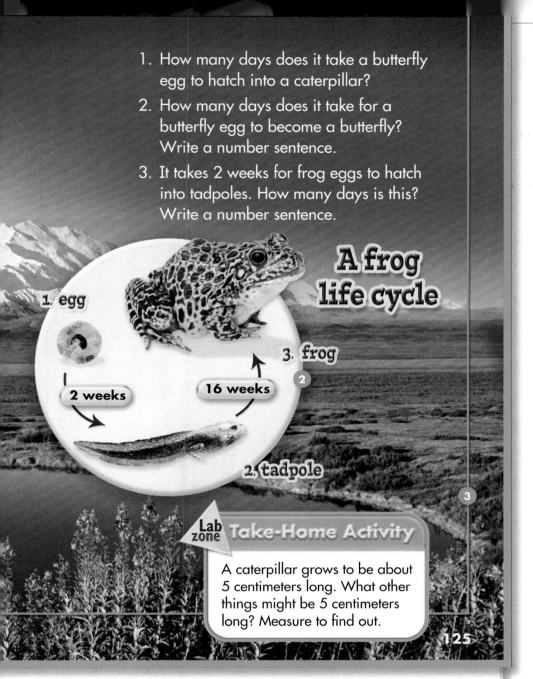

A frog life cycle

1. egg

2 weeks

3. frog

16 weeks

2. tadpole

Lab zone Take-Home Activity

A caterpillar grows to be about 5 centimeters long. What other things might be 5 centimeters long? Measure to find out.

125

Take-Home Activity

Tips for Success

- To prepare children for the activity, have them draw a line they think is 5 centimeters long. Then have them measure the line. Ask: **Was your line about 5 centimeters long?**

- Ask children to measure different things in the classroom. They should make a list of things that are about 5 centimeters long.

- Tell children they should now have an idea about how long 5 centimeters are. Based on this idea, they should be able to choose things to measure that are about that length. Tell children to continue their lists by measuring different things at home.

- Review children's lists as a class and make a class list of things that are about 5 centimeters long.

- Children can share their lists with their families.

Chapter 4 Review and Test Prep

Vocabulary

1. B
2. D
3. A
4. C

What did you learn?

5. Alike: People grow and change. Different: People have different heights, eye color, hair color, and skin color.
6. They both grow, have offspring, and die. Dragonflies are insects that begin as eggs and go through a nymph stage. Horses are mammals that grow inside their mother's body and look like small adults when they are born.
7. To start to grow

Chapter 4 Review and Test Prep

Vocabulary

Which picture goes with each word?

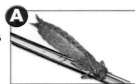

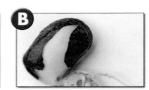

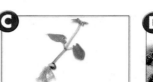

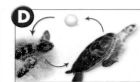

1. seed coat
2. life cycle
3. nymph
4. seedling

A
B
C
D

What did you learn?

5. How are people alike and different?
6. Compare the life cycles of a dragonfly and a horse. How are they alike and different?
7. What does germinate mean?

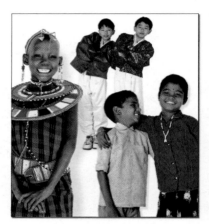

Assessment Resources

Name ______________ Chapter 4 Test

Read each question and choose the best answer. Then fill in the circle next to the correct answer.

1. Which is a living thing that can grow and be a parent?
   - Ⓐ rock
   - Ⓑ cloud
   - Ⓒ toy turtle
   - Ⓓ sea turtle

2. Look at the picture. Think about how the animals are alike and different.

Which sentence is true?
   - Ⓕ The mother and baby do not look alike.
   - Ⓖ The mother and baby look exactly alike.
   - Ⓗ The baby looks like its mother, but its spots are different.
   - Ⓘ The baby looks like its mother, but it will grow up to look like another animal.

Assessment Book Chapter 4 Test 13

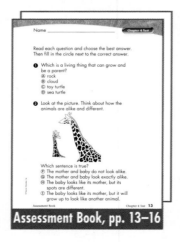

Assessment Book, pp. 13–16

MindPoint Quiz Show

MindPoint enables children to test their knowledge of the chapter in a game format.

ExamView® Use ExamView as a print or online assessment tool.

Success Tracker

Data management system to track Adequate Yearly Progress (AYP) and provide intervention online at **pearsonsuccessnet.com/successtracker**

Take-Home Book

Children can make a Take-Home Booklet using Workbook pp. 53–54.

8. **Infer** Why does a baby turtle's special tooth fall out after it hatches from the egg?

 Infer

9. People are wearing heavy coats and hats outside. They are wearing gloves and scarves. What can you **infer** about the weather?

I know	I can infer
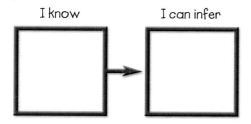

Test Prep

Fill in the circle next to the correct answer.

10. What kind of animal changes from an egg to a nymph?

Ⓐ mammal
Ⓑ insect
Ⓒ reptile
Ⓓ bird

11. **Writing** in Science How might living things be like their parents? Make a list.

127

 Process Skills

8. **Infer**
   It no longer needs the tooth.

9. **Infer** It is cold outside.

Test Prep

10. B

11. **Writing** in Science Answers will vary.

Intervention and Remediation

			Teacher Edition Resources			Ancillary Resources		
Science Objectives	**Review Item**	**Student Edition Pages**	**Guide Comprehension**	**Extend Vocab**	**Diagnostic Check**	**Vocab Cards**	**Quick Study**	**Workbook Pages**
The student understands that living things can reproduce, and nonliving things cannot reproduce.		102–105, 116–117	103, 105, 109, 111, 113	111	103, 105		103, 117	44, 49
The student understands that plants and animals produce offspring with similar characteristics, but individual differences (for example, kittens in a litter may be colored differently).	5, 11	106–107, 112–113, 116–117	107, 111, 113, 115, 117, 121			106	111, 113, 117, 119	16, 47, 49, 50
The student knows that some organisms have adaptations that enable them to move from one medium to another (for example, dragonflies begin life in water, move to land, and then fly in the air).	9	108–109		105		108	109	45
The student describes how organisms change as they grow and mature.	6, 7, 8, 10	114–115, 118–119	107, 109, 111, 115, 117, 119	103, 107, 115, 117, 119	119	114	115, 119	48, 50

Biography

Meet Mario J. Mota

 Science Objective

* Explore and identify career opportunities in marine biology.

1 Introduce

Build Background

Ask children: **What types of turtles have you seen before? Where did you see these turtles?** Children may have seen turtles in their communities or in zoos and theme parks. Have children draw a picture of a turtle they have seen.

2 Teach

Quick SUMMARY

* Dr. Mario J. Mota is a NASA marine biologist who studies sea turtles.
* Sea turtles lay their eggs on or near the same beach where they hatched.

Read page 128 with children. Have children look at the photograph of the sea turtle shown on page 128. Ask children: **Where does a sea turtle egg hatch?** The beach. **Where does a sea turtle spend most of its life?** The ocean. Children may have the misconception that NASA is made up only of astronauts. Explain to children that many people who work for NASA, including Dr. Mota, do other important jobs including studying animals. Explain to children that a marine biologist is a scientist who studies plants and animals that live in the ocean.

3 Explore

Ask children: **What do you think sea turtles eat for food?** List children's answers on the board. Explain to children that most sea turtles are meat eaters, but some turtles eat only plants. Tell children that sea turtles eat crabs, lobster, shrimp, clams, oysters, jellyfish, small fish, snails, and seaweed. Have children look at their list on the board to see how many food items are correct.

Biography

SAVE the Sea Turtles

Meet Mario J. Mota

Dr. Mota

Read Together

Dr. Mario Mota is a marine biologist. He works at NASA. Dr. Mota studies turtle biology. He uses some of the tools used on the space shuttle to study the turtles.

Dr. Mota was born in Africa. When Dr. Mota was young, he liked to fish. Dr. Mota always loved the ocean. He knew he wanted to work by the ocean.

Sea turtles lay their eggs on or near the same beach where they hatched. They lay more than 100 eggs in each nest!

Lab zone Take-Home Activity

Baby sea turtles hatch from eggs. Work with your family. Make a list of other animals that hatch from eggs.

128

Take-Home Activity

Tips for Success

* Make sure children clearly understand the assignment before they leave school. Children may ask family members to help them write their lists during their discussion at home. Children may wish to draw pictures of some of the animals on their lists.
* Have children share their lists with classmates.

Find Important Words

There are important words in science questions. These words help you understand the questions.

Megan lives near a big pond where lots of frogs live. One day, Megan sat on the grass by the pond. She liked watching the frogs. Megan saw one frog sitting very still. The frog's tongue zipped out. It caught a tasty insect to eat.

Read the question.

What is one thing that frogs eat?

Ⓐ ponds
Ⓑ sandwiches
Ⓒ grass
Ⓓ insects

First, find important words in the question. The most important words are **frogs** and **eat.** Next, find important words in the text that match the important words in the question. Use the words to answer the question.

129

Test Talk

 **Test-Taking Strategies**

Find Important Words

Teach children this strategy to help them improve their scores on multiple-choice tests.

• Have children read each sentence in the story on p. 129 to find important words.

• Children may use sticky notes or their fingers to flag words they think are important. Tell them that important words are words that give information.

• Guide children with questions to find out what the sentences are about.

• Ask children which word is found in different forms in each sentence except the last one. (Frog)

• Ask children to read the question to identify important words in the question that match the important words in the story. Then have children complete the exercise.

Assess: Find Important Words

D

Wrap-Up

 Science Objective

- The student increases comprehension by rereading, retelling, and discussion.

1 | Chapter Summaries

Group Summarize

- Use the chapter summaries on p. 130 to make a class summary chart about Life Science. Include a section on the chart for each chapter.
- Divide children into groups. Each group should work as a team to review one chapter. Children should reread and review their assigned chapter together. Encourage group discussions. Each group should present an oral report to the class.
- As each group presents, help children organize information into clear summary statements on the class summary chart.

2 | Performance Assessment

- Have children work individually or in pairs to complete the task.
- Provide children with safety scissors and old magazines, calendars, or other texts for cutting out pictures of animals.
- Encourage children to cut out many different kinds of animals that live on land, in water, and in the air.
- Children may sort animals into various valid groups. Have children describe how they sorted the animals and talk about the characteristics of each group.
- You may challenge children to sort their groups further (for example, sort a group of insects into insects that fly and insects that do not fly).
- Children should be able to identify animals with backbones and animals without backbones. If children have difficulty with this concept, review Chapter 2 Lessons 1 and 7.

Unit A Wrap-Up

Chapter 1

How do plants live in their habitats?

- Plants have adaptations that help them live in different environments.

Chapter 2

How are animals different from each other?

- Animals can be put into two groups. One group of animals has backbones. The other group of animals does not have backbones.

Chapter 3

How do living things help each other?

- Living things help each other in different ways. Animals and plants that need each other for food are part of a food chain.

Chapter 4

How do living things grow in different ways?

- Living things have different life cycles. A life cycle is the way a living thing grows and changes. Plants and animals have life cycles.

130

Science Background

Invertebrates

Animals without backbones are called invertebrates. Invertebrates make up more than 90 percent of living animals. There are many types of invertebrates. Some animals without backbones, such as grasshoppers and lobsters, have a hard outer shell. Other invertebrates, such as worms and jellyfish, are filled with fluid.

Performance Assessment

How Can You Sort Animals?

- Cut out pictures of different animals that live on the land, in water, and in the air.
- Put the animals into groups.
- Tell which animals have backbones and which animals...

Read More About Life Science!

Look for books like these.

131

3 | Extend Knowledge

- Organize the class into three groups.
- Explain that they are going to find out about animals that live on the land, in water, and in the air.
- Assign a different habitat to each group. For example, one group can find animals that live on land, another group can find animals that live in water, and the third group can find animals that live in the air.
- Ask children to work... assigned habitats... ...backbones. Children... information in the library or on the Internet.
- Each group should prepare a poster/mural to present to the class.
- ...children to draw animals they don't... ...children to include the... ...background and put their animals... ...two groups on their poster/mural.
- After all posters/murals have been presented, lead the class in a discussion of similarities and differences in adaptations to life in each habitat.

My Science Journal

Alike and Different

Ask children to choose two animals and write about how they are alike and different. Sentences should identify each living thing's habitat and describe how it is adapted to live in its habitat.

Read More About Life Science!

Literature Library

- *Why Do Cats Meow?* by Joan Holub ISBN: 0-14-056788-7
- *Feathers, Flippers, and Feet* by Deborah Lock ISBN: 0-7566-0264-5
- *AB Sea* by Bobbie Kalman ISBN: 0-86505-725-7

Big Book Collection

- *Jump Into the Jungle* by Theresa Volpe ISBN: 0-328-11789-7

Experiment **Which bird beak can crush seeds?**

⭐ **Science Objectives**

- The student knows that animals and plants can be associated with their environment by an examination of their structural characteristics.
- The student knows that people use scientific processes including hypothesis, making inferences, and recording and communicating data when exploring the natural worlds.

1 Build Background

Children will conduct an experiment to find out which birds have beaks that will crush seeds. This experiment helps children learn how birds may differ from one another.

Managing Time and Materials

Time: 20 minutes

Groups: small groups

Materials: 2 *spring-type clothespins*; 2 *craft sticks*; 4 pieces of *plastic straw* (each 1 cm long); glue

Materials listed in *italic* are kit materials.

Advanced Preparation

Cut 4 pieces of plastic straw for each group. Each piece should be 1 cm long.

Teaching Tip

You may wish to have children glue craft sticks to clothespins ahead of time in order to allow time for the glue to dry. Remind children to be careful not to use too much glue and to clean up spills right away.

heron   cardinal

Experiment Which bird beak can crush seeds?

Look at the heron's beak. Look at the cardinal's beak. How are the beaks alike? How are they different?

Materials

2 clothespins

2 craft sticks

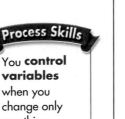

glue

straw pieces

Process Skills

You **control variables** when you change only one thing.

Ask a question.
Which bird uses its beak to crush seeds? **Use models** to learn more.

Make a hypothesis.
Which crushes better, a model of a heron's beak, or a model of a cardinal's beak? Tell what you think.

Plan a fair test.
Be sure to use the same kind of clothespins.

Do your test.

❶ Make a model of a heron's beak. Glue 2 craft sticks to a clothespin. Let the glue dry. Use the other clothespin as a model of a cardinal's beak. Use a piece of straw as a model of a seed.

Activity Resources

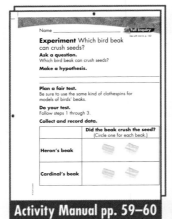

Activity Manual pp. 59–60   **Activity Rubric**

 Use Activity DVD Segment 9 to preview this activity.

 Call 1-888-537-4908 with activity questions.

 **More** Lab zone **Activities** **Take It to the Net** pearsonsuccessnet.com

Find more about this activity at our Web site.

- See the **Teacher's Activity Guide** for more support.
- An alternative activity is also available to download.

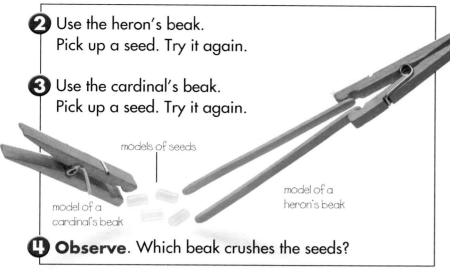

2 Use the heron's beak.
Pick up a seed. Try it again.

3 Use the cardinal's beak.
Pick up a seed. Try it again.

models of seeds

model of a
heron's beak

model of a
cardinal's beak

4 **Observe**. Which beak crushes the seeds?

Collect and record data.

	Did the beak crush the seed? (Circle one for each beak.)	
Heron's beak		
Cardinal's beak		

Tell your conclusion.
Which model crushes a straw?
Infer Which bird uses its beak to crush seeds?

┌─ **Go Further** ─┐
Which beak will pick up seeds faster? Try it and find out.
└────────────────┘

133

ELL Support

Access Content Before beginning the activity, conduct an inventory of materials with children. Solicit other names for each item. Accept labels in English and children's home languages.

Science Background

• When children do this Full Inquiry Experiment, they use the Steps of the Scientific Method:

1. Ask a question.
2. Make a hypothesis.
3. Plan a fair test.
4. Do your test.
5. Collect and record data.
6. Tell your conclusion.
7. Go further.

---

2 | What to Do

Encourage Full Inquiry Preview the activity, the materials, and the scientific method with children. Have each child rephrase his or her hypothesis as an If,... then... statement, such as: If the beak models are used to pick up pieces of straw, then both models will crush the straw.

Engage Point to the pictures of the cardinal and the heron. Discuss how the beaks are alike and different.

Explore Give each group their materials. Help children create the model of the heron's beak and the model of the cardinal's beak. Have children compare their models to the pictures. Encourage children to examine the pieces of straw.

Explain As each group picks up straws with their beak models, have group members identify the beak model that crushes the straws. Ask children to predict which bird crushes seeds and explain why. (A cardinal will crush seeds with its beak.)

Extend Encourage children to learn more about the differences in bird's beaks by using their models to find out which beak will pick up seeds faster.

Evaluate Ask children what type of food a cardinal would need in its environment. (A cardinal would need seeds from certain plants that produce seeds.) Have children review their hypothesis. Would they change their hypothesis if they did the experiment again?

3 | Assess

Tell Your Conclusion

Children should conclude that the model of a heron's beak (clothespin with craft sticks attached) will pick up a model of a seed (straw piece) without crushing it. The model of a cardinal's beak (clothespin only) will crush a straw piece. Children should infer that a cardinal uses its beak to crush seeds.

Go Further Children may propose a solution about which model will pick up seed models faster. Guide children to sort questions into those that can be answered with the materials available in the classroom and those that cannot. Then have children select a question to inquire further. Post other children's questions about birds. Encourage children to use the Steps of the Scientific Method to investigate on their own.

◤ **Process Skills** ◢

Fair Test

Discuss the meaning of a fair test with children. Talk about how scientists use fair tests when they conduct experiments. Why is it important that scientists use fair tests?

End with a Poem

End with a Poem

 Science Objectives

- The student predicts what a passage is about based on its title and illustrations.
- The student uses prior knowledge, illustrations, and text to make predictions.
- The student makes inferences based on text and prior knowledge (for example, regarding a character's traits, feelings, or actions).
- The student reads aloud familiar stories, poems, or passages with a beginning degree of fluency and expression.

1 | Introduce

Preview

Read and point to the title of the poem. Point out the author's name. Ask children to predict what the poem is about based on the pictures and the title.

Access Prior Knowledge

Ask children if they have ever picked vegetables in a garden. Have them describe the experience, including what vegetables they picked and what season it was.

2 | Teach

Read the poem aloud to children. Encourage children to picture the poem in their heads as they listen.

Explain to children that the word *sow* means to scatter seed on the ground.

Ask: **In what season do we plant seeds?** Spring

What do the seeds grow into in the summer and fall? Vegetables (carrots, peas, beans, tomatoes, pumpkins, squash, greens)

Why aren't seeds planted in winter? Possible answer: Because it is too cold for plants to grow.

Have children listen for rhyming words at the ends of the phrases as you read the poem to them a second time.

Little Seeds
by Else Holmelund Minarik

Little seeds we sow in spring,
growing while the robins sing,
give us carrots, peas and beans,
tomatoes, pumpkin, squash and greens.

134

Reading Link

Rhyming words

Have pairs of children find and write pairs of rhyming words from *Little Seeds* (*spring* and *sing*, *beans* and *greens*, *all* and *fall*, *then* and *again*). Have children add other words to each rhyming pair. Allow children to share their rhyming word lists.

And we pick them,
one and all,
through the summer,
through the fall.

Winter comes, then spring, and then
little seeds we grow again.

135

- Organize children into groups of 3. Have children choose roles: seeds, vegetable planter/picker, and narrator. Let the children act out the poem for their classmates as the narrator reads the poem. If possible, children may enjoy creating props to use in their dramatic reading.

- Write a whole class poem following the author's style. Write about planting seeds that become flowers, grass, or trees. Help children discover rhyming words that work in their version of the poem. If time permits, have students act out their whole class poem.

Explore Further

Poems About Plants and Animals

Children might enjoy reading other poems about plants and animals, such as:

- *Tommy* by Gwendolyn Brooks
- *The Bug* by Marjorie Barrows
- *Caterpillars* by Aileen Fisher

 Science Objectives

- The student knows that people use scientific processes including hypothesis, making inferences, and recording and communicating data when exploring the natural world.
- The student uses the senses, tools, and instruments to obtain information from his or her surroundings.

1 | Introduce

Build Background

Place five objects with different properties into five brown bags. Have children use their sense of touch to describe each object. Repeat with the same five objects in clear plastic bags so that children use only their sense of sight. Compare touch and sight descriptions of the same object.

2 | Plan and Experiment

As children develop their hypotheses, discuss

- possible hazards involved in conducting Science Fair projects.
- how investigations do not always produce the expected result.
- how to develop the experiment in order to correctly test the hypothesis.

3 | Communicate

Encourage students to use different media (pictures, drawings, numbers, written statements) to represent their information and data.

Students may communicate their experimental plans and/or results in a variety of forums (pair and share, class discussion, oral report, written lab report, poster, science fair day).

Discovery CHANNEL SCHOOL **Science Fair Projects**

Full Inquiry

Using Scientific Methods
1. Ask a question.
2. Make a hypothesis.
3. Plan a fair test.
4. Do your test.
5. Collect and record data.
6. Tell your conclusion.
7. Go further.

Idea 1
Temperature and Seeds
Plan a project. Find out if seeds will grow faster in a warm place or a cold place.

Idea 2
Jumping Insects
Plan a project. Find out if crickets or grasshoppers are better jumpers.

136

EC CRU I0 9 8 7 6 5 4 3 2 1

Science Background

- Scientist use magnifying lenses to observe detail about the size, shape, and characteristics of objects that are difficult or impossible to see with only the eye. Magnifying lenses have been incorporated into eyeglasses, microscopes, telescopes, and binoculars. Magnifying lenses are convex (outwardly curving) in shape.
- The word "lens" derives from the Latin word *lentil,* meaning biconvex shape and in the shape of the lentil bean.

Unit B
Earth Science in Illinois

ILLINOIS

Did you know that you can see Sue, the world's largest *Tyrannosaurus rex* skeleton, in Chicago? Sue is at the Field Museum of Natural History.

Earth Science in Illinois

How are minerals, wild weather, and dinosaur fossils alike? They can all be found in Illinois. You will learn more about the science behind them in Unit B.

Rocks and Minerals

Fluorite is the state mineral in Illinois. It has many colors. It glows too. You will learn more about rocks and minerals in Chapter 5.

Wild Weather

Illinois can have thunderstorms, tornadoes, and snowstorms. An exhibit called "Midwest Wild Weather" shows wild weather in Illinois and other states. The exhibit moves from museum to museum. You will learn more about weather in Chapter 6.

Illinois Tornadoes from 1997 to 2000	
Year	Number
2000	55
1999	64
1998	99
1997	29

The table shows the number of tornadoes in Illinois from 1997 to 2000.

2 • Earth Science in Illinois

Illinois Dinosaurs and Fossils

Dinosaurs lived a long time ago. The Hadrosaur lived in what is now Illinois. A group called B.I.G. looks for dinosaur fossils in Illinois. B.I.G. stands for Basics in Geology. You will learn more about dinosaurs and fossils in Chapter 7.

ISAT Prep

Answer the questions below. Write your answers on a separate sheet of paper.

Multiple-Choice Questions

1 What is the state mineral of Illinois?
- **A.** fossil
- **B.** tornado
- **C.** Hadrosaur
- **D.** fluorite

2 Which is an example of wild weather?
- **A.** clouds
- **B.** sunshine
- **C.** fog
- **D.** tornadoes

3 Which are two dinosaurs?
- **A.** *Tyrannosaurus rex* and hadrosaur
- **B.** *Tyrannosaurus rex* and fluorite
- **C.** Fluorite and fluorescent
- **D.** Hadrosaur and fluorite

Short-Response Questions

4 What does the group B.I.G. do in Illinois?

5 Were there more tornadoes in Illinois in 2000 or 1998?

Earth Science in Illinois • 3

Field Trip
The Field Museum of Natural History

The Field Museum of Natural History in Chicago has many exhibits about rocks and fossils. It has rocks that fell from space. There are big fossils and little fossils. You can even see how people learn about fossils.

Find out more:

Research to find out more about fossils.
- Make a fossil model. Make some clay into a block. Push a leaf into the block. Take away the leaf.
- What can you learn about fossils from your model?
- What do you know about dinosaurs from fossils?

4 • Earth Science in Illinois

Answers to ISAT Prep

1. D
2. D
3. A

4. B.I.G. looks for dinosaur fossils in Illinois.
5. There were more tornadoes in 1998.

ILLINOIS

Field Trip
The Field Museum of Natural History

Find out more:

- Children's leaf prints should resemble a fossil and allow the children to see how objects, such as plants or animals, can leave an impression in the clay.

- Children may note that their impressions let them see the size and shape of the leaf and some of its details.

- Children may realize that a fossil from a dinosaur can tell them about size, shape, and details of the dinosaur.

Math in Science

- Have children look at the chart on page 2 and find out how many tornadoes were recorded in Illinois from 1997 to 2000. (247)

- Ask children about how many tornadoes on average happened per year? (about 60)

Set Up Unit B

Getting Started	B2
Activity Connections	B4
Professional Development	B6
Reaching All Learners	B8

Chapter Pages

5 Earth's Land, Air and Water · 137–168

Planning Chapter 5	137A
Directed Inquiry **Explore** How are soils different?	140
Lesson 1 What are natural resources?	143
Lesson 2 What are rocks and soil like?	146
Lesson 3 How do people use plants?	150
Lesson 4 How does Earth change?	152
Lesson 5 How can people help protect Earth?	154
Guided Inquiry **Investigate** How do worms change the soil?	160

6 Earth's Weather and Seasons · 169–200

Planning Chapter 6	169A
Directed Inquiry **Explore** How much rain falls?	172
Lesson 1 What are some kinds of weather?	175
Lesson 2 What is the water cycle?	178
Lesson 3 What is spring?	180
Lesson 4 What is summer?	182
Lesson 5 What is fall?	184
Lesson 6 What is winter?	186
Lesson 7 What are some kinds of bad weather?	188
Guided Inquiry **Investigate** How can you measure weather changes?	194

7 Fossils and Dinosaurs · 201–224

Planning Chapter 7	201A
Directed Inquiry **Explore** Which fossils match the plants and animals?	204
Lesson 1 How can we learn about the past?	207
Lesson 2 What can we learn from fossils?	210
Lesson 3 What were dinosaurs like?	212
Lesson 4 What are some new discoveries?	216
Guided Inquiry **Investigate** How can you make a model of a fossil?	218

Wrap-Up Unit B

Test-Taking Strategies	225
Unit B Wrap-Up	226
Full Inquiry **Experiment** Does gravel, sand, or soil make the best imprint?	228
Full Inquiry **Science Fair Projects**	232

Unit B
Earth Science

Bulletin Board Kit

Includes:
- illustrated border
- punch-out picture
- label cards in English and Spanish
- suggestions for use

Big Book Collection

- *My Visit to the Dinosaurs* by Aliki ISBN 0-328-11790-0

Literature Library

- *Let's Go Rock Collecting* by Roma Gans, illustrated by Holly Keller. ISBN 0-064-45170-4
- *Tornado Alert* by Franklyn M. Branley ISBN 0-064-45904-5
- *A Year Goes Round: Poems for the Months* by Karen B. Winnick ISBN 1-563-97898-9

Earth Science

Fossils and Dinosaurs

extinct

Earth's Land, Air, and Water

recycle

paper

plastic

metal can

Earth's Weather and Seasons

lightning

lightning

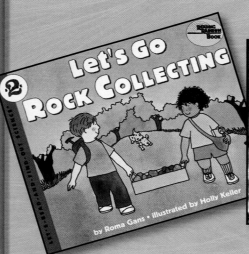

Let's Go Rock Collecting

by Roma Gans · illustrated by Holly Keller

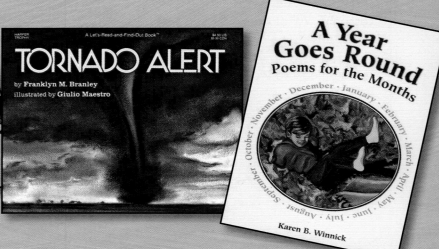

TORNADO ALERT

by Franklyn M. Branley
illustrated by Giulio Maestro

A Let's-Read-and-Find-Out Book™

A Year Goes Round
Poems for the Months

Karen B. Winnick

Integrating Your Day

Integrate the following cross-curricular ideas into your lessons as you teach this Earth Science unit.

Social Studies in Science

Gold, TE, p. 148
Tsunamis, TE, p. 153
The Iceman, TE, p. 209

Math in Science

Math in Science, SE/TE, pp. 147, 217
Recycling Bar Graph, pp. 162–163
Charting Favorite Seasons, pp. 196–197
Measuring Fossil Leaves, pp. 220–221
Recycling Count, TE, p. 156
How Much Rain?, TE, p. 177
The Sound of Thunder, TE, p. 189
Number Prefixes, TE, p. 214

Reading and Writing in Science

My Science Journal, TE, pp. 145, 187, 189, 191, 203, 227, 232
Writing in Science, SE/TE, pp. 145, 153, 165, 181, 187, 191, 199, 213, 215, 223
Reading Strategy, Picture Clues, pp. 141, 149, 151
Reading Strategy, Draw Conclusions, pp. 173, 179, 185, 193
Reading Strategy, Retell, pp. 205, 209, 211

Technology in Science

Technology in Science, SE/TE, pp. 159, 177
NSTA SciLinks, SE, pp. 178, 206
Discovery Channel School DVD
Students may access the Online Student Edition at **pearsonsuccessnet.com**

Health in Science

Health in Science, SE/TE, p. 155

Art in Science

Art in Science, SE/TE, pp. 157, 183, 189
Dinosaur Drawings, TE, p. 215

Unit B
Activity Connections

Scaffolded Inquiry

Levels of Inquiry

Find three levels of inquiry in the pages of the Student Edition. All three levels of inquiry in Scott Foresman Science engage students in activities that build a strong science foundation.

Equipment Kit

Includes:

- materials in chapter bags
- mobile storage carts
- activity placemats and trays
- Teacher's Activity Guides

	Student/Teacher Role	What Happens
Directed Inquiry 	Students learn process skills and follow step-by-step instructions. Teacher directs the activity.	Students are introduced to the process of inquiry through Directed Inquiry activities. A Directed Inquiry activity is explicitly directed by the teacher. As students are engaged in the activity, they learn process skills. They also have a positive inquiry experience they can draw upon as they move toward more independence.
Guided Inquiry 	Students take more ownership of the inquiry process. Teacher guides the activity.	Teachers provide structure, and students take more ownership in Guided Inquiry activities. The teacher's role is that of a guide rather than a leader. Students are encouraged to think about variables, and they learn to plan for variables that may affect the outcome of an investigation
Full Inquiry 	Students take the lead in planning and conducting the experiment. Teacher facilitates the inquiry.	Students apply the skills and knowledge developed in Directed and Guided Inquiry to Full Inquiry activities. Students follow the steps of the scientific method as they conduct the experiment shown. Then students are encouraged to identify new answerable questions, plan for variables, and develop their own experiments using available materials.

Materials List

	Activities	Kit Materials	School-supplied Materials
Chapter 5	**p. 140** How are soils different?	potting soil sandy soil paper plates hand lenses droppers plastic cups	water
	pp. 160–161 How do worms change the soil?	earthworms (coupon) potting soil resealable plastic bags plastic gloves	crumbled dried leaves hole punch
Chapter 6	**p. 172** How much rain falls?	tall plastic jars	masking tape metric rulers black pencils
	pp. 194–195 How can you measure weather changes?	thermometer (alcohol) rain gauge	
Chapter 7	**p. 204** Which fossils match the plants and animals?		Activity Masters 10–11 safety scissors crayons or markers glue construction paper
	pp. 218–219 How can you make a model of a fossil?	modeling clay seashells	small classroom objects
Unit B Experiment Activity	**pp. 228–229** Does gravel, sand, or soil make the best imprint?	paper plates gravel sand potting soil scallop shells plastic cups	safety goggles index cards

Essential Questions

- overarching questions that tie topics and concepts together
- cannot be answered in single sentence
- help children develop a richer understanding of science

Chapter 5

What are Earth's natural resources?

Sunlight, water, and air are natural resources that can never be used up. Oil and coal are natural resources that can be used up. Rocks and minerals are natural resources that come from Earth. Plants are natural resources used for food, shelter, and clothing.

Facilitate Understanding

- Help children create a T-chart to compare renewable and nonrenewable natural resources.

renewable natural resources	nonrenewable natural resources

Chapter 6

How does weather change?

Weather can be hot or cold, wet or dry. Rain, sleet, hail, and snow are types of wet weather. A drought can occur when rain does not fall. The water cycle follows the flow of water from Earth, to the atmosphere, and back to Earth again. Weather changes throughout the seasons of spring, summer, fall, and winter. Some types of bad weather include thunderstorms, tornadoes, and hurricanes.

Facilitate Understanding

- Write the words *spring, summer, fall,* and *winter* on the board. Have children describe the possible weather conditions that occur where they live during each season.

- Have children watch a portion of a previously videotaped weather forecast, preferably from a season other than the one they are currently in. Ask children to infer which season the broadcast is describing and why they think this is so.

Chapter 7

How can people learn about the Earth long ago?

We learn about the past by studying fossils. Scientists who study fossils are called paleontologists. Some fossils are of plants and animals that are extinct, or no longer living on Earth. Dinosaurs were animals that lived long ago. All dinosaurs are now extinct. Paleontologists found fossil eggs from the dinosaur Oviraptor. The paleontologists studied the fossil eggs to learn more about the life of the Oviraptor.

Facilitate Understanding

- Have children examine pictures of different plant and animal fossils. Ask children to infer what types of living things made these fossils and where they might have lived.

- Have children look at the pictures of the Barosaurus and Dilophosaurus shown on pages 212–213. Help children create a Venn diagram to compare and contrast the physical characteristics of these two dinosaurs.

Barosaurus   **Dilophosaurus**

big
long neck
tiny head

long
tail

medium
short neck
big head

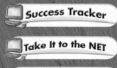

Unit B
Reaching All Learners

Meeting Individual Needs

These suggested strategies can help you customize instruction for children with individual needs.

English Learners

Have children draw the meaning of words in Word Collection Books.

Speaking of Science

 10 minutes whole class

Word Collection Books

Have children draw and, if possible, label pictures in Word Collection Books. The pictures and words may be collected on personal note cards or entered in a binder or spiral notebook. You may supplement Word Collection Book activities with any of the following:

- demonstration or pantomime
- conversation in pairs or groups
- use of the senses to explore visuals, sounds, or textures
- discussion of synonyms
- modeling basic English sentences, word patterns, verb tenses, and high

frequency words such as *the/these, and/or,* and *if/then.*

- **Beginning** Ask children to draw what a word means on one side of a card or page.
- **Intermediate** Ask children to draw what a word means on one side of a card or page. Help children write the word under the picture.
- **Advanced** Ask children to draw what a word means on one side of a card or page and write the word. Ask volunteers to hold up a labeled drawing and say the word.

Advanced Learners

Help children extend their thinking as they focus on essential questions for Earth Science.

Essential Question: How can we recycle everyday things?

Be creative.

 20 minutes small groups

- Have children look at examples of items that can be recycled, such as a plastic bag, newspaper, glass jar, plastic milk carton, cardboard box, and aluminum can.

- Have children name three ways that each of the items mentioned above can be reused instead of being thrown away.

- Have children share their ideas with other groups. Ideas will vary, but children should come to realize that many things we automatically throw away can be used for other purposes. This will reduce the pollution we add to the environment.

Special Needs

Utilize visuals to reinforce concepts throughout the unit. Select a variety of visuals, such as pictures, graphic organizers, and real objects.

Compare and Contrast

 20 minutes small groups

- Have groups study two visuals related to the same topic, such as pictures of a hurricane and  tornado, summer day and winter day, or gold and silver metal.

- Have children work together to describe how the visuals are alike and how they are different. You may have them use Graphic Organizer 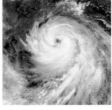 Transparency 2 (T-chart) to list the similarities and differences.

Leveled Readers and Leveled Practice

Leveled Readers deliver the same concepts and skills as the chapter. Use Leveled Readers for original instruction or for needed reteaching.

Below-Level

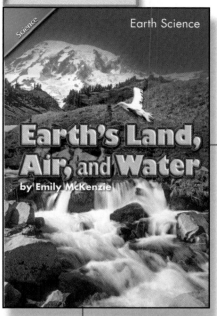

Science — Earth Science
Earth's Land, Air, and Water
by Emily McKenzie

Leveled Practice

Leveled Reader Teacher's Guide

On-Level

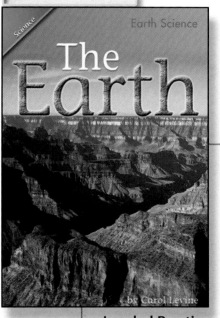

Science — Earth Science
The Earth
by Carol Levine

Leveled Practice

Leveled Reader Teacher's Guide

Advanced

Science — Earth Science
Crystals and Gems
by Joyce Churchill

Leveled Practice

Leveled Reader Teacher's Guide

Below-Level Leveled Reader has the same content as Chapter 5, but is written at a less difficult reading level.

On-Level Leveled Reader has the same concepts as Chapter 5, and it is written at grade level.

Advanced Leveled Reader is above grade level and enriches the chapter with additional examples and extended ideas.

Leveled Reader Database
Scott Foresman
pearsonsuccessnet.com

Use the online database to search for additional leveled readers by level, title, content, and skill.

Key Content and Skill in Leveled Readers and Chapter 5

Content	Vocabulary		Target Reading Skill	Graphic Organizer
Earth's Land, Air, and Water	boulder sand erosion pollution	weathering minerals natural resource recycle	🎯 Picture Clues	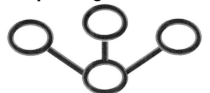

Lesson/Activity	Pacing	Science Objectives
Build Background pp. 137–139	20 minutes	• The student identifies words and constructs meaning from text, illustrations, graphics, and charts using the strategies of phonics, word structure, and context clues.
Lab zone **Flip Chart Activity** How does erosion affect land?		
Lab zone **Flip Chart Activity** How can you reuse something?		
Lab zone Directed Inquiry		• The student knows that scientists and technologists use a variety of tools (e.g., thermometers, magnifiers, rulers, and scales) to obtain information in more detail and to make work easier.
Explore How are soils different? p. 140	15 minutes	
How to Read Science p. 141	20 minutes	• The student uses a variety of context clues (for example, illustrations, diagrams, information in the story, titles and headings, sequence) to construct meaning (meaning cues).
1 What are natural resources? pp. 142–145	30 minutes	• The student knows selected resources used by people for water, food, and shelter are limited and necessary for their survival.
2 What are rocks and soil like? pp. 146–149	30 minutes	• The student extends and refines knowledge that the surface of the Earth is composed of different types of solid materials that come in all sizes.
3 How do people use plants? pp. 150–151	20 minutes	• The student knows selected resources used by people for water, food, and shelter are limited and necessary for their survival.
4 How does Earth change? pp. 152–153	20 minutes	• The student understands the processes of weathering and erosion.
5 How can people help protect Earth? pp. 154–159	40 minutes	• The student knows that human beings cause changes in their environment, and these changes can be positive or negative. • The student knows ways that human activity affects the environment.
Lab zone Guided Inquiry		• The student keeps science records.
Investigate How do worms change the soil? pp. 160–161	15 minutes initially	
Wrap-Up Chapter 5 pp. 162–168	20 minutes	• The student displays solutions to problems by generating, collecting, organizing, and analyzing data using simple graphs and charts.
Math in Science: Recycling Bar Graph	20 minutes	
Chapter 5 Review and Test Prep	20 minutes	
NASA Feature: Looking out for Earth	20 minutes	
Career: Forester		

Vocabulary/Skills	Assessment/Intervention	Resources/Technology
Process Skills: Infer Observe Estimate and Measure	• Chapter Review, SE, pp. 164–165	• Science Content Transparency 5 • Workbook, p. 55 • Graphic Organizer Transparency 1 • Vocabulary Cards • Activity Book, pp. 65–66
Process Skill: Observe Target Reading Skill: **Picture Clues**	• Explain Your Results, SE, p. 140 • Activity Rubric 🎯 **Picture Clues,** SE, p. 141	• Activity Book, pp. 61–62 • Workbook, pp. 56–57 • Every Student Learns Guide, p. 31 • Activity DVD • Activity Placemat 10
natural resource	• Scaffolded Questions, TE, pp. 143, 145 • Checkpoint Questions, SE, p. 144 • Chapter Review, SE, pp. 164–165 (7, 10)	• Workbook, p. 58 • Quick Study, pp. 54–55 • Every Student Learns Guide, p. 32
boulder sand minerals	• Scaffolded Questions, TE, pp. 147, 149 • Checkpoint Questions, SE, pp. 147, 149 • Chapter Review, SE, pp. 164–165 (1, 2, 4, 9) 🎯 **Picture Clues**, SE, p. 149	• Workbook, p. 59 • Quick Study, pp. 56–57 • Every Student Learns Guide, p. 33
	• Scaffolded Questions, TE, p. 151 • Checkpoint Questions, SE, p. 151 • Chapter Review, SE, pp. 164–165 (7, 11) 🎯 **Picture Clues**, SE, p. 151	• Workbook, p. 60 • Quick Study, pp. 58–59 • Every Student Learns Guide, p. 34
erosion weathering	• Scaffolded Questions, TE, p. 153 • Checkpoint Questions, SE, p. 153 • Chapter Review, SE, pp. 164–165 (3, 8)	• Workbook, p. 61 • Quick Study, pp. 60–61 • Every Student Learns Guide, p. 35
pollution recycle	• Scaffolded Questions, TE, pp. 155, 157, 159 • Checkpoint Questions, SE, pp. 155, 157, 159 • Chapter Review, SE, pp. 164–165 (5, 6, 12)	• Workbook, p. 62 • Quick Study, pp. 62–63 • Every Student Learns Guide, p. 36
Process Skill: Collect Data	• Explain Your Results, SE, p. 161 • Chapter Review, SE, pp. 164–165 • Activity Rubric	• Activity Book, pp. 63–64 • Activity DVD • Activity Placemat 11
Math Skill: Read a Bar Graph	• Scaffolded Questions, TE, p. 163 🎯 **Picture Clues**, SE, p. 165 ⊙ **ExamView®** Chapter 5 Test 💻 **Success Tracker** pearsonsuccessnet.com/ successtracker	• Workbook, pp. 63, 65–66 • Assessment Book, pp. 31–34

Quick | **Teaching Plan**

If time is short . . .
• Build Background, pp. 138–139
• Explore Activity, p. 140
• How to Read Science, p. 141
• Lesson 1, pp. 142–145
• Lesson 3, pp. 150–151
• Lesson 5, pp. 154–159

Other quick options . . .

Quick ACTIVITY

TE pp. 138, 142, 146, 150, 152, 154, 162

TRANSPARENCIES 27, 28, 29, 30, 31

Quick SUMMARY

TE pp. 142, 144, 146, 148, 150, 152, 154, 156, 158

Chapter 5 Activity Guide

 Children learn to ask and answer scientific questions as they progress to greater independence in scaffolded inquiry.

Directed Inquiry A Directed Inquiry activity begins each chapter.

Guided Inquiry A Guided Inquiry activity closes each chapter.

Full Inquiry Experiments and Science Fair Projects at the end of each unit provide opportunities for Full Inquiry.

Lab zone Directed Inquiry

 Explore **How are soils different?** p. 140

Time 15 minutes

Grouping small groups

Advance Preparation Measure 2 tbsp potting soil and 2 tbsp of sandy soil for each group. Place each sample on a paper plate. Pour $\frac{1}{3}$ c water into each group's plastic cup.

Materials *2 paper plates; hand lens; plastic cup, (9 oz.); plastic dropper; potting soil (2 tbsp); sandy soil (2 tbsp); water (about $\frac{1}{3}$ cup)*

Alternative Materials Instead of potting soil, you can use rich garden soil.

What to Expect Children will find that sandy soil is coarser, rougher, lighter in color, and absorbs water more slowly than potting soil.

Safety Notes Caution children not to inhale soil. Have children wash hands immediately after completing the activity.

 Activity DVD Unit B, Chapter 5

 Activity Placemat Mat 10

Lab zone Guided Inquiry

 Investigate **How do worms change the soil?** pp. 160–161

Time 15 minutes initially, and 10 minutes once a week for 3 weeks

Grouping small groups

Advance Preparation Use the live materials coupon to order earthworms 2 weeks in advance. Collect dried leaves and break them into smaller pieces. Fill each bag with 3 c damp potting soil. Punch holes in each bag so that air can get in.

Materials *2 resealable plastic bags, (10 × 12 in.); potting soil (6 c); 3 earthworms (live materials coupon); plastic gloves (1 pair per child); crumbled leaves ($\frac{1}{4}$ c); hole punch (teacher use)*

Alternative Materials If tree or garden leaves are not available, use dead leaves from houseplants, fresh celery tops, or lettuce. Damp garden soil can be used instead of potting soil.

Science Center This activity can be set up in your Science Center for children to work on throughout the day.

What to Expect After 2 to 3 weeks, the compost bag with worms will have fewer leaves on top than the compost bag without worms.

Safety Note Be sure children wash hands after handling worms. To protect native wildlife, do not release the living organisms into the environment.

 Activity DVD Unit B, Chapter 5

 Activity Placemat Mat 11

Other Resources
The following Resources are available for activities found in the Student Edition.

Demonstration Kit If you wish to rehearse or demonstrate the Chapter 5 activities, use the materials provided in the Demonstration Kit.

Classroom Equipment Kit Materials shown in *italic print* are available in the Classroom Equipment Kit.

Activity Placemats The Equipment Kit includes an Activity Placemat for each activity, a work surface which identifies the materials that need to be gathered.

Quick **ACTIVITY**

Transparencies Each lesson starts with a Quick Activity. Use the Quick Activity Overhead Transparencies to focus children's attention on each task.

Teacher's Activity Guide For detailed information about Inquiry Activities, access the Teacher's Activity Guide at **pearsonsuccessnet.com**.

Activity Flip Chart

How does erosion affect land?

Use this center activity after teaching Lesson 4 of the chapter.

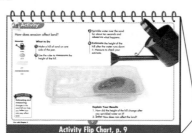

Activity Flip Chart, p. 9

Process Skill Estimate and measure, infer, observe

 Time 10 minutes

 Grouping Individual or pairs

Materials water in a small watering can; sand; plastic pan; metric ruler

Procedure
- Review with children the correct way to measure with a metric ruler. Have children **measure** the height of the sand hill they have made.
- Have children **estimate** the height of the sand hill after they have poured the water over it. Have children measure the height of the hill to check their estimate.
- Children should **infer** that the sand hill becomes shorter after the water is poured over it because the water washes away some of the sand.

What to Expect Children will observe that water washes away sediment and wears down hills. The sediment accumulates elsewhere.

Think About It
1. The height of the hill decreased after water fell on it.
2. Rain washes away the soil and drops it someplace else.

Activity Flip Chart

How can you reuse something?

Use this center activity after teaching Lesson 5 of the chapter.

Activity Flip Chart, p. 10

Process Skill Observe, infer

 Time 20 minutes

 Grouping Individual or pairs

Materials clean, empty milk and juice containers (a variety of sizes and shapes); clean, empty metal can; scissors; markers of assorted colors; construction paper of assorted colors; craft materials for decoration (such as buttons, sequins, and beads); white glue; white drawing paper

Procedure
- Leave the original labels on the containers so that students can better **observe** the original purpose of the container.
- Have children **infer** how to change the original container before they begin to make the actual changes. Encourage students to repeat this activity for another container.

What to Expect Children will likely create a variety of reusable items from the containers. Examples include a planter, a scoop, a small bucket, a coin bank, a pencil holder, and so on.

Think About It
1. To reuse something means to use it again for the same or a different purpose.
2. Answers should describe a specific purpose such as filling with soil and putting a plant in it.

Chapter 5
Workbook Support

online Teacher's Edition
pearsonsuccessnet.com

Use the following Workbook pages to support content and skill development as you teach Chapter 5. You can also view and print Workbook pages from the Online Teacher's Edition.

Use with Build Background, pp. 138–139

Name _____ **Vocabulary Preview**
Use with Chapter 5.

Draw a picture or write a sentence to go with each word.

boulder	erosion
weathering	natural resource
sand	pollution
minerals	recycle

Directions: Read the words and draw pictures to illustrate them or write sentences about them. Cut out the boxes to use as word cards.
Home Activity: Give clues to the vocabulary words, such as *Old cans made into new cans* and *Dirty air, land, or water,* and have your child say the correct words.

Workbook   Vocabulary Preview **55**

Workbook, p. 55

Use with How to Read Science, p. 141

Name _____ **How to Read Science**
Use with Chapter 5.

Ⓒ Picture Clues
Read the science article.

Collect and Recycle
People can help keep Earth clean. One way is to collect newspaper, metal cans, and plastic bottles. These things can be recycled, or changed and used again.

56 How to Read Science   Workbook

Workbook, pp. 56–57

Use with Lesson 1, pp. 142–145

Name _____ **Think, Read, Learn**
Use with pages 143–145.

What are natural resources?
Before You Read Lesson 1

Read each sentence. Do you think it is true? Do you think it is not true? Circle the word or words after each sentence that tell what you think.

1. Sunlight is a natural resource.   True   Not True
2. Oil is a natural resource that can
   be replaced.   True   Not True
3. Water and air will never be used up.   True   Not True

After You Read Lesson 1

Read each sentence again. Circle the word or words after each sentence that tell what you think now. Did you change any answers? Put an **X** by each answer that you changed.

1. Sunlight is a natural resource.   (True)   Not True
2. Oil is a natural resource that can
   be replaced.   True   (Not True)
3. Water and air will never be used up. (True)   Not True

Home Activity: Together talk about your child's answers. Have your child explain why his or her answers may have changed after reading the lesson.

Workbook   Think, Read, Learn **58**

Workbook, p. 58

Use with Lesson 2, pp. 146–149

Name _____ **Think, Read, Learn**
Use with pages 146–149.

What are rocks and soil like?
Before You Read Lesson 2

Read each sentence. Do you think it is true? Do you think it is not true? Circle the word or words after each sentence that tell what you think.

1. A boulder is a small rock.   True   Not True
2. Sand is made of tiny pieces of rock. True   Not True
3. Rocks are made of minerals.   True   Not True
4. Soil is always dark, hard, and wet.   True   Not True

After You Read Lesson 2

Read each sentence again. Circle the word or words after each sentence that tell what you think now. Did you change any answers? Put an **X** by each answer that you changed.

1. A boulder is a small rock.   True   (Not True)
2. Sand is made of tiny pieces of rock. (True)   Not True
3. Rocks are made of minerals.   (True)   Not True
4. Soil is always dark, hard, and wet.   True   (Not True)

Home Activity: Together talk about your child's answers. Have your child explain why his or her answers may have changed after reading the lesson.

Workbook   Think, Read, Learn **59**

Workbook, p. 59

Name _____

Think, Read, Learn

Use with pages 150–151.

How do people use plants?

Before You Read Lesson 3

Read each sentence. Do you think it is true? Do you think it is not true? Circle the word or words after each sentence that tell what you think.

1. Plants can be used as food.   True   Not True
2. Plants cannot be used to make
   clothes.   True   Not True
3. A newspaper is made from plants.   True   Not True

After You Read Lesson 3

Read each sentence again. Circle the word or words after each sentence that tell what you think now. Did you change any answers? Put an **X** by each answer that you changed.

1. Plants can be used as food.   (True) Not True
2. Plants cannot be used to make
   clothes.   True   (Not True)
3. A newspaper is made from plants.   (True) Not True

 Home Activity: Together talk about your child's answers. Have your child explain why his or her answers may have changed after reading the lesson.

Workbook   Think, Read, Learn **60**

Workbook, p. 60

Name _____

Think, Read, Learn

Use with pages 152–153.

How does Earth change?

Before You Read Lesson 4

Read each sentence. Do you think it is true? Do you think it is not true? Circle the word or words after each sentence that tell what you think.

1. Erosion can change Earth.   True   Not True
2. Plant roots can help stop erosion. True   Not True
3. Weathering is when rocks or soil
   are moved by water or wind.   True   Not True

After You Read Lesson 4

Read each sentence again. Circle the word or words after each sentence that tell what you think now. Did you change any answers? Put an **X** by each answer that you changed.

1. Erosion can change Earth.   (True) Not True
2. Plant roots can help stop erosion. (True) Not True
3. Weathering is when rocks or soil
   are moved by water or wind.   True   (Not True)

Home Activity: Together talk about your child's answers. Have your child explain why his or her answers may have changed after reading the lesson.

Workbook   Think, Read, Learn **61**

Workbook, p. 61

Name _____

Think, Read, Learn

Use with pages 154–159.

How can people help protect Earth?

Before You Read Lesson 5

Read each sentence. Do you think it is true? Do you think it is not true? Circle the word or words after each sentence that tell what you think.

1. People can help reduce pollution.   True   Not True
2. Paper and plastic can be recycled. True   Not True
3. Trees cannot be replaced.   True   Not True
4. Plants and animals are safe in
   a refuge.   True   Not True

After You Read Lesson 5

Read each sentence again. Circle the word or words after each sentence that tell what you think now. Did you change any answers? Put an **X** by each answer that you changed.

1. People can help reduce pollution.   (True) Not True
2. Paper and plastic can be recycled. (True) Not True
3. Trees cannot be replaced.   True   (Not True)
4. Plants and animals are safe in
   a refuge.   (True) Not True

Home Activity: Together talk about your child's answers. Have your child explain why his or her answers may have changed after reading the lesson.

Workbook   Think, Read, Learn **62**

Workbook, p. 62

Name _____

Math in Science

Use with Chapter 5.

Bird Count

Mrs. Sung's second-grade class visited a bird refuge last week. The students counted the number of ducks, cranes, and geese they saw on a pond. They made a bar graph to show how many of each kind of bird they saw.

Number of Birds that Students Saw

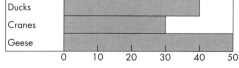

Use the bar graph to answer these questions.

1. How many ducks did the students see? ___40___
2. How many more geese than cranes did the students see? ___20___
3. Write a number sentence that shows how many ducks and cranes the students saw. ___40 + 30 = 70___

Directions: Look at the bar graph and note how many of each kind of bird the students saw. Then use those numbers to answer the questions.
Home Activity: Your child learned how to interpret a bar graph. Together count how many glasses, mugs, and dinner plates you have and make a bar graph like the one on this page. Then ask your child questions about the bar graph.

Workbook   Math in Science **63**

Workbook, p. 63

Chapter 5 Assessment Support

Use the following Assessment Book pages and ExamView to assess Chapter 5 content. You can also view and print Assessment Book pages from the Online Teacher's Edition.

Assessment Options

Formal Assessment

- Chapter Review and Test Prep, SE pp. 164–165
- Assessment Book, pp. 31–34
- Prescriptions for remediation are shown on TE p. 165

Performance Assessment

- Unit Wrap-Up, SE pp. 226–227

Ongoing Assessment

- Diagnostic Check, TE pp. 143, 147, 155
- Scaffolded Questions, TE pp. 143, 145, 147, 149, 151, 153, 155, 157, 159, 163

Portfolio Assessment

- My Science Journal, TE p. 145

Success Tracker

- Data management system to assess Adequate Yearly Progress (AYP) and provide intervention

ExamView®

- Alternative test formats are available online or through ExamView CD-ROM

Chapter 5 Test

Name _____   Chapter 5 Test

Read each question and choose the best answer. Then fill in the circle next to the correct answer.

1 Complete the sentence. Many _____ are a mixture of clay, sand, and humus.
Ⓐ soils
Ⓑ rocks
Ⓒ sands
Ⓓ boulders

2 Which sentence is true about natural resources?
Ⓕ They are useful to people.
Ⓖ They come from Earth.
Ⓗ Some can be replaced when they are used.
Ⓘ All of the sentences are true about natural resources.

3 What is sand made up of?
Ⓐ soil
Ⓑ boulders
Ⓒ gold and silver
Ⓓ tiny pieces of rock

Assessment Book   Chapter 5 Test **31**

Assessment Book, p. 31

Chapter 5 Test

Name _____   Chapter 5 Test

4 Look at the picture below.

Think about what you learned from the picture.
What natural resource is the chair made of?
Ⓕ soil
Ⓖ wood
Ⓗ cotton
Ⓘ minerals

5 What is erosion?
Ⓐ a kind of soil
Ⓑ a kind of rock
Ⓒ when roots of plants keep soil in place
Ⓓ when rocks and soil are moved by water or wind

32 Chapter 5 Test   Assessment Book

Assessment Book, p. 32

Chapter 5 Test

Name _____   Chapter 5 Test

6 What happens when people add harmful things to land, water, or air?
Ⓕ reusing
Ⓖ pollution
Ⓗ recycling
Ⓘ protection

7 Read the chart. Use what you learn to answer the question.

Taking Care of Earth	
Problem	**How People Can Help**
Litter	Pick up trash
Too much trash	Recycle and reuse things
People cut down trees	Plant new trees

What is this chart about?
Ⓐ problems caused by litter
Ⓑ problems caused by people
Ⓒ how animals are hurt by pollution
Ⓓ how people can help take care of Earth

Assessment Book   Chapter 5 Test **33**

Assessment Book, p. 33

Chapter 5 Test

Name _____   Chapter 5 Test

8 What is a refuge?
Ⓕ a place where people build their homes
Ⓖ a place where all the trees are cut down
Ⓗ a safe place for people to work and live
Ⓘ a safe place for plants and animals to live

Write the answers to the questions on the lines.

9 How do people use air? (2 points)
Children should write one or two sentences about how people use air. For example: People breathe air, use air to inflate balls, balloons. Wind moves boats.

10 Look at the forest shown in the picture below.

What can people do to help the plants and animals that live in the forest? (2 points)
People can plant new trees.

34 Chapter 5 Test   Assessment Book

Assessment Book, p. 34

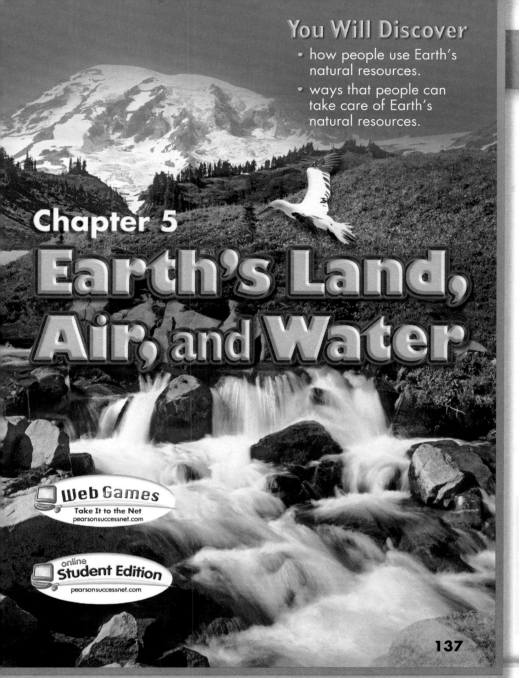

You Will Discover

* how people use Earth's natural resources.
* ways that people can take care of Earth's natural resources.

Chapter 5

Earth's Land, Air, and Water

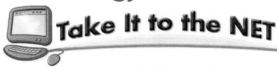
Web Games
Take It to the Net
pearsonsuccessnet.com

online Student Edition
pearsonsuccessnet.com

137

Chapter 5

Earth's Land, Air, and Water

 Science Objectives

* The student recognizes that the solid materials making up the Earth come in all sizes, from boulders to grains of sand.
* The student knows that life occurs on or near the surface of the Earth in land, air, and water.
* The student understands that people influence the quality of life of those around them.
* The student knows that the activities of humans affect plants and animals in many ways.
* The student knows that people use scientific processes including hypothesis, making inferences, and recording and communicating data when exploring the natural world.

Quick | TEACHING PLAN

If time is short...
Use Build Background page to engage children in chapter content. Then do Explore Activity, How to Read Science, and Lessons 1, 3, and 5.

Professional Development

To enhance your qualifications in science:

* preview content in Earth Science DVD Segments *Earth's Weather and Water* and *Earth's Changing Surface*.
* preview activity management techniques described in Activity DVD Unit B, Chapter 5.

Technology Link

 **Take It to the NET**

To access student resources:
1. Go to **www.pearsonsuccessnet.com.**
2. Click on the register button.
3. Enter the access code **frog** and your school's zip code.

Chapter 5 Concept Web

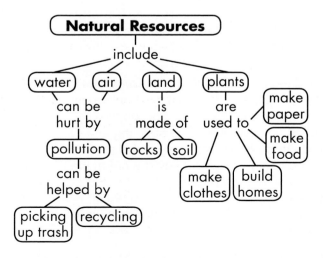

Children can create a concept web to organize ideas about Earth's land, air, and water.

Build Background

 Science Objective

- The student identifies words and constructs meaning from text, illustrations, graphics, and charts, using the strategies of phonics, word structure, and context clues.

Chapter 5 Vocabulary Words

natural resource, p. 143
boulder, p. 146
sand, p. 146
minerals, p. 147
erosion, p. 152
weathering, p. 153
pollution, p. 154
recycle, p. 156

1 | Introduce the Concept

Quick ACTIVITY

Tell children: ***Draw a picture of an outdoor place you have visited.*** Then have children share their pictures with a partner. Ask the artists to identify and describe the location of the outdoor place. For example, you might show children a picture of a lake and say, "This is Lake Scott. It is a big lake with a beach and lots of trees around it." Use all of the pictures to create a classroom display that shows some of Earth's natural resources.

Discuss Essential Question

Many science vocabulary words are abstract. Use the pictures and labels on these pages to help you open a discussion about science concepts and build academic language.

Read the Chapter 5 Essential Question to children, **What are Earth's natural resources?** Explain to children that resources are supplies of things we use. A natural resource is anything that comes from Earth that people can use. Earth's resources are called natural because they are not made by people. Help children brainstorm a list of natural resources. Be sure to include land, air, and water. As children list these natural resources, ask them to tell why they think each natural resource is important.

Revisit the essential question with children as they work through this chapter.

Build Background Resources

Workbook, p. 55

Graphic Organizer Transparency 1

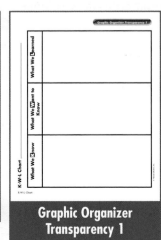

Vocabulary Cards

ELL Support

Access Content Before reading the chapter text, lead children on a picture/text walk.

Chapter 5 Vocabulary

natural resource
page 143

boulder page 146

sand page 146

minerals page 147

erosion page 152

weathering
page 153

pollution page 154

recycle page 157

boulder

pollution

recycle

139

Science Background

Fossil Fuels

The fossil fuels crude oil, coal, and natural gas were formed within Earth's crust. Millions of years ago, the bodies of prehistoric sea animals and plants became trapped in sediment. Over a long period of time, heat and pressure changed the sediment containing these bodies into crude oil, coal, and natural gas.

Science Misconception

Running Out of Fossil Fuels

Some children might not realize that fossil fuels are not being made as quickly as we are using them. Most of our fossil fuels were made long ago, before the time of the dinosaurs. If we do not conserve these natural resources, they may run out.

Use the following K-W-L chart provided on **pearsonsuccessnet.com** or Graphic Organizer Transparency 1.

Word	K What I Know	W What I Want to Know	L What I Learned
natural resource			
boulder			
sand			
minerals			
erosion			
weathering			
pollution			
recycle			

On Graphic Organizer Transparency 1, list vocabulary words under the first column. Explain to children that you will fill in the "K" and "W" columns of the chart together.

- Pronounce each word. Solicit information from children as you fill in the "K" column. For example, children may have prior knowledge of what recycling is and what they do at home to contribute to community recycling efforts.

- Guide children as you fill in the "W" column of the chart. A possible question might be, "What natural resources are found in your community?"

- Encourage students to add a note in the "W" column when they learn what they wanted to know.

- Tell children they will work as a class to fill in the last column, "L," as they read the chapter.

Word Recognition Use the Vocabulary Cards to reinforce recognition of each written word and its definition.

3 | Practice

Vocabulary Strategy: Which Word?

Using the Vocabulary Cards, read the definition of each vocabulary word aloud. Have children point to each word on pages 138–139. Then have pairs of children work together to create simple riddles that have vocabulary words as their answers. Have children take turns asking and answering riddles.

SCAFFOLDED INQUIRY

1 Explore How are soils different?

⭐ **Science Objective**

- The student knows that scientists and technologists use a variety of tools (e.g., thermometers, magnifiers, rulers, and scales) to obtain information and to make work easier.

1 Build Background

Children compare and contrast two types of soil.

Managing Time and Materials

Time: 15 minutes
Groups: small groups
Materials: *2 paper plates; hand lens; plastic cup (9 oz.); plastic dropper; potting soil (2 tbsp); sandy soil (2 tbsp);* water (about $\frac{1}{3}$ c)

Materials listed in *italic* are kit materials.

2 What to Do

Engage Ask children: ***What is soil and why is it important?*** Accept all logical responses.

Explore Have children compare the soils.

Explain Ask groups to discuss similarities and differences in the two types of soil.

Extend Have children examine soil samples from their schoolyards, home yards, or gardens.

Evaluate Discuss how well the soils absorb water.

3 Explain Your Results

Both are made of tiny particles. Potting soil has a stronger smell. Sandy soil is coarser, lighter in color, and absorbs water more slowly than potting soil.

Process Skills

Have children compare and contrast the two soils.

Explore How are soils different?

Materials

plates with soils

hand lens

dropper

cup with water

What to Do

1 Observe the soils. Look, smell, and touch.

2 Use the hand lens. Observe the smallest bits of soil.

3 Add water. Observe how the soils soak up the water.

Label the plates.

sandy soil

potting soil

Process Skills

You **observe** when you look, smell, and touch.

Explain Your Results

Observe How are the soils alike? How are they different?

Activity Resources

Activity Book pp. 61–62

Activity Rubric

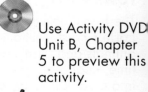

Use Activity DVD Unit B, Chapter 5 to preview this activity.

Call 1-888-537-4908 with activity questions.

🖥 More Lab zone **Activities** **Take It to the Net** pearsonsuccessnet.com

Find more about this activity at our Web site.

- See the **Teacher's Activity Guide** for more support.
- An alternative activity is also available to download.

Reading Skills

 Picture Clues

Pictures can give you clues about what you read.

Science Article

Soil

There are many kinds of living things in soil. Plants live in soil. Worms and other animals live in soil too.

Apply It!
Observe What lives in the soil? Look for clues in the picture.

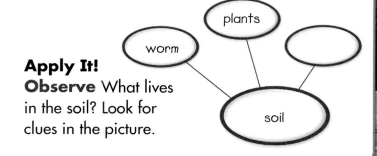

plants

worm

soil

141

How to Read Science Resource

Workbook, pp. 56–57

ELL Support

For more practice on **Picture Clues**, use **Every Student Learns Teacher's Guide,** p. 31

 Picture Clues

⭐ **Reading Objective**

- The student uses a variety of context clues (for example, illustrations, diagrams, information in the story, titles and headings, sequence) to construct meaning (meaning cues).

About the Target Skill

The target skill for *Earth's Land, Water, and Air* is **Picture Clues.** Children are introduced to the skill as you guide them through this page.

1 Introduce

Hold up a picture for children to see. The picture should show a single object, such as a tree or a bird. Ask children: *What is one thing you can learn about* (name topic) *from this picture?* Children's answers will vary, but they should identify something shown in the picture.

2 Model the Skill

Look together at page 141. Read the Science Article as a class. Look at the picture together.

Say: *This article is about soil. This picture gives us clues about soil. What can soil look like?* Soil can be dark and made of small particles. *What else does the picture show?* There are things in the soil.

3 Practice

Graphic Organizer

Look at the Graphic Organizer together. Work with children to complete the Graphic Organizer using the facts from the Science Article.

Apply It!

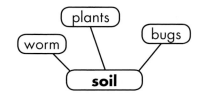

plants

worm

bugs

soil

What are natural resources?

 Science Objective

- The student knows some of Earth's natural resources, including land, air, and water; and identifies renewable and nonrenewable resources.

1 Introduce

Quick ACTIVITY | TRANSPARENCY 27 |

Provide magazines that have pictures of natural resources (such as travel, and nature magazines). Have children cut out pictures of resources that come from Earth, such as water, rocks, and trees. Then have them paste the pictures on a large piece of construction paper. Children can work in pairs or small groups. Have children tell how people use these resources.

Access Prior Knowledge

Have children recall rocks they have seen. Invite them to describe briefly where they saw the rocks. How are those rocks like the ones pictured? How are they different? Mention that rocks are one kind of natural resource.

Set Purpose

Tell children they are going to read about Earth's natural resources. Help them set a **purpose for reading**, such as to discover how important natural resources are to living things.

2 Teach

Quick SUMMARY

- Natural resources are useful materials that come from Earth.
- Some natural resources, such as oil and coal, cannot be replaced. Others, such as trees, can be replaced.
- Sunlight, water, and air can never be used up.

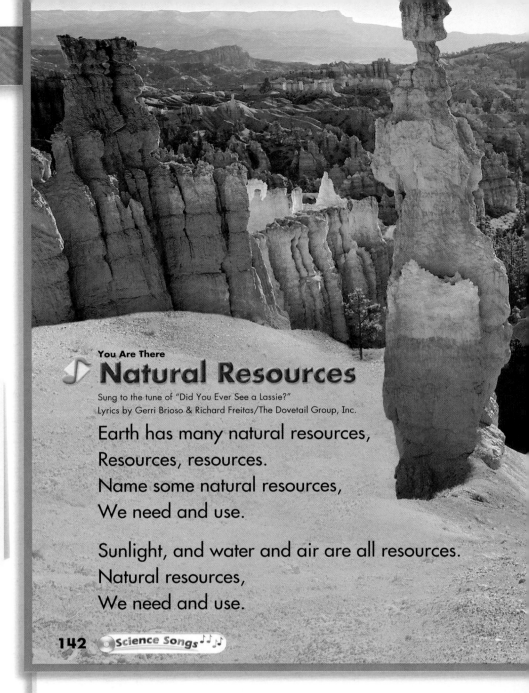

You Are There

♪ Natural Resources

Sung to the tune of "Did You Ever See a Lassie?"
Lyrics by Gerri Brioso & Richard Freitas/The Dovetail Group, Inc.

Earth has many natural resources,

Resources, resources.

Name some natural resources,

We need and use.

Sunlight, and water and air are all resources.

Natural resources,

We need and use.

142 Science Songs ♪♪♫

Lesson 1 Resource

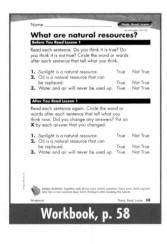

Workbook, p. 58

 Science Songs ♪♪♫

Use the Science Songs CD to play "Natural Resources" for the class.

Lesson 1

What are natural resources?

Sunlight, water, and forests are natural resources. A **natural resource** is a useful thing that comes from nature. Oil and coal are natural resources too.

Some natural resources cannot be replaced after they are used up. Oil and coal cannot be replaced.

Some natural resources can be replaced after they are used. New trees can be planted to replace trees that are cut down for wood.

Some natural resources can never be used up. Sunlight, water, and air will never be used up.

143

Sing or play "Natural Resources" for children. Then read page 143 together. Look at the picture of the canyon and have children name a natural resource that they cannot see in the picture but that they know is present. (Air, sunlight)

Assign Quick Study pp. 54–55 to children who need help with lesson content.

Guide Comprehension

Ask children the following scaffolded questions to assess understanding.

Scaffolded Questions

 Define What is a natural resource?
A useful material that comes from Earth

2 List List some natural resources.
Sunlight, water, air, oil, coal, forests

3 Classify Which of the following natural resources can be replaced and which can never be used up: sunlight, trees, water? Trees can be replaced. Sunlight and water can never be used up.

Extend Vocabulary

Write the words *nature* and *natural* on the board. Circle the *-al* ending. Explain that *nature* names something; it is a noun. When the ending *-al* is added, the new word *natural* describes something; it is an adjective. Tell children that the two words are closely related. Write the term natural resource on the board and explain that a **natural resource** is a resource from nature.

Diagnostic Check

If… children have difficulty understanding what a natural resource is,

then… list examples of different natural resources on the board. Review each natural resource, making sure children understand that it comes from Earth and is important to people's lives.

ELL Leveled Support

Nature/Natural

Beginning Show children a picture of a human-made thing (such as a car) and a picture of a natural thing (such as a tree). Say, for example: ***People make cars. People do not make trees. Trees are found in nature. They are natural.*** Ask volunteers to say whether other pictured items are natural or made by people.

Intermediate Build on the above. Make a two-column chart on the board with the headings *Made by People* and *Natural*. Ask volunteers: ***What other things are made by people? What other things are natural?*** Record children's answers on the chart.

Advanced Ask children: ***What is a resource?*** Guide children to understand that a resource is something that we use to meet a need. For example, money is a resource. Then say: ***A natural resource is a resource that is not made by people. For example, trees are natural resources.*** Write *Natural Resources* on the board and ask volunteers to give other examples of resources that are not made by people. (Possible answers may include air, water, sunlight, plants, space.)

Science Objective

- The student knows selected resources used by people for water, food, and shelter are limited and necessary for their survival.

2 | Teach (continued)

Quick SUMMARY

- Water, both fresh and salt, is a natural resource that plants, animals, and people need to live.
- People use water to drink, cook, and clean. Water provides people with fish for food.
- Air is a natural resource that plants, animals, and people need to live.

Read pages 144–145 with children. Have children describe the different types of water resources (lakes, rivers, oceans, and so on) found in and near their community. Ask: **How do people, plants, and animals use these resources?** Possible answers: swimming, watering, drinking **How would our lives be different if these resources weren't here?** Possible answer: People and animals would be thirsty; plants would die.

Water and Air

Water is a natural resource. Plants, animals, and people need water to live. Ponds, rivers, streams, and lakes have fresh water. Oceans **1** have salt water.

People use water in many ways. People drink **2** water. People use water to cook and clean.

Air is a natural resource. Plants, animals, and people need air to live. Air is all around us. Wind is moving air.

✔ Lesson Checkpoint

1. Name some natural resources.

2. **Writing in Science** Make a list. What are some ways you use water every day?

144

Science Background

Earth's Water and Natural Resources

- Approximately three-fourths of Earth is covered by water. The different types of freshwater sources include rivers, lakes, ponds, and groundwater. Most of Earth's salt water is found in the oceans. Some water sources, such as marshes, wetlands, and bays, can be either freshwater or salt water.
- Renewable natural resources are those that are replaced constantly in nature. Sunlight, water, air, and food and cloth crops are all examples of renewable natural resources. Some natural resources are used up more quickly than they can be replaced. These are nonrenewable natural resources. Coal, oil, natural gas, minerals, and metals are all examples of nonrenewable natural resources. Coal is renewable over millions of years, but the time scale is so great that for human purposes, coal is considered to be a nonrenewable resource.

Plants need water to live.

Air is used to fill this soccer ball.

This fishing boat brings fish from the ocean for people to eat.

Hot air fills this balloon.

145

My Science Journal

Making a Word Web

Have children write a word web for the term *natural resource*. Tell them to include a definition, some examples, one or two examples of things that are not natural resources (nonexamples), and a sentence correctly using the term.

ELL Support

Vocabulary Focus

Make sure children understand the meaning of *replace*. Explain that it means "to put something back in its place again." Help children recognize that if trees are cut down, new trees can be planted. The new trees will *replace*, or take the place of, the ones that were cut down.

For scaffolded instruction about natural resources, use **Every Student Learns Teacher's Guide,** p. 32.

Guide Comprehension

Ask children the following scaffolded questions to assess understanding.

Scaffolded Questions

1 **Recall** *Name three places in nature where water is found.* Freshwater is found in ponds, rivers, streams, and lakes. Salt water is found in the ocean.

2 **Describe** *Describe three uses of water.* Water is used for drinking, cooking, cleaning, bathing, and swimming.

3 **Examine** *How is air important to us?* Possible answers: We need air to breathe. We fill some things with air to make them bigger. We use air to make things move.

Extend Vocabulary

Write the word *water* on the board. Explain that the word can be a noun that names something. It can also be used to describe an action: People water plants. They water horses or cattle. Discuss the verb's meaning. Then point out that water can also be used as an adjective that describes something. People enjoy water sports, such as swimming. Swimmers sometimes see water plants in a pond. Have children take turns using both the verb and the adjective *water* in oral or written sentences.

3 | Assess

✓ Lesson Checkpoint

1. Sunlight, water, air, trees, oil, coal

2. **Writing in Science** Have children write their answers in their science journals. Answers will vary but lists might include drinking, bathing, cooking, cleaning, swimming.

Lesson 2

What are rocks and soil like?

 Science Objective

• The student extends and refines knowledge that the surface of the Earth is composed of different types of solid materials that come in all sizes.

1 Introduce

Quick ACTIVITY | TRANSPARENCY 28

Have children examine different types of rocks and soil. You can bring in samples or show Quick Activity Transparency 21. Ask: *Where might you find rocks and soil like these?* Have children make a T-chart with *rocks* and *soil* written at the top. Have them list characteristics that show how rocks are different from soil.

Access Prior Knowledge

Ask children to think of a place they may have been that is rocky, sandy, or contains soil. Have children write about their experiences in these places in their science journals. Have them describe the rocks and soil.

Set Purpose

Tell children they are going to read about rocks and soil. Help them set a **purpose for reading,** such as being able to tell how rocks and soil are alike and how they are different.

2 Teach

Quick SUMMARY

• Rocks are natural resources that can have many shapes, sizes, and colors.

• A very big rock is called a boulder.

• Sand is made up of tiny pieces of rock broken off larger rocks by wind, rain, and ice.

• Rocks are made of minerals.

Read pages 146–147 with children. Discuss ways in which people use rocks and sand.

What are rocks and soil like?

Rocks are natural resources. Rocks come in many shapes, colors, and sizes. A very big ①rock is called a **boulder.** People use rocks to build houses.

Wind, rain, and ice can break rocks into smaller pieces. **Sand** is made of tiny pieces of rock. Some rocks can be smaller than grains of sand. People use sand to build roads.

146

Lesson 2 Resource

Workbook, p. 59

Science Background

Boulders

By definition, a boulder is any rock 256 millimeters (10.1 inches) or more in diameter.

Minerals are a natural resource. **Minerals** are nonliving materials that come from Earth. Rocks are made of minerals. Gold, iron, and silver are minerals.

Quartz is a mineral used to make glass.

Copper is a mineral. Some pots are made from copper.

1. ✓ Checkpoint Name four minerals.
2. Math in Science Think about a boulder. Is the length of a boulder closer to 10 inches or 10 feet? Explain your answer.

147

ELL Leveled Support

Identifying Rocks

Beginning Show children three pictures: two depicting rocks and one showing a living object. Ask children to identify the rocks and explain how they knew they were rocks.

Intermediate Ask children to list two places where they would expect to find rocks. Have them tell why they would expect to find rocks in those places.

Advanced Have children write two or three sentences describing one of the rocks they examined in this lesson. Suggest that they include at least two facts, such as size and color.

For scaffolded instruction about rocks and soil, use **Every Student Learns Teacher's Guide,** p. 33.

Examine the pictures to identify the different minerals shown. Have children look again at the rocks and minerals that they measured earlier. This time, have them use magnifying glasses and describe the smaller materials in the rocks.

Assign Quick Study pp. 56–57 to children who need help with lesson content.

Guide Comprehension

Ask children the following scaffolded questions to assess understanding.

Scaffolded Questions

1 Recall *What is a rock?* A natural resource that can be almost any size, color, or shape

2 Compare and Contrast *How are rocks and sand alike and different?* Alike: Both are natural resources that are made of minerals; Different: Sand is made of tiny pieces of rock.

3 Appraise *Why are rocks important to us?* They are used to make houses and roads.

Extend Vocabulary

Explain to children that the word **sand** can be used as a noun or a verb. In this lesson, sand is a noun meaning tiny pieces of rock. When used as a verb, sand means to make something smooth by rubbing it with sand or sandpaper.

Diagnostic Check

If... children have difficulty understanding the difference between rocks and minerals,

then... remind children that all rocks are made of minerals and that they perhaps saw these minerals when they examined rocks.

3 Assess

1. ✓ Checkpoint Quartz, copper, gold, and silver
2. Math in Science 10 feet. Boulders are large rocks. Something that measures 10 feet is larger than something that measures 10 inches.

Science Objective

- The student extends and refines knowledge that the surface of the Earth is composed of different types of solid materials that come in all sizes.

2 Teach (continued)

Quick SUMMARY

- Soil is a natural resource.
- Soil covers most of the land.
- Soil is a mixture of clay, sand, and humus.
- Soils can be different, and plants need the right kind of soil to grow.

Read pages 148–149 with children. Discuss with children what soil contains and ways it can be different. Make sure that children understand that most soil consists of nonliving materials, such as minerals, and the living materials that form humus. Talk about how different plants grow best in different soils. Ask children if they can give any examples of this idea. (Children may know that cacti grow well in desert soil.)

Soil

Soil is a natural resource. Soil covers most of Earth's land. Many soils are a mixture of clay, sand, and humus. Soil contains air and water. Most plants grow in soil.

Soil can be different colors. Soil can be hard or soft. Soil can feel wet or dry.

Sandy soil is loose. It feels dry and rough.

Clay soil has very small pieces. Clay soil feels smooth. It feels soft and sticky.

148

Social Studies Link

Gold

Tell children that gold has always been considered an important resource. Today it is used not only to make jewelry but also in industry, medicine, and other fields. Many minerals, including gold, are not evenly spread around the world. Have children research three countries to find out which has the most gold and which has the least: South Africa (most), Canada (least), United States.

Humus is a part of soil that comes from living things.

②

Different kinds of plants grow best in different kinds of soil. Plants may grow well in one kind of soil. They may not grow as well in another kind of soil. ③

✓ **Lesson Checkpoint**

1. Describe sandy soil, clay soil, and humus.

2. 🎯 Use **picture clues.** Tell how sandy soil, clay soil, and humus are different.

149

Science Background

Humus

Explain that humus is dead plant or animal remains that can be found in soil. Plants and animals that can be found in the soil include bacteria, fungi, roundworms, mites, springtails, millipedes, centipedes, insects, plant roots, caterpillars, slugs, snails, larvae, and aphids. Tell children that the more humus there is in soil, the better plants will grow in that soil. Soil is a resource used to grow food and food is needed for survival. If your community has a composting program, you may be able to obtain a sample of humus to show children.

3 | Assess

✓ **Lesson Checkpoint**

1. Clay soil is soft, sticky, brown-colored, and has small grains. Sandy soil is usually light-colored with loose, large grains. Humus is a part of soil that comes from living things.

2. 🎯 Use **picture clues.** Sandy soil, clay soil, and humus are all types of soil. They are all made of smaller pieces.

Lesson 3

How do people use plants?

 Science Objective

- The student knows selected resources used by people for water, food, and shelter are limited and necessary for their survival.

1 Introduce

Quick ACTIVITY | TRANSPARENCY 29 |

Have children examine a variety of plant products such as bread, wooden pencils, cotton balls, a cotton T-shirt, and paper. Explain that all of these things come from plants or plant parts. Have children write on index cards what plant each item comes from. Have them switch cards with a partner and share their responses.

Access Prior Knowledge

Have children write a list of things that various plants have in common in their science journals. This list might include leaves, stems, flowers, green color, and the need for sunlight and water. Ask children how plants are different from animals.

Set Purpose

Tell children you are going to read to them about plants as natural resources. Help them set a **purpose for listening,** such as to find out the different uses of plants.

2 Teach

Quick SUMMARY

- Plants are natural resources.
- Plants are used to build homes, to make clothes, to make food, and to make paper.

Read pages 150–151 to children. Examine the pictures to identify some uses we have for plants. Brainstorm with children other uses for plants, including other food sources, other uses for wood and paper, and as homes to different animals.

Assign Quick Study pp. 58–59 to children who need help with lesson content.

Lesson 3

How do people use plants?

Plants are a natural resource. People use plants in many ways. Plants can be used to make food, shelter, and clothing. The pictures show some things you use every day that are made from plants.

People use cotton to make clothes. This T-shirt is made from cotton.

People use wood from pine trees to build houses.

150

Lesson 3 Resource

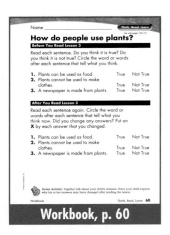

How do people use plants?

Before You Read Lesson 3

Read each sentence. Do you think it is true? Do you think it is not true? Circle the word or words after each sentence that tell what you think.

1. Plants can be used as food.   True   Not True
2. Plants cannot be used to make clothes.   True   Not True
3. A newspaper is made from plants.   True   Not True

After You Read Lesson 3

Read each sentence again. Circle the word or words after each sentence that tell what you think now. Did you change any answers? Put an **X** by each answer that you changed.

1. Plants can be used as food.   True   Not True
2. Plants cannot be used to make clothes.   True   Not True
3. A newspaper is made from plants.   True   Not True

Home Activity: Together talk about your child's answers. Have your child explain why his or her answers may have changed after reading the lesson.

Workbook   Think, Read, Learn **60**

Workbook, p. 60

1. What is one way that people use cotton plants?

2. 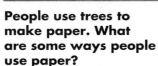 Use **picture clues.** What things are made from trees?

People use wheat to make food. This bread is made from wheat.

People use trees to make paper. What are some ways people use paper?

 ③

151

Science Background

Cotton Bolls and Maple Syrup

• Cotton fiber comes from the cotton boll, which is the seedpod of the plant. After being picked, seeds are removed from cotton bolls in a process called ginning. Then the bolls are shipped to textile mills and made into yarn (through cleaning, carding, combing, and spinning). The yarn is woven into cotton fabric on looms in factories.

• Maple syrup is made from the sweet-water sap of the sugar maple tree. Trees are tapped in the spring so the sap will run into buckets. Then the sap is cooked for a long time until it gets thick and sweet.

ELL Support

Listing Plants

Name all the plants pictured on pages 150–151. Ask children: **What else is made from cotton? What other trees can you name? What other foods come from plants? What other uses are there for paper?**

For scaffolded instruction about plants, use **Every Student Learns Teacher's Guide,** p. 34.

Guide Comprehension

Ask children the following scaffolded questions to assess understanding.

Scaffolded Questions

① **List** *What are some ways plants are important to us?* Plants provide us with shelter, clothing, paper, and food.

② **Describe** *How does cotton look on a cotton plant?* Cotton looks like fluffy white balls along the stem of the plant.

③ **Evaluate** *Would we be able to live without plants? Why or why not?* Possible answer: No, we would not be able to live without plants because we eat some plant parts and we need plants for shelter.

Extend Vocabulary

Tell children that the word *plant* has more than one meaning. It can be a noun that names a living thing, such as a tree. It can also be a noun that means "a building and machines used to make or produce articles." (The power plant operates 24 hours a day.) The word *plant* can also be a verb that means "to put something in the ground to grow" (I will plant a tree.) and "to set something firmly in or on." (I planted the candle on the cake.) Have children take turns creating oral or written sentences using the less familiar meanings of *plant.*

3 | Assess

√ **Lesson Checkpoint**

1. People use cotton plants to make clothing.

2. 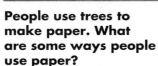 Use **picture clues.** Houses and paper are made from trees.

Lesson 4

How does Earth change?

 Science Objective

- The student understands the processes of weathering and erosion.

1 | Introduce

Quick ACTIVITY | TRANSPARENCY 30 |

Place a sugar cube or piece of hard candy in water. Have children see how long it takes the piece of candy to dissolve in the water. Tell children that the candy dissolving in water is similar to the process by which water in nature wears away, or weathers, rock over time. If possible, show children smooth, rounded weathered rocks.

Access Prior Knowledge

Ask children to remember a time when they washed dirt or mud off their hands, feet, or shoes. Ask: *Where did the soil go?* Discuss the fact that water can wash away soil. Point out that water can wash away soil on the surface of Earth.

Set Purpose

Tell children they are going to read about some changes that happen on the surface of Earth. Help them set a **purpose for reading,** such as to find out what causes the surface of Earth to change.

2 | Teach

Quick SUMMARY

- Erosion happens when rocks or soil are moved by water or wind.
- Plants can help prevent erosion.
- Weathering, caused by water and ice or temperature changes, is the breaking apart and changing of rocks.
- Digging animals can change Earth's surface.

Read pages 152–153 with children. As a class, use the illustration on page 152 to discuss the effects of erosion and how plants can help prevent erosion.

Lesson 4

How does Earth change?

Earth is always changing. Erosion can change Earth. **Erosion** happens when rocks or soil are moved by water or wind.

Plants can help prevent erosion. The roots on plants hold the soil in place.

Look at what erosion can do to a field!

152

Lesson 4 Resource

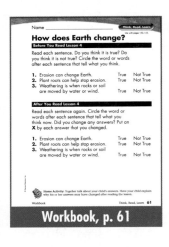

Workbook, p. 61

Weathering can change Earth too. **Weathering** is the breaking apart and changing of rocks. Water can cause weathering. Changes in temperature can cause weathering. ❶

✓ Lesson Checkpoint

1. How does weathering change Earth?

2. Writing in Science Look for erosion near where you live. Write about what you see.

Animals that dig homes in soil can change Earth too. Gophers change the shape of the land.

153

Social Studies Link

Tsunamis

A tsunami is a huge ocean wave formed by an underwater earthquake or volcano. As the waves approach shallow waters along the coast they grow and crash into the shore. A tsunami can travel up to 450 miles per hour and be as high as 100 feet. Tsunamis are sometimes referred to as "tidal waves," but tsunamis have nothing to do with tides. On December 26, 2004 a major tsunami struck a large area in Southeast Asia. Help children locate Southeast Asia on a map or globe. The tsunami caused an incredible amount of destruction. Tsunamis can cause Earth to change.

ELL Support

Weathering

Help children understand weathering by abrasion by having them rub sandpaper on soft rock specimens and observe the changes that occur.

For scaffolded instruction about weathering and erosion, use **Every Student Learns Teacher's Guide,** p. 35.

Discuss weathering, explaining that moving water can cut through soil and minerals over time. Explain to children that when temperatures drop below freezing, water in the soil and in rocks can freeze. When it freezes, it grows bigger, and this can move or break up soil. Ask children: **What other animals dig in soil?** Worms, moles, ants

Assign Quick Study pp. 60–61 to children who need help with lesson content.

Guide Comprehension

Ask children the following scaffolded questions to assess understanding.

Scaffolded Questions

❶ **Recall** *What is weathering?* Weathering is the breaking apart and changing of rocks.

❷ **Describe** *How do plants prevent erosion?* Plant roots hold soil in place.

❸ **Assess** *Which do you think would be changed more quickly by erosion, sand or rock? Why?* Possible answer: Sand, because the small pieces could easily be moved by wind or water.

Extend Vocabulary

Tell children that the word **weathering** is related to the word *weather*. Write both words on the board. Explain that weather refers to conditions of the air such as temperature, air pressure, winds, humidity, and precipitation. *Weathering* is the action of the weather conditions in changing the color, texture, composition, or form of rocks.

3 | Assess

✓ Lesson Checkpoint

1. By changing the shape and size of rocks.

2. Writing in Science Have children write their answers in their science journals. Answers will vary.

Lesson 5

How can people help protect Earth?

 Science Objectives

- The student knows ways that human activity affects the environment.
- The student knows that human beings cause changes in their environment, and these changes can be positive or negative.

1 | Introduce

Quick ACTIVITY

TRANSPARENCY 31

Tell children that pollution is the adding of harmful things to water, air, and land. Provide one example, such as throwing trash into a river. Ask children to brainstorm other possible causes of pollution, as well as ways of reducing it.

Access Prior Knowledge

Ask children to remember a place where they might have seen trash on the ground or in some other natural area. In their science journals, have children describe how they felt about this.

Set Purpose

Tell children they are going to read about ways to protect Earth. Help them set a **purpose for reading,** such as being able to understand what pollution is and how people can help reduce pollution.

2 | Teach

Quick SUMMARY

- Pollution is the adding of harmful things to land, air, or water.
- Pollution can affect living things.
- Many people are working together to reduce pollution and take care of Earth.

How can people help protect Earth?

People change the Earth by causing pollution. **Pollution** happens when something harmful is added to the land, air, or water. Pollution can cause some plants and animals to get sick or die.

Many people have started working together to help reduce pollution. They want to make sure plants and animals stay safe. They want to take care of the Earth.

This lake was once polluted.

154

Lesson 5 Resource

Name _____

Think, Read, Learn

Use with pages 154–155

How can people help protect Earth?

Before You Read Lesson 5

Read each sentence. Do you think it is true? Do you think it is not true? Circle the word or words after each sentence that tell what you think.

1. People can help reduce pollution.   True   Not True
2. Paper and plastic can be recycled.   True   Not True
3. Trees cannot be replaced.   True   Not True
4. Plants and animals are safe in a refuge.   True   Not True

After You Read Lesson 5

Read each sentence again. Circle the word or words after each sentence that tell what you think now. Did you change any answers? Put an **X** by each answer that you changed.

1. People can help reduce pollution.   True   Not True
2. Paper and plastic can be recycled.   True   Not True
3. Trees cannot be replaced.   True   Not True
4. Plants and animals are safe in a refuge.   True   Not True

Home Activity: Together talk about your child's answers. Have your child explain why his or her answers may have changed after reading the lesson.

Workbook   Think, Read, Learn **62**

Workbook, p. 62

People worked to clean up this lake. It is now safe for plants and animals.

1. ✓Checkpoint What is pollution?

2. **Health** in Science What are some ways clean water is important to people?

Science Background

Groundwater

- Groundwater fills cracks in rocks and sediments beneath Earth's surface. Most groundwater is naturally pure—more than 90 percent of the world's total supply of drinkable water is groundwater.

- Groundwater is vulnerable to pollutants that seep from landfills, septic systems, fertilized fields, leaking gasoline storage tanks, or household chemicals and pesticides that have been dumped down the drain or on the ground.

Science Misconception

Pollution Has Many Forms

Children may be surprised to learn that light can be a form of pollution. Explain that outdoor lights from parking lots, buildings, and homes make it difficult for people to get a good look at the stars. In the past, large telescopes have been built in areas where it is dark because there are very few businesses and homes. As cities have grown, however, light pollution has made it more difficult for scientists to use these telescopes to see the stars.

Read pages 154–155 with children. Discuss reasons why pollution is harmful. Point out that smokestacks once added dirty smoke to the air. Newer ones clean the smoke first. Point out that even plants and animals can be harmful in the wrong place. Discuss ways that people are working to reduce or reverse pollution: making changes in cars and smokestacks; cleaning up harbors and rivers; changing laws; and limiting the use of certain chemicals.

Assign Quick Study pp. 62–63 to children who need help with lesson content.

Guide Comprehension

Ask children the following scaffolded questions to assess understanding.

Scaffolded Questions

1 **Recall** *What is pollution?* Adding harmful things to land, air, or water

2 **Explain** *Why do people want to reduce pollution?* Pollution is harmful to plants and animals.

3 **Plan** *What can people do at home to reduce pollution?* Answers may include picking up trash, recycling, using fewer paper towels or facial tissues.

Extend Vocabulary

Write the word **pollution** on the board. Tell children that it has its derivation in Latin words meaning "through mud." Define pollution as a noun meaning "the act or process of dirtying any part of the environment." Ask children to write one sentence using the word.

Diagnostic Check

If... children have difficulty understanding the concept of pollution,

then... have them look at pictures of polluted areas and identify things they think are harmful to the environments shown.

1. ✓**Checkpoint** Pollution is adding something harmful to the land, air, or water.

2. **Health** in Science Drinking polluted water can harm people.

Science Objectives

- The student knows ways that human activity affects the environment (for example, land fills for disposal of wastes, land development for homes and industry, dams to control rivers or generate electricity).
- The student knows that human beings cause changes in their environment, and these changes can be positive or negative (for example, introducing exotic organisms, deforestation, littering, contaminating water and air).

2 Teach (continued)

Quick SUMMARY

- Trash on the ground is called litter.
- Reducing amounts of things used and reusing things are ways to prevent pollution.
- Recycling reduces pollution by changing something so it can be used again.

Read pages 156–157 with children. Explain that things thrown into a trash can eventually get taken to a landfill. The fewer things people throw away, the less quickly the landfill will fill up.

Discuss what life would be like if the water, air, and soil were dirty. Help children recognize that their quality of life would suffer. Explain to children that it is important to develop respect and responsibility for the environment. They can do that by engaging in conservation practices such as recycling, reusing, cleaning up trash, and using less power and water whenever possible. Make sure children understand their role in these processes. Make sure children understand that recycled objects may not be identical to the original objects; old tires may be recycled into roadways, for example, and plastic bottles may wind up as cloth.

Reduce, Reuse, Recycle

What are some ways people can take care of Earth? People can pick up litter on the ground. People can reduce the amount of what they use. ❸ *Reduce* means to use less. How can you reduce the amount of water you use each day?

People can reuse things. *Reuse* means to use again. How could you reuse a shoe box?

Plastic milk cartons can be recycled to make new objects.

156

Science Background

Landfills

Landfills are places where trash is dumped. Cans, bottles, plastic containers, and paper cannot be broken down quickly or at all. They remain in the ground for a very long time. Some communities cover trash with soil, allow the contents to settle, and eventually plant the area with vegetation. This allows the landfill to be used for building.

Math Link

Recycling Count

If your community has a recycling program, someone from the community may be available to speak to children about the benefits of recycling. Have children count the number of plastic, glass, and metal containers their family recycles in one day. Explain how important this effort is over periods of weeks, months, and years.

People can recycle. **Recycle** means to change something so it can be used ❶ again. Cans, glass, paper, plastic, and ❷ metal can all be recycled. Some parts of this playground were made from recycled plastic milk bottles!

1. ✓**Checkpoint** What can you do to help take care of Earth?

2. **Art** in Science Collect empty containers and other trash. Use them to make art.

157

ELL Support

Language Detectives: Compound Words

- Draw children's attention to compound words in this lesson: *something*, *shoebox*, and *playground*. Write the words on the board, explaining that each is a compound word, a word made from two smaller words. Draw a vertical line between *shoe* and *box*. Ask a volunteer to read each. Discuss the meaning of the individual words and the compound word they form. Then have children identify the words that make up *something* and *playground*.

- Ask children to have a word hunt and look for other compound words in the chapter. List several on the board, and use the word parts to figure out what each compound word means.

For scaffolded instruction about pollution and recycling, use **Every Student Learns Teacher's Guide,** p. 36.

Ask children the following scaffolded questions to assess understanding.

Scaffolded Questions

❶ **Define** *What does it mean to recycle?* Change something so it can be used again

❷ **Classify** *What kinds of things can be recycled?* Cans, glass, paper, plastic, and metal

❸ **Infer** *Why is reducing good for the environment?* If people use less, they will throw away less and keep Earth cleaner.

Extend Vocabulary

Write *cycle* and *recycle* on the board. Tell children that a cycle is a circle of events, like the life cycles of plants and animals they learned about earlier. The word **recycle** means to go through the circle of events again. When people recycle, they treat or process something again so that it can be reused. Write *use* and *reuse* on the board. Point out that reuse means to use again. Explain that the letters *re-* are a prefix, a word part that changes the meaning of the word to which it is added. Provide additional examples, such as *read/reread*, *heat/reheat*, and *build/rebuild*.

3 | Assess

1. ✓**Checkpoint** Possible answers: Pick up litter, recycle, reuse things, and reduce the amount of what is used

2. **Art** in Science Art projects will vary.

Science Objectives

- The student knows ways that human activity affects the environment.
- The student knows that human beings cause changes in their environment, and these changes can be positive or negative.

2 | Teach (continued)

Quick SUMMARY

- People cut down trees, and new trees can be replanted to replace cut trees.
- Wind and fire can kill trees, which then grow back over time.
- When people build on land, plants and animals lose their homes.
- A refuge is a safe place for plants and animals to live.

Read pages 158–159 with children. Ask children to brainstorm a list of animals that live in or near trees. Have children think about what might happen to these animals if the trees are not replanted.

Point out that fires can be started by people or by lightning that happens during a thunderstorm. Ask what happens to trees that are destroyed by wind and fire. (They grow back.) Ask how else humans can change land. (They can build on it.) If possible, mention local areas that were once wild but are now built upon.

Protecting Plants and Animals

Chop! People cut down trees. Some animals live in trees. People plant new trees. Animals can make their homes in the new trees.

Campfires can turn into forest fires. Always put out campfires.

Wind and fire can kill trees. New trees start to grow back after a forest fire. These new trees might grow big and tall.

158

Science Background

Wildfire Prevention Tips

Tell children that forest fires can be started by people who are careless with campfires. Sparks from running cars, fireworks, and burning trash can also cause forest fires. Discuss how fires can cause habitat destruction. Explain that people can replant forests after a fire, which is called reforestation. This is one way of taking care of Earth.

Provide these wildfire prevention tips.

- Build the campfire on bare soil away from overhanging branches, dry grass, and leaves.
- Circle the campfire pit with rocks and keep a bucket of water and a shovel nearby.
- To put out a campfire, drown it in water, stir it, and then drown it again.
- Never leave a campfire unattended.
- Never play with matches.

People build homes and factories on land. Plants and animals that lived on the land may have no place to go. People take plants and animals to a refuge. A refuge is a safe place to live. People cannot build on a refuge. ③

This bird lives in a refuge in Florida. People can see plants and animals at the refuge.

✓ **Lesson Checkpoint**

1. What are some ways people can help protect plants and animals?

2. **Technology** in Science Read an article about wildfires on the Internet.

SCAFFOLDED INQUIRY

Investigate How do worms change the soil?

★ **Science Objective**

- The student keeps science records.

1 | Build Background

This activity encourages children to observe worms processing compost.

Managing Time and Materials

Time: 15 minutes initially, and 10 minutes once a week for 3 weeks

Groups: small groups

Materials: *2 resealable plastic bags, (10 × 12 in); potting soil (6 c); 3 earthworms (live materials coupon); plastic gloves (1 pair per child); crumbled dried leaves ($\frac{1}{4}$ c);* hole punch (teacher use)

Materials listed in *italic* are kit materials.

Advance Preparation

Use the live materials coupon to order earthworms 2 weeks in advance. For each group, prepare 2 bags with 3 c of damp soil in each. Collect enough dried leaves so that each group has about $\frac{1}{4}$ cup crumbled leaves. Use a hole punch or scissors to make holes near the top of each bag.

Safety Notes

Be sure children wash hands after handling worms. To protect native wildlife, do not release the living organisms into the environment.

2 | What to Do

Encourage Guided Inquiry

Preview the activity and the materials with children. Ask: ***What would happen if you observed compost bags with worms and compost bags without worms for 3 weeks?***

Guide children to write an If.../then...statement such as: **If I observe a compost bag with worms and a compost bag without worms for 3 weeks, then fewer leaves will appear in the bag with worms.**

Investigate How do worms change the soil?

Compost is a mixture of soil with other things like leaves and grass. How will worms change compost?

Materials

plastic gloves

bags with soil

leaves

worms

Process Skills

Filling in a chart can help you **collect data**.

What to Do

❶ Wear gloves. Put leaves in both bags.

❷ Put worms in one bag.

Be sure to close the bags.

Activity Resources

Name _____

Investigate How do worms change the soil?

❶ **Collect Data** Draw what happens inside the bags.

Compost Bags

	Bag With Worms	Bag Without Worms
Week 1		
Week 2		
Week 3		

Activity Book   Guided Inquiry **63**

Name _____

Activity Rubric

Investigate: How do worms change the soil?

Scoring Criteria	1	2	3	4
Student followed directions to complete this activity.				
Student **observed** the compost bags for three weeks.				
Student **collected data** by making drawings in chart for three weeks.				
Student **inferred** that worms "ate" the leaves and incorporated the leaves into the soil.				
Student reported that the bag without worms had more leaves after three weeks.				

Scoring Key

4 points correct, complete, detailed
3 points partially correct, complete, detailed
2 points partially correct, partially complete, lacks some detail
1 point incorrect or incomplete, needs assistance

Activity Book   Guided Inquiry **175**

Activity Book, pp. 63–64

Activity Rubric

Use Activity DVD Unit B, Chapter 5 to preview this activity.

Call 1-888-537-4908 with activity questions.

More Lab zone **Activities** **Take It to the Net** pearsonsuccessnet.com

Find more about this activity at our Web site.

- See the **Teacher's Activity Guide** for more support.
- An alternative activity is also available to download.

3 **Observe** the bags for 3 weeks.

The worms are alive! Handle with care.

4 **Collect Data** Draw a chart like the one below to show what happens inside the bags.

Compost Bags		
	With Worms	**Without Worms**
Week 1		
Week 2		
Week 3		

Explain Your Results

1. Which bag had more leaves after 3 weeks?
2. **Infer** What happened to the leaves?

┌─ **Go Further** ─┐
What will happen if you use more worms? Investigate to find out.
└─────────────┘

161

Engage Have children look at a photograph of an earthworm and discuss its physical characteristics.

Explore Have children follow the steps to set up the compost bags. As children are setting up the bags, ask them to explain why composting is a good thing for the environment. Children should observe the bags for 3 weeks and record their data in the data chart.

Explain Children should understand that as the worms burrow through the soil, leaves may be mixed into the soil. Parts of some leaves may be eaten and digested by the worms.

Extend Have the class make one large compost bin with all of their worms in a large plastic tub. This way, children can see composting on a larger scale.

Evaluate Have students summarize the changes and possible causes for the changes in the compost bag with worms.

3 | Explain Your Results

Use the "Explain Your Results" questions to help children review evidence and develop explanations.

- Give children an opportunity to reflect on the data, or evidence, they have gathered in the investigation.

- Have children use the evidence gathered to develop their explanations. Accept reasonable, logical explanations.

1. The bag without worms.
2. **Infer** The worms may have mixed the leaves in the soil, and may have eaten parts of the leaves.

Go Further

Children may propose any number of changes to the activity to fully understand how worms are useful in the creation of compost. Children may modify the number of worms placed in the compost bag to see how this will change the composition of the compost.

Process Skills

Collect Data

Discuss the importance of being able to collect data. Remind children that the goal of science is to help us understand the world around us. Scientists can use data they have collected to help explain things they observe. You can use the Process Skills sheet on Collecting Data at this time.

Science Background

Earthworms

Earthworms eat organic material left in the soil. The waste from the worms becomes compost. Each worm's waste contains nitrogen and other nutrients necessary for plant growth. When added to the soil, worm compost increases nutrient availability and improves soil structure and drainage. In addition to making the soil fertile, earthworms are natural soil tillers. They mix layers of soil while producing tunnels in the soil to help air and water reach plant roots.

ELL Support

Access Content Before beginning the activity, conduct an inventory of materials with children. Solicit other names for each item. Accept labels in English and children's home languages.

Math in Science

Recycling Bar Graph

Science Objective

• The student displays solutions to problems by generating, collecting, organizing, and analyzing data using simple graphs and charts.

1 | Introduce

Quick ACTIVITY

Place two similar but unequal piles of small objects, such as game counters or pennies, on a table. Each pile should contain just enough items so children cannot instantly tell which is larger. Ask children to guess which pile contains more. Then lay out the objects in two rows. Discuss why it is easier to determine quantity when the information is organized.

2 | Teach the Skill

Read pages 162–163 with children.

Before children do this activity, have them identify the different parts of the graph and what each represents. Have volunteers read aloud the title, the labels, and the numerals. Ask what the numerals represent.

Demonstrate how children can determine the number of cans that Mrs. Lee's class recycled.

Math in Science

Recycling Bar Graph

Nelson School wants to help keep the environment clean. The second graders decided to recycle cans.

Read the bar graph to find out how many cans each second-grade class recycled in one week.

1. How many cans did Mr. Green's class recycle?
2. How many more cans did Mrs. Hill's class recycle than Mr. Green's class? Write a number sentence.

162 **e Tools** Take It to the Net
pearsonsuccessnet.com

Activity Resource

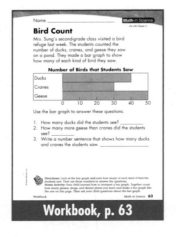

Bird Count

Mrs. Sung's second-grade class visited a bird refuge last week. The students counted the number of ducks, cranes, and geese they saw on a pond. They made a bar graph to show how many of each kind of bird they saw.

Number of Birds that Students Saw

Ducks
Cranes
Geese
0   10   20   30   40   50

Use the bar graph to answer these questions.

1. How many ducks did the students see? _____
2. How many more geese than cranes did the students see? _____
3. Write a number sentence that shows how many ducks and cranes the students saw.

Workbook, p. 63

e Tools Take It to the Net
pearsonsuccessnet.com

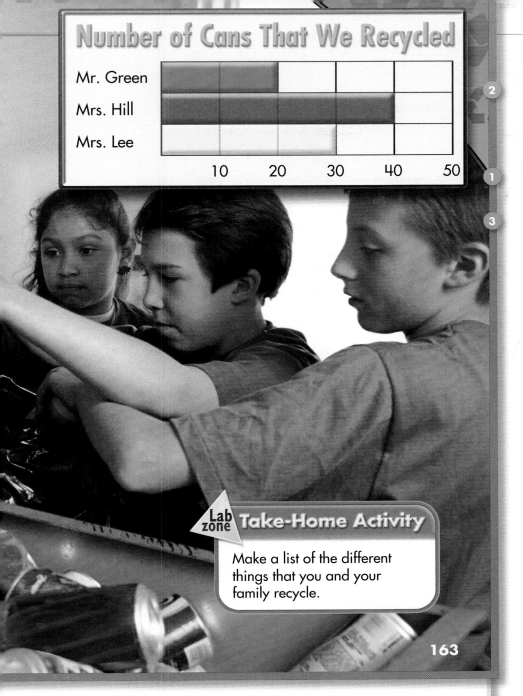

Number of Cans That We Recycled

	10	20	30	40	50
Mr. Green					
Mrs. Hill					
Mrs. Lee					

Lab zone **Take-Home Activity**

Make a list of the different things that you and your family recycle.

163

Vocabulary

1. D
2. B
3. E
4. C
5. A
6. F

What did you learn?

7. Possible answers: sunlight, water, soil, minerals, trees, oil, coal, and air
8. Erosion changes Earth by moving rocks or soil.

Chapter 5 Review and Test Prep

Vocabulary
Which picture goes with each word?

1. boulder
2. mineral
3. erosion
4. sand
5. recycle
6. pollution

What did you learn?

7. Name some of Earth's natural resources.
8. How does erosion change Earth?

Assessment Resources

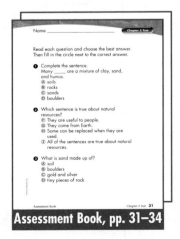

Assessment Book, pp. 31–34

 MindPoint Quiz Show

MindPoint enables students to test their knowledge of the chapter in a game format.

 **ExamView** Use ExamView as a print or online assessment tool to create alternative tests for students.

Success Tracker

Data management system to track Adequate Yearly Progress (AYP) and provide intervention online at **pearsonsuccessnet.com/ successtracker**

Take-Home Booklet

Children can make a Take-Home Booklet using Workbook pp. 65–66.

9. **Observe** Look at a plant outside. Describe the soil.

⊙ Picture Clues

10. **Use picture clues** Tell how people use air.

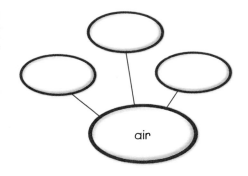

air

Test Prep

Fill in the circle next to the correct answer.

11. What do people make from cotton?

Ⓐ furniture
Ⓑ maple syrup
Ⓒ clothes
Ⓓ playgrounds

12. **Writing** in Science List some things people throw away. Tell how you could reuse one of those things.

165

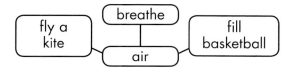
9. **Observe** Possible answer: The soil is made of sand and humus. If necessary, have children review the physical characteristics of sand, humus, and clay.

10. ⊙ **Picture Clues**

fly a kite — breathe — air — fill basketball

Test Prep

11. C

12. **Writing** in Science Answers will vary, but might include paper, cans, and milk bottles. Paper could be reused as scrap paper if it was turned over.

Intervention and Remediation

⭐ Science Objectives	Review Item	Student Edition Pages	Teacher Edition Resources				Ancillary Resources		
			Guide Comprehension	Extend Vocab	Diagnostic Check	Vocab Cards	Quick Study	Workbook Pages
The student knows some of Earth's natural resources, including land, air, and water; and identifies renewable and nonrenewable sources.	7	142–143	143, 145, 147	143	143	•	143	58
The student knows selected resources used by people for water, food, and shelter are limited and necessary for their survival.		144–145	143, 145, 151		143			
The student extends and refines knowledge that the surface of the Earth is composed of different types of solid materials that come in all sizes.	9	146–149	147, 149	149	147	•	147	59
The student knows some ways people use natural resources.	9, 11	150–151	145, 147, 151	147			150	60
The student describes ways that Earth changes.	8	152–153	153	153		•	153	61
The student knows ways that human activity affects the environment.	12	154–159	155, 159	155	155	•	155	62
The student knows that human beings cause changes in their environment, and these changes can be positive or negative.	12	154–159	155, 157, 159	155, 157, 159	155	•	155	62

Feature

Looking out for Earth

⭐ **Science Objective**

- The student knows that scientists and technologists use a variety of tools such as satellites.

1 | Introduce

Quick ACTIVITY

Look at the pictures on pages 166 and 167. Explain to children that a satellite is something that goes around Earth and sends and receives signals. Satellites allow us to send and receive signals and pictures from space.

2 | Teach

Quick SUMMARY

- NASA scientists send satellites into space on rockets.
- Satellites take pictures of Earth from space.
- Crops and forest fires can be tracked with satellites.

Read pages 166 and 167 together with children. Examine the pictures on page 166 to show children that satellites can take important pictures from space. Satellite pictures show plants growing, dirty air over cities, and forest fires. Tell children that satellites are also useful in tracking large storms like hurricanes.

Have children look at the pictures of the satellites shown on page 167. Ask children: **How are these satellites similar?** (They are metal, have antennas, and revolve around Earth.) **How are they different?** (They have different shapes and sizes.) You may wish to show children more pictures of different types of satellites.

Looking out for Earth

Many satellites move around Earth. NASA scientists send satellites to space. Scientists use satellites to take pictures of Earth's natural resources. Satellite pictures can show dirty air over cities. The satellite pictures can also show how well crops are growing. Spotting forest fires is easier from satellites too.

The smoky area shows a forest fire.

A satellite takes pictures of new plants.

166

Science Background

Sputnik

On October 4, 1957, the Soviet Union launched the first artificial satellite, Sputnik 1, into space. Sputnik 2 was launched less than a month later and was the first satellite to orbit Earth with a life form, a dog named Laika. Sputnik 3 was launched on May 15, 1958. The United States launched its first satellite, Explorer 1, on January 31, 1958. America quickly launched a wide variety of satellites, including the early Tiros weather satellite and communications satellites. Today there are thousands of satellites orbiting Earth at different heights.

Help from Satellites

Satellites provide firefighters with up-to-date maps and satellite images that help them plan their response to forest fires. The size of the fire is easier to see and watch from space. Satellites also provide information about floods, hurricanes, and volcanic eruptions.

Take-Home Activity

NASA satellites take pictures of Earth. Draw a picture of what you think Earth looks like from space.

167

3 | Explore

Tell children that there are other objects besides satellites that are revolving around Earth. The International Space Station (ISS) is a research station orbiting Earth that is dedicated to performing experiments in space. The ISS is a place where astronauts will learn how to live and work away from Earth's gravity. The 16 countries participating in the ISS program are the United States, Russia, Japan, Brazil, Canada, Belgium, Denmark, France, Germany, Italy, Netherlands, Norway, Spain, Sweden, Switzerland, and United Kingdom.

Take-Home Activity

Tips for Success

- Assist children in writing down the assignment and making sure they clearly understand the nature of the assignment.

- Encourage children to use colored pencils to make their drawings colorful and attractive.

- Have children bring their completed drawings to school to present to their classmates.

- Post children's work on a wall or bulletin board.

Forester

 Science Objective

- The student knows that human beings cause changes in their environment, and these changes can be positive (for example, creating refuges, replanting deforested regions, creating laws to restrict burning) or negative (for example, introducing exotic organisms, deforestation, littering, contaminating water and air).

1 | Introduce

Build Background

Ask children to think about a time that they visited or saw a forest. Ask children to describe the plants and animals they saw in the forest and draw a picture showing them.

2 | Teach

Quick SUMMARY

- Foresters help build roads in the forest, prevent forest fires, plant new trees, and decide how trees will be cut down in the forest.

Read page 168 together with children. Explain that many plants and animals live in the forest and that foresters play an important role in protecting them. Ask children to describe things people can do to help prevent forest fires.

3 | Explore

Look at a state or national map to identify areas close to children that contain forests. Show children pictures of different types of forests such as temperate, tropical rain, pine or redwood forests. Ask children: **How are these forests alike? How are they different?** (All contain trees and other plants, and animals, but these living things are different from one forest to another.) Explain to children that all states contain some forest land, and it is the job of the forester to make sure that each forest with its plants and animals is protected and healthy.

Career

Forester

Read Together

Foresters have many jobs. They build roads in forests. They work to prevent forest fires. They decide how many trees can be cut. They plant new trees.

Foresters study forests and learn how to keep them healthy. They help protect plants and animals that live in forests. Foresters teach other people how to be safe in the forest.

Lab zone Take-Home Activity

Tell what job you would like to do if you were a forester. Tell your family about how your job would help the forest.

168

Take-Home Activity

Tips for Success

- Assist children in writing down the assignment and making sure they clearly understand the nature of the assignment.
- Have children share their stories with classmates.

Leveled Readers and Leveled Practice

Leveled Readers deliver the same concepts and skills as the chapter. Use Leveled Readers for original instruction or for needed reteaching.

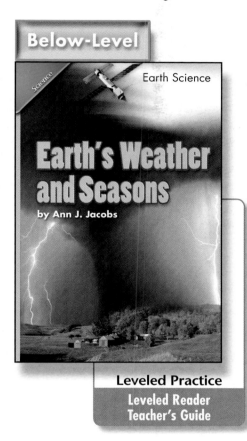

Below-Level

Earth Science

Earth's Weather and Seasons

by Ann J. Jacobs

Leveled Practice

Leveled Reader Teacher's Guide

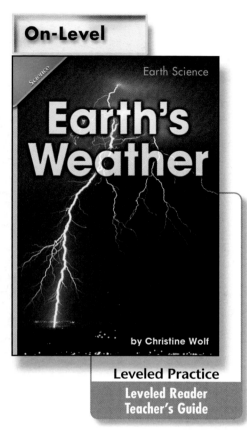

On-Level

Earth Science

Earth's Weather

by Christine Wolf

Leveled Practice

Leveled Reader Teacher's Guide

Advanced

Earth Science

How Clouds Are Made

by Marilyn Greco

Leveled Practice

Leveled Reader Teacher's Guide

Below-Level Leveled Reader has the same content as Chapter 6, but is written at a less difficult reading level.

On-Level Leveled Reader has the same concepts as Chapter 6, and is written at grade level.

Advanced Leveled Reader is above grade level and enriches the chapter with additional examples and extended ideas.

Leveled Reader Database

Scott Foresman
pearsonsuccessnet.com

Use the online database to search for additional leveled readers by level, title, content, and skill.

Key Content and Skill in Leveled Readers and Chapter 6

Content	Vocabulary		Target Reading Skill	Graphic Organizer
Earth's Weather and Seasons	water cycle condense hibernate tornado	evaporate migrate lightning hurricane	Draw Conclusions	I know → My conclusion

Chapter 6 Planning Guide

Essential Question: How does weather change?

Lesson/Activity		Pacing	Science Objectives
Build Background	pp. 169–171	20 minutes	• The student identifies words and constructs meaning from text, illustrations, graphics, and charts using the strategies of phonics, word structure, and context clues.
Lab zone Flip Chart Activity What happens when cold air meets warm air?			
Lab zone Flip Chart Activity How can you tell that water is moving?			
Lab zone Directed Inquiry			• The student knows that people use scientific processes including hypothesis, making inferences, and recording and communicating data when exploring the natural world.
Explore How much rain falls?	p. 172	15 minutes	
How to Read Science	p. 173	20 minutes	• The student makes connections and inferences based on text and prior knowledge.
1 What are some kinds of weather?	pp. 174–177	30 minutes	• The student knows that weather conditions occur in patterns over time.
2 What is the water cycle?	pp. 178–179	20 minutes	• The student knows that most natural events occur in patterns.
3 What is spring?	pp. 180–181	20 minutes	• The student knows that weather conditions occur in patterns over time.
4 What is summer?	pp. 182–183	20 minutes	• The student knows that weather conditions occur in patterns over time.
5 What is fall?	pp. 184–185	20 minutes	• The student knows that weather conditions occur in patterns over time.
6 What is winter?	pp. 186–187	20 minutes	• The student knows that weather conditions occur in patterns over time.
7 What are some kinds of bad weather?	pp. 188–193	40 minutes	• The student recognizes patterns in weather.
Lab zone Guided Inquiry			• The student keeps science records.
Investigate How can you measure weather changes?	pp. 194–195	10 minutes per day for 5 days	• The student uses a variety of tools to observe, measure, analyze and predict changes in size, mass, temperature, color, position, quantity, sound, and movement.
Wrap-Up Chapter 6	pp. 196–200		• The student uses mathematical language to read and interpret data on a simple concrete graph, pictorial graph, or chart.
Math in Science: Favorite Seasons		20 minutes	
Chapter 6 Review and Test Prep		20 minutes	
NASA Career: Atmospheric Scientist		20 minutes	

Vocabulary/Skills	Assessment/Intervention	Resources/Technology
Process Skills: Observe Interpret Data Communicate Infer	• Chapter Review, SE, pp. 198–199	• Science Content Transparency 6 • Workbook, p. 67 • Graphic Organizer Transparency 7 • Vocabulary Cards • Activity Book, pp. 73–74
Process Skill: Infer ⊙ Target Reading Skill: **Draw Conclusions**	• Explain Your Results, SE, p. 172 • Activity Rubric ⊙ **Draw Conclusions,** SE, p. 173	• Activity Book, pp. 69–70 • Activity DVD • Workbook, pp. 68–69 • Every Student Learns, p. 37 • Activity Placemat 12
	• Scaffolded Questions, TE, pp. 175, 177 • Checkpoint Questions, SE, p. 177 • Chapter Review, SE, pp. 198–199 (9)	• Workbook, p. 70 • Quick Study, pp. 64–65 • Every Student Learns, p. 38
water cycle evaporate condense	• Scaffolded Questions, TE, pp. 179 • Checkpoint Questions, SE, p. 179 • Chapter Review, SE, pp. 198–199 (7, 11) ⊙ **Draw Conclusions,** SE, p. 179	• Workbook, p. 71 • Quick Study, pp. 66–67 • Every Student Learns, p. 39
	• Scaffolded Questions, TE, p. 181 • Checkpoint Questions, SE, p. 180 • Chapter Review, SE, pp. 198–199 (12)	• Workbook, p. 72 • Quick Study, pp. 68–69 • Every Student Learns, p. 40
	• Scaffolded Questions, TE, p. 183 • Checkpoint Questions, SE, p. 182 • Chapter Review, SE, pp. 198–199 (8, 12)	• Workbook, p. 73 • Quick Study, pp. 70–71 • Every Student Learns, p. 41
migrate	• Scaffolded Questions, TE, p. 185 • Checkpoint Questions, SE, p. 184 • Chapter Review, SE, pp. 198–199 (12) ⊙ **Draw Conclusions,** SE, p. 184	• Workbook, p. 74 • Quick Study, pp. 72–73 • Every Student Learns, p. 42
hibernate	• Scaffolded Questions, TE, p. 187 • Checkpoint Questions, SE, p. 186 • Chapter Review, SE, pp. 198–199 (3, 12)	• Workbook, p. 75 • Quick Study, pp. 74–75 • Every Student Learns, p. 43
lightning tornado hurricane	• Scaffolded Questions, TE, pp. 189, 191, 193 • Checkpoint Questions, SE, pp. 188, 190, 192 • Chapter Review, SE, pp. 198–199 (1, 2, 5) ⊙ **Draw Conclusions,** SE, p. 192	• Workbook, p. 76 • Quick Study, pp. 76–77 • Every Student Learns, p. 44
Process Skills: Collect Data, Interpret Data	• Explain Your Results, SE, p. 195 • Activity Rubric	• Activity Book, pp. 71–72 • Activity DVD • Activity Placemat 13
Math Skill: Make a Graph	• Scaffolded Questions, TE, p. 197 ⊙ **Draw Conclusions,** SE, p. 199 **ExamView®** Chapter 6 Test **Success Tracker** pearsonsuccessnet.com/ successtracker	• Workbook, pp. 77, 79–80 • Assessment Book, pp. 35–38

Quick | Teaching Plan

If time is short . . .
- Build Background, pp. 170–171
- Explore Activity, p. 172
- How to Read Science, p. 173
- Lesson 1, pp. 174–177
- Lesson 2, pp. 178–179
- Lesson 7, pp. 188–193

Other quick options . . .

Quick ACTIVITY

TE pp. 174, 178, 180, 182, 184, 186, 188

TRANSPARENCIES 32, 33, 34, 35, 36, 37, 38

Quick SUMMARY

TE pp. 174, 176, 178, 180, 182, 184, 186, 188, 190, 192

Chapter 6
Activity Guide

 Children learn to ask and answer scientific questions as they progress to greater independence in scaffolded inquiry.

 Directed Inquiry   A Directed Inquiry activity begins each chapter.

 Guided Inquiry   A Guided Inquiry activity closes each chapter.

 Full Inquiry   Experiments and Science Fair Projects at the end of each unit provide opportunities for Full Inquiry.

Lab zone Directed Inquiry

 Explore   How much rain falls? p. 172

🕐 **Time**   15 minutes

🧍 **Grouping**   small groups

Advance Preparation   Cut a 14 cm piece of masking tape for each group.

Materials   *tall clear plastic jar (12 oz cylinder); masking tape (1½ in. wide); metric ruler; black pencil*

Alternative Materials   Tall plastic bottles with flat bottoms can be used instead of tall jars. Use scissors to cut off the top of each bottle. If 1½ in. wide masking tape is not available, use 2 strips of ¾ in. masking tape side by side.

Teaching Tips   The jar must be secured when it is put outside to make sure it doesn't tip over. You can tape an old wooden ruler or a dowel to the side of the jar with masking tape. Then stick the end of the ruler or dowel into the ground.

What to Expect   The completed rain gauge will show markings that will measure rainfall in centimeters. Children will infer that the marks indicate how much rain has fallen.

 Activity DVD   Unit B, Chapter 6

 Activity Placemat   Mat 12

Lab zone Guided Inquiry

 Investigate   How can you measure weather changes? pp. 194–195

🕐 **Time**   10 minutes per day for 5 days

🧍 **Grouping**   small groups

Materials   *rain gauge (whole class use); thermometer (alcohol)*

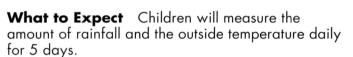

Alternative Materials   You may wish to use the rain gauges made in the Directed Inquiry activity.

What to Expect   Children will measure the amount of rainfall and the outside temperature daily for 5 days.

Safety Note   The thermometers do not contain mercury.

 Activity DVD   Unit B, Chapter 6

Activity Placemat   Mat 13

Other Resources

The following Resources are available for activities found in the Student Edition.

Demonstration Kit   If you wish to rehearse or demonstrate the Chapter 6 activities, use the materials provided in the Demonstration Kit.

Classroom Equipment Kit
Materials shown in *italic print* are available in the Classroom Equipment Kit.

Activity Placemats   The Equipment Kit includes an Activity Placemat for each activity, a work surface which identifies the materials that need to be gathered.

Quick ACTIVITY

Transparencies   Each lesson starts with a Quick Activity. Use the Quick Activity Overhead Transparencies to focus children's attention on each task.

Teacher's Activity Guide   For detailed information about Inquiry Activities, access the Teacher's Activity Guide at **pearsonsuccessnet.com**.

Activity Flip Chart

What happens when cold air meets warm air?

This center activity supports the chapter as a whole.

Activity Flip Chart, p. 11

Process Skills   Observe, interpret data, communicate

 Time   20 minutes

 Grouping   Individual or pairs

Materials   2 clear glass mason jars; warm water; cold water; red and blue food coloring; ice cubes; plastic spoon

Procedure

- Discuss what condensation is and what happens when warm and cold air meet.
- Ask children to **communicate** how they know the water on the outside of the jar did not come from the water inside the jar.
- Children should **interpret data** by explaining what they **observe**.

What to Expect   Children will observe that condensation forms on the outside of the cold jar (the one with blue water).

Think About It

1. Condensation formed on the outside of the jar with the blue (cold) water. The jar with the red (warm) water did not change or had only a small amount of condensation.

2. Water vapor in the warm air condensed onto the outside of the cold glass jar. The temperature difference was not as great with the warm jar so little or no water condensed there.

Activity Flip Chart

How can you tell that water is moving?

Use this center activity after teaching Lesson 2 of the chapter.

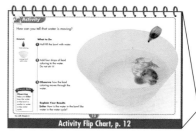
Activity Flip Chart, p. 12

Process Skills   Observe, infer

 Time   10 minutes

 Grouping   Individual or pairs

Materials   mixing bowl; green food coloring (or any color); water

Procedure

- Review the stages of the water cycle. Point out that this activity shows that water is always moving, even if it looks like it is not at first. The motion of water is a large part of every step of the water cycle.
- Make sure children do not shake or stir the water after adding the food coloring drops. Children will **observe** the movement of the green food coloring and **infer** that the water is moving in the bowl.

What to Expect   The green color will change shape and position within the water. Children will observe water moving in the bowl and infer how it is similar to the water in the water cycle.

Think About It   The water in the bowl is similar to the water in the water cycle because it is always moving.

Chapter 6 Workbook Support

Online Teacher's Edition
pearsonsuccessnet.com

Use the following Workbook pages to support content and skill development as you teach Chapter 6. You can also view and print Workbook pages from the Online Teacher's Edition.

Use with Build Background, pp. 170–171

Name _____

Vocabulary Preview
Use with Chapter 6.

Draw a picture or write a sentence to go with each word.

tornado	hurricane
water cycle	lightning
evaporate	migrate
condense	hibernate

Directions: Read the words and draw pictures to illustrate them or write sentences about them. Cut out the boxes to use as word cards.
Home Activity: Ask your child to explain the difference between a *tornado* and a *hurricane* and between animals that *migrate* and animals that *hibernate*. Have your child tell how *evaporate* and *condense* are related to the water cycle.

Workbook   Vocabulary Preview **67**

Workbook, p. 67

Use with How to Read Science, p. 173

Name _____

How To Read Science
Use with Chapter 6.

Draw Conclusions
Look at the picture.

Science Picture

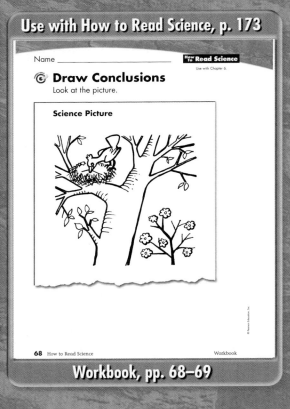

68 How to Read Science   Workbook

Workbook, pp. 68–69

Use with Lesson 1, pp. 174–177

Name _____

Think, Read, Learn
Use with pages 175–177.

What are some kinds of weather?

Before You Read Lesson 1

Read each sentence. Do you think it is true? Do you think it is not true? Circle the word or words after each sentence that tell what you think.

1. Weather can be hot or cold and wet or dry.   True   Not True
2. Sleet is one kind of wet weather.   True   Not True
3. Snow falls when the air is very warm. True   Not True

After You Read Lesson 1

Read each sentence again. Circle the word or words after each sentence that tell what you think now. Did you change any answers? Put an **X** by each answer that you changed.

1. Weather can be hot or cold and wet or dry.   (True)   Not True
2. Sleet is one kind of wet weather.   (True)   Not True
3. Snow falls when the air is very warm. True   (Not True)

Home Activity: Together talk about your child's answers. Have your child explain why his or her answers may have changed after reading the lesson.

Workbook   Think, Read, Learn **70**

Workbook, p. 70

Use with Lesson 2, pp. 178–179

Name _____

Think, Read, Learn
Use with pages 178–179.

What is the water cycle?

Before You Read Lesson 2

Read each sentence. Do you think it is true? Do you think it is not true? Circle the word or words after each sentence that tell what you think.

1. Clouds are not part of the water cycle.   True   Not True
2. Some water changes into water vapor.   True   Not True
3. Water vapor condenses when it gets cold.   True   Not True

After You Read Lesson 2

Read each sentence again. Circle the word or words after each sentence that tell what you think now. Did you change any answers? Put an **X** by each answer that you changed.

1. Clouds are not part of the water cycle.   True   (Not True)
2. Some water changes into water vapor.   (True)   Not True
3. Water vapor condenses when it gets cold.   (True)   Not True

Home Activity: Together talk about your child's answers. Have your child explain why his or her answers may have changed after reading the lesson.

Workbook   Think, Read, Learn **71**

Workbook, p. 71

Use with Lesson 3, pp. 180–181

Name _____

Think, Read, Learn
Use with pages 180–181.

What is spring?

Before You Read Lesson 3

Read each sentence. Do you think it is true? Do you think it is not true? Circle the word or words after each sentence that tell what you think.

1. Spring is one of the four seasons.   True   Not True
2. Spring days are very hot.   True   Not True
3. Many animals have babies.   True   Not True

After You Read Lesson 3

Read each sentence again. Circle the word or words after each sentence that tell what you think now. Did you change any answers? Put an **X** by each answer that you changed.

1. Spring is one of the four seasons.   (True)   Not True
2. Spring days are very hot.   True   (Not True)
3. Many animals have babies.   (True)   Not True

Home Activity: Together talk about your child's answers. Have your child explain why his or her answers may have changed after reading the lesson.

Workbook   Think, Read, Learn **72**

Workbook, p. 72

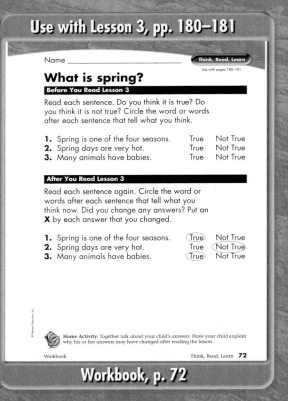

Use with Lesson 4, pp. 182–183

Name _____   **Think, Read, Learn**
Use with pages 182–183.

What is summer?

Before You Read Lesson 4

Read each sentence. Do you think it is true? Do you think it is not true? Circle the word or words after each sentence that tell what you think.

1. Summer is cooler than spring.   True   Not True
2. Summer has a lot of daylight hours.   True   Not True
3. Many trees grow green leaves
   in summer.   True   Not True

After You Read Lesson 4

Read each sentence again. Circle the word or words after each sentence that tell what you think now. Did you change any answers? Put an **X** by each answer that you changed.

1. Summer is cooler than spring.   True   (Not True)
2. Summer has a lot of daylight hours.   (True)   Not True
3. Many trees grow green leaves
   in summer.   (True)   Not True

 Home Activity: Together talk about your child's answers. Have your child explain why his or her answers may have changed after reading the lesson.

Workbook   Think, Read, Learn **73**

Workbook, p. 73

Use with Lesson 5, pp. 184–185

Name _____   **Think, Read, Learn**
Use with pages 184–185.

What is fall?

Before You Read Lesson 5

Read each sentence. Do you think it is true? Do you think it is not true? Circle the word or words after each sentence that tell what you think.

1. Fall is cooler than summer.   True   Not True
2. Fall has more daylight hours than
   summer.   True   Not True
3. Some animals start to get ready for
   the winter.   True   Not True

After You Read Lesson 5

Read each sentence again. Circle the word or words after each sentence that tell what you think now. Did you change any answers? Put an **X** by each answer that you changed.

1. Fall is cooler than summer.   (True)   Not True
2. Fall has more daylight hours than
   summer.   True   (Not True)
3. Some animals start to get ready for
   the winter.   (True)   Not True

 Home Activity: Together talk about your child's answers. Have your child explain why his or her answers may have changed after reading the lesson.

Workbook   Think, Read, Learn **74**

Workbook, p. 74

Use with Lesson 6, pp. 186–187

Name _____   **Think, Read, Learn**
Use with pages 186–187.

What is winter?

Before You Read Lesson 6

Read each sentence. Do you think it is true? Do you think it is not true? Circle the word or words after each sentence that tell what you think.

1. Winter is colder than fall.   True   Not True
2. Leaves change color in the winter.   True   Not True
3. Some animals sleep through the
   winter.   True   Not True

After You Read Lesson 6

Read each sentence again. Circle the word or words after each sentence that tell what you think now. Did you change any answers? Put an **X** by each answer that you changed.

1. Winter is colder than fall.   (True)   Not True
2. Leaves change color in the winter.   True   (Not True)
3. Some animals sleep through the
   winter.   (True)   Not True

Home Activity: Together talk about your child's answers. Have your child explain why his or her answers may have changed after reading the lesson.

Workbook   Think, Read, Learn **75**

Workbook, p. 75

Use with Lesson 7, pp. 188–193

Name _____   **Think, Read, Learn**
Use with pages 188–193.

What are some kinds of bad weather?

Before You Read Lesson 7

Read each sentence. Do you think it is true? Do you think it is not true? Circle the word or words after each sentence that tell what you think.

1. A thunderstorm has lightning.   True   Not True
2. Tornadoes are hard to predict.   True   Not True
3. Tornadoes have heavy rains but
   no winds.   True   Not True
4. Hurricanes have strong winds
   but no rain.   True   Not True

After You Read Lesson 7

Read each sentence again. Circle the word or words after each sentence that tell what you think now. Did you change any answers? Put an **X** by each answer that you changed.

1. A thunderstorm has lightning.   (True)   Not True
2. Tornadoes are hard to predict.   (True)   Not True
3. Tornadoes have heavy rains but
   no winds.   True   (Not True)
4. Hurricanes have strong winds
   but no rain.   True   (Not True)

Home Activity: Together talk about your child's answers. Have your child explain why his or her answers may have changed after reading the lesson.

Workbook   Think, Read, Learn **76**

Workbook, p. 76

Use with Math in Science, pp. 196–197

Name _____   **Math in Science**
Use with Chapter 6.

Weather Reports

Mr. Hanson's second-grade class did reports on kinds of bad weather. They made a graph to show how many students reported on each kind of bad weather.

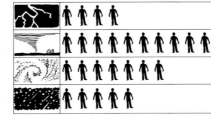

Look at the graph. Answer the questions.

1. How many students reported on hurricanes? ___7___
2. How many more students reported on tornadoes than
   on blizzards? ___5 more___
3. Use <, >, or =. Compare how many students reported
   on thunderstorms to how many students reported on
   hurricanes. ___4 < 7___

Directions: Look at the graph. Count how many students reported on each kind of bad weather. Use those numbers to answer the questions.
Home Activity: Your child learned how to use a graph. Ask family and friends which of the four kinds of bad weather they have experienced. With your child, make a graph like the one on the page to show the information.

Workbook   Math in Science **77**

Workbook, p. 77

Chapter 6 Assessment Support

Use the following Assessment Book pages and ExamView to assess Chapter 6 content. You can also view and print Assessment Book pages from the Online Teacher's Edition.

Assessment Options

Formal Assessment

- Chapter Review and Test Prep, SE pp. 198–199
- Assessment Book, pp. 35–38
- Prescriptions for remediation are shown on TE p. 199

Performance Assessment

- Unit Wrap-Up, SE pp. 226–227

Ongoing Assessment

- Diagnostic Check, TE pp. 175, 189
- Scaffolded Questions, TE pp. 175, 177, 179, 181, 183, 185, 187, 189, 191, 193, 197

Portfolio Assessment

- My Science Journal, TE pp. 187, 189, 191

 **Success Tracker**

- Data management system to assess Adequate Yearly Progress (AYP) and provide intervention

 **ExamView®**

- Alternative test formats are available online or through ExamView CD-ROM

Chapter 6 Test

Name _____ **Chapter 6 Test**

Read each question and choose the best answer. Then fill in the circle next to the correct answer.

1. What is the weather like when snow falls?
   Ⓐ dry
   Ⓑ cold
   Ⓒ warm
   Ⓓ windy

2. Which season does the picture show?

tulips and daffodils

   Ⓕ fall
   Ⓖ winter
   Ⓗ spring
   Ⓘ summer

Assessment Book — Chapter 6 Test **35**

Assessment Book, p. 35

Chapter 6 Test

Name _____ **Chapter 6 Test**

3. Think about the water cycle. What happens after the water evaporates?
   Ⓐ Nothing happens.
   Ⓑ The water turns to snow.
   Ⓒ The water flows into rivers and lakes.
   Ⓓ The water cools, condenses, and forms clouds.

4. Read the chart.

Spring	?
Buds on trees	Green leaves
Warm air	Hot air
Rain	Sunshine

What should be the title of the second column?
   Ⓕ Fall
   Ⓖ Winter
   Ⓗ Summer
   Ⓘ Seasons

36 Chapter 6 Test — Assessment Book

Assessment Book, p. 36

Chapter 6 Test

Name _____ **Chapter 6 Test**

5. When do the seasons repeat?
   Ⓐ never
   Ⓑ every day
   Ⓒ every year
   Ⓓ every summer

6. Look at the picture.

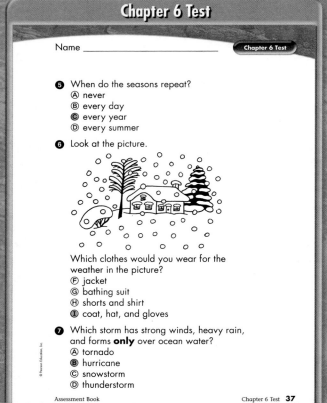

Which clothes would you wear for the weather in the picture?
   Ⓕ jacket
   Ⓖ bathing suit
   Ⓗ shorts and shirt
   Ⓘ coat, hat, and gloves

7. Which storm has strong winds, heavy rain, and forms **only** over ocean water?
   Ⓐ tornado
   Ⓑ hurricane
   Ⓒ snowstorm
   Ⓓ thunderstorm

Assessment Book — Chapter 6 Test **37**

Assessment Book, p. 37

Chapter 6 Test

Name _____ **Chapter 6 Test**

8. Which sentence is true of thunderstorms?
   Ⓕ They have lightning.
   Ⓖ They have heavy rain.
   Ⓗ They can be dangerous.
   Ⓘ All of the sentences are true of thunderstorms.

9. Why do some animals migrate in the fall?
   Ⓐ They grow heavier coats to keep them warm.
   Ⓑ They eat the food they stored for the winter.
   Ⓒ They go to colder places where they can find shelter.
   Ⓓ They go to warmer places where they can find food.

Write the answer to the question on the lines.

10. Think about the type of home you live in. Write what you would do if you were at home during a tornado. Write a sentence. (2 points)
   Answers will vary. Children should go to a basement, or to an inside hall, closet or bathroom on the first floor if there is no basement. They should keep away from windows. They should cover their heads.

38 Chapter 6 Test — Assessment Book

Assessment Book, p. 38

You Will Discover

- that there are patterns in the weather.
- how weather changes from season to season.

Chapter 6
Earth's Weather and Seasons

online
Student Edition
pearsonsuccessnet.com

169

Earth's Weather and Seasons

 Science Objectives

- The student recognizes patterns in weather.
- The student knows that people use scientific processes including hypothesis, making inferences, and recording and communicating data when exploring the natural world.
- The student knows that most natural events occur in patterns.

Quick | TEACHING PLAN

If time is short...

Use Build Background page to engage children in chapter content. Then do Explore Activity, How to Read Science, and Lessons 1, 2, and 7.

Professional Development

To enhance your qualifications in science:

- preview content in Earth Science DVD Segment *Earth's Weather and Water.*
- preview activity management techniques described in Activity DVD Unit B, Chapter 6.

Take It to the NET

To access student resources:
1. Go to **www.pearsonsuccessnet.com.**
2. Click on the register button.
3. Enter the access code **frog** and your school's zip code.

Chapter 6 Concept Web

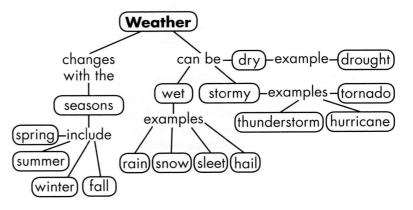

Children can create a concept web to organize ideas about Earth's weather and seasons.

Build Background

- The student identifies words and constructs meaning from text, illustrations, graphics, and charts, using the strategies of phonics, word structure, and context clues.

Chapter 6 Vocabulary Words

water cycle, p. 178
evaporate, p.179
condense, p. 179
migrate, p. 184
hibernate, p. 186
lightning, p. 188
tornado, p. 190
hurricane, p. 192

1 | Introduce the Concept

Quick ACTIVITY

Write several weather words on the board and read them aloud: *sunny, cloudy, hot, cold, rainy.* Tell children that these words and others describe weather. If possible, ask children to look outside and describe what they observe about the weather. Ask: **Is the weather the same every day?** Children should infer from past experience that weather varies from day to day and from one season to another.

Discuss Essential Question

Many science vocabulary words are abstract. Use the pictures and labels on these pages to help you open a discussion about science concepts and build academic language.

Read the Chapter 6 Essential Question to children, **How does weather change?** Ask leading questions to encourage children to identify seasonal changes as well as daily ones. For example, ask: **What kinds of clothes do you wear in summer? What kinds of clothes do you wear in winter?**

Revisit the essential question with children as they work through this chapter.

How does weather change?

tornado

water cycle

evaporate

condense

170

Build Background Resources

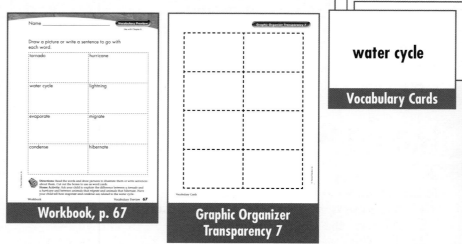

Workbook, p. 67

Graphic Organizer Transparency 7

water cycle

Vocabulary Cards

ELL Support

Access Content Before reading the chapter text, lead children on a picture/text walk.

Chapter 6 Vocabulary

water cycle page 178

evaporate page 179

condense page 179

migrate page 184

hibernate page 186

lightning page 188

tornado page 190

hurricane page 192

hurricane

lightning

migrate

hibernate

171

Science Background

Weather Instruments

- People who study weather use a number of different instruments. The most common include thermometers, which measure temperature; anemometers, which measure wind speed; and barometers, which measure air pressure.

- The barometer is a strong predictor of weather changes. A low barometric pressure is associated with clouds, rain, storms, and generally bad weather. A high barometric pressure indicates clear skies and sunny, warm, dry weather. A falling barometric pressure indicates that air pressure is dropping and bad weather is approaching; a rising barometric pressure indicates that air pressure is rising and good weather is on the way.

Science Misconception

Lightning Strikes

Ask children if they have heard the expression that "lightning never strikes twice in the same place." Explain to children that lightning can strike the same place more than once.

2 | Introduce Vocabulary

Use the following List-Group-Label chart provided on **pearsonsuccessnet.com** or Graphic Organizer Transparency 7.

water cycle	evaporate	condense
migrate	hibernate	lightning
tornado	hurricane	

Have children work in small groups. Provide each group with a copy of the Graphic Organizer. List the vocabulary words on the board. Tell children to copy the words, placing one word in each square. Have children cut out the eight word cards and place them on their workspace. Direct them to find words that are related to one another and to place those cards in groups. Tell children to determine a category name that can serve as a label for each group of words. On the board, record the results of each group of children. As a class, select the best category names for the word groups.

- Pronounce each word as you list it on the board. Solicit information about each word from children. For example, children may know that the words *hibernate* and *migrate* refer to animal behavior associated with the seasons.

- Guide children as they look for relationships among the words.

- Guide children in choosing a category name for each group of words.

- Tell children they will return to their word groups after reading the chapter and check to see if their groupings and labels are correct.

Word Recognition Use the Vocabulary Cards to reinforce recognition of each written word and its definition.

3 | Practice

Vocabulary Strategy: Word Map

Using the Vocabulary Cards, read the definition of a vocabulary word aloud. Reinforce the definition and identification of the word by creating a word map. Write the word in the center. Invite children to contribute descriptive words, synonyms, a sentence using the word correctly, and a picture that illustrates the word. Repeat with each vocabulary word.

Explore How much rain falls?

⭐ **Science Objective**

• The student knows that people use scientific processes including hypothesis, making inferences, and recording and communicating data when exploring the natural world.

1 Build Background

This activity encourages children to make a rain gauge and infer how it measures rainfall.

Managing Time and Materials

Time: 15 minutes

Groups: small groups

Materials: *tall clear plastic jar (12 oz cylinder); masking tape, (1½ in. wide); metric ruler; black pencil*

Alternative Materials: Tall plastic bottles with flat bottoms can be used in place of tall jars.

Materials listed in *italics* are kit materials.

Advance Preparation

Cut a 14 cm piece of masking tape for each group.

2 What to Do

Engage Ask **Why is rain important?** Answers might include helping plants grow, filling lakes, and providing drinking water.

Explore Have children make the rain gauge.

Explain Ask how the rain gauge works.

Extend Have each child make a rain gauge for home.

Evaluate Does each rain gauge around the school measure the same amount of rain? Why or why not?

3 Explain Your Results

Infer The jar's numbers will tell how much rain fell.

Process Skills

Children **infer** how a rain gauge measures rainfall.

Explore How much rain falls?

Make a tool to measure how much rain falls.

Materials

jar

tape

ruler

black pencil

What to Do

❶ Number each centimeter line up to 12. Start at the bottom of the tape.

❷ Fasten tape to the jar.

Process Skills

You can use what you know and what you have learned to **infer**.

Explain Your Results

Infer How could you use this tool to measure how much rain falls?

Activity Resources

Activity Book, pp. 69–70

Activity Rubric

Use Activity DV Unit B, Chapter 6 to preview this activity.

Call 1-888-537-490 with activity questions.

🖥 **More** Lab zone **Activities** **Take It to the Net** pearsonsuccessnet.com

Find more about this activity at our Web site.

• See the **Teacher's Activity Guide** for more support.

• An alternative activity is also available to download.

How to Read Science

Reading Skills

Draw Conclusions

You draw conclusions when you decide about something you see or read.

Science Picture

Apply It!
Look at the picture.
Infer What is the weather like outside?

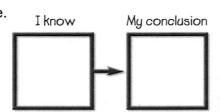

I know ⟶ My conclusion

173

How to Read Science Resource

Workbook, pp. 68–69

ELL Support

For more practice on **Draw Conclusions,** use **Every Student Learns Teacher's Guide,** p. 37.

Draw Conclusions

⭐ Reading Objective

- The student makes connections and inferences based on text and prior knowledge (for example, order of events, possible outcomes).

About the Target Skill

The target skill for *Earth's Weather and Seasons* is **Draw Conclusions.** Children are introduced to the skill as you guide them through this page.

1 | Introduce

Show children a picture of a person dressed in winter clothing. Ask: **What do you think the weather is like where this person is? What makes you think this?** Children should conclude that because the person is wearing so much clothing, the weather is probably cold.

2 | Model the Skill

Look together at the Science Picture and read the words that introduce it as a class.

Say: **This picture shows a child getting ready to go outside.** Ask: **What is she wearing?** A raincoat and rain boots **What is she planning to take with her?** An umbrella **What do you know about when people use such things?**

3 | Practice

Graphic Organizer

Look at the Graphic Organizer together. Work with children to complete the Graphic Organizer using the facts from the Science Picture.

Apply It!

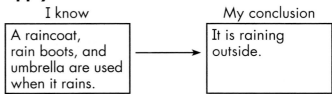

I know | My conclusion
| A raincoat, rain boots, and umbrella are used when it rains. | ⟶ | It is raining outside. |

What are some kinds of weather?

 Science Objective

- The student knows that weather conditions occur in patterns over time.

1 Introduce

Quick ACTIVITY | TRANSPARENCY 32

Ask: ***What are some words that describe different kinds of weather?*** Possible answers: sunny, cloudy, rain, snow, hot, cold. Ask: ***How might you dress for different kinds of weather?*** Discuss their answers. Then have children draw a picture of their favorite kind of weather.

Access Prior Knowledge

Ask children: ***What is the hottest time of the year? What is the coldest time of the year? How do you dress during those times of the year?*** Children should remember that summer is the hottest time of the year and winter is the coldest time of the year. Children will wear clothes such as T-shirts and shorts during the summer, but will wear heavier clothing, such as sweaters and jackets, during the winter.

Set Purpose

Tell children they are going to read about Earth's weather. Help them set a **purpose for reading,** such as to discover how different kinds of weather affect the environment.

2 Teach

Quick SUMMARY

- Weather is the condition of the air outside.
- Temperature and wind are both part of weather.
- Weather helps determine what people wear and do.

Sing or play "What's the Weather?" for children. Then read page 175 together.

You Are There

What's the Weather?

Sung to the tune of "Yankee Doodle"
Lyrics by Gerri Brioso & Richard Freitas/The Dovetail Group, Inc.

There's all kinds of weather and
Of that I'm really sure.
Just open up a window
Or peek out an open door.

174  Science Songs ♪♪♫

Lesson 1 Resource

Workbook, p. 70

 Science Songs ♪♪♫

Use the Science Songs CD to play "What's the Weather?" for the class.

What are some kinds of weather?

You wake up in the morning.
How do you know what to wear?
Check the weather!

Weather is what the air outside is 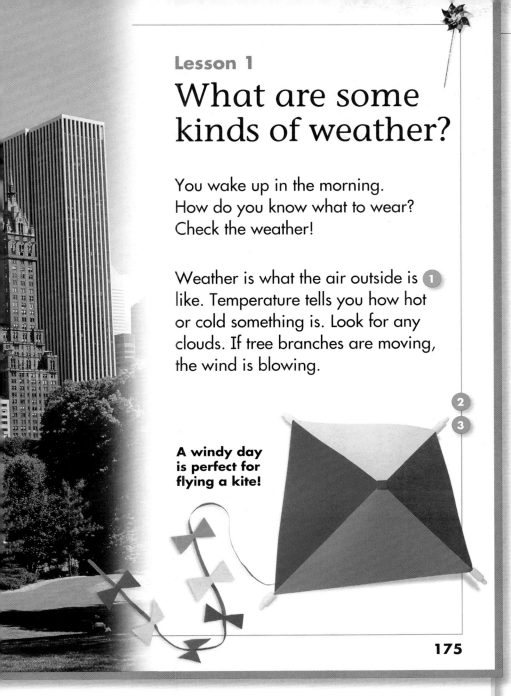 1
like. Temperature tells you how hot
or cold something is. Look for any
clouds. If tree branches are moving,
the wind is blowing.

2
3

**A windy day
is perfect for
flying a kite!**

175

ELL Leveled Support

Kinds of Weather

Beginning Point to the sky outside and ask: ***What is the weather today?*** Help children answer: *The weather is _____.* (*warm, cold, sunny, cloudy, rainy, snowy*) Point out the pictures on pages 174–177 and check for understanding of these weather words.

Intermediate Build on the above. Hand out paper and crayons or markers. Say: ***Draw a picture of the weather today.*** Help children label their pictures with *The weather is _____.* (*warm, cold, sunny, cloudy, rainy, snowy*)

Advanced Build on the above. Help children answer the questions: ***What is the weather today? What was the weather yesterday?*** Help children understand the meaning of *yesterday* by providing examples of "things we did yesterday" by saying: ***Yesterday, we _____.*** Then ask: ***What will the weather be tomorrow?***

Explain to children that they can learn a lot about weather just by observing it. They can feel the temperature and see if it is windy. Discuss other types of weather that children can identify from observing, such as rain, lightning, or snow.

Assign Quick Study pp. 64–65 to children who need help with lesson content.

Guide Comprehension

Ask children the following scaffolded questions to assess understanding.

Scaffolded Questions

1 **Review** *What is weather?* What the air outside is like

2 **Compare** *Compare today's weather to yesterday's weather.* Answers will vary.

3 **Appraise** *How does the weather affect some of the things you do?* Possible answer: Bad weather may keep children from doing outdoor activities.

Extend Vocabulary

Write the word *weather* on the board and have children read it and tell what it means. (What the air outside is like) Write the word *whether* on the board and explain that this word sounds the same but has a different meaning. It expresses a choice or can mean "if." Offer an example, such as "I don't know whether or not it will rain." Tell children that words that sound alike but have different meanings are called homophones. Provide other examples from the page: *some/sum; know/no.* Write these on the board and discuss their meanings. Explain that the words around a homophone can help children figure out its meaning.

Diagnostic Check

If... children have difficulty understanding the factors that make up weather,

then... ask children to describe the condition of the air outside: Is it hot, warm, cool, or cold? Is it cloudy or sunny? Is it windy or calm? Is it dry? Remind children that all of these conditions determine the weather in an area.

- The student knows that weather conditions occur in patterns over time.

2 | Teach (continued)

Quick SUMMARY

- Clouds can help tell what kind of weather is coming.
- Clouds are made of tiny drops of water, which may fall as rain if they get big or heavy enough. The drops can also fall as sleet or snow.
- Rain, sleet, and snow are different kinds of wet weather.
- A drought can happen when there is little rain.

Read pages 176–177 with children. Have children describe the types of precipitation that fall in the area where they live. Ask leading questions, such as ***Does much rain fall in our area? Does much snow or sleet fall in our area?*** Answers will vary. Point out that floods occur when there is too much rain. Droughts happen after periods of too little rain.

Heavy rains can fall in spring and summer. 3

Some places get snow in winter.

Hail is pieces of ice that fall from clouds.

Wet and Dry Weather

Clouds can help tell you what kind of weather is coming. Clouds are made up of drops of water and small pieces of ice. When the small pieces of ice join together, they start to fall.

Snowflakes fall in cold weather. Blizzards are snow storms with strong winds. In warm air, snow melts into rain as it falls. Sleet is rain that freezes as it falls. Snow, rain, and sleet are different kinds of wet weather.

176

Science Background

Annual Rainfall

- Some say the wettest place on Earth is Mount Waialeale, Hawaii, with annual rainfall averaging 11.7 meters (463 inches). Others say it is Cherapunjee, India, with 11.5 meters. Ironically, Cherapunjee is also plagued by drought. This is because all of the rain falls during the monsoon season, and the surrounding forest, which used to retain the water throughout the year, has been destroyed. The driest desert on Earth (according to the U.S. Geological Survey) is the Atacama Desert in Chile, where there are spots where no rain has ever been recorded.

Science Misconception

Snow Vocabulary

- It is a myth that Eskimos, or Inuit, have more words for *snow* in their language than English does. Examples of words in the English language that refer to snow include *blizzard, dusting, flurry, frost, hardpack, avalanche, powder, sleet, slush, snowman,* and *snowbank.*

The land is very dry in a drought.

A drought can happen when it does not rain for a long time. A drought is one kind of dry weather. There may not be enough water for many plants and animals during a drought.

Some plants may not be able to live in a drought.

✓ **Lesson Checkpoint**

1. What are three kinds of wet weather?

2. **Technology** in Science Go to www.nws.noaa.gov on the Internet. What will the weather be like tomorrow where you live?

177

Math Link

How Much Rain?

Tell children that people sometimes calculate the total rainfall in their area for a period of time. Give children the following information: January rainfall: 2 inches; February rainfall: 3 inches; March rainfall: 5 inches; April rainfall: 4 inches. Have children calculate the total rainfall. (14 inches) Then have them make a bar graph showing the monthly rainfall.

ELL Support

Language Detectives: Building Vocabulary

Provide the following sentence frames for children to complete:

• Water that falls from the sky is called _____.

• You cannot see _____, but you can feel if it is hot or cold.

• On some days, the sky is filled with fluffy white _____.

For scaffolded instruction about different kinds of weather, use **Every Student Learns Teacher's Guide,** p. 38.

Guide Comprehension

Ask children the following scaffolded questions to assess understanding.

Scaffolded Questions

1 **List** *List four different types of water that falls from the sky.* Rain, sleet, snow, and hail

2 **Contrast** *How is sleet different from rain?* Sleet is rain that freezes as it falls.

3 **Infer** *How could too much rain be dangerous?* It could cause floods.

Extend Vocabulary

Explain to children that the words *rain* and *snow* appear in many compound words. Compound words are made from two smaller words. Write these words on the board: *rainbow, raincoat, raindrop, rainstorm, snowfall, snowflake, snowman, snowshoe,* and *snowstorm.* Have children discuss the meanings of words they know and try to guess the meanings of unfamiliar words. Then have them find the meanings of unfamiliar words in a dictionary.

3 | Assess

✓ **Lesson Checkpoint**

1. Rain, sleet, snow, and possibly hail

2. **Technology** in Science Answers will vary. Check children's work.

Lesson 2

What is the water cycle?

 Science Objective

- The student knows that most natural events occur in patterns.

1 | Introduce

Quick ACTIVITY

| TRANSPARENCY 33 |

Ask: ***What happens to water on wet clothes as they hang to dry?*** Do a demonstration to help explain how water goes into the air (evaporation). Place a bowl of water in the classroom and mark the water's level with a piece of tape. Have children predict how the water will change if the bowl is left out overnight. Explain that water from the bowl and from wet clothes goes into the air.

Access Prior Knowledge

Ask: ***The last time water fell in our area, in what form did it fall?*** Answers will vary. Remind children that water can fall to Earth in the form of rain, snow, hail, or sleet. Tell children that they are going to learn how water goes from Earth to the air and from the air to Earth.

Set Purpose

Tell children they are going to read about a process called the water cycle. Help them set a **purpose for reading,** such as to understand what the water cycle is.

2 | Teach

Quick SUMMARY

- The water cycle is the way water moves from clouds to Earth and back to clouds.
- Water from the clouds falls to Earth's land, rivers, lakes, and oceans.
- Energy from the Sun causes water to evaporate. The water changes into water vapor in the air. When the water vapor gets cold, it condenses into tiny drops of water. These drops form clouds, and the cycle starts again.

What is the water cycle?

The way water moves from the clouds to Earth and back to the clouds again is called the **water cycle.** Look at this picture. Follow the steps in the water cycle.

Water falls from the clouds. The water might be in the form of rain, snow, hail, or sleet.

Water flows into rivers, lakes, and oceans.

178 | **SciLinks** Take It to the Net | keyword: water cycle
pearsonsuccessnet.com | code: g2p178

Lesson 2 Resource

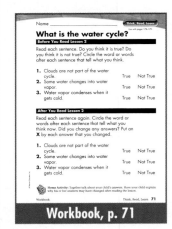

Workbook, p. 71

SciLinks Take It to the Net
pearsonsuccessnet.com

Technology Link

Children can go online to discover more about **water cycle** by using the NSTA *SciLink* available at **pearsonsuccessnet.com.**

When the water vapor in clouds gets cold, it condenses. **Condense** means to change into tiny drops of water. The tiny drops of water form clouds.

Energy from the Sun makes some of the water evaporate. Water **evaporates** when it changes into water vapor. *Water vapor* is water in the air. You cannot see water vapor.

2
3

✓ **Lesson Checkpoint**

1. What are the steps in the water cycle?

2. 🎯 **Draw Conclusions** How does energy from the Sun change water in water puddles?

179

Science Misconception

New Water

Some children may think that new water is constantly being formed on Earth. Explain to children that no new water is being created on Earth. The water that is already on Earth is being moved from one place to another through the process called the water cycle.

ELL Support

Dramatizing the Water Cycle

Ask children to express with their hands and bodies what happens during each step in the water cycle. Provide verbal prompts, saying, for example: **There is a lot of water in the clouds. What might happen?** Children might move their wiggling fingers downward to show rain falling.

For scaffolded instruction about the water cycle, use **Every Student Learns Teacher's Guide,** p. 39.

Read pages 178–179 with children. Explain to children that water vapor is a gas. It forms when water evaporates, or changes from a liquid into a gas. When water vapor cools, it condenses, or changes from a gas into a liquid.

Assign Quick Study pp. 66–67 to children who need help with lesson content.

Guide Comprehension

Ask children the following scaffolded questions to assess understanding.

Scaffolded Questions

1 **Recall** *What is the water cycle?* The movement of water from the clouds to Earth and back to the clouds again

2 **Comprehend** *How does water get into the air as a gas?* Water gets into the air as a gas when it evaporates.

3 **Value** *How does the water cycle affect the amount of water on Earth?* The water cycle keeps taking away water from the water supply and then putting it back.

Extend Vocabulary

Write the word *cycle* on the board. Explain that this word came into the English language from the Greek language. There it meant "circle or wheel." Discuss how the **water cycle** is like a wheel or circle. (It has no end.) Point out that *cycle* is part of many words that children already know, such as *bicycle*. Have them suggest other words. (*Tricycle, motorcycle, cyclone*)

3 | Assess

✓ **Lesson Checkpoint**

1. Water falls from a cloud as rain, snow, sleet, or hail. Water runs into lakes, rivers, and oceans. Water evaporates into the air as water vapor. The water vapor cools and condenses into water drops that make up clouds. The water drops fall to Earth again.

2. 🎯 **Draw Conclusions** Energy from the Sun causes the water in puddles to evaporate and become water vapor.

Lesson 3

What is spring?

 Science Objective

- The student knows that weather conditions occur in patterns over time.

1 | Introduce

Quick ACTIVITY | TRANSPARENCY 34

Write the months for each season on the board. Have children come to the board and write their name under the season that contains their birthdays. Ask children: **What kind of outdoor activities can you do on your birthday?** Explain to children that they are going to be learning about each of Earth's seasons. First they will learn about spring. Have children draw a picture of their favorite springtime activity.

Access Prior Knowledge

In their science journals, have children write the name of their favorite season. Have children list the favorite things they do during that season. Have volunteers read their lists to the class.

Set Purpose

Tell children you are going to read to them about the season of spring. Help them set a **purpose for listening,** such as to find out what things occur in the spring.

2 | Teach

Quick SUMMARY

- Weather in many places changes with the seasons. Seasons repeat every year.
- Spring days may be warm, cool, or rainy. Many animals have babies in the spring.

Read pages 180–181 to children. As children look at the pictures, explain that spring is the season in which many new things come into being: plants begin to grow leaves and flowers; many animals have babies.

Lesson 3

What is spring?

Weather in many places changes with the seasons. The four seasons are spring, summer, fall, and winter. The seasons ① repeat every year.

Some spring days are cool. Other spring days are warm. Spring days ② can be rainy. The rain helps plants grow. Many animals have babies in the spring.

✔ Lesson Checkpoint

1. Tell about two things that can happen in spring.

2. **Writing in Science**
   Write two sentences. What are some things you like to do in spring?

This mother deer had her baby in the spring.

180

Lesson 3 Resource

Workbook, p. 72

Holland, Michigan

Holland, Michigan is known for its beautiful tulips. Tulips bloom in the spring.

Spring can be very rainy.

New leaves start growing on trees in the spring.

③

Science Background

The Equinox

Although spring arrives in different places at different times, people in the Northern Hemisphere usually associate it with the vernal equinox. This is the time of year when day and night are of equal length on Earth. On the equinox, the Sun is directly overhead at noon at the equator. This takes place around mid-March.

ELL Support

What Is a Season?

Help students understand that the word *season* means a period of time. People divide the year into days and months; seasons are how nature divides a year.

For scaffolded instruction about the four seasons, use **Every Student Learns Teacher's Guide,** p. 40.

Remind children that plants must have sunlight and water in order to grow and spring often brings warmer temperatures and rain.

Assign Quick Study pp. 68–69 to children who need help with lesson content.

Guide Comprehension

Ask children the following scaffolded questions to assess understanding.

Scaffolded Questions

① **Recall *How often do the seasons repeat?*** Every year

② **Explain *Why do you see more plants growing in the spring than in the winter?*** Warm temperatures, longer days, and rain help plants grow.

③ **Evaluate *Why is spring an important season?*** Possible answers: Spring brings needed rain and warmth that help plants grow and bloom; spring is often the time in which animals have babies and plants grow new leaves; winter is over.

Extend Vocabulary

Tell children that the word *spring* has many meanings. In addition to naming a season, it can also name the following: a coiled object that stretches and then returns to its original size; a small stream of water that flows out of the ground; or an action. Invite children to use the various meanings of the word in oral sentences.

3 | Assess

✓ Lesson Checkpoint

1. Answers will vary but may include: there are more daylight hours than in winter, plants grow, animals have babies, and some days are cool while others are warm.

2. **Writing in Science** Have children write their answers in their science journals. Possible answers may include: riding bicycles, playing outside, flying kites.

What is summer?

Lesson 4

⭐ Science Objective

- The student knows that weather conditions occur in patterns over time.

1 | Introduce

Quick ACTIVITY | TRANSPARENCY 35

Show children pictures of people doing summer activities such as swimming, water-skiing, boating, riding amusement park rides, and eating ice cream or other cool treats. Ask children: **What do all of these pictures have in common?** Guide children to the idea that all of the pictures show activities that people do in the summer. Then have children make a list of things they like to do in the summer.

Access Prior Knowledge

Ask children: **What type of weather do we have in the summer?** Children should answer that it gets hotter, there is usually less rain, and thunderstorms are more common. In their science journals, have children write about their favorite summer activity.

Set Purpose

Tell children they are going to read about summer. Help them set a **purpose for reading,** such as to find out what weather changes occur during summer and how they affect plants and animals.

2 | Teach

Quick SUMMARY

- Summer often has long, hot days and warm nights.
- In most places, it is the hottest season of the year.
- During summer, leaves, flowers, fruits, and vegetables grow.

Read pages 182–183 with children. Explain to children that since the days are longer in the summer, they are able to do more outdoor activities during the daytime.

What is summer?

① Summer comes after spring. Summer has more daylight hours than spring. Summer often has hot days and warm nights. In most places, summer is the hottest season of the year. Green leaves grow on many trees and other plants. Flowers, fruits, and vegetables grow.

②

✓ Lesson Checkpoint

1. How are daylight hours in spring and summer different?

2. **Art in Science** Draw a picture of your neighborhood in summer.

You can see many animal families in the summer.

182

Lesson 4 Resource

Workbook, p. 73

Charleston, South Carolina

Parks can be beautiful in the summer. This park is in Charleston, South Carolina.

Many people like to grow vegetables in the summer.

The adult duck is swimming with her babies on a summer day.

3

Science Background
Summer
Earth is tilted on its axis at an angle of 23.5 degrees. When it is summer in the Northern Hemisphere, that hemisphere is tilted toward the Sun. The Sun's rays strike more directly.

Science Misconception
Sun and Summer
Children may think that when it is summer where they live, it is summer everywhere. When the Northern Hemisphere is enjoying summer, it is winter in the Southern Hemisphere.

ELL Support
Understanding Comparison Forms
Draw a line on the board. Write *coldest* at one end and *hottest* at the other. In between write *cold, warm,* and *hot.* Discuss each word.

For scaffolded instruction about summer, use **Every Student Learns Teacher's Guide,** p. 41.

Ask children to describe the kind of clothing they wear during the summer. Answers should include T-shirts, shorts, sandals, and bathing suits. Remind children that we wear this type of clothing during the summer because the days are hotter. Have children brainstorm a list of fruits and vegetables they see in the summer.

Assign Quick Study pp. 70–71 to children who need help with lesson content.

Guide Comprehension

Ask children the following scaffolded questions to assess understanding.

Scaffolded Questions
1 **Recall** *What is summer weather like?* Long, hot days and warm nights

2 **Identify** *What are two activities you can do in the summer?* Possible answer: Go to the beach or on a picnic

3 **Evaluate** *Why is summer an important season?* Possible answers: going on vacations and doing other outdoor activities, growing flowers, fruits, and vegetables.

Extend Vocabulary

Tell children that just as the year can be divided into seasons, so can the day be divided into parts. The parts of a day form a pattern, just as the seasons of the year do. Draw a circle on the board. Around it write these words: *morning, noon, afternoon, evening, night.* Discuss the meaning of each term, since a few may be unfamiliar. Then invite children to tell what kinds of activities they usually do at each time of day.

3 | Assess

✓ Lesson Checkpoint

1. The daylight hours increase from the first day of winter to the first day of summer. Then they start to decrease throughout summer and fall.

2. Art in Science Drawings will vary.

Lesson 5

What is fall?

Science Objective

- The student knows that weather conditions occur in patterns over time.

1 | Introduce

Quick ACTIVITY ・ TRANSPARENCY 36

Have children look at pictures of fall leaves that are red, orange, yellow, or brown. Ask children: **How are these leaves different from the leaves you see in the summer?** Children should say that summer leaves are green. **What is about to happen to leaves that turn different colors?** They will fall off the trees. In their science journals, have children describe the difference between summer and fall leaves. Have them draw and color fall leaves.

Access Prior Knowledge

Ask children to raise their hands to the question: **How many of you know the season in which a new school year begins?** Ask children to describe what happens to the weather at this time of year. Help them recognize that the days are becoming cooler and shorter.

Set Purpose

Tell children you are going to read to them about fall. Help them set a **purpose for listening,** such as to find out what happens to plants and animals during fall.

2 | Teach

Quick SUMMARY

- Fall days have fewer hours of daylight than summer and are cooler, although many are still warm.
- In some places during fall, some leaves turn different colors and fall off the trees.
- In fall, some animals store food for winter, while others migrate.

Lesson 5
What is fall?

1. Fall comes after summer. There are fewer hours of daylight in fall than in summer. The air begins to get cooler.

The leaves on some trees turn different colors in fall. Then the leaves fall to the ground.

Some animals, such as chipmunks and squirrels, begin to store food for the winter. Other animals 2. **migrate,** or move to a different place.

✓ Lesson Checkpoint

1. What are two things animals might do in fall?

2. **Draw Conclusions** Suppose you see many groups of geese flying south in the fall. What do you think is happening?

In fall, some animals gather food for the winter.

184

Lesson 5 Resource

Name _____
Think, Read, Learn
What is fall?
Before You Read Lesson 5
Read each sentence. Do you think it is true? Do you think it is not true? Circle the word or words after each sentence that tell what you think.
1. Fall is cooler than summer. True Not True
2. Fall has more daylight hours than summer. True Not True
3. Some animals start to get ready for the winter. True Not True
After You Read Lesson 5
Read each sentence again. Circle the word or words after each sentence that tell what you think now. Did you change any answers? Put an X by each answer that you changed.
1. Fall is cooler than summer. True Not True
2. Fall has more daylight hours than summer. True Not True
3. Some animals start to get ready for the winter. True Not True
Home Activity: Together talk about your child's answers. Have your child explain why his or her answers may have changed after reading the lesson.
Workbook Think, Read, Learn **74**

Workbook, p. 74

Bloomington, Indiana

Look at the trees in Bloomington, Indiana. The leaves have turned different colors.

Sandhill cranes migrate every fall.

In fall, farmers harvest crops.

185

Science Background

Animal Adaptations

- The bird with the longest migration path is the Arctic tern. When it flies south, winters in Antarctica, and flies north again, it goes about 36,000 kilometers (21,600 miles). Because an Arctic tern lives about 20 years, its lifetime migration distance is about 720,000 kilometers (432,000 miles), or the equivalent of a round trip to the Moon!

ELL Support

Winter Conditions

Discuss reasons why animals have a hard time finding food in winter: frozen ground, snow covering the ground, fewer sources of food. Help children understand that some animals gather and store food, some eat a great deal so they can survive periods without food, and some migrate to places where it is easier to find food.

For scaffolded instruction about fall, use **Every Student Learns Teacher's Guide,** p. 42.

Read pages 184–185 to children. Discuss the pictures. Explain that the colored leaves they see on the trees are dying. These leaves will fall off the trees and the trees will not have new leaves until the spring. Ask: **What are the birds doing, and why?** (Migrating to warmer places, where they can get food) Discuss how the farmers are harvesting crops, just as many animals gather food. All are getting ready for winter.

Assign Quick Study pp. 72–73 to children who need help with lesson content.

Guide Comprehension

Ask children the following scaffolded questions to assess understanding.

Scaffolded Questions

1 **Compare** *How is fall weather different from summer weather?* There are fewer hours of daylight during fall, and the air gets cooler.

2 **Infer** *Why do birds migrate in fall?* To find food

3 **Evaluate** *What do you think is the biggest difference between summer and fall?* Possible answers: Animals migrate; plants stop growing and may lose their leaves.

Extend Vocabulary

Write the word **migrate** on the board. Explain that this word has different forms. Write *migrated, migrating,* and *migration.* Have children identify the ending added to the word *migrate.* Then tell children the meaning of the words. Point out that migrating can be both a verb and an adjective. For example, "Birds are migrating; migrating birds may fly for days."

3 | Assess

✓ Lesson Checkpoint

1. Some animals store food for the coming winter. Other animals migrate to warmer places.

2. **Draw Conclusions** The geese flying south are migrating.

What is winter?

 Science Objective

- The student knows that weather conditions occur in patterns over time.

1 Introduce

Quick ACTIVITY | TRANSPARENCY 37

Have children look at winter scenes. Ask: ***What do you think the air is like in these places?*** Children should recognize that it would be cold.

Access Prior Knowledge

Ask children: ***How do we dress in winter?*** Children should know that in most places people put on more clothes in the winter. Have children brainstorm activities that they and others do in the winter.

Set Purpose

Tell children they are going to read about winter. Help them set a **purpose for reading,** such as to find out what weather changes occur during winter and how this affects plants and animals.

2 Teach

Quick SUMMARY

- In some places winter can be very cold and may have snow and ice.
- Winter has fewer hours of daylight than fall.
- Many trees have no leaves and grow little. Animals may hibernate.

Read pages 186–187 with children. Explain to children that some people have very cold winters and others do not. That depends on whether people live in northern areas or southern areas.

What is winter?

1 Winter comes after fall. In some places, winter can be very cold. It may even snow. Ponds and streams may turn to ice.

Winter has fewer daylight hours than fall. Many trees have no leaves.

Some animals hibernate in winter. **Hibernate** means to have a long, deep sleep. Animals that hibernate come out in spring to look for food.

2
3

Most bears hibernate in winter.

✓ Lesson Checkpoint

1. What happens when an animal hibernates?

2. Writing in Science Write in your journal about winter where you live. What is the weather like?

Lesson 6 Resource

Workbook, p. 75

Adirondack, New York

There can be heavy snowstorms in Adirondack, New York.

You can see many trees and roofs covered with snow in winter.

It is fun to play in the snow. Be sure to wear coats and hats.

187

My Science Journal

My Favorite Season

Have children think about the information about seasons they have learned. Have them determine which season is their most favorite and which season is their least favorite. Have children draw a T-chart and label the columns appropriately. Then have them list three reasons for their choice of each season as most or least favorite.

ELL Support

Winter Activities

Show children pictures of people doing winter activities such as skiing, sledding, ice-skating, and ice fishing. Ask children: **What do all of these pictures have in common?** Guide children to the idea that the pictures show activities that people do in winter.

For scaffolded instruction about winter, use **Every Student Learns Teacher's Guide,** p. 43.

Show children a map of the United States and discuss which places are very cold. Explain to children that in these places, plants stop growing and some animals hibernate so they do not need to search for food. Discuss reasons why food would be scarce in winter.

Assign Quick Study pp. 74–75 to children who need help with lesson content.

Guide Comprehension

Ask children the following scaffolded questions to assess understanding.

Scaffolded Questions

1 **Describe** *What can the weather be like in winter in some places?* Winter can be very cold and snowy.

2 **Compare** *How does winter weather compare to summer weather?* Summer weather has long, hot days and warm nights, and winter weather has shorter, cold days and nights.

3 **Evaluate** *Why is it important for some animals to hibernate during winter?* In some places food is scarce during the winter months and animals that hibernate do not need to hunt for food.

Extend Vocabulary

Explain to children that **hibernate** comes from the Latin word for "winter." Write the word on the board. Next to it, write *hibernating* and *hibernation.* Ask children what they think each word means before providing the definition. To illustrate how each word can be used, provide sentences such as, "The chipmunks are hibernating now; the hibernating chipmunks will become active again in spring." "Hibernation means spending the winter sleeping or resting."

3 | Assess

✓ Lesson Checkpoint

1. The animal sleeps or rests through the winter.

2. Writing in Science Have children write their answers in their science journals. Answers will vary. Check children's work.

Lesson 7

What are some kinds of bad weather?

 Science Objective

- The student recognizes patterns in weather.

1 | Introduce

Quick ACTIVITY | TRANSPARENCY 38 |

Ask children which they think comes first: thunder or lightning. Tally their answers on the board. Then tell them that lightning comes before thunder. Have children imitate the sound of thunder.

Access Prior Knowledge

Ask children to recall and describe thunderstorms, if they have seen any. Explain that while thunderstorms can bring much-needed rain, it is important to stay safe during a storm.

Set Purpose

Tell children they are going to read about thunderstorms and lightning. Help them **set a purpose for reading,** such as understanding how to be safe if such storms come.

2 | Teach

Quick SUMMARY

- Thunderstorms have heavy rains with thunder and lightning. Some have high winds and hail.
- Lightning is a flash of light in the sky. Thunder is the loud sound that follows.
- During a thunderstorm, find indoor shelter and stay away from water, metal, telephones, trees, and objects that use electricity.

Read pages 188–189 with children. Explain that thunderstorms tend to develop during the warmer months of spring and summer. Have children look at the picture on page 189 and explain that lightning is a huge amount of electricity in the sky. Lightning is one thing that happens during a thunderstorm.

Lesson 7

What are some kinds of bad weather?

A thunderstorm is a kind of bad weather. A thunderstorm has heavy rain with thunder and lightning.
① **Lightning** is a flash of light in the sky. Thunder is the loud sound that **②** you hear after lightning flashes. Sometimes thunderstorms have hail **③** and strong winds.

1. ✓**Checkpoint** What is lightning?

2. **Art** in Science Make a safety poster. Show how to stay safe during a thunderstorm.

Lesson 7 Resource

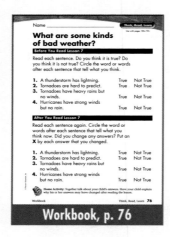

Workbook, p. 76

A lot of rain can fall during a thunderstorm.

Thunderstorm Safety

- Find shelter in a building or car.

- Stay away from water.

- Stay away from metal objects.

- Do not stand under a tree.

- Do not use telephones.

- Keep away from objects that use electricity.

189

My Science Journal

Describing a Thunderstorm

Ask children if they have ever experienced a thunderstorm. In their science journals, have children write what they saw, heard, and felt during the storm. Have children draw and label a picture of what they saw during the storm. Have volunteers share their stories with the class.

Science Misconception

Lightning Paths

Children may think that lightning travels only from the sky to the ground. During lightning storms, lightning often travels from cloud to cloud, and on rare occasions, lightning will travel from the ground to the sky.

Math Link

The Sound of Thunder

Tell children that the sound of thunder can travel a great distance. It travels about one kilometer every 3 seconds (one mile every 5 seconds). Have children determine how many seconds it will take the sound of thunder to travel two kilometers (6 seconds) and three kilometers (9 seconds).

Explain to children that lightning is dangerous, so they need to find shelter immediately if they are outside when a thunderstorm arrives. Because lightning tends to strike tall objects, they should avoid these. Tell children that lightning travels quickly through metal objects, water, and electrical wires, so they should avoid these too.

Assign Quick Study pp. 76–77 to children who need help with lesson content.

Guide Comprehension

Ask children the following scaffolded questions to assess understanding.

Scaffolded Questions

1 Recall *What is a thunderstorm?* Heavy rain with thunder and lightning

2 Describe *What things can happen during a thunderstorm?* Lightning, thunder, rain, strong winds, and hail

3 Infer *Why can thunderstorms be dangerous?* Lightning can strike an object or person, and strong winds and hail can cause damage to buildings or people.

Extend Vocabulary

Explain to children that the word **lightning** means a flash of light in the sky. Because lightning occurs so quickly and suddenly, the word is sometimes used as an adjective to mean "with speed and suddenness." Provide this example: The runner moved with lightning speed.

Diagnostic Check

If... children have difficulty understanding how to stay safe during a thunderstorm,

then... have them develop a plan to follow if a thunderstorm occurs near their homes.

3 Assess

1. **✓ Checkpoint** A flash of light in the sky

2. **Art in Science** Children's posters should include at least some of the safety tips from page 189.

- The student understands some impacts of tornadoes.
- The student understands ways to stay safe in tornadoes.

2 | Teach (continued)

Quick SUMMARY

- A tornado has strong, funnel-shaped winds that come down from clouds and touch the ground.
- A tornado that touches the ground can destroy things.
- During a tornado, find indoor shelter, preferably in a basement or a closet or room in the middle of the first floor of a building, and keep the head covered. If a shelter is not available, lie flat in a low place.

Explain to children that thunderstorms can sometimes produce large funnel-shaped winds called tornadoes. Have children look at the picture on pages 190–191 and explain that tornadoes can form quickly and can be very dangerous.

Read pages 190–191 with children. Explain to children that tornadoes often carry small pieces of metal or broken glass that travel very fast. It is very important to get inside a building if a tornado appears. Tell children to go to the basement of the building if it has one. If it does not, tell children to move to a room on the first floor that is in the middle of the building and has no windows. A closet is often the safest place to be during a tornado. If a shelter is not available, tell children they should lie flat in a low place.

Tornadoes

Tornadoes can happen during thunderstorms. A **tornado** has very strong winds that come down from clouds in the shape of a funnel.

Tornadoes form quickly. It is hard to predict when a tornado will happen. A tornado that touches the ground can destroy things.

1. ✓Checkpoint What is one way to stay safe during a tornado?
2. Writing in Science Tell what a tornado is like.

190

Tornadoes can happen in spring or summer.

Science Background

The Fujita Scale

In 1971, tornado expert Theodore Fujita developed a scale for determining the damage done by a tornado. According to Dr. Fujita's scale:

- an F0 tornado has wind speeds less than 116 km/hr (73 mph) and does light damage
- an F1 tornado has wind speeds between 116–180 km/hr (73–112 mph) and does moderate damage
- an F2 tornado has wind speeds between 181–253 km/hr (113–157 mph) and does considerable damage
- an F3 tornado has wind speeds between 254–332 km/hr (158–206 mph) and does severe damage
- an F4 tornado has wind speeds between 333–419 km/hr (207–260 mph) and does devastating damage
- an F5 tornado has wind speeds between 420–512 km/hr (261–318 mph) and does incredible damage

Tornado Safety

- Go to the basement or an inside hall, closet, or bathroom.

- Sit under the stairs or near an inner wall.

- Keep away from windows, water, metal, and objects that use electricity.

- Cover your head.

- If you cannot get to shelter, lie flat in a low place.

191

Guide Comprehension

Ask children the following scaffolded questions to assess understanding.

Scaffolded Questions

1 Define *What does a tornado have?* Strong, funnel-shaped winds that come down from clouds

2 Appraise *Why should you be inside during a tornado?* To keep from being hit by flying material

3 Plan *Where in this school might be a safe place if a tornado hit?* Answers will vary, but should be a basement or an inside room in the middle of the first floor.

Extend Vocabulary

Write the word **tornado** on the board. Tell children that there are several other words that mean almost the same thing. Then write *twister, cyclone, whirlwind,* and *waterspout.* Pronounce each word and point out that a waterspout is a tornado that takes place over water.

3 | Assess

1. **✓ Checkpoint** Possible answer: Go inside and to the basement or an inside hall, closet, or bathroom.

2. **Writing in Science** Have children write their answers in their science journals. Children should mention strong winds.

My Science Journal

A Tornado-Safety Plan

Tell children to make a tornado-safety plan for themselves or for people living in areas where tornadoes occur. Have them base their plan on what they have read about tornado safety and on what they know about their homes or homes in general. Have them decide which place would be safest during a tornado. Have them tell what they would do there.

Science Background

How Tornadoes Form

Tornados sometimes form along the southwest side of a severe thunderstorm. There the warm air is forced upward rapidly, and the result is a drop in air pressure. Winds start to rotate rapidly around the area of low pressure, forming a tornado. Air rushes into the tornado from all directions and spirals upward (updrafts).

Tornado Trivia

On average, about 1,000 tornadoes occur in the United States each year. About 75 percent of the world's reported tornadoes occur in the United States and 5 percent occur in Canada.

- The student understands some impacts of hurricanes.
- The student understands ways to stay safe in hurricanes.

2 Teach (continued)

Quick SUMMARY

- A hurricane is a large storm that forms over warm ocean water.
- A hurricane has heavy rains and strong winds.
- If a hurricane approaches, move to a safe place inland.
- Make a home safe during a hurricane by boarding up windows, bringing belongings inside, storing extra water, and checking batteries in flashlights and radios.
- During a hurricane, stay inside and away from windows.

Explain to children that hurricanes are large, watery storms that form over the ocean during the summer and fall. Have children look at the picture on page 193 and tell them that this picture of the eye of a hurricane was taken from a weather satellite that orbits Earth. The eye is a calm area in the center of the storm.

Read pages 192–193 with children. Explain to children that because hurricanes contain heavy rain and very strong winds, it is important that people prepare for them. Since hurricanes form slowly and we have excellent ways of tracking them, people usually have a great deal of time to protect themselves.

Hurricanes

A **hurricane** is a large storm that starts over warm ocean water. A hurricane has heavy rains. The rains can cause floods.

A hurricane has very strong winds. The winds can knock down trees and buildings.

✓ Lesson Checkpoint

1. What is a hurricane?
2.  **Draw Conclusions** What might happen to objects left outside during a hurricane?

192

ELL Leveled Support

Comparing Storms

Beginning On the board, write the words *thunderstorm, tornado,* and *hurricane.* Have children list one characteristic for each storm.

Intermediate Have children compare the storms and tell ways in which they are alike. For example, they all may have strong winds; all can be dangerous.

Advanced For each type of storm listed on the board, have children describe two things they should do to be safe if that storm occurs.

For scaffolded instruction about bad weather, use **Every Student Learns Teacher's Guide,** p. 44.

Hurricane Safety

- **Move away from the ocean if you can.**

- **Board up windows.**

- **Bring loose objects inside.**

- **Keep extra water on hand for drinking.**

- **Check the batteries in your flashlights and radio.**

- **During the storm, stay inside. Stay away from windows.**

This picture shows the eye of a hurricane. The eye is a calm area in the center of the storm.

Science Background

The Saffir-Simpson Hurricane Scale

The Saffir-Simpson Hurricane Scale is a rating system based on a hurricane's intensity. In this system:

- a Category 1 hurricane (119–153 km/hr winds) does minimal damage

- a Category 2 hurricane (154–177 km/hr winds) does mild damage

- a Category 3 hurricane (178–209 km/hr winds) does considerable damage

- a Category 4 hurricane (210–249 km/hr winds) does extensive damage

- a Category 5 hurricane (249 km/hr winds) does severe damage

Recent Hurricanes

In 2004, nine out of 15 tropical storms in the North Atlantic became hurricanes. Four of those hurricanes struck the state of Florida during the months of August and September: Charley, Frances, Ivan, and Jeanne. The hurricanes caused considerable damage throughout the state.

Guide Comprehension

Ask children the following scaffolded questions to assess understanding.

Scaffolded Questions

1 **Describe** *What is a hurricane?* A large storm with heavy rain and strong winds that starts over warm ocean water

2 **Contrast** *How is a hurricane different from a tornado?* A tornado is a quick-forming wind storm and a hurricane is a slow-forming wind and water storm.

3 **Plan** *How can you prepare your home for a hurricane?* Board up windows, bring in belongings, store water, and check batteries in flashlights and radios

Extend Vocabulary

Explain to children that the word **hurricane** comes from the Taino Indian culture. The Taino lived in Central America and on islands in the warm waters of the Caribbean Sea. Their word *huracan* was the basis for our word *hurricane*. Tell children that other Taino words we have borrowed include *hammock*, *barbecue*, and *canoe*.

3 | Assess

✓ Lesson Checkpoint

1. A hurricane is a large storm that starts over warm ocean water.

2. ○ **Draw Conclusions** Accept reasonable answers.

SCAFFOLDED INQUIRY

▮▮ Investigate How can you measure weather changes?

⭐ **Science Objectives**

- The student keeps science records.
- The student uses a variety of tools to observe, measure, analyze and predict changes in size, mass, temperature, color, position, quantity, sound, and movement.

1 | Build Background

This activity encourages children to use a rain gauge and outdoor thermometer to measure the precipitation and temperature for one week and record their findings in a chart.

Managing Time and Materials

Time:	10 minutes per day for 5 days
Groups:	small groups
Materials:	*rain gauge (whole class use); thermometer (alcohol)*
Alternative: Materials	You may wish to use the rain gauges made in the Directed Inquiry activity on p. 172 in the Student Edition.

Materials listed in *italic* are kit materials.

Safety Note

The thermometers do not contain mercury.

Teaching Tip

If it is a dry week, assure children that the data are valuable and worth collecting.

2 | What to Do

Encourage Guided Inquiry

Preview the activity and the materials with children. Ask: **How are a rain gauge and a thermometer used to measure changes in the weather?**

Guide children to write an If.../then... statement such as: **If I use a rain gauge and a thermometer to measure weather changes for 5 days, then I will observe changes in rainfall and temperature.**

Investigate How can you measure weather changes?

There are many tools for measuring weather. A rain gauge measures rainfall. A thermometer measures temperature.

Materials

rain gauge

thermometer

What to Do

① Put the weather tools outside.

② Check them every day for one week.

③ Write how much rain fell each day. Write the temperature for each day.

Process Skills

You can use a chart to help **classify** weather.

Activity Resources

Name _____

Guided Inquiry

Investigate How can you measure weather changes?

② Collect Data Write how much rain fell each day. Write the temperature for each day.

Rain and Temperature for One Week

Day of the Week	rain gauge (centimeters)	thermometer (°C)
Monday		
Tuesday		
Wednesday		
Thursday		
Friday		

Activity Book   Guided Inquiry **71**

Name _____

Guided Inquiry

Activity Rubric

Investigate: How can you measure weather changes?

Scoring Criteria	1	2	3	4
Student checked the rain gauge and thermometer for one week.				
Student **collected data** on a chart to show daily rainfall and temperatures for one week.				
Student summarized the weather for the week.				
Student **classified** each day as rainy or not rainy.				
Student **interpreted data** by telling weather changes from day to day.				

Scoring Key
4 points correct, complete, detailed
3 points partially correct, complete, detailed
2 points partially correct, partially complete, lacks some detail
1 point incorrect or incomplete, needs assistance

Activity Book   Guided Inquiry **177**

Activity Book, pp. 71–72 | **Activity Rubric**

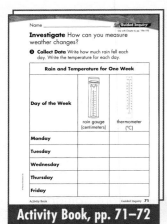

Use Activity DVD Unit B, Chapter 6 to preview this activity.

Call 1-888-537-490 with activity questions.

🖥 **More** Lab zone **Activities** **Take It to the Net** pearsonsuccessnet.com

Find more about this activity at our Web site.

- See the **Teacher's Activity Guide** for more support.
- An alternative activity is also available to download.

Temperature and Rain for One Week		
Day of the Week	rain gauge	thermometer
Monday		
Tuesday		
Wednesday		
Thursday		
Friday		

Explain Your Results

1. **Classify** each day as rainy or not rainy. What does your chart tell you about the weather for one week?

2. Tell how the weather changed from day to day.

Go Further

How much rain do you think might fall in 5 days? Measure to find out.

195

Science Background

Meteorologists

A meteorologist is a person who studies or predicts the weather. A television meteorologist presents current weather information and weather forecasts to the surrounding community. A television meteorologist works with computer programs that produce the interesting weather graphics that people at home can see.

ELL Support

Access Content Before beginning the activity, conduct an inventory of materials with children. Solicit other names for each item. Accept labels in English and children's home languages.

Engage Hold up a rain gauge. Ask children to review how a rain gauge works. Hold up a thermometer. Ask children: **What does a thermometer measure?** (temperature)

Explore Have children follow the steps of the activity. As children observe rainfall amounts and temperature each day, have them record their results in the data table.

Explain After completing the activity, have children explain how a rain gauge and thermometer are used to determine weather changes.

Extend Have children record temperature and rainfall each month and discuss weather changes from month to month. Ask children which months of the year have the most rainfall or snowfall and which months are the hottest or coldest.

Evaluate Ask children to examine their data. How did rainfall and temperature change from the first day of the activity to the last day?

3 | Explain Your Results

Use the "Explain Your Results" questions to help children review evidence and develop explanations.

- Give children an opportunity to reflect on the data, or evidence, they have gathered in the investigation.
- Have children use the evidence gathered to develop their explanations. Accept reasonable, logical explanations.

Classify

1. Check children's work for accuracy.
2. Children should write about their observations of the weather for the week.

Go Further

Have children determine the total rainfall around the school for a 5-day period. Children may wish to use additional weather measuring instruments such as a barometer (measures air pressure) or a wind vane (measures wind direction).

Post other questions children have about weather measurement. Encourage children to investigate on their own.

Process Skills

Interpret Data

Remind children that data are any information they can collect. Tell children that after data are collected, they can be used to answer questions. This is called interpreting data. You can use the Process Skills sheet on Interpreting Data at this time.

Math in Science

Charting Favorite Seasons

⭐ Science Objective

- The student uses mathematical language to read and interpret data on a simple concrete graph, pictorial graph, or chart.

1 | Introduce

Quick ACTIVITY

Ask children to identify interesting activities that they could do in each season. List their responses on the board. Encourage children to consider both indoor and outdoor activities. Challenge children to figure out a way to determine and display what season is the most/least favorite among the class.

2 | Teach the Skill

Read pages 196–197 with children. Go over the chart carefully. Have children identify the part of the chart that shows the seasons. Then have children identify what each stick figure represents. (A child) Demonstrate how children can determine how many children liked spring best. Ask: **How many figures do you see next to the word spring?** Three

Math in Science

Charting Favorite Seasons

Nan wanted to find out what her classmates' favorite seasons were. She made a chart to show this information.

196 ⚙ **Tools** Take It to the Net
pearsonsuccessnet.com

Activity Resource

Workbook, p. 77

⚙ **Tools** Take It to the Net
pearsonsuccessnet.com

Look at the chart. Answer the questions.

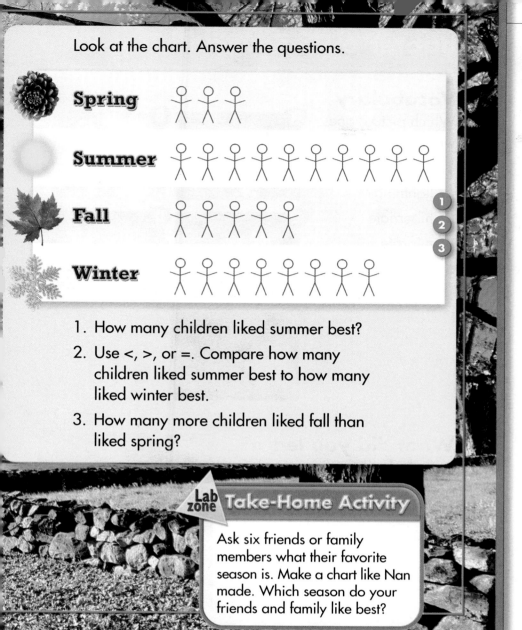

Spring

Summer

Fall

Winter

1. How many children liked summer best?

2. Use <, >, or =. Compare how many children liked summer best to how many liked winter best.

3. How many more children liked fall than liked spring?

Lab zone Take-Home Activity

Ask six friends or family members what their favorite season is. Make a chart like Nan made. Which season do your friends and family like best?

197

Guide Comprehension

Ask children the following scaffolded questions to assess understanding.

Scaffolded Questions

1 Compare *Which season was the favorite of the largest number of children?* Summer

2 Categorize *Which were the two most favorite seasons?* Summer and winter

3 Propose *What are some other ways Nan could have presented the same information?* Possible answers: She could have written a paragraph. She could have made a different kind of graphic, such as a pie chart.

3 | Assess

1. 10
2. 10 > 8
3. 2

Take-Home Activity

Tips for Success

• Assist children in creating a chart and writing in the correct headings. Also, review how to fill in the chart.

• Have children bring their completed charts to school to present to their classmates. Check children's charts for accuracy. The total number of people should add up to 6.

• As an extension, have children work in teams to create other ways of showing the information from their charts.

• Encourage children to share their charts with their family or friends.

Vocabulary

1. C
2. A
3. B
4. D
5. E

What did you learn?

6. Water falls from clouds as rain, snow, sleet, or hail. Water runs into lakes, rivers, and oceans. Water evaporates into the air as water vapor. The water vapor cools and condenses into water drops that makes up clouds. The water drops fall to Earth again.

7. Summer has the most daylight hours.

Chapter 6 Review and Test Prep

Vocabulary

Which picture goes with each word?

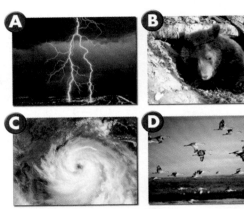

1. hurricane
2. lightning
3. hibernate
4. migrate
5. tornado

What did you learn?

6. Tell what happens in each step of the water cycle.

7. Which season has the most daylight hours?

Assessment Resources

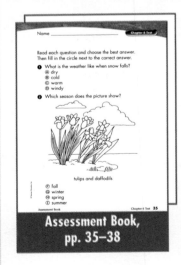

Assessment Book, pp. 35–38

MindPoint Quiz Show

MindPoint enables students to test their knowledge of the chapter in a game format.

ExamView® Use ExamView as a print or online assessment tool to create alternative tests for students.

Success Tracker

Data management system to track Adequate Yearly Progress (AYP) and provide intervention online at **pearsonsuccessnet.com/successtracker**

Take-Home Booklet

Children can make a Take-Home Booklet using Workbook pp. 79–80.

8. Collect Data Observe the weather for 10 days. Record the number of days that are sunny, cloudy, and rainy.

Draw Conclusions

9. Look at the picture. Which season do you think it is?

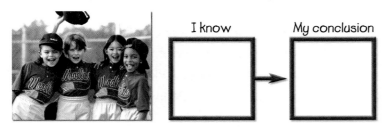

I know	My conclusion

Test Prep

Fill in the circle next to the correct answer.

10. When water vapor changes to liquid it _____.

Ⓐ evaporates

Ⓑ hibernates

Ⓒ condenses

Ⓓ migrates

11. **Writing** in Science

Write four sentences. Describe what the weather is like where you live in each of the four seasons.

199

---

8. Collect Data Check children's work for accuracy.

Draw Conclusions

9.

I know	My conclusion
People play baseball in summer.	It is summer.

Test Prep

10. C

11. **Writing** in Science   Check children's work for accuracy.

Intervention and Remediation

Science Objectives	Review Item	Student Edition Pages	Teacher Edition Resources			Ancillary Resources		
			Guide Comprehension	Extend Vocab	Diagnostic Check	Vocab Cards	Quick Study	Workbook Pages
The student knows that weather conditions occur in patterns over time.	6, 7, 8, 9, 10, 11	174–177, 180–187	181, 183, 185, 187	181		•	175, 181, 183, 185, 187	70, 72, 73, 74, 75
The student understands that most natural events occur in comprehensible, consistent patterns.	6, 7, 8, 11	178–179	179, 181, 183, 185, 187	179, 181, 183, 185, 187		•	179	71, 75
The student knows some impacts of bad weather.		188–189	177, 189	189		•	189	76
The student knows ways to stay safe in bad weather.		188–189			189	•	189	76
The student knows some impacts of tornadoes.		190–191	191			•		
The student knows some ways to stay safe in tornadoes.		190–191	191			•		
The student knows some impacts of hurricanes.		192–193	193			•		
The student knows some ways to stay safe in hurricanes.		192–193	193			•		

Career

Atmospheric Scientist

 Science Objective

- The student knows that men and women of all ethnic and social backgrounds make contributions to science and technology, practice science and technology.

1 Introduce

Build Background

Review with children the characteristics of a hurricane. Remind children that hurricanes are large storms that start over the ocean and bring high winds and much rain.

2 Teach

Quick SUMMARY

- Atmospheric scientists study the weather.
- By studying hurricanes, NASA scientists learn how to predict when and where a hurricane is likely to occur.

Read page 200 together with children. Explain that atmospheric scientists study hurricanes to learn more about them. Tell children hurricanes move slowly. This gives scientists time to decide if the hurricanes will be dangerous enough to move people out of the way. Remind children that satellites can also be used to track the path of hurricanes from space (pages 166–167).

3 Explore

Tell children that all hurricanes are given names. The names alternate back and forth between men's and women's names and follow the letters of the alphabet (except *Q, U,* and *Z*). Have children look at the hurricane names for the current year and propose a "new" list of names.

Career

Robbie Hood works as an Atmospheric Scientist at NASA.

Atmospheric Scientist

Read Together

Atmospheric scientists study the weather. Some atmospheric scientists who work at NASA study hurricanes. They want to learn more about how hurricanes work and what is the best way to use satellites to observe them.

Studying hurricanes has helped NASA scientists learn how to predict when and where a hurricane is likely to occur. This way, warnings can be given sooner and more people can move to places where they can stay safe.

Lab zone Take-Home Activity

Talk with your family about hurricanes. Make a list of reasons why atmospheric scientists are important people.

200

Take-Home Activity

Tips for Success

- Assist children in writing down the assignment and making sure they clearly understand it.
- Children may ask family members to help them make their lists during their discussion at home.
- Have children bring their completed lists to school to share with their classmates.

Leveled Readers and Leveled Practice

Leveled Readers deliver the same concepts and skills as the chapter. Use Leveled Readers for original instruction or for needed reteaching.

Below-Level

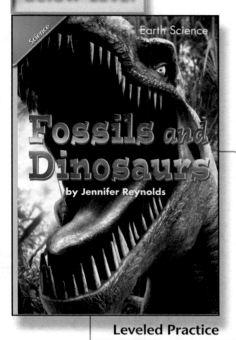

Earth Science

Fossils and Dinosaurs
by Jennifer Reynolds

Leveled Practice

Leveled Reader Teacher's Guide

On-Level

Earth Science

Dinosaur Fossils
by Kim Borland

Leveled Practice

Leveled Reader Teacher's Guide

Advanced

Earth Science

Tyrannosaurus Rex
by Susan Jones Leeming

Leveled Practice

Leveled Reader Teacher's Guide

Below-Level Leveled Reader has the same content as Chapter 7, but is written at a less difficult reading level.

On-Level Leveled Reader has the same concepts as Chapter 7, and is written at grade level.

Advanced Reader is above grade level and enriches the chapter with additional examples and extended ideas.

Leveled Reader Database
Scott Foresman
pearsonsuccessnet.com

Use the online database to search for additional leveled readers by level, title, content, and skill.

Key Content and Skill in Leveled Readers and Chapter 7

Content	Vocabulary	Target Reading Skill	Graphic Organizer
Fossils and Dinosaurs	fossil extinct paleontologist dinosaur	Retell	

Chapter 7 Planning Guide

Lesson/Activity	Pacing	Science Objectives
Build Background pp. 201–203	20 minutes	• The student identifies words and constructs meaning from text, illustrations, graphics, and charts using the strategies of phonics, word structure, and context clues.
Lab zone **Flip Chart Activity** How do paleontologists dig for fossils?		
Lab zone **Flip Chart Activity** How can you tell what made the tracks?		
Lab zone Directed Inquiry		• The student knows ways objects can be grouped according to similarities or differences of their physical characteristics.
Explore Which fossils match the plants and animals? p. 204	20 minutes	
How to Read Science p. 205	20 minutes	• The student uses a variety of strategies to comprehend text.
1 How can we learn about the past? pp. 206–209	30 minutes	• The student describes how fossils are formed.
2 What can we learn from fossils? pp. 210–211	20 minutes	• The student explains how fossils give information about plants and animals that lived on Earth long ago.
3 What were dinosaurs like? pp. 212–215	30 minutes	• The student describes different dinosaurs that lived on Earth long ago.
4 What are some new discoveries? pp. 216–217	20 minutes	• The student explains how new discoveries are made by paleontologists.
Lab zone Guided Inquiry		• The student knows that people use scientific processes including hypothesis, making inferences, and recording and communicating data when exploring the natural world.
Investigate How can you make a model of a fossil? pp. 218–219	20 minutes	
Wrap-Up Chapter 7 pp. 220–224	20 minutes	• The student uses customary and metric units to measure, compare, and order objects according to their lengths, weights, or capacities.
Math in Science: Measuring Fossil Leaves	20 minutes	
Chapter 7 Review and Test Prep	20 minutes	
Biography: Susan Hendrickson	20 minutes	

Vocabulary/Skills	Assessment/Intervention	Resources/Technology
Process Skills: Use a Model Interpret Data Infer	• Chapter Review, SE, pp. 222–223 (1–3)	• Science Content Transparency 7 • Workbook, p. 81 • Graphic Organizer Transparency 3 • Vocabulary Cards • Activity Book, pp. 75–76
Process Skill: Communicate Target Reading Skill: **Retell**	• Explain Your Results, SE, p. 204 • Activity Rubric • Retell, SE, p. 205	• Activity Book, pp. 77–78 • Activity DVD • Workbook, pp. 82–83 • Every Student Learns, p. 45 • Activity Placement 14
fossil paleontologists	• Scaffolded Questions, TE, pp. 207, 209 • Checkpoint Questions, SE, p. 209 • Chapter Review, SE, pp. 222–223 (1, 2, 6) • Retell, SE, p. 209	• Workbook, p. 84 • Quick Study, pp. 78–79 • Every Student Learns, p. 46
extinct	• Scaffolded Questions, TE, p. 211 • Checkpoint Questions, SE, p. 211 • Chapter Review, SE, pp. 222–223 (4, 6, 7) • Retell, SE, p. 211	• Workbook, p. 85 • Quick Study, pp. 80–81 • Every Student Learns, p. 47
dinosaurs	• Scaffolded Questions, TE, pp. 213, 215 • Checkpoint Questions, SE, pp. 213, 215 • Chapter Review, SE, pp. 222–223 (3, 7, 8, 9)	• Workbook, p. 86 • Quick Study, pp. 82–83 • Every Student Learns, p. 48
	• Scaffolded Questions, TE, p. 217 • Checkpoint Questions, SE, p. 217 • Chapter Review, SE, pp. 222–223 (7)	• Workbook, p. 87 • Quick Study, pp. 84–85 • Every Student Learns, p. 49
Process Skills: Make Models, Infer	• Explain Your Results, SE, p. 219 • Activity Rubric	• Activity Book, pp. 79–80 • Activity DVD • Activity Placemat 15
Math Skill: Make a Bar Graph	• Scaffolded Questions, TE, p. 221 • Retell, SE, p. 223 • ExamView® Chapter 7 Test • Success Tracker pearsonsuccessnet.com/successtracker	• Workbook, p. 88 • Assessment Book, pp. 39–42

Wrap-Up Unit B

Lab zone Full Inquiry

Experiment How strong is the wind? pp. 128–129

Lab zone Full Inquiry

Science Fair Project p. 131a

Quick Teaching Plan

If time is short . . .
• Build Background, pp. 202–203
• Explore Activity, p. 204
• How to Read Science, p. 205
• Lesson 1, pp. 206–209
• Lesson 3, pp. 212–215

Other quick options . . .

Quick ACTIVITY

TE pp. 202, 206, 210, 212, 216, 220

TRANSPARENCIES 39, 40, 41, 42

Quick SUMMARY

TE pp. 206, 208, 210, 212, 214, 216

Chapter 7 Activity Guide

Children learn to ask and answer scientific questions as they progress to greater independence in scaffolded inquiry.

Directed Inquiry A Directed Inquiry activity begins each chapter.

Guided Inquiry A Guided Inquiry activity closes each chapter.

Full Inquiry Experiments and Science Fair Projects at the end of each unit provide opportunities for Full Inquiry.

Lab zone Directed Inquiry

Explore **Which fossils match the plants and animals?** p. 204

 Time 15 minutes

 Grouping individuals

Advance Preparation Make copies of the puzzle cards for each child. Use Activity Masters 10–11 from the Activity Book Teacher's Guide, pp. T33–T34.

Materials Puzzle Cards 1 and 2 (Activity Masters 10–11); safety scissors; crayons or markers; glue; construction paper (2 sheets)

Teaching Tips Explain to children that the fossils and organisms are scrambled on the puzzle sheets and that they are to match them correctly.

What to Expect Children will use picture clues to match each fossil picture to the picture of the correct plant or animal.

 Activity DVD Unit B, Chapter 7

 Activity Placemat Mat 14

Lab zone Guided Inquiry

Investigate **How can you make a model of a fossil?** pp. 218–219

 Time 30 minutes

 Grouping pairs

Advance Preparation You may wish to gather a variety of small classroom objects that will make good impressions when pressed into clay.

Materials *modeling clay (1 stick, ½ stick for each partner); seashell; 2 small classroom objects (paper clip, Snap Cube®, eraser, etc.)*

Science Center This activity can be set up in your Science Center for students to work on throughout the day.

What to Expect Children will make a model of a fossil by pressing a shell into clay. Children will then make another "fossil" using a small classroom object and have a partner guess what object made the fossil.

Safety Note Remind children not to choose sharp or breakable classroom objects for their fossils.

 Activity DVD Unit B, Chapter 7

 Activity Placemat Mat 15

Lab zone Full Inquiry

Experiment **Does gravel, sand, or soil make the best imprint?** pp. 228–229

Time 30 minutes

Grouping small groups

Advance Preparation For each group, fill 3 clear plastic cups with ½ c sand, ½ c gravel, and ½ c potting soil respectively.

Safety Note Remind children to wear safety goggles during this activity. Have children wash their hands after handling the materials.

Teaching Tips Children may need to wipe off the shell with a paper towel after making each imprint. Have children gently press the shell into the sand so that sand particles do not fall into the imprint.

Materials *sand (½ c); gravel (½ c); potting soil (½ c); 3 clear plastic cups (9 oz); 3 paper plates; scallop shell; safety goggles (1 per child); 3 index cards*

Alternative Materials Any combination of materials may be used in place of sand, gravel, and potting soil as long as the textures vary. Other possible materials include clay soil, sandy soil, and small rocks.

What to Expect The scallop shell will make the best imprint in sand, a partial imprint in soil, and no imprint in gravel.

 Activity DVD Unit Experiment

 Activity Placemat Mat 16

Other Resources

The following Resources are available for activities found in the Student Edition.

Demonstration Kit If you wish to rehearse or demonstrate the Chapter 7 activities, use the materials provided in the Demonstration Kit.

Classroom Equipment Kit Materials shown in *italic print* are available in the Classroom Equipment Kit.

Activity Placemats The Equipment Kit includes an Activity Placemat for each activity, a work surface that identifies the materials that need to be gathered.

Quick ACTIVITY

Transparencies Use a transparency to focus children's attention on the Quick Activity for each lesson.

Teacher's Activity Guide For detailed information about Inquiry Activities, access the Teacher's Activity Guide at **pearsonsuccessnet.com**.

Activity Flip Chart

How do paleontologists dig for fossils?

Use this center activity after teaching Lesson 2 of the chapter.

Activity Flip Chart, p. 13

Process Skill Use a model

 Time 20 minutes

 Grouping individual or pairs

Materials Use a 9×13 inch aluminum pan for each group. Fill the pan with sand. Dampen the sand. Fossils can be made from a variety of items.

Procedure

- When burying the fossils, you might want to leave one or two partly exposed. This would **model** the way scientists often come upon fossils.
- Emphasize that they should act slowly, as if they were **modeling** the uncovering of an actual rare fossil and did not want to break it.

What to Expect Children will dig slowly and carefully as they unearth model fossils.

Think About It

1. It is important to dig carefully and slowly so that you don't accidentally break the fossils.
2. Paleontologists have to dig for fossils and clean them carefully so that they don't break them. The fossils should be as complete as possible so that we can learn as much as possible from them.

Activity Flip Chart

How can you tell what made the tracks?

This center activity supports the chapter.

Activity Flip Chart, p. 14

Process Skills Interpret data, infer

 Time 20 minutes

 Grouping pairs

Materials small objects such as a pencil, paper clip, erasers, clay; hand lens

Procedure

- Make tracks, using the side of a quarter and the side of a nickel. Children can **infer** that these tracks were made from different coins.
- Model how to use part of an item and at different angles to make a track. Suggest that children make some of their tracks easy to identify and some more difficult for **interpreting data.**

What to Expect Children will find out that it can sometimes be difficult to figure out what object made a fossil track.

Think About It

1. The tracks that show only a small part of the item were probably the most difficult to match.
2. The track doesn't always show a lot about the thing that made it. Some tracks may look the same even though they were made by different things.

Chapter 7
Workbook Support

online Teacher's Edition
pearsonsuccessnet.com

Use the following Workbook pages to support content and skill development as you teach Chapter 7. You can also view and print Workbook pages from the Online Teacher's Edition.

Use with Build Background, pp. 202–203

Name _____ **Vocabulary Preview**

Use with Chapter 7.

Draw a picture or write a sentence to go with each word.

dinosaur	fossil
extinct	paleontologist

Directions: Read the words and draw pictures to illustrate them or write sentences about them. Cut out the boxes to use as word cards.
Home Activity: Have your child pretend to be a paleontologist and explain what he or she does using all the vocabulary words.

Workbook   Vocabulary Preview **81**

Workbook, p. 81

Use with How to Read Science, p. 205

Name _____ **How To Read Science**

Use with Chapter 7.

◉ Retell

Trilobite
Millions of years ago, this small animal lived in Earth's oceans. It had a shell and three body parts. The middle part had many legs.

Trilobite

82 How to Read Science   Workbook

Workbook, pp. 82–83

Use with Lesson 1, pp. 206–209

Name _____ **Think, Read, Learn**

Use with pages 207–209.

How can we learn about the past?

Before You Read Lesson 1

Read each sentence. Do you think it is true? Do you think it is not true? Circle the word or words after each sentence that tell what you think.

1. Fossils were once plants or animals.   True   Not True
2. Fossils form very quickly.   True   Not True
3. Paleontologists study fossils.   True   Not True

After You Read Lesson 1

Read each sentence again. Circle the word or words after each sentence that tell what you think now. Did you change any answers? Put an **X** by each answer that you changed.

1. Fossils were once plants or animals.   (True)   Not True
2. Fossils form very quickly.   True   (Not True)
3. Paleontologists study fossils.   (True)   Not True

Home Activity: Together talk about your child's answers. Have your child explain why his or her answers may have changed after reading the lesson.

Workbook   Think, Read, Learn **84**

Workbook, p. 84

Use with Lesson 2, pp. 210–211

Name _____ **Think, Read, Learn**

Use with pages 210–211.

What can we learn from fossils?

Before You Read Lesson 2

Read each sentence. Do you think it is true? Do you think it is not true? Circle the word or words after each sentence that tell what you think.

1. Fossils give clues about long-ago living things.   True   Not True
2. Extinct animals have disappeared from Earth forever.   True   Not True
3. Only animals can become extinct.   True   Not True

After You Read Lesson 2

Read each sentence again. Circle the word or words after each sentence that tell what you think now. Did you change any answers? Put an **X** by each answer that you changed.

1. Fossils give clues about long-ago living things.   (True)   Not True
2. Extinct animals have disappeared from Earth forever.   (True)   Not True
3. Only animals can become extinct.   True   (Not True)

Home Activity: Together talk about your child's answers. Have your child explain why his or her answers may have changed after reading the lesson.

Workbook   Think, Read, Learn **85**

Workbook, p. 85

Name _____

Think, Read, Learn
Use with pages 212–215.

What were dinosaurs like?

Before You Read Lesson 3

Read each sentence. Do you think it is true? Do you think it is not true? Circle the word or words after each sentence that tell what you think.

1. Not all dinosaurs are extinct.   True   Not True
2. Dinosaurs with big, flat teeth ate plants.   True   Not True
3. Some dinosaurs ate other dinosaurs.   True   Not True

After You Read Lesson 3

Read each sentence again. Circle the word or words after each sentence that tell what you think now. Did you change any answers? Put an **X** by each answer that you changed.

1. Not all dinosaurs are extinct.   True   (Not True)
2. Dinosaurs with big, flat teeth ate plants.   (True)   Not True
3. Some dinosaurs ate other dinosaurs.   (True)   Not True

Home Activity: Together talk about your child's answers. Have your child explain why his or her answers may have changed after reading the lesson.

Workbook   Think, Read, Learn **86**

Workbook, p. 86

Name _____

Think, Read, Learn
Use with pages 216–217.

What are some new discoveries?

Before You Read Lesson 4

Read each sentence. Do you think it is true? Do you think it is not true? Circle the word or words after each sentence that tell what you think.

1. Oviraptors were one kind of dinosaur.   True   Not True
2. Oviraptors laid eggs.   True   Not True
3. Oviraptors ate their own eggs.   True   Not True

After You Read Lesson 4

Read each sentence again. Circle the word or words after each sentence that tell what you think now. Did you change any answers? Put an **X** by each answer that you changed.

1. Oviraptors were one kind of dinosaur.   (True)   Not True
2. Oviraptors laid eggs.   (True)   Not True
3. Oviraptors ate their own eggs.   True   (Not True)

Home Activity: Together talk about your child's answers. Have your child explain why his or her answers may have changed after reading the lesson.

Workbook   Think, Read, Learn **87**

Workbook, p. 87

Name _____

Math in Science
Use with Chapter 7.

How long are dinosaur teeth?

Look at the dinosaur teeth. Estimate how long each tooth is. Measure the teeth.
Fill in the bar graph to show how long each dinosaur tooth is. Use the bar graph to answer the questions.

Dinosaur Teeth

15
14
13
12
11
10
9
8
7
6
5
4
3
2
1
0
     1   2   3
Teeth

1. Which tooth is the shortest?   3
2. Which tooth is the longest?   1
3. How much shorter is Tooth 2 than Tooth 1?   7 cm shorter

Directions: Use a ruler to measure each dinosaur tooth. Record each measurement by filling in the appropriate number of boxes in the graph. Use the information in the graph to answer the questions.
Home Activity: Your child learned how to record data on a bar graph. Have your child measure middle fingers on family members' hands and record the measurements on a bar graph like the one on the page.

Workbook   Math in Science **88**

Workbook, p. 88

Chapter 7 Assessment Support

online
Teacher's Edition
pearsonsuccessnet.com

Use the following Assessment Book pages and ExamView to assess Chapter 7 content. You can also view and print Assessment Book pages from the Online Teacher's Edition.

Assessment Options

Formal Assessment
- Chapter Review and Test Prep, SE pp. 222–223
- Assessment Book, pp. 39–42
- Prescriptions for remediation are shown on TE p. 223

Performance Assessment
- Unit Wrap-Up, SE pp. 226–227

Ongoing Assessment
- Diagnostic Check, TE pp. 207, 213
- Scaffolded Questions, TE pp. 207, 209, 211, 213, 215, 217, 221

Portfolio Assessment
- My Science Journal, TE p. 203

Success Tracker
- Data management system to assess Adequate Yearly Progress (AYP) and provide intervention

ExamView®
- Alternative test formats are available online or through ExamView CD-ROM

Chapter 7 Test

Name _____ Chapter 7 Test

Read each question and choose the best answer. Then fill in the circle next to the correct answer.

❶ Look at the picture.

Which word goes with the picture?
- Ⓐ fossil
- Ⓑ extinct
- Ⓒ dinosaur
- Ⓓ paleontologist

❷ What do paleontologists study?
- Ⓕ fossils
- Ⓖ people
- Ⓗ weather
- Ⓘ museums

Assessment Book   Chapter 7 Test **39**

Assessment Book, p. 39

Chapter 7 Test

Name _____ Chapter 7 Test

❸ What does the word **extinct** tell about?
- Ⓐ what an animal looked like
- Ⓑ how a fossil forms in a lake in mud
- Ⓒ when the weather on Earth changes over a long time
- Ⓓ when a plant or animal disappears from Earth forever

❹ Look at the picture. Think about this dinosaur's teeth.

What did this dinosaur probably eat?
- Ⓕ fruit
- Ⓖ eggs
- Ⓗ meat
- Ⓘ plants

40 Chapter 7 Test   Assessment Book

Assessment Book, p. 40

Chapter 7 Test

Name _____ Chapter 7 Test

❺ What is the name of this dinosaur?

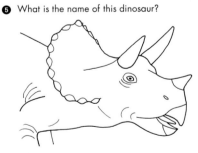

- Ⓐ Barosaurus
- Ⓑ Triceratops
- Ⓒ Compsognathus
- Ⓓ Tyrannosaurus rex

❻ What did iguanodons eat?
- Ⓕ fruit
- Ⓖ eggs
- Ⓗ meat
- Ⓘ plants

Assessment Book   Chapter 7 Test **41**

Assessment Book, p. 41

Chapter 7 Test

Name _____ Chapter 7 Test

❼ Read the chart. Use what you learn to answer the question.

New Discoveries	
Paleontologists Found	**Paleontologists Thought**
An Oviraptor near some eggs	The Oviraptor was stealing the eggs to eat them
An Oviraptor sitting on the same kind of eggs	The Oviraptor was protecting its own eggs

What is this chart about?
- Ⓐ how Oviraptors find food
- Ⓑ how Oviraptors sit on eggs
- Ⓒ how paleontologists learned about Oviraptors
- Ⓓ how paleontologists discovered what Oviraptors eat

Write the answers to the questions on the lines.

❽ How are footprint fossils formed? (2 points)
An animal makes a footprint in mud. The mud turns to rock.
_____

❾ What can fossils tell us about plants and animals? (2 points)
Answers may vary slightly. Children may respond that fossils can tell us the size and shape of plants and animals, or what animals ate.

42 Chapter 7 Test   Assessment Book

Assessment Book, p. 42

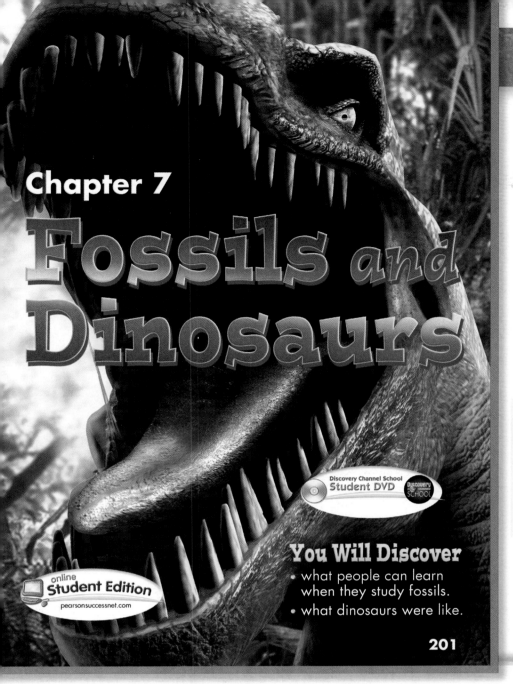

Chapter 7
Fossils and Dinosaurs

Discovery Channel School Student DVD

online Student Edition
pearsonsuccessnet.com

You Will Discover
- what people can learn when they study fossils.
- what dinosaurs were like.

201

Chapter 7

Fossils and Dinosaurs

 Science Objectives

- The student knows that fossils provide evidence about the plants and animals that lived long ago.
- The student can describe how fossils are formed.
- The student recognizes that scientists such as paleontologists use technology in scientific research.
- The student can describe the characteristics of different dinosaurs.

Quick | TEACHING PLAN

If time is short...
Use Build Background page to engage children in chapter content. Then do Explore Activity, How to Read Science, and Lessons 1 and 3.

Professional Development

To enhance your qualifications in science:
- preview content in Earth Science DVD Segments *Earth's Geologic History* and *Earth's Changing Crust.*
- preview activity management techniques described in Activity DVD Unit B, Chapter 7.

 **Technology Link**

For additional information on the topics covered in this chapter, have children view the Discovery Channel School DVD *Dinosaurs and Fossils.*

**ake It to the NET**

To access student resources:
1. Go to **www.pearsonsuccessnet.com.**
2. Click on the register button.
3. Enter the access code **frog** and your school's zip code.

Chapter 7 Concept Web

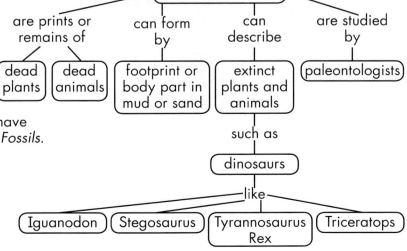

Children can create a concept web to organize ideas about fossils and dinosaurs.

Build Background

 Science Objective

- The student identifies words and constructs meaning from text, illustrations, graphics, and charts, using the strategies of phonics, word structure, and context clues.

Chapter 7 Vocabulary Words

fossil, p. 207
paleontologist, p. 207
extinct, p. 210
dinosaur, p. 212

1 | Introduce the Concept

Quick ACTIVITY

Have children look at the picture of the dinosaurs shown on pages 202–203. Ask children: **Do dinosaurs still live on Earth?** Children should answer no. **Do you think there are other living things besides dinosaurs that used to live on Earth but no longer do?** Children should answer yes.

Discuss Essential Question

Many science vocabulary words are abstract. Use the pictures and labels on these pages to help you open a discussion about science concepts and build academic language.

Read the Chapter 7 Essential Question to children, **How can people learn about Earth long ago?** Explain to children that the plants and animals that lived on Earth long ago are different from the plants and animals that live on Earth now. Ask children to brainstorm a list of animals they would find at a zoo. Explain to children that the zoo animals they listed would not have lived on Earth during the time of the dinosaurs.

Revisit the essential question with children as they work through this chapter.

How can people learn about the Earth long ago?

dinosaur

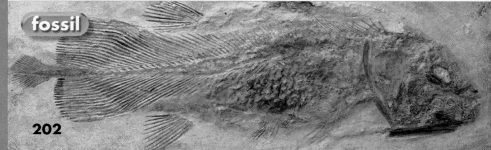
fossil

202

Build Background Resources

Workbook, p. 81

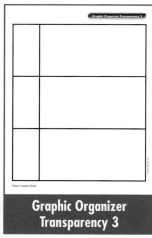

Graphic Organizer Transparency 3

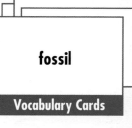
fossil

Vocabulary Cards

ELL Support

Access Content Before reading the chapter text, lead children on a picture/text walk.

Chapter 7 Vocabulary

fossil page 207

paleontologist page 207

extinct page 210

dinosaur page 212

extinct

paleontologist

203

Science Misconception

Museum Fossils

Children may assume that when they see dinosaur bones or skeletons in a museum, they are looking at the real bones of the dinosaur. Explain to children that dinosaur bones can be very large and heavy and not in good enough condition to be rebuilt into a skeleton. Many museums make copies of the bones out of fiberglass or other artificial materials that are lighter than real bone, and these artificial bones are built into the dinosaur skeletons they see.

My Science Journal

Dinosaur Description

Children have most likely seen pictures or models of a dinosaur in books, movies, or museums. Encourage children to think about what they have seen. Then have them draw a picture of that dinosaur or what they suppose a dinosaur would have looked like. Have them write a sentence describing the dinosaur.

2 | Introduce Vocabulary

Use the following Prediction/Confirmation chart provided on **pearsonsuccessnet.com** or Graphic Organizer Transparency 3.

Word	What I Predict	What I Know
fossil		
paleontologist		
extinct		
dinosaur		

Give a copy of Graphic Organizer Transparency 3 to each child. Write the vocabulary words on pages 202–203 on the board and have children copy the words under the first column.

- Pronounce each word carefully as you write it. The word *paleontologist* may be unfamiliar to children. Ask children to repeat each word.

- In the second column of the chart, have children write what they predict is the definition of each word. Some children may have prior knowledge of one or more words that can help them do this. To stimulate thinking, ask: **What does it mean if an animal is extinct?**

- Tell children they will fill out the third column of this chart as they read the lessons in the chapter.

- As they add definitions to the third column of the chart, have children compare their predicted definitions of the vocabulary words to the actual definitions.

Word Recognition Use the Vocabulary Cards to reinforce recognition of each written word and its definition.

3 | Practice

Vocabulary Strategy: Using Picture Clues

Remind children that it can be helpful to use picture clues to determine the definition of a word. Have children look at the picture under the word *paleontologist* on page 203. Ask children: **What are the people in this picture doing?** Answers should include working in the field, examining bones or other fossils, digging in the rocks, roping off an area. **Do you think a paleontologist might do these things?** Explain to children that by looking carefully at this picture, they might be able to guess that a paleontologist is a scientist who studies fossils.

SCAFFOLDED INQUIRY

Explore Which fossils match the plants and animals?

⭐ **Science Objective**

• The student knows ways objects can be grouped according to similarities or differences of their physical characteristics.

1 | Build Background

This activity encourages children to use fossil clues to match fossils with organisms.

Managing Time and Materials

Time:	15 minutes
Groups:	individuals
Materials:	Puzzle Cards 1 and 2 (Activity Masters 10–11); safety scissors; crayons or markers; glue; construction paper (2 sheets)

2 | What to Do

Engage Ask children: **What is a fossil?** A part or print of a plant or animal that lived long ago.

Explore Have children match the fossil pictures to the correct plant or animal and glue the puzzles on a piece of construction paper.

Explain Explain to children that scientists use real fossils to study living things from long ago.

Extend Have children look at actual fossils and draw pictures of what they think the plants or animals that made these fossils might look like.

Evaluate Ask children: **Why do scientists study fossils?** To learn more about plants and animals that lived long ago.

3 | Explain Your Results

Children should look for similar characteristics to match the correct fossil to the plant or animal.

Process Skills

Have children **communicate** by answering questions about how they did the matching.

Explore Which fossils match the plants and animals?

A fossil is a print or remains of a plant or animal that lived long ago.

Materials

puzzle cards

crayons or markers

scissors and glue

paper

What to Do

❶ Cut out the cards.

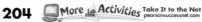

Be careful! Be careful with scissors.

Color the pictures.

❷ Put the cards together. Match each fossil to an animal or a plant.

❸ Glue the puzzles on paper.

Process Skills

You **communicate** when you answer questions.

Explain Your Results

Communicate How did you match fossils to plants and animals?

Activity Resources

Activity Book, pp. 77–78

Activity Rubric

Use Activity DVD Unit B, Chapter 7 to preview this activity.

Call 1-888-537-490 with activity questions.

🖥 More **Lab zone** Activities **Take It to the Net** pearsonsuccessnet.com

Find more about this activity at our Web site.

• See the **Teacher's Activity Guide** for more support.
• An alternative activity is also available to download.

How to Read Science

Retell

Retell means to tell what you learned in your own words.

Science Story

Fossil Shell

Long ago, an animal lived in this huge fossil shell. The animal had long arms. Scientists think the arms had rows of suction cups just like an octopus.

Apply It!
Communicate
Tell what you learned about the animal in the fossil shell.

Retell

205

How to Read Science Resource

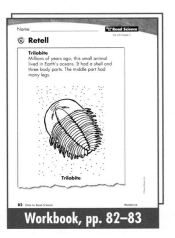

Workbook, pp. 82–83

ELL Support

For more practice on **Retell,** use **Every Student Learns Teacher's Guide,** p. 45.

Retell

⭐ Reading Objective

• The student uses a variety of strategies to comprehend text (for example, self-monitoring, predicting, retelling, discussing, restating ideas).

About the Target Skill

The target skill for *Fossils and Dinosaurs* is **Retell.** Children are introduced to the skill as you guide them through this page.

1 | Introduce

Tell children that you are going to describe something scary that happened to you when you were a child. Slowly describe a short, scary situation to children. Have volunteers retell the story using their own words.

2 | Model the Skill

Look together at the picture on page 205. Read the Science Story as a class. Ask children: **What kind of arms did this animal have?**

3 | Practice

Graphic Organizer

Look at the Graphic Organizer together. Work with children to complete the Graphic Organizer using the facts from the Science Story.

Apply It!

Retell

It had long arms.
Scientists think the arms had rows of suction cups.

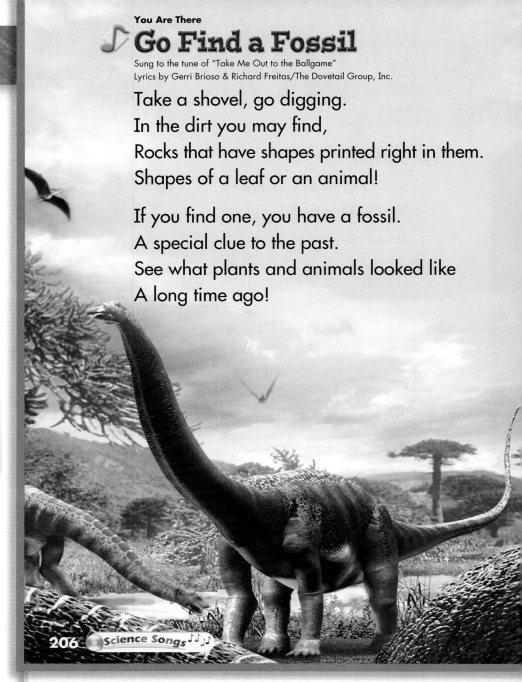

Chapter 7 **Lesson 1**

How can we learn about the past?

 Science Objective

• The student describes how fossils are formed.

1 Introduce

Quick ACTIVITY | TRANSPARENCY 39

Have children examine pictures of different plant and animal fossils. Ask: **How is a plant fossil like a plant? How is it different?** Discuss their answers. Then have children draw a picture of an animal and a picture of what its fossil would look like.

Access Prior Knowledge

Have children look at the picture on pages 206–207. Ask children: **What are these animals called?** Dinosaurs **How do we know what these animals looked like?** From fossils that scientists have found

Set Purpose

Tell children they are going to read about fossils. Help them set a **purpose for reading,** such as to discover how fossils are made.

2 Teach

Quick SUMMARY

• A fossil is the print or remains of a plant or animal that lived long ago.

• Paleontologists are scientists who study fossils.

Sing or play "Go Find a Fossil" for children. Then read page 207 together. Explain to children that fossils were formed from plants and animals that lived many years ago. Fossils are usually an imprint left by the plant or animal. Sometimes real plant or animal parts can be found as fossils. Tell children dinosaur bones are examples of fossils.

Tell children that a paleontologist is a scientist who studies fossils and helps us understand what plants and animals looked like long ago. Have children brainstorm tools paleontologists might use. (Map, charts, digging instruments, and rulers)

You Are There

♪ Go Find a Fossil

Sung to the tune of "Take Me Out to the Ballgame"
Lyrics by Gerri Brioso & Richard Freitas/The Dovetail Group, Inc.

Take a shovel, go digging.
In the dirt you may find,
Rocks that have shapes printed right in them.
Shapes of a leaf or an animal!

If you find one, you have a fossil.
A special clue to the past.
See what plants and animals looked like
A long time ago!

206 **Science Songs** ♪♪♪

Lesson 1 Resources

Workbook, p. 84

Science Songs ♪♪♪

Use the Science Songs CD to play "Go Find a Fossil" for the class.

SciLinks **Take It to the Net**
pearsonsuccessnet.com

Technology Link

Children can go online to discover more about **fossil** by using the NSTA *SciLink* available at **pearsonsuccessnet.com.**

Lesson 1

How can we learn about the past?

A **fossil** is a print or remains of a plant or animal that lived long ago. ①
Some fossils are very old bones. Other fossils are shapes left in rocks. ②

Scientists who study fossils are called **paleontologists.** Paleontologists use fossils to learn what plants and animals looked like long ago. ③

SciLinks Take It to the Net
keyword: fossil
pearsonsuccessnet.com
code: g2p207

207

ELL Leveled Support

Dinosaurs!

Beginning Point to pictures on pages 208–211. Say: **These are fossils.** Then point to the dinosaur on page 206. Ask: **What is this?** Some children may be able to tell you: *This is a dinosaur.* Point to a picture of dinosaur bones; one can be found on page 215. Say: **Bones—these are the bones of the dinosaur.** Point to one of your arm bones and to other bones to convey the meaning of the word *bone.* Ask a volunteer to point to a bone in his or her arm.

Intermediate Build on the above. Ask: **Who likes dinosaurs?** Ask children to name some dinosaurs they know. Preview the lesson by turning to pages 212–213 to show different kinds of dinosaurs. Have children repeat some of the names after you and enter them in their Word Collection Books.

Advanced Build on the above. Ask: **Why do we study fossils?** Discuss with children how studying fossils can help people learn about plants and animals that lived a long time ago. Do not expect correct English, but model correct English as you restate and respond to what children say.

Assign Quick Study pp. 78–79 to children who need help with lesson content.

Guide Comprehension

Ask children the following scaffolded questions to assess understanding.

Scaffolded Questions

① **Recall** **What is a fossil?** A print or remains of a plant or animal that lived long ago

② **Describe** **What are some types of fossils?** Very old bones and shapes that have been left in rocks

③ **Value** **Why do scientists look for fossils?** To learn about plants and animals that lived long ago

Extend Vocabulary

Write the words **paleontologist** and *geologist* on the board. Explain to children that the suffix *-gist* means "a scientist who studies." The prefix *paleo-* means "ancient," so a paleontologist is a scientist who studies ancient, or very old, things. The prefix *geo-* means "Earth," so a *geologist* studies Earth. Ask: **If the prefix bio- means "life," what does a biologist do?** Studies living things **If the prefix zoo- means "animal," what does a zoologist do?** Studies animals

Diagnostic Check

If... children have difficulty understanding what a fossil is,

then... show children examples of fossils (actual ones or pictures of) and point out what type of plant or animal part is represented in each fossil.

Science Objective

- The student describes how fossils are formed.

2|Teach (continued)

Quick SUMMARY

- Some fossils formed when a plant or animal was covered by sand or mud that turned to rock.
- Fossils can show the shape of a plant or animal.
- Fossils can show an animal's footprint.

Read pages 208–209 with children. Explain to children that fossils are usually formed in mud or sand that has turned to rock. This happens over a long time. The plants or animals die and their body parts decay, but a print is left behind in the solidifying mud or sand. Once the mud or sand has turned to rock, the print is in the rock permanently.

How Fossils Form

A fossil of a lizard has been left in a rock. The pictures on the next page show how one kind of fossil formed. Look at the other kinds of fossils on these pages.

This fossil shows the shape of another lizard that lived long ago.

2 Long ago, an animal made this footprint in the mud. The mud turned to rock. The footprint is another kind of fossil.

208

Science Misconception

Making New Fossils

Children may think no new fossils are being formed. Explain that plants and animals continue to die and their bodies may settle to the bottom of lakes or oceans. Mud and sand may bury them and the process of fossilization will begin.

ELL Support

Fossil Models

Have children carefully push leaves into blocks of clay and then carefully remove them. Have children look at the imprints. Tell children these imprints are similar to the imprints fossils make in rock.

For scaffolded instruction about fossils, use **Every Student Learns Teacher's Guide,** p. 46.

This shell is a fossil.

This fossil is of a plant that lived long ago.

A Fossil Is Formed

A lizard dies.

The lizard is covered by sand and mud.

The sand and mud become rock. The print of the lizard is a fossil.

✓ Lesson Checkpoint

1. What are fossils?

2. ↻ **Retell** how fossils are formed.

209

Science Background

More About Fossils

- Many fossils are not actual plant or animal parts. Petrified fossils are mineral copies of the original fossils. For example, water and minerals can flow through tiny holes in a buried dinosaur bone. When the water evaporates, the minerals are left in the bone, turning it into stone.

- Fossils are not always found in rocks. Insect fossils have been found in hardened tree sap called amber. Organisms that die in dry places can sometimes dry out so fast their soft parts do not decay. This process is called mummification. Organisms have also been preserved in large pieces of ice or in tar pits.

Social Studies Link

The Iceman

In September 1991, a couple hiking in the Alps Mountains in Italy discovered a mummified human. He is called the Iceman and is thought to date back to approximately 3300 B.C. He had tattoos and wore a grass cloak and leather clothes. Other items found with the Iceman included a copper ax, arrows with flint heads, and an unfinished bow. The Iceman is now on display at the Museum of Archaeology in Bolzano, Italy.

Ask children the following scaffolded questions to assess understanding.

Scaffolded Questions

1 **Recall** *What are fossils made from?* Dead plant or animal bodies

2 **Compare** *How is a footprint you make in the mud similar to a fossil? How is it different?* Both are impressions in soft mud or sand. A human footprint is new and an animal or plant that lived many years ago made a fossil.

3 **Infer** *Why might animals with shells make good fossils?* The hard shell makes a deep impression in the mud or sand.

Extend Vocabulary

Point out to children the word *footprint*. Tell children it is a compound word made up of the words "foot" and "print." Ask children what each word means. (Foot: part of the body; print: a mark made by pressing) Ask children to tell you a definition of the word based on the meanings of its parts. (A mark left by the pressure of a foot) Ask: *Who can tell me the meaning of the word fingerprint? Can you give some other examples of compound words?*

3 | Assess

✓ Lesson Checkpoint

1. Fossils can be parts of plants and animals that have turned into rock. Fossils can be marks left by animals.

2. ↻ **Retell** The plants or animals died and were quickly covered by sand and mud. The sand and mud turned into rock.

Lesson 2

What can we learn from fossils?

 Science Objective

- The student explains how fossils give information about plants and animals that lived on Earth long ago.

1 | Introduce

Quick ACTIVITY | TRANSPARENCY 40

Have children look at the pictures of fossils on pages 208 and 209. Then have them draw a picture of what they think one of the fossils might have looked like when it was alive. Have them tell whether the fossil was a plant or an animal.

Access Prior Knowledge

Ask children why fossils are clues to the past. (They tell us about plants and animals that lived long ago but are no longer on Earth.) Have them tell what things about plants and animals from the past we can learn from fossils. (Size, shape, where they lived) Write the responses on the board.

Set Purpose

Tell children they are going to read about what fossils can tell about the plants and animals that lived long ago. Help them set a **purpose for reading,** such as to understand the importance of fossils.

2 | Teach

Quick SUMMARY

- Fossils show the size and shape of plants and animals that lived long ago.
- An extinct plant or animal no longer lives on Earth.

Read pages 210–211 with children. Explain that plants and animals no longer found on Earth are called extinct. Remind children that dinosaurs are extinct animals. Tell children that plants and animals become extinct for many reasons.

210 | **UNIT B • Earth Science**

Lesson 2

What can we learn from fossils?

③ Fossils show the size and shape of plants and animals that lived long ago. Some fossils are of plants and animals that are extinct. An **extinct** ① plant or animal no longer lives on Earth.

The Archaeopteris is an extinct plant that looked like a tree. This fossil shows the shape of its leaves.

Sometimes plants and animals no longer get what they need from their habitat. The plants and animals cannot live. They may disappear from Earth forever.

210

Lesson 2 Resource

Workbook, p. 85

For scaffolded instruction about extinct species and the work of paleontologists, use **Every Student Learns Teacher's Guide,** p. 47.

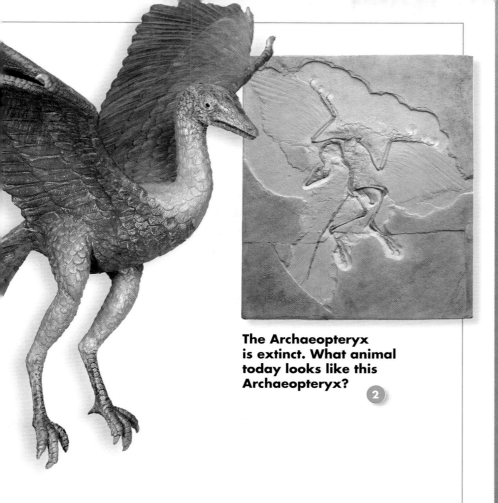

The Archaeopteryx is extinct. What animal today looks like this Archaeopteryx? ②

✓ **Lesson Checkpoint**

1. What do paleontologists learn from fossils?

2. 🎯 **Retell** What can happen to plants and animals when they no longer get what they need from their habitat?

Science Background

Extinction

There are many suggested reasons for extinction. One is climate change. Another is a natural catastrophe such as a meteor strike or an asteroid colliding with Earth. The Alvarez theory suggests that a giant asteroid hit Earth around 65 million years ago, sending huge amounts of hot ash and other debris into the atmosphere. This debris may have lingered in the atmosphere for months, blocking sunlight needed by plants to grow. This possibly caused the extinction of dinosaurs and other species that no longer had a food source.

ELL Support

Language Detectives: Building Vocabulary

Provide the following sentence frames for children to complete:

• _____ give clues about the past.

• An _____ plant or animal is no longer living on Earth.

• A change in a plant's or animal's _____ can cause the plant or animal to disappear forever.

One reason plants and animals become extinct is that their habitats no longer meet their needs. Another reason is that the environment changes. When the environment changes, some plants and animals survive and reproduce, and others die or move to new locations.

Have children look at the picture of the Archaeopteryx on page 211 and respond to the question in the caption. (A bird)

Assign Quick Study pp. 80–81 to children who need help with lesson content.

Guide Comprehension

Ask children the following scaffolded questions to assess understanding.

Scaffolded Questions

① **Describe** *What is an extinct plant or animal?* One that no longer lives on Earth.

② **Compare** *How does an Archaeopteryx compare to a bird of today?* Answers may include that the Archaeopteryx is larger, scalier, and has larger claws than many of today's birds.

③ **Value** *Why are fossils important?* Fossils give clues about what extinct plants and animals looked like. This helps people learn more about Earth's history.

Extend Vocabulary

Write the word **extinct** on the board. Tell children the word comes from a Latin verb meaning "no longer burning" or "no longer active." Explain that when used to describe plants or animals, the word means "no longer alive on Earth." Help children see the relationship between meanings. Ask: *Do you know what an extinct volcano is?* One no longer erupting Tell children that the word extinguish means "to stop from burning or put out."

3 | Assess

✓ **Lesson Checkpoint**

1. Paleontologists learn about the size and shape of plants and animals that lived long ago.

2. 🎯 **Retell** They cannot live. They become extinct.

Lesson 3

What were dinosaurs like?

 Science Objective

- The student describes different dinosaurs that lived on Earth long ago.

1 | Introduce

Quick ACTIVITY   `TRANSPARENCY 41`

Have children look at plastic models or pictures of dinosaurs. Then have them make a list of all the things they know about dinosaurs. Have children share their lists with the class. Ask: *Are there any animals on Earth now that look like dinosaurs?* Accept logical answers.

Access Prior Knowledge

In their science journals, have children make a list of all of the things they know about dinosaurs. Have children share their lists with the class. Have volunteers describe well-known dinosaurs portrayed in movies, television, or stories.

Set Purpose

Tell children you are going to read to them about dinosaurs. Help them set a **purpose for listening,** such as learning about the different types of dinosaurs.

2 | Teach

Quick SUMMARY

- Dinosaurs were animals that lived long ago and are now extinct.
- Dinosaurs varied in size and in what they ate.

Read pages 212–213 to children. Explain that the first dinosaurs appeared on Earth millions of years ago and then disappeared. Tell children that people and dinosaurs never lived on Earth at the same time.

As children look at the dinosaurs on pages 212–213, review the physical characteristics of each type of dinosaur.

Lesson 3

What were dinosaurs like?

Dinosaurs were animals that lived long ago. Some dinosaurs were very big. Other dinosaurs were small. Some dinosaurs ate plants. Some dinosaurs ate other animals. All dinosaurs are extinct.

A Compsognathus was about the same size as a chicken.

212

Lesson 3 Resource

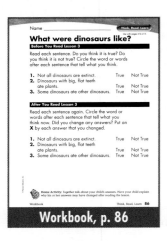

Workbook, p. 86

The Barosaurus was very tall. ②

Crunch!
The Iguanodon's big, flat teeth helped it chew plants.

Gulp!
A Dilophosaurus caught and ate other dinosaurs. ③

1. ✓**Checkpoint** What did an Iguanodon eat?

2. **Writing** in Science Write about some ways dinosaurs were different. Tell how they are the same.

213

ELL Leveled Support
Describing Dinosaurs

Beginning Show children a picture of a dinosaur. Have children describe its physical characteristics.

Intermediate Have children look at a picture that shows the teeth of that dinosaur. Ask children to decide what kind of food that dinosaur probably ate. Have children give support for their answers.

Advanced Show children pictures of two dinosaurs with different characteristics. Have children write a brief description of each dinosaur, including what it might possibly have eaten.

For scaffolded instruction about dinosaurs, use **Every Student Learns Teacher's Guide,** p. 48.

Explain to children that some dinosaurs ate plants, and others ate other animals.

Assign Quick Study pp. 82–83 to children who need help with lesson content.

Guide Comprehension

Ask children the following scaffolded questions to assess understanding.

Scaffolded Questions

① **Recall** *What is a dinosaur?* An animal that lived long ago

② **Contrast** *How is a Compsognathus different from a Barosaurus?*
Compsognathus was small, Barosaurus was big.

③ **Infer** *Which dinosaur was more likely to eat a Compsognathus, a Dilophosaurus or an Iguanodon? Why?*
A Dilophosaurus because it ate animals and an Iguanodon ate plants.

Extend Vocabulary

Explain to children that the word **dinosaur** comes from the Greek word *deinos* meaning "terrible" and the Greek word *sauros* meaning "lizard." Have children compare the physical characteristics of dinosaurs to those of lizards.

Diagnostic Check

If... children have a hard time learning the characteristics of different types of dinosaurs,

then... draw a five-column chart on the board. Write the names of the dinosaurs discussed in the first column. Label the next four columns *Big, Small, Plant eater,* and *Meat eater.* Have children tell you where to place checkmarks for each dinosaur. Have them use the information on pages 212–213 to help them.

3 | Assess

1. ✓**Checkpoint** Plants

2. **Writing** in Science Have children write in their science journals. Check children's work for accuracy.

Science Objective

- The student describes different dinosaurs that lived on Earth long ago.

2 | Teach (continued)

Quick SUMMARY

- Fossils give paleontologists clues about what dinosaurs looked like.
- Different dinosaurs had different physical features, which allowed them to survive in their environments.

Read pages 214–215 to children. Have children look at the pictures of the Stegosaurus on page 215. Have children note how small the Stegosaurus's head was in comparison to its body. Ask children what the spikes found on the end of the Stegosaurus's tail might have been used for. (Protection If another dinosaur attacked the Stegosaurus, it could swing its tail and hit the other dinosaur with the spikes.)

Explain to children that paleontologists will often look at dinosaur teeth to determine what the dinosaur ate. Ask: **What did the Stegosaurus eat?** Plants Have children look at the Tyrannosaurus rex on page 214. Ask: **What do the Tyrannosaurus rex's teeth look like? What did the Tyrannosaurus rex eat?** They are long and sharp and were probably used to tear meat.

Have children look at the picture of the Triceratops on page 214. Ask: **How did the Triceratops use its horns?** To defend itself against other dinosaurs

Learning About Dinosaurs

Paleontologists study fossils of dinosaur bones. They want to know what dinosaurs looked like. The Stegosaurus had a large body. Its head and mouth were small. Paleontologists think this dinosaur ate plants. A Stegosaurus needed an environment with lots of plants.

A Triceratops had three horns on its head! The horns may have helped stop other animals from attacking.

What big teeth! A Tyrannosaurus rex probably used its sharp teeth to eat meat.

214

Science Misconception

Dinosaur Features

After looking at the pictures of the dinosaurs on pages 212–215, children may think scientists know exactly what dinosaurs looked like. While scientists are sure about the skeletal structures of many species of dinosaurs, information about skin type, skin color, and other physical features is open to interpretation. Artists sometimes draw features such as lips and eyelids on dinosaurs to make them look familiar.

Math Link

Number Prefixes

Explain to children that the prefix *tri-* means "three." Remind children that a Triceratops has three horns on its head. Ask children to brainstorm words that contain the prefix *tri-* when it represents the number three. Answers might include triple (something done 3 times), tricycle (3 wheels), triathlon (3 sporting events), and triplets (3 children). If time permits, this activity can be done with other number prefixes.

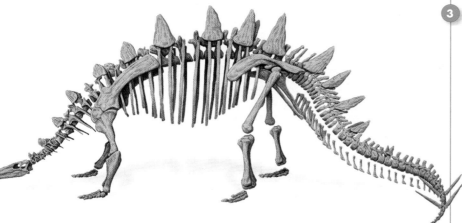

Look at the skeleton of a Stegosaurus. Scientists used the skeleton to make a model of how the Stegosaurus may have looked.

③

✓ Lesson Checkpoint

1. What did paleontologists learn about a Stegosaurus by looking at its bones?

2. **Writing** in Science Write one sentence. Tell which dinosaur is your favorite and why.

215

Science Background

More About Dinosaurs

• Tyrannosaurus rex was a fierce predator that walked on two huge, powerful back legs. This meat-eating dinosaur had a large head with sharp, pointed teeth and well-developed jaw muscles. It had tiny, almost useless, forearms, each with two fingers. Tyrannosaurus rex could be 40 feet long, 20 feet tall, and weigh 14,000 pounds. Tyrannosaurus rex had a stiff, pointed tail that it used as a counterbalance for its huge head and for making rapid turns.

• Stegosaurus was 26–30 feet in length, about 9 feet tall, and weighed about 6,800 pounds. The Stegosaurus's back legs were twice as long as its front legs. The Stegosaurus had a very small brain—about the size of a walnut.

Art Link

Dinosaur Drawings

Ask children to suppose they have discovered a new type of dinosaur. Have children draw, color, and label the body parts of this dinosaur. Have volunteers share their drawings with the class. Display children's work on a bulletin board or wall.

Ask children the following scaffolded questions to assess understanding.

Scaffolded Questions

① **Describe** *How would you describe a Stegosaurus?* It had a large body and a small head and mouth.

② **Compare** *Compare the diet of the Stegosaurus to the diet of the Tyrannosaurus rex.* A Stegosaurus ate plants and a Tyrannosaurus rex ate meat.

③ **Infer** *What can fossils tell us about dinosaurs?* Fossils can be used to describe a dinosaur's size, shape, diet, and behaviors.

Extend Vocabulary

Point out the word *skeleton* on page 215. Ask children: *What is a skeleton?* Accept reasonable answers and try to elicit the idea that a skeleton is a framework of bones inside the body. Relate this to children's study of animals with backbones in Chapter 2, saying: *A skeleton is the framework of bones inside the body that supports the muscles and organs of any animal having a backbone.* Then ask: *What animals with backbones can you name?*

3 | Assess

✓ Lesson Checkpoint

1. They learned that the Stegosaurus had a big body, but a small head and mouth.

2. **Writing** in Science Have children write their answers in their science journals. Check children's work.

Lesson 4

What are some new discoveries?

 Science Objective

- The student explains how new discoveries are made by paleontologists.

1 | Introduce

Quick ACTIVITY | TRANSPARENCY 42

Have children think about chicken eggs and brainstorm a list of physical characteristics of the shell of the egg. Ask: **What do you think is the purpose of the chicken eggshell?** To protect the developing chicken **What will happen to the developing chicken if the eggshell breaks before the baby chick is fully grown?** The chick will die.

Access Prior Knowledge

In their science journals, have children make a list of animals that lay eggs. Have volunteers share their lists with the class. Children should list different types of birds and reptiles. Children may also list fish and amphibians.

Set Purpose

Tell children they are going to read about a dinosaur called the Oviraptor. Help them set a **purpose for reading,** such as to find out what paleontologists have discovered about the Oviraptor.

2 | Teach

Quick SUMMARY

- Paleontologists think that the fossils of a small dinosaur called the Oviraptor and its eggs show that the dinosaur was keeping its eggs safe.

Read pages 216–217 with children. Explain to children that sometimes it is difficult for paleontologists to know what happened so many years ago.

What are some new discoveries?

An Oviraptor was a small dinosaur. Paleontologists found fossils of an Oviraptor near some eggs. They thought the Oviraptor was stealing the eggs to eat them.

1 **Oviraptor eggs were twice as long as chicken eggs.**

Later, another Oviraptor fossil was found. It was sitting on the same kind of eggs. Now paleontologists think that the Oviraptor was not stealing the eggs. They think the Oviraptor was keeping its own eggs safe.

216

Lesson 4 Resource

Workbook, p. 87

Paleontologists now think that Oviraptors kept their eggs safe from other animals. ②

✓ Lesson Checkpoint

1. What did paleontologists learn about the Oviraptor?

2. **Math in Science** Oviraptor eggs were about 20 centimeters long. Find something in your classroom that you think is about 20 centimeters long. Measure it.

217

One example to tell children about is the Oviraptor. When paleontologists first discovered the Oviraptor near some eggs, they thought the dinosaur was stealing the eggs. With more discoveries, they realized that the Oviraptor was keeping her eggs safe.

Assign Quick Study pp. 84–85 to children who need help with lesson content.

Guide Comprehension

Ask children the following scaffolded questions to assess understanding.

Scaffolded Questions

① **Describe** *How large are Oviraptor eggs?* About twice as long as chicken eggs

② **Infer** *Why was it important for the Oviraptor to stay close to her eggs?* To keep them safe from other animals

③ **Synthesize** *How did paleontologists change their opinions about the Oviraptor?* At first, paleontologists thought that Oviraptors were stealing eggs. They later realized that Oviraptors were keeping their eggs safe from predators.

Extend Vocabulary

Point out the word *Oviraptor* on page 217. Tell children that the Latin word *ova* means *eggs*. Ask: **What other word for a shape sounds like it comes from the same word?** Oval. Ask children to draw and label a nest of oval eggs.

3 | Assess

✓ Lesson Checkpoint

1. It protected its own eggs from predators.

2. **Math in Science** Answers will vary. Check children's work.

Science Background

Nurturing Dinosaurs

For many years scientists believed that like most modern-day reptiles, dinosaurs did not nurture their young. Dinosaur remains found more recently have led paleontologists to change their view. Some paleontologists now believe that at least some dinosaurs protected their eggs, actively nurtured their young, and even brought them food in a birdlike fashion.

ELL Support

Comparing Egg Sizes

Show children pictures of chicken eggs. Have children think about the size of an Oviraptor's eggs when you describe them as being two times the size of chicken eggs. Ask children to suggest an object that would be about the size of an Oviraptor's egg.

For scaffolded instruction about the Oviraptor, use **Every Student Learns Teacher's Guide,** p. 49.

Lab zone Guided Inquiry

SCAFFOLDED INQUIRY

■■ Investigate How can you make a model of a fossil?

⭐ **Science Objective**

- The student knows that people use scientific processes including hypothesis, making inferences, and recording and communicating data when exploring the natural world.

1 | Build Background

This activity encourages children to make impressions of a shell in clay that will show details of the shell's surface and shape.

Managing Time and Materials

Time:	30 minutes
Groups:	pairs
Materials:	*modeling clay* (1 stick; ½ each partner); *seashell;* 2 small classroom objects (paper clip, Snap Cube®, eraser)

Materials listed in *italics* are kit materials.

Advance Preparation

You may wish to gather a variety of small classroom objects that will make good impressions when pressed into clay.

Safety Note

Remind children not to choose sharp or breakable classroom objects for their fossils.

2 | What to Do

Encourage Guided Inquiry

Preview the activity and the materials with children. Ask: **How are modeling clay, seashells, and classroom objects used to make models of fossils?**

Guide children to write an If…/then… statement such as: **If a seashell or other object is pressed into modeling clay, an imprint will be formed.**

Investigate How can you make a model of a fossil?

Materials

shell

clay

2 classroom objects

What to Do

❶ **Make a model** of a fossil. Press a shell into clay.

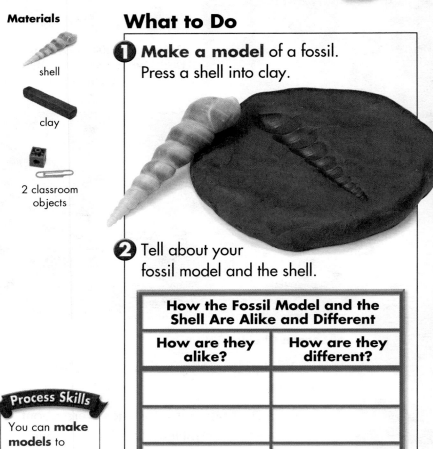

❷ Tell about your fossil model and the shell.

Process Skills

You can **make models** to understand how things happen.

How the Fossil Model and the Shell Are Alike and Different	
How are they alike?	**How are they different?**

Activity Resources

Activity Book, pp. 79–80

Activity Rubric

Use Activity DVD Unit B, Chapter 7 to preview this activity.

Call 1-888-537-4908 with activity questions.

More Lab zone Activities Take It to the Net pearsonsuccessnet.com

Find more about this activity at our Web site.

- See the **Teacher's Activity Guide** for more support.
- An alternative activity is also available to download.

3 Now pick an object in your classroom. Make a fossil model of the object.

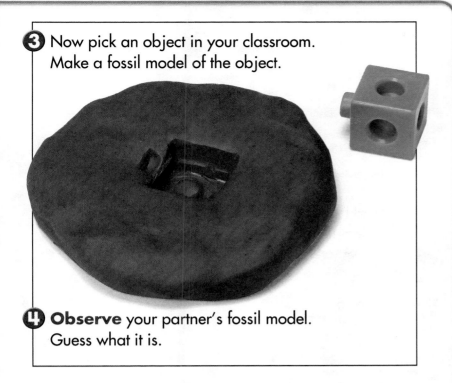

4 **Observe** your partner's fossil model. Guess what it is.

Explain Your Results

1. How did you **infer** what your partner's fossil model was?

2. How do fossils give clues about living things?

Go Further

What else could you do to make models of fossils? Make a plan and try it.

Science Background

Digging for Fossils

After being found, a fossil must be carefully removed from the rock that surrounds it. First, a fossil is labeled and photographed before it is removed from rock. Most of the rock that surrounds a fossil is removed with large tools such as picks or shovels. The 2–3 inches of rock closest to a fossil is removed with small hand tools such as a trowel, hammer, whisk, or dental tool. Before removing a crumbling or fragile fossil from rock, a quick-setting glue can be applied to it. Fossils are carefully packed before they are moved to a lab for study.

ELL Support

Access Content Before beginning the activity, conduct an inventory of materials with children. Solicit other names for each item. Accept labels in English and children's home languages.

Engage Hold up a stick of modeling clay. Ask children: *How can modeling clay be used?* Remind children that they will be using modeling clay to make models of fossils.

Explore Have children follow the steps of the activity. As children observe similarities and differences between the model and the shell, have them record their observations in the data table.

Explain After completing the activity, have children explain how they made models of fossils.

Extend Children may want to make fossil models of organisms other than mollusks. Discuss other objects children might use and play the guessing game again.

Evaluate Ask children to examine their data. How were the model and the shell alike? different?

3 | Explain Your Results

Use the "Explain Your Results" questions to help children review evidence and develop explanations.

- Give children an opportunity to reflect on the data, or evidence, they have gathered in the investigation.

- Have children use the evidence gathered to develop their explanations. Accept reasonable, logical explanations.

1. **Infer** Check children's work for accuracy.
2. The marks on the fossils are the same as parts of the real things. The fossils help you picture what the real thing looked like.

Go Further

Children may propose any number of changes to the activity to fully understand how to make models of fossils.

Post other questions children have about making models of fossils. Encourage children to investigate on their own.

Process Skills

Make Models

Discuss the importance of making models. Remind children that science is a way of learning about the world around us. Many questions in science have been answered by making models of a real-life thing. Remind children that when they look at a globe or map, they are looking at a model of Earth. You can use the Process Skills sheet on Modeling at this time.

Math in Science

Measuring Fossil Leaves

 Science Objective

- The student uses customary and metric units to measure, compare, and order objects according to their lengths, weights, or capacities.

1 | Introduce

Quick ACTIVITY

Hold up a metric ruler. Ask children: **What is this tool?** A ruler **What is this tool used for?** To measure lengths or distances Remind children that during science class, they will measure in metric units. Tell children that when they run a 100-meter dash in a track-and-field event or drink juice from a 2-liter bottle, they are using metric units.

2 | Teach the Skill

Read pages 220–221 with children. Hold up a meterstick. Remind children that the meter is the basic unit of length in the metric system. Tell children that if a meterstick is divided into 100 equal parts, each part is called a centimeter. Use an overhead projector, common objects, and a clear metric ruler to review with children how to measure the length of an object in centimeters. Using the objects you measured on the overhead projector, review with children how to make a bar graph.

After children have reviewed measurement, have them use a metric ruler to measure each leaf shown on page 220. Have children use these lengths to complete the bar graph on page 221.

Math in Science

Measuring Fossil Leaves

Look at the fossils of 3 leaves. Estimate how long each leaf is in centimeters. Measure the leaves.

220 **Tools** Take It to the Net
pearsonsuccessnet.com

Activity Resource

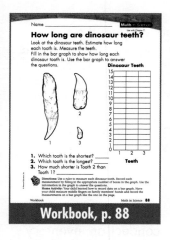

Workbook, p. 88

Tools Take It to the Net
pearsonsuccessnet.com

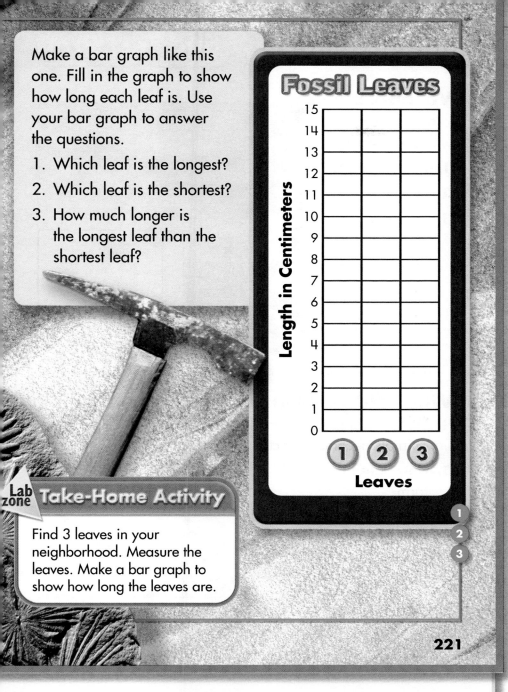

Make a bar graph like this one. Fill in the graph to show how long each leaf is. Use your bar graph to answer the questions.

1. Which leaf is the longest?
2. Which leaf is the shortest?
3. How much longer is the longest leaf than the shortest leaf?

Fossil Leaves

Length in Centimeters

15
14
13
12
11
10
9
8
7
6
5
4
3
2
1
0

① ② ③

Leaves

Lab zone Take-Home Activity

Find 3 leaves in your neighborhood. Measure the leaves. Make a bar graph to show how long the leaves are.

221

Scaffolded Questions

① Recall *What is the purpose of a ruler?* To measure length or distance

② Calculate *How many centimeters are in 1 meter?* 100

③ Measure *To the nearest whole centimeter, how long is your shoe?* Answers will vary.

3 | Assess

1. 3
2. 1
3. 6.5 cm

Take-Home Activity

Tips for Success

- Assist children in creating a bar graph and writing in the correct headings. Also, review how to fill in the bar graph.

- Review the instructions for finding three leaves to measure. Review how to use a metric ruler to measure in centimeters.

- Have children bring their leaves and completed bar graphs to school to present to their classmates. Check children's measurements for accuracy.

- As an extension, have children spread their fingers as far apart as they can and measure their hand span from their little finger to their thumb. Have children compare their measurements with other members of the class.

- Children can share their bar graphs with their family or friends.

Chapter 7 Review and Test Prep

Vocabulary

1. B
2. A
3. C

What did you learn?

4. Some plants and animals become extinct because their habitats can no longer meet their needs.
5. A dead leaf is quickly covered by mud and sand. After many years, everything turns to rock.
6. People can use fossils to learn what plants and animals looked like long ago, what animals ate, and what some of the animal behaviors were.

Chapter 7 Review and Test Prep

Vocabulary

Which picture goes with each word?

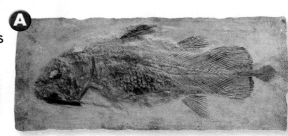

1. paleontologist
2. fossil
3. dinosaur

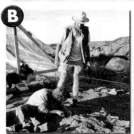

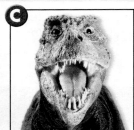

A

B

C

What did you learn?

4. Why do some plants and animals become extinct?
5. How does a leaf fossil form?
6. How can people use fossils to learn about the past?

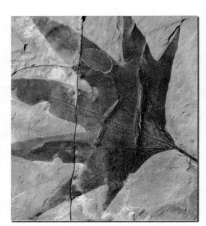

Assessment Resources

Name ____________ Chapter 7 Test

Read each question and choose the best answer. Then fill in the circle next to the correct answer.

1 Look at the picture.

Which word goes with the picture?
Ⓐ fossil
Ⓑ extinct
Ⓒ dinosaur
Ⓓ paleontologist

2 What do paleontologists study?
Ⓕ fossils
Ⓖ people
Ⓗ weather
Ⓘ museums

Assessment Book — Chapter 7 Test 39

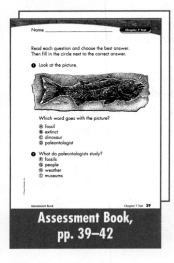

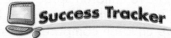

Assessment Book, pp. 39–42

MindPoint Quiz Show

MindPoint enables students to test their knowledge of the chapter in a game format.

ExamView® Use ExamView as a print or online assessment tool to create alternative tests for students.

Success Tracker

Data management system to track Adequate Yearly Progress (AYP) and provide intervention online at **pearsonsuccessnet.com/successtracker**

Take-Home Booklet

Children can make a Take-Home Booklet using Workbook pp. 89–90.

Process Skills

7. Communicate Tell how fossils help us learn what some dinosaurs were like.

◉ Retell

8.

A Triceratops' head could grow up to 7 feet long. It had a bird-like beak to help it eat plants.

Retell what you learned about the Triceratops.

Retell

Test Prep

Fill in the circle next to the correct answer.

9. Which dinosaur was as tall as a chicken?

Ⓐ Tyrannosaurus

Ⓑ Barosaurus

Ⓒ Compsognathus

Ⓓ Archaeopteryx

10. Writing in Science Write two sentences. Tell what you learned about paleontologists.

223

7. Communicate Possible answer: Fossils tell the size and shape of dinosaurs, what they ate, and how some took care of their eggs.

◉ Retell

8.   Retell

> A Triceratops had a very big head. It ate plants with its birdlike beak.

Test Prep

9. C

10. Writing in Science Check children's work for accuracy.

Intervention and Remediation

			Teacher Edition Resources			**Ancillary Resources**		
⭐ **Science Objectives**	**Review Item**	**Student Edition Pages**	**Guide Comprehension**	**Extend Vocab**	**Diagnostic Check**	**Vocab Cards**	**Quick Study**	**Workbook Pages**
The student describes how fossils are formed.	5	206–209	207, 209		207	•	207	84
The student explains how fossils give information about plants and animals that lived on Earth long ago.	4, 6, 7, 8	210–211	207, 209, 211, 215		207	•	211	85
The student describes different dinosaurs that lived on Earth long ago.	7, 8, 9	212–215	211, 213, 215, 217	213	213	•	213, 217	86
The student explains how new discoveries are made by paleontologists.	10	216–217	217	207				87

Biography

Susan Hendrickson

 Science Objective

• The student knows that men and women of all ethnic and social backgrounds make contributions to science and technology, practice science and technology, investigate the world around them, and can answer scientific questions.

1 Introduce

Build Background

Review with children that a Tyrannosaurus rex was a large dinosaur that walked on 2 legs and had sharp teeth for eating meat.

2 Teach

Quick SUMMARY

• Sue Hendrickson is a paleontologist, or fossil hunter.

Read page 224 together with children. Susan Hendrickson is a paleontologist who found the fossil bones of a Tyrannosaurus rex. She named the fossil skeleton Sue. Sue is now on display at the Field Museum in Chicago.

Have children look at the Tyrannosaurus rex skeleton shown on page 224. Ask children to infer how useful the front limbs of the Tyrannosaurus rex would have been. Children should infer that, due to their very small size, the front limbs would not have been very useful.

3 Explore

Have children look at a map of the world. Tell children that only about 30 Tyrannosaurus rex fossils have been found around the world. In the US, Tyrannosaurus rex fossils have been found in the states of Montana, Wyoming, Utah, Texas, and South Dakota (where Sue was found). Tyrannosaurus rex fossils have also been found in the Canadian provinces of Alberta and Saskatchewan, and in the Asian country of Mongolia.

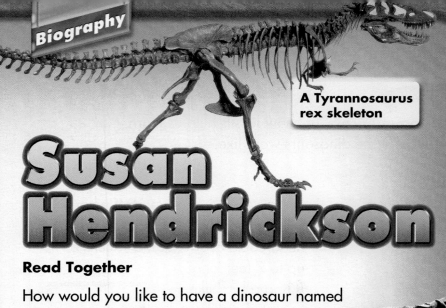

A Tyrannosaurus rex skeleton

Biography

Susan Hendrickson

Read Together

How would you like to have a dinosaur named after you? This Tyrannosaurus rex is named Sue. It is named after Susan Hendrickson. Susan Hendrickson is a paleontologist. She looks for extinct animals to show in museums.

Susan Hendrickson found the fossil bones of this Tyrannosaurus rex. You can see Sue the Tyrannosaurus rex if you visit the Field Museum in Chicago.

Sue, the Tyrannosaurus rex skeleton

Lab zone **Take-Home Activity**

Use pipe cleaners to make a model of a Tyrannosaurus rex skeleton. Share your model with your family.

224

Take-Home Activity

Tips for Success

• Assist children in writing down the assignment and making sure they clearly understand it.

• Children may ask family members to help them make their models.

• Have children bring their completed models to school to present to their classmates.

• Display children's work in the classroom.

Use Information from Text and Graphics

You can use information from text and charts to help you answer science questions.

Month	Rainfall
March	1 inch
April	4 inches
May	3 inches

March had the least rain. The months of April and May had more rain than March.

Use the information from the text and the chart to answer the question.

Which month had the most rain?

Ⓐ March
Ⓑ April
Ⓒ May
Ⓓ June

The text tells that April and May had more rain than March. Look at the chart. Which month had the most rain?

225

Test Talk

Test-Taking Strategies

Science Objective

- The student uses tables and graphs to represent and interpret data.

Use Information from Text and Graphics

Teach children this strategy to help them improve their scores on multiple-choice tests.

- Have children read the text on p. 225 and look at the chart.
- Help children read and understand the chart. Ask them to point to the column labeled "Month" and the column labeled "Rainfall."
- Guide children to read the information in each row of the chart by using their finger to point to each month and then moving it across to the right to read the rainfall.
- Children may also locate a rainfall and then move across to the left to identify the month. Ask children to use the chart to find which month had the least amount of rain. (March)
- Ask children to read the question. Tell them to reread the text and use the chart to help them answer it. Then have children complete the exercise.

Assess: Use Information from Text and Graphics

B

Wrap-Up

Science Objective

- The student increases comprehension by rereading, retelling, and discussion.

1 | Chapter Summaries

Group Summarize

- Use the chapter summaries on p. 226 to make a class summary chart about Earth Science. Include a section on the chart for each chapter.
- Divide children into groups. Each group should work as a team to review one chapter. Encourage group discussions. Allow each group to present information about the chapter to the class.
- As each group presents, help children organize information into clear summary statements on the class summary chart.

2 | Performance Assessment

- Have children work individually or in pairs to complete the task.
- Provide children with sand, a cookie pan, and water for making their models of water erosion. Have children adapt their models to show how erosion could be slowed down.
- Have children share their information with classmates.

Unit B Wrap-Up

Chapter 5

What are Earth's natural resources?
- Sunlight, air, and water are some of Earth's natural resources.

Chapter 6

How does weather change?
- Weather can change from day to day.
- Different seasons have different kinds of weather.

Chapter 7

How can people learn about Earth long ago?
- People study fossils to learn about plants and animals that lived on Earth long ago.

226

Science Background

The Grand Canyon

One of the most dramatic examples of rock erosion in the United States is the Grand Canyon. During the past five or six million years, the Colorado River and its tributaries have carved away rock in the Grand Canyon. Even though the Grand Canyon rarely receives more than 15 inches of rain each year, the rain can come suddenly in the form of violent storms, increasing the effects of water erosion. The Grand Canyon continues to grow and change as the Colorado River and its tributaries flow through it. As long as rain and snow continue to fall in northern Arizona, upriver from the Grand Canyon, the forces of erosion will continue to shape it.

Performance Assessment

Make a model of water erosion.

- Put some sandbox sand on a cookie pan.
- Tilt the pan slightly.
- Slowly pour water from a cup at the top of the pan.
- Watch the water erode the sand.
- Tell how you could keep the sand from eroding.

Read More about Earth Science!

227

- Organize the class into groups.
- Explain that they are going to find out about different ways that wind, water, and sunlight can be used to produce energy. This helps us save Earth's natural resources.
- Ask children to work together to find examples of alternative energy sources.
- Each group should prepare a poster/mural to present to the class.
- Encourage children to draw or cut out/paste pictures showing their type of alternative energy source and identify how it affects people.
- After all posters/murals have been presented, lead the class in a discussion of similarities and differences in the types of alternative energy sources presented.

My Science Journal

What do you do on a rainy, snowy, windy, or sunny day?

Ask children to write about or draw pictures showing activities that they can do in different types of weather. Have children share their stories or pictures with classmates.

Read More about Earth Science!

Literature Library

- *Let's Go Rock Collecting* by Roma Gans ISBN: 0-064-45170-4
- *Tornado Alert* by Franklyn M. Branley ISBN: 0-064-45904-5
- *A Year Goes Round: Poems for the Months* by Karen B. Winnick ISBN: 1-563-97898-9

Big Book Collection

- *My Visit to the Dinosaurs* by Aliki ISBN: 0-328-11790-0

Experiment Does gravel, sand, or soil make the best imprint?

 Science Objectives

- The student participates in groups to conduct experiments and solve problems.
- The student understands that, through the use of science processes, people can solve problems and make decisions.

1 | Build Background

In this full inquiry experiment, students review ideals of a fair test, and use scientific thinking processes.

After students conduct the experiment shown, they may be ready to engage in the thinking processes of Full Inquiry. Suggestions for Full Inquiries that students can do independently are listed in Go Further.

This experiment helps children perform a test to see if the clearest fossil imprints are made in sand, gravel, or potting soil.

Managing Time and Materials

Time: 30 minutes

Groups: small groups

Materials: *gravel ($\frac{1}{2}$ c); sand ($\frac{1}{2}$ c); potting soil ($\frac{1}{2}$ c); 3 clear plastic cups (9 oz); 3 paper plates; scallop shell; 3 index cards; safety goggles (1 per child)*

Materials listed in *italics* are kit materials.

Advance Preparation

For each group, fill 3 clear plastic cups with $\frac{1}{2}$ c gravel, $\frac{1}{2}$ c sand, and $\frac{1}{2}$ c potting soil, respectively.

Safety Note

Children should wear safety goggles during the activity and wash their hands when they finish.

Teaching Tips

- Children may need to wipe off the shell after making each imprint. Have paper towels on hand.
- Have children gently press the shell into the sand so that sand particles do not fall into the imprint.

Experiment Does gravel, sand, or soil make the best imprint?

Sometimes sand can slowly change to rock. An imprint made by a plant or animal can become a fossil in the rock.

Materials

safety goggles

3 paper plates

3 index cards

cup with gravel, cup with sand, cup with soil

shell

Process Skills

A **hypothesis** answers a question that you can test.

Ask a question.
Which will make the best imprint?

Make your hypothesis.
Is the best imprint made in gravel, sand, or soil? Tell what you think.

Plan a fair test.
Use the same amount on each plate.

Do your test.

1 Put gravel, sand or soil on each plate.

Label each plate.

sand

soil

gravel

Activity Resources

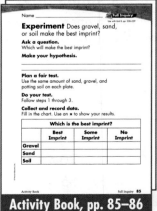

Use Activity DVD Unit B to preview this activity.

Call
1-888-537-4908
with activity questions.

 More Lab Activities **Take It to the Net** pearsonsuccessnet.com

Find more about this activity at our Web site.

- See the **Teacher's Activity Guide** for more support.
- An alternative activity is also available to download.

2 Press the shell into the gravel, sand, or soil.

Wash your hands when you are finished.

3 **Observe** the imprint in each pile.

Collect and record data.
Fill in the chart. Use an **X**.

Which is the best imprint?			
	Best Imprint	**Some Imprint**	**No Imprint**
Gravel			
Sand			
Soil			

Tell your conclusion.
Does gravel, sand, or soil make the best imprint? Which would make the best imprint fossil?

Go Further
What might happen if you use wet sand, soil, and gravel? Try it and find out.

Science Background

- Scallops are mollusks with two hinged shells (bivalves), which filter their food from the surrounding water. Scallops are different from oysters, clams, and mussels because they have the ability to move short distances by rapidly opening and closing their shells. Most scallops have a creamy, beige, light blonde color. Scallops are primarily harvested by dredging and are shucked soon after capture. They cannot hold their shells closed; therefore, once they are out of the water, they lose moisture quickly and die.

- When children do this Full Inquiry Experiment, they use the Steps of the Scientific Method:

  1. Ask a question.
  2. Make a hypothesis.
  3. Plan a fair test.
  4. Do your test.

  5. Collect and record data.
  6. Tell your conclusion.
  7. Go further.

---

2 | What to Do

Encourage Full Inquiry Preview the activity, the materials, and the scientific method with children. Guide them to rephrase their hypotheses as If.../then... statements such as: *If sand, gravel, and soil are used to make imprints of a shell, then sand will make the best imprint.*

Engage Ask children: *Why are fossils important to us?* (They can tell us things about plants and animals that lived on Earth long ago).

Explore As children experiment, they should collect and record their data in the data table.

Explain Have each group share its data. Ask children: *Was the best imprint made in gravel, sand, or soil?* (Sand)

Extend Have children hypothesize what they think would happen if they dampen the soil before putting the fossil into it. Have children dampen the soil and press the scallop shell into it.

Evaluate Have students review their hypotheses and tell their conclusion. Did the experimental results support their hypotheses or not?

3 | Assess

Tell your conclusion.
Children should conclude that a scallop shell will leave a clear impression in sand, a partial imprint in potting soil, and no imprint in gravel. Children should explain how they modeled fossil imprinting and how they came to their conclusion.

Go Further Children may propose a solution about what might happen if wet gravel, sand, and soil were used. Guide children to develop questions that can be answered by modifying the activity. Then have children select a question to inquire further. Post other chidren's questions about imprint fossils. Encourage children to investigate on their own.

Process Skills

Hypothesis
Scientists often gather information about a question and then suggest a possible answer to the question. This possible answer is called a hypothesis. After scientists develop a hypothesis, they can perform an experiment to see if the hypothesis is correct or incorrect.

Language Arts Objectives

- The student predicts what a passage is about based on its title and illustrations.
- The student uses prior knowledge, illustrations, and text to make predictions.
- The student makes inferences based on text and prior knowledge (for example, regarding a character's traits, feelings, or actions).
- The student reads aloud familiar stories, poems, or passages with a beginning degree of fluency and expression.

1 | Introduce

Preview

Read and point to the title of the poem. Point out the author's name. Ask children to predict what the poem is about based on the pictures and the title.

Access Prior Knowledge

Ask children to describe a time they have been outside on a windy day. Guide children to use their senses to describe the experience by asking questions such as: What did the wind feel like on your face? Was it warm or cold? Could you see the wind? What did the wind do to trees and other plants? How did the wind affect other objects?

2 | Teach

Read the poem aloud to children. Encourage children to think about a windy day as they listen.

Explain to children that the word *mischievous* means teasing or full of tricks. The wind can be mischievous because it can move objects from one place to another.

Ask: **Why do you think the author wrote "brushing the world with feathery wings?"** Because the wind moves softly over objects like feathers.

The Spring Wind

by Charlotte Zolotow

The summer wind
is soft and sweet
the winter wind is strong
the autumn wind is mischievous
and sweeps the leaves along.

230

Reading Link

Rhyming words

Tell children to listen for rhyming words at the ends of the phrases as you read the poem *The Spring Wind* to them a second time. Ask children to name the rhyming word pairs and write them on the board (*strong* and *along*; *things*, *wings*, and *sings*). Have children say other words that rhyme with each pair and make a class word list.

The wind I love the best
comes gently after rain
smelling of spring and growing things
brushing the world with feathery wings
while everything glistens, and
    everything sings
in the spring wind
after the rain.

231

Explore Further

Poems About Weather and Dinosaurs

Children might enjoy reading other poems about land, water, air, and weather, such as:

- *Stegosaurus* by Robert Byrd
- *Lines on a Small Potato* by Margaret Fishback
- *Who Has Seen the Wind* by Christina Rossetti
- *Winter Morning* by Ogden Nash
- *In the Fog* by Lilian Moore

3 | Assess

- Organize children into groups of 3. Have children choose roles: wind, leaves, rain, and narrator. Let the children act out the poem for their classmates as the narrator reads the poem. If possible, children may enjoy creating props to use in their dramatic reading.

- Write a whole class poem following the author's style. Write about a different kind of weather, such as snow or long, summer days. Help children discover rhyming words that work in their version of the poem.

Science Objectives

- The student knows that scientists and technologists use a variety of tools (e.g. thermometers) to obtain information in more detail and to make work easier.
- The student knows that people use scientific processes including hypothesis, making inferences, and recording and communicating data when exploring the natural world.

1 | Introduce

Build Background

Remind children that scientists try to explain puzzling events and test their ideas through experiments. Tell children that they have the opportunity to explore their own questions by conducting an independent research project.

2 | Plan and Experiment

As children develop their hypotheses, discuss

- possible hazards involved in conducting Science Fair projects.
- how investigations do not always produce the expected result.
- how to develop the experiment in order to correctly test the hypothesis.

3 | Communicate

Encourage children to use different media (pictures, drawings, numbers, written statements) to represent their information and data.

Children may communicate their experimental plans and/or results in a variety of forums (pair and share, class discussion, oral report, written lab report, poster, science fair day).

Science Fair Projects

Full Inquiry

Using Scientific Methods
1. Ask a question.
2. Make a hypothesis.
3. Plan a fair test.
4. Do your test.
5. Collect and record data.
6. Tell your conclusions.
7. Go further.

Idea 1
How Fast Water Evaporates

Plan a project. Find out if water evaporates faster in a cold place or a warm place.

Idea 2
Measuring Temperature

Plan a project. Find out how the temperature outside changes during the day.

232

My Science Journal

In their science journals, have children write about the hottest and coldest places they ever visited. Have children draw pictures of these places. Have volunteers share their stories and pictures with classmates.

Graphic Organizers . . . . **EMi–EMxv**

    K-W-L Chart . . . . EMi
    T chart . . . . EMii
    Three-Column Chart . . . . EMiii
    Word Web . . . . EMiv
    Vocabulary Cards . . . . EMv
    List-Group-Label . . . . EMvi
    Alike and Different . . . . EMvii
    Picture Clues . . . . EMviii
    Draw Conclusions . . . . EMix
    Predict . . . . EMx
    Cause and Effect . . . . EMxi
    Put Things in Order . . . . EMxii
    Important Details . . . . EMxiii
    Retell . . . . EMxiv
    Infer . . . . EMxv

Bibliographies . . . . **EMxvi–EMxxv**

    Leveled Reader Bibliography . . . . EMxvi–EMxvii
    Unit A Bibliography . . . . EMxviii–EMxix
    Unit B Bibliography . . . . EMxx–EMxxi
    Unit C Bibliography . . . . EMxxii–EMxxiii
    Unit D Bibliography . . . . EMxxiv–EMxxv

Professional Development Articles . . . . **EMxxvi–EMxliii**

    Tim Cooney: *The Standards Movement in Science Education* . . . . . EMxxvi–EMxxvii
    M. Jenice Goldston: *Professional Development: A Lifelong Journey* . . . EMxxviii
    Karen L. Ostlund: *Scaffolded Inquiry and the Inquiry Continuum* . . . EMxxix–EMxxxi
    Nancy Romance: *How Meaningful Science Learning Supports*
       Reading Comprehension: What the Research Says to the Classroom Teacher . . EMxxxii–EMxxxiii
    James Flood and Diane Lapp: *Vocabulary Instruction in Science* . . . EMxxxiv–EMxxxv
    Jim Cummins: *Supporting ESL Students in Learning the Language of Science* . . . . EMxxxvi–EMxxxvii
    Shirley Gholston Key: *Diversity in Science Education* . . . . . EMxxxviii–EMxxxix
    Michael P. Klentschy: *Student Science Notebooks and the*
       Science-Literacy Connection . . . . EMxl–EMxli
    William F. Tate IV: *Science and the Role of Mathematical Models* . . . EMxlii
    Jack A. Gerlovich: *Teaching Safety in the Classroom* . . . . EMxliii

Scott Foresman Science Grade Level Scope and Sequence: . . . . **EMxliv–EMxlv**

Scott Foresman Science Program Scope and Sequence . . . . **EMxlvi–EMxlvii**

Credits for Teacher's Edition . . . . **EMxlviii**

Metric and Customary Measurement **EM1**

Glossary **EM2–EM21**

Index **EM22–EM28**

Credits for Student Edition **EM29–EM31**

Resources for Teachers and Children

K-W-L Chart

What We **K**now	What We **W**ant to Know	What We **L**earned

T Chart

Three-Column Chart

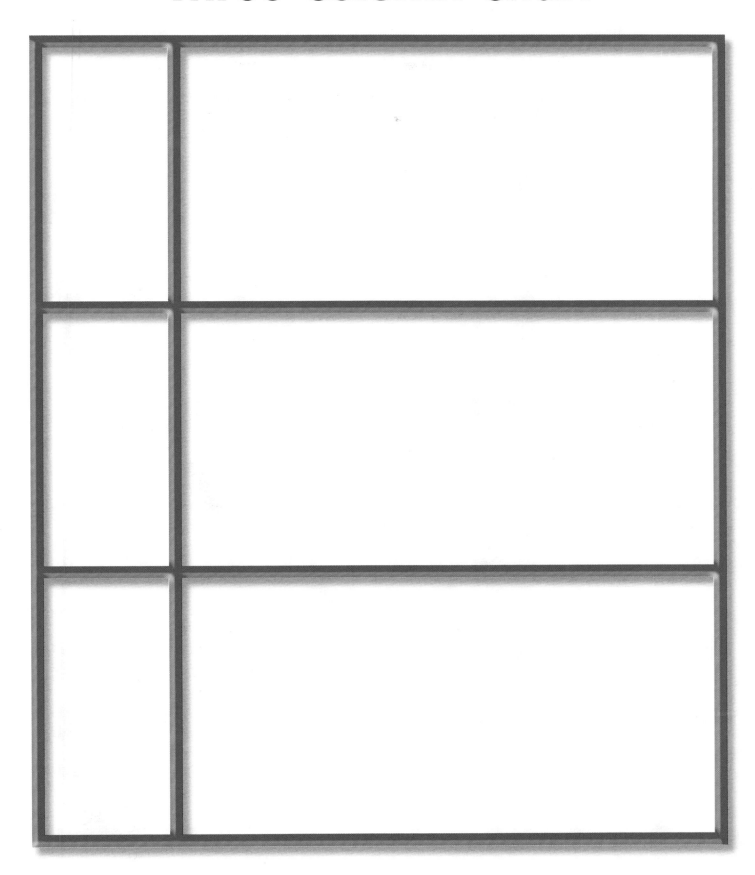

Word Web

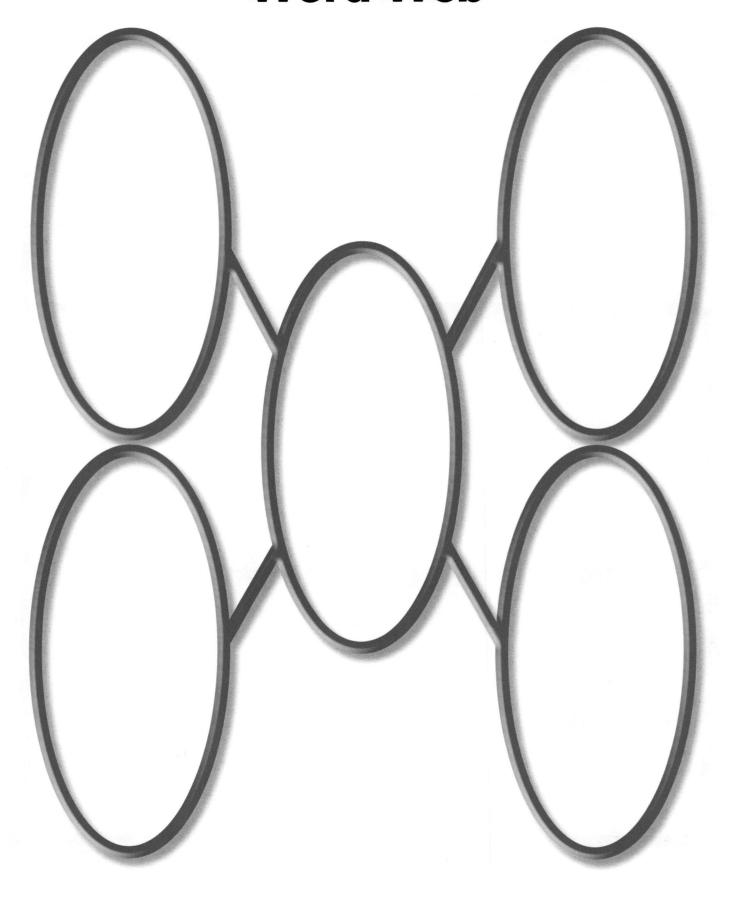

Vocabulary Cards

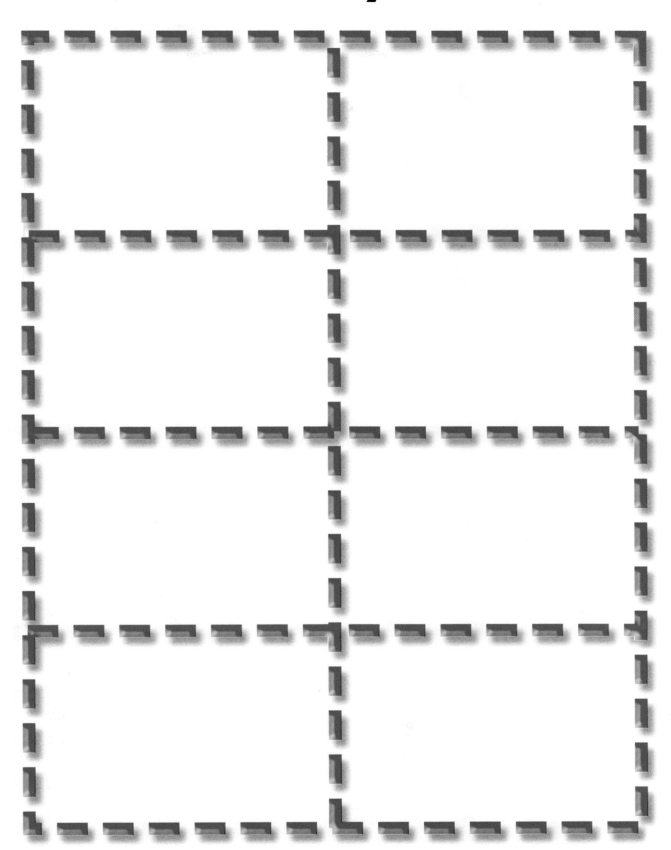

List-Group-Label

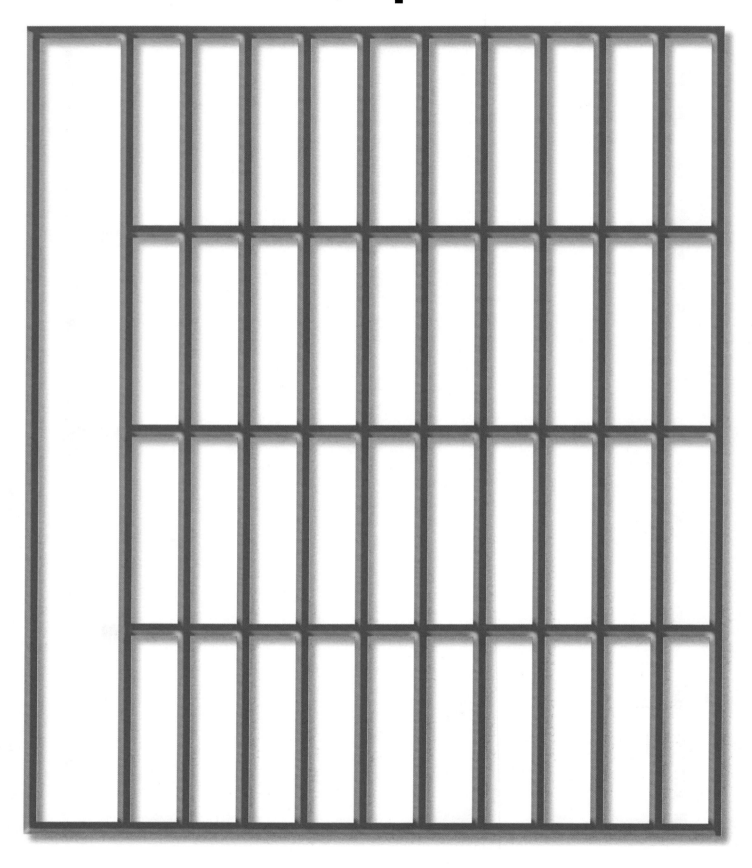

Alike and Different

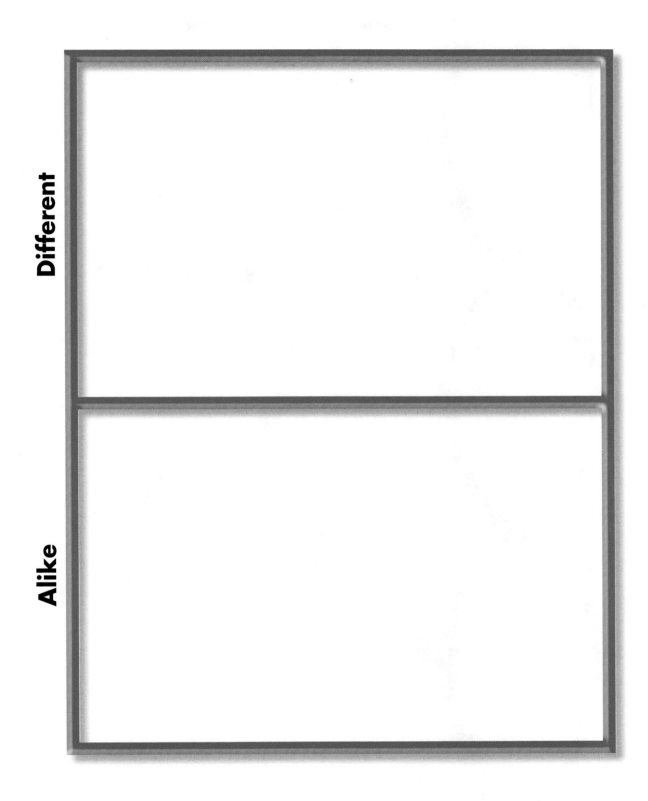

Different

Alike

Picture Clues

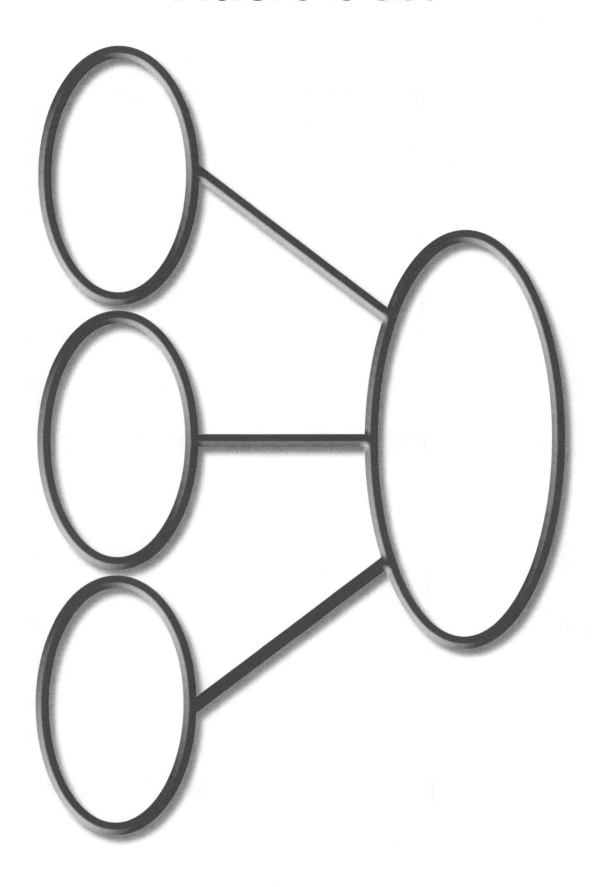

Draw Conclusions

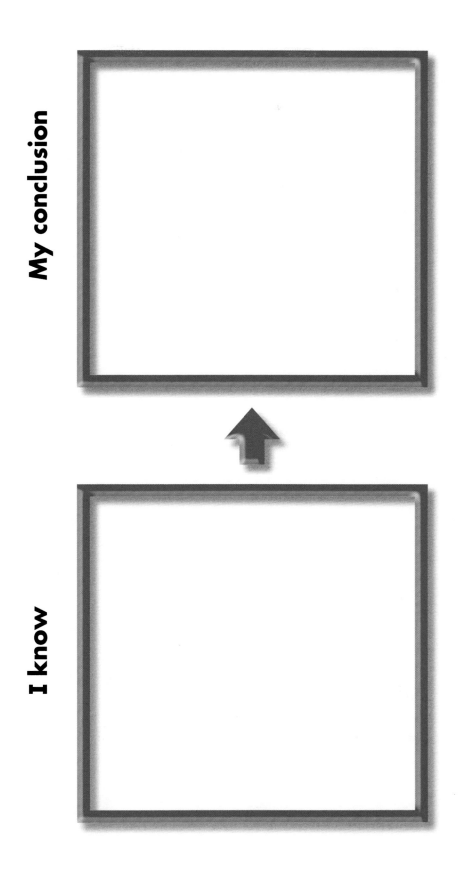

My conclusion

I know

Predict

I predict

I know

Cause and Effect

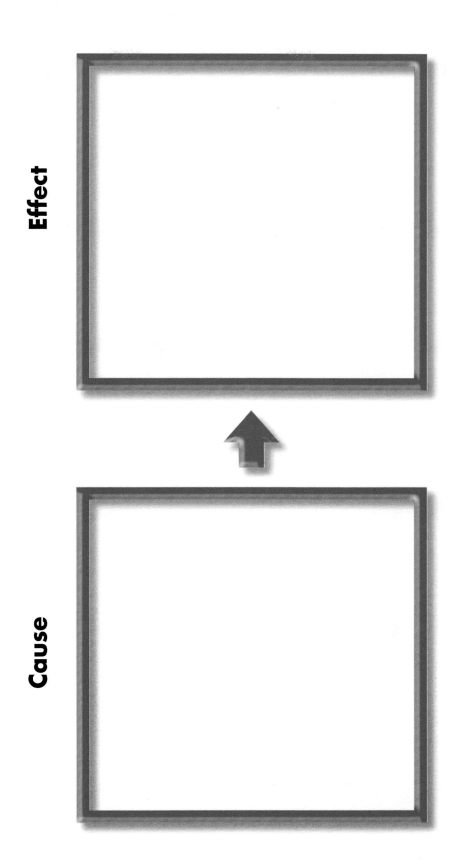

Effect

Cause

Put Things in Order

First

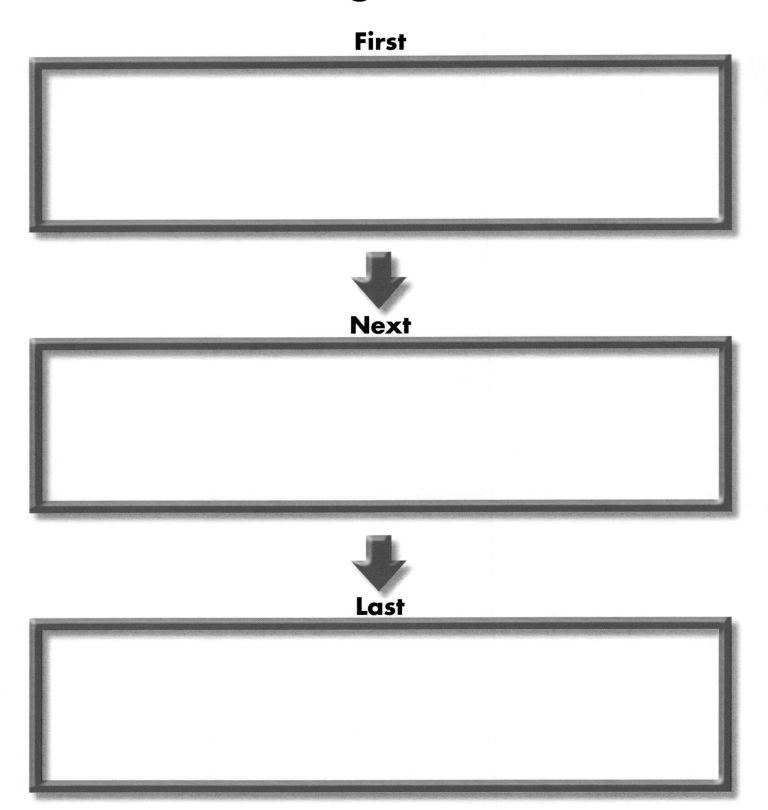

Next

Last

Important Details

Retell

Retell

Infer

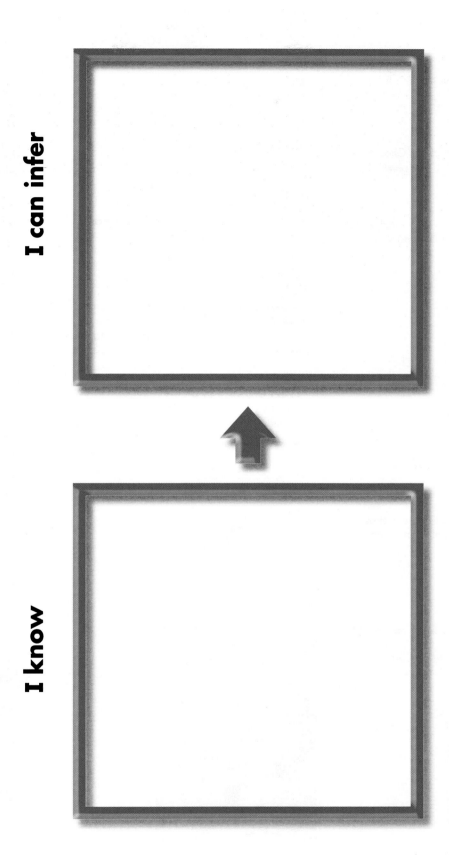

I can infer

I know

Leveled Reader Bibliography

Chapter 1

All About Plants
(ISBN 0-328-13769-3)
This book has the same content as Chapter 1 but is written at a less difficult reading level.
[Below-Level]

Plants
(ISBN 0-328-13770-7)
This book has the same concepts as Chapter 1 and is written at grade level. [On-Level]

Desert Plants
(ISBN 0-328-13771-5)
This book is above grade level and enriches the chapter with additional examples and ideas.
[Advanced]

Chapter 2

All About Animals
(ISBN 0-328-13772-3)
This book has the same content as Chapter 2 but is written at a less difficult reading level.
[Below-Level]

Animal Groups
(ISBN 0-328-13773-1)
This book has the same concepts as Chapter 2 and is written at grade level. [On-Level]

Nocturnal Animals
(ISBN 0-328-13774-X)
This book is above grade level and enriches the chapter with additional examples and ideas.
[Advanced]

Chapter 3

How Plants and Animals Live Together
(ISBN 0-328-34216-5)
This book has the same content as Chapter 3 but is written at a less difficult reading level.
[Below-Level]

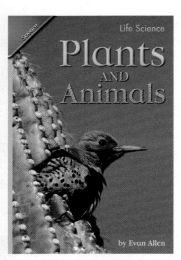

Plants and Animals
(ISBN 0-328-13776-6)
This book has the same concepts as Chapter 3 and is written at grade level. [On-Level]

Life in a Rain Forest
(ISBN 0-328-13777-4)
This book is above grade level and enriches the chapter with additional examples and ideas.
[Advanced]

Chapter 4

How Living Things Grow and Change
(ISBN 0-328-34217-3)
This book has the same content as Chapter 4 but is written at a less difficult reading level.
[Below-Level]

Growing and Changing
(ISBN 0-328-13779-0)
This book has the same concepts as Chapter 4 and is written at grade level. [On-Level]

Animal Eggs
(ISBN 0-328-13780-4)
This book is above grade level and enriches the chapter with additional examples and ideas.
[Advanced]

Chapter 5

Earth's Land, Air, and Water
(ISBN 0-328-34218-1)
This book has the same content as Chapter 5 but is written at a less difficult reading level.
[Below-Level]

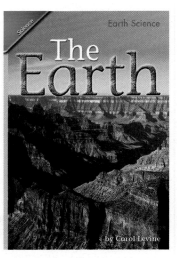

The Earth
(ISBN 0-328-13782-0)
This book has the same concepts as Chapter 5 and is written at grade level. [On-Level]

Crystals and Gems
(ISBN 0-328-13783-9)
This book is above grade level and enriches the chapter with additional examples and ideas.
[Advanced]

Chapter 6

Earth's Weather and Seasons
(ISBN 0-328-34219-X)
This book has the same content as Chapter 6 but is written at a less difficult reading level.
[Below-Level]

Earth's Weather
(ISBN 0-328-34220-3)
This book has the same concepts as Chapter 6 and is written at grade level. [On-Level]

How Clouds are Made
(ISBN 0-328-13786-3)
This book is above grade level and enriches the chapter with additional examples and ideas.
[Advanced]

Chapter 7

Fossils and Dinosaurs
(ISBN 0-328-34221-1)
This book has the same content as Chapter 7 but is written at a less difficult reading level.
[Below-Level]

Dinosaur Fossils
(ISBN 0-328-13788-X)
This book has the same concepts as Chapter 7 and is written at grade level. [On-Level]

Tyrannosaurus rex
(ISBN 0-328-13789-8)
This book is above grade level and enriches the chapter with additional examples and ideas.
[Advanced]

Chapter 8

Properties of Matter
(ISBN 0-328-34222-X)
This book has the same content as Chapter 8 but is written at a less difficult reading level.
[Below-Level]

Matter
(ISBN 0-328-13791-X)
This book has the same concepts as Chapter 8 and is written at grade level. [On-Level]

Air is Everywhere
(ISBN 0-328-13792-8)
This book is above grade level and enriches the chapter with additional examples and ideas.
[Advanced]

Chapter 9

Energy
(ISBN 0-328-13793-6)
This book has the same content as Chapter 9 but is written at a less difficult reading level.
Below-Level

What is Energy?
(ISBN 0-328-13794-4)
This book has the same concepts as Chapter 9 and is written at grade level. **On-Level**

Ships and Boats
(ISBN 0-328-13795-2)
This book is above grade level and enriches the chapter with additional examples and ideas.
Advanced

Chapter 10

Forces and Motion
(ISBN 0-328-34223-8)
This book has the same content as Chapter 10 but is written at a less difficult reading level.
Below-Level

Motion and Force
(ISBN 0-328-13797-9)
This book has the same concepts as Chapter 10 and is written at grade level. **On-Level**

Magnet Fun
(ISBN 0-328-13798-7)
This book is above grade level and enriches the chapter with additional examples and ideas.
Advanced

Chapter 11

Sound
(ISBN 0-328-13799-5)
This book has the same content as Chapter 11 but is written at a less difficult reading level.
Below-Level

All About Sound
(ISBN 0-328-13800-2)
This book has the same concepts as Chapter 11 and is written at grade level. **On-Level**

How Sound Travels
(ISBN 0-328-13801-0)
This book is above grade level and enriches the chapter with additional examples and ideas.
Advanced

Chapter 12

Earth and Space
(ISBN 0-328-34224-6)
This book has the same content as Chapter 12 but is written at a less difficult reading level.
Below-Level

Exploring Earth and Space
(ISBN 0-328-34225-4)
This book has the same concepts as Chapter 12 and is written at grade level. **On-Level**

Guide to the Constellations
(ISBN 0-328-34226-2)
This book is above grade level and enriches the chapter with additional examples and ideas.
Advanced

Chapter 13

Technology in Our World
(ISBN 0-328-13805-3)
This book has the same content as Chapter 13 but is written at a less difficult reading level.
Below-Level

Technology
(ISBN 0-328-13806-1)
This book has the same concepts as Chapter 13 and is written at grade level. **On-Level**

Then and Now: Flying Machines
(ISBN 0-328-13807-X)
This book is above grade level and enriches the chapter with additional examples and ideas.
Advanced

Unit A Bibliography

For Children

- *At Home in the Tide Pool,*
  by Alexandra Wright
  (Charlesbridge Publishing,
  ISBN 0881064823, 1999)
  With colorful illustrations and
  informative text, this book draws
  children close to the details of life in a
  tide pool. **Easy**

- *Birds Build Nests,*
  by Yvonne Winer
  (Charlesbridge Publishing,
  ISBN 1570915008, 2002)
  In this poetic introduction to birds'
  nesting habits, each spread features
  a brief poem about the places where
  various species nest–in logs, among
  the lily pads, on beach cliffs, capping
  chimneys. **Easy**

- *Crafty Chameleon,*
  by Mwenye Hadithi
  (Little, Brown & Company,
  ISBN 0316337714, 1998)
  A chameleon bedeviled by a leopard
  and a crocodile uses his wits to get them
  to leave him alone. **Easy**

- *Dandelion Adventures,*
  by L. Patricia Kite
  (Lerner Publishing Group,
  ISBN 0761303774, 1998)
  This book follows seven dandelion seed
  parachutes as they land in different
  circumstances to show examples of
  the way in which common plants
  regenerate. **Easy**

- *From Seed to Plant,*
  by Gail Gibbons
  (Holiday House, ISBN 0823410250,
  1993)
  The author presents a simple introduction
  to how plants reproduce, discussing
  pollination, seed dispersal, and growth
  from seed to plant. **Easy**

- *Sea Turtles,*
  by Gail Gibbons
  (Holiday House, ISBN 082341373X,
  1998)
  Soft watercolor illustrations amplify
  brief descriptions of the eight species
  of sea turtles. Unique characteristics
  are described in a few carefully chosen
  words, and pictures draw readers into
  the creatures' underwater world. **Easy**

- *Animal Lives: The Rabbit,*
  by Sally Tagholm
  (Kingfisher, ISBN 0753456079, 2003)
  This story depicts the realities of life
  in the wild for the rabbit, including
  discussions of predators, mating, and
  reproduction, as well as the growth and
  defenses of young rabbits. **On-Level**

- *Brilliant Bees,*
  by Linda Glaser
  (Lerner Publishing Group,
  ISBN 0761319433, 2003)
  In this picture book, a young girl
  shares her observations on honeybees,
  including physical and behavioral
  characteristics of the insects, various
  functions that the workers and the
  queen perform within the hive, and their
  importance as pollinators. **On-Level**

- *How a Seed Grows,*
  by Helene J. Jordan
  (HarperTrophy, ISBN 0064451070,
  1992)
  This simple introduction leads young
  readers through a series of steps that
  result in a basic understanding of how
  seeds grow. **On-Level**

- *How Do Animals Adapt?,*
  by Bobbie Kalman
  (Crabtree Publishing Company,
  ISBN 0865059578, 2000)
  This book examines ways that animals'
  bodies and/or behavior help them
  survive in particular habitats. Types
  of adaptation include camouflage,
  hibernation, and migration. **On-Level**

- *Something Is Growing,*
  by Walter Lyon Krudop
  (Simon & Schuster Children's,
  ISBN 0689319401, 1995)
  Nobody notices the boy Peter planting
  a seed in a small patch of dirt by a
  busy street, but the result—an unusual,
  towering plant that quickly starts
  spreading out of control—attracts a
  great deal of attention. **On-Level**

- *Who Eats What? Food Chains and
  Food Webs,*
  by Patricia Lauber
  (HarperTrophy, ISBN 0064451305,
  1995)
  This book explains how every link in
  a food chain is important because
  each living thing depends on others for
  survival. **On-Level**

Claws, Coats and Camouflage: The Ways Animals Fit into Their World,
by Susan E. Goodman
(Millbrook Press, ISBN 0761318658, 2001)
How well different animals from insects to humans are adapted for surviving in their environments is described and illustrated in this book. **Challenge**

Coyote and Badger: Desert Hunters of the Southwest,
by Bruce Hiscock
(Boyds Mills Press, ISBN 1563978482, 2001)
This fictionalized portrait of animals desperate for food reveals the instinctive predatory nature of a coyote and the patient skill of a badger; the two creatures form a bond and hunt together in Chaco Canyon, New Mexico. **Challenge**

Following the Coast,
by Jim Arnosky
(HarperCollins, ISBN 0688171184, 2004)
In a picture-book essay for older children, renowned naturalist, author, and illustrator Arnosky explores Atlantic coast salt marshes, noting the flora, fauna, and landmarks that he sees. **Challenge**

Jellies: The Life of Jellyfish,
by Twig C. George
(Lerner Publishing Group, ISBN 0761316590, 2000)
Gorgeous full-color underwater photos and a simple, readable text provide a fascinating introduction to these little-known and often unheralded marine organisms. **Challenge**

Plants with Seeds,
by Elaine Pascoe
(Rosen Publishing Group, ISBN 0823963144, 2003)
This book details the life cycles and characteristics of plants that use seeds to reproduce. **Challenge**

Seeds, Stems, and Stamens: The Ways Plants Fit into Their World,
by Susan E. Goodman.
(Lerner Publishing Group, ISBN 0761318747, 2001)
This book about the ways plants survive in their various habitats discusses fitting into the environment; getting Sun, water, and food; inherent defenses; and propogating the species. **Challenge**

For Teachers

Access Nature,
by Bethe Gilbert Almeras and David Heath
National Wildlife Federation, ISBN 0945051727, 2001)
An inclusive outdoor-education curriculum published by the National Wildlife Foundation. A useful and extensive collection of activities for exploring nature to supplement units about habitats.

Experiments in Science: How Do Things Grow?,
by David Glover
(Dorling Kindersley, Inc., ISBN 078947848X, 2001)
Children discover the answers to this question and more in these experiments that cover everything from finding out how different animals use their senses to making a pond viewer.

Mother Opossum and Her Babies,
by Jean C. Echols, Jaine Kopp, Ellen Blinderman, and Kimi Hosoume
(Graywolf Press, ISBN 0924886218, 1999)
Children meet the opossum in a series of creative science and math activities. The many interesting attributes and behaviors of the opossum make it a great animal to learn about. Activities interweave science, math, and language arts with role-playing, drama, and art.

Nature Smart: Awesome Projects to Make with Mother Nature's Help,
by Gwen Diehn, Terry Krautwurst, Alan Anderson, Joe Rhatigan, and Heather Smith
(Sterling Publishing Co., Inc., ISBN 1402705158, 2003)
Kids will get in touch with nature with 150 illustrated, nature-friendly projects. There are things to do for every season of the year, crafts that use recycled materials, and activities that encourage youngsters to investigate the natural world.

Unit B Bibliography

For Children

Flash, Crash, Rumble and Roll,
by Franklyn M. Branley
(HarperTrophy, ISBN 0064451798, 1999)
This book describes and demystifies one of nature's most powerful atmospheric events, the thunderstorm. **Easy**

Four Stories for Four Seasons
by Tomie dePaola
(Aladdin, ISBN 0671886339, 1994)
Four friends—Missy Cat, Master Dog, Mistress Pig, and Mister Frog—explore the pleasures and the small problems of friendship in four seasonal tales. **Easy**

Weather: Poems for All Seasons
selected by Lee Bennett Hopkins, illustrated by Melanie Hall
(HarperTrophy, ISBN 0064441911, 1995)
This collection of poems describes various weather conditions, by such authors as Christina G. Rossetti, Myra Cohn Livingston, and Aileen Fisher. **Easy**

What Will the Weather Be?
by Lynda DeWitt and Carolyn Croll
(HarperTrophy, ISBN 0064451135, 1993)
Changes in the weather are not always predictable. This book explains what the scientists know—and what they sometimes can't know—about our changing weather. **Easy**

Where Do Puddles Go?
by Fay Robinson
(Children's Press, ISBN 0516460366, 1995)
This book about the water cycle encourages children to learn about evaporation and condensation by observing things in their daily life. **Easy**

Where Does the Garbage Go?
by Paul Showers and Randy Chewning
(HarperCollins Children's Books, ISBN 0064451143, 1993)
The book gives simple, succinct, and clear explanations of how recycling conserves energy and reduces pollution as it decreases waste. **Easy**

Fossils Tell of Long Ago,
by Aliki
(HarperCollins Children's Books, ISBN 0064450937, 1990)
In clear, precise language, the author explains how dinosaur tracks are cast in mud, how insects trapped in sticky tree sap harden into amber, and how fossils of tropical plants are found in very cold places. **On-Level**

The Lorax,
by Dr. Seuss
(Random House Books for Young Readers, ISBN 0394823370, 1971)
Whimsical rhymes, delightfully original creatures, and weirdly undulating illustrations deliver a powerful message about the environment that Dr. Seuss implores readers to heed. **On-Level**

New Dinos: The Latest Finds! The Coolest Dinosaur Discoveries!
by Shelley Tanaka
(Atheneum, ISBN 0689851839, 2003)
High-powered electron microscopes, CT scans, and computer models are helping scientists discover new dinosaur species and reevaluate long-held ideas about dinosaur behavior. **On-Level**

Rachel Carson, Friend of the Earth,
by Francene Sabin
(Troll Communications, ISBN 0816745579, 1998)
This biography of the well-known conservationist discusses Carson's childhood, her love of nature, her influences, and her stellar career. **On-Level**

Water, Water Everywhere,
by Mark J. Rauzon and Cynthia Overbeck Bix
(Sagebrush Bound, ISBN 0613771214, 1995)
This simple book examines the forms of water on earth. Stunning full-color photographs are interspersed with poetic yet informative descriptions of what water is and why it is important. **On-Level**

What Happened to the Dinosaurs?
by Franklyn M. Branley and Marc Simont
(HarperTrophy, ISBN 0064451054, 1991)
The author provides clear, easy-to-understand explanations of several possible causes for the dinosaurs' extinction. **On-Level**

Dinosaur Parents, Dinosaur Young: Uncovering the Mystery of Dinosaur Families,
by Kathleen Weidner Zoehfeld
(Clarion Books, ISBN 0395913381, 2001)
The book draws from the very latest findings to describe how scientists are continually making new discoveries and drawing new conclusions about what life was like for dinosaurs and their young. **Challenge**

Global Change,
by Theodore P. Snow
(Children's Press, ISBN 0516011057, 1990)
This book describes some of the changes people are inflicting on the world, such as the cutting down of tropical forests, the destroying of ozone, oil spills, and acid rain. **Challenge**

The Great Kapok Tree: A Tale of the Amazon Rain Forest,
by Lynne Cherry
(Gulliver Green, ISBN 015200520X, 1990)
This modern fable takes look at what the Kapok tree means to the creatures that live near it—and what rain forests mean to the world's ecology. **Challenge**

The Kids' Natural History Book: Making Dinos, Fossils, Mammoths & More!
by Judy Press
(Williamson Publishing, ISBN 1885593244, 2000)
This idea-packed book focuses on animal life on Earth during the last 570 million years (the Cambrian period to the present), covering sea creatures, insects, dinosaurs, reptiles, amphibians, birds, and mammals. **Challenge**

Life in a Bucket of Soil,
by Alvin Silverstein
(Dover Publications, ISBN 0486410579, 2000)
This book describes the various animals that live within the soil under our feet, including earthworms, roundworms, snails, mites, beetles, and ants. **Challenge**

Rocks and Fossils,
by Chris Pellant
(Kingfisher, ISBN 0753456192, 2003)
Packed with crisp photography, engaging activities, and clear explanations, this book is an authoritative and fun guide to this favorite subject. **Challenge**

For Teachers

Earth Book for Kids: Activities to Help Heal the Environment,
by Linda Schwartz
(Learning Works, ISBN 0881601950, 1990)
Creative ideas with easy-to-follow instructions show kids how to make their own paper, compare phosphate levels in detergents, test the effects of oil pollution, conduct a recycling survey, create a trash sculpture, redesign a package, chart a flush, measure acidity, and make a difference in many other exciting ways.

First Science Experiments: Wonderful Weather,
by Shar Levine and Leslie Johnstone
(Sterling Publishing Co., Inc., ISBN 0806972491, 2003)
Offers hands-on experiences that focus on five elements of weather: air and temperature, water, ice and snow, wind, and thunder and lightning.

Water, Stones & Fossil Bones,
by Karen Lind
(National Science Teachers Association, ISBN 087355101X, 1991)
51 hands-on earth science activities include background information to introduce each activity, descriptions of concepts and skills to be developed, step-by-step procedures, questions keyed to the procedure to help guide student discussion and probe understanding, and suggestions for further investigations.

Weatherwatch,
by Valerie Wyatt
(Scott Foresman Addison Wesley, ISBN 0921103638, 1990)
Experiments teaching about weather are presented clearly, each with a list of necessary materials involving common household items, and warnings to involve adults in certain procedures are included. Youngsters learn to make a rainbow, a cloud, lightning, and thunder, to note the effects of cold and hot weather on living things, and to create smog.

Unit C Bibliography

For Children

- *Energy from the Sun,*
  by Allan Fowler
  (Scholastic Library Publishing, ISBN 0516262556, 1998)
  This book defines energy and examines how energy from the Sun provides us with heat, light, plants, food, and other things necessary for life on Earth. **Easy**

- *Energy Makes Things Happen,*
  by Kimberly Brubaker Bradley
  (HarperTrophy, ISBN 0064452131, 2002)
  Using familiar, everyday examples, this book begins to explain the concept of energy and how it is used. **Easy**

- *Sounds All Around,*
  by Wendy Pfeffer
  (HarperTrophy, ISBN 0064451771, 1999)
  This book provides a simple explanation of sounds and hearing. Beginning with snaps, claps, and whistles, it describes how sound waves vibrate through the air, and how tiny bones in the ear vibrate. **Easy**

- *Switch On, Switch Off,*
  by Melvin Berger
  (HarperTrophy, ISBN 006445097X, 2001)
  An easy-to-understand, informative, and accurate science concept book that uses clear, succinct language to explain how electricity is produced and transmitted, and how generators, light bulbs, and electrical plugs work. **Easy**

- *What Happened?,*
  by Rozanne Lanczak Williams
  (Creative Teaching Press, ISBN 0916119475, 1994)
  This book presents changes in the state of matter through the eyes of a child. **Easy**

- *What Is the World Made Of? All About Solids, Liquids, and Gases,*
  by Kathleen Weidner Zoehfeld
  (HarperTrophy, ISBN 0064451631, 1998)
  In simple text, this book presents the three states of matter, solid, liquid, and gas, and describes their attributes. **Easy**

- *All About Sound,*
  by Melvin Berger
  (Scholastic, ISBN 0590467603, 1994)
  Hands-on experiments and fascinating facts introduce young readers to the world of sound. **On-Level**

- *The Book of Pitch Exploration: Can Your Voice Do This?*
  by John M. Feierabend
  (GIA Publications, ISBN 157999265X, 2004)
  The imaginative and effective activities in this book invite children to discover the sounds they can make with their voices. **On-Level**

- *Bouncing and Bending Light,*
  by Barbara Taylor
  (Watts Franklin, ISBN 0531140148, 1990)
  This book offers experiments that demonstrate the reflection, refraction, interference, and dispersion of light by mirrors, lenses, and other materials. **On-Level**

- *Experiment with Movement,*
  by Bryan Murphy
  (Lerner Publishing Group, ISBN 0822524511, 1991)
  This book presents simple experiments demonstrating the basic scientific principles of movement. **On-Level**

- *Forces,*
  by Graham Peacock
  (Steck-Vaughn, ISBN 1568471920, 1994)
  Illustrated with color photographs and artwork, this book examines different types of forces at work in various everyday environments, describing their properties, their effects on objects, and how they feature in typical contexts. **On-Level**

- *Simple Machines,*
  by Adrienne Mason, Deborah Hodge, The Ontario Science Centre
  (Kids Can Press, ISBN 1550743996, 2000)
  In this book, the lever, wheel, wheel and axle, gears, pulleys, inclined plane, screw, and combinations of basic machines are explored through simple and fun experiments. **On-Level**

Bending Light: An Exploratorium Toolbook,
by Pat Murphy, Jenefer Merrill, and Paul Doherty
(Little, Brown & Company, ISBN 0316258512, 1993)
Simple experiments introduce the basic principles of light and lenses. **Challenge**

Electricity and Magnets,
by Sarah Angliss
(Houghton Mifflin Company, ISBN 0753453495, 2001)
This book explores science in action with a wide variety of exciting experiments. Scientific principles and fascinating facts are brought to life using everyday materials. **Challenge**

Eyewitness: Matter,
by Christopher Cooper
(DK Publishing Inc., ISBN 0789448866, 1999)
This book examines the elements that make up the physical world and the properties and behavior of different kinds of matter. **Challenge**

Forces and Motion,
by John Graham and David Le Jars
(Kingfisher, ISBN 0753453487, 2001)
This book explores gravity, friction, centrifugal force, and the underlying laws of physics that help machines work. **Challenge**

Lifting by Levers,
by Andrew Dunn
(Thomson Learning, ISBN 1568470169, 1993)
This book describes simple machines that utilize the principle of levers to move heavy objects, cut material, and make music. **Challenge**

Sound,
by Bobbi Searle
(Copper Beech, ISBN 0761317376, 2002)
A thought-provoking look at sound provides instructions for a variety of experiments that explore the properties of sound, including vibrations, echoes, music, and sounds in nature. **Challenge**

For Teachers

Awesome Experiments in Light & Sound,
by Michael A. Dispezio and Catherine Leary
(Sterling Publishing, ISBN 0806998237, 1999)
Presents over seventy experiments designed to demonstrate the properties of light and sound and explain the science behind them, covering such topics as wavelengths, color spectrums, vibration, and air particles.

Janice VanCleave's Physics for Every Kid: 101 Easy Experiments in Motion, Heat, Light, Machines, and Sound,
by Janice VanCleave
(Wiley, ISBN 0471525057, 1991)
Presents 101 experiments relating to physics using materials readily available around the house.

Science Experiments with Sound & Music,
by Shar Levine and Leslie Johnstone
(Sterling, ISBN 0806976977, 2002)
This thorough look at sounds and music offers 34 easy-to-do activities that demonstrate the scientific concepts behind sound waves, pitch, acoustics, and scales.

Unit D Bibliography

For Children

Communication Then and Now,
by Robin Nelson
(Lerner Publications, ISBN 0822546388, 2003)
This book provides a brief, photographic overview of advances in communication technology. **Easy**

The Moon Seems to Change,
by Franklyn M. Branley
(HarperTrophy, ISBN 0064450651, 1987)
Children can read about the phenomena of the Moon's phases and with an experiment using an orange, a pencil, and a flashlight, they can see why the Moon looks different at different times of the month. **Easy**

The Sky Is Full of Stars,
by Franklyn M. Branley
(HarperTrophy, ISBN 0064450023, 1983)
Young stargazers learn about different star colors and brightness, how to locate major constellations, and how to make mini planetariums by using coffee cans and flashlights. **Easy**

The Sun Is Always Shining Somewhere,
by Allan Fowler
(Children's Press, ISBN 9996318621, 1992)
This book provides an introduction to basic facts about the nearest star, including why it looks so much bigger than other stars and why there is night and day. **Easy**

There's No Place Like Space: All About Our Solar System,
by Tish Rabe
(Random House Books for Young Readers, ISBN 0679891153, 1999)
Beginning readers and budding astronomers are launched Dr. Seuss style on a trip to visit the nine planets in our solar system along with the Cat in the Hat, Thing One, Thing Two, and Dick and Sally. **Easy**

What Makes Day and Night,
by Franklyn M. Branley
(HarperTrophy, ISBN 0064450503, 1986)
Accompanied by NASA photos and colorful drawings, the text explains the Earth's rotation in clear and simple terms. An experiment using a lamp as the "Sun" further clarifies the principles introduced. **Easy**

Eyewitness: Media & Communications,
by Clive Gifford
(DK Publishing, Inc., ISBN 078946294X, 2000)
This volume is packed with information and photos about the important inventions and advances in this rapidly changing field, including the printing press, radio, telegraph, telephone, and television. **On-Level**

The Moon Book,
by Gail Gibbons
(Holiday House ISBN 0823413640, 1998)
This book offers a great deal of information about the Moon: its orbits and phases, eclipses, tides, history of lunar exploration, as well as the legends and myths it has inspired in various cultures. **On-Level**

Moon, Sun, and Stars,
by John Bryan Lewellen
(Scholastic Library Publishing, ISBN 0516416375, 1990)
A brief introduction to astronomy, with emphasis on the relationship between the Moon, the Earth, and the Sun. **On-Level**

Paint a Sun in the Sky: A First Look at the Seasons,
by Claire Llewellyn and Amanda Wood (Illustrator)
(Picture Window Books, ISBN 1404806598, 2004)
Using illustrations and text, this book describes the relationship between the Sun and the seasons. **On-Level**

Seasons,
by Robyn Supraner
(Troll Communications L.L.C., ISBN 0816747199, 1998)
Young readers will experience the seasons of the northern hemisphere, learning what causes them and how people, animals, and plants are affected by them. **On-Level**

Alexander Graham Bell and the Telephone,
by Steve Parker
(Chelsea House Publishers, ISBN 0791030040, 1995)
This is a biography of the man who invented the telephone and revolutionized the way we communicate. **Challenge**

Technology,
by Roger Bridgman
(DK Publishing, Inc., ISBN 0789448874, 1999)
Packed with sharp color illustrations and fascinating facts, this highly informative guide explores all aspects of technology, from ancient artifacts to the latest advances in computer-aided design. **Challenge**

Find the Constellations,
by Hans Augusto Rey
(Houghton Mifflin Company, ISBN 0395245095, 1976)
From the creator of *Curious George* comes this colorfully illustrated, informative beginner's guide to locating and identifying constellations in the northern hemisphere, with an extensive index, glossary, and time table for sky viewing. **Challenge**

From Radio to the Wireless Web,
by Joanne Mattern
(Enslow Publishers, ISBN 0766018938, 2002)
This book traces the history and development of wireless communication from Marconi's invention of the telegraph in 1895 to the arrival of satellite radio in cars in 2001. **Challenge**

Neil Armstrong: Meet the Famous Astronaut,
by Barbara Kramer
(Enslow, ISBN 07660200, 2003)
The early days of space exploration are explored through the life and experiences of the first man to set foot on the Moon. **Challenge**

What a Great Idea: Inventions That Changed the World,
by Steve Tomecek
(Scholastic, ISBN 0590681443, 2003)
From the hand ax and mathematics to IC chips and the laser, each technological touchstone in human history is described and placed in historical context. The time span is 3500 B.C. to today. **Challenge**

For Teachers

Inventeering: A Problem-Solving Approach to Teaching Technology,
by Bob Corney and Norm Dale
(Trifolium Books, Inc., ISBN 1552440141, 2000)
This book covers the design process; classroom safety and organization; basic and specialized tools; and choosing and using materials for building structures, creating machines, and learning about energy.

Moon Journals: Writing, Art, and Inquiry Through Focused Nature Study,
by Gina Rester-Zodrow and Joni Chancer
(Heinemann, ISBN 0435072218, 1997)
Primary school teachers recount how their students observed the Moon's transit for 28 days and recorded their impressions in journals of poetry, prose, and art, and offer advice and instructions for art and writing exercises.

Space Book: Activities For Experiencing The Universe and The Night Sky,
by Marc McCutcheon
(John Wiley And Sons, Inc., ISBN 047116142X, 2002)
Readers take an imaginary journey through our solar system and outer space. Each stop on the journey features information about that particular celestial body and an activity that can easily be performed in any classroom or home.

Take A Technowalk to Learn About Mechanisms and Energy,
by Peter Williams and Saryl Jacobson
(Trifolium Books, Inc., ISBN 1552440044, 2000)
10 mini field trips focus on the applications of technology in the everyday world. Activities engage students and teach them to make the connection between concepts of mechanisms and energy and the inventions, tools, and machines that employ these concepts.

Dr. Timothy Cooney
Professor of Earth Science and Science Education
University of Northern Iowa (UNI)
Cedar Falls, Iowa

The Standards Movement in Science Education

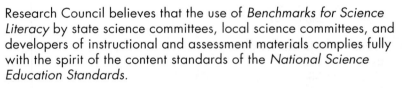

Over a decade ago, the American Association for the Advancement of Science (AAAS), through Project 2061, published Benchmarks for Science Literacy. Developers of *Benchmarks for Science Literacy* based their work on the belief that all students should and can learn science. *Benchmarks for Science Literacy* is an effort to teach all students a basic core of scientific knowledge. This effort was a departure from earlier reform-minded efforts that had as their goals the production of scientists and engineers—an idea that made science in schools regarded as a specialized subject to be taught to special students.

Not long after the release of *Benchmarks for Science Literacy (BSL)*, a second major effort to focus our nation's attention on science education started when the National Research Council of the National Academy of Sciences organized a committee to develop national standards for K–12 science. The National Committee on Science Education Standards and Assessment (NCSESA) also had "Science for All" as its guiding principle.

"In particular, the commitment to 'Science for All' implies inclusion not only of those who traditionally have received encouragement and opportunity to pursue science, of women and girls, all racial and ethnic groups, the physically and educationally challenged, and those with limited English proficiency. Further, it implies attention to various styles of learning and differing sources of motivation. Every person must be brought into and given access to the ongoing conversation of science."

—NCSESA, 1992

The National Research Council acknowledged the influence of the *Benchmarks for Science Literacy* on the work of the NCSESA, including its final product, the *National Science Education Standards (NSES)*, which was first published in 1996. In fact the National

Research Council believes that the use of *Benchmarks for Science Literacy* by state science committees, local science committees, and developers of instructional and assessment materials complies fully with the spirit of the content standards of the *National Science Education Standards*.

Before *Benchmarks for Science Literacy* and the *National Science Education Standards* were developed, few resources provided direction for a comprehensive K–12 science curriculum. Benchmarks and Standards are criteria by which judgment can be made. They are broad, general statements of what is possible and do not define one universal best approach.

National Science Education Standards

National Science Education Standards exist for 1) content, 2) teaching, 3) assessment, 4) program, and 5) system.

- *Content Standards* define what ALL students should understand and be able to do as a result of their school learning experiences.

- *Teaching Standards* provide a vision of what teachers need to understand and do to provide for students learning experiences that are aligned with content standards.

- *Assessment Standards* identify essential characteristics of fair and accurate student assessments and program evaluations that are consistent with content standards at the school district, state, and national levels.

- *Program Standards* describe how content, teaching, and assessment are coordinated in school practice over a full range of schooling to provide all students the opportunity to learn science.

- *System Standards* describe how policies and practices outside of the immediate learning environment support high quality science programs.

Content Standards

Perhaps of most immediate concern to the classroom teacher are the content standards. These ultimately shape what will be taught in the classroom. The NSES and BSL have an extensive overlap of what content should be taught in schools. The Content Standards of NSES for grade spans K–4, 5–8, and 9–12 are divided into seven categories. BSL breaks down content standards for grade spans K–2, 3–5, 6–8, and 9–12 into 10 chapters directly related to science content. In spite of this difference, one could easily integrate the areas of content standards from BSL into the NSES content standards.

BSL chapters are:

Nature of Technology, Historical Nature of Science, Habits of Mind, Common Themes, Physical Setting, Living Environment, Human Organism, Human Society, and *Designed World.*

In comparison, the NSES categories are:

Science as Inquiry, Physical Science, Life Science, Earth and Space Science, Science and Technology, Science in Personal and Social Perspectives, and *the History and Nature of Science.* An eighth category, *Unifying Concepts and Processes,* should be developed over the entire K–12 science experience.

As you read the synopses of the NSES standards below, you should be able to see the link with the categories in the BSL.

- *Science as Inquiry Standards* are the basic and controlling principles in the organization and experiences in students' science education. The standards on inquiry highlight the ability to do inquiry, which goes well beyond just using process skills. The Science as Inquiry standards include the "processes of science," but go beyond by requiring that students combine process skills and scientific knowledge as they incorporate scientific reasoning and critical thinking to help develop their understanding of science.

- *Physical, Life, and Earth and Space Science Standards* express the primary subject matter of science. Science subject matter focuses on those science concepts, principles, and theories that are fundamental for all students to know and to be able to use.

- *Science and Technology Standards* establish useful connections between the natural world and the designed world and offer essential decision-making abilities.

- *Science in Personal Perspective Standards* connect students with their social and personal world. In the elementary grades, these standards include personal health, environmental change, and science and technology in local challenges and in society.

- *History and Nature of Science Standards* include an understanding of the nature of science and uses history in school science programs to clarify different aspects of scientific inquiry, science in society, and the human aspects of science.

- *Unifying Concepts and Processes Standards* provide students with powerful ideas that help them understand the natural world. These conceptual and procedural schemes are integral to students' science learning experiences and include concepts and processes such as systems, organization, interactions, change, measurement, models, scale, adaptation, and explanation.

Scott Foresman Science and Science Standards

States now have strong science frameworks for school districts to use to develop science curricula. Most states considered *Benchmarks for Science Literacy* and/or *National Science Education Standards* as useful guidelines for development of their state standards. In addition to the typical subject-oriented standards, states use statements such as: "Students understand that science, technology, and society are interwoven and interdependent" and "Students understand and use the science process skills and habits of mind to solve problems." These types of statements are exactly what is recommended by BSL and NSES.

Scott Foresman *Science* aligns with content standards. At each grade level, the subject matter is divided into four units: Life Science, Earth Science, Physical Science, and Space and Technology. In addition to the content standards, Scott Foresman *Science* supports the science inquiry standards using an inquiry continuum from Directed Inquiry through Guided Inquiry to Full Inquiry. As students gain experience and confidence in their ability to do science, they are given greater responsibility to determine how they investigate as well as what original questions to ask.

References

American Association for the Advancement of Science (1993). *Benchmarks for Science Literacy.* New York: Oxford University Press.

Hoffman, K. M., and E. K. Stage. 1993. *Science for all students.* Momentum Volume 24. September/October.

National Research Council (1996). *National Science Education Standards.* Washington, DC: National Academy Press.

National Research Council, NCSESA. *National Science Education Standards: Discussion Summary.* Prepared for the Sigma Xi Conference. April 14–15, 1994.

Dr. M. Jenice Goldston
Associate Professor of Science Education
Department of Elementary Education Programs
University of Alabama
Tuscaloosa, Alabama

Professional Development: A Lifelong Journey

> *"The deeper we search, the more we find there is to know, and as long as human life exists I believe that it will always be so."*
> —Albert Einstein

Professional development of teachers of elementary science means many things to many individuals, but if the point of teaching is to cultivate learning, then learning should be at the center of the discussion. The "learning" that is meant here is not isolated, devoid of context and experience, nor is it mind-numbing information jammed into the minds of individuals assigned to chairs in a classroom. Rather it is the learning that involves the interests and the unquenchable curiosity that captures the psyche of a child who becomes engrossed with how a remote control car allows him/her to manipulate its motion and begins to think about motion, forces, momentum, and forms of energy. For this type of learning to occur, teachers of elementary science must be able to draw upon their pedagogical knowledge to foster meaningful understanding that lasts.

Although many agree that "Science for All" is important, science is infrequently thought of as a "core discipline" in the elementary curriculum. Teachers feel increasing pressure to minimize, if not eliminate, science instruction in order to focus on math and literacy skills. Many elementary teachers find science difficult to teach or feel they are unprepared to teach it. As a result, professional development is crucial if elementary teachers are to teach science in ways that foster meaningful student learning and achievement.

According to Guskey (2000, p. 4), professional development includes "processes and activities designed to enhance the professional knowledge, skills, and attitudes of educators" to improve student learning. The breadth of this definition opens the doors to many possibilities for professional development.

No matter what type of professional development activity one chooses, professional development must begin with the teacher whose interests form a nexus with the new processes, ideas, and activities designed to extend their knowledge. How can students learn to do science if they rarely have the opportunity? It takes time and practice for students to learn inquiry skills. They must have opportunities to use inquiry skills when "doing" science. Commonly recognized types of professional development include attending science workshops; taking science courses; enrolling in an online science institute; forming study groups with colleagues; conducting action research; joining professional organizations; or attending a science conference.

Whatever form professional development takes, research findings suggest that high-quality professional development activities

a) provide opportunities for teachers to build skills and knowledge

b) use strategies that teachers will use with their students

c) build learning communities

d) support teachers to serve in leadership roles, and

e) provide links to other parts of the education system (Loucks-Horsley et al. 1998).

Finally, serving as a framework for the ongoing professional development of science teachers is a set of Professional Development Standards for teachers of science that provides a vision of "learning and teaching science in which all students have an opportunity to become scientifically literate." (National Reseach Council, p. 55)

These standards present guidelines in the development of knowledge and skills for teachers of elementary science. In brief, the professional development standards for which teachers of elementary science should strive include:

- The learning of science content through inquiry;
- The integration of knowledge about science with knowledge about learning, teaching, and students;
- The development of the understanding and ability for lifelong learning;
- The coherence and integration of a professional development program.

The overarching premise for making this vision a reality is that teachers are responsible for their own professional development and that it is a lifelong, continuous process of learning.

References

Guskey, T. R. (2000). *Evaluating Professional Development.* Thousand Oaks, CA: Corwin Press.

Loucks-Horsley, S., Hewson, P., Love, N., Stiles, K. (1998). *Designing Professional Development for Teachers of Science and Mathematics.* Thousand Oaks, CA: Corwin Press.

National Research Council (1996). *The National Science Education Standards.* Washington, D.C.: National Academy Press.

Karen L. Ostlund, Ph.D.
UTeach Specialist
College of Natural Sciences
The University of Texas at Austin
Austin, Texas

Scaffolded Inquiry

The **Continuum of Inquiry** is a series of developmental stages. Students progress through these stages to learn the skills and knowledge necessary to engage in inquiry. The sequence of the stages in the Continuum of Inquiry is described below.

Directed Inquiry

- The beginning stage, **Directed Inquiry,** is teacher- or materials-directed. It provides a structured model of the inquiry process. Without this type of support and guidance, students cannot progress to asking and answering scientific questions independently.

- Directed Inquiry introduces students to the essential features of inquiry, and helps students reflect on the characteristics of the processes in which they are engaged.

- Directed Inquiry provides the foundation upon which subsequent stages of inquiry are built. These explorations are designed to provide students with the experiences necessary to learn and practice the processes of inquiry.

Guided Inquiry

- In the second stage, **Guided Inquiry,** the teacher moves from the role of director to facilitator. Students continue to refine their inquiry skills based on the foundation developed during the Directed Inquiry explorations.

- During Guided Inquiry, students have the opportunity to practice skills of inquiry with greater independence. Students are encouraged to think about variables, and they learn to plan for all the variables that may affect the outcome of an investigation.

- Guided Inquiry focuses student attention on learning particular science concepts. Students build science literacy and improve confidence in their abilities to do inquiry.

Full Inquiry

- **Full Inquiry** is one of the ultimate goals of science literacy. To conduct full inquiry, students must be able to apply the skills and knowledge developed in the previous stages in the Continuum of Inquiry.

- According to the National Research Council (1996), Full Inquiry takes place if the following essential features of inquiry are present.
  - Questions are scientifically oriented
  - Learners use evidence to evaluate explanations
  - The explanations answer the questions
  - Alternative explanations are compared and evaluated
  - Explanations are communicated and justified
  - Full Inquiry is modeled in Scott Foresman *Science* to provide a framework so that students can conduct their own investigations. After practicing the thinking processes as they follow the model of a full inquiry experiment, students are encouraged to pose scientifically oriented questions and investigate independently.

Because Scott Foresman *Science* provides scaffolded inquiry, students will be able to attain the goal of conducting independent inquiry. Without the framework provided by scaffolded inquiry, an unrealistic burden rests on the teacher (Colburn, 2004). Moving from teacher-directed to teacher-facilitated to student-directed inquiries allows for a continuously deepening understanding of the skills and knowledge fundamental to conducting inquiry. Therefore, the cycle of Directed, Guided, and Full Inquiry is repeated throughout the Scott Foresman *Science* program.

The Inquiry Continuum

Students must be provided with the scaffolding to engage in full inquiry. They need to practice how to plan and conduct an investigation. Planning begins with posing a question or problem that can be investigated. Then the conditions of the investigation need to be set up (which variables will remain the same, which will be changed, and what outcome or effects will provide the results). Next the investigation is conducted, data is collected and analyzed, an explanation is formulated and compared to scientific knowledge, and the explanation is communicated and justified.

References

Colburn, Alan (2004). *Inquiring Scientists Want to Know. Educational Leadership,* 62(1), 63–66.

National Research Council (1996). *National Science Education Standards.* Washington, DC: National Academy Press.

National Research Council (2000). Steve Olson and Susan Loucks-Horsley, eds. Committee on the Development of an Addendum to the National Science Education Standards on Scientific Inquiry, National Research Council. *Inquiry and the 'National Science Education Standards': A Guide for Teaching and Learning.* Washington, DC: National Academy Press.

Karen L. Ostlund, Ph.D.
UTeach Specialist
College of Natural Sciences
The University of Texas at Austin
Austin, Texas

The Inquiry Continuum

The chart below shows stages in the development of the processes of inquiry. Classrooms may be at different stages in this developmental process, but the ultimate goal is to reach Full Inquiry.

Students: The Beginning Stage has the least amount of student self-direction and Final Stage has the most student self-direction.

Teachers: The Beginning Stage indicates the most direction from the teacher and/or material and Final Stage indicates the least direction from the teacher and/or materials.

The Processes of Inquiry	Question	Predict or Formulate Hypotheses	Investigate
Beginning Stage **Directed Inquiry**	Students use question provided by the teacher, materials, or some other source.	Students are given a prediction for conducting a descriptive investigation or a hypothesis for conducting an experiment.	Students are given the procedures and materials to conduct an investigation (descriptive investigation or experiment).
Transitional Stage **Guided Inquiry**	Students are guided to refine and clarify questions developed with input from the teacher, materials, or some other source.	Students are guided to make a prediction for descriptive investigations or construct a hypothesis for experiments and revise predictions and/or hypotheses if necessary.	Students are given suggestions for procedures and materials that could be used to conduct an investigation (descriptive investigation or experiment).
Final Stage **Full Inquiry**	Students investigate a question that can be answered by doing descriptive investigations or experiments.	Students develop logical/reasonable predictions and/or hypotheses.	Students devise a plan that takes all the variables into account and conduct an investigation (descriptive investigation or experiment).

The Inquiry Continuum

Collect & Organize Data	Analyze and Draw Conclusions	Formulate Explanations	Propose Scientific Explanations	Communicate Findings
Students follow step-by-step procedures provided by the teacher, materials, or some other source to collect and organize data into tables, graphs, and/or charts.	Students are given instructions on how to analyze the data, and guided to draw a conclusion to answer the question being investigated.	Students take synthesized data and are given step-by-step directions to formulate their explanation.	Students are given scientific explanations.	Students are given step-by-step procedures for communicating findings and justifying a provided explanation with evidence from the investigation.
Students are given instructions to collect data and tables, graphs, and/or charts are recommended to organize the data collected.	Students are given suggestions on how to analyze the data on their own and draw conclusions to answer the question being investigated.	Students are guided in the process of formulating explanations from the data they collected, analyzed, and synthesized.	Students are guided to reliable sources of scientific explanations and asked to compare this information to their explanations and make any necessary revisions.	Students are given guidelines for communicating findings and justifying their explanations with evidence from their investigation.
Students decide how and what data to collect and construct tables, graphs, and/or charts to organize the data collected.	Students determine what evidence is needed, analyze the collected data ,and draw conclusions to answer the question being investigated.	Students formulate their explanation after analyzing and synthesizing the data they collected.	Students independently examine scientific explanations from reliable sources and use the information to revise and strengthen their explanations.	Students use logical reasoning to communicate findings and justify their explanations with evidence from their investigation.

Dr. Nancy Romance
Professor of Science Education & Principal Investigator
NSF/IERI Science IDEAS Project
Charles E. Schmidt College of Science
Florida Atlantic University
Boca Raton, Florida

How Meaningful Science Learning Supports Reading Comprehension: What the Research Says to the Classroom Teacher

Two major educational goals:

1. **Increase student motivation for doing and learning science.**

2. **Improve student reading comprehension proficiency.**

While educators acknowledge the continuing crisis in both science and reading, most are less aware of the powerful relationship between meaningful science learning and reading comprehension. These curriculum areas support and enhance each other. In addressing the complementary nature of science learning and reading comprehension, this article will provide both a framework for understanding the relationship and some how-to strategies for the classroom.

There are basically three major considerations that will help teachers increase the quality of and time allocated for elementary science while achieving important literacy (reading comprehension) goals. The first consideration results from a synthesis of twenty years of research on learning (Bransford, 1999). It provides the dynamic framework for key decisions about teaching science and reading. The second consideration translates those findings into meaningful curricular decisions directly applicable in the classroom. Third, consensus research in terms of student achievement outcomes supports integrating science learning with reading comprehension instruction which, in turn, supports teachers and principals when making such curricular revisions.

First, emphasize relevant prior knowledge as the basis for all subsequent learning. Second, organize concepts and concept relationships that students must learn around big ideas that allow learners to construct conceptual understanding necessary to retrieve that knowledge and support further learning. Third, provide students with opportunities to think about and apply knowledge to other contexts and problems. These findings parallel suggestions from reading research (Snow, 2002) which identify the need for adequate background knowledge, technical vocabulary, motivation, and reading strategies to comprehend informational text. Because these underlying principles and findings are, in effect, addressing the same cognitive abilities, they provide a strong basis for connecting science learning with reading comprehension.

What can classroom teachers do?

This section addresses the importance of (a) using guided and open-ended inquiry to actively engage all students, (b) integrating writing to help students learn science (while promoting literacy), and (c) applying reading comprehension strategies (summarization, questioning, prior knowledge, graphic organizers, and text features) to informational passages which are related to concepts introduced through opening hands-on experiences. In turn, relating the hands-on experience with writing and reading is synergistic. That is, their combined value is far greater than their value as separate instructional approaches. (This is precisely why science learning and reading comprehension enhance each other in terms of student learning.)

Use guided and open-ended inquiry to actively engage all students.

In planning your lessons, consider how your teacher's edition, which is based upon current research in learning, provides a well thought out guide for instruction. Consider the concept(s) to be learned by the students and whether students possess the adequate prior knowledge in order to benefit from the lesson. Because we understand the importance of building student prior knowledge, plan for and engage students in well-designed inquiry-based hands-on science activities and explorations which serve to introduce the concept and important vocabulary (building prior knowledge). Doing science (active engagement) has repeatedly been shown to be an essential motivator for learning. In effect, such learning experiences scaffold student learning, especially for high need students most apt to be missing such experiences both in and out of school.

Integrate writing to help students learn science (while promoting literacy).

A key instructional strategy which clearly increases science learning and literacy development is to integrate numerous opportunities for students to write in science. Opportunities for writing include using it to record and explain ideas as part of all inquiry-based learning. In accessing relevant prior knowledge, students can answer questions about what they know or they can pose questions about the topic they would like to learn. Finally, journaling as an integral part of a science course provides a record of learning and a key organizational skill for students.

Apply reading comprehension strategies (summarization, questioning, prior knowledge, graphic organizers, and text features) to informational passages.

Classroom teachers can integrate key reading comprehension strategies as part of guided reading using informational texts. This integration promotes both learning science concepts and general reading comprehension proficiency.

Several key strategies:

- Take advantage of text features to help learners visualize and organize the concepts.
- Explore how the author has organized the concepts.
- Apply critical cognitive skills such as inferring, predicting, and generalizing while discussing passages in the text.

Other valuable comprehension strategies which complement and scaffold science learning:

- Use context clues to determine the meaning of key vocabulary.
- Identify cause and effect relationships.
- Summarize information to identify the main idea and supporting detail.
- Identify how objects or events are alike (compare) or different (contrast).

As students become more proficient in using these strategies, and as they continue to deepen their understanding of science, there is an obvious increase in student interest. They read further, pursuing their interests, and they share what they are learning. When learning and enjoyment increase, the broad goals of science and literacy are achieved.

Finally, consensus research findings (Amaral, et al, 2002; Duke, et al, 2003; Guthrie et al, 2004; Romance & Vitale, 1992 and 2001) clearly indicate the positive effect of integrating science learning and reading comprehension (including writing) on student achievement outcomes in both science and reading. The integration engenders positive student attitudes toward reading and motivation to learn science. The power is in the combination, and it's easy to do. A quality elementary science program is a powerful resource to achieve these goals.

References

Amaral, O. M., Garrison, L. & Klentschy, M. (2002). *Helping English learners increase achievement through inquiry-based science instruction.* Bilingual Research Journal, 26(2), 213-239.

Bransford, J. D., Brown, A. L., & Cocking, R. R. (1999). *How people learn.* Washington, DC: National Academy Press.

Duke, N. K., Bennett-Armistead, S., & Roberts, E. M. (2003). *Filling the non-fiction void.* American Educator, 27(1), 30-35.

Guthrie, J. T., Wigfield, A., & Perencevich, K. C. (2004). *Motivating reading comprehension: Concept oriented reading instruction.* Mahwah, NJ: Lawrence Erlbaum Associates.

Romance, N. R., & Vitale, M. R. (2001). *Implementing an in-depth expanded science model in elementary schools: Multi-year findings, research issues, and policy implications.* International Journal of Science Education, 23, 373-404.

Romance, N. R., & Vitale, M. R. (1992). *A curriculum strategy that expands time for in-depth elementary science instruction by using science-based reading strategies: Effects of a year-long study in grade 4.* Journal of Research in Science Teaching, 29, 545-554.

Snow, C. E. (2002). *Reading for understanding: Toward a research and development program in reading comprehension (Rand Report).* Santa Monica, CA: Rand.

Dr. James Flood
Distinguished Professor of Literacy and Language
School of Teacher Education
San Diego State University
San Diego, California

Dr. Diane Lapp
Distinguished Professor of Reading and Language
Arts in Teacher Education
San Diego State University
San Diego, California

Vocabulary Instruction in Science

Vocabulary knowledge, arguably one of the most important hallmarks of an educated person, is essential for comprehending science texts at all levels. It plays a vital role in every aspect of reading from understanding the gist of a simple text to interpreting and appreciating the most complex texts (Beck, McKeown and Kucan, 2002; Brassell and Flood, 2004; Lapp, Flood, Brock and Fisher, 2005; Nagy and Anderson, 1988).

The Most Frequently Asked Questions About Vocabulary Instruction

How many words can I teach in a year?

While estimates vary, Beck et al. (2002) concluded that 400 words per year was a reasonable estimate of the number of words that could be taught and learned in one school year.

How many words can I teach in one lesson?

There is an easy answer: five to seven new, unfamiliar words per lesson. When we try to extend this number by preteaching difficult words that children will encounter in a new text (and the list grows to 10–20 words), we are courting disaster. For each new word introduced beyond five to seven, we can count on memory overload, which negatively affects the learning of the target words.

However, not all children know the same words, so some of the words you designate as new will not be new for every child. Moreover, new words may be introduced through known words.

How many encounters/exposures to words are needed?

Some researchers (Lapp, Flood, Brock and Fisher, 2005; Scott, 1988) have suggested that at least 8 to 10 exposures are needed before a new word begins to become part of a child's lexicon. The real answer to this question depends upon the child's background as well as the word itself. Some words clearly take time "to own." As Brassell and Flood (2004) note: vocabulary development is incremental. We never really own most words; we just grow in our understanding of the concepts they represent.

What words should I teach?

Anyone who has stopped to ponder this question has been immediately overwhelmed by the myriad of choices: 1) content-area words like *matter, force, gravity, energy;* 2) grade level high frequency words; 3) high utility (but less frequent) words like *imaginative, design, adjustable, creative*. Although the list of possibilities seems endless, as teachers we must make sensible choices that are based on sound criteria.

Criteria for Selecting Vocabulary Words to be Taught

In an attempt to sort out the words that should be taught, Graves (2000) advises teachers to distinguish between *teaching new concepts* and *teaching new labels for familiar concepts*. Words may be divided into four very useful categories:

1. **high frequency words (car, driver);**
2. **domain specific technical vocabulary (raceway);**
3. **low frequency words (carburetor); and**
4. **high utility words (gasoline)**

Beck and her colleagues (2002) provide another framework for organizing words into three general categories: Tier I words are almost universally known **(tree, leaf);** Tier II includes almost all of the words we need to teach students; and Tier III words are infrequent and technical **(photosynthesis)** that are best learned at their point of need.

A sensible set of criteria for selecting Tier II words includes the following:

1. **Choose words that have high utility in the child's life**
2. **Choose words that will lead students to other words**
3. **Choose words that are needed in a particular content area**

How can I proactively teach vocabulary?

There is no one best way to teach vocabulary to every child. Children learn word meanings in multiple ways ranging from learning words incidentally, e.g. from Read Alouds, to robust, explicit, effective instruction.

Instructional Strategies

Well-researched instructional strategies can help teachers instruct their students in the vocabulary they will need to comprehend science books. While there are many excellent strategies that teachers can use effectively (for a review, see Brassell and Flood, 2004), we will include just an example of—perhaps the most effective—strategy for helping children learn science words.

Semantic Mapping

Semantic maps are particularly useful for visually representing new word meanings and the relationship between the new word and other known words (Blachowicz & Fisher, 2002; Brassell and Flood, 2004). **Semantic Mapping,** which is also known as "semantic webbing" and "semantic networking," often uses a graphic organizer resembling a spider web to connect information.

In the classroom example that we present below, the teacher presents the word *dinosaur,* which is a Tier I word for most children; it is not a new concept, therefore, it does not count as one of our 400 words for the year; it may be a new written word for many children, but it is probably not an unknown word. In this lesson, *dinosaur* is the topic word that leads to three new words that the teacher wants to teach—extinct, survival and fossil. The words linking *dinosaur* with the target words are all Tier I words (lived, earth, water, land) which are the 'glue' that keeps the network operating. The linking words *lived* and *became* are critical for understanding the relationships among the words that are included in the semantic map; they become review words that help children place the new words in a functioning network.

Classroom Example:

Rogelio Martinez's second graders were beginning a unit on dinosaurs. He wanted his students to understand how scientists could prove dinosaurs' existence and why the dinosaurs became extinct. Mr. Martinez wrote the word "dinosaurs" on the chalkboard and asked students to organize into groups of 3–4. Next, he asked each group to brainstorm all of the words that they could think of associated with dinosaurs. He told the groups to pay attention to characteristics words shared so that they could categorize them under subheadings. After about five minutes, Mr. Martinez asked the groups to dictate their words which he then wrote on the chalkboard. He encouraged students to place words under categories. For example, when students shared the words "ancient" and "old," Mr. Martinez explained that dinosaur remains were also known as "fossils" and placed the terms under that category. Later, when students said that dinosaurs had lived on "land" and in "water," a student suggested that Mr. Martinez categorize those terms under "Earth." After further discussion, students asked Mr. Martinez to connect categories with the key word "dinosaur" by writing relationship words on the connecting lines. For example, one student asked Mr. Martinez to connect "dinosaurs" with "food" with the word "ate." Finally, Mr. Martinez told students to add words and categories to the semantic map as they learned more about dinosaurs.

Semantic Map

Concept/Key Word: Dinosaurs

The following standards were met as this lesson was presented:

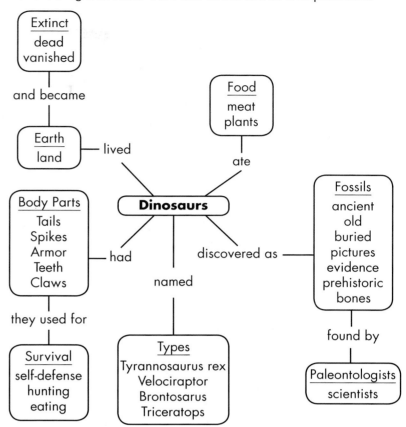

Grade Two Science Goals

After unit lesson, students will be able to:

- say that fossils provide evidence about the plants and animals that lived long ago on Earth;
- list characteristics of dinosaurs;
- describe conditions that may cause a species to become extinct; and
- explain how scientists learn about the past history of the Earth

Notes

Academic Professional Development (APD Press) has granted permission to reprint the classroom example that is presented in this paper. The example appears in Brassell, D. and Flood, J. (2004) *Vocabulary Strategies Every Teacher Should Know.* San Diego, CA: APD Press.

References

Beck, I, McKeown M. and Kucan, L. (2002). *Bringing Words to Life.* New York: Guilford Press.

Blachowicz, C., & Fisher, P. J. (2002). *Teaching vocabulary in all classrooms (2nd ed.).* Upper Saddle River, NJ: Merrill/Prentice Hall.

Brassell, D., & Flood, J. (2004). *Vocabulary strategies every teacher needs to know.* San Diego, CA: Academic Professional Development.

Graves, M. (2000). A vocabulary program to complement and bolster a middle-grade comprehension program. In B. Taylor, M. Graves, & P. van den Broek (Eds.), *Reading for meaning: Fostering comprehension in the middle grades* (pp. 116-135). Newark, DE: International Reading Association.

Lapp, D, Flood, J., Brock,C., Fisher,D (2005) *Teaching Reading to Every Child (4th ed.),* Mahwah, NJ: Lawrence Erlbaum.

Nagy, W. (1988). *Teaching vocabulary to improve reading comprehension.* Newark, DE: International Reading Association.

Scott, J., Jamieson-Noel, D. & Asselin, M. (2003). *Vocabulary Instruction Throughout the School Day in 23 Canadian Upper-Elementary Classrooms.* The Elementary School Journal, 103(3), 269-286.

Dr. Jim Cummins, Professor
Department of Curriculum, Teaching, and Learning
University of Toronto
Toronto, Canada

Supporting ESL Students in Learning the Language of Science

Because language is infused into all aspects of the teaching of science, students whose knowledge of English is limited are likely to have difficulty accessing scientific concepts and expressing their understanding of these concepts in oral and written language. Therefore, teachers are faced with the challenge of modifying their instruction in ways that will assist ESL students.

Effective academic language instruction for ESL students across the curriculum is built on three fundamental pillars:

1. **Activate Prior Knowledge/Build Background Knowledge**

2. **Access Content**

3. **Extend Language**

In developing scientific knowledge through language, and language abilities through science, we can apply these three instructional principles in powerful ways.

1. Activate Prior Knowledge/Build Background Knowledge

Prior knowledge is the foundation of learning. When students read a scientific text, they construct meaning by bringing their prior knowledge of language, science, and of the world in general to the text. Students may not explicitly realize what they know about a particular topic or issue. Activating their prior knowledge brings it to consciousness and facilitates learning.

Activating prior knowledge and building background knowledge are important for all students, but particularly for ESL students who may be struggling with unfamiliar vocabulary and grammatical structures in addition to complex new concepts. Building this context permits students to understand more complex language and to pursue more cognitively demanding activities. It lessens the cognitive load of the text and frees up brain power.

Activation of prior knowledge enables teachers to validate ESL students' background experiences and affirm their cultural knowledge. Inviting students to contribute what they already know to the class discussion communicates to students that the cultural and linguistic knowledge they are bringing into the classroom is valuable.

Strategies for activating prior knowledge and building background knowledge.

A variety of strategies to activate students' prior knowledge are embedded in Scott Foresman *Science.*

- *Brainstorming/discussion* This type of language interaction can happen in the context of a whole class, in small groups, or in pairs; for example, students can interview a partner to find out what each one knows about a particular topic. Discussion can also be highly effective in making abstract concepts more concrete and comprehensible.

- *Use of graphic organizers* These can be used to capture the results of brainstorming and discussion. For example, K-W-L- charts can be used to record what students already **K**now, what they **W**ant to know, and, after the lesson, what they have **L**earned. Word webs and many other graphic organizers enable students to record and organize their information.

- *Visuals in texts* Photographs, charts, and graphs can be used to stimulate discussion about aspects of what is depicted and to encourage students to predict what the text is likely to be about.

- *Short-term direct experiences* Quick activities that begin each lesson provide opportunities for students to observe science-related phenomena and can stimulate discussion of what students have observed. Teachers help students relate their observations or experiences to the content of the science lesson.

- *Long-term direct experiences* Class projects and formal inquiry activities provide opportunities for students to deepen their knowledge of abstract concepts.

- *Writing about what we know* Dialogue journals for note taking and responses to written prompts are useful means for the student to both record information and review it later.

2. Access Content

We can also support or *scaffold* students' learning by modifying the input itself. We provide this scaffolding by embedding the content in a richly redundant context with multiple routes to the meaning in addition to the language itself. Building this redundancy enables ESL students to access the content despite any limitations in English language proficiency.

Strategies that improve student access to academic content.

The following methods, which you will find embedded in Scott Foresman *Science,* can help students more effectively get access to meaning.

- **Use Visuals** Visuals enable students to "see" the basic concept we are trying to teach much more effectively than if we rely only on words.

- **Dramatize/Act Out** For beginning ESL students, *Total Physical Response,* where students physically represent a phenomenon or act out commands, can be highly effective.

- **Clarify Language** Language-oriented activities aim to clarify the meanings of new words and concepts. Teachers can modify their language by paraphrasing ideas and explaining new concepts and words. They explain new words by providing synonyms, antonyms, and definitions either in English or in the home language of students. Important vocabulary can be repeated and recycled as part of the paraphrasing of ideas. The meaning can also be communicated and/or reinforced through gestures, body language, and demonstrations.

- **Make Personal and Cultural Connections** Notes in the Scott Foresman *Science* Teacher's Edition suggest ways to link content to students' everyday experiences. These content connections validate students' sense of identity and make the learning more meaningful.

- **Make Cross-Curricular Connections** The more cognitive operations students perform related to a particular issue or problem, the deeper their comprehension becomes.

- **Provide Hands-on Experiences** The more we can contextualize or personalize abstract concepts by embedding them in students' hands-on experiences, the more comprehensible they will become for students. Hands-on projects also allow students link the conversational language they use in the "real" world and the more abstract and specialized language they are learning in science. Discussions about concrete phenomena and problems demystify the language of Science. The abstract concepts we learn in science help us understand what we see with our very own eyes and vice-versa.

- **Encourage Learning Strategies** Learning strategies are useful for all students, but particularly for ESL students who face obvious challenges in accessing curricular content. Examples of strategies included in Scott Foresman *Science* are: planning tasks or activities, visualization, grouping and classifying information, taking notes and summarizing information, questioning for clarification, and using multiple resources and reference materials to find information or complete a task.

3. Extend Language

A systematic focus on and exploration of language is essential if students are to develop knowledge of the specific vocabulary and text structures that are used in scientific discourse. Students can systematically collect the meanings of words and phrases they encounter in science texts in a personal or group *language bank.*

Strategies that help students accelerate their acquisition of academic language.

A variety of strategies to extend students' language knowledge and awareness are embedded in Scott Foresman *Science.*

- **Explore Etymology** Paradoxically, the complexity of scientific language provides some important opportunities for language exploration. A large percentage of the less frequent academic and technical vocabulary of English derives from Latin and Greek roots. So word formation often follows some very predictable patterns.

- **Identify Rules and Conventions** When students know some of the rules or conventions of how academic words are formed, they have an edge in extending their vocabulary. It helps them not only figure out the meanings of individual words but also how to form different parts of speech from these words.

- **Relate Academic Words to Students' First Language** This encourages students to relate the English word to their prior knowledge of the word (or related words in their first language). It also provides students with an opportunity to display and feel proud of their first language linguistic expertise.

- **Identify and Practice Conjugates** When we demystify how academic language works, students are more likely to recognize parts of speech in their reading of complex text across the curriculum and to become more adept at inferring meanings from context. For example, the student who recognizes that acceleration is a noun (rather than a verb or adjective), has taken a step closer to the meaning of the term in the context of a particular sentence or text.

- **Model Appropriate Academic Language** If teachers provide good models, then students can extend their own command of more formal registers of language. In addition, students must be given the opportunity and incentive to use academic language in both oral and written modalities. For example, after a concrete hands-on group experience or project, students are asked to report back to the class orally about what they did and what they observed and then to write about it.

Conclusion

Science will assume relevance to students and be learned much more effectively when students can relate the content of instruction to their prior experience and current interests. In addition to activating students' prior knowledge and building background knowledge, we may need to modify our instruction in specific ways to make the content accessible to ESL students who are still in the process of catching up to native-speakers in academic English language proficiency.

These supports should focus not only on making the scientific content comprehensible to students but also on extending their awareness of how the language of science works. In this way, students can develop insights about academic language that will bear fruit in other areas. When we integrate these active uses of language with the science curriculum, students benefit both with respect to their knowledge of scientific content and language abilities.

References

Chamot, A. U. & O'Malley, J.M. (1994). *The CALLA Handbook: Implementing the Cognitive Academic Language Learning Approach.* Reading, MA: Addison-Wesley.

Collier, V. P. and Thomas, W. P. (1999). *Making U.S. schools effective for English language learners, Part 1.* TESOL Matters, 9:4 (August/September), pp. 1 & 6.

Cummins (2001). *Negotiating identities: Education for empowerment in a diverse society.* 2nd edition. Los Angeles: California Association for Bilingual Education.

Díaz-Rico, L. & Weed, K. Z. (2002). *The crosscultural, language, and academic development handbook: A complete K-12 reference guide.* 2nd edition. Boston: Allyn & Bacon.

Gibbons, P. (1991). *Learning to learn in a second language.* Newtown, Australia: Primary English Teaching Association.

Meyer, L. (2000). *Barriers to meaningful instruction for English learners.* Theory into Practice, 34(2), 228-236.

Neuman, S. B. (1999). *Books make a difference: A study of access to literacy.* Reading Research Quarterly, 34(3), 286-311.

Dr. Shirley Gholston Key
Associate Professor of Science Education
Instruction and Curriculum Leadership Department
College of Education
University of Memphis
Memphis, Tennessee

Diversity in Science Education

Multicultural education is an educational reform movement and philosophy designed to change the total educational environment so that students from diverse racial and ethnic groups, both gender groups, exceptional students, and students from each social-class group will experience equal educational opportunities in schools, colleges, and universities (Banks, 1995).

Science curricula and science classrooms have been devoid of relevant cultural inclusion or multicultural education. Many science educators believe "science is pure" and thus escapes the influences of current pedagogy, trends, and especially cultural influences. Even though science processes are generic or "culture free," if students cannot and do not identify with information that are "processing," they may internalize the notion that they cannot perform science or are not expected to process scientific information. The process of validating and/or correcting perceived notions depends on one's culture. Multicultural science or culturally inclusive science is believed to be an enhancement for students of color.

What is sought and needed in science classrooms is a model which integrates the learning of the traditional science with the cultures within the classroom. **Culturally inclusive science** integrates the learner's culture into the academic and social context of the science classroom to aid and support science learning (Baptiste & Key, 1996). The culturally inclusive model demonstrates that the equity pedagogy and the content integration dimensions are not mutually exclusive (Key, 1999).

Student achievement is influenced by student attitudes, interests, motivation, type of curricula, relevancy of materials, and the culture of the students. To understand how culture may influence science and other disciplines, one must be aware of the five dimensions of multicultural education (Banks & Banks, 1995).

- *Content integration* encompasses the extent to which teachers use culturally relevant examples, data, and information from a variety of cultures and groups to illustrate key concepts, principles, generalizations, and theories in their subject areas or disciplines.

- *Knowledge construction* involves the procedure by which social, behavioral, and natural scientists create knowledge, and the manner in which the implicit cultural assumption, frames of reference, perspective, and biases influence the ways that knowledge is constructed within each discipline.

- *Prejudice reduction* describes the characteristics of children's racial attitudes and suggests strategies that can help students develop more democratic attitudes and values.

- *Equity pedagogy* uses methods that facilitate the academic achievement of students from diverse racial, ethnic, and social class groups.

- *Empowering school culture and social structure* describes the process of restructuring the school's culture so that students from diverse groups will experience educational equality (Banks & Banks, 1995).

Some strategies that enhance the science learning and achievement of students of color are cooperative learning and inquiry. Other concepts that also enhance students of color achievement when addressed properly are congruency, locus of control, and field dependency.

Cooperative Learning

Cooperative learning is advantageous for all students. African American students' achievement is enhanced when cooperative learning groups incorporate group rewards based on group members' individual learning (Irvine and York, 1995). The following cooperative learning strategies make learning more personable and less threatening for many students.

- *Strategically mix students to form groups.* Group students of different backgrounds, academic achievement levels, and social skill levels. A mixture of different abilities, ethnic backgrounds, learning styles, and personal interests works best for productive student teams. One of the benefits of cooperative teams is the mixing of students who have not interacted before (Johnson, et. al. 1986).

- *Demand group responsibility.* Group members should be interdependent, working to accomplish a common goal. The teacher structures the assignment so each member must contribute to successfully meet the group's goal. Allowing one or two to dominate the activity does not result in greater understanding for all.

- *Demand individual accountability.* Assignments should be structured so each member accomplishes a specific task. Try to provide opportunities for every group member to make a unique contribution. Students who work together in groups without differentiated tasks (for example, to prepare a single worksheet) have not shown significant achievement benefits. Therefore the teacher should use assessments which measure group and individual achievement.

- *Introduce students to social or interpersonal skills.* Skills such as making eye contact, encouraging fellow group members, using quiet voices, and disagreeing without hostility are habits which will become part of the cooperative group's repertoire.

Inquiry

Inquiry is the most appropriate vehicle for accommodating all learning modalities. Inquiry teaching is a means by which all children are able to construct processes, products, and attitudes in unique and valid ways that result in meaningful and lasting learning. Constructivism says that all children learn in different ways and inquiry provides the means. Inquiry methodology allows children to develop their own investigations to address questions they raise themselves. It encourages children to take charge of their own learning and children who take charge of their own learning have a greater tendency to develop an internal locus of control. The teacher can implement inquiry methodology by allowing students to figure out what caused what (cause and effect activities), to recognize and name variables, and define them operationally, and by employing discovery learning methodologies.

Congruency

Congruency is the alignment between a student's learning style and the teacher's teaching style. Multicultural advocates and experts believe that the closer the match between a student's learning style and a teacher's instructional methods, the more likely the student will experience academic success (Irvine & York, 1995).

Students of color were less successful when assimilation vs. accommodation of their learning styles occurred. They are more successful when accommodation of the teaching style is made to their learning styles (Irvine & York, 1995).

Locus of Control

Locus of control is the concept or belief about the source of one's fate. It is a powerful predictor of academic achievement (Brookover, et. al., 1979). A student with an internal locus of control believes personal successes or failures are due largely to his/her own abilities and efforts. A student with an external locus of control believes their successes or failures are due largely to external factors, luck, other people's actions, or difficult situations. Many students of color have been found to have an external locus of control. Teachers can help students to convert to an internal locus of control by encouraging students to evaluate the outcomes of investigations, encouraging students to suggest ways of changing variables, and by encouraging them to suggest additional ways of investigating a given phenomenon. Students can also suggest topics for investigation and set their own goals and evaluate their own progress. These strategies encourage students to trust their judgement, become more independent, and establish an internal locus of control.

Field Dependency

Field dependency is the inability of persons to recognize camouflaged information. Students with field dependency see things holistically. They tend to rely on external cues and are less able to differentiate part of a field as discrete from the field as a whole. In contrast, the field independent persons have the ability to recognize camouflaged information very easily. The field independent student has the ability to ignore unnecessary details and surrounding camouflaging information.

Science teachers can use several strategies to enhance the skills of a field dependent student. Well-organized, structured materials help to enhance the understanding of field dependent learners. They can use constructivistic method, process-inquiry methodology, puzzles and board games, and computer games, organizers for science lessons, concept maps, and process skills (Martin, 1996).

Graphic organizers are tools for organizing science information to help make concepts easier for different types of learners. There are various styles and are concept driven. They are very helpful to the

field dependent learners. Some graphic organizers include charts, tables, graphs, concept maps, different types of webs, T-charts, KWL charts, and many others.

Graphic organizers can aid all learners to organize, analyze, and reflect upon science concepts. They have been extremely effective in helping the field dependent learner to focus on key patterns and issues, to look at background information that is normally missed, and to ask questions that lead students to discover properties or qualities (Jonassen & Grabowski, 1993).

To begin to address diversity in your science classroom:

- Plan your science lessons or topics as usual.
- Include the researching of persons of color and/other cultures that have contributed to the lesson topic or concept as one of your objectives.
- Use appropriate strategies to help accomplish the lesson with maximum achievement for the students, e.g. use cooperative learning, inquiry and graphic organizers.
- Integrate this information "into" the guided practice, independent practice, and/or assessment of the lesson.
- Use the names and information within the lesson text as well as in the questions and assessment materials.
- Assign authentic assessments to discuss and use this culturally rich information.
- Use the cultural inclusion typology (Baptiste & Key, 1996), culturally inclusive science model (Key, 1999), and multicultural education dimensions (Banks, 1995) to vary the methods and increase students' knowledge.
- Repeat this with all lessons on a daily basis

© KEYCON (Used with the permission of Dr. Shirley Key)

References

Banks, J. (1995). *Multiethnic Education: Theory and practice (4th ed.).* Boston: Allyn and Bacon.

Banks, J., & Banks, C. (Eds.). (1995). *Handbook of Research on Multicultural Education,* New York: Macmillan.

Baptiste, P. & Key, S. (1996). *Cultural Inclusion: Where does your program stand?* The Science Teacher, 63(2) 32-35.

Brookover, W., Beady, C., Flood, P., Schweitzer, J. & Wisenbaker, J. (1979). *School social systems and student achievement: Schools can make a difference.* New York: Praeger.

Dunn, R. & Dunn, K. (1979). *Teaching students through their individual learning styles.* Englewood Cliffs, New Jersey: Prentice Hall.

Gregorc, A. F. (1979). *Learning/teaching styles: Potent forces behind them.* Educational Leadership, 36 (4), 234-36.

Hollins, E., & Spencer, K. (1990). *Restructuring schools for cultural inclusion: Changing the schooling process for African American youngsters.* Journal of Education, 172 (2), 89-100.

Irvine, J. & York, D. (1995). *Learning Styles and Culturally Diverse Students: A Literature Review. In Handbook of Research on Multicultural Education.* 484–497. New York: Macmillan.

Johnson, D., Johnson, R. & Holubec, E. (1986). *Circles of Learning.* Edina, Minnesota: Interaction Book Company.

Jonassen, D. & Grabowski, B. (1993). *Handbook of Individual Differences: Learning & Instruction.* Mahwah, New Jersey: Lawerence Erlbaum Associates.

Key, S. (1999). Using Culture to Enhance African-American Students' Interest in Science. In Ed Hines, M., Kincheloe, & Steinberg (Eds.), *Multicultural Science Education: Critical Essays, Research, and Practice.* New York: Lang Publishing Company.

Key, S. (1995). African American eighth grade science students' perceived interest in topics taught in traditional and nontraditional science curricula. *Dissertation Abstract International,* A56 (5), 1725.

Martin, D. (1996). *Elementary Science Methods: A Constructivist Approach.* New York: Delmar Publishing.

Mintzes, J., Wandersee, J., & Novak, J. (1998). *Teaching Science for Understanding: A Human Constructivist View.* New York: Academic Press.

Dr. Michael P. Klentschy
Superintendent
El Centro Elementary School District
El Centro, California

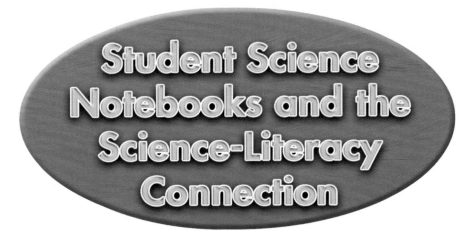

Student Science Notebooks and the Science-Literacy Connection

Learning science helps children develop an understanding of the world around them. To do this they must develop concepts that help them link their experiences together and learn ways to collect and organize information and apply and test ideas. This learning not only contributes to children's ability to make better sense of things around them, but also prepares them to deal more effectively with wider decision-making and problem-solving in their lives. When literacy skills are linked to science content, students have a personal, practical motivation to master language as a tool that can help them answer their questions about the world around them. Language becomes the primary avenue that students use to arrive at scientific understanding. Scientific literacy should emphasize scientific ways of knowing and the process of thinking critically and creatively about the natural world.

The Learning Research and Development Center at the University of Pittsburgh and the National Center on Education and the Economy identifies reciprocal skills associated with science and literacy (2000). These reciprocal skills include the following:

Literacy	*Science*
note details	observe and retain minute details
compare and contrast	how are things different and how they are the same
predict	what will happen next
sequence of events	process of logic and analysis
link cause and effect	what causes things to react in a particular way
distinguish fact from opinion	the use of evidence to support claims
link words with precise meanings	develop operational definitions of a concept though experiences
make inferences	based upon observation and evidence
draw conclusions	by combining data from various sources

This analysis of the reciprocal nature of science and literacy strengthens the view that effective science teaching is a powerful means to connect science and literacy.

This form of communication is both oral and written in the form of student science notebooks. Words and language are used as a way of trying out a framework for understanding—learners need to have to reflect on ideas. Through writing students can generate a personal response to experiences, for clarifying ideas, and for constructing knowledge. Writing enables the learner to understand first and to communicate second.

Science and literacy also have another strong point of connection through the desire of many educators to develop metacognitive awareness in children. Cognition is an interactive-constructive process and metacognition is a conscious awareness and control of this process that results in verifying, rethinking, reflecting, and reshaping information into meaningful knowledge networks. Research has demonstrated that children can be taught these strategies, including the ability to predict outcomes, explain oneself in order to improve understanding and to plan ahead. Teaching metacognitive strategies in context has been shown to improve student content understanding, written composition and problem solving, especially when language skills and science are taught in the context of each other (National Research Council, 1999).

Student Science Notebooks

The design of an effective program of instruction links science and literacy through the use of student science notebooks. An effective program of science instruction is based upon the belief that students need to be provided with an opportunity to develop "voice" in their personal construction of meaning of the science phenomena. This "voice" comes in the form of their science notebooks. The science notebook is utilized during their science experiences, in social interactions, as a tool for reflection, and as a tool for constructing meaning (Klentschy and Molina-De La Torre, 2004). All students participating in effective programs of instruction in science showed a pattern of significant growth in student achievement in both science achievement and in reading and writing achievement (Amaral et al, 2002; Jorgenson and Vanosdall, 2002). This research also indicates that writing enables students to express their current ideas about science content in a form that they can examine and think about. Achievement in science is directly proportional to the student's ability to use language (Fellows, 1994).

This form of expository writing through the use of student science notebooks may also help students link new information with prior knowledge (Rivard, 1994). Science notebooks can also contain drawings, tables or graphs that are essential for the child to form meaning from the science experience. The use of student science notebooks in class discussions helps students construct meaning of the science phenomena. The student science notebook then becomes more than a record of data that students collect, facts they learn, and procedures they conduct. The science notebook also becomes a record of students' reflections, questions, speculations, decisions and conclusions all focused on the science phenomena. As such, a science notebook becomes a central place where language, data, and experience operate jointly to form meaning for the student.

Knowledge-Transforming

The act of writing by its very nature may enhance thinking. Writing may achieve this by demanding the learner to organize language. Frequently classroom writing in science is directed at communicating what the student knows to the teacher, filling in the blanks or producing short responses to teacher-generated questions, and recording observations and information. Simply listing the procedures for experiments and writing a narrative of the results limits students in the construction of true meaning from the phenomena and reduces the experience to retelling knowledge.

The use of student science notebooks is effective for most students when the teacher is more concerned with establishing a dialogue with students to monitor learning, emphasizing the thinking and learning processes involved in learning the content. Teachers should consider posing questions which students might ask themselves in knowledge-transforming writing in their science notebooks such as:

What evidence do I have?

What claims should I make?

What are alternative explanations?

Santa and Havens (1991) suggested that meaningful writing should bridge new information and prior knowledge, provide authentic authoring tasks for an uninformed audience, encourage minds-on learning, facilitate conceptual organization and restructuring, and promote metacognition. Writing should allow the transformation of vague ideas to clear conceptions and stimulate the construction of meaning. This belief is also based on the importance of establishing student "voice" in science notebook writing.

Marzano (1991) has argued that fostering higher order thinking demands instructional activities in which the learner's existing knowledge is restructured through activities that are complex and long term. He argues that writing is appropriate to induce knowledge transformation.

Feedback

One of the most important strategies a teacher can use is to provide students with feedback on their work. Teacher feedback plays an important role in the knowledge-transformational process of using student notebooks in science instruction. Marzano et al (2001) reported in a review of nine research studies that feedback that guides students, rather than merely telling them what is right or wrong could attain significant differences in student achievement. The most appropriate form of feedback in a knowledge-transforming mode of instruction is one of asking guiding questions to the student or writing guiding questions in their science notebooks.

The timing of feedback also appears to be critical to its effectiveness. In general, the more delay that occurs in giving feedback, the longer it takes students to eliminate misconceptions (Marzano et al, 2001). Perhaps this is especially true for science misconceptions.

Research on feedback also indicates that students can effectively monitor their own progress. The use of student feedback in the form of self-evaluation has been strongly advocated by researcher Grant Wiggins (1993). This self-evaluating form of feedback is also important in the construction of meaning by the students.

Summary

A growing body of evidence indicates that a strong relationship between student participation in effective inquiry-based science instruction programs not only improves their achievement in science, but also in reading, language arts and mathematics (Amaral et al, 2002, Jorgenson and Vanosdall, 2002). An extensive examination of this body of evidence indicates a strong connection between science and literacy. The disciplines are mutually reinforcing in a reciprocating process. This connection appears to be the strongest where student science notebooks play a pivotal role in the instructional program. This connection also has the potential to assist students in developing their metacognitive abilities in science.

The student science notebook serves as the important link between science and literacy when used in the classroom as a knowledge-transforming form of writing. It provides the appropriate opportunity for students to develop "voice" in the process of constructing meaning from their experiences with the science phenomena. Coupled with appropriate and timely feedback from the classroom teacher, the science notebook has strong potential to provide the improvement in student achievement educators are seeking.

References

Amaral, Olga, Garrison, Leslie, and Klentschy, Michael. (Summer, 2002). Helping English learners increase achievement through inquiry-based science instruction. *Bilingual Research Journal,* 26:2, 213-239.

Fellows, Nancy. (1994). A window into thinking: Using student writing to understand conceptual change in science learning. *Journal of Research in Science Teaching,* 31(9), 985-1001.

Jorgenson, Olaf and Vanosdall, Rick (2002). The death of science? What are we risking in our rush toward standardized testing and the three R's? *Phi Delta Kappan,* 83(8), 601- 605.

Klentschy, M. and Molina-De La Torre, E. (2004). Students' science notebooks and the inquiry process. In W. Saul (Ed.). *Crossing Borders in Literacy and Science Instruction: Perspectives on Theory and Practice.* Newark, DE: International Reading Association Press.

Learning Research and Development Center at the University of Pittsburgh and the National Center on Education and the Economy. (2000). *New standards: Performance standards and assessments for schools.* Pittsburgh, PA: Learning Research and Development Center.

Marzano, Robert. (1991). Fostering thinking across the curriculum through knowledge restructuring. *Journal of Reading,* 34, 518-525.

Marzano, Robert, Pickering, Debra, and Pollock, Jane. (2001). *Classroom instruction that works: Research-based strategies for increasing student achievement.* Alexandria, VA: Association for Supervision and Curriculum Development.

National Research Council. (1999). How people learn: Bridging research and practice. In Susan Donovan, John Bransford, and John Pellegrino (Eds.), *Committee on Learning Research and Education.* Washington, DC: National Academy Press.

Rivard, Leonard. (1994). A review of writing to learn in science: Implications for practice and research. *Journal of Research in Science Teaching,* 31(9), 969-983.

Santa, C.M., & Havens, L.T. (1991). Learning through writing. In C.M. Santa & D.E Alvermann (Eds.), *Science learning: Processes and applications* (pp. 122–133). Newark, DE: International Reading Association.

Wiggins, Grant. (1993). *Assessing student performances: Exploring the purpose and limits of testing.* San Francisco, CA: Jossey-Bass.

Dr. William Tate
Chair and Professor of Education
and Applied Statistics
Department of Education
Washington University
St. Louis, Missouri

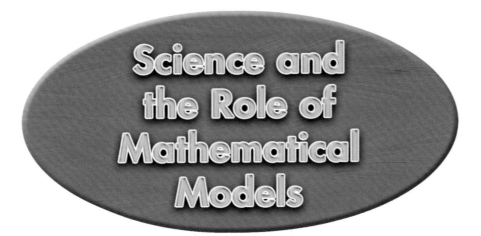

Science and the Role of Mathematical Models

"Mathematical modeling, the process of describing scientific phenomena in a mathematical framework, brings the powerful machinery of mathematics—its ability to generalize, to extract what is common in diverse problems, and to build effective algorithms—to bear on characterization, analysis, and prediction in scientific problems . . . Through modeling, speculations about a system are given a form that allows them to be examined qualitatively and quantitatively from many angles; in particular, modeling allows the detection of discrepancies between theory and reality."

The problems faced by scientists and engineers are so complex that many challenges can be solved only with the participation of mathematicians. The ability to follow scientific arguments as a citizen or to engage in science as a participant is enhanced by more advanced mathematical skills and conceptual understanding. It is a great advantage for students in grades K–6 to see mathematics as integral to science (National Council of Teachers of Mathematics, 2000). Elementary students with significant mathematical preparation in their school science programs have more opportunities to learn mathematics and to advance to the academic level required to understand the complexity of today's scientific enterprise (Tate and Johnson, 1997). Many research problems involve systems that are not transparent and thus demand exploration with new mathematical tools (Wright and Chorin, 1999).

The use of and the process of learning to create mathematical models are vital to both scientific education and the practice of science. Model building can begin in kindergarten (National Research Council, 1999). Numerous opportunities exist in Scott Foresman *Science* for students to engage in the model development cycle: model construction, model evaluation, and model revision. This cycle mirrors the process many in the scientific community implement.

Each kind of science uses the language of mathematics to communicate about data and the process of data analysis. At one level the term *data* refers to presentational aspects of the phenomenon under study. The data of phenomena are mapped onto words or numbers. This mapping is called *measurement.*

The quality of all data analysis depends on the quality of the measurements. Good science requires that scientists measure in a variety of ways. Technology helps the scientist to measure. Often the scientist must measure large amounts of data, and thus an aim of analysis is to reduce the data to a summary that makes sense. Calculating measures of central tendency (mean, median, or mode), variability (e.g., range), and shape (graphic representations) can effectively reduce 700 data points to a handful, often without losing the essential characteristics of data. Scientists come to understand that the trade-off between precision and richness of data is folded into categories. The error in this process is also quantified in mathematical terms and factored into scientific findings.

Mathematics helps scientists break down and reassemble data into models. Mathematics is the language used by scientists to model change in the world. Understanding change is a vital part of the inquiry process. Moreover, scientific advancement in all branches of science requires considered investment in the mathematical enterprise; good science and mathematics are complementary. In the Scott Foresman Science program, students have a real opportunity to learn about the interrelationship between science and mathematics. Models, computation, and problem solving are central themes of the mathematics component of this science textbook series, reflecting the goal of providing a scientific education consistent with the practice of science.

References

National Council of Teachers of Mathematics (2000). Principles and standards for school mathematics. Reston, VA: National Council of Teachers of Mathematics.

National Research Council (1999). How people learn: Brain, mind, experience and school. Washington, DC: National Academy Press.

Tate, W. F. & Johnson, H. C. (1999). Mathematical reasoning and educational policy: Moving beyond the politics of dead language. In L .V. Stiff (ed.), *Developing mathematical reasoning in grades K–12.* Reston, VA: National Council of Teachers of Mathematics.

Wright, M. & Chorin, A. (1999). Mathematics and Science. Report to the Division of Mathematical Sciences. Arlington, VA: National Science Foundation.

Dr. Jack A. Gerlovich
Professor of Science Education/Safety
Drake University
Des Moines, Iowa

Teaching Safety in the Classroom

> *"Safety is a fundamental concern in all experimental science. Teachers of science must know and apply the necessary safety regulations in the storage, use, and care of the materials used by students. They adhere to safety rules and guidelines that are established by national organizations…as well as by local and state regulatory agencies. They work with the school and district to ensure implementation and use of safety guidelines for which they are responsible, such as the presence of safety equipment and appropriate class size. Teachers also teach students how to engage safely in investigations inside and outside the classroom."*
> —National Science Education Standards, 1996

Safe procedure is part of sound scientific inquiry. Activities in Scott Foresman *Science* reinforce and extend science concepts using materials and procedures that are generally safe when used as directed. Students learn not only how to safely investigate the topics at hand; they also develop safety habits that will serve them well in future endeavors in science and otherwise.

Throughout Scott Foresman *Science,* students learn that simple, safe materials can be used effectively to investigate science concepts. Safety reminders regarding procedure are given in the Student's Edition whenever appropriate. These include "Be careful!" symbols and references to cover goggles on appropriate pages. The Teacher's Edition includes specific safety tips for activities and demonstrations. If properly implemented, these guidelines can help assure a safe science teaching and learning setting for teacher and students.

General safety tips for the elementary science classroom

- Teachers should conduct annual audits of safety problems and inform the administration of problems in writing.

- All emergency telephone numbers (police, fire department, nurse, hospital, poison control center, and so on) should be posted with a telephone easily and quickly accessible.

- Safety should be incorporated into all teacher lesson plans and student lab/activity reports.

- Prior to using any equipment or substances, teachers should be certain they understand the proper function and hazards associated with the use of those items. This information should be communicated to the students.

- The proper use of appropriate eye protective equipment that meets the American National Standards Institute (ANSI Z87.1) standards should be demonstrated to students. These should be worn whenever the potential for eye injury exists, including but not restricted to: use of caustic chemicals, equipment, glassware, or projectiles. Even relatively safe items such as rubber bands and balloons can cause eye injury and warrant the use of eye protection. All protective eye equipment should be sanitized before it is worn by students.

- To prevent students from interfering with each other and to assist the safe exit of students from the room in case of an emergency, teachers should assure that rooms are not overcrowded, that students understand exit procedures, and that aisles are kept uncluttered.

- Teachers should periodically conduct practice drills with students. For example, students might practice exiting the room due to an emergency, coping with a fire, and aiding a chemical splash victim.

- Unless you know the outcome is safe, you should never mix substances "just to see what happens." No hazardous substances are used in Scott Foresman *Science.* However, certain substances, when combined, might pose safety problems. Notes about the dangers of mixing chemicals are included on the appropriate pages throughout the program.

- All equipment should be properly stored. Dangerous items should be kept in a locked storage area.

- Whenever possible, plastic items should replace glass. If glass containers are essential, temperature- and break-resistant glassware should be used.

- To prevent slipping and falls, any liquids spilled on floors should be wiped up immediately.

- If the teacher is not satisfied that all foreseeable dangers have been reduced to an acceptable level, the activity should be altered or eliminated.

- To verify that science safety issues are understood, the teacher may want to have students state them or write them in their own words.

Teachers should be aware of applicable federal, state, and local laws, codes, professional science education standards, and relevant guidelines from professional organizations that apply to the activities being performed.

Resources

Biehl, J.T.; L.L. Motz; S. S., West (1999). *NSTA Guide to School Science Facilities,* National Science Teachers Association, Arlington, VA.

Kwan, T.; J. Texley. (2002). *Exploring Safely: A Guide for Elementary Teachers,* National Science Teachers Association, Arlington, VA.

National Science Teachers Association (1997). *NSTA Pathways to the Science Standards, Elementary School Edition,* National Science Teachers Association, Arlington, VA.

National Research Council (1996). *National Science Education Standards,* National Academy Press, Washington, D.C.

Scope and Sequence
Grade 2

Unit A Life Science	Unit B Earth Science

National Science Education Standards
- The characteristics of organisms
- Life cycles of organisms
- Organisms and environments
- Characteristics and changes in populations
- Personal health

National Science Education Standards
- Properties of earth materials
- Types of resources
- Changes in environments
- Abilities to distinguish between natural objects and objects made by humans

Chapter 1 All About Plants
Lesson 1 What are the parts of a plant?
Lesson 2 How are seeds scattered?
Lesson 3 How are plants grouped?
Lesson 4 How are some woodland plants adapted?
Lesson 5 How are some prairie plants adapted?
Lesson 6 How are some desert plants adapted?
Lesson 7 How are some marsh plants adapted?

Chapter 2 All About Animals
Lesson 1 What are some animals with backbones?
Lesson 2 What are some ways mammals are adapted?
Lesson 3 What are some ways birds are adapted?
Lesson 4 What are some ways fish are adapted?
Lesson 5 What are some ways reptiles are adapted?
Lesson 6 What are some ways amphibians are adapted?
Lesson 7 What are some animals without backbones?

Chapter 3 How Plants and Animals Live Together
Lesson 1 What do plants and animals need?
Lesson 2 How do plants and animals get food in a grassland?
Lesson 3 How do plants and animals get food in an ocean?
Lesson 4 What can cause a food web to change?
Lesson 5 How do plants and animals help each other?

Chapter 4 How Living Things Grow and Change
Lesson 1 How do sea turtles grow and change?
Lesson 2 What is the life cycle of a dragonfly?
Lesson 3 What is the life cycle of a horse?
Lesson 4 How are young animals like their parents?
Lesson 5 What is the life cycle of a bean plant?
Lesson 6 How are young plants like their parents?
Lesson 7 How do people grow and change?

Chapter 5 Earth's Land, Air, and Water
Lesson 1 What are natural resources?
Lesson 2 What are rocks and soil like?
Lesson 3 How do people use plants?
Lesson 4 How does Earth change?
Lesson 5 How can people help protect Earth?

Chapter 6 Earth's Weather and Seasons
Lesson 1 What are some kinds of weather?
Lesson 2 What is the water cycle?
Lesson 3 What is spring?
Lesson 4 What is summer?
Lesson 5 What is fall?
Lesson 6 What is winter?
Lesson 7 What are some kinds of bad weather?

Chapter 7 Fossils and Dinosaurs
Lesson 1 How can we learn about the past?
Lesson 2 What can we learn from fossils?
Lesson 3 What were dinosaurs like?
Lesson 4 What are some new discoveries?

Unit C Physical Science

National Science Education Standards
- Properties of objects and materials
- Position and motion of objects
- Light, heat, electricity, and magnetism

Chapter 8 Properties of Matter
Lesson 1 What is matter?
Lesson 2 What are the states of matter?
Lesson 3 How can matter be changed?
Lesson 4 How can cooling and heating change matter?

Chapter 9 Energy
Lesson 1 What is energy?
Lesson 2 How do living things use energy?
Lesson 3 What are some sources of heat?
Lesson 4 How does light move?
Lesson 5 What are other kinds of energy?

Chapter 10 Forces and Motion
Lesson 1 How do objects move?
Lesson 2 What is work?
Lesson 3 How can you change the way things move?
Lesson 4 How can simple machines help you do work?
Lesson 5 What are magnets?

Chapter 11 Sound
Lesson 1 What is sound?
Lesson 2 What is pitch?
Lesson 3 How does sound travel?
Lesson 4 How do some animals make sounds?
Lesson 5 What are some sounds around you?

Unit D Space and Technology

National Science Education Standards
- Objects in the sky
- Changes in the earth and sky
- Science and technology in local challenges
- Abilities of technological design
- Understanding about science and technology

Chapter 12 Earth and Space
Lesson 1 What is the Sun?
Lesson 2 What causes day and night?
Lesson 3 What causes seasons to change?
Lesson 4 What can you see in the night sky?
Lesson 5 Why does the Moon seem to change?
Lesson 6 What is the solar system?

Chapter 13 Technology in Our World
Lesson 1 What is technology?
Lesson 2 How does technology help us?
Lesson 3 How do we use technology to communicate?
Lesson 4 What are some other ways we use technology?
Lesson 5 How do people make things?

Scott Foresman *Science* Scope and Sequence

National Science Education Standards

	Grade K	Grade 1

Unit A Life Science

Grades K–4
- The characteristics of organisms
- Life cycles of organisms
- Organisms and environments
- Characteristics and changes in populations
- Personal health

Grades 5–6
- Structure and function in living systems
- Reproduction and heredity
- Regulation and behavior
- Populations and ecosystems
- Diversity and adaptations of organisms
- Personal health

Grade K
Chapter 1
Needs of Plants and Animals
Chapter 2
Growing and Changing
Chapter 3
Plants and Animals All Around

Grade 1
Chapter 1
Living and Nonliving
Chapter 2
Habitats
Chapter 3
How Plants and Animals Live
Chapter 4
Life Cycles
Chapter 5
Food Chains

Unit B Earth Science

Grades K–4
- Properties of earth materials
- Types of resources
- Changes in environments
- Abilities to distinguish between natural objects and objects made by humans

Grades 5–6
- Structure of the earth system
- Earth's history
- Natural hazards
- Risks and benefits

Grade K
Chapter 4
Our Land, Water, and Air
Chapter 5
Weather and Seasons

Grade 1
Chapter 6
Land, Water, and Air
Chapter 7
Weather

Unit C Physical Science

Grades K–4
- Properties of objects and materials
- Position and motion of objects
- Light, heat, electricity, and magnetism

Grades 5–6
- Properties and changes of properties in matter
- Motions and forces
- Transfer of energy

Grade K
Chapter 6
Matter
Chapter 7
Heat and Light
Chapter 8
How Things Move

Grade 1
Chapter 8
Observing Matter
Chapter 9
Movement and Sound
Chapter 10
Learning About Energy

Unit D Space and Technology

Grades K–4
- Objects in the sky
- Changes in the earth and sky
- Science and technology in local challenges
- Abilities of technological design
- Understanding about science and technology

Grades 5–6
- Earth in the solar system
- Abilities of technological design
- Understandings about science and technology
- Science and technology in society

Grade K
Chapter 9
Day and Night
Chapter 10
How Things Work

Grade 1
Chapter 11
Day and Night Sky
Chapter 12
Science in Our World

Grade 2	Grade 3	Grade 4	Grade 5	Grade 6
Chapter 1 All About Plants **Chapter 2** All About Animals **Chapter 3** How Plants and Animals Live Together **Chapter 4** How Living Things Grow and Change	**Chapter 1** Plants and How They Grow **Chapter 2** How Animals Live **Chapter 3** Where Plants and Animals Live **Chapter 4** Plants and Animals Living Together	**Chapter 1** Classifying Plants and Animals **Chapter 2** Energy from Plants **Chapter 3** Ecosystems **Chapter 4** Changes in Ecosystems **Chapter 5** Systems of the Human Body	**Chapter 1** Classifying Organisms **Chapter 2** Cells to Systems **Chapter 3** Human Body Systems **Chapter 4** Plants **Chapter 5** Interactions in Ecosystems **Chapter 6** Changes in Ecosystems	**Chapter 1** Classification **Chapter 2** Cells **Chapter 3** Reproduction **Chapter 4** Body Systems **Chapter 5** Plants **Chapter 6** Biomes **Chapter 7** Ecosystems
Chapter 5 Earth's Land, Air, and Water **Chapter 6** Earth's Weather and Seasons **Chapter 7** Fossils and Dinosaurs	**Chapter 5** Water **Chapter 6** Weather **Chapter 7** Rocks and Soil **Chapter 8** Changes on Earth **Chapter 9** Natural Resources	**Chapter 6** Water Cycle and Weather **Chapter 7** Hurricanes and Tornadoes **Chapter 8** Minerals and Rocks **Chapter 9** Changes to Earth's Surface **Chapter 10** Using Natural Resources	**Chapter 7** Water on Earth **Chapter 8** Weather Patterns **Chapter 9** Earth's Changing Surface **Chapter 10** Protecting Earth's Resources	**Chapter 8** Plate Tectonics **Chapter 9** Rocks and Minerals **Chapter 10** Reshaping Earth's Surface **Chapter 11** Earth's Resources **Chapter 12** Climate and Weather
Chapter 8 Properties of Matter **Chapter 9** Energy **Chapter 10** Forces and Motion **Chapter 11** Sound	**Chapter 10** Matter and Its Properties **Chapter 11** Changes in Matter **Chapter 12** Forces and Motion **Chapter 13** Energy **Chapter 14** Sound	**Chapter 11** Properties of Matter **Chapter 12** Heat **Chapter 13** Electricity and Magnetism **Chapter 14** Sound and Light **Chapter 15** Objects in Motion **Chapter 16** Simple Machines	**Chapter 11** Matter and Its Properties **Chapter 12** Changes in Matter **Chapter 13** Forces and Motion **Chapter 14** Changing Forms of Energy **Chapter 15** Electricity	**Chapter 13** Matter **Chapter 14** Building Blocks of Matter **Chapter 15** Forces and Motion **Chapter 16** Machines **Chapter 17** Changing Energy Forms **Chapter 18** Thermal and Light Energy
Chapter 12 Earth and Space **Chapter 13** Technology in Our World	**Chapter 15** Patterns in the Sky **Chapter 16** The Solar System **Chapter 17** Science in Our Lives	**Chapter 17** Earth's Cycles **Chapter 18** Inner and Outer Planets **Chapter 19** Effects of Technology	**Chapter 16** Stars and Galaxies **Chapter 17** Earth in Space **Chapter 18** Technology in Our Lives	**Chapter 19** Earth, Sun, and Moon **Chapter 20** The Universe **Chapter 21** Impacts of Technology

Credits for Teacher's Edition

Illustrations

B1 Big Sesh Studios; C6 Laura Ovresat; C6 Stacey Schuett; C7 Sue Williams; D6 Philomena O'Neill; D7 Katherine Potter; D2, D6, 361B, 361C Bob Kayganich.

Photographs

Every effort has been made to secure permission and provide appropriate credit for photographic material. The publisher deeply regrets any omission and pledges to correct errors called to its attention in subsequent editions.

Unless otherwise acknowledged, all photographs are the property of Scott Foresman, a division of Pearson Education.

Photo locators denoted as follows: Top (T), Center (C), Bottom (B), Left (L), Right (R), Background (Bkgd).

Cover: (C) ©Chase Swift/Corbis, (B) ©Walter Hodges/ Corbis, (Bkgd) ©Ralph A. Clevenger/Corbis, ©George Grall/ NGS Image Collection; **Unit A:** A1 (BC, Bkgd) ©Brandon D. Cole/Corbis; A2 (TC, TR, BL, BR) ©DK Images, (CR) ©The Image Bank/Getty Images, (CL) © Randy Morse/Animals Animals/Earth Scenes, (C) Stephen Frink/Corbis, (C) Sanford/ Agliolo/Corbis, (CR) Amos Nachoum/Corbis, (BC) Jonathan Blair/Corbis, (BR) © Soames Summerhays/Photo Researchers, Inc., (TR) ©Joseph Van Os/Getty Images; A4 ©David Aubrey/ Corbis; A6 (TR) Ted Levin/Animals Animals/Earth Scenes, (BL, TC) ©DK Images; A7 (TC) Pete Atkinson/NHPA Limited, (BC) Tim Davis/Corbis; A8 ©Comstock Inc.; 1B (BL) Image Quest 3-D/NHPA Limited, (TL, CL) ©DK Images, (CL) ©Pat O'Hara/ Corbis, (BL) ©Steve Kaufman/Corbis; 1C ©Eric Crichton/ Corbis; 1D ©DK Images; 1F Peter Anderson/©DK Images; 1G Brand X Pictures; 33B (TL) W. Perry Conway/Corbis, (TL) Joe McDonald/Corbis, (CL, BL) ©DK Images, (CL) Daniel Heuclin/NHPA Limited; 33C ©DK Images; 33D ©DK Images; 33G ©Stephen Dalton/NHPA Limited; 58 (TL, TR) ©Rubberball Productions; 59 ©Rubberball Productions; 65B (BL, CL) ©DK Images, (TL) ©Clem Haagner/Gallo Images/Corbis, (CL) ©Andrew J. Martinez/Photo Researchers, Inc., (BL) ©Sanford/ Agliolo/Corbis; 65C ©Eric and David Hosking/Corbis; 65D Brand X Pictures; 65F ©Richard Murphy; 65G ©Ian Beames/ Ecoscene/Corbis; 97B (CL) ©Tim Davis/Corbis, (TL) Courtesy of Digital Dragonflies, (TL) ©Tom Brakefield/Corbis, (CL) Bob Langrish/©DK Images, (BL) Brand X Pictures; 97C ©DK Images; 97D ©The Image Bank/Getty Images; 97F ©Julie Habel/Corbis; 97G ©Kevin Schafer/NHPA Limited; 134B (CL) Getty Images, (CL) ©Howard Kingsnorth/Taxi/Getty Images, (BL) ©Justin Pumfrey/Taxi/Getty Images; 134C ©Royalty-Free/ Corbis; **Unit B:** B1 Natural History Museum /©DK Images; B2 Hemera Technologies; B4 Giuliano Fornari/©DK Images; B6 ©Comstock Images/Getty Images; B7 ©The Natural History Museum, London; B8 (CL) © DK Images, (CR) ©Annie Griffiths Belt/NGS Image Collection; 137B (TL) Getty Images, (CL) Hemera Technologies, (CL) ©Joe McDonald/Animals Animals/ Earth Scenes, (BL) ©ThinkStock/SuperStock; 137C ©Photodisc Red/Getty Images; 137F ©DK Images; 137G ©DK Images; 156B ©Stone/Getty Images; 156C Getty Images; 169B (TL, CL, BL) Hemera Technologies, (TL) ©Corbis, (BL) ©DK Images; 169C ©Gary W. Carter/Corbis; 173A Getty Images; 173D ©Comstock Inc.; 174B ©Gen Nishino/Taxi/ Getty Images; (TL) ©Bruce Burkhardt/Corbis; (CL) Brand X Pictures/©Royalty-Free/Corbis, (CL) ©Manfred Danegger/ Photo Researchers, Inc., (BL) ©DK Images; 195A ©Ariel Skelley/Corbis; 201B (TL) Stephen Oliver/©DK Images, (CL) Hemera Technologies, (CL) ©DK Images, (BL) ©Francois Gohler/Photo Researchers, Inc.; 201C ©DK Images; 201F (TC, TR) ©DK Images; 201G ©DK Images; 201B ©Jody Dole/ The Image Bank/Getty Images; 208B (TL) ©D. Boone/Corbis, (CL) ©Stone/Getty Images, (CL) ©Lee Frost/Robert Harding Picture Library Ltd.; 208I ©Jet Propulsion Laboratory/NASA; 209A ©HQ/GRIN/NASA Image Exchange; 225A (T) Getty Images, (B) ©Jim Cummins/Taxi/Getty Images, (CC) ©DK Images, (TC) Corbis; 225B Getty Images; 225D ©DK Images; 226B ©Brand X Pictures/Getty Images; 226C ©DK Images; 227A ©DK Images; **Unit C:** C1 (Bkgd) ©Kelly-Mooney Photography/Corbis, (Bkgd) Corbis, (TL) ©Royalty-Free/Corbis; C2 ©Kathryn Russell/FoodPix; C7 ©Image Quest 3-D/NHPA Limited; C8 (BC) Rubberball Productions, (BL) ©Chris Carroll/ Corbis, (CR) ©Photodisc Green/Getty Images; 233B (CL) Hemera Technologies, (CL) Brand X Pictures, (BL) ©Brand X Pictures/Getty Images; 233C (BR) Getty Images, (BR) Brand X Pictures; 245A (BC) ©Gary Buss/Taxi/Getty Images, (T) ©Bettmann/Corbis; 245B ©Royalty-Free/Corbis; 245F (BL) ©Jet Propulsion Laboratory/NASA, (BR) ©Royalty-Free/Corbis; 251A ©D. Boone/Corbis; 251B (TR) Brand X Pictures, (CR) ©Royalty-Free/Corbis; 265B (TL, CL) Hemera Technologies, (CL) Dave King/Pitt Rivers Museum/University of Oxford, Oxford/©DK Images, (BL) ©Steven Gorton and Gary Ombler/ ©DK Images; 265C ©Steven Gorton and Gary Ombler/©DK Images; 265F ©Tom Stewart/Corbis; 297F ©Gary Ombler/ DK Images; 297B (TL) ©DK Images; (CL) Getty Images, (CL) Hemera Technologies; 329B (TL, CL) Getty Images, (CL) ©Taxi/ Getty Images, (CL) ©Ingram/Creatas, (BL) DK Images; 329C ©Royalty-Free/Corbis; 329F ©Thinkstock; **Unit D:** D1 (Bkgd) ©Reuters NewMedia Inc./Corbis, (Bkgd) ©Richard Cummins/ Corbis, (Bkgd) ©Taxi/Getty Images, (BR) ©DK Images, (CR) Getty Images; D4 Brand X Pictures; D7 Getty Images; D8 (BL) ©DK Images, (BL) ©LWA-Dann Tardif/Corbis; 361B (CL) ©Roger Ressmeyer/Corbis, (CL) ©John Sanford/Photo Researchers, Inc.; 393B (TL, CL) Hemera Technologies, (BL) Getty Images, (BL) ©Photodisc Green/Getty Images; 393C (BR) Getty Images, (BR) ©DK Images.

Metric and Customary Measures

Science uses the metric system to measure things. Metric measurement is used around the world. Here is how different metric measurements compare to customary measurement.

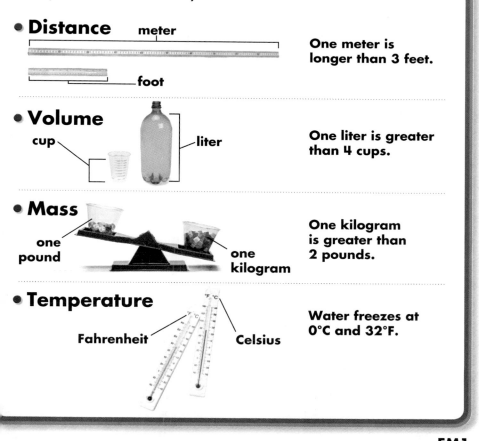

- **Distance** — meter / foot

  One meter is longer than 3 feet.

- **Volume** — cup / liter

  One liter is greater than 4 cups.

- **Mass** — one pound / one kilogram

  One kilogram is greater than 2 pounds.

- **Temperature** — Fahrenheit / Celsius

  Water freezes at 0°C and 32°F.

EM1

Science Background

The Metric System

- The metric system is also referred to as the International System of Units, or SI.

- The metric system is a decimal system, which means it is based on the number 10 and multiples of 10.

- The metric system uses prefixes with units of measure to express multiples of 10 larger and smaller than the unit. Some common prefixes used in the metric system include: deci- = 1/10; centi- = 1/100; milli- = 1/1000; kilo- = 1000.

Tell children that the metric system of measurement is used by scientists throughout the world. It is part of the "language" scientists use to communicate with one another. By using the metric system, scientists are able to compare and analyze data.

Tell children that the measurement units they usually use are called customary units. Have children name some customary units. Tell children that the same tools are used to measure in metric units, but the units are different.

Explain to children that they will be using both customary (English) and metric units to measure. Customary and metric units are considered standard units. Tell children that they will also use nonstandard units, such as paper clips.

Distance

Draw a thick line on the board that measures 60 centimeters. Give half the class rulers and the other half meter sticks, and have children measure the line you have drawn. Have them state its length in meters, centimeters, inches, and feet.

Volume

Display a liter container and a quart container. Ask children to estimate how many quart containers a liter container can fill. Fill the liter container with rice or beans. Pour the rice or beans into the quart container. Children should realize that you have to empty the quart container in order to continue filling it from the liter container. Follow this procedure until all the rice or beans from the liter container has been poured into the quart container. Ask children to compare their estimates to the actual number.

Mass

Provide groups of children with two objects of varying masses. Have children take turns holding one object in each hand and telling which is heavier. Then have children place the objects on a balance and observe what happens. Ask children to identify the heavier object and the lighter object.

Temperature

Fill three cups with cold, room temperature, and warm water. Label the cups A, B, and C. Arrange the cups in random order. Have children place a finger in each cup in quick succession and tell which is the coldest and warmest. Record their estimates. Then use a thermometer to determine the actual temperatures. Discuss with children how temperatures can be relative.

Glossary

The glossary uses letters and signs to show how words are pronounced. The mark ′ is placed after a syllable with a primary or heavy accent. The mark ′ is placed after a syllable with a secondary or lighter accent.

To hear these words pronounced, listen to the AudioText CD.

A

adapt (ə dapt′) To change. Animals are **adapted** to live in their environment. (page 16)

amphibian (am fib′ē ən) An animal with bones that lives part of its life on land and part of its life in water. My pet frog is an **amphibian.** (page 41)

attract (ə trakt′) To pull toward. The opposite poles of two magnets will **attract** one another. (page 318)

axis (ak′sis) An imaginary line around which a planet turns. Earth spins on an **axis.** (page 370)

EM2

B

bird (bėrd) An animal with a backbone that has feathers, two legs, and wings. The **bird** flew from place to place searching for food. (page 40)

boulder (bōl′der) A very big rock. The **boulder** is by the water. (page 146)

C

camouflage (kam′ə fläzh) A color or shape that makes a plant or an animal hard to see. Some animals use **camouflage** to hide themselves from danger. (page 42)

condense (kən dens′) To change from a gas to a liquid. Water vapor **condenses** on the outside of my glass of juice. (page 179)

conductor (kən duk′tər) Something that lets heat easily move through it. Metal is a **conductor.** (page 281)

constellation (kon′sta lā′shen) A group of stars that form a picture. I like to search the night sky for **constellations.** (page 376)

consumer (kən sü′mər) A living thing that cannot make its own food. Animals are **consumers.** (page 71)

crater (krā′tər) A hole that is shaped like a bowl. There are many **craters** on the surface of the Moon. (page 378)

D

dinosaur (dī′nə sôr) An extinct animal that lived millions of years ago. **Dinosaurs** are large animals that lived on Earth long ago. (page 212)

E

energy (en′ər jē) The ability to do work or make change. You need **energy** to play soccer. (page 271)

engine (en′jən) A machine that changes energy into force or motion. Cars, trains, and airplanes have an **engine** that helps them run. (page 400)

environment (en vī′rən mənt) Everything that surrounds a living thing. A cactus is a plant that grows in a desert **environment.** (page 16)

erosion (i rō′zhən) Process by which rocks and soil are moved from one place to another. Heavy rains can cause **erosion.** (page 152)

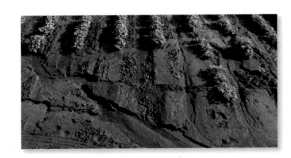

evaporate (i vap′ ə rāt) To change from a liquid to a gas. The puddle of water will **evaporate** and turn into water vapor. (page 179)

extinct (ek stingkt′) An animal or plant no longer living on Earth. Dinosaurs are **extinct.** (page 210)

 F

fish (fish) An animal with bones that lives in water and has gills. Many types of **fish** live in an ocean. (page 40)

flower (flou′ər) The part of a plant that makes seeds. Some plants have many **flowers.** (page 9)

EM6

food chain (füd chān) Plants use sunlight, air, and water to make food. Animals eat the plants. Other animals eat those animals. This is called a food chain. A coyote and a mountain lion are part of a **food chain.** (page 74)

food web (füd web) A food web is made up of the food chains in a habitat. Corn, voles, and coyotes are part of a **food web.** (page 76)

force (fôrs) A push or pull that makes something move. You use **force** to move the wagon. (page 304)

fossil (fos′əl) A print or remains of a plant or animal that lived long ago. Dinosaur **fossils** are in the museum. (page 207)

friction (frik′shən) A force that slows down or stops moving objects. A bicycle's brakes use **friction** to slow down. (page 312)

fuel (fyü′əl) Anything that is burned to make heat or power. We use wood as **fuel**. (page 279)

G

gas (gas) Matter that always takes the size and shape of its container. Bubbles are filled with **gas.** (page 246)

germinate (jėr′mə nāt) To begin to grow into a young plant. The plant seeds will soon **germinate.** (page 114)

gills (gilz) Special body parts that get oxygen from water. Fish have **gills**. (page 46)

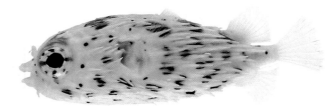

EM8

gravity (grav′ə tē) A force that pulls things toward the center of Earth. **Gravity** will pull the leaves back to Earth. (page 306)

hibernate (hī′bər nāt) To spend all winter sleeping or resting. Some animals **hibernate**. (page 186)

hurricane (hėr′ə kān) A storm that starts over warm ocean waters that has hard rain and very strong winds. A **hurricane** causes heavy rain and strong winds. (page 192)

insect (in′sekt) An animal without bones that has three body parts and six legs. It's fun to watch **insects.** (page 52)

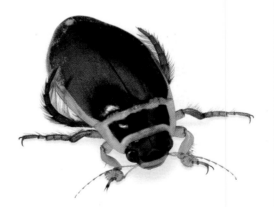

invent (in vent´) To make
something for the first time.
Alexander Graham Bell
invented the telephone.
(page 399)

leaves (lēvz) Parts of a plant that
use sunlight, air, nutrients, and
water to make food for the plant.
The **leaves** on the plant are long
and thin. (page 8)

life cycle (līf sī´kəl) The way a
living thing grows and changes.
We studied the **life cycle** of a
turtle. (page 106)

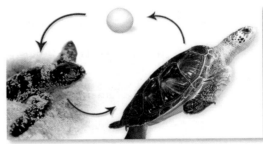

lightning (līt´ning) A flash of
electricity in the sky. We watched
lightning flash across the sky.
(page 188)

EM10

liquid (lik′wid) Matter that does not have its own shape, but does have its own mass. **Liquids** take the shape of their containers. (page 244)

loudness (loud′nəs) How loud or soft a sound is. The **loudness** of some sounds can change. (page 336)

M

mammal (mam′əl) An animal with bones that usually has hair or fur on its body and feeds milk to its young. Chipmunks are **mammals.** (page 40)

manufacture (man′yə fak′chər) To make by hand or machine. Many countries in the world **manufacture** clothing. (page 408)

mass (mas) The amount of matter in an object. I use a balance to measure **mass.** (page 239)

meteorologist (mē′tē ə rol′ə jist) A person who studies weather. The **meteorologist** predicted sunny weather. (page 407)

migrate (mī′grāt) To move from one place to another in a regular pattern. Many types of birds **migrate** in the winter. (page 184)

mineral (min′ər əl) A nonliving solid that comes from Earth. Copper is a **mineral.** (page 147)

mixture (miks′chər) Something made up of two or more kinds of matter that do not change. Fruit salad is a **mixture** of different fruits. (page 250)

motion (mō′shen) Motion is the act of moving. A merry-go-round moves in a circular **motion.** (page 303)

natural resource (nach′ər əl rē′sôrs) A useful thing that comes from nature. Rocks are **natural resources.** (page 143)

nutrients (nü′trē ənt) Materials that living things need to live and grow. People get **nutrients** from the food they eat. (page 7)

nymph (nimf) A young insect that looks like its parent and grows wings as it changes. We found a dragonfly **nymph** in the pond by our school. (page 108)

EM13

orbit (ôr′bit) The path around something. It takes Earth about one year to orbit the Sun one time. (page 374)

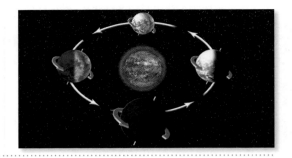

paleontologist (pā′lē on tol′ə jist) A scientist who studies fossils. **Paleontologists** study fossils to learn about life long ago. (page 207)

phase (fāz) The shape of the lighted part of the Moon. The Moon's **phases** can be seen best at night. (page 381)

pitch (pich) How high or low a sound is. The sound from the bullfrog had a low **pitch.** (page 338)

pollution (pə lü′ shən) Anything harmful added to land, air, or water. Many people work hard to reduce **pollution.** (page 154)

prairie (prâr′ē) Flat land covered with grasses and having few trees. A **prairie** has a lot of grass and few trees. (page 20)

predator (pred′ə tər) An animal that catches and eats another animal for food. A lion is a **predator.** (page 75)

prey (prā) An animal that is caught and eaten for food. Sea stars are the **prey** of sea otters. (page 75)

producer (prə dü′sər) A living thing that makes its own food. A kelp is a **producer.** (page 71)

property (prop′ər tē) Something about an object that you can observe with your senses. An object's color is one kind of **property.** (page 240)

recycle (rē sī′kəl) To change something so that it can be used again. My family **recycles** plastic bottles. (page 156)

reflect (ri flekt′) To bounce off of something. A mirror can **reflect** light. (page 282)

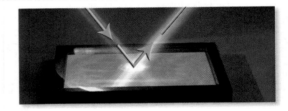

repel (ri pel′) To push away. The north ends of magnets will **repel** one another. (page 318)

reptile (rep′tīl) An animal with bones that has dry, scaly skin. Snakes are **reptiles.** (page 41)

EM16

roots (rüts) Parts of a plant that hold the plant in place and that take in water and nutrients from the soil. The **roots** of the old oak tree are deep inside the ground. (page 8)

rotation (rō tā′shən) Spinning on an axis. Earth makes one complete **rotation** each day. (page 370)

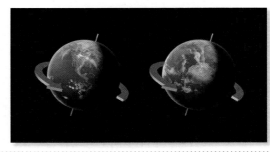

S

sand (sand) Tiny pieces of rock. People use **sand** to build roads. (page 146)

satellite (sat′l īt) An object that revolves around another object. Meteorologists study pictures taken by **satellites** to predict weather. (page 407)

EM17

seed coat (sēd kōt) The hard outer covering of a seed. The **seed coat** protects the seed. (page 114)

seedling (sēd′ling) A young plant. The tree **seedling** grows into a tree. (page 114)

shadow (shad′ō) A shadow is made when something blocks the light. The tree makes a **shadow.** (page 284)

simple machine (sim′pəl mə shēn) A tool with few or no moving parts that makes work easier. Workers often use **simple machines** to help them build things. (page 314)

solar energy (sō′lər en′ərjē) Solar energy is heat and light from the Sun. The house is heated by **solar energy.** (page 272)

solar system (sō′lər sis′tem)
The Sun, the planets and their
moons, and other objects that
orbit the Sun. Earth is in our
solar system. (page 382)

solid (sol′id) Matter that has its
own shape and takes up space.
The case that hold the supplies is
a **solid.** (page 242)

source (sôrs) A place from which
something comes. A lamp is one
source of light. (page 278)

states of matter (stāts uv mat′ər)
The three states of matter are
solids, liquids, and gases. Water
is a liquid **state of matter.**
(page 242)

stem (stem) Part of a plant that
holds it up and that carries water
and nutrients to the leaves. The
stem is long and green. (page 8)

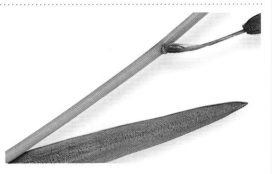

EM19

technology (tek nol′ə jē) Using science to help solve problems. People use **technology** every day. (page 399)

tornado (tôr nā′ dō) Very strong wind that comes down from clouds in the shape of a funnel. A **tornado** touched down near our town. (page 190)

transportation (tran′spər tā′ shən) Ways to move people or things from place to place. Today, **transportation** makes travel easier and faster than ever before. (page 400)

V

vaccine (vak sēn′) Medicine that can help prevent a disease. Mia got a shot of the flu **vaccine.** (page 402)

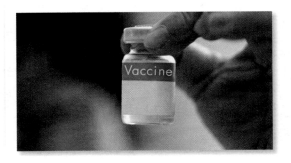

vibrate (vī′brāt) To move back and forth very fast. A flute makes the air **vibrate** to make sounds. (page 335)

 W

water cycle (wȯ′tər sī′kəl) The way water moves from the clouds to Earth and back to the clouds. Water condenses and evaporates during the **water cycle.** (page 178)

weathering (weŦH′ər ing) The breaking apart and changing of rocks. **Weathering** causes sharp rocks to become smooth. (page 153)

work (wėrk) When force moves an object. It took a lot of **work** to push the sled up the hill. (page 308)

Page numbers after a *p* refer to a photograph or drawing. Page numbers after a *c* refer to a chart, graph, or diagram.

Boldface page numbers indicate pages in the Teacher's Edition. Other page numbers indicate pages in the Student Edition.

Absolute zero, 257
Access prior knowledge, 10, 12, 16, 20, 46, 50, 62, 82, 84, 112, 114, 142, 146, 150, 152, 174, 178, 180, 182, 184, 186, 188, 242, 248, 278, 282, 286, 302, 308, 310, 314,318, 334, 338, 340, 342, 344, 366, 370, 374, 376, 380, 382, 398, 402, 404, 406, 408
Activities
  Activity Flip Chart, **1E, 33E, 65E, 97E, 137E, 169E, 201E, 233E, 265E, 297E, 329E, 361E, 393E**
  Activity Guides, **1D–1E, 33D–33E, 65D–65E, 97D–97E, 137D–137E, 169D–169E, 201D–201E, 233D–233E, 265D–265E, 297D–297E, 329D–329E, 361D–361E, 393D–393E**
  Activity Rubrics, **4, 26, 36, 56, 68, 90, 100, 122, 140, 160, 172, 194, 204, 218, 236, 256, 268, 290, 300, 322, 332, 346, 364, 384, 396, 410**
  directed inquiry, explore. *See* **Directed Inquiry, Explore**
  forming hypotheses, 228–229
  full inquiry, experiment. *See* **Full Inquiry, Experiment**
  guided inquiry, investigate. *See* **Guided Inquiry, Investigate**
  quick. *See* **Quick activities**
  resources, **26, 36, 56, 92, 100, 122, 160, 194, 196, 204, 218, 220, 236, 256, 258, 268, 290, 300, 322, 332, 346, 348, 364**
  take-home. *See* **Take-home activities**
Adapt, adaptation, 16–25
Advanced-level readers, 1A, 33A, 65A, 97A, 137A, 169A, 201A, 233A, 265A, 297A, 329A, 361A, 393A
Air
  as a gas, **247**
  as natural resource, 142–145
Airplanes, 328
Alike and different, 37, **38,** 41, 45, **61,** 117, 120–121, 131, 140, 218–219, 365, 369, **383,** 389
Atmospheric scientist, 200
Amphibians, *p35, p41, p50, p51*
Analyze, 11, 45, 53, 290, 401
Anemometer, 171

Animal scientist, 352
Animals, 33–64
  adaptations of, **185**
  classifying, **35, 58, 59, 79**
  functions, of body parts, 316–317
  grouping, **54,** 58–59, 131
  growth and change, 102–113
  interdependence, 84–89
  needs of, **7, 70,** 71–73, 274–277
  and plants, 84–86, **88, 90–91**
  protecting, **46, 88,** 158–159
  sounds of, 342–343, **352**
  warm-blooded, **72**
Antarctica, 62–63, **185**
Ants, *p84*
"Apple Shadows" (poem), 358–359
Apply information, 15, 75, 125, 275, 285
Appraise, 47, 125, 147, 175, 413
Arctic tern, 185
Arizona, 22
Art in Science, 14, **15, 43, 75, 117,** 157, 182, **183,** 188, **189,** 251, 283, 319, 341, 379, **A3, B3, C3, D3**
Art link, 47, 215, 249, 273, 371, 373
  habitats, **18**
Assessment, 29, 59, 93, 125, 197, 221, 251, 253, 259, 273, 293, 325, 349, 387
  diagnostic check, **7, 13, 17, 39, 53, 71, 75, 79, 85, 87, 103, 105, 119, 147, 155, 175, 189, 207, 213, 239, 243, 245, 249, 253, 271, 275, 279, 283, 287, 303, 305, 311, 315, 319, 335, 367, 377, 399**
  lesson checkpoints, **9, 11, 13, 15, 17, 19, 23, 25, 41, 43, 45, 47, 49, 51, 53, 73, 75, 81, 85, 87, 89, 105, 107, 109, 111, 113, 115, 117, 145, 147, 149, 151, 153, 157, 159, 177, 179, 181, 183, 187, 191, 211, 215, 217, 241, 245, 247, 249, 251, 253, 255, 273, 277, 279, 281, 283, 285, 287, 289, 305, 307, 309, 311, 313, 315, 317, 319, 321, 337, 341, 345, 369, 373, 375, 379, 383, 401, 403, 405, 409**
  resources, **30, 60, 94, 126, 164, 198, 222, 260, 294, 350, 388, 414**
Astronauts, 262–263
Astronomer, 392
Atmosphere, on Earth, 67, 407
Atmospheric scientist, 200
Attract, attraction, *p299,* 318, *p319, p320, p321*
Attributes. *See* **Alike and different; Color; Mass; Opaque; Sound; Temperature; Translucent; Viscosity; Volume; Weight**
Axis, *p362, p370, p371*
  Moon, **380–381**

Backbones
  animals with, **38,** 39–51, **59**
  animals without, 52–55, **59**

Bar graph, 348–349
Barometer, 171
Below-level readers, 1A, 33A, 65A, 97A, 137A, 169A, 201A, 233A, 265A, 297A, 329A, 361A, 393A
Bicycles, invention of, 397
Binoculars, 377
Biographies
  Chase, Mary Agnes, 32
  Hendrickson, Susan, 224
  Jenkins, Luther, 328
  Mota, Mario J., 128
  Purgue, Alejandro, 352
  Wright, Shonte, 416
Birds, 35, *p40, p44, p45*
  migration, **185**
Bones, 38–39
Boulders, *p138, p146*
Build background, 2–3, **26,** 34–35, **36, 56,** 66–67, **68,** 98–99, **122, 128,** 138–139, **140, 160,** 170–171, **194,** 202–203, **204, 218,** 234–235, **236, 256, 264,** 266–267, **268, 290, 296,** 298–299, **300, 304, 322, 328,** 330–331, **346,** 362–363, **364, 384, 392,** 394–395
  resources, **66, 138, 170, 202, 234, 266, 298, 330, 362**
Butterflies, life cycle, **122, 124–125**

Cactus, *p13, p23, p116*
Calculating, 221, 371, 375
Calendar patterns, 371
Calories, 276
Camouflage, *p35, p42,* **43,** *p44,* **45,** *p52*
Careers, 328
  astronomer, 392
  atmospheric scientist, 200
  farmer, 96
  forester, 168
  lighting operator, 296
  marine biologist, 128
  material scientist, 264
  wildlife rehabilitator, 64
Categorizing, 197
Cause and effect, 69, 73, 83, 95
Chameleon, *p48,* 49
Chapter reviews. *See* **Reviews, chapter**
Chase, Mary Agnes, 32
Chipmunks, *p43*
Classifying, 12–15, 35, 55, 58, 79, 143, 157, 281, 305
Clay soil, *p148,* 149
Color
  and heat, **268, 283**
  and light, **27, 296**
Communicating, 56–57, **61,** 131, 204, 205, 223, 300, 301, 327, **379,** 389, 396, 397, 411
Communication, and technology, 404–405, **412**

Compare and contrast, 11, 17, 39, 41, 45, 55, 73, 79, 103, 109, 113, 140, 147, 149, 175, 177, 185, 187, 197, 211, 213, 215, 239, 241, 243, 247, 253, 255, 259, 293, 349, 401, 405, 413

Compasses, 319

Compound words, 45, 157, 255

Comprehend information, 15, 71, 73, 83, 113, 179

Computers, 395

Concept webs, 1, 33, 65, 97, 137, 169, 201, 233, 265, 297, 329, 361, 393

Condense, condensation, p179

Conduction, 281

Conductor, p267, p280, 281

Comprehend, 15

Conservation, 83, 88, 154–159

Constellations, p376, p377, 384–385

Consumers, p71

Contact forces, 299

Cooling matter, 251

Copernicus, 383

Cotton bolls, 151

Craters, Moon, p378–379

Cross-circular link, 91

Data
collecting, 100, 122–123, **161,** 194–195, 199, 228–229
interpreting, 194–195, 322–323
recording, 122–123, 229

Day and night, 364, 370–371

De Mestral, George, 11

Decomposers, 79

Deer, p42, p58

Defining, 111, 143, 157, 243, 245, 271, 303, 307, 313, 335, 383, 385, 403, 409

Density, 245

Department of Agriculture, United States, 277

Describing, 153, 207, 211, 215, 217, 241, 247, 249, 251, 253, 255, 283, 285, 303, 343, 369

Desert, p23

Diagnostic check. See **Assessment, diagnostic check**

Dinosaurs, p202–203, 212–217, 223

Directed Inquiry, Explore, 1D, 4, **33D,** 36, **65D,** 68, **97D,** 100, **137D,** 140, **169D,** 172, **201D,** 204, **233D,** 236, **265D,** 268, **297D,** 300, **329D,** 332, **361D,** 364, **393D,** 396

Discovery Channel School DVD, 97, 201, 329, 361

Diving beetle, p52–53, p58

Dragonfly, p108, p109

Drawing conclusions, 25, 173, 179, 184, **185,** 192, **193,** 199, 237, 247, 249, 261, 290

Drought, p177

Earth, 152–157, p382, 386
axis of, **370, 371, 374–375**
changes, **152–154**
rotation of, **370, 371, 372–373, 374–375**
and space, **361–389**

Effect, and cause, See **Cause and effect**

Electricity, 288–289

ELL (English language learners) support, 2, 5, 8, 10, 11, 14, 19, 20, 25, 27, 34, 37, 41, 43, 44, 45, 46, 47, 48, 50, 51, 54, 69, 73, 79, 83, 87, 89, 98, 101, 105, 107, 109, 110, 111, 112, 113, 115, 116, 117, 119, 138, 145, 151, 153, 157, 161, 170, 173, 177, 179, 183, 185, 187, 195, 202, 205, 208, 217, 219, 234, 237, 241, 246, 249, 257, 269, 272, 281, 283, 287, 298, 301, 304, 313, 315, 319, 323, 330, 333, 336, 339, 341, 345, 347, 362, 369, 372, 375, 379, 383, 385, 394, 397, 403, 405, 407, 409

access content, **57, 66**
English Learners, **A8, B8, C8, D8**

ELL Leveled Support, 7, 9, 39, 55, 71, 76, 103, 121, 143, 147, 175, 192, 207, 213, 239, 253, 271, 275, 303, 309, 335, 343, 367, 381, 399, 400

Energy, 74, **265,** p266–267, **268–270,** 271, **272–273,** 274–277, **278–295**
definition, **271**
types of, **267, 286–287**

Engine, p400, **401**

Engineer, 328

Environment. 16, 42, 50. Also See **Conservation; Earth; Natural resources; Pollution**

Environment, of plants, 16

Equinox, 181

Erosion, p152, 153

Estimating and measuring, 17, 89, 92–93, **117,** 124–125, 147, **162,** 217, 220–221, 232, 243, 256–257, 258–259, 292–293, 300, 311, 324–325

Evaluating, 39, 43, 57, 105, 151, 181, 183, 185, 187, 399

Evaporate, evaporation, 179, 251, 254–255

Examples, giving, 279, 287, 303, 305, 311, 315, 321, 337, 341, 345

Experiment. See **Full Inquiry, Experiment**

Experimenting. See **Directed inquiry, explore; Full inquiry, experiment; Guided inquiry, investigate**

Explain, 9, 23, 36, 41, 47, 51, 55, 93, 117, 155, 159, 181, 271, 289, 325, 367, 369, 377, 381

Explore. See **Directed Inquiry, Explore**

Extinct, extinction, 210, 211

Fair test, plan a, 132–133, 136, 228–229, 232, 356–357, 360, 420–421, 424

Fall season, p184, 185, **374–375**

Farmer, 96

Fasteners, clothing, 11

Ferns, 14, p15

Fire prevention, wilderness, 158

Fish, 35, p40, p46–47

Flight, air and spacecraft, 328

Flowers, p2, p9, 12, 13, **25,** p117

Flying squirrels, p42–43

Food
as energy, **96,** 276–277
in space, 262–263

Food chain, p67, 74–75, 78–79, **275**

Food pyramid, 277

Food web, p67, 76–83, **91**
changing, 82–83
ocean, 80–81

Force, 304–305, 308, 310
and distance, **312**
and heat, **312–313**
measuring, **300**
and motion, **297–305**
in sports, **311**

Forces, contact, 299

Forces in nature, 306

Forester, 168

Formulating, 293

Fossil fuels, 139

Fossil, 201, p202, **203–206,** 207–211, 218–221, 223
formation of, **206–208**

Foxgloves, 117

Freeze-dried foods, 262

Freezing, 252–253, **256**

Freezing point, 255

Friction, 278, p312–313

Frog, p41, p50, p51
life cycles, **124–125**

Fruit, p12

Fuel, p279
fossil, **139**

Fujita scale, 190

Fujita, Theodore, 190

Full Inquiry, Experiment, 97D, 132–133, **201D,** 228–229, **329D,** 356–357, **393D,** 420–421

Gaffer, 296

Galileo, 378

Gas, 246–247, **248,** 253, 254–255

Generalizing, 273, 289, 335

Geography, 85

Germinate, 99, p114

Gills, p34, p46

Giraffe, p71, **113**

Gold, 148

Grade level expectations, *See* Intervention and remediation

Graphic organizers, 3, 5, 34, 37, 67, 69, 99, 101, 141, 171, 173, 205, 235, 237, 246, 267, 269, 299, 301, 333, 365, 397

Graphing and charting, 58–59, 100, **163**, **177**, 220–221, 348–349, **386**

Grassland, 74–77

Gravity, p306, p307
and the solar system, **363**

Groundwater, 155

Growth and change, 103
animals, **98**, 102–113
human beings, **118–121**
insects, 108–109, 122–123
plants, **98**, 114–117

Guide comprehension, see Scaffolded questions

Guided Inquiry, Investigate, 1D, 26–27, **33D**, 56–57, **65D**, 90–91, **97D**, 122–123, **137D**, 160–161, **169D**, 194–195, **201D**, 218–219, **233D**, 256–257, **265D**, 290–291, **297D**, 322–323, **329D**, 346–347, **361D**, 384–385, **393D**, 410–411

Habitats, 72–73

Handedness, **100**, 101

Health in Science, 13, **91**, 155, 276, **277**, 402–403, **A3, B3, C3, D3**

Heat, 278–281, **286–287**
and color, **268, 283**
sources of, **278–279, 312–313**

Heating matter, **251**, 254, p255

Hendrickson, Susan, 224

Heredity
human beings, **118–121**
plants, **116–117**

Hibernate, hibernation, 43, p171, p186, **187**

Homophones, 49

Horse, p110–111

How to Read Science
alike and different, 37, 365
cause and effect, 69
drawing conclusions, 173, 237
important details, 333
infer, 101, 269
picture clues, 141
predict, 5
put things in order, 301
resources, **5, 37, 69, 101, 141, 173, 205, 237, 269, 301, 333, 365, 397**
retell, 205, 397

Hubble space telescope, 392

Human beings
growth and change, 118–121
heredity, **118–121**
needs of, 274–277
prehistoric, **209**

Hummingbirds, p44, **45**

Humus, p148–149

Hurricanes, p171, p192–193

Hypothesis, make a, 26, 51, 71, 132–133, 228–229, 356–357, 420–421

Ice, 242

Iceman, 209

Identify, 23

Identifying, 53, 183, 317, 349, 379

Iguana, p49

Important details, 333, 338, **339**, 343, 351

Inclined plane, p315

Indiana, p185

Inferring, 26–27, 31, **43, 47**, 68, 90–91, 100, **101, 103, 107**, 109, **115, 119, 121**, 122–123, 127, **157, 159**, 172, 173, **177, 185, 189, 213, 215, 217**, 236, 237, **247, 249, 251, 253, 255**, 268, 269, **271**, 274, **275, 283, 287**, 289, 290–291, 295, **371, 373, 375, 377, 381, 387**, 415

Insect, p35, p52–53, 55
life cycles, p108–109, 122–123

Inspecting, 29

Internet resources, 16, 26, 68, 100, 114, 122, 137, 140, 159, **160**, 177, **178, 194, 204, 206, 218, 236, 268, 290, 300, 304, 322, 332, 338, 346, 364, 381, 384**, 387, **390, 398**

Interpreting, 121, 195, 277, 313, 317, 323, 337, 345

Intervention and remediation, 31, 61, 95, 127, 165, 199, 223, 261, 295, 327, 351, 389, 415

Invent, 287, 398, 399

Invertebrates, 57, 59

Investigate, *See* **Guided Inquiry, Investigate**

Jenkins, Luther, 328

Journal, 8, 11, 14, 17, 19, 23, 35, 40, 45, 54, 67, 72, 75, 81, 83, 86, 88, 99, 104, 106, 145, 187, 189, 191, 235, 273, 281, 285, 289, 305, 311, 317, 321, 337, 339, 369, 373, 378, 382, 401, 409

Judge, 53, 281, 403

Jupiter, p382, **383**

Kepler, Johannes, 383

Krill, p63

Landfills, 156

Language detectives, 157, 177, 249, 281, 315, 372, 403, 405

Lasers, 328

Leaves, p3, p8, 14, p28–29

Less than or greater than, 113, 412

Leveled readers, *See* **Advanced–level readers; Below–level readers; On–level readers**

Lever, p314, p316

Life cycle, 114
bean plant, p114–115
butterfly, p122, p124
dragonfly, p108–109
frog, p125
horse, p110–111
sea turtle, p104–107

Life on Earth, 67

Light, **27,** 272, 282–283, **284, 286, 290, 328**

Light pollution, 377

Lighting operator, 296

Lightning, p188–189

Liquids, p244–245, **246**, p252, p253, 254, p255, 340–341

List, 163, 277, 279

Living things, vs. nonliving things, 3, 99, 99–102

Locating, 15, 105, 325

Loudness, p336, p337, **345**

Magnet, 318–321, 322–323, **322–323**

Mammal, p34, **35,** 38–39, p40, p42–43, **110**

Manufacture, 395, p408, p409

Map, locator, c181, c183, c185, c187

Marine biologist, 128

Mars, p382, 383, 386–387, p390–391

Marsh, 24–25

Mass, 239, **240**, p242
vs. weight, **306**

Matching, 315

Material scientist, 264

Math in Science, 17, 47, 55, 77, 89, 105, 115, 147, 217, 241, 243, 253, 285, 311, 381, 405, **A3, B3, C3, D3,** *See also* **Math link**
bar graph, 162–163, 348–349
comparing numbers, 412–413
estimating and measuring, 92–93, 124–125, 220–221, 258–259, 292–293, 324–325, 348–349
graphing and charting, 162–163, 196–197, 220–221, 258–259, 292–293, 348–349, 386–387, 412–413
grouping and sorting, 58–59
number sentences, 162–163, 324–325
patterns, 28–29

Math link, 53, 81, 88, 312
  adding, **117**
  counting, **156**
  estimating and measuring, **189**
  food webs, **81**
  graphing, **177**
  less than or greater than, **113**
  measuring, **88**
  number prefixes, **214**
  sorting, **243**
  symmetry, **17**
Matter, 233–261
  changing, 248–255
  measuring, **258–259**
  properties of, **236, 238–239,** p240–241
  states of, 242–249, 353
Maze, making a, 410–411
Measuring and estimating. See
  Estimating and measuring
Medical science. See **Health in science**
Melting, 101, 252, 254, p255, **256**
Mercury (planet), p382, **383,** p386, 387
Metamorphosis, 122
Meteorologist, 195, p407
Meteorology, 407
Metric system, 236, 324–325
Microscopes, 243
Migrate, migration, 184, p185
Mineral, 3, p147
Mixture, p250, p251
Modeling, 91
Models, making and using, 36, 90–91,
  123, 218–219, **364,** 365, 384–385
Moon, the, 378–381
Mosses, 14, p15
Mota, Mario J., 128
Motion, p303, p313, **396**
  and force, **297–305,** 310–311
  and gravity, **306–307**
  kinds of, **302–303**
  and magnets, **318–319**
  measuring, 324–325
Mount Waialeale, Hawaii, 176
Music link, 336

Naming, 49, 125, 273, 399
**NASA (National Aeronautics and Space
  Administration),** 62
  careers at, 128, 200, 264, 328, 416
  mission to Mars, 390–391
  satellites, 62, p63, p166–167
  space food, 262–263
  studies penguins, 62–63
Natural resources, **137–142,** 143–151
  plants as, **150–151**
  renewable vs. nonrenewable, **144**
Neptune, 382, p383, 386, p387
Nests, building, p86, p87
Nettles, 18
Newton, Sir Isaac, 383
Night and day, **364,** p370–371
  sky at night, **376–379**

Nightjar bird, 45
Nitrogen, 25
**NOAA (National Oceanic and
  Atmospheric Administration)
  Web site,** 177
Non-living things, vs. living things, 3,
  99–102, 214
Number prefixes, 214
Number sentences, 413
Nutrients, **6,** 7, 8, 24
Nutrition, 91, 96, See also **Food,
  as energy**
Nymph, 99, p108, 109

Observe, xxii, xxvii, 26–27, 132–133, 140,
  141, 160–161, 165, 218–219, 256–257,
  261, 290–291, 295, 322–323, 332, 333,
  351, 356–357, 384–385, 410–411
Ocean habitats, 78–81
Octopus, p54, **55,** 56–57, p58
Oil spill, p82, p83
On-level readers, 7, 39, 71, 103, 143,
  175, 207, 239, 271, 303, 335, 367,
  399
Onomatopoeia, 345
Opaque, 284
Operational definitions, making,
  384–385
Opportunity (space rover), p391
Orbit, p374–375, c386, 387

Paleontologist, p207, 224
Patterns, p28, p29
Penguins, p45, p58, p62–63
Performance assessments, 131, 227,
  355, 419
Peticolas, Laura, 392
Phases, Moon, p380–381
Photosynthesis, 368
Picture clues, 141, 148–149, 150–151, 165
Pinecones, 14, p15
Pitch, p338–339, **346, 347**
Plant scientist, 32
Plants, 10
  and animals, 84–87, **88, 90–91**
  classifying, 12–15
  environment, 16–17
  heredity, **116–117**
  life cycles, p114–115, 116–117
  as natural resource, p150–151
  needs of, **3,** 4, **6, 7, 8,** 26–27, **70,** 71–73,
    144–145, 274–275, **368**
  parts of, **6,** p8–9, **10**
  protecting, 158–159
  woodland, 16–19
Poems, 134–135, 230–231, 358–359,
  422–423
Pollution, **83, 88,** p154–155, **400,** 401
  light, **377**

Polynas, 62
Porcupine fish, 47
Prairie, plants in, p20–21
Predator, p75
Predict, 4, 5, **7,** 10, **17, 23, 25, 29,** 31,
  89, 149, 256–257, **273, 283, 290,
  309, 319,** 322–323, **341,** 346–347,
  403, 410–411
Prehistoric man, 209
Prey, p75
Prism, 282
Producer, 71
Professional development, 1, 33, 65, 97,
  137, 169, 201, 233, 265, 297, 329, 361,
  393
Properties, of matter, 238–239,
  p240–241
Protecting Earth, See **Conservation**
Pull, 302, 303, 304
Pulley, p315
Purgue, Alejandro, 352
Push, 302, 303, 304
Put things in order, **17, 281,** 301, 307, 312,
  313, 327. See also Sequencing

Quick activities, 2, 6, 10, 12, 16, 20, 22,
  38, 42, 44, 46, 48, 50, 52, 58, 62,
  66, 70, 74, 78, 82, 84, 92, 98, 102,
  108, 112, 114, 116, 118, 124, 138,
  142, 146, 152, 154, 162, 166, 170,
  174, 178, 180, 182, 184, 186, 188,
  202, 206, 210, 212, 216, 220, 234,
  238, 242, 248, 252, 258, 262, 266,
  270, 274, 278, 282, 286, 292, 298,
  302, 310, 314, 324, 330, 334, 338,
  340, 342, 344, 348, 362, 366, 370,
  374, 376, 386, 394, 398, 402, 404,
  406, 408
Quick summary, 6, 8, 10, 12, 14, 16, 18,
  20, 22, 32, 38, 40, 42, 44, 46, 48, 50,
  52, 62, 64, 70, 72, 74, 76, 78, 80, 82,
  84, 86, 88, 96, 102, 104, 106, 108,
  110, 112, 114, 116, 118, 120, 128, 142,
  144, 146, 148, 150, 152, 154, 156,
  158, 166, 168, 174, 176, 178, 180,
  182, 184, 186, 188, 190, 192, 200,
  206, 208, 210, 212, 214, 216, 224,
  238, 240, 242, 244, 246, 248, 250,
  252, 254, 262, 270, 272, 274, 278,
  280, 282, 284, 286, 288, 296, 302,
  304, 306, 308, 310–311, 312, 314,
  316, 318–319, 320, 328, 334, 338,
  340, 342, 344–345, 366, 366–367,
  368, 370, 372, 374–375, 378, 382,
  390, 392, 398, 400, 402–403,
  404–405, 406–407, 408
Quick teaching plans, 1, 33, 65, 97, 137,
  169, 201, 233, 265, 297, 329, 361, 393

Rainfall, 172, **176**
Reaching All Learners
    Advanced Learners, **A8, B8, C8, D8**
    English Learners, **A8, B8, C8, D8**
    Meeting Individual Needs, **A8, B8, C8, D8**
    Special Needs, **A8, B8, C8, D8**
**Reading and Writing in Science, A3, B3,
    C3, D3**
Reading link, 307, 377
Reading skills. See **How to read science**
Recalling, 17, 25, 41, 51, 59, 73, 85, 87,
    89, 115, 119, 145, 147, 149, 153, 155,
    179, 181, 183, 189, 207, 213, 221, 239,
    241, 249, 251, 259, 275, 293, 343, 407
Recognizing, 371, 383, 399
Recycling, p156–157, 162–163
Reflect, reflection, p282–283
Remediation. See **Intervention and
    remediation**
Repel, 318, p319, **320**
Reptiles, p41
    adaptations of, p48–49
Resource. See **Natural Resources**
Restating, 309, 373
Retell, 205, 209, 211, 223, 397, 403, 409, 415
Reviewing, 311
Reviews, chapter, 30–31, 60–61, 94–95,
    126–127, 164–165, 198–199, 222–223,
    260–261, 294–295, 326–327, 350–351,
    388–389, 414–415
Reviews, unit
    Performance Assessment, 131, 227,
        355, 419
    Test Talk, 129, 225, 353, 417
    Wrap-Up, 130, 226, 354, 418
Rock, p146, 147
Roots, p8, 14
Rotation, of planets, 370, p371, **374–375**

Safety, and electricity, 289
Sand, p138, 146
Satellites, space, 62, p63, 166, p167, p407
Saturn, 382, p383, 386–387
Scaffolded inquiry, A4, B4, C4, D4
Scaffolded questions, 81, 213
    analyze, **11, 45, 53, 401**
    apply information, **75, 125, 275, 285**
    appraise, **47, 125, 147, 175, 191, 413**
    assess, **153**
    assign value, **239, 243, 245**
    calculate, **221, 371, 375**
    categorize, **197**
    cause and effect, **83**
    choose, **311, 367**
    classify, **55, 281, 305**
    classifying, **79, 143, 157**
    communicate, **379**
    compare, **11, 17**

compare and contrast, **39, 41, 79, 103,
    109, 113, 147, 149, 175, 177, 185,
    187, 197, 211, 213, 215, 239, 241,
    243, 245, 247, 253, 255, 259, 293,
    349, 381, 401, 405, 413**
comprehend, **15, 71, 73, 113, 179,
    309, 317, 321, 335**
conclude, **307**
define, **7, 107, 111, 143, 157, 191,
    243, 245, 271, 303, 307, 313,
    335, 383, 403, 409**
describe, **145, 151, 153, 187, 189,
    207, 211, 215, 217, 241, 247,
    249, 251, 253, 255, 283, 285,
    303, 343, 369**
determine, **409**
differentiate, **409**
discover, **285**
dissect, **407**
draw conclusions, **25**
estimate, **117, 221, 259**
evaluate, **39, 43, 105, 151, 181, 183,
    185, 187, 399**
examine, **145, 325**
examples, giving, **279, 287, 303, 305**
explain, **9, 23, 41, 47, 51, 55, 93, 117,
    155, 159, 181, 271, 289, 325, 367,
    369, 377, 381, 387, 413**
formulating, **293**
generalize, **273, 289, 335**
give examples, **311, 315, 321, 337,
    341, 345**
hypothesize, **51, 71**
identify, **9, 23, 53, 183, 317, 349, 379**
infer, **43, 47, 103, 107, 109, 115,
    119, 157, 159, 177, 185, 189,
    213, 215, 217, 247, 249, 251,
    253, 255, 271, 283, 287, 371,
    373, 375, 377, 381, 387**
inspect, **29**
interpret, **121, 277, 313, 317, 337, 345**
invent, **287**
judge, **53, 281, 403**
label, **319**
list, **7, 103, 121, 143, 151, 163, 177,
    277, 279, 401**
locate, **15, 105, 325**
match, **315**
measure, **117, 221**
name, **39, 43, 49, 79, 109, 125, 273,
    337, 367, 369, 375, 377, 383,
    387, 399**
plan, **155, 191**
predict, **7, 13, 23, 25, 29, 89, 149, 273,
    283, 309, 319, 341, 403**
propose, **197**
put things in order, **281**
rank, **163**
recall, **17, 25, 41, 45, 51, 55, 59, 73,
    85, 87, 89, 115, 119, 145, 147, 149,
    153, 155, 179, 181, 183, 189, 207,
    213, 221, 239, 241, 249, 251, 259,
    275, 293, 343, 407**
recognize, **349, 371, 383, 399**
recommend, **277**
relate, **275, 379**
restate, **309, 373**
review, **175, 311, 341**
sequence, **17, 111, 115, 305**
state, **289, 319**
state opinion, **407**

summarize, **315**
summarizing, **279**
synthesizing, **217**
tell, **321**
understanding, **119**
value, appreciating, **179, 207, 211**
Science background, 75, 77
    absolute zero, **257**
    air, **247**
    animal adaptations, **185**
    animals, classifying, **35**
    annual rainfall, **176**
    boulders, **146**
    butterflies, **123**
    calories, **276**
    clothing fasteners, **11**
    compasses, **319**
    constellations, **385**
    contact forces, **299**
    cotton bolls, **151**
    decomposers, **79**
    dinosaurs, **215, 217**
    dragonfly, **109**
    earthworms, **161**
    electrical conductivity, **289**
    energy, types of, **267**
    equinox, **181**
    extinction, **211**
    flowers and plants, **25**
    food chains and food webs, **77, 91**
    food pyramid, **277**
    forces in nature, **306**
    fossil fuels, **139, 279**
    fossils, **209**
    fossils and dinosaurs, **219**
    foxgloves, **117**
    freeze-dried foods, **262**
    frogs, **51**
    Fujita scale, **190**
    giraffes, **113**
    gravity, **307**
    gravity and the solar system, **363**
    horses, **111**
    humus, **149**
    insects, **53**
    interdependence, of plants and animals, **85**
    landfills, **156**
    life on earth, **67**
    light, **27**
    light pollution, **377**
    living things, vs. nonliving things, **99**
    magnetic field, **320**
    magnets, **323**
    maple syrup, **151**
    matter, changing, **251**
    meteorology, **407**
    meteorology, meteorologists, **195**
    microscopes, **243**
    minerals in soil, **3**
    mission to Mars, **390–391**
    the Moon, **378**
    natural resources, **144**
    nests, **86**
    nettles, **18**
    objects, and light transmission, **284**
    octopi, **54, 57**
    penguins, **45**
    pitch, sound, **347**
    polynas, **62**
    porcupine fish, **47**
    prairies, **21**

rating storm intensity, **193**
saguaro cactus, **13**
satellites, **166**
seeds, **115**
sequoia trees, **15**
simple machines in the human body, **316**
solar energy, **272**
sound properties, **337**
sound waves, **331**
summer, **183**
sun as plant need, **368**
tornadoes, **191**
turtles, **104, 106**
twins, identical, **120**
viscosity, **244**
warm-blooded animals, **72**
water, **254**
weather instruments, **171**
wildfire prevention, **158**

Science Fair Projects, 136, 232, 360, 424

Science misconceptions, 3, 8, 40, 49, 375
density, **245**
dinosaurs, **214**
electricity as invention, **288**
energy use, of living things, **276**
force, **305**
friction, **313**
keeping warm, **280**
lightning, **171**
lightning paths, **189**
mass and weight, **240**
mixtures, **251**
museum fossils, **203**
new fossils, **208**
new water, **179**
pollution, **155**
reflection, **283**
snow vocabulary, **176**
sound and telephones, **341**
sun and summer, **183**
technology, **395**
vaccines, **402**
weight, **306**

Science process skills
classify, 194–195
collect data, 100, 122–123, 199, 229
communicate, 56–57, 61, 204, 205, 223, 300, 301, 327, 389, 396, 397, 411
control variables, 132–133
estimate and measure, 68, 256, 300, 421
experiment. *See* **Full inquiry, experiment**
explore. *See* **Directed inquiry, explore**
infer, 27, 31, 68, 69, 90–91, 95, 100, 101, 123, 127, 133, 161, 172, 173, 219, 236, 237, 268, 269, 346–347, 415
interpret data, 322–323
investigate. *See* **Guided inquiry, investigate**
make and use models, 36, 37, 90, 91, 132, 218–219, 364, 365, 384
make hypotheses, 132, 228–229, 356, 420
make operational definitions, 384–385
observe, 26, 27, 133, 140, 141, 161, 165, 219, 229, 236, 256, 261, 290–291, 295, 323, 332, 333, 356, 385, 410
plan a fair test, 132, 228, 356, 420
predict, 4, 5, 56, 123, 256–257, 322, 346–347, 410–411

Scientific methods, using, xxvi, 136, 232, 360, 424
Sea otter, p79
Seasons, 180–187, 196–197, 199, 374–375
changing, **374–375**
and science misconceptions, **375**
Seed coat, p114, 115
Seedling, 114, p115
Seed, p9, 10, p11, **13,** 14, **98, 99,** 114, **115**
Semantic map, 267
Sequencing, 111, 115, 305. *See also* **Put things in order**
Sequoia trees, 15
Sequoyah (Cherokee leader), 15
Shadow, p284–285, 292–293, **296**
Shelter, 84–85, p86, p87
Simple machines, p314–315, **316–317**
Skunks, p38, p39
Sky, 376–379
Snake, p37, p48
Social Studies in Science, 18, **19,** 22, **23,** 85, 107, 279, 286, **287,** 315, 374, **375, A3, B3, C3, D3**
Social studies link, 13, 80, 111, 120, 148, 153, 209, 250, 383, 405
Soil, 140, 141, p148, p149, 228–229
Solar energy, p272, p273
Solar system, p382, p383
concept web, **361**
and gravity, **363**
Solid, 242–243, 252–253, 340–341
Songs
"Go Find a Fossil," 206
"Good Partners," 70
"Hi Little Turtle!," 102
"Listen to the Sounds," 334
"Natural Resources," 142
"Plants," 6
"Technology Helps Us All," 398
"The Sun," 366
"They're All Matter!," 238
"Use Some Force!," 302
"What Has Backbones?," 38
"What's the Weather?," 174
"Where Do We Get Energy?," 270
Sound, 336–345
graphing and charting, **348–349**
properties of, **336–339, 346–347**
traveling, 340–341
Sound waves, 331
Sounds
animal, 342–343, **352**
identifying, **344–345**
loudness and softness, **336–337,** 345
Source, of heat, p278
Space exploration. *See* **NASA (National Aeronautics and Space Administration)**
Space food, 262–263
Space rovers, 390, p391, p416
Space-time relationships, 105
Spiders, p55
Sports, force in, 311

Spring season, 180, p181, **374–375**
Sputnik space satellite, 166
Stars, p376–377
Statement, making, 289, 319, 407
States of matter, 235
Stems, p9, 14
Storms, types of, 188–193
Summarizing, 279, 315
Summer, 182, p183, **374–375**
Sun, energy from the. *See* **Solar energy**
Sun, the, 366, 367–375, **380–381**
Sunlight, 364
Sunlight, as plant need, 368
Symmetry, in nature, 17, 28
Synonyms, 249
Synthesizing, 217

Take-home activities, 29, 32, 59, 63, 64, 93, 96, 125, 128, 163, 167, 168, 197, 200, 221, 224, 259, 263, 264, 293, 296, 325, 328, 349, 352, 387, 391, 392, 413, 416
Take-home booklet, 60, 94, **126, 164, 198, 222, 260, 294, 326, 350, 388, 414**
Target Reading Skills
alike and different, 37, 41, 45, 61, 365, 369, 383, 389
cause and effect, 69, 73, 83, 95
draw conclusions, 173, 179, 184, 192, 199, 237, 247, 249, 261
important details, 333, 338, 343, 351
infer, 101, 109, 111, 121, 127, 269, 274, 289, 295
picture clues, 141, 149, 151, 165
predict, 5, 10, 24, 31
put things in order, 301, 307, 312, 327
retell, 205, 209, 211, 223, 397, 403, 409, 415
Teaching plans, quick. *See* **Quick teaching plans**
Technology, 393–415, 399
and communication, **404–405**
concept web, **393**
defining, **395, 398–399**
medical, **402–403**
other uses, **406–407**
and transportation, **400–401**
Technology in Science, 53, 159, 177, 317, 376, **377, A3, B3, C3, D3**
Technology link, 85, 201, 304, 338, **361, 381**
Telephones, and sound, 341
Telephones, using, 398–399
Telescope, 377, 392
Telling, 321
Temperature, measuring, 171, 256–257, **268**
Test Talk, 129, 225, 353, 417
Thawing. *See* **Melting**
Thermometer, 171, 268
"This Happy Day" (poem), 422

Thunderstorm, p188–189
Time, measuring, 124–125
Toads, p51
Tornadoes, p190–191
Translucent, 284
Transparencies, 3, 99, 139, 210, 216, 235, 246, 267, 338, 340, 342, 398, 402, 404, 406
Transparent, 284
Transportation, p400, p401, **412**
Trees, p12, p16, p17
   sequoia, **15**
Tsunamis, 153
Turtles, p64, 102–107, **102, 103, 104, 106, 128**
   life cycle, 104–107
   song, 102

Understanding, 317, 321, 335
Unit reviews, See **Reviews, unit**
United States Department of Agriculture, 277
Uranus, 382, p383, 386–387

Vaccine, p402, **403**
Value, assigning, 239, 243, 245
Vapor, 253
Venus, p382, 383, 386–387
Venus's flytrap, 25
Vertebrates, 38, 39, 39–51, 59

Vibrate, vibration, 332, 334, 335, **346, 352**
Viscosity, 244
Vocabulary
   extending, **7, 9, 11, 13, 19, 23, 25, 39, 41, 43, 45, 47, 49,** 51, **53, 55, 71, 73, 75, 79, 81, 83, 85, 89, 103, 105, 107, 109, 111, 113, 115, 117, 119, 121, 143, 145, 147, 149, 151, 153, 155, 157, 159, 175, 177, 179, 181, 183, 185, 187, 189, 191, 193, 207, 211, 213, 215, 217, 239, 241, 247, 249, 251, 253, 271, 273, 275, 277, 279, 281, 283, 285, 289, 303, 305, 307, 311, 313, 315, 317, 319, 321, 335, 337, 341, 345, 367, 369, 371, 373, 399, 401, 403, 405**
   introducing, **3, 35, 67, 99, 139, 171, 203, 235, 267, 299, 331, 363, 395**
   lists, **234, 266, 298, 330, 362, 394**
Vocabulary lists, 2, 3, **34,** 35, **66,** 67, **98,** 99, **138,** 139, **170,** 171, **202,** 203, **234,** 235, **266,** 267, **298,** 299, **330,** 331, **362,** 363, **384,** 395
Vocal cords, 352
Voles, 74, 75
Volume, of sound. See **Loudness**

Water, as natural resource, 144–145, **254**
   pollution, **155**
Water cycle, p178–179
Water vapor, 179, 252–253
Weather, 169–174, 175–197, **407**
   kinds of, **174–175, 188–193**

Weather instruments, 171, 194–195
Weathering, 153
Wedge, p134, **315,** p316
Weight, 240
   vs. mass, **306**
Wheel and axle, p314–315
Wildfire prevention, 158
Wildlife rehabilitator, 64
Winter, p186, 187, **374–375**
Woodland habitat, p16, p17, p18–19
Word recognition, 34
Word wall words. See **Vocabulary**
Word web, 35, 145
Work, p308–309
Worms, 161
Wrap-Up, Unit, 130–131, 226–227, 354–355, 418–419
Wright, Shonte, 416
Writing in science, 9, 20, 31, 49, 51, 61, 79, 81, 87, 95, 111, 113, 127, 144, **145,** 153, 165, 180, 186, **187,** 190, **191,** 199, 213, 215, 223, 245, 255, 261, 273, 281, 295, 305, 309, 321, 327, 337, 344, **345,** 351, 371, 373, 389, 401, 407, 415
Writing link, 51, 345

Yeast, p68, 69

Zebras, p72

Credits

Text

"Little Seeds" from *The Winds that Come From Far Away and Other Poems* by Else Holmelund Minarik. Copyright ©1964 by Else Holmelund Minarik. Used by permission of HarperCollins Publishers.

"The Spring Wind" from *River Winding: Poems* by Charolotte Zolotow; Copyright ©1970 by Charlotte Zolotow. Reprinted by permission of S©ott Treimel, NY.

"This Happy Day" from *The Little Hill* by Harry Behn (Harcourt Brace, 1949).

"Apple Shadows" reprinted from *Black Earth, Gold Sun* by Patricia Hubbell with permission of Marshall Cavendish. Copyright ©2001 by Cavendish Children's Books.

Illustrations

29, 301, 327, 362, 367–368, 370–374, 376, 378, 380, 382, 388 Bob Kayganich; 69 Patrick Gnan; 201–203, 205-208 Big Sesh Studios; 344 Philip Williams; 365 Mary Teichman.

Photographs

Every effort has been made to secure permission and provide appropriate credit for photographic material. The publisher deeply regrets any omission and pledges to correct errors called to its attention in subsequent editions.

Unless otherwise acknowledged, all photographs are the property of Scott Foresman, a division of Pearson Education.

Photo locators denoted as follows: Top (T), Center (C), Bottom (B), Left (L), Right (R), Background (Bkgd).

Cover: (C) ©Chase Swift/Corbis, (B) ©Walter Hodges/Corbis, (Bkgd) ©Ralph A. Clevenger/Corbis, (Bkgd) ©George Grall/NGS Image Collection

Title Page: ©Tom Brakefield/Corbis

Front Matter: ii ©DK Images; iii (TR, BR) ©DK Images; v ©DK Images; vi (CL) ©David Middleton/NHPA Limited, (CL) ©Stephen Dalton/NHPA Limited; vii (CR) Tom Brakefield/Corbis, (B) Geoff Moon; Frank Lane Picture Agency/Corbis; viii (CL) Nigel J. Dennis/NHPA Limited, (B) William Bernard/Corbis; ix Andy Rouse/NHPA Limited; x (CL) ©Stone/Getty Images, (CL) ©Steve Terrill/Corbis, (B) ©DK Images; xi ©Jim Zuckerman/Corbis; xiii ©DK Images; xiv ©Charles Gupton/Corbis; xv ©Kelly-Mooney Photography/Corbis; xvi (CL) ©Lester Lefkowitz/Corbis, (CL) Getty Images; xvii (CR) ©John Gillmoure/Corbis, (Bkgd) ©Handout/Reuters/Corbis; xviii (CL, B) NASA Image Exchange, (CL) Getty Images, (BC) ©NASA/JPL/Handout/Reuters/Corbis; xix ©Reuters/Corbis; xxiv NASA; xxv Getty Images; xxix ©Royalty-Free/Corbis; xxxi ©Ed Bock/Corbis.

Unit A: Divider: (Bkgd) Digital Vision, (CC) Digital Vision; **Chapter 1:** 1 (C) ©David Middleton/NHPA Limited, (BR) ©Stephen Dalton/NHPA Limited, (TR) Brand X Pictures; 2 (BR) ©DK Images, (T) Corbis; 3 (BL) ©DK Images, (BR) Richard Hamilton Smith/Corbis; 5 (Bkgd) Corbis, (TR) ©Stephen Dalton/NHPA Limited, (CL) ©Eric Crichton/Corbis; 6 (C) Corbis, (TR) ©Stephen Dalton/NHPA Limited; 7 (BR) Brand X Pictures, (TR) Hemera Technologies; 8 (TL, BL, BC) ©DK Images; 10 Brand X Pictures; 11 (CL) ©Ted Mead/PhotoLibrary, (TR, BR) ©DK Images, (TL) ©Michael Boys/Corbis, (CR) ©ChromaZone Images/Index Stock Imagery, (BL) ©Scott Camazine/Photo Researchers, Inc.; 12 (TL) Peter Anderson/©DK Images, (CR) ©Cosmo Condina/Getty Images; 13 (CL) Steve Kaufman/Corbis, (CR) Ted Levin/Animals Animals/Earth Scenes; 14 Getty Images; 15 (TR, CR) ©DK Images, (TL) ©Bill Ross/Corbis, (CL) ©Ed Reschke/Peter Arnold, Inc., (BL) ©Ted Mead/PhotoLibrary, (BR) Getty Images; 16 (CR) ©M.P. Kahl/DRK Photo, (TL) ©DK Images; 17 (CL)©Royalty-Free/Corbis, (TR) ©DK Images; 18 (TL) ©Medford Taylor/NGS Image Collection, (BR) ©Eric Crichton/Corbis; 19 (TR, BR) ©DK Images, (C) ©Bob Wickham/PhotoLibrary; 20 (TL) ©Pat O'Hara/Corbis, (BR) Neil Fletcher and Matthew Ward/©DK Images; 21 (C) Getty Images, (TR) ©Pat O'Hara/Corbis, (BR) ©David Muench/Corbis; 22 (BR) ©Ronald Martin, (TL) Getty Images; 23 (C) Randall Hyman Photography, (BR) ©Patti Murray/Animals Animals/Earth Scenes, (TR) ©Steve Kaufman/Corbis; 24 (TL, BR) Brand X Pictures; 25 (TR) Image Quest 3-D/NHPA Limited, (BR) ©OSF/Animals Animals/Earth Scenes, ©David Muench/Corbis; 26 ©George D. Lepp/Corbis; 28 (CL, BL) Matthew Ward/©DK Images, (T) Hemera Technologies; 29 ©Klein/Hubert/Peter Arnold, Inc.; 30 (BR) ©Pat O'Hara/Corbis, (TR) ©Richard Hamilton Smith/Corbis, (TL, CL, CC, CR) ©DK Images; 31 (TR) ©DK Images, (CL) ©Roy Rainford/Robert Harding Picture Library, Ltd.; 32 (BL) Getty Images, (TL, CL) Hunt Institute for Botanical Documentation/Carnegie Mellon University, Pittsburgh, PA; **Chapter 2:** 33 (C) Tom Brakefield/Corbis, (CR) Brand X Pictures; 34 (BL) ©Don Enger/Animals Animals/Earth Scenes, (TC) ©Alan G. Nelson/Animals Animals/Earth Scenes, (BR) Getty Images; 35 (CR) ©Tom Brakefield/Corbis, (TR) ©Joe McDonald/Corbis, (BR) ©Buddy Mays/Corbis, (BL) ©Jean-Louis Le Moigne/NHPA Limited; 37 (Bkgd) ©Alan G. Nelson/Animals Animals/Earth Scenes, (TR) Brand X Pictures, (CL) ©Breck P. Kent/Animals Animals/Earth Scenes, (BCL) ©Joe McDonald/Animals Animals/Earth Scenes; 38 ©Alan G. Nelson/Animals Animals/Earth Scenes; 39 (BR) ©W. Perry Conway/Corbis, (TL) ©DK Images; 40 (BL) ©Joe McDonald/Corbis, (BC) ©George D.Lepp/Corbis, (BR) Getty Images, (TL) Hemera Technologies; 41 (BL) Getty Images, (BR) ©Tom Brakefield/Corbis; 42 (BL) ©Royalty-Free/Corbis, (TR) ©Joe McDonald/Corbis, (TL) Getty Images, (BR) ©D. Robert & Lorri Franz/Corbis; 43 ©Breck P. Kent/Animals Animals/Earth Scenes; 44 (TR) ©Jean-Louis Le Moigne/NHPA Limited, (B) ©Kent Wood/Photo Researchers, Inc., (TL) ©DK Images; 45 ©DK Images; 46 (CR, BL) ©DK Images, (TL) ©Comstock; 47 (TR, CR) ©DK Images; 48 (C) ©Stephen Dalton/NHPA Limited, (BL) ©Daniel Heuclin/NHPA Limited, (TL) Hemera Technologies; 49 ©Zig Leszczynski/Animals Animals/Earth Scenes; 50 (B) ©Carmela Leszczynski/Animals Animals/Earth Scenes, (TL) Hemera Technologies; 51 (CL) Getty Images, (C) ©Kim Taylor/Bruce Coleman Collection; 52 (TL, C) ©DK Images, (BL) ©Geoff Moon/Frank Lane Picture Agency/Corbis; 53 ©OSF/D. Clyne/Animals Animals/Earth Scenes; 54 (TL, C) ©DK Images; 55 (CR) ©Niall Benvie/Corbis, (TR, CR)©DK Images; 56 ©Dale Sanders/Masterfile Corporation; 58 (C, BC, BR) ©DK Images, (BL) ©Royalty-Free/Corbis, (CL) ©Carmela Leszczynski/Animals Animals/Earth Scenes; 59 (BL) ©DK Images, (BR) ©Daniel Heuclin/NHPA Limited; 60 (TR, CL, BR) Getty Images, (TL) ©Tom Brakefield/Corbis, (TCL) ©DK Images, (TCR) ©Joe McDonald/Corbis, (CR) ©Don Enger/Animals Animals/Earth Scenes; 61 (TR) ©DK Images, (CL, CR) Hemera Technologies; 62 (Bkgd) Map Resources, (C) ©Marian Bacon/Animals Animals/Earth Scenes, (B) Getty Images; 63 (TR) ©Andrew Syred/Photo Researchers, Inc., (T)©Royalty-Free/Corbis, (BR) MFSC/NASA, (C) ©Orbital Sciences Corporation/Photo Researchers, Inc.; 64 (BL) ©Niall Benvie/Corbis, (CL)©George Grall/National Geographic/Getty Images, (TR) ©Raymond Gehman/NGS Image Collection; **Chapter 3:** 65 (TC) ©Nigel J. Dennis/NHPA Limited, (TR) Getty Images; 66 (TC) ©Clem Haagner/Gallo Images/Corbis, (B) ©Kennan Ward/Corbis; 67 (BR) ©Randy Morse/Animals Animals/Earth Scenes, (CR) ©Stephen Frink/Corbis, (BR) ©James Watt/Animals Animals/Earth Scenes, (CR) ©Steve Bein/Corbis, (CR) ©Andrew J. Martinez/Photo Researchers, Inc., (TR) ©Sanford/Agliolo/Corbis, (TR) ©Amos Nachoum/Corbis; 69 (Bkgd) ©Clem Haagner/Gallo Images/Corbis, (TR) Getty Images; 70 Clem Haagner/Gallo Images/Corbis; 71 (R) ©Peter Johnson/Corbis, (TR) Hemera Technologies; 72 (TL) Getty Images, (B) ©Clem Haagner/Gallo Images/Corbis; 73 ©Ian Beames/Ecoscene/Corbis; 74 (BL) ©Royalty-Free/Corbis, (BR) ©Joe McDonald/Corbis, (TL) Frank Greenaway/©DK Images; 75 (BR) ©William Bernard/Corbis, ©Gaoil Shumway/Getty Images, (CR) ©Royalty-Free/Corbis; 76 (TR) ©DK Images, (TL, CR) ©Joe McDonald/Corbis, (BR) ©Stephen Krasemann/NHPA Limited, (CL)©Royalty-Free/Corbis; 77 (CL) ©Gaoil Shumway/Getty Images, (TC) ©Jim Zipp/Photo Researchers, Inc.; 78 (CL) ©Randy Morse/Animals Animals/Earth Scenes, (BC) ©Stephen Frink/Corbis, (CR) ©Andrew J. Martinez/Photo Researchers, Inc., (TL) Brand X Pictures; 79 ©Kennan Ward/Corbis; 80 (TC) ©James Watt/Animals Animals/Earth Scenes, (BR) ©Andrew J. Martinez/Photo Researchers, Inc., (CR) ©Stephen Frink/Corbis, (CL) ©Randy Morse/Animals Animals/Earth Scenes, (TL) ©Andrew J. Martinez/Photo Researchers, Inc.; 81 (T) ©Amos Nachoum/Corbis, (CR) ©Sanford/Agliolo/Corbis, (BC) ©Steve Bein/Corbis; 82 (T) ©Sanford/Agliolo/Corbis, (BL) ©Bettmann/Corbis; 83 ©Sanford/Agliolo/Corbis; 84 (B) ©Michael and Patricia Fogden/Corbis, (TL) ©DK Images; 85 ©Fred McConnaughey/Photo Researchers, Inc.; 86 (BL) ©Darrell Gulin/Corbis, (TL) Getty Images, (BR) ©Farrell Grehan/Corbis; 87 ©DK Images; 88 (CL) ©Pete Atkinson/NHPA Limited, (TL) NHPA Limited; 89 (CC) ©Eric and David Hosking/Corbis, (TC) ©Rob C. Nunnington/Gallo Images/Corbis, (TR) ©Richard Murphy; 90 ©Kennan Ward/Corbis; 92 (TR) ©Joe McDonald/Corbis, (BR) ©D. Robert and Lorri Franz/Corbis, (BL) Frank Greenaway/©DK Images, (Bkgd) ©William Manning/Corbis, (BL) Getty Images, (CL) Jane Burton/©DK Images; 94 (BR) ©Clem Haagner/Gallo Images/Corbis, (TC) ©Stephen Krasemann/NHPA Limited, (TR) ©Randy Morse/Animals Animals/Earth Scenes, (CL, CR) ©Royalty-Free/Corbis, (C) ©Joe McDonald/Corbis; 95 (CL) ©George H. H. Huey/Corbis, (CR) ©Norbert Rosing/NGS Image Collection, (TR) ©Andrew J. Martinez/Photo Researchers, Inc.; 96

Notes